格列佛游记

GULLIVER'S TRAVELS

英国文学卷

中英对照全译本

[英] 乔纳森·斯威夫特 著

Jonathan Swift

盛世教育西方名著翻译委员会 译

世界图书出版公司

上海·西安·北京·广州

图书在版编目（CIP）数据

格列佛游记 ：英汉对照 / (英) 斯威夫特(Swift,J.) 著 ；盛世教育西方名著翻译委员会译.—上海：上海世界图书出版公司，2012.1（2016.4重印）

ISBN 978-7-5100-3668-2

Ⅰ. ①格… Ⅱ. ①斯… ②盛… Ⅲ. ①英语－汉语－对照读物②长篇小说－英国－近代 Ⅳ. ①H319.4：I

中国版本图书馆 CIP 数据核字(2011)第 179174 号

格列佛游记

[英] 乔纳森·斯威夫特 著

盛世教育西方名著翻译委员会 译

上海世界图书出版公司 出版发行

上海市广中路 88 号

邮政编码 200083

杭州恒力通印务有限公司印刷

如发现印刷质量问题，请与印刷厂联系

（质检科电话：0571－88506965）

各地新华书店经销

开本：880×1230 1/32 印张：14.5 字数：520 000

2016年 4 月第 1 版第 4 次印刷

ISBN 978-7-5100-3668-2/H·1151

定价：26.80 元

http://www.wpcsh.com.cn

http://www.wpcsh.com

通过阅读文学名著学语言，是掌握英语的绝佳方法。既可接触原汁原味的英语，又能享受文学之美，一举两得，何乐不为？

对于喜欢阅读名著的读者，这是一个最好的时代，因为有成千上万的书可以选择；这又是一个不好的时代，因为在浩繁的卷帙中，很难找到适合自己的好书。

然而，你手中的这套丛书，值得你来信赖。

这套精选的中英对照名著全译丛书，未改编改写、未删节削减，且配有权威注释、部分书中还添加了精美插图。

要学语言、读好书，当读名著原文。如习武者切磋交流，同高手过招方能渐明其间奥妙，若一味在低端徘徊，终难登堂入室。积年流传的名著，就是书中“高手”。然而这个“高手”，却有真假之分。初读书时，常遇到一些挂了名著名家之名改写改编的版本，虽有助于了解基本情节，然而所得只是皮毛，你何曾真的就读过了那名著呢？一边是窖藏了50年的女儿红，一边是贴了女儿红标签的薄酒，那滋味，怎能一样？“朝闻道，夕死可矣。”人生短如朝露，当努力追求真正的美。

本套丛书的英文版本，是根据外文原版书精心挑选而来；对应的中文译文以直译为主，以方便中英文对照学习，译文经反复推敲，对忠实理解原著极有助益；在涉及到重要文化习俗之处，添加了精当的注释，以解疑惑。

读过本套丛书的原文全译，相信你会得书之真意、语言之精髓。

送君“开卷有益”之书，愿成文采斐然之人。

CONTENTS
目 录

PART I. A VOYAGE TO LILLIPUT

第一部分 利利普特国游记

CHAPTER 1

第一章

The Author gives some Account of himself and Family: his first Inducements to travel. He is shipwrecked, and swims for his Life, gets safe ashore in the Country of LILLIPUT; is made a prisoner, and carried up the Country.

My father had a small estate in *Nottinghamshire*; I was the third of five sons. He sent me to *Emanuel College* in *Cambridge*, at fourteen years old, where I resided three years, and applied myself close to my studies: but the charge of maintaining me, (although I had a very scanty allowance) being too great for a narrow fortune, I was bound apprentice to Mr. *James Bates*, an eminent surgeon in *London*, with whom I continued four years; and my father now and then sending me small sums of money, I laid them out in learning navigation, and other parts of the mathematics, useful to those who intend to travel, as I always believed it would be some time or other my fortune to do. When I left Mr. *Bates*, I went down to my father; where, by the assistance of him and my uncle *John*, and some other relations, I got forty pounds, and a

作者对自己及其家庭做了简略的介绍：促使他开始旅行的最初原因。他遭遇海难，游水自救，终于脱险，到达利利普特国岸边；被俘，然后被押到利利普特国境内。

我的父亲在诺丁汉郡有一处地产。我们家有 5 个兄弟，我排行老三。在我 14 岁时，父亲把我送到剑桥大学的伊曼纽尔学院。我在那里度过了 3 年的时间，潜心学习。虽然家里会给少量的零用钱，但对于拮据的家庭来说还是负担太重，于是我立约成了詹姆斯·贝茨先生的学徒。他是伦敦城里一位有名的外科医生，我跟随了他 4 年。父亲偶尔会给我寄点小钱，我便把这些钱花在了学习航海知识和数学上，这对于打算旅行的人来说是大有用处的。我一直相信总有一天我会有幸扬帆远行。在贝茨先生那里学成后，我便回到父亲的家。父亲和约翰叔叔，还有其他几位亲戚为我筹到了 40 英镑去莱顿大学读书，还答应每年给我 30 英镑解决生活开支。我在那里花了两年零 7 个月的时间学习物理学，我知道物理学

promise of thirty pounds a year to maintain me at *Leiden*:. There I studied physic two years and seven months, knowing it would be useful in long voyages.

对远程航行是很有帮助的。

Soon after my return from *Leiden*, I was recommended by my good master Mr. *Bates*, to be surgeon to the *Swallow*, *Captain Abraham Pannell* commander; with whom I continued three years and a half, making a voyage or two into the *Levant*, and some other parts. When I came back, I resolved to settle in *London*, to which Mr. *Bates*, my master, encouraged me, and by him I was recommended to several patients. I took part of a small house in the *Old Jewry*; and being advised to alter my condition, I married Mrs. *Mary Burton*, second daughter to Mr. *Edmond Burton*, hosier in *Newgate Street,* with whom I received four hundred pounds for a portion.

一从莱顿回来，我的师傅贝茨先生便举荐我到亚伯拉罕·潘奈尔船长的"飞燕"号担任外科医生。我在"飞燕"号上工作了3年半，航行到黎凡特[1]一两次，也去了些其他的地方。回来后，我决定在伦敦安顿下来，恩师贝茨先生也支持我的决定，还介绍给我几个病人。我在老朱瑞街上的一栋小房子里租了几个房间。大家都劝我该改变一下生活方式，于是我娶了新门街针织品商埃德蒙德·伯顿的二女儿玛丽·伯顿为妻，也因此得到了她价值400英镑的嫁妆。

But, my good master *Bates* dying in two years after, and I having few friends, my business began to fail; for my conscience would not suffer me to imitate the bad practice of too many among my brethren. Having, therefore consulted with my wife, and some of my acquaintance, I determined to go again to sea. I was surgeon successively in two ships, and made several voyages, for six years, to the

恩师贝茨两年后驾鹤西去，而我几乎也没有什么朋友，于是事业开始走了下坡路。我的很多同行医德败坏，但如果我也效仿他们，必然会遭受良心的谴责。于是在与太太和几个熟人商议之后，我决定再次踏上航海之行。6 年来我先后在两艘航船上担任外科医生，航行了许多次，曾到过东印度群岛和西印度群岛，在那里我也赚得了不少财

[1] 黎凡特：包括地中海东部附近诸岛和沿岸附近诸国在内的地区。

East and *West Indies*, by which I got some addition to my fortune. My hours of leisure I spent in reading the best authors, ancient and modern, being always provided with a good number of books; and when I was ashore, in observing the manners and dispositions of the people, as well as learning their language, wherein I had a great facility by the strength of my memory.

富。我总会随身带着很多书籍，每逢闲暇便会拜读这些古今最著名的作家的作品。一上岸，我便会观察当地的风俗习惯和风土人情，学习当地语言，因为我有着很强的记忆力，所以学习语言并非难事。

The last of these voyages not proving very fortunate, I grew weary of the sea, and intended to stay at home with my wife and family. I removed from the *Old Jury* to *Fetter Lane*, and from thence to *Wapping*, hoping to get business among the sailors; but it would not turn to account. After three years' expectation that things would mend, I accepted an advantageous offer from Captain *William Prichard*, master of the *Antelope*, who was making a voyage to the *South Sea*. We set sail from *Bristol May* 4th, 1699, and our voyage at first was very prosperous.

最后几次航行不太顺利，于是我就不想出海了，而是希望能跟太太和家人待在一起。我从老朱瑞街搬到了费达巷，之后又搬到了沃平，本来想能在水手圈子里做做生意，但结果事与愿违。就这样过了3 年，情况都没有好转，我就接受了“羚羊”号船长威廉·普里查德的待遇优厚的聘请，准备扬帆驶往南海。我们于 1699 年 5 月从比利斯托起航，起初的航行称得上一帆风顺。

It would not be proper, for some reasons, to trouble the reader with the particulars of our adventures in those seas: Let it suffice to inform him, that in our passage from thence to the *East Indies*, we were driven by a violent storm to the northwest of *Van Diemen's* Land. By an observation, we found ourselves in the latitude of 30 degrees 2 minutes south.

由于某些原因，我不便事无巨细地将我们在那片海域上的冒险经历告诉读者，以免带来困扰，因此以下的叙述就足够了：在驶往东印度群岛的途中，我们遭遇了一场恶劣的风暴，被吹到了梵·戴门地的西北方向。经过观测，我们得知我们所在的位置是南纬 30°02′。12 个水手因为过度疲劳以及饮食恶

Twelve of our crew were dead by immoderate labour, and ill food, the rest were in a very weak condition. On the fifth of *November*, which was the beginning of summer in those parts, the weather being very hazy, the seamen spied a rock, within half a cable's length of the ship; but the wind was so strong, that we were driven directly upon it, and immediately split. Six of the crew, of whom I was one, having let down the boat into the sea, made a shift to get clear of the ship, and the rock. We rowed by my computation about three leagues, till we were able to work no longer, being already spent with labor while we were in the ship. We, therefore trusted ourselves to the mercy of the waves and in about half an hour the boat was overset by a sudden flurry from the north. What became of my companions in the boat, as well as of those who escaped on the rock, or were left in the vessel, I cannot tell; but conclude they were all lost. For my own part, I swam as fortune directed me, and was pushed forward by wind and tide. I often let my legs drop, and could feel no bottom: but when I was almost gone, and able to struggle no longer, I found myself within my depth; and by this time the storm was much abated. The declivity was so small, that I walked near a mile before I got to the shore, which I conjectured was about

劣而丧命，其他的也都极度虚弱，奄奄一息。11月5日，正当那个地区进入夏季的时候，海面上下起了茫茫大雾。水手们在离船半缆的地方发现一块礁石，由于风势太猛，我们被直直地刮向那块礁石，船体顷刻间被撞裂。包括我在内的6名船员放下救生艇，拼命划离大船和礁石。就我估算，我们划出了9英里就精疲力竭了，因为在大船上，我们就已经体力不支了，于是便任凭海浪载着我们在海面上漂流。漂了大概半小时，我们的小船就被一阵从北面刮来的疾风吹翻了。我无从得知救生艇上其他5个人以及当初爬到礁石上或留在大船里的同伴们后来怎样了，但我推断他们肯定难逃一劫。而我呢，只能奋力地游水，顺从命运的指引，任凭风浪的推拥。我时不时地将腿向下伸直，但都够不到底。就在我快要无力自救，再也挣扎不动的时候，我的脚探到了地面，这时的风暴也减弱了很多。因为海底坡度太小，所以我差不多走了一英里才走上岸，据我估计那时的时间是晚上8点钟左右。我又朝前走了差不多半英里，但还是没发现任何房屋或居民的影子。起码是我没看见，因为我实在太虚弱了。本来就已经精疲力竭，天气又炎热，再加上离船前还喝了半品脱白兰地，我已经困到支持不住了，于是就在草地上躺了下

eight o'clock in the evening. I then advanced forward near half a mile, but could not discover any sign of houses or inhabitants; at least I was in so weak a condition, that I did not observe them. I was extremely tired, and with that, and the heat of the weather, and about half a pint of brandy that I drank as I left the ship, I found myself much inclined to sleep. I lay down on the grass, which was very short and soft, where I slept sounder than ever I remembered to have done in my life, and as I reckoned, above nine hours; for when I awaked, it was just daylight. I attempted to rise, but was not able to stir: for as I happened to lie on my back, I found my arms and legs were strongly fastened on each side to the ground; and my hair, which was long and thick, tied down in the same manner. I likewise felt several slender ligatures across my body, from my *Armpits* to my thighs. I could only look upwards, the sun began to grow hot, and the light offended my eyes. I heard a confused noise about me, but in the posture I lay, could see nothing except the sky. In a little time I felt something alive moving on my left leg, which advancing gently forward over my breast, came almost up to my chin; when bending my eyes downward as much as I could, I perceived it to be a human creature not six inches high, with a bow and arrow in his

来。草叶不长还很柔软，就这样我睡了记忆中最酣甜的一觉。据推算我应该是睡了 9 个小时，因为我醒来时差不多正是拂晓。我想坐起身来，但却动弹不得：我刚好是仰面躺在草地上，我发现我的胳膊和腿都被牢牢地捆在了地上，而我浓密的长头发也同样被系在了地上。我还感觉到我的身上从腋窝到大腿都被捆上了细长的绳索，因此只能仰面朝上。太阳开始烧灼，光线刺痛了我的双眼，我听到周围一片嘈杂的声音，但由于我只能躺着动弹不得，所以除了天空我什么都看不见。不一会儿我感觉有活物在我的左腿上移动，这个东西轻轻地走到了我的胸膛，几乎就要走到我的下巴前了。我使劲让眼睛向下朝我的前胸方向看去，隐约看见一个不足 6 英寸的小人，他手里拿着弓箭，背上还挎着一个箭袋。这时，我感觉至少有 40 个（据我推测）这样的小人跟着带头的这位走了上来。我惊愕不已，大声地吼了起来，他们立刻吓得掉头就跑。后来我得知有些小人还因为从我身上跳下去而摔伤了自己。但他们不久又折了回来，还有一个壮着胆子走到能看清我整张脸的位置，举着双手，满眼崇拜地望着我，尖着嗓子清楚地喊出“海金那·德古尔”几个字，其他人也跟着他喊了起来，但我不知道那是什么意思。就像读者所能

hands, and a quiver at his back. In the mean time, I felt at least forty more of the same kind (as I conjectured) following the first. I was in the utmost astonishment, and roared so loud, that they all ran back in a fright; and some of them, as I was afterwards told, were hurt with the falls they got by leaping from my sides upon the ground. However, they soon returned, and one of them, who ventured so far as to get a full sight of my face, lifting up his hands and eyes by way of admiration, cried out in a shrill, but distinct voice, *Hekinah degul*: the others repeated the same words several times, but I then knew not what they meant. I lay all this while, as the reader may believe, in great uneasiness: At length, struggling to get loose, I had the fortune to break the strings, and wrench out the pegs that fastened my left arm to the ground; for, by lifting it up to my face, I discovered the methods they had taken to bind me; and, at the same time, with a violent pull, which gave me excessive pain, I a little loosened the strings that tied down my hair on the left side, so that I was just able to turn my head about two inches. But the creatures ran off a second time, before I could seize them; whereupon there was a great shout in a very shrill accent, and after it ceased, I heard one of them cry aloud, *Tolgo phonac*; when in an instant I

想象到的，我一直局促不安地躺在那里。最后我拼命挣扎，幸运地将绳索挣断，拔出了把我左臂捆在地上的钉子。我把左臂举到眼前，这才看明白他们捆绑我的方式。同时，我把头猛力向右一扭，把将我左边头发系在地上的绳索拉松了些，疼得我够戗，这样我的脑袋就能转动两英寸左右了。还没等我抓住这些小人，他们就又一次跑开了。然后我听到一声刺耳的喊叫，紧接着又听到一个小人高喊了一句“托尔古·冯纳克”。我的左手应声感到差不多有100支像针一样的箭从远处朝我射来。他们又向空中发射了一轮弓箭，就像我们在欧洲投弹那样，我估计有很多箭落在了我身上（虽然我没什么感觉），有些朝我的脸上飞来，我便立刻用左手护住了脸。他们这样一番射箭，让我疼得大叫了起来，我拼命挣脱绳索，但他们又开始了新一轮更猛烈的进攻，有些小人还拼命地用长矛刺向我的两肋。幸运的是，我正穿着那件黄色软皮上衣，因此就算他们再怎么使劲也无济于事。我想我最明智的做法就是躺着不动，于是打算就这样躺到晚上，既然我的左手上的绳子已经松了，那整个身子挣脱开绳索也就不是什么难事了。至于这些当地的小人，只要他们都像我看到的那样矮小，我就绝对相信自己能敌得过他们

felt above an hundred arrows discharged on my left hand, which pricked me like so many needles; and besides they shot another flight into the air, as we do bombs in *Europe*, whereof many, I suppose, fell on my body (though I felt them not) and some on my face, which I immediately covered with my left hand. When this shower of arrows was over, I fell a groaning with grief and pain, and then striving again to get loose, they discharged another volley larger than the first, and some of them attempted with spears to stick me in the sides; but, by good luck, I had on me a buff jerkin, which they could not pierce. I thought it the most prudent method to lie still, and my design was to continue so till night, when my left hand being already loose, I could easily free myself and as for the inhabitants, I had reason to believe I might be a match for the greatest Armies they could bring against me, if they were all of the same size with him that I saw. But fortune disposed otherwise of me. When the people observed I was quiet, they discharged no more arrows: but, by the noise I heard increasing, I knew their numbers were greater; and about four yards from me, over against my right ear, I heard a knocking for above an hour, like that of people at work; when turning my head that way, as well as the pegs and

最强大的军队。但命运却偏偏跟我作对。等这些小人看到我不再挣扎的时候，他们就不再放箭了，但我听到周围越来越嘈杂，我估计他们的队伍一定更庞大了。我听到他们在离我右耳4码的地方敲敲打打了一个钟头，像是在忙着做活儿。我扯着钉子和绳索把脑袋扭过去，看到他们已经搭起了一个台子，离地大概一英尺半的高度，上面差不多能站4个小人，侧面还架着两三把梯子。他们中间一个看上去有些身份的小人对我长篇大论了一通，但我一个字都听不懂。我要提到的是，在这个“大人物”演说前，他大声喊了三声“兰格鲁·德布尔·桑”（后来他们向我解释了这句话和先前那些话的意思）。话音一落，就有差不多50个小人立刻朝我走了过来，砍断了捆着我左边头发的绳索。这样一来，我的脑袋就能转向右边，看着这个要发表演说的小人了。他看起来正值中年，比他3个随从长得高些。其中一个男侍从为他扯着裙裾，身材比我的中指长不了多少。另外两个则站在他两旁扶持着他。他全然一副演说家的派头，我能感受到他演讲中所表达出的威胁、承诺、可怜和仁慈。我恭顺地作出回应，还举起左手，眼睛看着太阳，做出一副向天发誓的样子。我在弃船前几个小时就没怎么吃东西，因此现在更是饿昏了

strings would permit me, I saw a stage erected, about a foot and a half from the ground, capable of holding four of the inhabitants, with two or three ladders to mount it: from whence one of them, who seemed to be a person of quality, made me a long speech, whereof I understood not one syllable. But I should have mentioned, that before the principal person began his oration, he cried out three times *Langro Debul san* (these words and the former were afterwards repeated and explained to me). Whereupon immediately about fifty of the inhabitants came, and cut the strings that fastened the left side of my head, which gave me the liberty of turning it to the right, and of observing the person and gesture of him that was to speak. He appeared to be of a middle age, and taller than any of the other three who attended him, whereof one was a page who held up his train, and seemed to be somewhat longer than my middle finger; the other two stood one on each side to support him. He acted every part of an orator, and I could observe many periods of threatenings, and others of promises, pity, and kindness. I answered in a few words, but in the most submissive manner, lifting up my left hand and both my eyes to the sun, as calling him for a witness; and being almost famished with hunger, having not eaten a morsel for some hours

头，饥肠辘辘，这种饥饿感让我也顾不得耐着性子了，我不断地用手指指着嘴巴（这种做法可能有些不成体统），向他们示意我想吃东西。那位赫古（我后来得知这是他们对地位尊贵的人的称呼）看懂了我的意思。他从台子上走了下去，命令他们把梯子搭在我的身体两侧，就这样差不多有100个小人提着装满肉的篮子顺梯而上把食物送到我嘴边。这些食物是这位大人理解我的意思后立刻命令下人送过来的。这里面有不少动物的肉，但我分辨不出来具体是哪些动物。这些肉的形状像羊肩肉、羊腿和胸排，加工很精细，但对我来说这些肉比百灵鸟的翅膀还小。这样的肉我一口能吃两三块，还有步枪子弹大小的面包我一口也能吃上3块。他们不停地给我运来食物，我的大块头和大食量让他们大为惊奇。接着我又示意他们我想喝水。由于见识到我吃东西的架势，他们便知道小分量对我来说是不够的，于是这些聪明机灵的小人便找来他们最大的酒桶，把酒桶滚到我手上，再把桶盖打开。我举起木桶一饮而尽，因为这桶酒还不到半品脱，所以一口喝光并非难事。这种酒的味道尝起来有点像勃艮第产的淡酒，但味道要更香一些。他们又给我搬来一桶酒，我同样一饮而尽，向他们示意我还想再喝一些，但他们已经拿不出更

before I left the ship, I found the demands of nature so strong upon me, that I could not forbear showing my impatience (perhaps against the strict rules of decency) by putting my finger frequently to my mouth, to signify that I wanted food. The *hurgo* (for so they call a great lord, as I afterwards learned) understood me very well. He descended from the stage, and commanded that several ladders should be applied to my sides, on which above an hundred of the inhabitants mounted, and walked towards my mouth, laden with baskets full of meat, which had been provided, and sent thither by the king's orders, upon the first intelligence he received of me. I observed there was the flesh of several animals, but could not distinguish them by the taste. There were shoulders, legs, and loins, shaped like those of mutton, and very well dressed, but smaller than the wings of a lark. I eat them by two or three at a mouthful, and took three loaves at a time, about the bigness of musket bullets. They supplied me as they could, showing a thousand marks of wonder and astonishment at my bulk and appetite. I then made another sign that I wanted drink. They found by my eating that a small quantity would not suffice me, and being a most ingenious people, they slung up with great dexterity one of their largest hogsheads, then rolled

多的酒给我了。我的一举一动在他们看来都是奇迹一般，因此在我吃过喝过后，他们高兴地大喊了起来，在我胸膛上跳起了舞，嘴里还不停地重复喊着一开始的那句“海金那·德古尔”。他们大喊了一句“波拉彻·米沃拉”提醒站在下面的人躲开，然后示意我可以将那两只木桶扔下去。当他们看见两个从天而降的酒桶时，都不禁发出了“海金那·德古尔”的呼声。我承认当看到这些小人在我身上来回走动时，我常常会忍不住想要一手逮住我所能够得着的四五十个小人，再把他们扔到地上。但想起他们始终没打算把我置之死地，而且我也曾向他们保证过要以礼相待，我便依旧保持着恭顺的态度，没多久我就完全把刚刚的念头抛到九霄云外去了。而且这些人还如此大费周章地热情款待我，我自然不能以怨报德。但我实在对这些小人的大无畏精神感到吃惊，我的一只手已经松了绑，而他们居然还敢爬到我身上并在上边走来走去，看到如此庞然大物竟也没有发抖。等看到我不再要肉吃之后，一位钦差大臣就向我走来。这位阁下爬上我的右腿，向前一直走到我面前，身边还跟着十来个随从。他把盖着玉玺的圣旨举到我眼前，对我讲了十来分钟的话。他的言语中没有愤怒的迹象，而是在宣布一个决定。他不时

it towards my hand, and beat out the top; I drank it off at a draught, which I might well do, for it did not hold half a pint, and tasted like a small wine of *Burgundy*, but much more delicious. They brought me a second hogshead, which I drank in the same manner, and made signs for more, but they had none to give me. When I had performed these wonders, they shouted for joy, and danced upon my breast, repeating, several times as they did at first, *Hekinah degul*. They made me a sign that I should throw down the two hogsheads, but first warned the people below to stand out of the way, crying aloud, *Borach Mivola*, and when they saw the vessels in the air, there was an universal shout of *Hekinah degul*. I confess I was often tempted, while they were passing backwards and forwards on my body, to seize forty or fifty of the first that came in my reach, and dash them against the ground. But the remembrance of what I had felt, which probably might not be the worst they could do, and the promise of honour I made them, for so I interpreted my submissive behavior, soon drove out those imaginations. Besides, I now considered myself as bound by the laws of hospitality to a people who had treated me with so much expense and magnificence. However, in my thoughts I could not sufficiently wonder at the intrepidity of these diminutive mortals,

地朝前指着，后来我才知道他是在指着前方的都城。都城离这里差不多有一英里的距离，他们的皇帝下令要把我运过去。我回应了几句话，但他们丝毫听不懂，于是我就用已经松绑的左手指了指我的右手（我把手抬起，高过那位阁下的头顶，唯恐伤到他和他的随从），接着又指指我的脑袋和身体，向他们示意我希望可以松绑。看来他明白了我的意思，因为他摇了摇头表示不同意，还用手摆出一个姿势，意思是说我必须像俘虏那样被押运进城。但他还比画着告诉我肉酒管够，他们会好好款待我。于是我再次试图挣脱捆绑，但我立刻感觉到脸上和手上之前被箭刺伤的疼痛，那些箭头还都扎在里面，所以伤口处都起了水泡。而且我发现他们的人数又增加了，便比画着告诉他们就按他们的意思处置我好了。这位赫古和他的随从便和悦有礼地从我身上退了下去。我听到他们不断齐声喊着“拍普罗姆·瑟兰”这几个字，紧接着我感觉到我左侧有一大群小人把绳索松开了些，这样我就可以向右翻翻身，也能方便小解。我大大地尿了一泡。当这些小人看懂我想要撒尿的手势时，他们惊得赶紧向两侧闪开，好躲开这股激流和随之而来的声响和破坏。但在这之前他们往我脸上和双手上涂上了一种味道很好闻的药膏，

who durst venture to mount and walk upon my body, while one of my hands was at liberty, without trembling at the very sight of so prodigious a creature as I must appear to them. After some time, when they observed that I made no more demands for meat, there appeared before me a person of high rank from his imperial majesty. His excellency having mounted on the small of my right leg, advanced forwards up to my face, with about a dozen of his retinue. and producing his credentials under the signet-royal, which he applied close to my eyes, spoke about ten minutes, without any signs of anger, but with a kind of determinate resolution, often pointing forwards, which, as I afterwards found, was towards the capital city, about half a mile distant, whither it was agreed by his majesty in council that I must be conveyed. I answered in few words, but to no purpose, and made a sign with my hand that was loose, putting it to the other (but over his excellency's head, for fear of hurting him or his train) and then to my own head and body, to signify that I desired my liberty. It appeared that he understood me well enough, for he shook his head by way of disapprobation, and held his hand in a posture to show that I must be carried as a prisoner. However, he made other signs to let me understand that

过了几分钟那些被箭刺伤的地方就不痛了。再加上刚刚的酒足饭饱，我便感到昏昏欲睡。后来我才知道自己一觉睡了8个小时，原来是皇帝命令医生在我的酒里下了安眠药。

I should have meat and drink enough, and very good treatment. Whereupon I once more thought of attempting to break my bonds, but again, when I felt the smart of their arrows upon my face and hands, which were all in blisters, and many of the darts still sticking in them, and observing likewise that the number of my enemies increased, I gave tokens to let them know that they might do with me what they pleased. Upon this the *hurgo* and his train withdrew with much civility and cheerful countenances. Soon after I heard a general shout, with frequent repetitions of the words, *Peplom selan*, and I felt great numbers of the people on my left side relaxing the cords to such a degree, that I was able to turn upon my right, and to ease myself with making water; which I very plentifully did, to the great astonishment of the people, who conjecturing by my motions what I was going to do, immediately opened to the right and left on the side to avoid the torrent which fell with such noise and violence from me. But before this, they had daubed my face and both my hands with a sort of ointment very pleasant to the smell, which in a few minutes removed all the smart of their arrows. These circumstances, added to the refreshment I had received by their victuals and drink, which were very nourishing, disposed me to sleep. I slept about eight hours, as I was afterwards assured; and it was no wonder, for the physicians, by the emperor's order, had mingled a sleepy potion in the hogsheads of wine.

It seems that upon the first moment I was discovered sleeping on the ground after my landing, the emperor had early notice of it by an express, and determined in council that I should be tied in the manner I have related (which was done in the night while I slept) that plenty of meat and drink should be sent me, and a machine prepared to carry me to the capital city.

This resolution perhaps may appear very bold and dangerous, and I am confident would not be imitated by any prince in *Europe* on the like occasion. However, in my opinion it was extremely prudent, as well as generous. for supposing these people had endeavored to kill me with their spears and arrows while I was asleep, I should certainly have awaked with the first sense of smart, which might so far have roused my rage and strength, as to have enabled me to break the strings wherewith I was tied; after which, as they were not able to make resistance, so they could expect no mercy.

These people are most excellent mathematicians, and arrived to a great

看来，当时他们一发现我躺在海边睡觉时，就有人禀报了皇帝。皇帝立刻召开议会决定在那晚用我睡觉时捆绑我的方式用器械将我绑着运进首都，还下令要供给我足够的酒肉。

这个决定可能显得大胆而危险，我敢说任何一位欧洲的君主在这种情况下都不会效仿此做法的。但在我看来这种做法非常明智谨慎，又很宽宏大量。如果他们打算在我熟睡时用长矛和弓箭杀死我，那我一感到疼痛就会惊醒过来，愤怒地挣脱开捆绑我的绳索，到时候他们不管怎样反抗都是无济于事的，而我对他们也绝不会心慈手软的。

在皇帝的支持鼓励和大力赞助下，这些小人的数学都学得极

perfection in mechanics, by the countenance and encouragement of the emperor, who is a renowned patron of learning. The prince hath several machines fixed on wheels for the carriage of trees and other great weights. He often builds his largest men of war, whereof some are nine foot long, in the woods where the timber grows, and has them carried on these engines three or four hundred yards to the sea. Five hundred carpenters and engineers were immediately set to work to prepare the greatest engine they had. It was a frame of wood raised three inches from the ground, about seven foot long and four wide, moving upon twenty-two wheels. The shout I heard was upon the arrival of this engine, which it seems set out in four hours after my landing. It was brought parallel to me as I lay. But the principal difficulty was to raise and place me in this vehicle. Eighty poles, each of one foot high, were erected for this purpose, and very strong cords of the bigness of packthread were fastened by hooks to many bandages, which the workmen had girt round my neck, my hands, my body, and my legs. Nine hundred of the strongest men were employed to draw up these cords by many pulleys fastened on the poles, and thus in less than three hours, I was raised and slung into the engine, and there tied fast.

好，也掌握了精湛的力学知识。皇帝有很多安着轮子的大型机械用来运送大树和其他重物。他还在森林里就地取材建造最大的军舰，差不多有 9 英尺长，建好后就放在这些器械上运到三四百码外的海上。500 个工匠和工程师立刻遵旨去着手准备他们最大的器械。这是一个高 3 英尺，长 7 英尺，宽 4 英尺的木架，装有 22 个轮子。机械一运达我就听到他们的欢呼声，看来在我上岸后 4 个小时他们就动身了。他们把这个机械平行放在了我身旁，但最大的麻烦是怎样把我抬起来弄上去。他们竖起了 80 根一英尺高的柱子，然后用绷带缠在我的脖子，双手，身体和双腿上，再把系着结实绳索的钩子钩在绷带上。他们将柱子顶端安上滑轮再将绳子穿过来，900 个最强壮的小人被雇来拉绳索，就这样，不到 3 个小时他们就把我抬了起来放到了那个器械上，然后又将我紧紧地绑在上面。以上这些都是他们后来告诉我的，因为这整个过程中我都因喝了下在酒里的安眠药而睡得正酣。他们征用了 1500 匹个头最大的御马——每匹差不多有 4 英寸半高——将我拉到半英里远的都城。

All this I was told, for while the whole operation was performing, I lay in a profound sleep, by the force of that soporiferous medicine infused into my liquor. Fifteen hundred of the emperor's largest horses, each about four inches and an half high, were employed to draw me towards the metropolis, which, as I said, was half a mile distant.

About four hours after we began our journey, I awaked by a very ridiculous accident; for the carriage being stopt a while to adjust something that was out of order, two or three of the young natives had the curiosity to see how I looked when I was asleep: They climbed up into the engine, and advancing very softly to my face, one of them, an officer in the guards, put the sharp end of his half-pike a good way up into my left nostril, which tickled my nose like a straw, and made me sneeze violently; whereupon they stole off unperceived, and it was three weeks before I knew the cause of my awaking so suddenly. We made a long march the remaining part of the day, and rested at night with five hundred guards on each side of me, half with torches, and half with bows and arrows, ready to shoot me, if I should offer to stir. The next morning at sunrise we continued our march, and arrived within two hundred yards of the city gates about noon. The emperor, and

大概 4 小时后我们就上路了，突然发生的一个滑稽事件将我弄醒了——在抬着我往都城走的路上，队伍停下了一阵子来调整绳索机械。有两三个年轻的小人好奇心作祟想看看我睡着是什么样子，于是就钻进大拖车，轻轻爬到我的脸上。他们中有一个是护卫队的军官，这个军官用他短矛尖锐的一头插进了我的左鼻孔，这一下子就像稻草那样把我的鼻子弄痒了，我狠狠打了一个喷嚏，他们就悄悄溜走了，3 个星期后我才知道为什么当时我会醒来得那么突然。调整完后我们又走了很久，晚上休息时，500 个护卫分别守在我的两侧，一半拿着火炬，另一半拿着弓箭，准备在我想要挣脱的时候随时向我射箭。第二天黎明我们又开始赶路，到中午时离城门已经不足 200 码了。皇帝与他的满朝文武全部出来迎接我们，但大臣们唯恐皇帝会遭到什么危险，都劝谏皇帝不要爬到我的身体上去。

all his court came out to meet us, but his great officers would by no means suffer his majesty to endanger his person, by mounting on my body.

At the place where the carriage stopped, there stood an ancient temple, esteemed to be the largest in the whole kingdom, which having been polluted some years before by an unnatural murder, was, according to the zeal of those people, looked upon as profane, and therefore had been applied to common use, and all the ornaments and furniture carried away. In this edifice it was determined I should lodge. The great gate fronting to the north was about four foot high, and almost two foot wide, through which I could easily creep. On each side of the gate was a small window not above six inches from the ground: into that on the left side, the king's smith conveyed fourscore and eleven chains, like those that hang to a lady's watch in *Europe*, and almost as large, which were locked to my left leg with six and thirty padlocks. Over against this temple, on t'other side of the great highway, at twenty foot distance, there was a turret at least five foot high. Here the emperor ascended with many principal lords of his court, to have an opportunity of viewing me, as I was told, for I could not see them. It was reckoned that above an hundred thousand inhabitants came out

拖车停在了一座古庙前。这座古庙是全国最大的庙宇，但几年前这里曾发生一起杀戮，虔诚的人们认为这场杀戮是对庙宇的亵渎，于是便将此庙宇降为公用，撤去了原来的装饰和摆设。皇帝决定就让我在这个大建筑物里寄住。大门正对北面，差不多有 4 英尺高，两英尺宽，够我爬着进出。大门两边分别有一个小窗户，离地不到 6 英寸。御用铁匠从左边的窗口拉进去 91 根铁链——这些铁链很像欧洲女士手表上的链子，粗细也差不多——拴住我的左腿，再用 36 个挂锁固定住。古庙正对着大路的一端，距离 20 英尺的地方有一个大约 5 英尺高的炮塔，皇帝和大臣随从们登上了炮台一睹我的形象。这都是后来别人告诉我的，因为当时我是看不见他们的。据估计当时有 10 万个当地居民万人空巷赶来参观。尽管有护卫队看守，但我敢说至少有 1 万个小人好几次顺着梯子爬到了我身上。于是皇帝马上宣布禁止此行为，违者将以死论处。等工匠确定锁链不会被我挣脱开后，他们便砍断了所有捆着我的绳索。我站起身来，情绪从未有过的低落。但这些小人看到我站起来走动，以及听

of the town upon the same errand; and in spite of my guards, I believe there could not be fewer than ten thousand, at several times, who mounted my body by the help of ladders. But a proclamation was soon issued to forbid it upon pain of death. When the workmen found it was impossible for me to break loose, they cut all the strings that bound me; whereupon I rose up with as melancholy a disposition as ever I had in my life. But the noise and astonishment of the people at seeing me rise and walk are not to be expressed. The chains that held my left leg were about two yards long, and gave me not only the liberty of walking backwards and forwards in a semicircle, but being fixed within four inches of the gate, allowed me to creep in, and lie at my full length in the temple.

到这些动作发生的声音时，惊讶之情溢于言表。拴住我左腿的铁链差不多有两码长，这样我不仅能够在这个距离半径内自由走动，而且因为铁链固定的地方离大门不到4英寸，我还能爬进大门，伸直身子躺在庙里。

CHAPTER 2

第二章

The Emperor of Lilliput, attended by several of the Nobility, comes to see the Author in his Confinement. The Emperor's Person and Habit described. Learned Men appointed to teach the Author their Language. He gains Favour by his mild Disposition. His Pockets are searched, and his Sword and Pistols taken from him.

利利普特国的皇帝在许多大臣的陪同下来到监禁处看望作者。对皇帝外貌和性格的描写。当地学者奉命向作者教授他们的语言。作者因性格温和而大受喜爱。衣袋被搜查，剑和手枪被没收。

When I found myself on my foot, I looked about me, and must confess I never beheld a more entertaining prospect. The country round appeared like a continued garden, and the enclosed fields, which were generally forty foot square, resembled so many beds of flowers. These fields were intermingled with woods of half a stang, and the tallest trees, as I could judge, appeared to be seven foot high. I viewed the town on my left hand, which looked like the painted scene of a city in a theatre.

我站起身来环顾四周，我得说我从没看过如此令人愉悦的景色。田野就像无尽的花园，每块田地都有差不多 40 平方英尺，就像一个个花坛。田地里点缀着树林，树林差不多有 1/8 英亩。据我估计，这里最高的树大概有 4 英尺高。我向镇子的左边放眼望去，景色像极了城里戏院里的油画布景。

I had been for some hours extremely pressed by the necessities of nature; which was no wonder, it being almost two days since I had last disburthened myself. I was under great difficulties between urgency and shame. The best expedient I could

几个小时以来，我一直很难受地憋着大便，这也不足为奇，我差不多已经两天没有大便了。我又急又羞。我所能想到的权宜之计就是爬进庙里，而我也这么做了。我关上大门，一直爬到铁链扯不动的位

think on, was to creep into my house, which I accordingly did; and shutting the gate after me, I went as far as the length of my chain would suffer, and discharged my body of that uneasy load. But this was the only time I was ever guilty of so uncleanly an action; for which I cannot but hope the candid reader will give some allowance, after he hath maturely and impartially considered my case, and the distress I was in. From this time my constant practice was, as soon as I rose, to perform that business in open air, at the full extent of my chain, and due care was taken every morning before company came, that the offensive matter should be carried off in wheelbarrows, by two servants appointed for that purpose. I would not have dwelt so long upon a circumstance to the world; which I am told some of my maligners have been pleased, upon this and other occasions, to call in question.

置，排出了这些让我焦躁不安的负担。这种不卫生的事情我只做过这一次，我只希望公正的读者能在充分而公平地考虑我当时的情况和忍受的痛苦后对我宽宏大量些。从那以后我都会在起床后，有人来之前跑到铁链所允许的最远的户外解手。而排出的粪便也要有人用手推车运走，于是他们为此派来了两个仆人。我没办法住在不干净的环境里，但有些人就愿意诽谤中伤我，总是就此问题表示质疑。

When this adventure was at an end, I came back out of my house, having occasion for fresh air. The emperor was already descended from the tower, and advancing on horseback towards me, which had like to have cost him dear; for the beast, though very well trained, yet wholly unused to such a sight, which appeared as if a mountain moved before him, reared up on his hinder foot: But that prince, who is an excellent horseman, kept

方便完后我就来到房子外面，好呼吸些新鲜空气。皇帝已经从塔上下来了，骑在马背上朝我走了过来，为此付出的代价也不小——这匹马虽然受过良好训练，但看到我像一座山那样在它眼前移动，便受到惊吓，直起后腿暴跳了起来。但这位皇帝也是个出色的骑手，一直稳住没掉下来，直到他的仆人跑过去拉住了缰绳皇帝才下了马。下马后皇帝便围着我边走边惊羡地打

his seat, till his attendants ran in, and held the bridle, while his majesty had time to dismount. When he alighted, he surveyed me round with great admiration, but kept without the length of my chain. He ordered his cooks and butlers, who were already prepared, to give me victuals and drink, which they pushed forward in a sort of vehicles upon wheels untill I could reach them. I took these vehicles, and soon emptied them all; twenty of them were filled with meat? And ten with liquor each of the former afforded me two or three good mouthfuls, and I emptied the liquor of ten vessel, which was contained in earthen vials, into one vehicle, drinking it off at a draught, and so I did with the rest. The empress, and young princes of the blood, of both sexes, attended by many ladies, sat at some distance in their chairs; but upon the accident that happened to the emperor's horse, they alighted, and came near his person, which I am now going to describe. He is taller, by almost the breadth of my nail, than any of his court, which alone is enough to strike an awe into the beholders. His features are strong and masculine, with an *Austrian* lip and arched nose, his complexion olive, his countenance erect, his body and limbs well proportioned, all his motions graceful, and his deportment majestic. He was then past his prime, being

量我，但还是保持着铁链长度以外的距离。御厨和仆役长早已奉命为我准备好了酒和肉，皇帝命令下人用小车将这些食物送到我手能够到的地方。我拿起这些小车，很快就将里面的食物吃了个精光。其中20辆小车装满了肉，10辆装着酒，我两三口就能吃完一辆车上的肉，小车上的酒也每10桶合倒在一个容器里一口喝光，就这样我喝光吃光了所有酒肉。皇后和皇家子嗣们，不论男女都在很多侍女的陪同下远远地坐在马车上，但看到皇帝的坐骑受惊后他们就都下了马车，走到皇帝身边。现在我就来描述一下皇帝的形象。他个头比他的随从们要高出我一个指甲那么长，这样的优势足以让人肃然起敬。他身材强壮，很有阳刚之气，长着酷像奥地利人的嘴唇和拱形鼻，有着橄榄色的皮肤，五官立体坚毅，身材比例极佳，他的一举一动都有着皇家的优雅与庄严。他已经过了风华正茂的年纪，现年28岁过9个月，在位执政已7年，国家正值太平盛世，战无不胜。为了更能便于瞻仰皇帝的容貌，我就侧身躺了下来，这样我的脸就和皇帝平行了起来，但他站在离我3码远的地方。不过后来我也曾多次将他托在手中，也有了更细致入微的观察。他的穿着简单朴素，风格既像亚洲又像欧洲；他头上戴着一顶金头盔，上面

twenty-eight years and three quarters old, of which he had reigned about seven, in great felicity, and generally victorious. For the better convenience of beholding him, I lay on my side, so that my face was parallel to his, and he stood but three yards off: However, I have had him since many times in my hand, and therefore cannot be deceived in the description. His dress was very plain and simple, and the fashion of it between the *Asiatic* and the *European*; but he had on his head a light helmet of gold, adorned with jewels, and a plume an the crest. He held his sword drawn in his hand, to defend himself, if I should happen to break loose; it was almost three inches long, the hilt and scabbard were gold enriched with diamonds. His voice was shrill, but very clear and articulate, and I could distinctly hear it when I stood up. The ladies and courtiers were all most magnificently clad, so that the spot they stood upon seemed to resemble a petticoat spread on the ground, embroidered with figures of gold and silver. His imperial majesty spoke often to me, and I returned answers, but neither of us could understand a syllable. There were several of his priests and lawyers present (as I conjectured by their habits) who were commanded to address themselves to me, and I spoke to them in as many languages as I had the least smattering of, which

装饰着珠宝，顶端还插着一根羽毛。他手中握着已经出鞘的宝剑，以备在我挣脱开束缚时保护自己。这把剑有3英寸长，剑柄和剑鞘都镶有宝石。皇帝的声音尖锐而清晰，就算我站起身来也依然能听得清。贵妇和朝臣们衣着都非常华丽光鲜，所以他们所站的地方仿佛一条有着金色银色刺绣图案的裙子铺在地上。皇帝时不时地跟我说话，我也会作出回答，但我们俩都不知道对方在讲些什么。在场的还有他的牧师和律师们（我通过他们的行为作出的猜测），他们奉命向我讲话，我把但凡我有点一知半解的语言都用了一遍，什么高地德语，低地德语，拉丁语，法语，西班牙语，意大利语，我都试了，但他们还是一种也听不懂。两个小时后他们就离开了，只留下一支强大的护卫队来阻止有人上前无礼或乌合之众的预谋，这些小人都耐不住性子壮着胆尽可能近地向我围过来，其中一些还很冒失无礼地在我挨着大门坐下时向我射箭。其中一支箭还差一点点就刺到我的左眼。于是护卫队的上校下令逮住了这些危险分子中的6个头目，决定对他们最好的惩罚就是把他们捆起来送到我手里，士兵们就用长矛无尖的一端把他们赶到了我能够得到的地方。我把他们全都放在右手上，将其中5个放进了大衣口袋，

were *High* and *Low Dutch*, *Latin, French, Spanish, Italian,* and *Lingua Franca*; but all to no purpose. After about two hours the court retired, and I was left with a strong guard, to prevent the impertinence, and probably the malice of the rabble, who were very impatient to crowd about me as near as they durst, and some of them had the impudence to shoot their arrows at me as I sat on the ground by the door of my house, whereof one very narrowly missed my left eye. But the colonel ordered six of the ring leaders to be seized, and thought no punishment so proper as to deliver them bound into my hands, which some of his soldiers accordingly did, pushing them forwards with the butt-ends of their pikes into my reach; I took them all on my right hand, put five of them into my coat-pocket, and as to the sixth, I made a countenance as if I would eat him alive. The poor man squalled terribly, and the colonel and his officers were in much pain, especially when they saw me take out my penknife: but I soon put them out of fear; for, looking mildly, and immediately cutting the strings he was bound with, I set him gently on the ground, and away he ran; I treated the rest in the same manner, taking them one by one out of my pocket, and I observed both the soldiers and people were highly obliged at this mark of my

对着第六个扮出一副要活活把他吃掉的样子。这个可怜的小人声嘶力竭地哭喊着，上校和官兵们也吓得不轻，尤其当他们看到我拿出了我的小刀后更是惶恐万分，但我马上打消了他们的恐惧——我温和地看着这个小人，一下子割断了捆着他的绳索，轻轻将他放到地上，一着陆他就跑开了。对剩下的 5 个小人我也是这样。我把他们一个个从口袋里拿了出来，看到官兵和小人们都很感激我的仁慈，这后来也为我在朝中获得认可起到了很大作用。

clemency, which was represented very much to my advantage at court.

Towards night I got with some difficulty into my house, where I lay on the ground, and continued to do so about a fortnight; during which time the emperor gave orders to have a bed prepared for me. Six hundred beds of the common measure were brought in carriages, and worked up in my house; an hundred and fifty of their beds sewn together made up the breadth and length, and these were four double, which however kept me but very indifferently from the hardness of the floor, that was of smooth stone. By the same computation they provided me with sheets, blankets, and coverlets, tolerable enough for one who had been so long inured to hardships as I.

到了晚上，我好不容易才爬进屋，躺在地上。就这样过了两个星期，在这期间，工匠们奉皇上旨意忙着给我制造床铺。他们用车运来了600张床，在我的屋子里拼装了起来，照着床的尺寸把150条褥子缝到一起，这样铺了4层，但对我来说这和硬邦邦的地面也没什么区别。他们又照同样的尺寸给我缝制了床单，毯子和被单，对于我这样一个吃惯了苦的人这些都是可以将就的。

As the news of my arrival spread through the kingdom, it brought prodigious numbers of rich, idle, and curious people to see me; so that the villages were almost emptied, and great neglect of tillage and household affairs must have ensued, if his imperial majesty had not provided by several proclamations and orders of state against this inconvenience. He directed that those, who had already beheld me, should return home, and not presume to come within fifty yards of my house without license from court; whereby the secretaries of

我到来的消息传遍了整个王国，于是就有数不尽终日无所事事的达官贵人好奇地前来一睹我的容貌。各个村落的人也都全体出动，要不是皇帝向全国颁布了相关法令，农活和家务准会被耽误。他还命令那些已经看到我的人赶紧打道回府，我的房子50码以内不准近前，除非持有朝廷批准的许可证。于是朝廷也因此捞到了一大笔税款。

state got considerable fees.

In the mean time, the emperor held frequent councils to debate what course should be taken with me; and I was afterwards assured by a particular friend, a person of great quality, who was looked upon to be as much in the secret as any, that the court was under many difficulties concerning me. They apprehended my breaking loose, that my diet would be very expensive, and might cause a famine. Sometimes they determined to starve me, or at least to shoot me in the face and hands with poisoned arrows, which would soon dispatch me: but again they considered, that the stench of so large a carcase might produce a plague in the metropolis, and probably spread through the whole kingdom. In the midst of these consultations, several officers of the army went to the door of the great council-chamber; and two of them being admitted, gave an account of my behavior to the six criminals above-mentioned, which made so favourable an impression in the breast of his majesty and the whole board in my behalf, that an imperial commission was issued out, obliging all the villages nine hundred yards round the city, to deliver in every morning six beeves, forty sheep, and other victuals for my sustenance; together with a proportionable quantity of bread, and

但同时，皇帝也定期召开议会讨论该如何处置我。后来我一个地位显赫的特别朋友向我证实朝廷的确因为我而伤透了脑筋，他也被视为参与了这次机密事件。他们担心我会挣开铁链，而且我的饮食也可能引发饥荒。他们还曾决定将我饿死，或是用毒箭射死，但他们又害怕庞大的尸体会让都城产生瘟疫，可能还会蔓延到国家的其他地方。就在朝廷讨论商议的时候，几位官兵来到会议室大门前，其中两个人叙述了我对之前提到的那6个罪犯的行为，于是皇帝和满朝官员对我一下子改观，立刻颁布了法令，命令都城周边900码内的村庄每天早晨都要给我送来6头牛，40头羊和其他食物，还要送来相应数量的面包，酒和其他饮料，所需费用由国库承担。皇帝平时靠自己领地的收入维持生活，几乎不向人民征税，除非赶上重大事件。如果遇到战乱，人们就要随他出征，费用自己掏。皇帝为我雇了600个用人，付给他们伙食费以维持生计，下令让他们在我大门两侧驻扎帐篷以方便服侍我。他还吩咐300个裁缝为我缝制了一套本国样式的衣服，6个知识最渊博的学者教我他们的语言。最后，皇帝还下令定期让所有御马和战马在我面前操练，好让它们熟悉我。所有命令都按部就班

wine, and other liquors: for the due payment of which, his majesty gave assignments upon his treasury. For this prince lives chiefly upon his own demesnes, seldom except upon great occasions, raising any subsidies upon his subjects, who are bound to attend him in his wars at their own expense. An establishment was also made of six hundred persons to be my domestics, who had board-wages allowed for their maintenance, and tents built for them very conveniently on each side of my door. It was likewise ordered, that three hundred tailors should make me a suit of clothes after the fashion of the country: that six of his majesty's greatest scholars should be employed to instruct me in their language: and, lastly, that the emperor's horses, and those of the nobility, and troops of guards should be frequently exercised in my sight, to accustom themselves to me. All these orders were duly put in execution, and in about three weeks I made a great progress in learning their language; during which time, the emperor frequently honoured me with his visits, and was pleased to assist my masters in teaching me. We began already to converse together in some sort; and the first words I learnt were to express my desire that he would please give me my liberty, which I every day repeated on my knees. His

地执行了起来。3 个星期后，我的语言进步了许多，皇帝也时常会在侍者的陪同下来看望我，还会饶有兴致地和学者们一起教我语言。我们已经可以有一些交流了，我所学说的第一句话就是向皇帝表达我希望重获自由，我每天都跪在地上重复着这个渴求。皇帝的回答就我所能听懂的内容是，这还需要时间，得等国会商议后才能做决定，首先我得“路莫斯，莱尔敏，佩索，戴斯马尔，隆，安姆坡所”，意思是我要发誓与他和他的臣民和睦相处。但他们都对我很好，皇帝还让我耐心一些，行为谨慎些，好博得他和他的臣民的好感。他还希望如果他派官员来给我搜身我不要介意，因为我身上可能会带着武器，而就我这样一个庞然大物来说，我的随身物件对他们来说也肯定很具危险性。我边比画边对皇帝说我可以满足他的要求，我已经做好了准备脱下衣服，翻出口袋让他检查。他回答说，根据国家的法令，需要由两个军官来为我搜身，还说他知道如果我不同意配合的话，这个任务就不可能完成，但他认为我为人宽厚公正，放心把他的手下交给我，而从我身上搜出的东西在我离开王国的时候也会原样奉还，或按我要求的价格如数赔偿。我用手托起两位军官，先把他们放进大衣口袋，然后再依次放进其他所有的

answer, as I could apprehend it, was, that this must be a work of time, not to be thought on without the advice of his council, and that first I must *lumos kelmin pesso desmar lon emposo*; that is, swear a peace with him and his kingdom. However, that I should be used with all kindness, and he advised me to acquire by my patience, and discreet behavior, the good opinion of himself and his subjects. He desired I would not take it ill, if he gave orders to certain proper officers to search me; for probably I might carry about me several weapons, which must needs be dangerous things, if they answered the bulk of so prodigious a person. I said, his majesty should be satisfied, for I was ready to strip myself and turn up my pockets before him. This I delivered part in words, and part in signs. He replied, that by the laws of the kingdom I must be searched by two of his officers; that he knew this could not be done without my consent and assistance; that he had so good an opinion of my generosity and justice, as to trust their persons in my hands; that whatever they took from me should be returned when I left the country, or paid for at the rate which I should set upon them. I took up the two officers in my hands, put them first into my coat-pockets, and then into every other pocket about me, except my

口袋里，只有裤子上两个表袋和一个秘密口袋我认为没有检查的必要，因为里面只是放着些只对我自己有用的东西。一个表袋里放着一块银表，另一个里面有一个装着一小块金子的布袋。两位军官拿走了我的钢笔，墨水和纸张，然后做了详细记录。等他们工作完成后便请我把他们放下去，他们要将这些物品呈给皇帝。后来我将这份详细记录逐字译成了英语，内容如下：

two fobs, and another secret pocket I had no mind should be searched, wherein I had some little necessaries that were of no consequence to any but myself. In one of my fobs there was a silver watch, and in the other a small quantity of gold in a purse. These gentlemen, having pen, ink, and paper about them, made an exact inventory of everything they saw; and when they had done, desired I would set them down, that they might deliver it to the emperor. This inventory I afterwards translated into *English*, and is word for word as follows.

IMPRIMIS, In the right coat-pocket of the *great man-mountain* (for so I interpret the words *quinbus flestrin*) after the strictest search, we found only one great piece of coarse cloth, large enough to be a foot-cloth for your majesty's chief room of state. In the left pocket we saw a huge silver chest, with a cover of the same metal, which we the searchers were not able to lift. We desired it should be opened, and one of us stepping into it, found himself up to the mid leg in a sort of dust, some part whereof flying up to our faces, set us both a sneezing for several times together. In his right waistcoat-pocket, we found a prodigious number of white thin substances, folded one over another, about the bigness of

我们对"巨人山"(这是我对"昆布斯·弗莱斯特润"一词的翻译)进行了严格的搜查，在他的大衣右口袋里只找到了一大块粗布，大小足能做陛下大殿的地毯。在左边口袋里我们找到一个巨大的银质箱子，盖子也是银质的。我们抬不动，便想打开它，我们其中一个走了进去，结果里面的尘埃没过了膝盖，尘埃扑面而来，让我们俩打了好几个喷嚏。在他右边的背心口袋里，我们找到了一大堆白色的东西，一层层紧紧地用粗缆绳捆在一起，足有3个人那个大，上面还画着黑色的图形。臣不才，猜想那就是他们的文字，他们的每个字母都差不多有我们的手掌大小。在左边的口袋里我们发现了一个装置，它

three men, tied with a strong cable, and marked with black figures; which we humbly conceive to be writings, every letter almost half as large as the palm of our hands. In the left, there was a sort of engine, from the back of which were extended twenty long poles, resembling the palisado's before your majesty's court; wherewith we conjecture the *man-mountain* combs his head, for we did not always trouble him with questions, because we found it a great difficulty to make him understand us. In the large pocket on the right side of his middle cover (so I translate the word *ranfu-lo*, by which they meant my breeches) we saw a hollow pillar of iron, about the length of a man, fastened to a strong piece of timber, larger than the pillar; and upon one side of the pillar were huge pieces of iron sticking out, cut into strange figures, which we know not what to make of. In the left pocket, another engine of the same kind. In the smaller pocket on the right side, were several round flat pieces of white and red metal, of different bulk; some of the white, which seemed to be silver, were so large and heavy, that my comrade and I could hardly lift them. In the left pocket were two black pillars irregularly shaped: we could not without difficulty, reach the top of them as we stood at the bottom of his pocket. One of them was covered, and

的背面伸出 20 根柱子，就像陛下皇宫外的栅栏，我们猜想那是巨人山用来梳头发的东西。我们不能老拿这些问题去麻烦他，因为我们发现他不太能听懂我们的话。在中衣（这是我对“兰福一罗”一词的翻译，他们指的是我的马裤）右侧的大口袋里，我们找到一个铁质的空柱子，差不多有一人高，紧紧系在一块比柱子还要高大的木头上，柱子的一边上面还伸出很多大铁片，奇形怪状的，我们不知道是做什么用的。左边的口袋里也有个一样的装置。右边的小口袋里有几个白色或红色的扁平圆形金属片，每个大小都不一样，有些白色的，像是银子做的，又大又沉，我俩都几乎抬不动。在左边口袋里有两个形状不规则的黑色柱状物，由于我们站在口袋底部，所以费了很大劲才爬到柱顶。其中一个柱顶有东西盖着，像是一体的，另一个柱子的顶端有一个白色的圆形装置，差不多有我们两个脑袋大。每个柱子上都镶着巨大的金属片，我们担心这是危险装置，所以命令他打开，他便将这两个装置从外壳里拿了出来，告诉我们说在他的国家这两个柱状物一个用来刮胡子，一个用来切肉。还有两个口袋是我们不能进入的，他将这两个口袋称作表袋，右边表袋外悬挂着一条很粗的银链子，底部拴着一个很精致的装置。我们让

seemed all of a piece: but at the upper end of the other, there appeared a white round substance, about twice the bigness of our heads. Within each of these was enclosed a prodigious plate of steel; which, by our orders, we obliged him to show us, because we apprehended they might be dangerous engines. He took them out of their cases, and told us, that in his own country his practice was to shave his beard with one of these, and to cut his meat with the other. There were two pockets which we could not enter: these he called his fobs. Out of the right fob hung a great silver chain, with a wonderful kind of engine at the bottom. We directed him to draw out whatever was fostened to that chain, which appeared to be a globe, half silver, and half of some transparent metal: for on the transparent side we saw certain strange figures circularly drawn, and thought we could touch them, till we found our fingers stopped by that lucid substance. He put this engine to our ears, which made an incessant noise like that of a water-mill. and we conjecture it is either some unknown animal, or the god that he worships: but we are more inclined to the latter opinion, because he assured us (if we understood him right, for he expressed himself very imperfectly) that he seldom did anything without consulting it. He called it his oracle, and said it pointed out

他把拴在链子上的东西从口袋里抽出来，结果发现那是一个球形的装置，一半是银子做的，一半是某种透明的金属做的。我们在透明的那面看到一圈奇怪的图案，本以为能触到这些图案，结果手指却被这些透明的物质挡住了。他将这个装置拿到我们耳边，我们听到里面像水车那样不断有声音发出，我们猜想这可能是一种不知名的动物，或者是他崇拜的神明——我们更倾向于后一种猜想，因为他跟我们说（但愿我们正确理解了他的意思，因为他的表达能力实在够戗）他不管干什么几乎都要请教这个东西。他将它叫做“预言”，说他每干一件事它都会为他指明时间。他从左边表袋里拿出了一张几乎有渔网大小的网子，但能够像钱包那样打开关闭，用途也是一样的：我们在里面找到几片厚重的黄色金属，如果是纯金，那绝对价值连城。

the time for every action of his life. From the left fob he took out a net almost large enough for a fisherman, but contrived to open and shut like a purse, and served him for the same use: we found therein several massy pieces of yellow metal, which if they be real gold, must be of immense value.

Having thus, in obedience to your majesty's commands, diligently searched all his pockets, we observed a girdle about his waist made of the hide of some prodigious animal; from which, on the left side, hung a sword of the length of five men; and on the right, a bag or pouch divided into two cells, each cell capable of holding three of your majesty's subjects. In one of these cells were several globes or balls of a most ponderous metal, about the bigness of our heads, and required a strong hand to lift them: the other cell contained a heap of certain black grains, but of no great bulk or weight, for we could hold above fifty of them in the palms of our hands.

This is an exact inventory of what we found about the body of the *man-mountain*, who used us with great civility, and due respect to your majesty's commission. Signed and sealed, on the fourth day of the eighty-ninth moon of your majesty's auspicious reign.

Clefrin Freloc, Marsi Freloc.

遵照陛下的旨意，我们严格地搜查了他所有的口袋，我们还发现他腰上系着一条兽皮制成的腰带，在腰带的左侧，挂着一条有 5 个人长的剑，右侧挂着一个包，这个包隔有两部分，每个隔间里能站 3 个陛下的臣民；其中一个隔间里放着几个很有重量的球状物，大约有我们的脑袋那么大，力气很大的人才能举得起来；另一个隔间堆着些黑色的谷物，但不多也不沉，我们双手差不多能捧起 50 粒。

以上就是我们从巨人山身上搜出物品的详细清单。巨人山对待我们态度极为礼貌，对陛下的命令也表现出了应有的尊敬。签名盖章。吾皇登基第八十九月零四天。

克莱夫林·弗莱洛克，马尔

When this inventory was read over to the emperor, he directed me, although in very gentle terms, to deliver up the several particulars. He first called for my scimitar, which I took out, scabbard and all. In the meantime he ordered three thousand of his choicest troops (who then attended him) to surround me at a distance, with their bows and arrows just ready to discharge: but I did not observe it, for my eyes were wholly fixed upon his majesty. He then desired me to draw my scimitar, which, although it had got some rust by the sea-water, was in most parts exceeding bright. I did so, and immediately all the troops gave a shout between terror and surprise; for the sun shone clear, and the reflection dazzled their eyes as I waved the scimitar to and fro in my hand. His majesty, who is a most magnanimous prince, was less daunted than I could expect; he ordered me to return it into the scabbard, and cast it on the ground as gently as I could, about six foot from the end of my chain. The next thing he demanded was one of the hollow iron pillars, by which he meant my pocket-pistols. I drew it out, and at his desire, as well as I could, expressed to him the use of it; and charging it only with powder, which, by the closeness of my pouch happened to escape wetting in the

斯·弗莱洛克

详细清单宣读完毕后，皇帝虽言辞婉转，但还是命令我将这些物件交出来。他先命令我交出我的短弯刀，我就连同刀鞘一起取了下来。就在我取刀的同时，皇帝命令3000御前卫士将他层层围起，他们就立即上前，手里握着弓箭随时准备向我发射，但我并没注意到这些，眼睛只顾着看着皇帝了。接着，皇帝要求我将刀拔出。虽然在海水里泡得有些生锈，但整体看来刀面还是熠熠生辉的。我一拔出刀，所有的御前侍卫又惊又怕，立刻尖叫了起来。阳光明晃晃地照在刀面上，我拿着刀前后挥舞了起来，折射出的耀眼光芒让他们眼花缭乱。皇帝果真是个很有胆识的人，比我想象的要镇定得多。他命令我将刀入鞘，然后轻轻放到离拴着我铁链的那端6英尺的地上。然后他又命令我拿出其中一个空的铁柱子，他指的是我的小手枪。我遵命拿了出来，并向他解释了这个东西的用途。我把手枪里装上火药（我的火药袋没有被海水浸湿，所有谨慎的水手都会想办法避免这样糟糕的情况发生），提醒皇帝不要受惊后朝空中放了一枪。这一枪把大家吓得够呛，比短弯刀带来的惊慌更甚。几百个人摔倒在地，就好像被枪击中毙命一般。虽然皇帝没有摔倒，但他也花了好长时间才回过神

sea (an inconvenience against which all prudent mariners take special care to provide), I first cautioned the emperor not to be afraid, and then I let it off in the air. The astonishment here was much greater than at the sight of my scimitar. Hundreds fell down as if they had been struck dead; and even the emperor, although he stood his ground, could not recover himself in some time. I delivered up both my pistols in the same manner, as I had done my scimitar, and then my pouch of powder and bullets; begging him that the former might be kept from fire, for it would kindle with the smallest spark, and blow up his imperial palace into the air. I likewise delivered up my watch, which the emperor was very curious to see, and commanded two of his tallest yeomen of the guards to bear it on a pole upon their shoulders, as draymen in *England* do a barrel of ale. He was amazed at the continual noise it made, and the motion of the minute-hand, which he could easily discern; for their sight is much more acute than ours: and asked the opinions of his learned men about it, which were various and remote, as the reader may well imagine without my repeating; although indeed I could not very perfectly understand them. I then gave up my silver and copper money, my purse with nine large pieces of gold, and some smaller

来。我把我的两把手枪和火药子弹像上缴短弯刀那样放到了地上。我请求皇帝千万要把火药放到远离火源的地方，因为一个小火花就能将其引爆，把他的宫殿炸飞。接着我又上缴了我的手表。皇帝对手表好奇得不得了，命令侍卫队中最高的两个人用杆子扛在肩上，就像英国的运货车夫扛酒桶那样。皇帝对手表不断发出的声响惊讶不已，也很容易就看清了分针是在移动的，因为他们的眼力比我们的要更加敏锐些。他询问他的大学士们有何看法，尽管我听不太懂他们的话，但不用我说读者也能想象得出他们的意见有多五花八门，分歧有多大。然后我又上缴了银币，铜币，装着9个大金块和几小块金子的钱包，小刀，剃刀，梳子，银烟盒，手帕和日记本。皇帝下令将我的短弯刀、手枪和火药袋存放在皇家仓库里，剩下的则都还给了我。

ones; my knife and razor, my comb and silver snuff-box, my handkerchief and journal book. My scimitar, pistols, and pouch, were conveyed in carriages to his majesty's stores; but the rest of my goods were returned me.

I had, as I before observed, one private pocket, which escaped their search, wherein there was a pair of spectacles (which I sometimes use for the weakness of my eyes) a pocket perspective, and several other little conveniences; which being of no consequence to the emperor, I did not think myself bound in honour to discover, and I apprehended they might be lost or spoiled if I ventured them out of my possession.

之前我提到过我还有一个隐蔽的口袋，这个口袋逃过了这次搜查，里面放着一副眼镜（眼睛看不清的时候我会用到它），一个袖珍望远镜和一些别的小玩意儿。这些对皇帝来说都是无足轻重的东西，我也就觉得没必要拿出来接受检查，而且我估计如果我上缴了这些东西，那它们很可能被遗失或弄坏。

CHAPTER 3

第三章

The Author diverts the Emperor and his Nobility of both Sexes in a very uncommon Manner. The Diversions of the Court of LILLIPUT described. The Author has his Liberty granted him upon certain Conditions.

作者以一种不同寻常的方式为皇帝与贵族们表演了节目。对利利普特国朝中的娱乐活动进行了描述。在接受了一些条件后作者重获自由。

My gentleness and good behaviour had gained so far on the emperor and his court, and indeed upon the army and people in general, that I began to conceive hopes of getting my liberty in a short time. I took all possible methods to cultivate this favourable disposition. The natives came by degrees to be less apprehensive of any danger from me. I would sometimes lie down, and let five or six of them dance on my hand. and at last the boys and girls would venture to come and play at hide and seek in my hair. I had now made a good progress in understanding and speaking their language. The emperor had a mind one day to entertain me with several of the country shows, wherein they exceed all nations I have known, both of dexterity and magnificence. I was diverted with none so much as that of the rope-dancers, performed upon a slender

由于我品性温顺举止得体，我渐渐获得了皇帝，朝廷，以及军民的好感，于是我开始寄希望于在短时间内重获自由。我想尽一切办法表现出我温和的性情，当地人也渐渐不把我视为危险人物了。我有时会躺下来，让五六个小人在我手上跳舞，再后来男孩女孩们都会壮起胆子在我的头发里玩捉迷藏。这时我在语言方面已经进步了许多，能听懂他们的话也能表达出自己的意见。一天皇帝想请我欣赏几场他们国家的演出，他们的表演比我所知道的所有国家的表演都要精彩，演员们动作灵活，布景华丽宏伟。我最喜欢的表演非绳上舞蹈莫属了，这个节目由演员在一根白色细绳上表演，绳子大约两英尺长，离地 12 英寸。这么一来让我更加渴望自由了，请读者耐心往下看。

white thread, extended about two foot, and twelve inches from the ground. Upon which I shall desire liberty, with the reader's patience, to enlarge a little.

This diversion is only practised by those persons who are candidates for great employments and high favour, at court. They are trained in this art from their youth, and are not always of noble birth, or liberal education. When a great office is vacant either by death or disgrace (which often happens) five or six of those candidates petition the emperor to entertain his majesty and the court, with a dance on the rope, and whoever jumps the highest without falling, succeeds in the office. Very often the chief ministers themselves are commanded to show their skill, and to convince the emperor that they have not lost their faculty. Flimnap, the treasurer, is allowed to cut a caper on the strait rope, at least an inch higher than any other lord in the whole empire. I have seen him do the summerset several times together upon a trencher fixed on the rope, which is no thicker than a common packthread in England. My friend Reldresal, principal secretary for private affairs, is, in my opinion, if I am not partial, the second after the treasurer; the rest of the great officers are much upon a par.

These diversions are often attended

这些娱乐表演的演员全部是朝中高层的候选人。他们从小就学习这类表演，他们不一定出身名门，也不一定受过良好的教育。当担任重要职务的人因去世或失宠（这种情况时有发生）而空缺时，就会有五六个候选人请求皇帝允许他们为皇帝和大臣们表演绳上舞蹈，跳得最高又不会从绳子上掉下来的人就会赢得该职位。皇帝还会不时要求朝中各位重臣当众展示他们的技巧，证明他们的技艺没有生疏。大家一致认为，财务大臣福利姆奈普能在比别的朝中大臣的绳子高出一英寸的绳子上舞蹈。我曾见过他在一个固定在绳子上的木盘上一口气翻好几个跟斗，那根绳子比英国的麻绳粗不到哪儿去。如果我没有有失公允，那在我看来，我的朋友，内务大臣瑞尔德瑞萨尔的水平仅次于那个财务大臣。其他大臣的水平彼此间相差不大。

这些娱乐活动过程中常常会

with fatal accidents, whereof great numbers are on record. I myself have seen two or three candidates break a limb. But the danger is much greater when the ministers themselves are commanded to show their dexterity; for by contending to excel themselves and their fellows, they strain so far, that there is hardly one of them who hath not received a fall, and some of them two or three. I was assured that a year or two before my arrival, Flimnap would have infallibly broke his neck, if one of the king's cushions, that accidentally lay on the ground, had not weakened the force of his fall.

发生死亡事故，已经有很多被记录在案了。我就亲眼见过有两三个候选人摔断了胳膊。在任部长们被要求展示他们的技艺时是最为危险的时候，因为他们要与同僚竞争，想要优胜于他人，所以他们会把绳子拉得很紧，几乎每个人都会摔下来一次，有些人还会摔上两三次。他们告诉我说在我来到这里的一两年前，福利姆奈普就曾从绳上摔下来过，要不是皇帝的垫子碰巧放在地上在他落地时起到了缓冲作用，他准会摔断自己的脖子。

There is likewise another diversion, which is only shown before the emperor and empress, and first minister, upon particular occasions. The emperor lays on the table three fine silken threads of six inches long. one is blue, the other red, and the third green. These threads are proposed as prizes for those persons whom the emperor hath a mind to distinguish by a peculiar mark of his favour. The ceremony is performed in his majesty's great chamber of state, where the candidates are to undergo a trial of dexterity very different from the former, and such as I have not observed the least resemblance of in any other country of the old or the new world.

还有另一个娱乐项目，只在特定场合为皇帝，皇后和国务大臣表演。皇帝会在桌子上放上 3 根长为 6 英寸，分别为蓝，红，绿色的精美丝线。这 3 根丝线作为表演者的奖品分别代表了皇帝对各表演者不同的恩宠。这个仪式会在陛下的皇宫大殿内举行，候选人要接受一个灵巧度的考验，这个考验的方式同之前的大为不同，也是就我所知从古到今各国都不曾有过的。

The emperor holds a stick in his hands,

皇帝会用手举着一根手杖，手

both ends parallel to the horizon, while the candidates advancing one by one, sometimes leap over the stick, sometimes creep under it backwards and forwards several times, according as the stick is advanced or depressed. Sometimes the emperor holds one end of the stick, and his first minister the other; sometimes the minister has it entirely to himself. Whoever performs his part with most agility, and holds out the longest in leaping and creeping, is rewarded with the blue colored silk; the red is given to the next, and the green to the third, which they all wear girt twice round about the middle; and you see few great persons about this court, who are not adorned with one of these girdles.

杖与地面保持平行，候选人依次走上前来，根据手杖升高或降低来回从上面跳过或从下面爬过。有时会由皇帝拿着手杖的一端，国务大臣拿着另一端，有时则是国务大臣全权负责。动作最灵活，跳上爬下坚持时间最长的人奖励蓝丝线；第二名奖励红丝线，第三名绿丝线。他们所有人都把丝线在腰上缠上两圈，几乎所有朝中大臣都是这副打扮。

The horses of the army, and those of the royal stables, having been daily led before me, were no longer shy, but would come up to my very foot without starting. The riders would leap them over my hand as I held it on the ground and one of the emperor's huntsmen, upon a large courser, took my foot, shoe and all; which was indeed a prodigious leap.

战马和皇家御马每天都会被牵到我面前训练，所以它们不再害怕了，甚至还会泰然地跑到我脚边。当我把手放到地上时骑手们就会策马从我手上跳过去，有一位皇家猎手还能驾着一匹骏马从我的鞋子上一跃而过，实在让人赞叹不已。

I had the good fortune to divert the emperor one day after a very extraordinary manner. I desired he would order several sticks of two foot high, and the thickness of an ordinary cane, to be brought me; whereupon his majesty

有一天我有幸为皇帝表演了一个很特别的节目以资消遣。我请求皇帝下令为我准备几根两英尺高的木棍，一般手杖粗细就可以，皇帝便命令负责树林的官员照我的意思去办。第二天早上6个伐木

commanded the master of his woods to give directions accordingly; and the next morning six woodmen arrived with as many carriages, drawn by eight horses to each. I took nine of these sticks, and fixing them firmly in the ground in a quadrangular figure, two foot and a half square, I took four other sticks, and tied them parallel at each corner, about two foot from the ground; then I fastened my handkerchief to the nine sticks that stood erect, and extended it on all sides till it was as tight as the top of a drum; and the four parallel sticks rising about five inches higher than the handkerchief, served as ledges on each side. When I had finished my work, I desired the emperor to let a troop of his best horse, twenty-four in number, come and exercise upon this plain. His majesty approved of the proposal, and I took them up one by one in my hands, ready mounted and armed, with the proper officers to exercise them. As soon as they got into order, they divided into two parties, performed mock skirmishes, discharged blunt arrows, drew their swords, fled and pursued, attacked and retired, and in short discovered the best military discipline I ever beheld. The parallel sticks secured them and their horses from falling over the stage; and the emperor was so much delighted, that he ordered this entertainment to be repeated

工人便驾着马车把木棍送了来，每辆马车都由 8 匹马拉着。我从中拿了 9 根木棍，将它们牢牢插在地里围成一个四边形，面积为两英尺半平方英尺。我又拿了 4 根木棍离地两英尺平行绑在 4 个角上，然后将我的手帕系在这 9 根竖立的木棍上，各边拉紧直至手帕紧绷得像鼓面那样。最后，我将 4 根平行的木棍抬高到比手帕高出 5 英寸的位置作为各个方向的边缘。我完成了这些工作后就请求皇帝命令他最优秀的 24 匹战马来这个平台上训练。皇帝批准了我的请求后，我便用手将这些套好马鞍、武装完毕的战马和训练人员依次放了上去。他们各就各位后便立即分成两个阵营，发射钝箭，拔出刀剑，或逃跑或追赶，或进攻或退兵地模拟起了小型战斗。简而言之，这是我见过的最出色的军事训练。平行的木棍起到了保护作用，防止了训练人员或战马从台子上摔下的危险。皇帝也兴高采烈，下令重复表演了多日，有一次兴致勃勃地命令人们将他抬起，好指挥军队作战。他甚至还费劲唇舌劝说皇后允许我将她连人带椅举到离台子两码的地方观战，这个位置能让她将演习一览无余。

several days, and once was pleased to be lifted up, and give the word of command; and, with great difficulty, persuaded even the empress herself to let me hold her in her close chair within two yards of the stage, from whence she was able to take a full view of the whole performance.

It was my good fortune that no ill accident happened in these entertainments, only once a fiery horse that belonged to one of the captains pawing with his hoof struck a hole in my handkerchief, and his foot slipping, he overthrew his rider and himself; but I immediately relieved them both, and covering the hole with one hand, I set down the troop with the other, in the same manner as I took them up. The horse that fell was strained in the left shoulder, but the rider got no hurt, and I repaired my handkerchief as well as I could; however I would not trust to the strength of it any more in such dangerous enterprises.

对我来说很幸运的是，在整个演习过程中没有任何人发生事故。只有那么一次，一个队长的战马暴躁起来，用蹄子不停地扒着我的手帕，结果扒出一个洞，害得它自己和它的骑手从手帕上翻滚了下来，但我立即接住了他们俩，用一只手盖住了手帕上的洞，另一只手将军队送下台子。摔下来的战马伤到了左肩，但骑手毫发无伤。我尽量缝补好了手帕，但发生了这样危险的事故后我便不敢再冒险让手帕承受这样的强度了。

About two or three days before I was set at liberty, as I was entertaining the court with these kind of feat, there arrived an express to inform his majesty that some of his subjects riding near the place where I was first taken up, had seen a great black substance lying on the ground, very oddly shaped, extending its edges round as wide as his majesty's bedchamber, and rising up in the middle as high as a man; that it was no living creature, as they at first

就在我重获自由的两三天前，我正向皇帝和大臣们表演刚才的节目的时候，来了一个专使向皇帝报告说他的部下在骑马路过我上岸的地方时在地上发现了一个大大的黑色的东西，形状很奇怪，边是圆形的，整体有陛下的卧房那么大，中间还凸起有一人高。起初他们以为那是一种动物，但看到它在地上一动不动就围着它走了几圈，才确定这不是活物。他们一个踩着

apprehended, for it lay on the grass without motion, and some of them had walked round it several times: that by mounting upon each others shoulders, they had got to the top, which was flat and even, and stamping upon it they found it was hollow within; that they humbly conceived it might be something belonging to the man-mountain, and if his majesty pleased, they would undertake to bring it with only five horses. I presently knew what they meant, and was glad at heart to receive this intelligence. It seems upon my first reaching the shore after our shipwreck, I was in such confusion, that before I came to the place where I went to sleep, my hat which I had fastened with a string to my head while I was rowing, and had stuck on all the time I was swimming, fell off after I came to land; the string, as I conjecture, breaking by some accident which I never observed, but thought my hat had been lost at sea. I entreated his imperial majesty to give orders it might be brought to me as soon as possible, describing to him the use and nature of it: and the next day the waggoners arrived with it, but not in a very good condition; they had bored two holes in the brim, within an inch and a half of the edge, and fastened two hooks in the holes; these hooks were tied by a long cord to the harness, and thus my hat was dragged

一个的肩膀爬到它又扁又平的顶端，在上面用力踩了踩，发现里面是空的，于是他们斗胆猜想这估计是巨人山的东西，如果皇帝愿意的话，他们会派 5 匹马将这个东西运过来。我不一会儿就听明白了他们的意思，也很高兴得知了这个消息。估计是在我们的船翻了以后，我挣扎上岸时意识太过模糊，在走到我睡觉的地方之前把帽子搞丢了，因为在划船的时候我把帽子用绳子系在了脑袋上，在游水时帽子也还一直戴在头上。我估计那根绳子一定是不小心被弄断了，因为我没再找到它，而帽子就遗失在海上了。我恳求皇帝能下令将我的帽子尽快运还给我，我还向他解释了帽子的用途和特性。于是第二天御夫就把我的帽子运送了过来，但运送方式不算太好——他们在离帽檐一英寸半的位置上钻了两个孔，在孔里拴上了两个钩子，钩子上又系着一根长长的绳索，绳索的另一头连着马具，我的帽子就这样在地上拖了半英里。但利利普特国的地面非常光滑平整，因此帽子的损伤比我预期的要轻一些。

along for above half an English mile: but the ground in that country being extremely smooth and level, it received less damage than I expected.

Two days after this adventure, the emperor having ordered that part of his army which quarters in and about his metropolis to be in a readiness, took a fancy of diverting himself in a very singular manner. He desired I would stand like a colossus, with my legs as far asunder as I conveniently could. He then commanded his general (who was an old experienced leader, and a great patron of mine) to draw up the troops in close order, and march them under me, the foot by twenty-four in a breast, and the horse by sixteen, with drums beating, colours flying, and pikes advanced. This body consisted of three thousand foot, and a thousand horse. His Majesty gave orders, upon pain of death, that every soldier in his march should observe the strictest decency, with younger officers from turning up their eyes as they passed under me. And, to confess the truth, my breeches were at that time in so ill a condition, that they afforded some opportunities for laughter and admiration.

I had sent so many memorials and petitions for my liberty, that his majesty at length mentioned the matter first in the cabinet, and then in a full council; where it

发生这件事的两天后，皇帝下令驻扎在京城和京城周边的军队做好研习准备，因为他又想出一个娱乐消遣的奇异点子。他命令我像巨像那样站着，把腿尽最大能力分开，然后命令他的大将军——这位将军是位上了年纪，经验丰富的领导者，也是我的一个大恩人——将部队整编成密集的队形，在我的胯下行军。步兵 24 个人成一排，骑兵 16 个人成一排，要擂战鼓，升战旗，手持长矛向前行进。整个队伍由 3000 步兵和 1000 骑兵组成。皇帝下达命令说，行进中每个士兵都必须遵守最严格的军中礼仪，违者将被处以死刑。但就算这样，还是有几个年轻的军官在经过我胯下时将眼睛向上望了望。我得承认，我的马裤那个时候已经非常破旧了，因此他们向上看的时候都忍不住笑了出来，但也都惊羡不已。

为了重获自由，我向皇帝上书请愿了多次，终于有一天皇帝总算在内阁上提到了这个事情，然后又在全体国务委员会上提及此事。除

was opposed by none, except Skyresh Bolgolam, who was pleased, without any provocation, to be my mortal enemy. But it was carried against him by the whole board, and confirmed by the emperor. That minister was galbet, or admiral of the realm, very much in his master's confidence, and a person well versed in affairs, but of a morose and sour complexion. However, he was at length persuaded to comply; but prevailed that the articles and conditions upon which I should be set free, and to which I must swear, should be drawn up by himself. These articles were brought to me by Skyresh Bolgolam in person, attended by two under-secretaries, and several persons of distinction. After they were read, I was demanded to swear to the performance of them; first in the manner of my own country, and afterwards in the method prescribed by their laws; which was to hold my right foot in my left hand, to place the middle finger of my right hand on the crown of my head, and my thumb on the tip of my right ear.

了斯奇瑞史·博尔格莱姆外没有一人反对。我从未得罪过这个人，但他偏偏就喜欢当我的死对头。但除了他的一票反对以外，国会的其他成员都支持此决定，于是皇帝最终还是决定还我自由。这位大臣的官衔称为“盖尔贝特”，是位海军上将，深得皇帝宠信，精通国家事务，但个性阴郁，面色愠怒。然而他最后还是在大家的劝说下顺从了这一决定，但他还是坚持要我答应一些条款和条件后才能获得自由。这些条款和条件的内容由他亲自起草，而且我必须要照此宣誓。斯奇瑞史·博尔格莱姆在两位副官和几位显赫的人物的陪同下将这些条款亲自送达。他们将条款通读一遍后，命令我重复这些内容。第一遍要用我自己国家的方式宣誓，然后再用他们的法定方式宣誓一遍——用左手抓着右脚，右手中指置于头顶，大拇指置于右耳顶端。

But because the reader may perhaps be curious to have some idea of the style and manner of expression peculiar to that people, as well as to know the articles upon which I recovered my liberty, I have made a translation of the whole instrument word for word, as near as I was able,

读者可能会好奇这里的人特有的表达方式，以及我为了恢复自由所要答应的条件，我便尽力把整个文件的意思尽可能精准地逐字翻译了过来，以供大家过目：

which I here offer to the public.

GOLBASTO MOMAREN EVLAME GURDILO SHEFIN MULLY ULLY GUE, most Mighty Emperor of Lilliput, delight and terror of the universe, whose dominions extend five thousand blustrugs (about twelve miles in circumference) to the extremities of the globe; monarch of all monarchs, taller than the sons of men; whose foot press down to the centre, and whose head strikes against the sun: at whose nod the princes of the earth shake their knees; pleasant as the spring, comfortable as the summer, fruitful as autumn, dreadful as winter. His most sublime majesty proposeth to the man-mountain, lately arrived to our celestial dominions, the following articles, which by a solemn oath he shall be obliged to perform.

First, The man-mountain shall not depart from our dominions, without our license under our great seal.

2d, He shall not presume to come into our metropolis, without our express order; at which time the inhabitants shall have two hours warning to keep within doors.

3d, The said man-mountain shall confine his walks to our principal high roads, and not offer to walk or lie down in a meadow or field of corn.

4th, As he walks the said roads, he shall

高尔巴斯托·默玛仁·伊芙莱姆·高尔帝罗·佘芬·穆力·阿利·古，利利普特国至高无上的君王，举世拥戴敬畏，疆土延绵5000布拉斯特拉格（相当于12英里），直达地极，万王之王，比任何人类之子都要高大，脚立于地，头直指太阳，点点头就令世上所有君王双膝颤抖，如春般温暖，如夏般怡人，如秋般丰硕，如冬般威严。至高无上的陛下向近来到达我天朝疆域的巨人山提出如下条款，巨人山须当照此庄严宣誓：

一、通关文牒加盖玉玺后，巨人山才准离开我国领土。

二、除非专使通报，否则巨人山不准擅自进入我国都城。巨人山进城时本国居民应在两小时前接到警报足不出户。

三、巨人山只准在大路上行走，不准在草坪或田地上随意行走躺卧。

四、当巨人山行走在所规定的

take the utmost care not to trample upon the bodies of any of our loving subjects, their horses, or carriages, nor take any of our said subjects into his hands, without their own consent.

大路上时，必须谨小慎微，避免踩踏到我国忠诚的子民或他们的马匹和马车身上，不经他们同意，也不准将任何人放在自己手上。

5th, If an express requires extraordinary dispatch, the man-mountain shall be obliged to carry in his pocket the messenger and horse a six days journey once in every moon, and return the said messenger back (if so required) safe to our imperial presence.

五、如果有专使需要发派急件，巨人山应当将专使与专使的马匹放入衣袋，一月一次跑完6天的路程。如有必要，还需将此专使安全带回到陛下面前。

6th, He shall be our ally against our enemies in the island of Blefuscu, and do his utmost to destroy their fleet, which is now preparing to invade us.

六、巨人山应与我们同仇敌忾，联合抗击我们的敌人不来福斯库国，付出最大的力量摧毁他们的舰队，而该舰队正在准备对我们发起进攻。

7th, That the said man-mountain shall, at his times of leisure, be aiding and assisting to our workmen, in helping to raise certain great stones, towards covering the wall of the principal park, and other our royal buildings.

七、巨人山当在闲暇时候帮助工匠抬运巨石，协助他们修建国家公园的围墙和其他皇家建筑。

8th, That the said man-mountain shall, in two moons time, deliver in an exact survey of the circumference of our dominions, by a computation of his own paces round the coast.

八、巨人山要在两个月内精确勘测我国疆域，根据自己的步幅计算我国海岸线的长度。

Lastly. That upon his solemn oath to observe all the above articles, the said man-mountain shall have a daily allowance of meat and drink sufficient for the support of 1728of our subjects, with free access to our royal person, and other

最后，巨人山要就所有条文庄严宣誓，而他每天也会得到相当于维持我国 1728 个臣民生活所需的肉食与饮料。可随时朝见吾皇，并享受到浩荡皇恩。吾皇登基第九十一月十二日于拜尔法波拉克宫。

marks of our favour. Given at our palace at Belfaborac, the twelfth day of the ninety-first moon of our reign.

I swore and subscribed to these articles with great cheerfulness and content, although some of them were not so honourable as I could have wished; which proceeded wholly from the malice of Skyresh Bolgolam the high admiral: whereupon my chains were immediately unlocked, and I was at full liberty; the emperor himself in person did me the honour to be by at the whole ceremony. I made my acknowledgments by prostrating myself at his majesty's foot: but he commanded me to rise; and after many gracious expressions, which, to avoid the censure of vanity, I shall not repeat, he added, that he hoped I should prove a useful servant, and well deserve all the favours he had already conferred upon me, or might do for the future.

我心甘情愿地接受了这些条文并照此宣誓，尽管有些内容并没有我希望的那么公允，但那都是海军上将斯奇瑞史·博尔格莱姆存心不良想出的鬼主意。就这样我的锁链立即被解开了，我的行动完全自由了，这还是皇帝在大典上亲自为我松的绑。我俯身于皇帝脚前以感谢隆恩，他让我免礼平身，又亲切地对我说了很多话，为了避免大家觉得我虚荣，我就不赘述陛下所说的内容了。他后来还说，他希望我能成为一个有帮助的仆人，不要辜负他现在对我的宠信和将来可能赐予我的恩典。

The reader may please to observe, that in the last article for the recovery of my liberty, the emperor stipulates to allow me a quantity of meat and drink sufficient for the support of 1728 Lilliputians. Some time after, asking a friend at court how they came to fix on that determinate number; he told me, that his majesty's mathematicians, having taken the height of my body by the help of a quadrant, and

读者可能会注意到我重获自由条款中的最后一条，皇帝规定赐我相当于维持 1728 个小人生活的肉食和饮料。过了一段时间我询问了一位朝中的朋友他们是如何得出这个数字的，他告诉我说，陛下的数学家们曾用象限仪计算过我的身高，得出与他们身高的比例是 12:1，因为我们的身体结构都差不多，所以他们算出一个我顶 1728

finding it to exceed theirs in the proportion of twelve to one, they concluded from the similarity of their bodies, that mine must contain at least 1728 of theirs, and consequently would require as much food as was necessary to support that number of Lilliputians. By which, the reader may conceive an idea of the ingenuity of that people, as well as the prudent and exact economy of so great a prince.

个小人，因此要提供给我 1728 个小人所需的酒肉。通过这件事读者便能看出这些小人的智慧机灵以及这位伟大的君王的精明节俭。

CHAPTER 4

第四章

MILENDO, the Metropolis of LILLIPUT, described together with the Emperor's Palace. A Conversation between the Author and a principal Secretary, concerning the Affairs of that Empire. The Author's offers to serve the Emperor in his Wars.

对利利普特国都城米勒恩多和皇宫进行了描写。记录了作者同一位大臣就帝国大事的对话内容。作者表示愿意为皇帝而战，同仇敌忾。

The first request I made after I had obtained my liberty, was, that I might have license to see Milendo, the metropolis; which the emperor easily granted me, but with a special charge to do no hurt, either to the inhabitants, or their houses. The people had notice by proclamation of my design to visit the town.

在获得自由后，我提出的第一个请求就是参观都城米勒恩多。皇帝很痛快地答应了我，但特别嘱咐我不要伤到当地居民和他们的房子。当地人也随后接到了我要参观城镇的通知。

The wall which encompassed it, is two foot and an half high, and at least eleven inches broad, so that a coach and horses may be driven very safely round it; and it is flanked with strong towers at ten foot distance. I stepped over the great western gate, and passed very gently, and sideling, through the two principal streets, only in my short waistcoat, for fear of damaging the roofs and eves of the houses with the skirts of my coat. I walked with the utmost circumspection, to avoid treading on any

都城的城墙有两英尺半高，至少 11 英寸宽，因此能很安全地驾着马车在上面绕行。城墙侧面 10 英尺远的地方还立着几座坚固的瞭望塔。我倾着身子迈过高大的西城门，轻手轻脚地走在大路上。我只穿着背心，因为担心如果穿大衣，衣角会弄坏他们的房顶和屋檐。我小心翼翼地前行，生怕踩到在外游荡的小人——尽管皇帝非常严格地命令他们待在屋子里避免发生危险，但还是有人在街上闲

stragglers, that might remain in the streets although the orders were very strict, that all people should keep in their houses, at their own peril. The garret windows and tops of houses were so crowded with spectators, that I thought in all my travels I had not seen a more populous place.

逛。阁楼的窗前和屋顶上都挤满了前来猎奇观望的人。我旅行到过很多地方，从没见过人口如此稠密的城市。

The city is an exact square, each side of the wall being five hundred foot long. The two great streets which run across and divide it into four quarters, are five foot wide. The lanes and alleys which I could not enter, but only viewed them as I passed, are from twelve to eighteen inches. The town is capable of holding five hundred thousand souls. the houses are from three to five storeys; the shops and markets well provided.

都城呈规则的四方形，城墙的每个边都有 500 英尺长。两条宽 5 英尺的大路径直穿过城区，将其分割成 4 部分。小路小巷是我不能进入的，我只能在路过时看看，它们的宽度 12 到 18 英寸不等。全市可容纳 50 万人，房屋有 3 到 5 层，商店市场应有尽有。

The emperor's palace is in the centre of the city, where the two great streets meet. It is enclosed by a wall of two foot high, and twenty foot distant from the buildings. I had his majesty's permission to step over this wall; and the space being so wide between that and the palace, I could easily view it on every side. The outward court is a square of forty foot, and includes two other courts: in the inmost are the royal apartments, which I was very desirous to see, but found it extremely difficult; for the great gates, from one square into another, were but eighteen inches high, and seven inches wide. Now the buildings

皇帝的宫殿位于城市中心，是两条大路相交的地方。宫殿围墙有两英尺高，离宫殿 20 英尺远。陛下允许我跨过围墙，围墙内非常宽敞，我能从各个角度欣赏宫殿。外院 40 英尺见方，里面还包含着两个宫院：最里面的是皇家公寓，我非常渴望一饱眼福，但发现几乎看不到，因为从一座宫院通往另一座宫院间设有一扇高约 18 英寸，宽约 7 英寸的大门。而外院的建筑至少有 5 英尺高，所以我是不可能迈得过去的，因为尽管城墙是用厚度为 4 英寸的坚固毛石建成的，但如果迈过去，我还是肯定会将这些建

of the outer court were at least five foot high, and it was impossible for me to stride over them, without infinite damage to the pile, although the walls were strongly built of hewn stone, and four inches thick. At the same time the emperor had a great desire that I should see the magnificence of his palace; but this I was not able to do till three days after, which I spent in cutting down with my knife some of the largest trees in the royal park, about an hundred yards distant from the city. Of these trees I made two stools, each about three foot high, and strong enough to bear my weight. The people having received notice a second time, I went again through the city to the palace, with my two stools in my hands. When I came to the side of the outer court, I stood upon one stool, and took the other in my hand: this I lifted over the roof, and gently set it down on the space between the first and second court, which was eight foot wide. I then stepped over the buildings very conveniently, from one stool to the other, and drew up the first after me with a hooked stick. By this contrivance I got into the inmost court; and, lying down upon my side, I applied my face to the windows of the middle storeys, which were left open on purpose, and discovered the most splendid apartments that can be imagined. There I saw the empress, and

筑损坏。同时皇帝还很希望让我参观他宏伟的宫殿，但直到3天以后我才得以参观，因为那3天我一直忙着在离都城100码远的皇家公园用小刀砍了几棵长得最为高大的树。我用这些树木做了两个托架，每个托架大约3英尺高，结构坚固，能承受得了我的体重。城里居民又接到通知后我就拿着这两个托架又一次进城往宫殿走去，当走到外院边时，我便站在一个托架上，手里拿着另一个托架，将它举过屋顶，轻轻放在第一个院落和第二个院落之间差不多有8英尺宽的空地上。就这样很轻松地从一个托架迈过了这些建筑到另一个托架上，然后再用顶端拴着钩子的木棒将第一个托架钩起。用这个办法我终于来到了内院，侧身躺下，从中层特意为我打开的窗户望了进去，看到了我所能想象出的最华丽精美的房间。我看到房间里的皇后，还有由侍从长们陪着待在各自房间里的小王子。皇后面带微笑优雅和蔼地看着我，并从窗户里伸出手来让我亲吻。

the young princes in their several lodgings, with their chief attendants about them. Her imperial majesty was pleased to smile very graciously upon me, and gave me out of the window her hand to kiss.

But I shall not anticipate the reader with further descriptions of this kind, because I reserve them for a greater work, which is now almost ready for the press, containing a general description of this empire, from its first erection, through a long series of princes, with a particular account of their wars and politics, laws, learning, and religion; their plants and animals, their peculiar manners and customs, with other matters very curious and useful; my chief design, at present, being only to relate such events and transactions as happened to the public, or to myself, during a residence of about nine months in that empire.

One morning, about a fortnight after I had obtained my liberty, Reldresal, principal secretary (as they style him) for private affairs, came to my house, attended only by one servant. He ordered his coach to wait at a distance, and desired I would give him an hour's audience; which I readily consented to, on account of his quality and personal merits, as well as the many good offices he had done me during my solicitations at court. I offered to lie down, that he might the more conveniently reach my ear; but he chose

但我不想过多为读者赘述皇宫的描写了，因为我将会在另一本书中着重叙述这些内容，现在这本书也马上就要出版了，内容大概包括帝国的最初建立和历代皇帝，特别介绍了他们的战争，政治，法律，学术和宗教信仰。另外还描述了他们的植物动物，特别的礼仪规矩和风俗习惯，以及其他奇闻逸事。现在我主要想着重讲述一下在这个国家生活的9个月中发生在我和公众身上的事件。

在我获得自由两个星期后的一个早晨，内务大臣瑞尔德瑞萨尔（人们这样称呼他）因为私事来到我住的地方，随同而来的只有一个仆人。他命令他的马车夫在远处等他，并希望我能拿出一个小时的时间同他谈话。因为他品德高尚，功绩斐然，再加上他曾为我在朝中说过不少好话，我便欣然答应了。我表示愿意躺下来，这样他就能更方便地冲着我的耳朵说话，但他却宁愿我将他捧在手上交谈。他首先祝贺我获得了自由，说在这件事上他

rather to let me hold him in my hand during our conversation. He began with compliments on my liberty, said he might pretend to some merit in it; but, however, added, that if it had not been for the present situation of things at court, perhaps I might not have obtained it so soon. For, said he, as flourishing a condition as we may appear to be in to foreigners, we labor under two mighty evils; a violent faction at home, and the danger of an invasion by a most potent enemy, from abroad. As to the first, you are to understand, that for above seventy months past, there have been two struggling parties in this empire, under the names of Tramecksan, and Slamecksan, from the high and low heels of their shoes, by which they distinguish themselves. It is alledged indeed, that the high heels are most agreeable to our ancient constitution: but however this be, his majesty hath determined to make use of only low heels in the administration of the government, and all offices in the gift of the crown, as you cannot but observe; and particularly, that his majesty's imperial heels are lower at least by a drurr than any of his court (drurr is a measure about the fourteenth part of an inch). The animosities between these two parties run so high, that they will neither eat nor drink, nor talk with each other. We compute the Tramecksan, or high-heels, to exceed us in number; but

的功劳可不小，但又说要不是因为朝廷现在的情况，我也不会这么早就获得自由。他告诉我说："在外国人眼里我们利利普特国国力昌盛，但我们其实正面对着两大危机：朝廷中激烈的明争暗斗、尔虞我诈和国外劲敌虎视眈眈、蓄势入侵的危险。你要知道，70 多个月以来，朝中一直分为两大对立阵营，一个叫特雷姆克桑，另一个叫斯雷姆克桑，区别在于他们鞋跟的高矮，他们自己也是这样辨别敌我的。事实上，高跟党是最合乎我们古代的体制的，但在朝中管理层，陛下却坚决起用低跟党，其他所有职位也是一样，这一点你肯定也注意到了。特别是陛下自己的鞋跟甚至比朝中大臣的鞋跟矮了一德鲁尔（德鲁尔是一种长度计量单位，一德鲁尔等于 1/14 英寸）。两党间的矛盾甚为激烈，因此他们从来不在一起吃饭喝酒，甚至彼此都不说话。我们估计特雷姆克桑，也就是高跟党的人数已经超过了我们的人数，但主要权势还是在我党手中的。我们很担心我们尊敬的陛下有些偏向高跟党的趋向，因为我们明显发现他的一个鞋跟比另一个要高出一些，走起路来一跛一跛的。国家正处于激烈的内讧，而一波未平一波又起。外敌不来福斯库国又在伺机乘虚而入。不来福斯库国也是一个国力强盛的大帝国，几乎与我国面积相当，势均力敌。我们之

the power is wholly on our side. We apprehend his imperial highness, the heir to the crown, to have some tendency towards the high-heels; at least, we can plainly discover one of his heels higher than the other, which gives him a hobble in his gait. Now, in the midst of these intestine disquiets, we are threatened with an invasion from the island of Blefuscu, which is the other great empire of the universe, almost as large and powerful as this of his majesty. For as to what we have heard you affirm, that there are other kingdoms and states in the world, inhabited by human creatures as large as yourself, our philosophers are in much doubt, and would rather conjecture that you dropped from the moon, or one of the stars, because it is certain, that an hundred mortals of your bulk would, in a short time, destroy all the fruits and cattle of his majesty's dominions. Besides, our histories of six thousand moons make no mention of any other regions, than the two great empires of Lilliput and Blefuscu. Which two mighty powers have, as I was going to tell you, been engaged in a most obstinate war for six and thirty moons past. It began upon the following occasion. It is allowed on all hands, that the primitive way of breaking eggs before we eat them, was upon the larger end: but his present majesty's grandfather, while he was a boy, going to eat an egg, and

前听你说过，这个世界上还有其他的王国和国家里住着同你一样高大的人类，对此我们的哲学家充满了疑惑，他们宁愿相信你是从月亮或其他星体上掉下来的，因为像你这样的庞然大物只要 100 个，短时间内就能吃光我们所有的水果和牲畜。另外，我们 6000 个月的历史记录中除了我们利利普特国和不来福斯库国以外从未提及过其他任何地方。这两个国家在过去的 36 个月里一直在激烈地战争，而引发两国矛盾的事就是接下来我要说的了。我们所有人都认为剥鸡蛋时要从较大的那头开始剥起，但陛下的爷爷在还是个孩子的时候，有一次按照老法子剥鸡蛋，结果不小心割伤了一根手指。于是他的父亲，也就是当时的皇帝立刻颁布了一个法令，命令所有臣民以后只能从较小的一端剥鸡蛋，违者将会受到严厉处罚。这条法令惹得民怨四起，历史记载人们曾为此发起了 6 次反抗，一位皇帝因此丧了命，还有一位因此丢了皇位。这些民间暴乱始终都是由不来福斯库国历届的国王煽动的。当暴乱终于被镇压平息，被驱逐流放的人通常都会去不来福斯库国寻求庇护。据计算，长久以来总共有 11000 人宁愿舍弃生命也不愿从较小的一端开始剥鸡蛋。就此争论还出版了好几百本大型著作，但大端派的著作长久以来都是被禁的，朝廷也发布法律，

breaking it according to the ancient practice, happened to cut one of his fingers. Whereupon the emperor his father published an edict, commanding all his subjects, upon great penalties, to break the smaller end of their eggs. The people so highly resented this law, that our histories tell us there have been six rebellions raised on that account; wherein one emperor lost his life, and another his crown. These civil commotions were constantly fomented by the monarchs of Blefuscu; and when they were quelled, the exiles always fled for refuge to that empire. It is computed, that eleven thousand persons have, at several times, suffered death, rather than submit to break their eggs at the smaller end. Many hundred large volumes have been published upon this controversy: but the books of the Big-endians have been long forbidden, and the whole party rendered incapable by law of holding employments. During the course of these troubles, the Emperors of Blefuscu did frequently expostulate by their ambassadors, accusing us of making a schism in religion, by offending against a fundamental doctrine of our great prophet Lustrog, in the fifty-fourth chapter of the Blundecral (which is their Alcoran). This, however, is thought to be a mere strain upon the text: for the words are these; That all true Believers break their Eggs at

禁止大端派的人担任任何职务。在这些争执的过程中，不来福斯库国的皇帝时常会派大使来指责我们，说我们犯了宗教分裂罪，违反了我们大先知拉斯特罗格写在《布朗德克拉尔经》（这个经书相当于他们的《古兰经》）第五十四章的一条基本教义。但我们以为这只不过是他们对经文的曲解，原文是这样写的：所有真正的信徒都应在便利的一端剥鸡蛋。依我浅见，所谓‘便利的一端’其实是由人们自己的良心决定的，或至少该由最高行政官来决定。如今这些大端派的流犯都得到了不来福斯库国皇帝的极大宠信，又受到我国内部党羽私下的援助和怂恿，因此两个帝国间残酷的战争就这样开始，并持续了 36 个月，双方各有胜负。在战争中我们已经损失了 40 艘主力舰，数量更为庞大的小型战舰和 3 万个优秀的水手和战士。据估计敌军的损失比我们更惨重。然而他们现在已经整编起一支力量雄厚的舰队，正准备对我们展开袭击。而吾皇圣上对你的勇猛和力量寄予了极大信心，派我来向你将此大事作出解释。”

the convenient End: And which is the convenient end, seems, in my humble opinion, to be left to every man's conscience, or at least in the power of the chief magistrate to determine. Now the Big-endian exiles have found so much credit in the emperor of Blefuscu's court, and so much private assistance and encouragement from their party here at home, that a bloody war hath been carried on between the two empires for six and thirty moons with various success; during which time we have lost forty capital ships, and a much greater number of smaller vessels, together with thirty thousand of our best seamen and soldiers; and the damage received by the enemy is reckoned to be somewhat greater than ours. However, they have now equipped a numerous fleet, and are just preparing to make a descent upon us; and his imperial majesty placing great confidence in your valour and strength, hath commanded me to lay this account of his affairs before you.

I desired the secretary to present my humble duty to the emperor, and to let him know, that I thought it would not become me, who was a foreigner, to interfere with parties; but I was ready, with the hazard of my life, to defend his person and state against all invaders.

我向这位内务大臣表示，我愿为陛下尽上自己的一份力量，请他转告陛下，虽然作为一个外国人，我不便干涉他们两党之间的事务，但我已做好了准备，愿意以死保卫陛下和陛下的王国，不让他们受到侵略者的伤害。

CHAPTER 5

第五章

The Author, by an extraordinary Stratagem, prevents an Invasion. A high Title of Honour is conferred upon him. Ambassadors arrive from the Emperor of BLEFUSCU, and sue for Peace. The Empress's Apartment on fire, by Accident; the Author instrumental in saving the rest of the Palace.

作者以卓越的谋略阻止了敌军的侵略，并被授予了高级荣誉头衔。不来福斯库国国王派来使者求和。皇后寝宫意外着火，作者帮忙援救了宫殿其他的部分。

The empire of *Blefuscu* is an island, situated to the north north-east said of *Lilliput*, from whence it is parted only by a channel of eight hundred yards wide. I had not yet seen it, and upon this notice of an intended invasion, I avoided appearing on that side of the coast, for fear of being discovered by some of the enemy's ships, who had received no intelligence of me, all intercourse between the two empires having been strictly forbidden during the war, upon pain of death, and an embargo laid by our emperor upon all vessels whatsoever. I communicated to his majesty a project I had formed of seizing the enemy's whole fleet; which, as our scouts assured us, lay at anchor in the harbour, ready to sail with the first fair wind. I consulted the most experienced

不来福斯库国是个岛国，位于利利普特国的东北方，两国之间只隔着一条宽 800 码的海峡。我以前从未见过这个岛国，而现在又要打算入侵，所以就更避免出现在海边，我担心在船上的敌军会发现我。他们还对我毫不知情，因为战争期间两国的往来被严格中断，违者将被处以死刑。而且皇帝还下达封港令，所有船只统统不准出海。我向陛下禀报了我制订的关于将敌军舰队一网打尽的计划，就侦察兵的情报，他们的舰队正停泊在海港里，只要刮起顺风就会扬帆起航。我向经验最丰富的水手打听了海峡的深度，他们告诉我，他们用铅锤测量的结果是海峡的中间部分在水位达到最高点时有 70 格朗姆格鲁夫那么深，换算成欧洲测量

seamen, upon the depth of the channel, which they had often plumbed, who told me, that in the middle at high water it was seventy *glumgluffs* deep, which is about six foot of *European* measure; and the rest of it fifty *glumgluffs* at most. I walked towards the north-east coast over against *Blefuscu*, and, lying down behind a hillock, took out my small pocket perspective-glass, and viewed the enemy's fleet at anchor, consisting of about fifty men of war, and a great number of transports: I then came back to my house, and gave order (for which I had a warrant) for a great quantity of the strongest cable and bars of iron. The cable was about as thick as packthread, and the bars of the length and size of a knitting-needle. I trebled the cable to make it stronger, and for the same reason I twisted three of the iron bars together, bending the extremities into a hook. Having thus fixed fifty hooks to as many cables, I went back to the north-east coast, and putting off my coat, shoes, and stockings, walked into the sea in my leathern jerkin, about half an hour before high water. I waded with what haste I could, and swam in the middle about thirty yards till I felt ground; I arrived at the fleet in less than half an hour. The enemy was so frightened when they saw me, that they leaped out of their ships, and swam to shore, where there

单位就是6英尺深，海峡其余部分最深的地方有 50 格朗姆格鲁夫。我走到直对着不来福斯库国的东北岸，趴在一个小山丘后，拿出我的袖珍望远镜，朝敌军正停泊在海港上的舰队望去，这支舰队差不多由 50 艘战舰和大量运输舰组成。侦察完毕回到住处，我下令（我有委任状）让他们准备大量最粗的缆绳和铁棒。缆绳要有麻绳那么粗，铁棒的长度和大小则与编织用针相同。我把3根缆绳拧成一股，这样就更结实了。同样的，我也把3根铁棒拧到一起，将末端弯成一个钩子。就这样，我在 50 条缆绳上系上 50 个铁钩后又回到了东北海岸，脱下大衣和鞋袜，只穿着皮背心走入水中，大约半个小时后我到达了最深水位。我尽可能快地在水里蹚行，到了中间位置又游了 30 码后脚才再次探到地面。没用半小时我就来到了舰队停泊的地方。敌军发现我时简直吓得魂都没了，跳船的跳船，游上岸的游上岸，总共差不多有3万人。接着，我拿出我的工具，把铁钩钩在每艘船船头的洞里，再把所有缆绳系在一起。就在我忙于上述动作时，敌军冲我射来几千支箭，很多射到了我的手上和脸上，由于刺痛难忍，我的工作受到了极大干扰。最让我担心的是我的眼睛，要不是我临时想出了应急之计，我的双眼非被刺瞎不可。

could not be fewer than thirty thousand souls. I then took my tackling, and fastening a hook to a hole at the prow of each, I tied all the cords together at the end. While I was thus employed, the enemy discharged several thousand arrows, many of which stuck in my hands and face; and, besides the excessive smart, gave me much disturbance in my work. My greatest apprehension was for my eyes, which I should have infallibly lost, if I had not suddenly thought of an expedient. I kept among other little necessaries a pair of spectacles in a private pocket, which, as I observed before, had escaped the emperor's searchers. These I took out and fastened as strongly as I could upon my nose, and thus armed went on boldly with my work in spite of the enemy's arrows, many of which struck against the glasses of my spectacles, but without any other effect, further than a little to discompose them. I had now fastened all the hooks, and taking the knot in my hand, began to pull; but not a ship would stir, for they were all too fast held by their anchors, so that the boldest part of my enterprise remained. I therefore let go the cord, and leaving the hooks fixed to the ships, I resolutely cut with my knife the cables that fastened the anchors, receiving above two hundred shots in my face and hands; then I took up the knotted

我之前提到过，我有一个秘密口袋之前躲过了搜身，里面备有几样必需品，其中就有我的眼镜。我把眼镜拿出来，牢牢地戴在了鼻梁上。有了这层武装，我便放开手脚大胆地干了起来。尽管敌军还是在不停放箭，但除了把镜片刮花一点以外没有任何其他效果。这时我已经将所有钩子都拴紧了，把缆绳打结后握在手里开始拉动舰队，但这些船却一动不动，原来是它们的锚扎得太稳，这就给我带来了艰巨的任务。我放开了绳索，但钩子还是固定在船上。我用小刀将拴着船锚的绳索一一割断，而这一任务付出的代价就是我的脸上和手上又被射中了200多支箭。然后我又拿起拴着钩子的缆绳，轻松地拖着敌军最强大的50艘战舰往回游去。

end of the cables to which my hooks were tied, and with great ease drew fifty of the enemy's largest men of war after me.

The *Blefuscudians*, who had not the least imagination of what I intended, were at first confounded with astonishment. They had seen me cut the cables, and thought my design was only to let the ships run adrift, or fall foul on each other: but when they perceived the whole fleet moving in order, and saw me pulling at the end, they set up such a scream of grief and despair, that it is almost impossible to describe or conceive. When I had got out of danger, I stopped a while to pick out the arrows that stuck in my hands and face, and rubbed on some of the same ointment that was given me at my first arrival, as I have formerly mentioned. I then took off my spectacles, and waiting about an hour, till the tide was a little fallen, I waded through the middle with my cargo, and arrived safe at the royal port of *Lilliput*.

The emperor and his whole court stood on the shore expecting the issue of this great adventure. They saw the ships move forward in a large half-moon, but could not discern me, who was up to my breast in water. When I advanced to the middle of the channel, they were yet more in pain because I was under water to my neck. The emperor concluded me to be drowned, and that the enemy's fleet was

不来福斯库人丝毫没有预料到我的计划，完全被我的出现吓到了。当看见我在砍断缆绳时，他们以为我是让战舰随波逐流，或互相碰撞，缠在一起。但等他们看到我拉着绳子将整个舰队整齐地向前拖动时，才一下子回过神来，悲痛绝望地大叫了起来，那种情形简直没法用语言形容。等游出了危险区域，我便停了下来，把脸上和手上的箭拔了出来，涂上药膏。这种药膏我之前曾提到过，就是刚来岛上时他们给我的那种。我摘下眼镜，等了差不多一个小时海潮慢慢退下，才拖着这些战利品往回蹚行，终于安全到达了利利普特国的皇家港口。

皇帝和他全部的大臣们站在海岸上等待我凯旋归来。他们看到半月形的舰队在海面上缓缓而来，但却没看到我，因为海面没过了我的胸膛。当我游到海峡中部的时候，他们更加担心了，因为我的脖子也没到了水面以下。皇帝断定我一定是淹死了，而敌军的舰队也就要向他们发起进攻。但没过多久他的恐惧就打消了，因为海峡越来越

approaching in a hostile manner: but he was soon eased of his fears, for the channel growing shallower every step I made, I came in a short time within hearing, and holding up the end of the cable by which the fleet was fastened, I cried in a loud voice, *Long live the most puissant emperor of Lilliput!* This great prince received me at my landing with all possible encomiums, and created me a *nardac* upon the spot, which is the highest title of honour among them.

浅，不一会儿我就走进了听力所及的距离。我举着钩着舰队的绳索的一端，大声喊道："最伟大的利利普特国王万岁！"这位伟大的国王在我上岸后热烈地欢迎了我，对我极尽褒奖之词，当场封我为"纳尔达克"，这是利利普特国的最高荣誉。

His majesty desired I would take some other opportunity of bringing all the rest of his enemy's ships into his ports. And so unmeasurable is the ambition of princes, that he seemed to think of nothing less than reducing the whole empire of *Blefuscu* into a province, and governing it by viceroy; of destroying the Big-endian exiles, and compelling that people to break the smaller end of their eggs, by which he would remain the sole monarch of the whole world. But I endeavoured to divert him from this design, by many arguments drawn from the topics of policy, as well as justice: And I plainly protested, that I would never be an instrument of bringing a free and brave people into slavery. And when the matter was debated in council, the wisest part of the ministry were of my opinion.

陛下要求我寻找时机把敌军其余的战船全部拖到他的港口，足以见得这位皇帝的勃勃野心。他好像打算将整个不来福斯库帝国收为一个省，然后派总督统治。他要将大端派的流犯一网打尽，强制人民在吃鸡蛋时从鸡蛋的小端剥起，继而统治整个世界。但是我竭力地从政治角度，还有公正的观点劝谏陛下取消这个计划。我坦率地提出反对意见，告诉陛下，我不会当一个将自由勇敢的人民变为奴隶的工具。而在国务委员会上就这个问题展开讨论时，朝中最智慧的大臣们都是同意我的观点的。

This open bold declaration of mine was

我这次公开大胆地反对陛下

so opposite to the schemes and politics of his imperial majesty, that he could never forgive it; he mentioned it in a very artful manner at council, where I was told that some of the wisest appeared, at least by their silence, to be of my opinion; but others, who were my secret enemies, could not forbear some expressions, which by a side-wind reflected on me. And from this time began an intrigue between his majesty, and a junto of ministers maliciously bent against me, which broke out in less than two months, and had like to have ended in my utter destruction. Of so little weight are the greatest services to princes, when put into the balance with a refusal to gratify their passions.

About three weeks after this exploit, there arrived a solemn embassy from *Blefuscu*, with humble offers of a peace; which was soon concluded upon conditions very advantageous to our emperor, wherewith I shall not trouble the reader. There were six ambassadors, with a train of about five hundred persons, and their entry was very magnificent, suitable to the grandeur of their master, and the importance of their business. When their treaty was finished, wherein I did them several good offices by the credit I now had, or at least appeared to have at court, their excellencies, who were privately told how much I had been their friend, made

的计划，他绝不可能再原谅我，而这一点他也在会议上非常婉转地表示了出来。还有人告诉我说，几位最智慧的大臣至少用沉默的方式对我的意见表示了赞成。但还有那些我的夙敌，借此机会更是对我恶意中伤，旁敲侧击地表示对我的怀疑。从那以后，我的夙敌便与皇帝一起密谋除掉我，不到两个月后，这个密谋以我差点送命而告终。对皇帝们来说，如果你不能满足他们的野心，那么就算你立下了汗马功劳也是可以一笔勾销的。

在我立下大功大约 3 个星期后，不来福斯库国派来使者谦恭求和，和约内容对吾皇陛下非常有利，不用说读者也能想象得出。来利利普特国的一共有 6 个使者，随行人员差不多有 500 个，他们的入关仪式非常浩大壮观，丝毫没丢他们国王的面子，也充分展现了他们的重视程度。和约签订过程中，我也借着我当时在朝中的威信——至少表面上看是这样——帮了他们不少忙，也有人私底下告诉到访的阁下们，我其实是他们的朋友，于是他们就顺应礼节来拜访了我。他们先是对我的勇猛和慷慨大加溢美之词，然后又代表他们的皇帝邀

me a visit in form. They began with many compliments upon my valour and generosity, invited me to that kingdom in the emperor their master's name, and desired me to show them some proofs of my prodigious strength, of which they had heard so many wonders; wherein I readily obliged them, but shall not trouble the reader with the particulars.

请我访问他们的国家。他们还请求我向他们展示我惊人的力量，因为他们已经听说了相关的许多奇迹。我欣然答应了他们，具体细节就不在此向读者一一赘述了。

When I had for some time entertained their Excellencies to their infinite satisfaction and surprise, I desired they would do me the honour to present my most humble respects to the emperor their master, the renown of whose virtues had so justly filled the whole world with admiration, and whose royal person I resolved to attend before I returned to my own country: Accordingly, the next time I had the honour to see our emperor, I desired his general license to wait on the *Blefuscudian* monarch, which he was pleased to grant me, as I could plainly perceive, in a very cold manner; but could not guess the reason, till I had a whisper from a certain person, that *Flimnap* and *Bolgolam* had represented my intercourse with those ambassadors as a mark of disaffection, from which I am sure my heart was wholly free. And this was the first time I began to conceive some imperfect idea of courts and ministers.

我向到访的阁下们表演了几个节目，令他们大饱眼福，惊讶不已。我请求他们代表我向他们的皇帝表示最崇高的敬意，他的声望美德誉满全世界，并向他转达在我回到自己的国家前一定会去拜见他。为此，在我后来有幸见到我们的皇帝时，我请求他准许我前往不来福斯库国拜会他们的国君。陛下倒是很痛快就准许了我的请求，但我能看得出，他的态度是相当冷淡的。我一直猜不到原因，直到有一次有人悄悄告诉我说，福利姆奈普和博尔格莱姆将我和使者的交谈内容汇报给了皇帝，说我心怀不轨。对此我绝对问心无愧。那是我第一次开始认为朝中大臣其实也不尽完美。

It is to be observed, that these

ambassadors spoke to me by an interpreter, the languages of both empires differing as much from each other as any two in *Europe*, and each nation priding itself upon the antiquity, beauty, and energy of theirs own tongues, with an avowed contempt for that of theirs neighbour; yet our emperor, standing upon the advantage he had got by the seizure of their fleet, obliged them to deliver their credentials, and make their speech in the *Lilliputian* tongue. And it must be confessed, that from the great intercourse of trade and commerce between both realms, from the continual reception of exiles, which is mutual among them, and from the custom in each empire to send their young nobility and richer gentry to the other, in order to polish themselves, by seeing the world, and understanding men and manners; there are few persons of distinction, or merchants, or seamen, who dwell in the maritime parts, but what can hold conversation in both tongues; as I found some weeks after, when I went to pay my respects to the Emperor of *Blefuscu*, which in the midst of great misfortunes, through the malice of my enemies, proved a very happy adventure to me, as I shall relate in its proper place.

在这里我需要说明一点，就是这些大使交谈时是有一位翻译在场的，因为两国的语言各有不同，区别程度就像欧洲各国的语言那样。每个国家都自诩自己的语言历久弥新，发音优美，铿锵有力，也都曾公开表示过他们对邻国语言的不屑。我们的皇帝则仗着夺取了对方舰队的优势，强行要求他们用利利普特语递交国书并当众演讲。还有一点必须要说明，由于两国有着频繁的商贸往来，互相也不断接受对方的流亡人员，而且根据习惯，两个国家都会派年轻的贵族和富家子弟去对方国内开阔眼界，了解风土人情以汲取知识。再加上居住在沿海的当地人，商人，水手，几乎所有人都通晓两国语言，交流不成问题。这一点在我几星期后去拜见不来福斯库国国王的时候就发现了。由于我正身陷囹圄，我的夙敌也对我心怀怨恨，这次不来福斯库之行还是相当愉快的，相关细节我会在合适的章节加以描述。

The reader may remember, that when I signed those articles upon which I recovered my liberty, there were some

读者可能还记得，在我签下那些恢复自由的条款时，有些内容是我非常反感的，因为那会让我像奴

which I disliked upon account of their being too servile, neither could anything but an extreme necessity have forced me to submit. But being now a *nardac,* of the highest rank in that empire, such offices were looked upon as below my dignity, and the emperor (to do him justice) never once mentioned them to me. However, it was not long before I had an opportunity of doing his majesty, at least as I then thought, a most signal service. I was alarmed at midnight with the cries of many hundred people at my door; by which being suddenly awaked, I was in some kind of terror. I heard the word *burglum* repeated incessantly: several of the emperor's court making their way through the crowd, entreated me to come immediately to the palace, where her imperial majesty's apartment was on fire, by the carelessness of a maid of honour, who fell asleep while she was reading a romance. I got up in an instant; and orders being given to clear the way before me, and it being likewise a moonshine night, I made a shift to get to the palace without trampling on any of the people. I found they had already applied ladders to the walls of the apartment, and were well provided with buckets, but the water was at some distance. These buckets were about the size of a large thimble, and the poor people supplied me with them as fast

隶一样卑躬屈膝，除非万不得已，不然我是坚决不会屈从的。但现在我身为一个纳尔达克，全国上下最高的头衔，再让我做那些事情未免有损威严。而且说句公道话，皇帝也再没向我提到过那些事情。但不久以后，我又得到一个效忠陛下的机会，至少我那时认为我立下了卓越功勋。有一天半夜，好几百人在我门前大声呼喊，将我一下子惊醒，这让我心里冒出几丝恐惧。我听到人们不停地喊着“博尔格朗姆”这个词，又有几个御前侍卫从人群中飞奔而来，恳请我赶紧进宫，因为一个女仆在读冒险故事时不慎睡着将烛台打翻，致使皇后寝宫着了火。我立刻起床，让他们帮我清道，然后趁着明亮的月光一边小心不要踩到行人，一边向皇宫赶去。我看到他们已经将梯子搭在了寝宫墙上，水桶也都准备好了，只是水源离皇宫还有一段距离。每只水桶有大号套筒那么大，这些可怜的小人以他们最快的速度将水桶一只只递给我，但由于火势太猛，这些水根本无济于事。我本可以用大衣将火扑灭，但不幸的是由于出门太急，我就只穿了那件皮背心出来。情况岌岌可危，再这样下去，这座雄伟的宫殿一定会被烧成平地。这时我镇定下来，突然灵机一动，想出一个应急之计。我那天晚上喝了很多酒，是我喝过的味道最

as they could; but the flame was so violent, that they did little good. I might easily have stifled it with my coat, which I unfortunately left behind me for haste, and came away only in my leathern jerkin. The case seemed wholly desperate and deplorable, and this magnificent palace would have infallibly been burnt down to the ground, if, by a presence of mind, unusual to me, I had not suddenly thought of an expedient. I had the evening before drank plentifully of a most delicious wine, call *Glimigrim* (the *Blefuscudians* call it *Flunec*, but ours is esteemed the better sort), which is very diuretic. By the luckiest chance in the world, I had not discharged myself of any part of it. The heart I had contracted by coming very near the flames, and by my laboring to quench them, made the wine begin to operate by urine; which I voided in such a quantity, and applied so well to the proper places, that in three minutes the fire was wholly extinguished, and the rest of that noble pile, which had cost so many ages in erecting, preserved from destruction.

为香醇的酒，叫做“格里米格瑞姆”（不来福斯库人则称之为“弗朗耐克”，比我们的酒味道更美），这种酒非常利尿。而更巧的是，我睡前还没有小解。我靠着火源很近，又在不停忙着救火，于是这些酒就在我体内慢慢形成了尿。我大大地撒了一泡，刚好也对准了正确的地方，于是3分钟后大火就完全熄灭了，而这花了多年时间建造的皇家建筑群的其余部分也免遭毁坏。

It was now daylight, and I returned to my house, without waiting to congratulate with the emperor; because, although I had done a very eminent piece of service, yet I could not tell how his majesty might resent the manner by which I had performed it: for, by the fundamental laws

我回到住处时已经是早晨了。我没有等着皇帝来祝贺我扑灭了大火，因为尽管我立下了大功，但我可说不准陛下会不会厌恶我的灭火方式，因为该国的基本法规中有一条这样写道，凡是在皇城之内随地小便者，不论身份高低，格杀

of the realm, it is capital in any person, of what quality soever, to make water within the precincts of the palace. But I was a little comforted by a message from his majesty, that he would give orders to the grand justiciary for passing my pardon in form; which, however, I could not obtain. And I was privately assured, that the empress conceiving the greatest abhorrence of what I had done removed to the most distant side of the court, firmly resolved that those building should never be repaired for her use; and, in the presence of her chief confidants, could not forbear vowing revenge.

勿论。但后来我安心了一些，因为皇帝派人捎来口信说他命令大司法部赦免我的过错，但赦免令不能给我。有人私底下告诉我，皇后本人对我的行为深恶痛绝，已经移驾到宫殿最远的那头居住了，而且坚决表示那座建筑永远不要为她修缮，还在几个亲信面前表示，一定要为此向我报复。

CHAPTER 6

第六章

Of the Inhabitants of Lilliput; their Learning, Laws, and Customs; the Manner of Educating their Children. The Author's Way of living in that Country. His Vindication of a great Lady.

对利利普特国的居民进行描述。介绍了他们的学术、法律和风土人情，以及他们教育孩童的方式。记录了作者在该国的生活方式，以及他为一位贵妇的辩护。

Although I intend to leave the description of this empire to a particular treatise, yet, in the mean time I am content to gratify the curious reader with some general ideas. As the common size of the natives is somewhat under six inches high, so there is an exact proportion in all other animals, as well as plants and trees: for instance, the tallest horses and oxen are between four and five inches in height, the sheep an inch and a half, more or less; their geese about the bigness of a sparrow, and so the several gradations downwards, till you come to the smallest, which, to my sight, were almost invisible; but nature hath adapted the eyes of the *Lilliputians* to all objects proper for their view: they see with great exactness, but at no great distance. And to show the sharpness of their sight towards objects that are near, I have been much pleased with observing a cook pulling a lark, which was not so

虽然我打算另外写一部专门对这个帝国进行介绍描写的专著，但我还是要满足一下读者们的好奇心，介绍一下大概的情况。由于当地人的普遍身高都不足6英寸，因此这里的动物、农作物和树木都是同比例的大小。比如，这里最高的马和牛高度在4英寸到5英寸之间，羊则差不多有一英寸到一英寸半那么高。当地的鹅有我们的麻雀那么大，以此类推，直到体型最小的种类——通常我的肉眼都几乎看不到它们。而利利普特人的眼睛也是适应此环境的，他们的视力能看清细微的东西，但却看不远。他们对观察周围细小事物有着非常敏锐的视力。我曾饶有兴致地看着一个厨子在给一只不足苍蝇大小的百灵鸟清理内脏，还见到过一个小姑娘在用一根细到我看不清的丝线往一枚细到我看不清的针里穿。他们最高的树差不多有7英尺高，

large as a common fly; and a young girl threading an invisible needle with invisible silk. Their tallest trees are about seven foot high; I mean some of those in the great royal park, the tops whereof I could but just reach with my fist clenched. The other vegetables are in the same proportion; but this I leave to the reader's imagination.

我所说的是皇家大公园里的那些，我握紧拳头向上伸直才能够得到顶。至于其他蔬菜，尺寸也都是同比例缩小的，这就留给读者自己去想象了。

I shall say but little at present of their learning, which for many ages hath flourished in all its branches among them: but their manner of writing is very peculiar, being neither from the left to the right, like the *Europeans'*; nor from the right to the left, like the *Arabians'*; nor from up to down, like the Chinese; nor from down to up, like the *cascagians'*; but aslant from one corner of the paper to the other, like our ladies in *England*.

经过世代发展，他们的学术在各个方面都非常发达，只是他们的书写方式很独特，他们既不像欧洲人那样从左往右写，也不像阿拉伯人那样从右往左写，也不像中国人那样从上往下写，更不像卡斯卡基人那样从下往上写，而是从纸的一角沿对角线斜着写，像我们英国的女士们那样。

They bury their dead with their heads directly downwards, because they hold an opinion that in eleven thousand moons they are all to rise again, in which period the earth (which they conceive to be flat) will turn upside down, and by this means they shall, at their resurrection, be found ready standing on their foot. The learned among them confess the absurdity of this doctrine, but the practice still continues, in compliance to the vulgar.

他们埋葬死人的方式是头朝下埋葬，因为他们认为到了第一万一千个月时他们会复活，在那时地球（他们以为地球是扁平的）会整个底朝天，这样头朝下的埋葬方法能让他们在复活时方便站立。他们的学者承认这种说法的荒谬，但这种方式却在一直延续，老百姓们依旧在沿袭此风俗。

There are some laws and customs in this empire very peculiar, and if they were

这个国家的法律和习惯非常独特，要不是与我亲爱的祖国的法

not so directly contrary to those of my own dear country, I should be tempted to say a little in their justification. It is only to be wished that they were as well executed. The first I shall mention relates to informers. All crimes against the state are punished here with the utmost severity; but if the person accused maketh his innocence plainly to appear upon his trial, the accuser is immediately put to an ignominious death; and out of his goods or lands, the innocent person is quadruply recompensed for the loss of his time, for the danger he underwent, for the hardship of his imprisonment, and for all the charges he hath been at in making his defence. Or, if that fund be deficient, it is largely supplied by the crown. The emperor does also confer on him some public mark of his favour, and proclamation is made of his innocence through the whole city.

律和习惯大相径庭的话，我一定会尽量为他们说些公道话的。只是希望能够充分执行就好。我首先要介绍的是对告密者的刑罚。一切背叛国家的罪行在这里都会受到极为严酷的刑罚。但如果被告最终证明了自己的清白无辜，那原告就会立即被判有罪处以死刑。同时，被告能从原告的财产或土地中为他损失的时间、蒙受的危险、牢狱之灾和在官司中为自己辩护所花费的所有费用获得四重赔偿。如果资金不足，则由朝廷负担。皇帝还要公开对被告赐予皇恩，在全城宣告其清白无罪。

They look upon fraud as a greater crime than theft, and therefore seldom fail to punish it with death; for they allege, that care and vigilance, with a very common understanding, may preserve a man's goods from thieves, but honesty has no fence against superior cunning: and since it is necessary that there should be a perpetual intercourse of buying and selling, and dealing upon credit, where fraud is permitted and connived at, or hath

在利利普特国，欺骗比偷窃的罪责更甚，通常会被判以死刑。因为他们普遍认为，只要谨慎警觉就能避免遭到小偷偷窃，但诚实的美德在面对魔高一丈的狡诈时防不胜防。因为人们始终处在买卖关系中，需要诚信交易，如果在买卖中纵容欺骗，而没有法律加以制裁，那么吃亏的就永远是诚实的一方，反而骗子无赖会大发不义之财。我记得有一次，我为一个罪犯向皇上

no law to punish it, the honest dealer is always undone, and the knave gets the advantage. I remember when I was once interceding with the king for a criminal who had wronged his master of a great sum of money, which he had received by order, and run away with; and happening to tell his majesty, by way of extenuation, that it was only a breach of trust; the emperor thought it monstrous in me to offer, as a defence, the greatest aggravation of the crime: and truly I had little to say in return, farther than the common answer, that different nations had different customs; for, I confess, I was heartily ashamed.

求情，这个人奉他主人的命令去收款，竟然携款潜逃，拐走了主人的大笔钱财。我向陛下求情，说这只是一种失信背叛的行为，而陛下却认为我的说辞荒谬到了极点，竟用最严重的罪责用作辩护借口。这让我立刻哑口无言，不知如何作答，只能含含糊糊地回答说各国习俗各有不同。我得承认，当时的我真是羞愧难当。

Although we usually call reward and punishment the two hinges upon which all government turns, yet I could never observe this maxim to be put in practice by any nation except that of *Lilliput*. Whoever can there bring sufficient proof that he hath strictly observed the laws of his country for seventy-three moons, hath a claim to certain privileges, according to his quality and condition of life, with a proportionable sum of money out of a fund appropriated for that use: he likewise acquires the title of *snillpall*, or *legal*, which is added to his name, but does not descend to his posterity. And these people thought it a prodigious defect of policy among us, when I told them that our laws

虽然我们常说，奖赏制度和处罚制度是政府运作的两个关键，但我从没见过哪个国家像利利普特国这样谨守这一格言，做到如此赏罚分明。只要有人能充分证明自己连续 73 个月严格地遵守了本国法律法规，他就会获得一定特权，会根据他的地位和生活条件从国家专用基金中得到相应比例的钱财。他还可能会获得“斯尼尔帕尔”或“里格尔”头衔，这两个名称会同他的名字写到一起，但不会沿袭给后代。当我告诉他们，我们的法律体系只有惩罚制度，没有奖励制度时，他们都觉得不可思议，认为我们的法律制度相当不完善。摆在他们司法厅里象征公正的塑像也很

were enforced only by penalties, without any mention of reward. It is upon this account that the image of Justice, in their courts of judicature, is formed with six eyes, two before, as many behind, and on each side one, to signify circumspection; with a bag of gold open in her right hand, and a sword sheathed in her left, to show she was more disposed to reward than to punish.

能解释他们严明的司法制度。这个塑像有6只眼睛，两只在前，两只在后，左右两边也各有一只，以此表现谨慎公允。她的右手托着一袋金子，开口是敞开着的，左手握着一把入了鞘的宝剑，表示比起惩罚她更愿意奖赏人。

In choosing persons for all employments, they have more regard to good morals than to great abilities; for, since government is necessary to mankind, they believe that the common size of human understandings is fitted to some station or other, and that Providence never intended to make the management of public affairs a mystery, to be comprehended only by a few persons of sublime genius, of which there seldom are three born in an age: but they suppose truth, justice, temperance, and the like, to be in every man's power; the practice of which virtues, assisted by experience and a good intention, would qualify any man for the service of his country, except where a course of study is required. But they thought the want of moral virtues was so far from being supplied by superior endowments of the mind, that employments could never be put into such dangerous hands as those of persons so

入仕选拔时，比起能力卓越的人，他们也更倾向于选择品行端正的人。他们认为，既然人们需要一个政府来总管国家事务，那么普通人的能力就足以胜任相关的管理任务，上天也从没打算将公共管理事务搞得神秘莫测，只赐予一部分天才理解其意义的能力，而这样的天才每代也出现不了几个。但他们认为，诚实、公正、谦和等品质是每个人都具备的能力，只要在行事为人中以这些美德为标准，加之以经验和良好的初衷，那么只要经过学习和训练，假以时日，任何人都有能力为国家效力。但他们认为，如果一个人天赋异禀但道德败坏，那这个人也是万万不能得到录用的。况且，品性忠良的人就算因愚昧无知犯了错误，对人民的安定幸福也不会造成什么致命的后果。相反，若是那些有能力的人存心腐败故意使坏，那他们就会加倍营私舞弊，并掩盖他们的腐败行径。

qualified; and at least, that the mistakes committed by ignorance in a virtuous disposition, would never be of such fatal consequence to the public weal, as the practices of a man whose inclinations led him to be corrupt, and had great abilities to manage, and multiply, and defend his corruptions.

In like manner, the disbelief of a Divine Providence renders a man uncapable of holding any public station; for, since kings avow themselves to be the deputies of Providence, the *Lilliputians* think nothing can be more absurd than for a prince to employ such men as disown the authority under which he acts.

同样，不信仰上帝的人也不能担任任何公共职务。历任皇帝都宣称君权神授，因此利利普特人认为，没有什么比皇帝录用否认至高权威的人更荒谬的事了。

In relating these and the following laws, I would only be understood to mean the original institutions, and not the most scandalous corruptions into which these people are fallen by the degenerate nature of man. For as to that infamous practice of acquiring great employments by dancing on the ropes, or badges of favour and distinction by leaping over sticks, and creeping under them, the reader is to observe, that they were first introduced by the grandfather of the emperor now reigning, and grew to the present height, by the gradual increase of party and faction.

我所介绍的这些和接下来我要说到的法律，指的都是最初始的制度，而不是经过人们的天性、经过世代堕落后蒙上了丑闻腐败的制度。至于那些为获取职位不惜声名狼藉的做法，像读者曾读到的绳上舞蹈，或是根据围着木棍跳上钻下的表现授予荣誉，都是从当今圣上的祖父那代开始兴起，一直沿袭至今的。究其原因就是朝中的党派纷争，内讧不和造成的。

Ingratitude is, among them a capital crime, as we read it to have been in some

在他们看来，忘恩负义是头等重罪，我们也在其他国家的法律中

other countries; for they reason thus, that whoever makes ill returns to his benefactor, must needs be a common enemy to the rest of mankind, from whom he hath received no obligation, and therefore such a man is not fit to live.

Their notions relating to the duties of parents and children differ extremely from ours. Their opinion is, that parents are the last of all others to be trusted with the education of their own children: and therefore they have in every town public nurseries, where all parents, except cottagers and laborers, are obliged to send their infants of both sexes to be reared and educated when they come to the age of twenty moons, at which time, they are supposed to have some rudiments of docility. These schools are of several kinds, suited to different qualities, and to both sexes. They have certain professors well skilled in preparing children for such a condition of life as befits the rank of their parents, and their own capacities as well as inclinations. I shall first say something of the male nurseries, and then of the female.

The nurseries for males of noble or eminent birth, are provided with grave and learned professors, and their several deputies. The clothes and food of the children are plain and simple. They are bred up in the principles of honour,

读到过类似的制度。理由如下，他们认为不论什么人对自己的恩人以怨报德，都会被视为人类的公敌，因为这种人不知感恩，没有资格活在这世上。

他们对为人父母与为人子女的义务的观念与我们的完全不同。他们认为，在教育子女的过程中，父母是最不可靠的人。因此在每个镇子里都设有公共学校，除了佃户和工人外，所有父母都要将年满20个月的子女，不论男孩女孩，送到那里接受教育。因为那么大的孩子应该已经基本具备了可塑性。学校的类型多种多样，适应于不同的社会等级和性别。学校里有经验丰富的老师，根据他们父母的社会地位和孩子自己的兴趣爱好帮助他们培养生活方式。接下来我要先介绍一下男校，然后再介绍女校。

为皇族之后和出身名门的孩子设立的男校配有严肃而博学的老师和他们的副手。孩子的衣服和膳食简单朴素。他们从小就被教育成为自尊，公正，勇敢，谦逊，温和，虔诚和热爱祖国的人。除了他

justice, courage, modesty, clemency, religion, and love of their country; they are always employed in some business, except in the times of eating and sleeping, which are very short, and two hours for diversions, consisting of bodily exercises. They are dressed by men till four years of age, and then are obliged to dress themselves, although their quality be ever so great; and the women attendants, who are aged proportionably to ours at fifty, perform only the most menial offices. They are never suffered to converse with servants, but go together in smaller or greater numbers to take their diversions, and always in the presence of a professor, or one of his deputies; whereby they avoid those early bad impressions of folly and vice to which our children are subject. Their parents are suffered to see them only twice a year; the visit is to last but an hour. they are allowed to kiss the child at meeting and parting; but a professor, who always stands by on those occasions, will not suffer them to whisper, or use any fondling expressions, or bring any presents of toys, sweetmeats, and the like.

们吃饭睡觉的时间——时间通常很短——和两小时包括运动的娱乐时间外，始终有事可做。4 岁前有男仆为他们穿衣，尽管他们身份显赫，但从那以后他们就要学会自己穿衣。女仆的年纪大都在 50 岁，她们只做最卑微的工作。孩子们从来不准跟仆人说话，只准几人一小组或一大组一起玩耍，通常会有老师或老师的副手陪同。这样他们就不会像我们的孩子那样，在年幼时就沾染上行事愚蠢等恶习。孩子的父母每年只能与孩子见两次面，而每次见面时间也只有一个小时。在见面和分离的时候他们可以亲吻孩子，但在见面过程中总会有老师在场，这样他们就不能窃窃私语或有任何爱抚行为，也不能给孩子们送玩具，糖果，等等。

The pension from each family for the education and entertainment of a child, upon failure of due payment, is levied by the emperor’s officers.

每个家庭必须缴纳孩子的教育及娱乐费用，如有拖欠，则由朝廷征收。

The nurseries for children of ordinary gentlemen, merchants, traders, and

为普通绅士，商人和工匠的孩子设立的学校也按照同样的方法

handicrafts, are managed proportionably after the same manner; only those designed for trades are put out apprentices at eleven years old, whereas those of persons of quality continue in their exercises till fifteen, which answers to one and twenty with us: but the confinement is gradually lessened for the last three years.

In the female nurseries, the young girls of quality are educated much like the males, only they are dressed by orderly servants of their own sex, but always in the presence of a professor or deputy, till they come to dress themselves, which is at five years old. And if it be found that these nurses ever presume to entertain the girls with frightful or foolish stories, or the common follies practised by chamber-maids among us, they are publicly whipped thrice about the city, imprisoned for a year, and banished for life to the most desolate part of the country. Thus the young ladies there are as much ashamed of being cowards and fools, as the men, and despise all personal ornaments beyond decency and cleanliness: neither did I perceive any difference in their education, made by their difference of sex, only that the exercises of the females were not altogether so robust, and that some rules were given them relating to domestic life, and a smaller compass of learning was

管理。只有那些打算从商的孩子要在 11 岁时出去当学徒，其他达官贵人家的孩子则继续留在学校学习直到 15 岁，也就是我们的 21 岁，但最后 3 年的管理就渐渐不那么严格了。

在女校里，地位显赫的家族的女儿们接受教育的方式同男孩们相同，只是帮她们穿衣的仆人是衣着整齐的女仆，老师和老师的副手通常也是在场的，一直到她们 5 岁可以自己穿衣了为止。如果发现女仆违反纪律擅自给女孩们讲吓人或愚蠢的故事，或是玩那些女仆们习惯玩的把戏给女孩们看，就要将她们绕城一周鞭打示众，然后关进监狱一年，最后流放到国内最荒无人烟的地方以作惩罚。因此这里的年轻小姐们和男人们一样，都会对胆怯或愚蠢的行为感到羞耻，也都看不起有失体统和拖沓冗繁的打扮。反正我是没看出对男孩和女孩的教育方式有什么不同之处，只是女孩的运动不像男孩的那么剧烈。女孩还要学习一些家务劳动，学习的范围也比男孩的稍小一些，因为他们的信条是，在名门望族中，妻子始终要保持温柔娴淑，通情达理，因为她们不可能永远年轻。当女孩到了 12 岁，到了可以谈婚论嫁的年纪，她们的父母或监护人就

enjoined them: for their maxim is, that among people of quality, a wife should be always a reasonable and agreeable companion, because she cannot always be young. When the girls are twelve years old, which among them is the marriageable age, their parents or guardians take them home, with great expressions of gratitude to the professors, and seldom without tears of the young lady and her companions.

来将她们接回家，对老师也是万般感谢，而女孩离开自己的同伴时往往都是泪流满面。

In the nurseries of females of the meaner sort, the children are instructed in all kinds of works proper for their sex, and their several degrees: those intended for apprentices are dismissed at nine years old, the rest are kept to thirteen.

在较低一等的女校里，女孩们根据自己的性别和身份学习所有适合她们做的工作，打算当学徒的在 9 岁那年离开学校，其余的则要在学校一直待到 13 岁。

The meaner families who have children at these nurseries, are obliged, besides their annual pension, which is as low as possible, to return to the steward of the nursery a small monthly share of their gettings, to be a portion for the child; and therefore all parents are limited in their expenses by the law. For the *Lilliputians* think nothing can be more unjust, than for people to leave the burden of supporting their children on the public. As to persons of quality, they give security to appropriate a certain sum for each child, suitable to their condition; and these funds are always managed with good husbandry, and the most exact justice.

孩子在学校接受教育的贫寒家庭每年要缴纳学费，学费的价格非常低，除每年学费外他们还要按月将所得的一部分交给学校膳务员，作为孩子的食宿费，因此所有家长的花费都是受法律限制的。因为利利普特人认为，父母将教育孩子的负担丢给公共学校是极为不公平的做法。至于地位显赫的大户人家，他们按自己的条件为每个孩子都缴纳一定的资金，这些资金通常会得到妥善使用，公平分配。

The cottagers and laborers keep their children at home, their business being only to till and cultivate the earth, and therefore their education is of little consequence to the public; but the old and diseased among them are supported by hospitals: for begging is a trade unknown in this kingdom.

佃户和工人的孩子留在家里，他们要学习的只有耕地播种而已，因此他们是否接受教育对公众影响不大。他们中年老或患病的人由议员供养，乞讨的行为在这个国家则是闻所未闻、见所未见的。

And here it may perhaps divert the curious reader, to give some account of my domestic, and my manner of living in this country, during a residence of nine months and thirteen days. Having a head mechanically turned, and being likewise forced by necessity, I had made for myself a table and chair convenient enough, out of the largest trees in the royal park. Two hundred sempstresses were employed to make me shirts, and linen for my bed and table, all of the strongest and coarsest kind they could get; which, however, they were forced to quilt together in several folds, for the thickest was some degrees finer than lawn. Their linnen is usually three inches wide, and three foot make a piece.

接下来我要讲的可能会让好奇的读者非常感兴趣——我要描述一下我在利利普特的9个月零13天的生活情况。由于我天生擅长机械物理，再加上生活所需，我就在皇家公园里砍了几棵最高大的树，自己做了一套还算舒适的桌椅。他们还雇了200个女裁缝为我缝制衬衫和亚麻床单桌布，布料选用了他们所能找到的最结实最粗糙的那种。但即便是这样，他们还必须要把好几层布缝到一起才行，因为他们最厚的布同我们的上等细麻布比还是要精细许多。他们一张亚麻布通常是3英寸宽，3英尺长。

The sempstresses took my measure as I lay on the ground, one standing at my neck, and another at my mid-leg, with a strong cord extended, that each held by the end, while the third measured the length of the cord with a rule of an inch long. Then they measured my right thumb, and desired no more; for by a

女裁缝测量我的尺寸时，我是躺在地上的，她们一个站在我脖子上，一个站在我小腿中部，两个人一人拿着一根结实绳索的一头，第三个人则用一根一英寸长的尺子测量绳索的长度。她们又量了量我右手大拇指的尺寸，至此测量工作就结束了。因为通过数学计算方

mathematical computation, that twice round the thumb is once round the wrist, and so on to the neck and the waist, and by the help of my old shirt, which I displayed on the ground before them for a pattern, they fitted me exactly. Three hundred tailors were employed in the same manner to make me clothes; but they had another contrivance for taking my measure. I kneeled down, and they raised a ladder from the ground to my neck; upon this ladder one of them mounted, and let fall a plumb-line from my collar to the floor, which just answered the length of my coat; but my waist and arms I measured myself. When my clothes were finished, which was done in my house (for the largest of theirs would not be able to hold them), they looked like the patch-work made by the ladies in *England*, only that mine were all of a colour.

法，手腕的周长是大拇指周长的两倍，以此类推就能计算出脖子和腰部的尺寸，我又把我的旧衬衫平铺在地上给她们作比照，就这样她们为我缝制出了一件极为贴身的衬衫。还有300个裁缝用相同的办法为我缝制了衣服，但他们测量我尺寸的方法更是奇特。我跪在地上，他们将梯子从地面搭到我的颈部，有一个人顺着梯子爬了上来，将铅垂线从我的领口放下直到地面，这样测量出的就是我的大衣长度。至于腰部尺寸和胳膊的长度则是我自己测量的。衣服是在我的住处缝制的，因为他们最大的屋子也放不下这么大的衣服。等衣服做好以后，样子很像英国妇女们做的百衲衣，只不过我的浑身上下只有一种颜色罢了。

I had three hundred cooks to dress my victuals, in little convenient huts built about my house, where they and their families lived, and prepared me two dishes apiece. I took up twenty waiters in my hand, and placed them on the table, an hundred more attended below on the ground, some with dishes of meat, and some with barrels of wine and other liquors, slung on their shoulders; all which the waiters above drew up as I wanted, in

差不多有 300 个厨师给我做饭，他们和他们的家人住在我住处周围搭建的临时营房里，每人给我做两道菜。我用手将 20 个侍者托起放在桌子上，另外 100 多个在地上服侍我，有些端着肉，有些把酒桶和饮料桶扛在肩上。侍者们想出了很聪明的办法，他们把我要吃喝的食物和饮料从下面用绳索吊着运上来，就像欧洲人从井里吊水桶那样。他们的一盘肉够我吃一口，

a very ingenious manner, by certain cords, as we draw the bucket up a well in *Europe*. A dish of their meat was a good mouthful, and a barrel of their liquor a reasonable draught. Their mutton yields to ours, but their beef is excellent, I have had a sirloin so large, that I have been forced to make three bits of it; but this is rare. My servants were astonished to see me eat it bones and all, as in our country we do the leg of a lark. Their geese and turkeys I usually eat at a mouthful, and I must confess they far exceed ours. Of their smaller fowl I could take up twenty or thirty at the end of my knife.

一桶酒也只够我喝一口。他们的羊肉没有我们的好吃，但牛肉却很美味。我还曾吃到过一块很大的牛脊肉，咬了3口才吃完，但这种情况是很少见的。我的仆人们看到我连骨头也一起吃掉，都很吃惊，但在我们的国家，那就像是在吃一条云雀腿。在这儿我通常能一口吃掉一只鹅或火鸡，但我得说，他们的鹅和火鸡远没有我们的好吃。至于他们小一点的家禽，我用刀尖一下子就能挑起二三十只。

One day his imperial majesty being informed of my way of living, desired that himself, and his royal consort, with the young princes of the blood of both sexes, might have the happiness (as he was pleased to call it) of dining with me. They came accordingly, and I placed them upon chairs of state on my table, just over-against me, with their guards about them. *Flimnap* the lord high treasurer attended there likewise, with his white staff; and I observed he often looked on me with a sour countenance, which I would not seem to regard, but eat more than usual, in honour to my dear country, as well as to fill the court with admiration. I have some private reasons to believe, that this visit from his majesty gave

有一天，皇帝陛下得知了我的生活情况，决定要同皇后和所有的儿女们跟我一起享受用餐的乐趣（陛下很喜欢这样说）。于是有一天他们就来到了我的住所，我把他们放到我桌子上正对着我的御椅，他们的侍卫则站在他们周围。财政大臣福利姆奈普也手持他那根白色的手杖在一旁服侍。我发现他不时地会用一副酸溜溜的表情瞅我两眼，但我懒得理会，比平时更大口地吃了起来，为了我亲爱的祖国，也为了让朝廷的人对我更加赞叹。我心底里觉得，这次陛下的来访又给了福利姆奈普诽谤中伤我的机会。这位大人一直以来都是我的死对头，虽然表面上他表现得对我很友好，但就他平时阴郁的性格

Flimnap an opportunity of doing me ill offices to his master. That minister had always been my secret enemy, though he outwardly caressed me more than was usual to the moroseness of his nature. He represented to the emperor the low condition of his treasury; that he was forced to take up money at a great discount; that exchequer bills would not circulate under nine *percent*, below par; that in short I had cost his majesty above a million and a half of *sprugs* (their greatest gold coin, about the bigness of a spangle); and upon the whole, that it would be advisable in the emperor to take the first fair occasion of dismissing me.

来看这么做是极反常的。他向皇帝报告说，当前的财政状况并不是很好，给下面拨款都要打折扣，国库券的价值比票面价值低 9%才能流通。简而言之就是我已经花掉了陛下超过 1 亿 5000 万斯布拉格（他们最值钱的金币差不多有我们小金属片那么大）。所以皇帝应该在合适的时机将我遣散回国。

I am here obliged to vindicate the reputation of an excellent lady, who was an innocent sufferer upon my account. The treasure took a fancy to be jealous of his wife, from the malice of some evil tongues, who informed him that her grace had taken a violent affection for my person, and the court-scandal ran for some time, that she once came privately to my lodging. This I solemnly declare to be a most infamous falsehood, without any grounds, father than that her grace was pleased to treat me with all innocent marks of freedom and friendship. I own she came often to my house, but always publicly, nor ever without three more in the coach, who were usually her sister and

在这里我还要为一位贤良淑德的女士的名声进行辩护，她因为我的关系蒙上了不白之冤。这位大人竟因听信谗言为他的妻子吃起了飞醋，有人告诉他，说她的妻子疯狂地爱上了我，朝中一时间流言四起，说她曾悄悄来过我的住处。关于这一点，我要严肃声明，这简直是最恶毒的诽谤，根本是毫无根据，无中生有。这位夫人只不过用最无邪的直率和友善对待我。我承认她偶尔会来我的住处，但都是堂堂正正的公开前往，每次都至少有 3 个人同乘马车而来，一般都是她的姐妹，小女儿和一些特别的朋友，但这种行为在朝中的妇女中很是常见。而且我也要呼吁我身边的

young daughter, and some particular acquaintance; but this was commom to many other ladies of the court. And I still appeal to my servants round, whether they at any time saw a coach at my door without knowing what persons were in it. On those occasions, when a servant had given me notice, my custom was to go immediately to the door; and after paying my respects, to take up the coach and two horses very carefully in my hands (for if there were six horses, the postillion always unharnessed four) and place them on a table, where I had fixed a moveable rim quite round, of five inches high, to prevent accidents. And I have often had four coaches and horses at once on my table full of company, while I sat in my chair learning my face towards them; and when I was engaged with one set, the coachmen would gently drive the others round my table. I have passed many an afternoon very agreeably in these conversations. But I defy the treasurer, or his two informers (I will name them, and let them make their best of it), clustril and drunlo, to prove that any person ever came to me incognito, except thr secretary reldresal, who was sent by express command of his imperial majesty, as I have before related. I should not have dwelt so long upon this particular, if it had not been a point wherein the reputation of

仆人们为我作证，让他们说明到底曾经是否见过不知来者何人的马车出现在我的家门口。每当有人来访，我的仆人就会来向我通报，然后我便立即来到门口，行过礼后将马车和两匹马（如果是6匹马的马车，那左马驭者一般都会解下其中的4匹马）一起小心地托在手中，然后放到桌子上。我在桌子上还装上了一圈可拆卸的桌边，高5英寸，目的是防止事故发生。通常我的桌子上会同时有4架马车，而我则会坐在面对他们的椅子里。当我和一架马车里的人交谈时，其他3辆马车的车夫就会驾着马慢慢地在桌面绕着散步。我有很多下午都是在这样愉快的交谈中度过的。但我要公开反抗这位大人和他的两个谣言制造者（我会说出他们的名字，看他们如何全身而退），他们就是克鲁斯特里尔和德郎罗，到底要让他们说说看除了我先前提到的内务大臣瑞尔德瑞萨尔奉陛下之命秘密来访过以外，还有谁曾经匿名来访过我的住处。要不是此事事关之前提到的那位品行高尚的夫人之名誉，我才不会为我自己花这么长的时间辩护。虽然我很荣幸地成为了一个“纳尔达克”，而这位大臣却还没得到此殊荣，大家都知道他只是个“克朗姆”，官位在我之下一级，相当于英国侯爵和公爵的关系。但我得承认，他在朝中的声

a great lady is so nearly concerned, to say nothing of my own; though I had then the honour to be a nardac, which the treasurer himself is not, for all the world knows he is only a clumglum, a title inferior by one degree, as that of a marquis is to a duke in England, although I allow he preceded me in right of his pos. These false informations, which I afterwards came to the knowledge of, by an accident not proper to mention, made flimnap the treasurer show his lady for some time an ill countenance, and me a worse; and although he were at least undeceived and reconciled to her, yet I lost all credit with him, and found my interest decline very fast with the emperor himself, who was indeed too much governed by that favourite.

望比我高。这个谣言是后来我无意中得知的，至于具体怎样得知我不方便透露，因为这个谣言，这位大人对他的妻子摆了很久的臭脸，对我的态度就更恶劣了。虽然最后他醒悟了过来，和他的妻子澄清了误会，但他对我依然信任全无了。而我也发现皇帝陛下对我的兴趣也渐渐冷却，他被他的宠臣们实在是影响得太深了。

CHAPTER 7

第七章

The Author, being informed of a Design to accuse him of High Treason, makes his Escape to Blefuscu. His Reception there.

作者得知有人阴谋指控他犯了叛国罪，于是逃到不来福斯库国，并受到接待。

Before I proceed to give an account of my leaving this kingdom, it may be proper to inform the reader of a private intrigue which had been for two months forming against me.

在接下来要解释我离开这个国家的原因前，我要向读者透露一个他们谋划了两个月想要击垮我的阴谋。

I had been hitherto all my life a stranger to courts, for which I was unqualified by the meanness of my condition. I had indeed heard and read enough of the dispositions of great princes and ministers; but never expected to have found such terrible effects of them in so remote a country, governed, as I thought, by very different maxims from those in Europe.

我在朝中一向是个局外人，因为地位低微，所以一向不过问政事。关于王公大臣的秉性我曾听说过很多，也读过不少相关的书籍，但我绝对没想到这样遥远的国度也会受到同样糟糕的影响，我本以为这里的统治理念同欧洲的完全不同呢。

When I was just preparing to pay my attendance on the emperor of *Blefuscu*, a considerable person at court (to whom I had been very serviceable, at a time when he lay under the highest displeasure of his imperial majesty) came to my house very privately at night in a close chair, and without sending his name, desired admittance: The chairmen were dismissed; I put the chair, with his lordship in it, into

就当我准备造访不来福斯库国时，一位朝中重臣（他曾得罪过皇帝，我因此帮助过他）一天晚上坐着轿子秘密来到我的住处，进门时也没通报姓名。他把车夫支开后，我就将他连同他的轿子放进了我的大衣口袋，吩咐一个可靠的仆人，如果有人来访就说我身体抱恙，已经睡下了。然后我像往常那样关紧屋子的大门，把轿子一起放

my coat-pocket; and giving orders to a trusty servant to say I was indisposed and gone to sleep, I fastened the door of my house, placed the chair on the table, according to my usual custom, and sat down by it. After the common salutations were over, observing his lordship's countenance full of concern, and inquiring into the reason, he desired I would hear him with patience, in a matter that highly concerned my honour and my life. His speech was to the following effect, for I took notes of it as soon as he left me.

在了桌子上，在他旁边坐了下来。我们按照礼节寒暄了几句后，我发现这位大人的表情满是忧愁。我问他为何愁容满面，他便说，让我耐心地听他慢慢道来，这事关乎我的尊严和生命。以下就是他跟我说的内容，他一离开我就用纸笔记了下来。

You are to know, said he, that several committees of council have been lately called in the most private manner on your account: and it is but two days since his majesty came to a full resolution.

他这样说道——你要知道，朝廷为了你的事最近秘密开了很多次大会，两天前陛下终于做出了决定。

You are very sensible that *Skyris Bolgolam* (*galbet,* or high-admiral) hath been your mortal enemy almost ever since your arrival. His original reasons I know not, but his hatred is much increased since your great success against *Blefuscu*, by which his glory, as admiral, is obscured. This lord, in conjunction with *Flimnap* the high treasurer, whose enmity against you is notorious on account of his Lady, *Limtoc* the general, *Lalcon* the chamberlain, and *Balmuff* the grand justiciary, have prepared articles of impeachment against you, for treason, and other capital crimes.

你肯定也明显感到斯奇瑞斯•博尔格拉姆（官衔“盖尔贝特”，海军上将）差不多从你一来就成了你的死对头。一开始他怨恨你的原因我不知道，但自从你立下大功，大败不来福斯库国以后，他对你就越发痛恨了，因为你的功劳盖过了他海军上将的风光，让他颜面尽失。于是这位大人便联合起财务大臣福利姆奈普，就是那位因为他妻子和你传出绯闻而对你恨之入骨的大人，以及大将军利穆托克，宫廷大臣拉尔肯和司法部大臣巴尔穆夫，准备联名上书，控告你犯了叛国罪及其他重罪。

This preface made me so impatient, being conscious of my own merits and innocence, that I was going to interrupt; when he entreated me to be silent, and thus proceeded.

这位大臣的开场白让我按捺不住想要打断，因为我认为我只有功没有过。但他请我静静听他讲完，接着说了下去：

Out of gratitude for the favours you have done for me, I procured information of the whole proceedings, and a copy of the articles, wherein I venture my head for your service.

因为你曾有恩于我，我万分感激，所以我冒死打听到了他们诉讼的所有信息，搞到了一份弹劾书原文。

Articles of Impeachment against Quinbus Flestrin, the Man-Mountain.

巨人山昆布斯·弗莱斯特林的弹劾书。

ARTICLE I.

WHEREAS, by a statute made in the reign of his Imperial Majesty *Calin Deffar Plune*, it is enacted, That whoever shall make water within the Precincts of the Royal Palace, shall be liable to the Pains and Penalties of High-Treason: Notwithstanding, the said *Quinbus Flestrin*, in open breach of the said Law, under colour of extinguishing the Fire kindled in the Apartment of his Majesty's dear Imperial Consort, did maliciously, traitorously, and devilishly, by discharge of his Urine, put out the said Fire kindled in the said Apartment, lying and being within the Precincts of the said Royal Palace, against the Statute in that Case provided, *ec*. Against the Duty, *ec*.

第一条

凯林·德法尔·普鲁尼皇帝陛下在位时曾颁布过这样一条法令，在皇宫境内随地小便者将以严重叛国罪论处。昆布斯·弗莱斯特林以为皇后寝宫救火为借口公然触犯该条法令，竟撒尿灭火，实为居心叵测，忤逆不忠之举，影响极为恶劣。另外还在皇宫内随意躺卧，不仅触犯相关法令，还有不恭之嫌。

ARTICLE II.

THAT the said *Quinbus Flestrin* having brought the imperial fleet of *Blefuscu* into the royal port, and being afterwards commanded by his imperial majesty to seize all the other ships of the said empire of *Blefuscu*, and reduce that empire to a province, to be governed by a viceroy from hence, and to destroy and put to death not only all the *Big-endian exiles*, but likewise all the people of that empire, who would not immediately forsake the *Big-endian* heresy: He the said *Flestrin*, like a false traitor against his most auspicious, serene, imperial majesty, did petition to be excused from the said service, upon pretence of unwillingness to force the consciences, or destroy the liberties and lives of an innocent people.

第二条

在昆布斯·弗莱斯特林将敌国不来福斯库国的舰队缴来我皇家港口后，皇帝陛下又命令他再将不来福斯库国其他所有的船只统统俘获来，继而将该国降为一省，从此派总督管理，并将所有大端派的流犯以及该国境内所有坚持大端派异端邪说的人全部处死。而叛徒弗莱斯特林却以不愿昧着良心亵渎自由、葬送无辜人性命为由，违抗了受上天庇护，无上尊贵的陛下的旨意。

ARTICLE III.

THAT, whereas certain ambassadors arrived from the court of *Blefuscu* to sue for peace in his majesty's court: he the said *Flestrin* did, like a false traitor, aid, abet, comfort, and divert the said ambassadors, although he knew them to be servants to a prince who was lately an open enemy to his imperial majesty, and in open war against his said majesty.

第三条

在不来福斯库国使者来我天朝向吾皇求和时，弗莱斯特林一副叛国贼嘴脸，向这些使者阿谀奉承，逢迎讨好，而他明知这些使者的主子正是与我天朝皇帝陛下为敌，并公然以武力相持的敌人。

ARTICLE IV.

THAT the said *Quinbus Flestrin*, contrary to the duty of a faithful subject, is now preparing to make a voyage to the court and empire of *Blefuscu*, for which he hath received only verbal license from his imperial majesty; and under colour of the said license, doth falsely and traitorously intend to take the said voyage, and thereby to aid, comfort, and abet the emperor of *Blefuscu*, so late an enemy, and in open war with his imperial majesty aforesaid.

第四条

昆布斯·弗莱斯特林身为本朝臣民，竟心怀不忠，准备造访不来福斯库国，而就这一点吾皇陛下只是口头应允了而已。他以陛下的口头准许为借口，还真打算将此访问付诸实现，然后辅佐帮助支持我国之死敌不来福斯库国皇帝，其叛国阴谋昭然若揭。

There are some other articles, but these are the most important, of which I have read you an abstract.

In the several debates upon this impeachment, it must be confessed that his majesty gave many marks of his great lenity, often urging the services you had done him, and endeavoring to extenuate your crimes. The treasurer and admiral insisted that you should be put to the most painful and ignominious death, by setting fire on your house at night, and the general was to attend with twenty thousand men armed with poisoned arrows to shoot you on the face and hands. Some of your servants were to have private orders to strew a poisonous juice on your shirts, which would soon make you tear your own flesh, and die in the utmost torture. The general came into the

除了这几条，还有几条其他的罪名，但以上这些罪名是最主要的，我已经概要念给你听了。

在关于此弹劾的多次讨论中，陛下也多次主张宽大处理，时常提到你的丰功伟绩，尽力为你减轻罪名。但财务大臣和海军上将坚持认为应该将你处以最严酷的死刑，遗臭万年，把你连人带房子一把火烧掉。大将军则提议由2万人朝你的脸和手发射毒箭，置你于死地。他们还密令你的几个仆人在你的衣衫上洒上毒汁，这样你不一会儿就会撕扯自己的皮肉，受尽痛苦折磨而死。因为大将军也同意将你弹劾处死，于是朝中大部分的大臣就都纷纷站到反对你的队伍中了。但皇帝陛下的意思还是尽可能留你一命，最后还争取到宫廷大臣的支持。

same opinion, so that for a long time there was a majority against you. But his majesty resolving, if possible, to spare your life, at last brought off the chamberlain.

Upon this incident, *Reldresal* principal secretary for private affairs, who always approved himself your true friend, was commanded by the emperor to deliver his opinion, which he accordingly did; and therein justified the good thoughts you have of him. He allowed your crimes to be great, but that still there was room for mercy, the most commendable virtue in a prince, and for which his majesty was so justly celebrated. He said the friendship between you and him was so well known to the world, that perhaps the most honourable board might think him partial: however, in obedience to the command he had received, he would freely offer his sentiments. That if his majesty, in consideration of your services, and pursuant to his own merciful disposition, would please to spare your life, and only give orders to put out both your eyes, he humbly conceived, that, by this expedient, justice might in some measure be satisfied, and all the world would applaud the lenity of the emperor, as well as the fair and generous proceedings of those who have the honour to be his counselors. That the loss of your eyes would be no

就这个问题皇帝还命令内务大臣瑞尔德瑞萨尔发表意见。这位大臣与你私交甚好，一直将自己称作你忠实的朋友，他随后的意见也证明了他没有辜负你对他的好印象。他承认你罪大恶极，但罪不至死，尚有可怜悯之处。而且皇帝最值得称道的美德就是宅心仁厚，而皇帝陛下也正是因为具备这一美德而被天下人所称颂。他说他同你之间的友谊举国皆知，尊敬的各位大人可能会认为他有偏袒之意，但皇帝陛下既然命令他阐述观点，那他也不妨坦诚地说出自己的观点——如果皇帝陛下还念你曾立下大功，愿意仁慈地对你网开一面，不妨就免你一死，只下令将你两眼刺瞎就好。他认为这是个权宜之计，既能在一定程度上彰显公正，举国上下都会赞颂陛下的慈悲心肠，又能体现有幸成为陛下谋臣的大人们的公平慷慨。而且就算你眼瞎，也不会妨碍你发挥身体的力量，因此你仍然能为皇帝陛下效力。失明还能为我们增添勇气，因为看不见危险。你在偷袭敌军舰队时最担心的也是你的眼睛，这也是后来你违抗皇帝让你再次出击的命令的原

impediment to your bodily strength, by which you might still be useful to his majesty. That blindness is an addition to courage, by concealing dangers from us; that the fear you had for your eyes, was the greatest difficulty in bringing over the enemy's fleet, and it would be sufficient for you to see by the eyes of the ministers, since the greatest princes do no more.

因，因此以后有大臣们做你的眼睛也就够了。

This proposal was received with the utmost disapprobation by the whole board. *Bolgolam*, the admiral, could not preserve his temper; but rising up in fury, said, he wondered how the secretary durst presume to give his opinion for preserving the life of a traitor: that the services you had performed, were, by all true reasons of state, the great aggravation of your crime; that you, who were able to extinguish the fire, by discharge of Urine in her Majesty's Apartment(which he mentioned with horror)might, at another time, raise an Inundation by the same Means, to drown the whole Palace; and the same strength which enabled you to bring over the enemy's fleet, might serve, upon the first discontent to carry it back: that he had good reasons to think you were a *Big-endian* in your heart; and as treason begins in the heart before it appears in overt acts, so he accused you as a traitor on that account, and therefore insisted you should be put to death.

而这个提议引起了全体大臣的反对。海军上将博尔格拉姆抑制不住心中怒火，愤慨地说道，他真是不明白内务大臣怎么敢为了保全叛徒的性命而提出这样的观点。你的所谓功劳从国家角度出发来看都只能更加重你的罪名。你既然能用撒尿的办法将皇后寝宫的大火扑灭（说到这儿他都惊得哆嗦了起来），那下次你就可能用同样的办法给整个皇宫引发洪水。你能有本事把敌军的舰队给俘获来，那没准你一个不开心就又把舰队给送回去了。他还说他坚持认为你本质上是个大端派，而叛国罪总是想法先于行动，因此他指控你犯了叛国罪，应当以死论处。

The treasurer was of the same opinion; he showed to what straits his majesty's revenue was reduced by the charge of maintaining you, which would soon grow insupportable: That the secretary's expedient of putting out your eyes was so far from being a remedy against this evil, that it would probably increase it, as is manifest from the common practice of blinding some kind of Fowl, after which they fed the faster, and grew sooner fat: That his sacred majesty and the council, who are your judges, were in their own consciences fully convinced of your guilt, which was a sufficient argument to condemn you to death without the formal proofs required by the strict letter of the law.

财务大臣的想法也是这样。他说为了供养你，皇帝的财政正面临巨大问题，马上就要负担不起了。内务大臣关于刺瞎你双眼的提议会更加剧国家的财政负担，因为事实证明，如果鸟儿失明，那它就会吃得更多，长得更胖。如果皇帝和大臣——你的判官——都坚持你有罪，那么不再需要什么法律所规定的证据就足够判你死罪。

But his imperial majesty fully determined against capital punishment, was graciously pleased to say, that since the council thought the loss of your eyes too easy a censure, some other may be inflicted hereafter. And your friend, the secretary humbly desiring to be heard again, in answer to what the treasurer had objected concerning the great charge his majesty was at in maintaining you, said, that his excellency, who had the sole disposal of the emperor's revenue, might easily provide against that evil, by gradually lessening your establishment; by which, for want of sufficient food, you

但皇帝陛下还是决定不对你用极刑，他宽厚仁慈地说，既然大臣们认为只赐你失明太便宜你了，那以后还是可以加刑的。但你的朋友内务大臣又谦逊地请求给他再一次发言的机会，针对财务大臣提出皇帝陛下供养你的花销太大的问题，他说既然财务大臣有权利支配皇帝的财政收支，那这个问题就很好办了，只要渐渐削减你的生活补给就行了。这样一来，由于没有足够的食物你就会日渐虚弱无力，几个月以后体力就会消耗殆尽。而且就算你尸体腐烂也不会带来多大危险，因为你的体重已经减掉了

would grow weak and faint, and lose your appetite, and consequently decay and consume in a few months; neither would the stench of your carcass be then so dangerous, when it should become more than half diminished; and immediately upon your death, five or six thousand of his majesty's subjects might, in two or three days, cut your flesh from your bones, take it away by cart-loads, and bury it in distant parts to prevent infection, leaving the skeleton as a monument of admiration to posterity.

一半。你一死掉，皇帝陛下的 5000 或 6000 个臣民就可以在两三天的时间里把你的肉从骨头上割下来用运货马车运走，埋到很远的地方避免传播疾病，你的骨架则会作为纪念物供后人瞻仰。

Thus by the great friendship of the secretary, the whole affair was compromised. It was strictly enjoined, that the project of starving you by degrees should be kept a secret, but the sentence of putting out your eyes was entered on the books; none dissenting except *Bolgolam* the admiral, who being a creature of the empress, was perpetually instigated by her majesty to insist upon your death, she having borne perpetual malice against you, on account of that illegal method you took to extinguish the Fire in her Apartment.

因为你好朋友内务大臣的关系，大家就都同意了这个解决方案。皇帝命令说，关于要渐渐饿死你的整件事情必须严格保密，但关于刺瞎你双眼的判决已经载入弹劾书里了。除博尔格拉姆以外所有官员全无异议。博尔格拉姆是皇后的亲信，因为皇后的教唆，他始终坚持要将你处以死刑。就因为你那次使用非法方法扑灭她寝宫的大火，她对你已经深恶痛绝了。

In three days your friend the secretary will be directed to come to your house, and read before you the articles of impeachment; and then to signify the great lenity and favour of his majesty and council, whereby you are only condemned

3 天后你的朋友内务大臣就会来到你的住处向你宣读弹劾书的条文。到时候，为了显示皇帝陛下和满朝大臣的宽厚慈爱，你只会被处以刺瞎双眼。对于这一点，皇帝陛下毫无异议地认为你会满心感

to the loss of your eyes, which his majesty doth not question you will gratefully and humbly submit to; and twenty of his majesty's surgeons will attend, in order to see the operation well performed, by discharging very sharp-pointed arrows into the balls of your eyes, as you lie on the ground.

I leave to your prudence what measures you will take; and, to avoid suspicion, I must immediately return in as private a manner as I came.

His lordship did so, and I remained alone, under many doubts and perplexities of mind.

It was a custom introduced by this prince and his ministry (very different, as I have been assured, from the practices of former times), that after the court had decreed any cruel execution either to gratify the monarch's resentment, or the malice of a favourite, the emperor made a speech to his whole council, expressing his great lenity and tenderness, as qualities known and confessed by all the world. This speech was immediately published through the kingdom; nor did anything terrify the people so much as those encomiums on his majesty's mercy; because it was observed, that the more these praises were enlarged and insisted on, the more inhuman was the punishment, and the sufferer more

激谦卑顺服地接受这一宣判。为了保证手术顺利，到时候会有 20 个御医到场，行刑人员会让你躺在地上，然后把锋利的箭刺进你的眼球里。

我要走了，至于怎样应对就要靠你自己慎重考虑了，为了不被怀疑，我必须马上像来时那样悄悄地回去。

大人走后，就剩我一个人在屋子里，心里充满了疑问和困惑。

皇帝和他的内阁都有这样一个习惯（有人跟我说这次同以往特别不同），那就是在朝廷因为皇帝泄愤或宠臣恶意预谋的缘故宣布任何一个判决后，皇帝就要在全体内阁会议上发表演说，表达出他有着举世公认的慈悲宽大和仁厚温和。这个演说很快就在全国传了开来，老百姓都对皇帝的溢美之词害怕到不行，因为就以往经验，皇帝越是坚定夸大地赞美，那刑罚就越是惨无人道，受害者就越是无辜蒙冤。至于我自己，我必须要承认，我从来就没有成为朝臣的天资，也没有受到同等的教育，我对事情的判断力也差强人意，因此对于给我的判决，我丝毫看不出有什么慈悲宽厚可言，反而觉得（也许是我的

innocent. And, as to myself, I must confess, having never been designed for a courtier either by my birth or education, I was so ill a judge of things, that I could not discover the lenity and favour of this sentence, but conceived it (perhaps erroneously) rather to be rigorous than gentle, I sometimes thought of standing my trial, for although I could not deny the facts alleged in the several articles, yet I hoped they would admit of some extenuations. But having in my life perused many state-trials, which I ever observed to terminate as the judges thought fit to direct, I durst not rely on so dangerous a decision, in so critical a juncture, and against such powerful enemies. Once I was strongly bent upon resistance, for while I had liberty, the whole strength of that empire could hardly subdue me, and I might easily with stones pelt the metropolis to pieces; but I soon rejected that project with horror, by remembering the oath I had made to the emperor, the favours I received from him, and the high title of *nardac* he conferred upon me. Neither had I so soon learned the gratitude of courtiers, to persuade myself that his majesty's present severities acquitted me of all past obligations.

想法有误）严苛至极。有时我想索性就去接受审判，因为我不能否认弹劾书里的罪名，但我还是希望他们能够对我酌情从轻发落。但就我详细考察过的许多国家的审判来看，判决往往是由法官从主观想法判定的，我可不敢在这么命悬一线的时候，并且还面对着这样强大的敌人来指望这么危险的决定方式。我还打算奋力反抗，因为目前我还是自由之身，就算使出倾国的力量他们也难将我制伏，我用石块就能将他们的皇城击个粉碎。但马上我又惶恐地打消了这个念头，因为我想起我曾向皇帝许下的誓言，他对我的宠爱以及他封给我的高级荣誉“纳尔达克”。我也没这么快就学到朝臣们那种善于感恩的心态，我劝自己说，既然皇帝现在这么严酷，那我也不必为以前所尽的义务而耿耿于怀。

At last I fixed upon a resolution, for which it is probable I may incur some censure, and not unjustly; for I confess I

终于我下定了决心。这样做可能会为我招致责难，但那倒也正常。因为坦白讲，我的双目仍然完

owe the preserving my eyes, and consequently my liberty, to my own great rashness and want of experience: because if I had then known the nature of princes and ministers, which I have since observed in many other courts, and their methods of treating criminals less obnoxious than myself, I should with great alacrity and readiness have submitted to so easy a punishment. But hurried on by the precipitancy of youth, and having his imperial majesty's license to pay my attendance upon the emperor of *Blefuscu*, I took this opportunity, before the three days were elapsed, to send a letter to my friend the secretary, signifying my resolution of setting out that morning for *Blefuscu* pursuant to the leave I had got; and without waiting for an answer, I went to that side of the island where our fleet lay. I seized a large man of war, tied a cable to the prow, and lifting up the anchors, I stripped myself, put my clothes (together with my coverlet, which I brought under my arm) into the vessel, and drawing it after me between wading and swimming, arrived at the royal port of *Blefuscu*, where the people had long expected me; they lent me two guides to direct me to the capital city, which is of the same name. I held them in my hands until I came within two hundred yards of the gate, and desired them to signify my arrival to one of the secretaries, and let

好无损，还最终获得了自由，这都是因为我的鲁莽和缺乏经验。要是我那时就看清了国王和大臣的本质——这一点是后来我在其他朝廷里学来的——以及他们对待罪责比我轻的罪犯的方法，我一定会欣然准备好接受这一轻微的刑罚。但因为年纪尚轻，性格鲁莽轻率，再加上皇帝陛下恩准我拜访不来福斯库国国王的机会，我就借机趁 3 天还没过去时给我的朋友内务大臣寄了一封信，告诉他当天早晨我就要赶往不来福斯库国以脱身。没等我的朋友给我回信，我就赶往小岛停泊舰队的那岸去了。我抓住一艘大型战舰，将绳索系在船头上，拔起锚，脱下衣服，将衣服和被单（我夹在胳膊下带出来的）一起扔上船，将船拖在身后，半游半蹚地来到了不来福斯库国的皇家港口，那里的人们早就在岸边等着迎接我了。他们派出了两个人领我去都城，都城的名字也是一样的，我将这两个小人托在手中走了一路，直到来到离城门还有 200 码的地方，我请他们去向里面通报我已来到的消息，并告诉他们，我正等着皇帝陛下的命令。大约一个小时后我接到回话，皇帝陛下正同他的皇室成员和朝中大臣赶来接见我。于是我就又往前走了 100 码。皇帝和他的随从从马上跳了下来，皇后和贵妇们也从马车里走出来，我丝毫没看出他们有丝毫恐惧或担心的神

him know, I there waited his majesty's command. I had an answer in about an hour, that his majesty, attended by the royal family, and great officers of the court, was coming out to receive me. I advanced a hundred yards. The emperor, and his train, alighted from their horses, the empress and ladies from their coaches, and I did not perceive they were in any fright or concern. I lay on the ground to kiss his majesty's and the empress's hand. I told his majesty that I was come according to my promise, and with the license of the emperor my master, to have the honour of seeing so mighty a monarch, and to offer him any service in my power consistent with my duty to my own prince; not mentioning a word of my disgrace, because I had hitherto no regular information of it, and might suppose myself wholly ignorant of any such design; neither could I reasonably conceive that the emperor would discover the secret while I was out of his power: wherein, however, it soon appeared I was deceived.

色。我躺在地上亲吻了皇帝和皇后的手，告诉皇帝陛下我履行了承诺，获得了利利普特国皇帝的准许，有幸来访问他这位伟大的君王，也愿意像效忠于我自己的皇帝那样施展力量为他服务。但对于我的失宠我只字未提，因为至今我都没收到正式的通知，也不能表现出丝毫我已知晓计划的迹象。我现在也不在皇帝的势力范围，所以估计他不会将密谋公诸于众。然而很快，我就发现我的想法是错误的。

I shall not trouble the reader with the particular account of my reception at this court, which was suitable to the generosity of so great a prince; nor of the difficulties I was in for want of a house and bed, being forced to lie on the ground, wrapped up in my coverlet.

关于我在不来福斯库国受到的接待细节我就不向读者赘述了，总之此接待不枉一位伟大君王的慷慨雅量。我也不想多说我在那里没有住处没有床，只能在地上裹着被单睡觉的窘境了。

CHAPTER 8

第八章

The Author, by a lucky Accident, finds Means to leave Blefuscu; and after some Difficulties, returns safe to his native country.

作者侥幸找到了逃出不来福斯库国的方法。在经历重重困难后终于安全返回了他的祖国。

Three days after my arrival, walking out of curiosity to the North-East coast of the island, I observed, about half a league off, in the sea, somewhat that looked like a boat overturned. I pulled off my shoes and stockings, and wading two or three hundred yards, I found the object to approach nearer by force of the tide, and then plainly saw it to be a real boat, which I supposed might, by some tempest, have been driven from a ship; whereupon I returned immediately towards the city, and desired his imperial majesty to lend me twenty of the tallest vessels he had left after the loss of his fleet, and three thousand seamen under the command of his vice-admiral. This fleet sailed round, while I went back the shortest way to the coast, where I first discovered the boat; I found the tide had driven it still nearer. The seamen were all provided with cordage, which I had beforehand twisted to a sufficient strength. When the ships

在我到达不来福斯库国的3天后，由于好奇，我走到了这个岛的东北岸想一探究竟。我发现半里格远的海上漂着一个像是倒扣着的船的东西。我脱下鞋袜，在水里蹚行了两三百码，而那个东西也随着海浪逐渐漂近，然后我清楚地看明白那真是一艘小船，我估计是遭遇暴风雨从大船上被卷来的。于是我立刻离开岸边回到城里，请求皇帝陛下借给我舰队损失后剩下的最高的船只和海军中将指挥的 3000 个水手。这支舰队绕道而行，我则抄最近的路赶到了我第一次发现小船的海岸。我看到海浪将这艘小船推得更近了。水手们全都带着绳索，而这些绳索我也事先牢牢地将它们拧在一起了。等舰队到了，我就脱下了衣服，在水中蹚行到离小船 100 码的位置，之后就不得不游过去了。水手们把绳索的一端扔给了我，我将绳索系在船头的洞里，绳索的另一端则系在一艘军舰上。

came up, I stripped myself, and waded till I came within a hundred yards of the boat, after which I was forced to swim till I got up to it. The seamen threw me the end of the cord, which I fastened to a hole in the fore-part of the boat, and the other end to a man of war: But I found all my labor to little purpose; for being out of my depth, I was not able to work. In this necessity, I was forced to swim behind, and push the boat forwards as often as I could, with one of my hands; and the tide favouring me, I advanced so far, that I could just hold up my chin and feel the ground. I rested two or three minutes, and then gave the boat another shove, and so on till the sea was no higher than my Armpits; and now the most laborious part being over, I took out my other cables which were stowed in one of the ships, and fastened them first to the boat, and then to nine of the vessels which attended me; the wind being favorable, the seamen towed, and I shoved till we arrived within forty yards of the shore, and waiting till the tide was out, I got dry to the boat, and, by the assistance of two thousand men, with ropes and engines, I made a shift to turn it on its bottom, and found it was but little damaged.

但我发现我所有的努力都是白费，因为脚踩不到水底，所以没法工作。因此我不得不游到小船后面，用一只手尽力将它向前推。海浪倒帮了我不小的忙，我一直往前游到脚能踩到水底的地方，那个地方的水刚刚没过我的下巴。我休息了两三分钟，然后才又接着开始推，一直推到海面没过我腋窝的地方。最费力气的工作到此结束，我拿出其他放在船里的绳索，将它们先系在小船上，然后再系到 9 艘支援我的军舰上。风向也正合我意，水手们在前面拖着，我在后面推着，就这样我们来到了离海岸 50 码远的地方，一直在那里等到海水退潮。我把小船拖上岸，在 2000 个随行水手的帮助下，借助绳索和器械将小船翻转了过来，发现这艘小船受到的损伤很小。

I shall not trouble the reader with the difficulties I was under by the help of certain paddles, which cost me ten days making, to get my boat to the royal port of

我就不多跟读者啰唆，我耗了 10 天时间做成的船桨将小船划到不来福斯库国的皇家码头花了多少力气了。我到达时那里已经人山

Blefuscu, where a mighty concourse of people appeared upon my arrival, full of wonder at the sight of so prodigious a vessel. I told the emperor that my good fortune had thrown this boat in my way, to carry me to some place from whence I might return into my native country, and begged his majesty's orders for getting materials to fit it up, together with his license to depart; which, after some kind expostulation, he was pleased to grant.

人海，他们看到这样大的一艘船时无不惊讶万分。我告诉皇帝说，上天赐给我这艘小船是我的运气，这样我就能乘着这艘小船出海，说不定就能回到我的祖国。我请求皇帝陛下能下令提供给我一些在船上用的装备和出关的通行证。他先是温和地劝说了我几句，但最后还是欣然恩准了我的请求。

I did very much wonder, in all this time, not to have heard of any express relating to me from our emperor to the court of *Blefuscu*. But I was afterwards given privately to understand that, his imperial majesty, never imagining I had the least notice of his designs, believed I was only gone to *Blefuscu* in performance of my promise, according to the license he had given me, which was well known at our court, and would return in a few days when the ceremony was ended. But he was at last in pain at my long absence; and, after consulting with the treasurer, and the rest of that cabal, a person of quality was dispatched with the copy of the articles against me. This envoy had instructions to represent to the monarch of *Blefuscu*, the great lenity of his master, who was content to punish me no further than the loss of my eyes; that I had fled from justice, and if I did not return in two

那些日子我一直想不明白，为什么没有利利普特国的使者为了我的事代表皇帝来不来福斯库国。但后来才有人私下告诉我说，皇帝陛下丝毫没想到我已经知悉了他的计划，以为我只是因为有了他给我的通行证，应约来不来福斯库国访问，这事全朝上下也都是知道的，还以为等我几天的访问结束后就会回去。但最后他发现我去了那么久却还没回来，就开始担心了。在跟他的财务大臣和阴谋集团商议过后，就派了一位颇有身份的人带着弹劾书副本去往不来福斯库国。这位使者奉命向不来福斯库国的国君说明了他主子的仁慈宽大，只是赐我双目失明的刑罚而已，然而我却畏罪潜逃，要是我两个小时内还不回去的话，就会革去我“纳尔达克”的头衔，并宣判我为叛国贼。这个使者还说，为了维护两国和平友好的关系，他的主子希望皇

hours, I should be deprived of my title of *nardac,* and declared a traitor. The envoy further added, that in order to maintain the peace and amity between both empires, his master expected, that his brother of *Blefuscu* would give orders to have me sent back to *Lilliput*, bound hand and foot, to be punished as a traitor.

兄能够下令将我手脚捆绑后遣送回利利普特国，接受叛国贼的刑罚。

The emperor of *Blefuscu* having taken three days to consult, returned an answer consisting of many civilities and excuses. *He* said, that as for sending me bound, his brother knew it was impossible; that although I had deprived him of his fleet, yet he owed great obligations to me for many good offices I had done him in making the peace. That however both their majesties would soon be made easy; for I had found a prodigious vessel on the shore, able to carry me on the sea, which he had given order to fit up with my own assistance and direction; and he hoped in a few weeks both empires would be freed from so insupportable an Encumbrance.

不来福斯库国的皇帝跟他的内阁商议了3天后谦和有礼地给出了回答，内容也多为我开脱之意。陛下说，诚如皇兄所知，要将我五花大绑起来是做不到的。尽管我拖走了他的舰队，但他也很感谢我在两国议和时给予他的帮助。而且他们双方马上也将不必烦恼我的事情了，因为我在海边找到了一艘巨大的船能够载我出海，并且他已下令在我的协助和指导下将那艘船装备完毕。他希望几个星期后两国就都能摆脱掉我这个他们供应不起的累赘。

With this answer the envoy returned to *Lilliput*, and the monarch of *Blefuscu* related to me all that had passed, offering me at the same time (but under the strictest confidence) his gracious protection, if I would continue in his service; wherein although I believed him sincere, yet I resolved never more to put any confidence in princes or ministers

于是使者就将此回话传到了利利普特国。不来福斯库国皇帝将这所有的过程告诉了我，并同时极其秘密地向我表示如果我愿意继续为他效劳，他愿意竭力保护我。对于他的好意，我虽然诚心地相信他，但我再也不愿推心置腹地相信这些王公大臣了，避之唯恐不及。因此我谢绝了他的好意，乞求他能

where I could possibly avoid it; and therefore, with all due acknowledgments for his favourable intentions, I humbly begged to be excused. I told him, that since fortune, whether good or evil, had thrown a vessel in my way, I was resolved to venture myself in the ocean, rather than be an occasion of difference between two such mighty monarchs. Neither did I find the emperor at all displeased; and I discovered by a certain accident, that he was very glad of my resolution, and so were most of his ministers.

原谅。我告诉他，命运将一艘小船赐给了我，虽然不知是吉是凶，但我愿意顺应命运就此出海一搏，这样一来两国也不用为了我而发生分歧。我没看出皇帝因我的回答有什么不满，后来我也偶然发现他对我的决定还是很高兴的，大部分他的大臣也是这样。

These considerations moved me to hasten my departure somewhat sooner than I intended; to which the court, impatient to have me gone, very readily contributed. Five hundred workmen were employed to make two sails to my boat, according to my directions, by quilting thirteen fold of their strongest linen together. I was at the pains of making ropes and cables, by twisting ten, twenty or thirty of the thickest and strongest of theirs. A great stone that I happened to find, after a long search by the sea-shore, served me for an anchor. I had the tallow of three hundred cows for greasing my boat, and other uses. I was at incredible pains in cutting down some of the largest Timber Trees for oars and masts, wherein I was, however, much assisted by his majesty's ship-carpenters, who helped me

这更让我加紧了离开的想法。而全朝上下也全巴不得我赶紧走，都来帮我殷勤地做准备工作。皇帝根据我的请求雇了500个工人用13层他们最结实的亚麻布缝在一起为我的小船做了两张帆。我也一直很卖力地制作绳索和缆绳，就是将他们最粗最结实的绳子 10 根，20 根或 30 根拧在一起。我用我在海边找了很久才找到的一块大石头当做船锚，用 300 头牛的脂油润滑船体并留作他用。我花了很大的力气砍了几棵他们最高的原木制作了船桨和桅杆，但这个过程中皇帝派来的造船木匠帮了我很大的忙，我将船桨和桅杆粗略打造成型后由他们帮我将木料打磨光滑。

in smoothing them, after I had done the rough work.

In about a month, when all was prepared, I sent to receive his majesty's commands, and to take my leave. The emperor and royal family came out of the palace; I lay down on my face to kiss his hand, which he very graciously gave me; so did the empress and young princes of the blood. His majesty presented me with fifty purses of two hundred *sprugs* apiece, together with his picture at full length, which I put immediately into one of my gloves, to keep it from being hurt. The ceremonies at my departure were too many to trouble the reader with at this time.

差不多一个月后，所有准备工作大致完成，我便去接受皇帝陛下的命令，准备出发。皇帝和所有皇族来到大殿外，我脸贴着地躺了下来亲吻了陛下的手，陛下向我伸出手时态度也非常和蔼仁慈。我也同样亲吻了皇后和年轻皇子的手。皇帝赐给了我 50 个钱袋，每个钱袋里装着 200“斯普拉格”，还有一幅他的全身画像。我立马将这幅画像塞进了一只手套里以防止它受到损坏。关于我的送别典礼我现在就不多向读者赘述了。

I stored the boat with the carcasses of a hundred oxen, and three hundred sheep, with bread and drink proportionable, and as much meat ready dressed as four hundred cooks could provide. I took with me six cows and two bulls alive, with as many ewes and Rams, intending to carry them into my own country, and propagate the breed. And to feed them on board, I had a good bundle of hay, and a bag of corn. I would gladly have taken a dozen of the natives, but this was a thing the emperor would by no means permit; and besides a diligent search into my pockets, his majesty engaged my Honour not to carry away any of his subjects, although

我在小船上储备了 100 只全牛，300 只全羊和同比例量的面包和饮料，还有 400 个厨子烹饪出的大量熟肉。我还随船带了 6 只活的乳牛和公牛，以及大群母羊和公羊，打算带回我自己的国家饲养繁殖。因为要在船上喂养它们，我还带了一大捆干草和一袋谷物。我本想再带上十几个当地人同行，但皇帝说什么也不同意。他还派人认认真真地搜了我的口袋，还让我发誓不会带走任何他的臣民，就算他们自己同意或很想去也不行。

with their own consent and desire.

Having thus prepared all things as well as I was able, I set sail on the twenty-fourth day of *September*, 1701, at six in the morning; and, when I had gone about four leagues to the northward, the wind being at South-East, at six in the evening, I descried a small island about half a league to the North-West. I advanced forward, and cast anchor on the Lee-side of the island, which seemed to be uninhabited. I then took some refreshment, and went to my rest. I slept well, and I conjecture at least six hours, for I found the day broke in two hours after I awaked. It was a clear night. I eat my breakfast before the sun was up; and heaving anchor, the wind being favourable, I steered the same course that I had done the day before, wherein I was directed by my pocket-compass. My intention was to reach, if possible, one of those islands, which I had reason to believe lay to the North-East of *Van Diemen's* Land. I discovered nothing all that day; but upon the next, about three in the afternoon, when I had by my computation made twenty-four leagues from *Blefuscu*, I descried a sail steering to the South-Eeast; my course was due east. I hailed her, but could get no answer; yet I found I gained upon her, for the wind slackened. I made all the sail I could, and

就这样我准备了我所需的所有物品，在1701年9月24日的早上6点扬帆起航了。我向北边航行了4里格，即傍晚6点的时候，天就开始刮起了东南风，我看见西北方向半里格远的地方有座小岛。我驶向前，在小岛的背风面停船抛锚，看样子这座小岛上是无人居住的。于是我补充了些食物和饮料就去休息了。我睡得很熟，估计至少睡了6个小时，因为在我醒来后两个小时天才破晓。那是一个很晴朗的夜晚。太阳升起来之前我吃了些面包，将船锚拉了上来，风向也正合我意，于是我又沿着前一天的路线照着指南针的方向开始了航行。我的打算是尽可能到达梵·戴门地东北岸的某个小岛。一整天我都没有任何发现，但第二天，差不多在下午3点的时候，我估计我已经从不来福斯库国驶出了 24 里格的距离，我远远地望见了一艘向东南方向航行的大船。我当时的航向是向东。我在船上向他们招手，但没得到回应。风势慢慢减弱，我发现我离那艘船越来越近了。我乘势鼓起风帆全速前进，半个小时后那艘船上的人就发现了我，升起了他们的旗子，并放了一枪。一想到我就要回到亲爱的祖国，见到那里的亲人，我便高兴得不知如何是好，欣喜之情溢于言表。这艘船放下了

in half an hour she spied me, then hung out her ancient, and discharged a gun. It is not easy to express the joy I was in upon the unexpected hope of once more seeing my beloved country, and the dear pledges I had left in it. The ship slackened her sails, and I came up with her between five and six in the evening, *September* 26; but my heart leapt within me to see her *English* colours. I put my cows and sheep into my coat-pockets, and got on board with all my little cargo of provisions. The vessel was an *English* Merchant-Man returning from *Japan* by the *North* and South-Seas; the captain, Mr. *John* Biddel of *Deptford*, a very civil man, and an excellent sailor. We were now in the latitude of 30 degrees south; There were about fifty men in the ship; and here I met an old comrade of mine, one *Peter Williams*, who gave me a good character to the captain. This gentleman treated me with kindness, and desired I would let him know what place I came from last, and whither I was bound; which I did in few words, but he thought I was raving, and that the dangers I underwent had disturbed my head; whereupon I took my black cattle and sheep out of my pocket, which, after great astonishment, clearly convinced him of my veracity. I then showed him the gold given me by the emperor of Blefuscu, together with his

帆，我就在 9 月 26 下午五六点钟的时候登上了这艘大船。看到船上的英国国旗，我的心兴奋得怦怦直跳。我把我的牛和羊放进大衣口袋，带着我不多的补给品上了船。这艘船是一艘英国货轮，刚刚从日本途经北海和南海返航。船长是德普特福的约翰·比戴尔先生，是个非常有礼的人，同时也是位出色的水手。我们当时是在南纬 30°的地方。船上有大约 50 个人。在船上我竟还碰到了一位老同事，名叫彼得·威廉姆斯，他还向船长夸赞我是个品格高尚的人。这位先生对我很好，问我是从哪里出发航行，又要驶向何处。我跟他大概说了一下，但他却觉得我在胡言乱语，还以为我的脑袋出了什么问题。于是我就从口袋里拿出了牛羊，大为惊叹后他才确定我所说的是实话。我还给他看了不来福斯库国国王赐给我的金币，他的全身画像和他们国家的一些其他的珍贵物品。我给了他两个钱袋，每个钱袋里装着 200 斯普拉格，还向他保证，等我们回了英国我会送给他一头公羊、一头母羊和一只羊羔作为礼物。

majesty's picture at full length, and some other Rarities of that country. I gave him two purses of two hundred *sprugs* each, and promised, when we arrived in England, to make him a present of a cow and a sheep big with young.

I shall not trouble the reader with a particular account of this voyage, which was very prosperous for the most part. We arrived in the *Downs* on the 13th of *April* 1702. I had only one misfortune, that the rats on board carried away one of my sheep; I found her bones in a hole, picked clean from the flesh. the rest of my cattle I got safe on shore, and set them a grazing in a bowling-green at *Greenwich*, where the fineness of the grass made them feed very heartily, although I had always feared the contrary: neither could I possibly have preserved them in so long a voyage, if the captain had not allowed me some of his best Biscuit, which rubbed to powder, and mingled with water, was their constant food. The short time I continued in *England*, I made a considerable profit by showing my cattle to many persons of quality, and others: and before I began my second voyage, I sold them for six hundred pounds. Since my last return, I find the breed is considerably increased, especially the sheep; which I hope will prove much to the advantage of the woollen manufacture, by the fineness of

关于这次航行我就不向读者过多赘述了，总之一切都很顺利。我们于1702年4月13日抵达唐斯。只有一件事让我觉得很难过——船上的老鼠抓走了我的一只羊，后来我在一个洞里发现了它的骨头，骨头上的肉被吃得干干净净。剩下的牲口我都安全带上了岸，我把它们放在格林威治的一个滚木球场上吃草。那里的草很细嫩，它们吃得也很痛快，但我还是有些担心，因为要不是船长给了我几块美味的饼干让我研成粉末伴着水给它们当饲料，那么长的航行我是绝对没办法将它们养活的。我在英国逗留的不长的时间里，我将这些牲口展览给达官贵人们，因此收入颇丰。第二次航行前，我将它们都卖掉了，换来了600英镑。到我下次回来的时候，我发现这些牲口的数量大为增加，特别是羊。我希望这些精细柔软的羊绒能够帮助带动羊毛产业的发展。

the fleeces.

I stayed but two months with my wife and family; for my insatiable desire of seeing foreign countries would suffer me to continue no longer. I left fifteen hundred pounds with my wife, and fixed her in a good house at *Redriff*. My remaining stock I carried with me, part in money, and part in goods, in hopes to improve my Fortunes. My eldest uncle *John*, had left me an estate in land, near *Epping*, of about thirty pounds a year; and I had a long lease of the Black-Bull, in Fetter-Lane, which yielded me as much more: so that I was not in any danger of leaving my family upon the parish. My son *Johnny*, named so after his uncle, was at the Grammar School, and a towardly child. My daughter *Betty* (who is now well married, and has children) was then at her Needle-Work. I took leave of my wife, and boy and girl, with tears on both sides, and went on board the *Adventure*, a Merchant-Ship of three hundred tons, bound for *Surat*, Captain *John Nicholas of Liverpool* commander. But my account of this voyage must be referred to the second part of my travels.

我在家只陪了我的妻子和家人两个月，因为我对旅行意犹未尽，还想去国外见见世面，所以就不能再住下去了。我给我妻子留下了 1500 英镑，还给她在瑞德利夫买下了一套不错的房子。我将剩下的财产带在了身上，一部分是钱，一部分是物品，希望这些东西能为我赚来更大的财富。我年迈的约翰叔叔在埃平附近留给了我一处地产，一年大概 30 英镑的收入。我还将费达巷的黑公牛旅馆长期租了出去，这样又大大增加了我的收入，所以我就不用担心我走以后我的家人要靠教区救济生活了。我的儿子约翰尼——他是以他叔叔的名字给他命名的——现在正就读于文法学校，这孩子大有可为。我的女儿贝蒂（已经步入了美满的婚姻生活，还生了几个孩子）则在家做些针线活。我和我的妻子，儿子跟女儿含着泪互相道别后，就登上了“冒险号”，这是一艘有着 300 吨载重量的货轮，航行目的地是苏拉特。指挥这艘船的船长是利物浦的约翰·尼古拉斯。关于这次航行的详细情况我会在游记的第二部分一一介绍。

PART II. A VOYAGE TO BROBDINGNAG

第二部分 布罗卜丁奈格游记

CHAPTER 1

第一章

A great Storm described; the long-boat sent to fetch Water; the Author goes with it to discover theCountry. He is left on shore, is seized by one of the Natives, and carried to a Farmer's House. His Reception, with several Accidents that happened there. A Description of the Inhabitants.

描述一场巨大的暴风雨；长舢板被派出取淡水；作者随长舢板前往以了解这个国家。作者被丢弃在岸边，被一个当地土著捉住后带到一个农民家里。他在那里受到的招待并遭遇了一些事故。关于当地居民的一些描述。

Having been condemned by nature and fortune to an active and restless life, in ten months after my return, I again left my native country, and took shipping in the *Downs* on the 20th day of June 1702 in the *Adventure*, Capt. *John Nicholas* a *Cornish* man commander, bound for *Surat*. We had a very prosperous gale till we arrived at the *Cape of Good Hope*, where we landed for fresh water, but discovering a leak we unshipped our goods and wintered there; for the captain falling sick of an ague, we could not leave the *Cape* till the end of *March*. We then set sail, and had a good voyage till we passed the *Straits of Madagascar*; but having got northward of that island, and to about five degrees south latitude, the winds, which in those seas are observed to blow a constant equal gale

天性和命运注定了我要过一种活跃而不安定的日子。回来不到 10 个月，我再一次离开了祖国。1702 年 6 月 20 日，我在唐斯登上了“冒险号”前往苏拉特，船长约翰·尼古拉斯上校是一名康沃尔郡男子。我们一路上都有风助推着前行，直到抵达好望角。我们上岸取淡水，却发现船身有一条裂缝，迫不得已只得卸下货物在那里过冬。由于船长得了疟疾，直到 3 月底我们才离开好望角。起航后一切顺利，直到行驶过马达加斯加海峡，我们遇到了麻烦。当时船行驶到马达加斯加岛北面，大约是南纬 5°。根据观测，那一片海域在 12 月初到 5 月初总是吹西北风。可是 4 月 19 日那天，风刮得比平日猛烈得多，也更偏西一些，这样的情况一

between the north and west from the beginning of *December* to the beginning of *May*, on the 19th *of April* began to blow with much greater violence, and more westerly than usual, continuing so for twenty days together, during which time we were driven a little to the east of the *Molucca* Islands, and about three degrees northward of the line, as our captain found by an observation he took the 2d *of May*, at which time the wind ceased and it was a perfect calm, whereat I was not a little rejoiced. But he being a man well experienced in the navigation of those seas bid us all prepare against a storm, which accordingly happened the day following: for the southern wind, called the southern *monsoon*, began to set in.

直持续了 20 天。我们就被一点点刮到了摩鹿加群岛的东边。根据船长在 5 月 2 日的观测，当风停下来时，我们的所在地大约是北纬 3°。这时海上风平浪静，我非常欢喜。可是船长凭借他在那一带非常丰富的航海经验，吩咐我们做好准备，全力迎接一场暴风雨。如他所说，第二天暴风雨来了，因为是南风，也被称为南季节风，到来了。

Finding it was like to overblow, we took in our sprit-sail, and stood by to hand the Fore-sail; but making foul weather, we looked the guns were all fast, and handed the Missen. The ship lay very broad off, so we thought it better spooning before the sea, than trying or hulling. We reefed the foresail and set him, we hauled aft the foresheet; the helm was hard a weather. The ship wore bravely. We belayed the fore down-haul; but the sail was split, and we hauled down the yard, and got the sail into the ship, and unbound all the things clear of it. It was a very fierce storm; the sea broke strange and dangerous. We

发现风似乎刮得太猛烈了些，我们就收起斜杠帆，然后站在一边准备收前桅帆。但天气太恶劣，我们检查了一下船上的枪栓是否牢固，把后帆也收了。这时船已经远远偏离了航道。与其这样艰难地缓慢行驶或者降帆漂流，还不如侧转船身驶回前海。于是，我们收起前桅帆并将其固定住，随后把前桅帆角索用力拖向船尾，船舵吃风很紧，整艘船迅速转身。我们把前桅帆的缆绳拴在系索栓上，可是帆被劈开了一个口子，我们把帆桁放下来，把帆收进船里，卸下上面所有的东西。这是一场非常猛烈的暴风

hauled off upon the lanyard of the whipstaff, and helped the man at helm. We would not get down our Top-Mast, but let all stand, because she scudded before the sea very well, and we knew that the Top-Mast being aloft, the ship was the wholesomer, and made better way through the sea, seeing we had sea room. When the storm was over, we set foresail and mainsail, and brought the ship to. Then we set the Missen, Maintop-Sail, and the Foretop-Sail. Our course was east North-East, the wind was at South-West. We got the starboard tacks aboard, we cast off our weather braces and lifts; we set in the Lee-braces, and hauled forward by the weather-bowlings, and hauled them tight, and belayed them, and hauled over the Missen tack to windward, and kept her full and by as near as she would lie.

During this storm, which was followed by a strong wind, west South-West, we were carried by my computation about five hundred leagues to the east, so that the oldest sailor on board could not tell in what part of the world we were. Our provisions held out well, our ship was staunch, and our crew all in good health; but we lay in the utmost distress for water. We thought it best to hold on the same course rather than turn more northerly, which might have brought us to the North-West parts of great *Tartary*, and into

雨。大海打破一贯的平静，变得陌生而危险。我们帮舵手用力拉住舵柄上的系索。我们没有把中桅降下来，而是让它继续挺立着，这利于船在前海顺风行驶，而且我们确信，中桅直立在最高处的话，船就能够顺利行驶，而且有足够宽广的海域令船更安全地穿过海面。暴风雨结束以后，我们升起了前桅帆和主帆，继续行驶。然后又升起后帆、中桅主帆、中桅前帆。航向是东北偏东，而风向是西南。我们采用了右舷抢风法，将右舷的上下角索解下来，同时解开迎风一面的转帆索和空中供应线，而背风一面的转帆索则通过上风滚筒朝前拉紧、拴牢，再把后帆上下角索拉过来迎着风，这样使船尽可能靠近航道满帆前进。

暴风雨伴随着一阵西南偏西的强风，据我估算，我们已经被向东吹了大约500里格，船上最老的水手也说不清楚我们当时身处世界何处。我们的给养还能维持，船很坚固，所有船员身体状况良好。但淡水严重缺乏。我们认为不能再向北行驶了，最好还是回到原来的航线，否则很可能进入大鞑靼的西北部，驶入冰冻的海洋。

the frozen Sea.

On the 16th day of June 1703, a boy on the Top-Mast discovered land. On the 17th, we came in full view of a great island or continent (for we knew not whether), on the south side whereof was a small neck of land jutting out into the sea, and a creek too shallow to hold a ship of above one hundred Tuns. We cast anchor within a league of this creek, and our captain sent a dozen of his men well armed in the long-boat, with vessels for water if any could be found. I desired his leave to go with them, that I might see the country, and make what discoveries I could. When we came to land we saw no river or spring, nor any sign of inhabitants. Our men therefore wandered on the shore to find out some fresh water near the sea, and I walked alone about a mile on the other side, where I observed the country all barren and rocky. I now began to be weary, and seeing nothing to entertain my curiosity, I returned gently down towards the creek; and the sea being full in my view, I saw our men already got into the boat, and rowing for life to the ship. I was going to hollow after them, although it had been to little purpose, when I observed a huge creature walking after them in the sea, as fast as he could: he waded not much deeper than his knees, and took prodigious strides: but our men

1703年6月16日，爬到中桅上的水手发现了陆地。17日，展现在我们眼前的是一座大岛或者是一片大陆（我们不知道是哪个），南边有一个小半岛伸入海中，还有一个小小的港湾，但对于百吨以上的船来说实在太浅了，无法停泊。于是，我们在离它一里格的地方抛锚。船长派出12名水手，带着武器和容器，乘坐长舢板登陆寻找淡水。我请求与他们同去，这样我或许可以参观一下这个国家，说不定能有所发现。上岸后，我们既没有发现任何河流、泉水，也没看到有居民生活的迹象。我们的人就在海边徘徊，试图寻找些淡水。我则独自向另一边走了大约1英里，发现这里全是荒地和岩石。看不到任何可以吸引我好奇心的东西，我开始有些厌倦了，于是慢慢朝小港湾走去。大海完全占据了我的视线。我看到我们的人已经坐上了长舢板，疯狂地划向大船。我正要喊他们，尽管叫喊没什么用，忽然我看到有个大怪物在海水中迈着飞快的步子追赶他们。他走在海里，海水还没不了他的膝盖，他的步幅大得惊人。但我们的人落他有半里格，而且那附近的海域遍布尖锐的礁石，所以那个巨人没能追上小船。这都是事后我听别人说的，我可不敢冒险待在那里目睹这个场面，我沿着

had the start of him half a league, and the sea thereabouts being full of sharp pointed rocks, the monster was not able to overtake the boat. This I was afterwards told, for I durst not stay to see the issue of that adventure; but ran as fast as I could the way I first went; and then climbed up a steep hill which gave me some prospect of the country. I found it fully cultivated; but that which first surprised me was the length of the grass, which in those grounds that seemed to be kept for hay, was about twenty foot high.

来时的路狂奔，爬上一个陡坡，终于看到了这里的全景。我发现这里到处是耕地，但最先令我惊讶的是草的高度，大约有 20 英尺，就生长在那片似乎是种着干草的土地上。

I fell into a high road, for so I took it to be, though it served to the inhabitants only as a foot path through a field of barley. Here I walked on for some time, but could see little on either side, it being now near harvest, and the corn rising at least forty foot. I was an hour walking to the end of this field, which was fenced in with a hedge of at least one hundred and twenty Foot high, and the trees so lofty that I could make no computation of their altitude. There was a stile to pass from this field into the next. It had four steps, and a stone to cross over when you came to the uppermost. It was impossible for me to climb this stile, because every step was six foot high, and the upper stone above twenty. I was endeavouring to find some gap in the hedge, when I discovered one of the inhabitants in the next field

我踏上一条大路，对我来说是条大路，不过对当地居民来说，那只是一条穿过大麦地的小径。我在这条路上走了一会儿，可在路边什么也没看到。当时已经接近收割的时节了，麦子至少有 40 英尺高。我差不多走了一个小时才走到这一片麦地的尽头。麦地四周围着一道篱笆，至少有 120 英尺高。树木高得让我无法估算出它们的高度。相邻的麦地之间有一段 4 级台阶的阶梯，最高一级上还有一块巨大的石头。我根本不可能爬上这些台阶，因为每一级都高达 6 英尺，而最上面那块石头则超过 20 英尺。我正竭力寻找篱笆间是否有缺口，突然，一个当地人正从相邻的麦地向台阶走来。和我见到的在海水中追赶我们小船的那个巨人一样，这个人也相当高大。他看起来有一座

advancing towards the stile, of the same size with him whom I saw in the sea pursuing our boat. He appeared as tall as an ordinary spire-steeple, and took about ten yards at every stride, as near as I could guess. I was struck with the utmost fear and astonishment, and ran to hide myself in the corn, from whence I saw him at the top of the stile, looking back into the next field on the right hand, and heard him call in a voice many degrees louder than a speaking trumpet; but the noise was so high in the air, that at first I certainly thought it was thunder. Whereupon seven monsters like himself came towards him with reaping-hooks in their hands, each hook about the largeness of six scythes. These people were not so well clad as the first, whose servants or Labourers they seemed to be. for, upon some words he spoke, they went to reap the corn in the field where I lay. I kept from them at as great a distance as I could, but was forced to move with extreme difficulty, for the stalks of the corn were sometimes not above a foot distant, so that I could hardly squeeze my body betwixt them. However, I made a shift to go forward till I came to a part of the field where the corn had been laid by the rain and wind. Here it was impossible for me to advance a step: for the stalks were so interwoven that I could not creep through, and the beards of the

普通教堂的尖塔那么高，每一步都有 10 码左右，这还是最保守的推测。我极度恐惧，情急之下跑到麦子中躲了起来。在麦子间的缝隙中，我看到他站在台阶的顶端回头看右边的那块麦地，又听到他喊人的声音比用喇叭还要响亮得多。由于声源的位置很高，最初我还以为是雷声。听到他的召唤，有 7 个像他一样的巨人拿着镰刀走过来，那镰刀的长度相当于我们的长柄大镰刀的 6 倍。这些人穿得不如第一个人好，像是他的用人或者雇工，因为听他说了几句话之后，他们就来到我藏身的这块麦田里收割了。我竭尽所能躲开他们，但是因为麦秆间的距离有时连 1 英尺都不到，我将自己的身体挤过去极其困难。尽管如此，我还是尽力设法往前挤，来到一部分被风雨吹倒的麦地。这次我再也无法向前踏出一步了，因为麦秆互相交织在一起，我不可能从它们之间爬过去，而落在地上的麦芒又硬又尖，戳穿我的衣服刺到了肉里。就在这时，我听到割麦子的人已经走到我身后 100 码之内了。我精疲力竭，被悲伤和绝望击倒在地。我躺在两道田垄间，真希望自己就这样死了。想到妻儿将要成为可怜的孤儿寡母，我心里充满了哀伤。我还为自己的愚蠢、任性感到难过，我当初对亲友的忠告置若罔闻，一心想着进行这第二

fallen ears so strong and pointed that they pierced through my clothes into my flesh. At the same time I heard the reapers not above an hundred yards behind me. Being quite dispirited with toil, and wholly overcome by grief and despair, I lay down between two ridges, and heartily wished I might there end my days. I bemoaned my desolate widow, and fatherless children. I lamented my own folly and wilfulness in attempting a second voyage against the advice of all my friends and relations. In this terrible agitation of mind I could not forbear thinking of *Lilliput*, whose inhabitants looked upon me as the greatest prodigy that ever appeared in the world: where I was able to draw an imperial fleet in my hand, and perform those other actions which will be recorded for ever in the chronicles of that empire, while posterity shall hardly believe them, although attested by millions. I reflected what a mortification it must prove to me to appear as inconsiderable in this nation as one single *Lilliputian* would be among us. But, this I conceived was to be the least of my misfortunes: for, as human creatures are observed to be more savage and cruel in proportion to their bulk, what could I expect but to be a morsel in the mouth of the first among these enormous barbarians that should happen to seize me? Undoubtedly philosophers are in the

次航海。在这样纠结痛苦的时刻，我又无法克制地想起利利普特国来。那里的居民全都把我视为世界上最大的庞然大物。在那里，我可以只用手就打败一支皇家舰队，我在那里所开创的奇迹将会永远载入那个帝国的史册。然而他们的后代子孙们肯定不会相信，就算有数百万人可以作证。我想这真是我的奇耻大辱，我对这个民族来说可能会成为一个微不足道的人，就像一个利利普特国居民对我们来说也同样微不足道。然而眼下，利利普特国的事情对我来说只能算是最微小的不幸了，因为根据观测，人类的野蛮和残暴与他们的身材是成正比的。此刻我还有什么可指望的呢？只要等着这帮体形庞大的野人碰巧抓到我，然后成为他们其中之一的美食。毫无疑问，哲学家是有道理的，他们告诉我们：大和小只是相对而言，没有比较也就无所谓大小了。命运之神很有可能某天也会大发慈悲，让利利普特国的人也找到一个民族，和他们相比，这个民族的人身材更小，就像他们和我们相比一样。而且谁也不知道，对眼前这个身材如此高大的民族来说，会不会在世界上某个遥远的不为人知的地方还生活着比他们更高大的人呢？

right when they tell us, that nothing is great or little otherwise than by comparison. It might have pleased fortune to let the *Lilliputians* find some nation, where the people were as diminutive with respect to them, as they were to me. And who knows but that even this prodigious race of mortals might be equally overmatched in some distant part of the world, whereof we have yet no discovery?

Scared and confounded as I was, I could not forbear going on with these reflections, when one of the reapers approaching within ten yards of the ridge where I lay, made me apprehend that with the next step I should be squashed to death under his foot, or cut in two with his reaping Hook. And therefore when he was again about to move, I screamed as loud as fear could make me. Whereupon the huge creature trod short, and looking round about under him for some time, at last espied me as I lay on the ground. He considered awhile with the caution of one who endeavours to lay hold on a small dangerous animal in such a manner that it shall not be able either to scratch or to bite him, as I myself have sometimes done with a *weasel* in *England*. At length he ventured to take me up behind by the middle between his forefinger and thumb, and brought me within three yards of his eyes, that he might behold my shape more

我充满恐惧，心乱如麻，无法克制地这样胡思乱想下去。一个割麦人已经到附近了，离我躺着的田垄不到 10 码远，我不禁担心他再向前走一步就会把我踩扁，或者用镰刀把我割成两截。因此，就在他又要向前走的时候，我吓得拼命大声尖叫起来。一听到叫喊声，巨人突然停下了脚步，他俯视了一会儿，终于发现了躺在地上的我。他考虑了片刻，那小心的样子就像努力想去捉住一只危险的小动物而又生怕被它抓伤或咬伤一样。我在英国时，如果偶尔遇见黄鼠狼，就会像他现在这样。终于，他鼓起勇气用拇指和食指从我背后捏住我的腰将我捏到离他眼睛不到 3 码的地方，他这样是为了更清楚地观察我的身形。我猜到了他的想法，幸好我当时还算清醒，下定决心绝不挣扎一下。尽管他把我捏在半空中，离地 60 英尺，又怕我从他的指缝中间滑下来，于是用力捏着我

perfectly. I guessed his meaning, and my good fortune gave me so much presence of mind, that I resolved not to struggle in the least as he held me in the air above sixty Foot from the ground, although he grievously pinched my sides, for fear I should slip through his fingers. All I ventured was to raise my eyes towards the sun, and place my hands together in a supplicating posture, and to speak some words in an humble melancholy tone, suitable to the condition I then was in. For I apprehended every moment that he would dash me against the ground, as we usually do any little hateful animal which we have a mind to destroy. But my good star would have it, that he appeared pleased with my voice and gestures, and began to look upon me as a curiosity, much wondering to hear me pronounce articulate words, although he could not understand them. In the mean time I was not able to forbear groaning and shedding tears, and turning my head towards my sides; letting him know, as well as I could, how cruelly I was hurt by the pressure of his thumb and finger. He seemed to apprehend my meaning; for, lifting up the lappet of his coat, he put me gently into it, and immediately ran along with me to his master, who was a substantial farmer, and the same person I had first seen in the field.

的腰部。我唯一敢冒险去做的，就是抬眼望着太阳，双手合拢做出一副哀求的可怜相，又低声下气、楚楚可怜地说了几句符合我当时处境的话，因为我每分每秒都在担心他会猛地把我扔到地上，就像我们通常对待存心想让它死掉的任何可恶的小动物一样。可是我真是福星高照，他看起来对我的声音和姿态很感兴趣，开始把我当做一个有意思的宝贝。他听到我发音清晰地说话，尽管不明白我说的是什么，但还是非常好奇。与此同时，我忍不住发出呻吟并流泪了。我把头扭向腰部两侧，尽我所能让他意识到，我被他的拇指和食指捏得很疼。他好像明白了我的意思，因为他随手撩起了上衣的下摆，轻柔地把我放在上面，然后兜着我立刻跑去见他的主人。他的主人是个富裕的农场主，也就是我在麦地里看到的第一个巨人。

The farmer having (as I suppose by their talk) received such an account of me as his servant could give him, took a piece of a small straw, about the size of a Walking Staff, and therewith lifted up the lappets of my coat; which it seems he thought to be some kind of covering that nature had given me. He blew my hairs aside to take a better view of my face. He called his hinds about him, and asked them (as I afterwards learned) whether they had ever seen in the fields any little creature that resembled me. He then placed me softly on the ground upon all four, but I got immediately up, and walked slowly backwards and forwards, to let those people see I had no intent to run away. They all sat down in a circle about me, the better to observe my motions. I pulled off my hat, and made a low bow towards the farmer. I fell on my knees, and lifted up my hands and eyes, and spoke several words as loud as I could: I took a purse of gold out of my pocket, and humbly presented it to him. He received it on the palm of his hand, then applied it close to his eye, to see what it was, and afterwards turned it several times with the point of a pin (which he took out of his sleeve), but could make nothing of it. Whereupon I made a sign that he should place his hand on the ground. I then took the purse, and opening it, poured all the

那个农场主听他的雇工报告完我的情况后（我根据他们谈话的样子猜想的），就捡起一根手杖一样粗细的小麦秆儿，挑起我上衣的下摆。他仿佛觉得我也许天生就长着一个这样的外壳。他把我的头发吹到两边，把我的脸看得更清楚。他把他的雇工们都叫到身边来，问他们有没有在麦地里发现像我一样的小动物。这是我后来才弄明白的。接下来他轻柔地把我平放在地上，不过我立刻爬了起来，慢慢地来来回回地踱步，好让他们明白我并没有企图逃走。他们在我周围围成一圈坐了下来，以便更清楚地观察我的动作。我摘下帽子，向那个农场主深深地鞠了一躬。然后双膝跪地，举起双手，抬起眼睛，尽可能大声地说了几句话。我从口袋里掏出一袋金币，恭恭敬敬地呈献给他。他接过来放到手心里，拿到眼前看了看到底是什么，后来又从自己衣袖上取下一只别针，用针尖拨弄了几下，还是弄不明白那究竟是什么东西。于是我向他示意，让他把手放在地上，我拿过钱袋并且打开，将金币全部倒入他的手心，除了二三十枚小金币以外，还有6枚西班牙大金币，每一枚价值4个皮斯托尔。我看到他用舌头将小指指尖润了润，捡起其中的一块大金币，接着又捡起一块，可是他似乎完全不明白这是些什么。他对我做

gold into his palm. There were six Spanish-Pieces of four Pistoles each, besides twenty or thirty smaller coins. I saw him wet the tip of his little finger upon his tongue, and take up one of my largest pieces, and then another, but he seemed to be wholly ignorant what they were. He made me a sign to put them again into my purse, and the purse again into my pocket, which after offering it to him several times, I thought it best to do.

了一个手势，让我把金币收进钱包，再把钱包放回我的衣袋。我又献给他几次，他都不肯收，我想最好还是先收起来吧。

The farmer by this time was convinced I must be a rational creature. He spoke often to me, but the sound of his voice pierced my ears like that of a water-mill, yet his words were articulate enough. I answered as loud as I could, in several languages, and he often laid his ear within two yards of me, but all in vain, for we were wholly unintelligible to each other. He then sent his servants to their work, and taking his handkerchief out of his pocket, he doubled and spread it on his left hand, which he placed flat on the ground, with the palm upwards, making me a sign to step into it, as I could easily do, for it was not above a foot in thickness. I thought it my part to obey, and for fear of falling, laid myself at length upon the handkerchief, with the remainder of which he lapped me up to the head for further security, and in this manner carried me home to his house. There he called his

到这时，那农场主已经相信我是一个有理性的动物了。他常常跟我说话，可是那声音在我听来大得像水磨一样刺耳，不过倒是挺清楚的。我尽量提高音量，用几种不同的语言回答他，他也总是把耳朵凑到离我不足两码的位置听，可这也是徒然，因为我们完全听不懂对方在说什么。他让雇工们回去干活，从口袋里掏出一块手帕，摊在自己左手上叠成两层，再将手心朝上平放在地上，示意我走上去。他的手和手帕的厚度加起来还不到一英尺，所以我很容易就走上去了。我想我只能顺从，又怕跌下来，于是就伸直了身子在手帕上躺了下来。他把手帕四周余下的部分叠起来，把我包得只露出个头，这样就更安全了。他就这样将我带回了家。一到家，他就喊来他的妻子，把我拿给她看。可她吓得尖叫起来，转身就跑，就跟英国的女子见了癞蛤蟆

wife, and showed me to her; but she screamed and ran back, as women in *England* do at the sight of a toad or a spider. However, when she had a while seen my Behaviour, and how well I observed the signs her husband made, she was soon reconciled, and by degrees grew extremely tender of me.

或蜘蛛的反应一样。过了一会儿，她观察了我一会儿，觉得我行为安祥，并且十分准确地听她丈夫手势指挥，很快也就放心了，还渐渐地对我越来越温柔起来。

It was about twelve at noon, and a servant brought in dinner. It was only one substantial dish of meat (fit for the plain condition of an Husband-Man) in a dish of about four and twenty Foot diameter. The company were the farmer and his wife, three children, and an old grandmother. When they were sat down, the farmer placed me at some distance from him on the table, which was thirty Foot high from the floor. I was in a terrible fright, and kept as far as I could from the edge for fear of falling. The wife minced a bit of meat, then crumbled some bread on a trencher, and placed it before me. I made her a low bow, took out my knife and fork, and fell to eat, which gave them exceeding delight. The mistress sent her maid for a small Dram-cup, which held about three gallons, and filled it with drink: I took up the vessel with much difficulty in both hands, and in a most respectful manner drank to her ladyship's health, expressing the words as loud as I could in *English*, which made the company laugh so

已经是中午 12 点了，仆人将饭菜送了上来。他们的菜是满满的一盘肉（和他们节约的生活习惯很相符），装在一个直径达 24 英尺的盘子里。坐在一起吃饭的有这个农场主、他的妻子、3 个孩子以及一位老祖母。他们坐下来之后，这个农场主把我放到桌子上，离他们有一段距离。那个桌子离地面约有 30 英尺高。我简直吓得魂飞魄散，很怕掉下去，于是能离桌子边缘多远就走多远。农场主的妻子切下了一小块肉，又在一只木盘子里把一些面包弄碎，然后一起放到了我的面前。我向她深深地鞠了一躬，表示感谢，之后拿出自己的刀叉吃了起来。这令大家非常高兴。女主人吩咐女佣取来一只容量约为 3 加仑的小酒杯，斟满了酒。我十分吃力地用两只手将酒杯捧起，十分恭敬有礼地把酒喝下，并竭力提高音量用英语说：为夫人的健康干杯！这让大家开怀大笑，我差点儿被他们的笑声震聋了。酒尝起来有点像淡淡的苹果酒，一点儿也不难喝。接着

heartily, that I was almost deafened with the noise. This liquor tasted like a small cider, and was not unpleasant. Then the master made me a sign to come to his Trencher side; but as I walked on the table, being in great surprise all the time, as the indulgent reader will easily conceive and excuse, I happened to stumble against a crust, and fell flat on my face, but received no hurt. I got up immediately, and observing the good people to be in much concern, I took my hat (which I held under my arm out of good manners) and waving it over my head, made three Huzza's, to show that I had got no mischief by my fall. But advancing forwards toward my master (as I shall henceforth call him), his youngest son who sat next him, an arch boy of about ten years old, took me up by the legs, and held me so high in the air, that I trembled in every limb; but his father snatched me from him, and at the same time gave him such a box on the left ear, as would have felled an *European* troop of horse to the earth, ordering him to be taken from the table. But, being afraid the boy might owe me a spite, and well remembering how mischievous all children among us naturally are to sparrows, rabbits, young kittens, and puppy dogs, I fell on my knees, and pointing to the boy, made my master to

主人做了一个手势让我走到他切面包的木盘子那边。相信宽容的读者很容易就能理解并且原谅我后面发生的事情。由于一直惊魂未定，我走在桌子上的时候，碰巧被一块面包屑绊了一跤，整个脸都撞到桌面上，不过幸好没有受伤。我立刻爬起来，发现这些好心的人们都很关切地看着我，我就拿起帽子（为了礼貌，我一直把帽子夹在胳膊下面），举过头顶挥了挥，喊了3声万岁，表示我并没有受伤。但就在我迈步向我的主人（从此以后我就这样称呼他）走去的时候，坐在他旁边的那个最小的儿子，一个10岁左右非常调皮的小男孩，一把抓住了我的两条腿把我高高地举到了半空中，吓得我四肢发抖。幸好他的父亲赶紧把我从他手里抢了过来，同时给了他左脸一记耳光，命人把他带走，让他立刻离开饭桌。这个耳光足以打倒一队欧洲骑兵。但是我担心这个小男孩可能会因此而记恨我，又想起我们所有的孩子天生都爱捉弄那些麻雀、兔子、小猫和小狗，就跪了下来，指了指这个小男孩，让我的主人尽可能地明白，希望他能原谅他的儿子。我的主人答应了，小男孩重新回到了他的座位上。我走到他身边，吻了吻他的手，我的主人也拉过他的手让他轻轻地抚摸我。

understand, as well as I could, that I desired his son might be pardoned. The father complied, and the lad took his seat again; whereupon I went to him and kissed his hand, which my master took, and made him stroke me gently with it.

In the midst of dinner, my Mistress's favourite cat leapt into her lap. I heard a noise behind me like that of a dozen stocking-weavers at work; and turning my head, I found it proceeded from the purring of this animal, who seemed to be three times larger than an ox, as I computed by the view of her head, and one of her paws, while her mistress was feeding and stroking her. The fierceness of this creature's countenance altogether discomposed me; though I stood at the further end of the table, above fifty Foot off, and although my mistress held her fast for fear she might give a spring, and seize me in her talons. But it happened there was no danger; for the cat took not the least notice of me when my master placed me within three yards of her. And as I have been always told, and found true by experience in my travels, that flying, or discovering fear before a fierce animal, is a certain way to make it pursue or attack you, so I resolved in this dangerous juncture to show no manner of concern. I walked with intrepidity five or six times before the very head of the cat, and came

饭吃到一半的时候，女主人最宠爱的猫跳到了她膝盖上。我听到身后闹哄哄的，就像是 10 几个织袜工人劳作时发出的声音。回头一看，原来是那只猫在喘气。我看到它的头和一只爪子，估计这只猫足有我们的 3 头公牛那么大。此刻它的女主人正一边喂它吃东西，一边轻轻地拍打着它。那只猫狰狞的面相还是让我十分不安。尽管我远远地站在桌子的另一头，与猫相距 50 多英尺，可我的女主人还是担心万一它跳过来，把我抓到它的爪子里，所以紧紧地抱住它。不过幸好没什么危险，我的主人把我放到离它不足 3 码的地方，它都没注意到我。我常听别人提到，也在旅行中亲身经历过，如果在猛兽的面前逃跑或者暴露出自己的恐惧，那么它一定会来追赶或者攻击你。因此，我下定决心，在这危急关头，我要表现得满不在乎。我在猫的头前方大着胆子来回走了五六趟，有时离它还不到半码远。那只猫倒好像更怕我似的，弓起身子缩了回去。至于狗，我就更不害怕了。这时候有三四条狗进了房间，这对农户来说

within half a yard of her; whereupon she drew herself back, as if she were more afraid of me: I had less apprehension concerning the dogs, whereof three or four came into the room, as it is usual in farmers' houses; one of which was a mastiff equal in bulk to four elephants, and a greyhound somewhat taller than the mastiff, but not so large.

When dinner was almost done, the nurse came in with a child of a year old in her arms, who immediately spied me, and began a squall that you might have heard from London-Bridge *to Chelsea*, after the usual oratory of infants, to get me for a plaything. The mother out of pure indulgence took me up, and put me towards the child, who presently seized me by the middle, and got my head in his mouth, where I roared so loud that the urchin was frighted, and let me drop, and I should infallibly have broke my neck if the mother had not held her apron under me. The nurse, to quiet her babe made use of a rattle, which was a kind of hollow vessel filled with great stones, and fastened by a cable to the child's waist: But all in vain, so that she was forced to happy the last Remedy by giving it suck. I must confess no Object ever disgusted me so much as the sight of her monstrous Breast, which I cannot tell what to compare with, so as to give the curious

是常见的事，其中有一条是獒犬，抵得上4头大象那么大，还有一只灰狗，比獒犬个头更高，却没有獒犬那么大。

午饭快吃完的时候，保姆抱着个一岁的小孩走了进来。他立刻看到了我，然后大声尖叫起来，那尖叫声你从伦敦桥到切尔西那么远也能够听到。他像平常孩子那样咿呀了半天，要把我当玩具。母亲出于对孩子的溺爱，真的就把我拿起来送到了孩子跟前。他立刻一把将我拦腰抓在手上，把我的头直往他嘴里塞。我大吼一声，这个淘气鬼被我吓了一跳，一松手把我扔了。要不是他母亲用围裙接住我，我的脖子肯定会被摔断。保姆为了让孩子安静下来，就拿起了一只拨浪鼓。那是用一个中空的盒子做的，里边装了几块大石头，用一根绳子拴在孩子的腰间。但所有这一切都不管用，她被逼无奈，只好使出最后一招，给孩子喂奶。不得不承认，我还从没见过比她那巨大无比的乳房更令我感到恶心的东西。它长得非常奇特，我真不知道拿什么来和它相比，所以也无法向好奇的读者详细地说明这乳房的大小、形状

Reader an Idea of its Bulk, Shape and Colour. It stood prominent six foot, and could not be less than sixteen in Circumference. The Nipple was about half the Bigness of my Head, and the Hue both of that and the Dug so varified with Spots, Pimples and Freckles, that nothing coule appear more nauseous: For I had a near sight of her, she sitting down the more conveniently to give Suck, and I standing on the table. This made me reflect upon the fair skins of our *English* ladies, who appear so beautiful to us, only because they are of our own size, and their defects not to be seen but through a magnifying glass, where we find by experiment that the smoothest and whitest skins look rough and coarse, and ill colored.

和颜色。她的乳房挺起来大约有 6 英尺高，周长少说也有 16 英尺，乳头大概有我的半个头那么大，上面布满了黑点、丘疹和雀斑，那样的颜色和样子真是再没有什么比它更令人作呕的了。因为她坐着喂奶更方便，而我站在桌子上离得近，所以这一切我看得一清二楚。这令我想起我们英国的女士们白皙柔嫩的皮肤在我们眼中是多么的漂亮。不过那也只是因为她们的身材大小和我们差不多罢了，有什么缺点瑕疵还得借助放大镜才能看得清。我们做过试验，从放大镜里看，最光滑、最白皙的皮肤也是粗糙不平、颜色难看的。

I remember when I was at *Lilliput*, the complexions of those diminutive people appeared to me the fairest in the world, and talking upon this subject with a person of learning there, who was an intimate friend of mine, he said that my face appeared much fairer and smoother when he looked on me from the ground than it did upon a nearer view when I took him up in my hand, and brought him close, which he confessed was at first a very shocking sight. He said he could discover great holes in my skin, that the stumps of my beard were ten times stronger than the bristles of a boar, and my complexion

我记得在利利普特国的时候，那些小人的肤色在我看来是世界上最美丽的了。有一次我同那里的一个至交，同时也是一位学者谈到过这个问题。他说，他从地面往上远看我的脸比在更近的位置来看要光滑、漂亮得多。当我把他放在自己手里，让他和我离得很近的时候，他不得不承认一开始确实觉得那种景象特别恐怖。他说在我的皮肤上可以看到巨大的坑洞，我的胡子楂比野公猪的鬃毛还要硬 10 倍，肤色也是由多种不同颜色混杂在一起。不过请允许我在这里为自己辩白一下，我的相貌其实和我国的

made up of several colours altogether disagreeable: although I must beg leave to say for myself, that I am as fair as most of my sex and country, and very little sunburnt by all my travels. On the other side, discoursing of the ladies of that emperor's court, he used to tell me, one had freckles, another too wide a mouth, a third too large a nose, nothing of which I was able to distinguish. I confess this reflection was obvious enough; which however I could not forbear, lest the reader might think those vast creatures were actually deformed: for I must do them justice to say they are a comely race of people; and particularly the features of my master's countenance, although he were but a farmer, when I beheld him from the height of sixty Foot, appeared very well proportioned.

大多数男同胞不相上下，这几次的旅行也并没有把我晒得很黑。另一方面，提起皇帝的那些妃嫔们的时候，他又常常告诉我说，这个人有雀斑，那个人的嘴太大，还有什么人的鼻子也太大了，可对我来说这些都是无法辨别的。我相信他的这一见解已经足够令大家明白了，而我还是忍不住要重申一遍，免得读者们认为那些巨人们真的都丑陋不堪。我得公正地替他们说句话，他们是一个美丽的民族，尤其是我的主人，虽然只是一个农民，但我从 60 英尺的高处观察他，他的相貌也是非常匀称端庄的。

When dinner was done, my master went out to his Labours, and as I could discover by his voice and Gcsturcs, gave his wife a strict charge to take care of me. I was very much tired and disposed to sleep which, my mistress perceiving, she put me on her own bed, and covered me with a clean white handkerchief, but larger and coarser than the Main Sail of a man of war.

吃完午饭，我的主人要出去监督他的雇工们了。从他的声音和手势，我可以推测出他正细细叮嘱妻子要小心照顾我。我非常疲惫，很想睡一觉，女主人注意到了，就把我放到了她自己的床上，还给我盖上了一条干净的白手帕，但那手帕比一艘战舰的主帆还要大，还非常粗糙。

I slept about two hours, and dreamed I was at home with my wife and children, which aggravated my sorrows when I awaked and found myself alone in a vast

我大约睡了两个小时，梦见自己在家与妻子和孩子们在一起。当我醒来的时候，发现自己孤零零地在一个两三百英尺宽、200 多英尺

room, between two and three hundred Foot wide, and above two hundred high, lying in a bed twenty yards wide. My mistress was gone about her household affairs, and had locked me in. The bed was eight yards from the floor. Some natural Necessities required me to get down: I durst not presume to call, and I had, it would have been in vain with such a Voice as mine at so great a distance from the Room where I lay to the Kitchen where the family kept. While Iwas under these Circumstances two Rats crept up the Curtains, and ran smelling backwards and forwards on the Bed. One of them came almost up to my face, whereupon I rose in a fright, and drew out my hanger to defend myself. These horrible animals had the boldness to attack me on both sides, and one of them held his Fore-foot at my collar; but I had the good fortune to rip up his Belly before he could do me any mischief. He fell down at my foot, and the other seeing the fate of his comrade, made his escape, but not without one good wound on the back, which I gave him as he fled, and made the blood run trickling from him. After this exploit I walked gently to and fro on the bed, to recover my breath and loss of spirits. These creatures were of the size of a large mastiff, but infinitely more nimble and fierce, so that if I had taken off my belt before I went to

高的大房间里，躺在一张 20 码宽的床上。这就更加剧了我的哀伤。因为要忙家务，女主人把我一个人锁在了房间里面。床有 8 码高。因为生理上的需要，我不得不下床去。可是我不敢随便喊他们过来，况且就算喊了，我睡觉的房间离那一家人所在的厨房很远，以我微弱的音量他们根本听不到。正当我处在这种情况下的时候，两只老鼠忽然沿着帐幔爬上床来，来来回回地乱嗅了一会儿，还有一只差点爬到了我的脸上，我吓了一跳，猛地翻身站了起来，抽出腰刀自卫。这两只可怕的老鼠竟敢对我两面夹攻，其中一只伸过前爪来抓我的衣领，不过幸好它还没来得及伤害我，我就将它的腹部剖开了。它倒在了我脚下。另一只看到它同伴的悲惨下场，拔腿就跑，但在它逃跑时我朝它背上狠狠地刺了一刀，血汩汩地流了出来。大功告成以后，我在床上轻轻地来回走动以平静呼吸、恢复精神。这两只老鼠有大獒犬那么大，但要敏捷、凶猛得多，所以如果我睡觉前解下了皮带，我肯定早就被它们撕成碎片吃掉了。我量了一下死老鼠的尾巴，差一英寸不到两码长。那只老鼠的尸体还躺在那里流着血，恶心至极，可我却没有办法把它扔下床去。我发现它还有点呼吸，就向它脖子猛砍一刀，这才把它送上了西天。

sleep, I must infallibly have been torn to pieces and devoured. I measured the tail of the dead rat, and found it to be two yards long wanting an inch; but it went against my stomach to draw the carcass off the bed, where it lay still bleeding; I observed it had yet some life, but with a strong slash across the neck I thoroughly dispatched it.

Soon after my Mistress came into the Room, who seeing me all bloody, ran and took me up in her Hand. I pointed to the dead *Rat*, smiling and making other Signs to show I was not hurt, wherat she was extremely rejoiced, calling the Maid to take up the dead *Rat* with a pair of Tongs, and throw it out of the Windows. Then she set me on a Table where I showed her my Hanger all bloody, and wiping it on the Lapper of my Coat, returned it to the Scabbard. I was pressed to do more than one Thing, which another could not do for me, and therefore endeavoured to make my mistress understand that I desired to be set down on the Floor; which after she had done, my Bashfulness would not suffer me to express myself further than by pointing to the Door, and bowing several times. The good Woman with much Difficulty at last perceived what I would be at, and taking me up again in her Hand, walked into the Garden whereshe set me down. I went on one side about two hundred

过了一小会儿，女主人走进房间，发现我浑身沾满了血，赶紧跑过来把我放在手里。我指了指那只死老鼠，又微笑着给她做手势，让她明白我并没有受伤。她开心极了，喊来女佣用火钳把这只死老鼠扔到了窗外。接着她把我放到了桌子上，我把我那沾着血的腰刀给她看，又用上衣的下摆把刀上的血擦干净，然后收回了刀鞘。这时我迫不及待地要做一件别人无法代劳的事情，于是竭力让女主人明白我的意思，把我放到地上。之后，我只能羞涩地指指门口，向她连鞠了几躬，此外再也想不出别的办法来进一步表明我的意图了。这个好心的女人费尽千辛万苦终于弄明白了我想干什么，就拿起我，走进花园，又把我放在了地上。我走到离她约有 200 码的地方，向她示意，不要看我或者跟过来，然后藏在两片酸模树叶之间解决了生理需求。

Yards, and beckoning to her not to look or to follow me, I hid myself between two leaves of Sorrel, and there discharged the Necessities of Nature.

I hope the gentle reader will excuse me for dwelling on these and the like particulars, which however insignificant they may appear to grovelling vulgar minds, yet will certainly help a philosopher to enlarge his thoughts and imagination, and apply them to the benefit of public as well as private life, which was my sole design in presenting this and other accounts of my travels to the world; wherein I have been chiefly studious of truth, without affecting any ornaments of learning or of style. But the whole scene of this voyage made so strong an impression on my mind, and is so deeply in my memory, that in committing it to paper I did not omit one material circumstance: However, upon a strict review, I blotted out several passages of less moment which were in my first copy, for fear of being censured as tedious and trifling, whereof travellers are often, perhaps not without justice, accused.

我希望敬爱的读者们能原谅我将这些琐碎之事描述得如此详细。在没有思想的平庸之人看来，这些也许没什么意义，然而它们确实有助于拓展哲学家的思维和想象空间，于社会或是个人都是有益的。这也就是我将这些游记公诸于世的唯一目的。我只是在陈述事实，丝毫没有在知识或风格上夸大其词。但这次航行中的每一幕都给我留下了非常深刻的印象，在我的记忆之中留下清晰的印记，用文字表述时才没有遗漏任何一个重要情形。不过经过严格的修改，我还是删除了初稿中相对不太重要的几个段落，生怕别人指责我的游记太过冗长和细碎。旅行家们常常受到这样的指责，不过有可能还有几分道理。

CHAPTER 2

第二章

A Description of the Farmer's Daughter. The Author carried to a Market-Town, and then to the metropolis. The Particulars of this Journey.

关于农场主女儿的描写。作者被带到一个集镇，接着被带到了大都市。旅途中的所见所闻。

My mistress had a daughter of nine years old, a child of towardly parts for her age, very dextrous at her needle, and skilful in dressing her baby. Her mother and she contrived to fit up the baby's cradle for me against night: the cradle was put into a small drawer of a cabinet, and the drawer placed upon a hanging shelf for fear of the *rats*. This was my bed all the time I stayed with these people, though made more convenient by degrees, as I began to learn their language, and make my wants known. This young Girl was so handy, that after I had once or twice pulled off my Clothes before her, she was able to dress and undress me, although I never gave her that Trouble when would let me do either myself. She made me seven shirts, and some other linen of as fine cloth as could be got, which indeed was coarser than sackcloth; and these she constantly washed for me with her own hands. She was likewise my school-mistress, to teach me the

我的女主人有一个女儿，作为一个 9 岁的孩子，她非常聪明，针线活儿熟练，能相当灵巧地给洋娃娃做衣服。她和她母亲做了个婴儿用的摇篮供我晚上睡觉。摇篮被放在一个衣柜的小抽屉里，她们担心有老鼠伤害到我，于是把抽屉又放在了一块悬空的吊板上。在我和这一家人一起生活的这段时间里，这就是我的床了。后来我开始学习他们的语言，令他们更明白我的需求以后，这张床也就被改造得更加方便舒适了。这个小姑娘非常聪明，在我当着她面脱过一两次衣服以后，她就学会给我换衣服了。当然，只要她肯让我自己动手，我是绝对不会去麻烦她的。她为我缝制了 7 件衬衫和一些内衣，用的都是当地最精致的布料，事实上这些料子比粗麻布还要粗糙。她经常亲自给我洗衣服。她还是我的老师，教我他们的语言，我每指一样东西，她就告诉我那种东西在他们当地语言里怎么称呼。之后的这些天里，我

language: When I pointed to anything, she told me the name of it in her own tongue, so that in a few days I was able to call for whatever I had a mind to. She was very good natured, and not above forty foot high, being little for her age. She gave me the name of *Grildrig*, which the family took up, and afterwards the whole kingdom. The word imports what the *Latins* call *nanunculus*, the *Italians homunceletino*, and the *English mannikin*. To her I chiefly owe my preservation in that country: We never parted while I was there; I called her my *Glumdalclitch*, or little nurse: and I should be guilty of great ingratitude if I omitted this honourable mention of her care and affection towards me, which I heartily wish it lay in my power to requite as she deserves instead of being the innocent but unhappy Instrument of her Disgrace, as I have too much reason to fear.

It now began to be known and talked of in the neighbourhood, that my master had found a strange animal in the field about the bigness of a *splacknuck*, but exactly shaped in every part like a human creature; which it likewise imitated in all its actions; seemed to speak in a little language of its own, had already learned several words of theirs, went erect upon two legs, was tame and gentle, would come when it was called, do whatever it was bid, had the finest limbs in the world,

就能叫出我所需要的东西的名字了。她脾气很好，身高不到 40 英尺，对她那个年龄来说算矮的了。她给我取了个名字，叫“格里尔特里格”，他们全家人都这样称呼我，后来全国的人也都这么喊我。这个词和拉丁文里的“nanunculus”，意大利文里的“homunceletino”，英文里的“mannikin”（侏儒，矮子）是同一个意思。要不是她，我也不可能在那个国度生存下来。在那里生活的日子里，我们未曾分开。我管她叫我的“格兰姆达尔克立契”，意思是小保姆。如果我不在这里郑重地提一下她对我的关心和照顾，那我真是太忘恩负义了。我衷心希望我有能力报答她的恩情，这是她应得的。可我总担心她会因为我而丢脸，而且我的担心也是有理由的。

这件事很快就传遍了街头巷尾，大家议论纷纷，说我的主人在麦地里发现了一头怪兽，有一只“斯泼拉克那克”大小，身形却酷似人类。它还能模仿人类的动作，它似乎有自己的语言，也学会了几句人类的话。它双腿直立行走，性情温和，懂礼仪，召之即来，听从命令，服从指挥。它拥有世上最完美的四肢，肤色比贵族家 3 岁的女儿还要白嫩。一个住在附近的农民，他是我主人的一位特殊的朋

and a complexion fairer than a nobleman's daughter of three years old. Another farmer who lived hard by, and was a particular friend of my master, came on a visit on purpose to inquire into the truth of this story. I was immediately produced and placed upon a table, where I walked as I was commanded, drew my hanger, put it up again, made my reverence to my master's guest, asked him in his own language how he did, and told him *he was* welcome, just as my little nurse had instructed me. This man, who was old and dim sighted, put on his spectacles to behold me better, at which I could not forbear laughing very heartily, for his eyes appeared like the full moon shining into a chamber at two windows. Our people, who discovered the cause of my mirth, bore me company in laughing, at which the old fellow was fool enough to be angry and out of countenance. He had the character of a great miser, and, to my misfortune he well deserved it by the cursed advice he gave my master to show me as a sight upon a market-day in the next town, which was half an hour's riding, about two and twenty miles from our house. I guessed there was some mischief contriving, when I observed my master and his friend whispering long together, sometimes pointing at me; and my fears made me fancy that I overheard and understood some of their words. But,

友，特地前来拜访，想弄清楚事情的真相。我的主人立即把我拿了出来，放到了一张桌子上，我按照他的指挥在桌子上走路，抽出腰刀又收回刀鞘。我向我主人的朋友致敬，用他们的语言问候他，又说欢迎他的到来，这些都是我的小保姆教我的。这个人老眼昏花，戴上眼镜想把我看个清楚。他这一戴，我忍不住哈哈大笑起来，因为他的眼镜就像两个透过窗户照进房间的满月。这一家人弄清楚我发笑的原因后，也和我一起大笑起来。老头子被戏弄了一番，非常窘迫。就我不幸的遭遇来说，说他是个守财奴真是一点儿也不冤枉他。他给我的主人出了个馊主意，让我主人在赶集时，把我带到附近镇上去表演。那个镇在离我的主人家约 22 英里的地方，骑马半个小时就到了。我看到主人和他的朋友在一边窃窃私语了许久，间或用手指指我，就料定他们肯定是在谋划什么坏事。我偷听到了他们一些话，还听懂了其中的几句，这令我非常恐惧，忍不住开始胡思乱想。可是第二天早上，我的小保姆格兰姆达尔克立契就将整件事从头到尾告诉了我，她是从她母亲那里巧妙地打探来的。这个可怜的小姑娘把我搂在怀里，悲羞交加地哭了起来。她担心那些人笨手笨脚的会把我弄伤。他们有可能把我拿在手里时不小心把我捏死或者捏断我的手脚。她又说我

the next morning *Glumdalclitch* my little nurse told me the whole matter, which she had cunningly picked out from her mother. The poor girl laid me on her bosom, and fell a weeping with shame and grief. She apprehended some mischief would happen to me from rude vulgar folks, who might squeeze me to death, or break one of my limbs by taking me in their hands. She had also observed how modest I was in my nature, how nicely I regarded my honour, and what an indignity I should conceive it to be exposed for money as a public spectacle to the meanest of the people. She said, her *papa* and *mamma* had promised that *Grildrig* should be hers, but now she found they meant to serve her as they did last year, when they pretended to give her a lamb, and yet, as soon as it was fat, sold it to a butcher. For my own part I may truly affirm that I was less concerned than my nurse. I had a strong hope which left me, that I should one day recover my liberty; and as to the ignominy of being carried about for a monster, I considered myself to be a perfect stranger in the country, and that such a misfortune could never be charged upon me as a reproach if ever I should return to *England*; since the king of *Great Britain* himself, in my condition, must have undergone the same distress.

的性情是那么朴实温和，那么彬彬有礼，现在要让我去给一帮最粗俗的人表演来赚钱，这简直是对我莫大的羞辱。她说她的爸爸妈妈已经答应“格里尔特里格”归她了，可现在她察觉到，他们又要故技重演欺骗她了。去年他们假装送给她一只小羊羔，但一旦这只小羊羔长得肥硕了，他们立刻将其卖给了屠户。我倒不像我的小保姆那么担心。因为我心里有一个牢固的信念，那就是我总有一天会恢复自由。至于被人当做怪物到处带着去表演的耻辱，我就把自己看做是这个国家里的一个彻头彻尾的异乡人。有这种不幸的遭遇也不能归咎于我。等哪一天我回到了英国，人们也决不可能因为我有过这样的不幸遭遇来羞辱我。因为就算是大不列颠国王本人，在我的处境中，也同样要遭遇这样的不幸的。

My master, pursuant to the advice of his friend, carried me in a box the next market

我的主人按照他那位朋友的建议，到了下一个赶集日，就把我

day to the neighbouring town, and took along with him his little daughter my nurse upon a pillion behind him. The box was close on every side, with a little door for me to go in and out, and a few Gimlet-holes to let in air. The girl had been so careful to put the quilt of her baby's bed into it, for me to lie down on. However, I was terribly shaken and discomposed in this journey, though it were but of half an hour. For the horse went about forty foot at every step, and trotted so high, that the agitation was equal to the rising and falling of a ship in a great storm, but much more frequent: our journey was somewhat further than from *London* to St. Albans. My master alighted at an inn which he used to frequent; and after consulting a while with the Inn-keeper and making some necessary preparations, he hired the *grultrud*, or cryer, to give notice through the town of a strange creature to be seen at the sign of the Horn and Crown, not so big as a *splacknuck* (an animal in that country very finely shaped, about six foot long) and in every part of the body resembling a human creature, could speak several words, and perform a hundred diverting tricks.

装在一个箱子里，带到了附近的镇上。他还带上了我的小保姆，也就是他的小女儿，让她坐在身后的马背上。箱子四面被封得严严实实，只有一个小门供我出入，另外还有几个透气的小孔。女孩儿心思细腻，她把婴儿床上的被褥拿来放到了我的箱子里，让我一路躺着。虽然只有半个小时的路程，但我却被摇晃得死去活来，因为那马每步要跨出 40 多英尺，而且上下起伏很大，箱子的震荡程度对我来说相当于一场强烈暴风雨中的船只，上下起伏，震荡得还远远比船只要频繁得多。我们的路程貌似比从伦敦到圣奥尔班还要远一点。我的主人在他经常光顾的一家小旅馆前下了马。他先和店主商量了一会儿，然后做好必要的准备，接着就雇了一名“格鲁特鲁德”，就是镇上的喊事员，用喇叭通知全镇到绿鹰旅馆来观赏一个奇异的动物。它还不及一头“斯泼拉克那克”（这是这个国家一种外形美观的动物，身长约 6 英尺）大，全身上下都酷似人，会说几个词，还能表演 100 种好玩的杂耍。

I was placed upon a table in the largest room of the inn, which might be near three hundred foot square. My little nurse stood on a low stool close to the table, to take

我被放到旅馆最大的房间里的一张桌子上，这个房间大约有 300 平方英尺。我的小保姆站在桌子旁边的一张矮凳子上，一边照顾

care of me, and direct what I should do. My master, to avoid a crowd, would suffer only thirty people at a time to see me. I walked about on the table as the girl commanded; She asked me questions as far as she knew my understanding of the language reached, and I answered them as loud as I could. I turned about several times to the company, paid my humble respects, said they were welcome, and used some other speeches I had been taught. I took up a thimble filled with liquor, which *Glumdalclitch* had given me for a cup, and drank their health. I drew out my hanger, and flourished with it after the manner of fencers in *England*. My nurse gave me part of a straw, which I exercised as a pike, having learnt the art in my youth. I was that day shown to twelve sets of company, and as often forced to go over again with the same fopperies, till I was half dead with weariness and vexation. For, those who had seen me made such wonderful reports, that the people were ready to break down the doors to come in. My master for his own interest would not suffer anyone to touch me except my nurse and, to prevent danger, benches were set round the table at such a distance as put me out of everybody's reach. However, an unlucky school-boy aimed a hazel Nut directly at my head, which very narrowly missed me; otherwise, it came with so much violence

我，一边指挥我表演。我的主人为了避免人群太过拥挤，每次只允许30个人进来看我。我按照小保姆的指令在桌子上来回踱步。她尽量只用我能听懂的有限的那几句话问我问题，我大声说出答案。我一边向观众致意，一边绕着桌子转圈，说欢迎光临，还说了一些其他我会说的话。格兰姆达尔克立契给了我一个像顶针那么大的酒杯，斟满了酒，我端起酒杯，说：为大家的健康干杯！我抽出腰刀，学着英国击剑家的样子舞弄了一番。我又拿过小保姆给我的麦秆当枪挥舞了一会儿。这项技艺我年轻时曾经学过。那天我一共表演了12场，被迫一遍又一遍地重复那些舞刀弄枪的愚蠢把戏，疲惫不堪，痛苦至极，直到累得半死才收工。由于人们对我的精彩表演赞不绝口，因此前来观赏的人越来越多，几乎要破门而入。主人为了维护自身的利益，除了我的小保姆外不允许任何人碰我。为了避免意外，他在桌子四周摆了一圈长凳，将我与众人远远地隔开，使他们碰不到我。可是，一个坏孩子拿起一颗榛子冲我的头扔过来，差点儿击中我。那榛子来势凶猛，果真被击中，我肯定早就脑浆迸裂，因为它几乎有一只小南瓜那么大。不过我很开心看到这小淘气鬼被痛打一顿，轰了出去。

that it would have infallibly knocked out my brains, for it was almost as large as a small pumpion: but I had the satisfaction to see the young rogue well beaten, and turned out of the room.

My master gave public notice, that he would show me again the next market-day, and in the mean time he prepared a more convenient vehicle for me, which he had reason enough to do; for I was so tired with my first journey, and with entertaining company for eight hours together, that I could hardly stand upon my legs, or speak a word. It was at least three days before I recovered my strength; and that I might have no rest at home, all the neighbouring Gentleman, from an hundred miles round, hearing of my fame, came to see me at my master's own house. There could not be fewer than thirty persons with their wives and children (for the country was very populous); and my master demanded the rate of a full room whenever he showed me at home, although it were only to a single family. so that for some time I had but little ease every day of the week (except *Wednesday*, which is their Sabbath) although I were not carried to the town.

主人向大家宣告，下一个赶集日再带我来表演。同时他也给我准备了一辆更方便的车子。他这样做的理由很充分，因为走这一趟我已经筋疲力尽，再加上连续 8 个小时为观众表演，两条腿都快支撑不住了，话也说不出来了。至少 3 天以后，我才恢复了体力。可是我在家里也无法休息，因为方圆 100 英里内的先生们听说我的名声后，都赶到我主人的家里来看我。当时带着妻子儿女来看我的人不下 30 个(乡下本来就人数众多)。每当在家里表演时，即使只有一家人观看表演，我的主人也要按照满满一屋子人来收取费用。虽然那一段时间我没有去镇上表演，但每天无法消停。只有星期三可以休息一下，因为那天是他们的安息日。

My master finding how profitable I was like to be, resolved to carry me to the most considerable cities of the kingdom. Having therefore provided himself with all things necessary for a long journey, and

主人发现带我到处表演如此有利可图之后，就决定带我去全国各大城市巡回表演。他将长途旅行的必需品准备妥当，又安排好了家里的事务，1703 年 8 月 17 日，也

settled his affairs at home, he took leave of his wife, and upon the 17th of *August* 1703 about two months after my arrival, we set out for the metropolis, situated near the middle of that empire, and about three thousand miles distance from our house: My master made his daughter *Glumdalclitch* ride behind him. She carried me on her lap in a box tied about her waist. The girl had lined it on all sides with the softest cloth she could get, well quilted underneath, furnished it with her baby's bed, provided me with linen and other necessaries, and made everything as convenient as she could. We had no other company but a boy of the house, who rode after us with the luggage.

就是我到这里两个月左右后，告别他的妻子，动身前往靠近整个国家中部，离家约 3000 英里的首都。主人让他女儿格兰姆达尔克立契骑在他身后的马背上。她把我装在一个箱子里系在腰间。她用能找到的最柔软的棉布贴在箱子的四面，棉布下面垫得厚厚的，然后把婴儿的小床放在里面，又给我准备了内衣和其他一些必需品，尽量把一切都安排得方便舒适。与我们同行的只有一个男仆，他带着行李骑马跟在后面。

My master's design was to show me in all the towns by the way, and to step out of the road for fifty or a hundred miles, to any village, or person of quality's house where he might expect custom. We made easy journeys of not above seven or eightscore miles a day: for *Glumdalclitch*, on purpose to spare me, complained she was tired with the trotting of the horse. She often took me out of my box at my own desire, to give me air, and show me the country, but always held me fast by a leading-string. We passed over five or six rivers many degrees broader and deeper than the *Nile* or the *Ganges*; and there was hardly a rivulet so small as the *Thames* at London-Bridge. We were ten weeks in our

我的主人计划让我在沿途所到的每个市镇表演，而且，只要有买卖，也可以离开大路走上 50 或 100 英里到村子上或者大户人家去演出。我们一路走得很慢，一天也走不到一百五六十英里。格兰姆达尔克立契为了保护我，就抱怨说她骑马骑累了。应我的要求，她常常把我拿出箱子，让我呼吸一下外面的新鲜空气，欣赏一下乡下的美景，不过总是用一根绳子紧紧地拴着我。我们穿过了五六条比尼罗河和恒河更宽更深的河，像伦敦桥畔的泰晤士河那样的小溪一条也看不到。我们一共走了 10 个星期，我像展品一样在 18 个大城市被展出，不包括沿途所到的许多村庄和

journey, and I was shown in eighteen large towns besides many villages and private families.

On the *26th* Day of *October*, we arrived at the metropolis, called in their language *Lorbrulgrud*, or *Pride of the Universe*. My master took a lodging in the principal street of the city, not far from the royal palace, and put out bills in the usual form, containing an exact description of my person and parts. He hired a large room between three and four hundred foot wide. He provided a table sixty foot in diameter, upon which I was to act my part, and palisadoed it round three foot from the edge, and as many high, to prevent my falling over. I was shown ten times a day to the wonder and satisfaction of all people. I could now speak the language tolerably well, and perfectly understood every word that was spoken to me. Besides, I had learned their alphabet, and could make a shift to explain a sentence here and there; for *Glumdalclitch* had been my instructor while we were at home, and at leisure hours during our journey. She carried a little book in her pocket, not much larger than a *Sanson's Atlas*; it was a common treatise for the use of young girls, giving a short account of their religion; out of this she taught me my letters, and interpreted the words.

私人家庭。

直到10月26日，我们才到达首都“洛布鲁格鲁德”，意思是“宇宙的骄傲”。我们住在离皇宫不远的一条大街上，按照惯例贴出广告，把我的情况详细描述了一番。他租下一间三四百英尺宽的大房间，准备了一张直径 60 英尺的圆桌要我在上面表演。为了防止我摔下桌子，他们在桌子上围了一圈 3 英尺高、距离桌边 3 英尺的护栏。我每天都有 10 场演出，我的表演令在座的观众赞不绝口，非常满意。我现在已经能把他们的语言说得相当流利了，基本上能听懂他们所说的每个词。而且，我还学会了他们的字母，偶尔还能自己解释某些句子。在家时格兰姆达尔克立契就一直指导我学习，旅途的闲暇中继续指导我。她的口袋里装着一本像《三松地图册》那么小的书。那是一本给小姑娘们看的普通读物，是关于他们宗教的概述。她就用这本书来教我字母，讲解单词。

CHAPTER 3

第三章

The Author sent for to Court. The Queen buys him of his Master the Farmer, and presents him to the King. He disputes with his Majesty's great scholars. An Apartment at Court provided for the Author. He is in high Favour with the Queen. He stands up for the Honour of his own Country. His Quarrels with the Queen's Dwarf.

作者进宫面圣。皇后将其从农场主手里买下来，献给国王。他舌战皇家学者。朝廷专门为他制作了一个房间。他受到皇后的宠爱。他极力维护祖国的荣誉。他和皇后的侏儒之间的争端。

The frequent labours I underwent every day made in a few weeks a very considerable change in my health: the more my master got by me, the more unsatiable he grew. I had quite lost my stomach, and was almost reduced to a skeleton. The farmer observed it, and concluding I soon must die, resolved to make as good a hand of me as he could. While he was thus reasoning and resolving with himself, a *slardral*, or gentleman Usher, came from court, commanding my master to carry me immediately thither for the diversion of the queen and her ladies. Some of the latter had already been to see me, and reported strange things of my beauty, Behaviour, and good sense. Her majesty and those who attended her were beyond

几个星期之内，每天如此繁重的劳动使我的身体发生了相当大的变化。我为主人赚到的钱越多，他就越发欲壑难填。我的肚子已经瘪下去，瘦得几乎只剩一把骨头了。主人见状，断定我活不了多长时间了，就决定从我身上尽可能多捞一笔。正当他谋划赚钱新方案的时候，从朝廷来了一个“斯拉德拉尔”，也就是引见官，命令主人即刻带我进宫给皇后和妃嫔们表演助兴。有几位妃嫔已经看过我的表演了，她们把我的美丽的外貌、得体的行为及正确的判断力当做离奇的事情报告给了皇后。皇后和她的侍从们非常喜爱我的举止。我双膝跪地，请求皇后允许我亲吻一下她的脚。然而我却被放到一张桌子上，之后这位亲切的皇后把她的一

measure delighted with my Demeanour. I fell on my knees and begged the honour of kissing her imperial foot; but this gracious princess held out her little finger towards me (after I was set on a table, which I embraced in both my arms, and put the tip of it, with the utmost respect) to my lip. She made me some general questions about my country and my travels, which I answered as distinctly and in as few words as I could. She asked whether I would be content to live at court. I bowed down to the board of the table, and humbly answered that I was my master's slave, but if I were at my own disposal, I should be proud to devote my life to her majesty's service. She then asked my master whether he were willing to sell me at a good price. He, who apprehended I could not live a month, was ready enough to part with me, and demanded a thousand pieces of gold, which were ordered him on the spot, each piece being the bigness of eight hundred moydores; but, allowing for the proportion of all things between that country and *Europe*, and the high price of gold among them, was hardly so great a sum as a thousand guineas would be in *England*. I then said to the queen, since I was now her majesty's most humble creature and vassal, I must beg the favour, that *Glumdalclitch*, who had always tended me with so much care and kindness, and understood to do it so well,

个小手指伸给了我。我立刻展开双臂将其抱住，以最恭敬的态度用我的嘴唇触碰了她的指尖。她问了我几个平常问题，是关于我的祖国和此次旅行情况的，我都简明扼要地回答了。她问我是否愿意住进皇宫。我深深鞠了一躬，一直鞠到桌面上，恭敬地答道，我是我主人的奴隶，但如果我能自己做主的话，能一辈子侍奉在皇后左右是我无上的光荣和幸运。她听完后问我的主人是否愿意将我以重金卖给她。主人正担心我可能熬不过这个月，巴不得赶紧脱手，于是出价 1000 金币。皇后当场下令付钱。每个金币都差不多有 800 个莫艾多那么大，但如果按照这个国家和欧洲的每一样东西之间的比例来看，再按照金子在他们那里的价值来计算一下，这 1000 金币几乎还不值英国的 1000 个畿尼。接下来我对皇后说，作为您最卑贱的奴仆，我想请求陛下开恩，也允许格兰姆达尔克立契留下，并允许她继续当我的保姆和老师。一直以来都是她照顾我，她对我关怀备至，非常亲切。她熟悉照顾我的各种细节。皇后答应了，也很容易就征得了那农场主的同意，自己的女儿能够入宫还有什么不高兴的？那个小姑娘也喜不自禁。我的旧主人同我告别，说他总算给我找到了一个好地方，然后就退了下去。我什么也没说，只向他浅浅地鞠了个躬。

might be admitted into her service, and continue to be my nurse and instructor. Her majesty agreed to my petition, and easily got the farmer's consent, who was glad enough to have his daughter preferred at court: and the poor girl herself was not able to hide her joy: My late master withdrew, bidding me farewell, and saying he had left me in a good service; to which I replied not a word, only making him a slight bow.

The queen observed my coldness, and when the farmer was gone out of the apartment, asked me the reason. I made bold to tell her majesty that I owed no other obligation to my late master, than his not dashing out the brains of a poor harmless creature found by chance in his field; which obligation was amply recompensed by the gain he had made in showing me through half the kingdom, and the price he had now sold me for. That the life I had since led, was laborious enough to kill an animal of ten times my strength. That my health was much impaired by the continual drudgery of entertaining the rabble every hour of the day, and that if my master had not thought my life in danger, her majesty perhaps would not have got so cheap a bargain. But as I was out of all fear of being ill treated under the protection of so great and good an empress, the ornament of nature, the darling of the world, the

皇后察觉到我对他的冷淡态度，农场主离开房间后就问我原因。我大胆对皇后说，我已经不欠我的旧主人什么情了。我唯一欠他的只是他没有将自己在麦地里碰巧发现的一只可怜无害的小动物打得脑浆飞迸。而这点人情我早已报答得淋漓尽致了。他让我在全国一半的地方表演，已经赚得不少了，如今又把我卖了个好价钱。我在他手里过着非常辛苦的生活，恐怕一个体力比我强 10 倍的动物也承受不了。从早到晚都忙着给一帮乌合之众卖力表演取乐，身体受到极大损伤。要不是他觉得我命不久矣，陛下很可能根本买不到这么一件便宜货。但是现在我一点也不害怕再会遭到那种虐待了，因为这位仁慈伟大、心地善良的皇后会保护我。大自然因她而增添了光彩，她是全世界的幸运儿、万民的福祉、不死的凤凰鸟。我以前的主人以为我命不久矣，恐怕他要失望了，因

delight of her subjects, the phoenix of the creation; so, I hoped my late master's apprehensions would appear to be groundless, for I already found my spirits to revive by the influence of her most august presence.

为我感觉到，在皇后陛下的庇护下，我的精神已经好多了。

This was the sum of my speech, delivered with great improprieties and hesitation; the latter part was altogether framed in the style peculiar to that people, whereof I learned some phrases from *Glumdalclitch*, while she was carrying me to court.

这就是我的大意。我说得吞吞吐吐，措辞也有不当之处，后半段完全是照那里人特有的语言风格来说的，有些词句还是格兰姆达尔克立契带我进宫时才学会的。

The queen giving great allowance for my defectiveness in speaking, was however surprised at so much wit and good sense in so diminutive an animal. She took me in her own Hands, and carried me to the king, who was then retired to his cabinet. His majesty, a prince of much gravity, and austere countenance, not well observing my shape at first view, asked the queen after a cold manner, how long it was since she grew fond of a *splacnuck*; for such it seems he took me to be, as I lay upon my breast in her majesty's right hand. But this princess, who hath an infinite deal of wit and humour, set me gently on my foot upon the scrutore, and commanded me to give his majesty an account of myself, which I did in a very few words; and *Glumdalclitch*, who attended at the cabinet door, and could not endure I

皇后对我所说的话的错误给予了极大的宽容，却非常惊讶这么微小的一个动物竟会有如此的判断力和见识。她亲手把我带到国王那里。国王这时已经摒退了众臣回到了内廷。他的表情非常庄重威严。他刚开始没有看清楚我的身形，我趴在皇后的右手里，他还以为是一只"斯泼拉克那克"呢，不冷不热地向皇后说，何时喜欢起"斯泼拉克那克"来了？但富有智慧和幽默的皇后把我轻轻地放在写字台上，让我向国王作自我介绍。我就简要地说了几句。在内宫门口侍候的格兰姆达尔克立契几乎跟我形影不离，这时就被召了进来，证实了我到她父亲家以来的全部经历。

should be out of her sight, being admitted, confirmed all that had passed from my arrival at her father's house.

The king, although he be as learned a person as any in his dominions, and had been educated in the study of philosophy, and particularly mathematics; yet when he observed my shape exactly, and saw me walk erect, before I began to speak, conceived I might be a piece of clockwork (which is in that country arrived to a very great perfection), contrived by some ingenious artist. But, when he heard my voice, and found what I delivered to be regular and rational, he could not conceal his astonishment. He was by no means satisfied with the relation I gave him of the manner I came into his kingdom, but thought it a story concerted between *Glumdalclitch* and her father, who had taught me a set of words to make me sell at a higher price. Upon this imagination he put several other questions to me, and still received rational answers, no otherwise defective than by a foreign accent, and an imperfect knowledge in the language, with some rustic phrases which I had learned at the farmer's house, and did not suit the polite style of a court.

His majesty sent for three great scholars who were then in their weekly waiting (according to the custom in that country). These gentlemen, after they had a while examined my shape with much nicety,

国王学识广博，不输给他领土上的任何一位学者。他曾经研究过哲学，特别是数学。尽管如此，他看清楚我的样子后，见我直立行走，在我开口说话之前他还是觉得我大概是哪位能工巧匠设计出来的一件钟表之类的机械，这种机械技术在那个国家已经很发达了。可是当他听到我的声音，发现我说话的内容十分有逻辑后，特别惊讶。我向他讲述我是怎么来到他的王国的，他却怎么听都不满意，以为格兰姆达尔克立契和她父亲事先编好了这一段故事。他们教我说这样一番话，就可以把我卖个好价钱。他猜想着，又问了我几个问题，得到的依然是合情合理的回答。我唯一的缺陷就是说话带点外国口音，对他们的语言运用得不够纯熟，还夹杂了一些在农民家里学到的乡下土话，与宫廷里的高雅格调不太相称。

国王传召了3位大学者前来觐见。这个星期轮到他们当值。学者轮流听候国王召见是这个国家的风俗。他们先是仔细打量了我一番，然后开始针对我各抒己见。他

were of different opinions concerning me. They all agreed that I could not be produced according to the regular laws of nature, because I was not framed with a capacity of preserving my life, either by swiftness, or climbing of trees, or digging holes in the earth. They observed by my teeth, which they viewed with great exactness, that I was a carnivorous animal; yet most quadrupeds being an overmatch for me, and field-mice, with some others, too nimble, they could not imagine how I should be able to support myself, unless I fed upon snails and other insects, which they offered by many learned arguments to evince that I could not possibly do. One of these Virtuosi seemed to think that I might be an Embryo, or abortive Birth. But this Opinion was rejected by the other two, who observed my Limbs to be perfect and finished, and that I had lived several Years, as it was manifested from my Beard, the Stumps whereof they plainly discovered through a Magnifying Glass. They would not allow me to be a dwarf, because my littleness was beyond all degrees of comparison; for, the queen's favourite dwarf, the smallest ever known in that kingdom, was nearly thirty foot high. After much debate, they concluded unanimously that I was only *relplum scalcath*, which is interpreted literally, *lusus naturae*; a determination exactly agreeable to the modern philosophy of

们一致认为，按照大自然的一般规律，不可能会有我这样的动物产生，因为我天生就不具备存活下来的能力，跑不快，不会爬树，也不会打洞。他们还非常认真地察看了我的牙齿，认为我属于肉食性动物。但是，我绝不是大多数四足动物的对手。而田鼠之类的动物又那么敏捷，他们根本无法想象我是如何生存下来的，除非我吃蜗牛或者其他昆虫。可他们又举出很多例证，说我也不可能吃那些东西。其中有一位似乎认为我或许是个胚胎，或者是一个早产儿。但是，这种说法马上遭到了另外两位的坚决反对。他们观察到我的四肢已发育成熟，从我的胡子观察出，我也有相当的年纪了。他们借助放大镜清清楚楚地看到了我的胡子楂。他们也不把我归入侏儒那一类，因为我的身材与他们国家的任何侏儒都无法相比，实在太小了。皇后最宠爱的那个侏儒是这个国家已知最矮小的了，身高也有 30 英尺左右。他们为此事争论了半天，最后得出一致结论，说我是“瑞尔普拉姆·斯盖尔卡斯”，也就是“lusus naturae”的意思。他们这种决断方法与欧洲现代哲学的做法完全一致。欧洲的现代哲学教授们很看不起不研究事理只懂得逃避问题的神秘学。亚里士多德的门徒们企图用老办法来掩饰他们的无知，可是又无法掩饰。欧洲的现代哲学教授

Europe, whose professors, disdaining the old evasion of occult causes, whereby the followers of *Aristotle* endeavour in vain to disguise their ignorance, have invented this wonderful solution of all difficulties to the unspeakable advancement of human knowledge.

们发明了这样一种可以解决所有困难的绝妙方法，使人类的知识得到了无法言喻的进步。

After this decisive conclusion, I entreated to be heard a word or two. I applied myself to the king, and assured his majesty that I came from a country which abounded with several millions of both sexes, and of my own stature; where the animals, trees, and houses were all in proportion, and where by consequence I might be as able to defend myself, and to find sustenance, as any of his majesty's subjects could do here; which I took for a full answer to those gentlemen's arguments. To this they only replied with a smile of contempt, saying, that the farmer had instructed me very well in my lesson. The king, who had a much better understanding, dismissing his learned men, sent for the farmer, who by good fortune was not yet gone out of town: having therefore first examined him privately, and then confronted him with me and the young girl, his majesty began to think that what we told him might possibly be true. He desired the queen to order that a particular care should be taken of me, and was of opinion, that *Glumdalclitch* should still continue in her

在他们果断得出这一结论之后，我恳请说两句。我向国王坦言，我确实来自某个国家，那里有很多像我这样身材的男男女女，那里的动物、树木和房屋的大小也都和我们具有相应的比例。因此，就和陛下的每一个臣民一样，我在自己的祖国也可以保护自己和维持生计。这就是我对那几位先生所有疑问的回答。他们对此嗤之以鼻，说那农场主把我调教得真好。国王毕竟见多识广，他摒退了那几位大学士，派人召来农场主。恰好农场主这时还没出城。国王先秘密地盘问他，然后又让他跟我和小姑娘对证，这才开始相信我们所说的话很可能是事实。他要皇后吩咐下去一定要对我特别关照，因为他看出我们俩的关系非常亲密，也同意格兰姆达尔克立契留下来继续做我的保姆。王宫给她安排了舒适的房间，一名为给她上课的女教师，一名服侍她梳妆更衣的宫女，还有另外两名为她做其他事情的仆人。但是照顾我的任务却由她一人全权负责。皇后命令为她制作家具的木工设计一个箱子以作我的卧室之

office of tending me, because he observed we had a great affection for each other. A convenient apartment was provided for her at court; she had a sort of governess appointed to take care of her education, a maid to dress her, and two other servants for menial offices; but the care of me was wholly appropriated to herself. The queen commanded her own cabinet-maker to contrive a box that might serve me for a bed-chamber, after the model that *Glumdalclitch* and I should agree upon. This man was a most ingenious artist, and according to my directions, in three weeks finished to me a wooden chamber of sixteen foot square and twelve high, with Sash windows, a door, and two closets, like a *London* bed-chamber. The board that made the ceiling was to be lifted up and down by two Hinges, to put in a bed ready furnished by her majesty's upholsterer, which *Glumdalclitch* took out every day to air, made it with her own hands, and letting it down at night, locked up the roof over me. A nice workman, who was famous for little curiosities, undertook to make me two chairs, with backs and frames, of a substance not unlike ivory, and two tables, with a cabinet to put my things in. The room was quilted on all sides, as well as the floor and the ceiling, to prevent any accident from the carelessness of those who carried me, and to break the force of a jolt when I

用，但样式得经过格兰姆达尔克立契和我的同意。那人的确是个能工巧匠，他按照我的要求，仅用 3 个星期的时间就为我做成了一间 16 英尺大小、12 英尺高的木头房子。上面还有可以推拉的窗户，有一扇门和两个衣橱，整个卧室类似于伦敦的风格。用作天花板的木板通过两个铰链来控制，可以打开或放下，皇后的家具商为我打造的小床，就是从屋顶放进去的。每天，格兰姆达尔克立契都会亲手把床拿出来晾一晾，晚上再放回去，然后再把我锁在里面。一名以制造各种稀奇玩意而闻名的工匠用一种类似象牙的材料，给我做了两把带靠背和扶手的椅子、两张桌子和几个柜子来存放零碎东西。房间的四壁，以及地板和天花板，都厚厚地垫上了柔软的东西，以防那些搬运我的人笨手笨脚酿成事故。就算我坐马车，也不至于被颠坏。为了防止老鼠闯进来，我让他们给我的门装了一把锁。铁匠反复尝试才打出了他们见所未见的一把小锁。据我了解，似乎英国有一位先生家的锁大小勉强能超过这把。我担心格兰姆达尔克立契会弄丢，想方设法自己装着钥匙。皇后又下令用最薄的丝绸为我缝制衣服。不过那丝绸的厚度也和英国的毛毯差不多，穿在我身上显得十分笨重，后来习惯了才好一些。衣服是按照这个国家的式样做的，一半像波斯风格一半像

went in a coach. I desired a lock for my door to prevent rats and mice from coming in: the smith after several attempts made the smallest that was ever seen among them for I have known a larger at the gate of a gentleman's house in *England*. I made a shift to keep the key in a pocket of my own, fearing *Glumdalclitch* might lose it. The queen likewise ordered the thinnest silks that could be gotten, to make me clothes, not much thicker than an *English* blanket, very cumbersome, till I was accustomed to them. They were after the fashion of the kingdom, partly resembling the *Persian*, and partly the *Chinese*, and are a very grave and decent habit.

The queen became so fond of my company, that she could not dine without me. I had a table placed upon the same at which her Majesty eat, just at her left elbow, and a chair to sit on. *Glumdalclitch* stood upon a stool on the floor, near my table, to assist and take care of me. I had an entire set of silver dishes and plates, and other necessaries, which in proportion to those of the queen, were not much bigger than what I have seen of the same kind in a *London* toy-shop, for the furniture of a baby-house: these my little nurse kept in her pocket, in a silver box, and gave me at meals as I wanted them, always cleaning them herself. No person dined with the queen but the two princesses royal, the elder sixteen years

中国风格，穿起来相当庄重大方。

皇后非常喜欢和我在一起。如果我不在她身边，她都不想用餐。她用餐时，会在自己左手边摆一张桌子和椅子给我用。格兰姆达尔克立契站在一张小凳子上，紧挨着我的桌子帮忙照顾我。我有一整套包括碗碟在内的银质餐具。和皇后的餐具比起来，它们就像我曾在伦敦一家玩具店看到的用来摆放在娃娃房里的餐具那么小。这套餐具被我的小保姆随身携带在她口袋里的一个银盒子里，当我吃饭的时候她就拿给我，平时她便亲手把它们洗得干干净净。和皇后一起吃饭的只有两位公主，大的 16 岁，小的那时才 13 岁过 1 个月。皇后总是把一小块肉放到我的盘子里，让我自己切着吃。她特别喜欢看我小口

old, and the younger at that time thirteen and a month. Her majesty used to put a bit of meat upon one of my dishes, out of which I carved for myself; and her diversion was to see me eat in miniature. for the queen (who had indeed but a weak stomach) took up at one mouthful, as much as a dozen *English* farmers could eat at a meal, which to me was for some time a very nauseous sight. She would craunch the wing of a lark, bones and all, between her teeth, although it were nine times as large as that of a full-grown turkey; and put a bit of bread in her mouth, as big as two twelvepenny loaves. She drank out of a golden cup, above a hogshead at a draught. Her knives were twice as long as a scythe set straight upon the handle. The spoons, forks, and other instruments were all in the same proportion. I remember when *Glumdalclitch* carried me out of curiosity, to see some of the tables at court, where ten or a dozen of these enormous knives and forks were lifted up together, I thought I had never till then beheld so terrible a sight.

吃东西的样子，将其视为乐趣。实际上皇后胃口并不大，但一顿饭也至少是 12 个英国农民的饭量。她吃饭的样子让我一度觉得非常恶心。她能将百灵鸟的一只翅膀连肉带骨头嚼得粉碎，而那翅膀足有 9 只长足的火鸡那么大。她随便往嘴里塞一小片面包，也有两个 12 便士的面包那么大。她用金杯喝饮料，在我看来一口就能喝掉一大桶。她餐刀的长度相当于两把拉直了的长柄大镰刀，汤匙、叉子和其他餐具也都这么大。记得有一次我因为好奇，就让格兰姆达尔克立契带我去宫里看那些人吃饭。10 几把如此巨大的刀叉同时举起，我觉得在那以前还从未见过如此恐怖的景象。

It is the custom that every *Wednesday* (which as I have before observed, was their Sabbath) the king and queen, with the royal issue of both sexes, dine together in the apartment of his majesty, to whom I was now become a great favourite; and at these times my little chair and table were placed at his left hand before one of the

我前面已经提到过，星期三是他们的安息日，到了这一天，国王、皇后、王子和公主们按照惯例都要在国王陛下的内廷聚餐。如今我已经是国王的宠臣了，每到星期三，他们就把我的小桌椅放在他左手边的一只盐瓶旁边。这位君王很喜欢和我交谈，询问我欧洲的风俗、

salt-cellars. This prince took a pleasure in conversing with me, inquiring into the manners, religion, laws, government, and learning of *Europe*, wherein I gave him the best account I was able. His apprehension was so clear, and his judgment so exact, that he made very wise reflections and observations upon all I said. But, I confess, that after I had been a little too copious in talking of my own beloved country, of our trade, and wars by sea and land, of our schisms in religion, and parties in the state; the prejudices of his education prevailed so far, that he could not forbear taking me up in his right hand, and stroking me gently with the other, after an hearty fit of laughing, asked me whether I were a *whig* or a *tory*. Then turning to his first minister, who waited behind him with a white staff, near as tall as the mainmast of the Royal *Sovereign*; he observed how contemptible a thing was human grandeur, which could be mimicked by such diminutive insects as I: and yet, said he, I dare engage, these creatures have their titles and distinctions of honour; they contrive little nests and burrows, that they call houses and cities; they make a figure in dress and equipage; they love, they fight, they dispute, they cheat, they betray. And thus he continued on, while my colour came and went several times, with indignation to hear our noble country, the mistress of arts and

宗教、法律、政治和学术方面的情况，我都尽量一一讲给他听。他反应敏捷，判断力很强，能针对我所说的内容发表十分睿智的感想和意见。不过我不得不承认，一旦涉及我亲爱的祖国，涉及我们的贸易、海战和陆战、宗教派别以及国内的不同政党，我就有点滔滔不绝了。他所受的教育使他对此深不以为然，最后忍不住问我是辉格党还是托利党，然后转身冲着他的首相说，人类的尊严实在不值一提，就连我这么小的昆虫都妄图效法。当时首相正侍奉在国王身后，手持一根白色权杖，几乎有“王权号”的主桅那么高。“不过话又说回来，”国王接着说，“我敢保证这些小东西肯定也有他们的爵位和官衔呢，他们建造一些小窝小洞，称其为房屋和城市，他们修饰打扮以炫人耳目，他们谈情说爱，他们发动战争，他们论辩、欺诈、背叛。”他就这样一口气说下去，我气得脸一阵红一阵白。我那高贵的祖国作为欧洲的仲裁人，它可与法国抗衡，是美德、虔诚、荣誉和真理的中心，是被全世界仰慕和我们自己引以为骄傲的地方。这样伟大的一个国家，竟遭到如此轻视。

arms, the scourge of *France*, the arbitress of Europe, the seat of virtue, piety, honour, and truth, the pride and envy of the world, so contemptuously treated.

But, as I was not in a condition to resent injuries, so, upon mature thoughts, I began to doubt whether I were injured or no. For, after having been accustomed several months to the sight and converse of this people, and observed every object upon which I cast my eyes to be of proportionable magnitude, the horror I had at first conceived from their bulk and aspect was so far worn off, that if I had then beheld a company of *English* lords and ladies in their finery and birthday clothes, acting their several parts in the most courtly manner of strutting, and bowing and prating; to say the truth, I should have been strongly tempted to laugh as much at them as this king and his grandees did at me. Neither indeed could I forbear smiling at myself, when the queen used to place me upon her hand towards a looking-glass, by which both our persons appeared before me in full view together; and there could nothing be more ridiculous than the comparison: so that I really began to imagine myself dwindled many degrees below my usual size.

但是以我当时的处境，面对这种伤害不能显出怨恨。经过一番深思熟虑之后，我甚至开始怀疑自己是否受了伤害。因为几个月下来，我已经看惯了这个国家的景象，听惯了人们的言谈，眼中所见的每一件事物也都大小比例协调，初次见到他们那庞大的身躯和面孔时的恐惧这时候已经渐渐消退。如果此时我看见一群英国的老爷太太们穿着华装丽服，在那里装腔作势，昂首阔步，点头哈腰，空谈闲聊，说实话，我也很有可能要嘲笑他们，就像这里的国王及其要员嘲笑我一样。皇后常常把我捧在手里站在镜子前，这样两个人在一起的样子就一览无余地映现在我的眼里。说心里话，这时我就忍不住笑自己。这种对比实在太悬殊了，显得很滑稽，我甚至开始想象自己的身材比原来缩小了好几倍。

Nothing angered and mortified me so much as the queen's dwarf, who being of the lowest stature that was ever in that country (for I verily think he was not full

最使我愤怒、屈辱的莫过于皇后的侏儒了。他是这个国家有史以来身材最矮小的人，我敢说他不到30英尺高。可是自从看到我比他还

thirty foot high) became so insolent at seeing a creature so much beneath him, that he would always affect to swagger and look big as he passed by me in the queen's Antechamber, while I was standing on some table talking with the lords or ladies of the court, and he seldom failed of a smart word or two upon my littleness; against which I could only revenge myself by calling him brother challenging him to wrestle, and such repartees as are usual in the mouths of *court pages*. One day at dinner this malicious little cub was so nettled with something I had said to him, that raising himself upon the frame of her majesty's chair, he took me up by the middle, as I was sitting down, not thinking any harm, and let me drop into a large silver bowl of cream, and then ran away as fast as he could. I fell over head and ears, and, if I had not been a good swimmer, it might have gone very hard with me; for *Glumdalclitch*, in that instant happened to be at the other end of the room, and the queen was in such a fright that she wanted presence of mind to assist me. But my little nurse ran to my relief, and took me out, after I had swallowed above a quart of cream. I was put to bed; however I received no other damage than the loss of a suit of clothes, which was utterly spoiled. The dwarf was soundly whipped, and as a further punishment, forced to

要矮小得多，他就表现得极其傲慢。在皇后的会客室里，每当我站在桌上和宫里的老爷太太们说话时，他总趾高气扬地从我身旁走过去，不说一两句俏皮话讽刺我矮小，就算万幸。每当这个时候，为了雪耻，我就冲他喊："兄弟，我们决斗吧！"或者学着宫廷侍从们的语气说几句俏皮话。一次晚饭时，我的一句话把他惹怒了，这个坏心眼的家伙竟然站到皇后的椅子上，一把将我拦腰抓起，扔进盛奶酪的大银碗里，谈后撒腿就跑。我当时刚想坐下去，没想到会发生什么不测。由于没有防备，一头栽进了碗里，要不是我擅长游泳，很可能就要倒大霉了。格兰姆达尔克立契正巧在房间的另一头，而皇后则被吓呆了，不知道该如何救我才好。幸好我的小保姆赶忙跑过来救了我，把我拎了出来，这时我早已经吞下了半夸脱的奶酪。她将我放到了床上。不过我并没有受什么伤，只是损失了一身衣服，那衣服是彻底没法再穿了。那个侏儒挨了一顿痛打。为了惩罚他，他们强迫他把我所掉进的那个碗里的奶酪全部喝了下去。这之后他被送给一名贵妇人，永远丧失了重新得宠的机会。因此我再也没有见过他，这使我感到非常满意，因为如果不是这样，我真不知道这个恶劣的家伙还会怎样来报复我呢。

drink up the bowl of cream, into which he had thrown me; neither was he ever restored to favour: for, soon after the queen bestowed him on a lady of high quality, so that I saw him no more, to my very great satisfaction; for I could not tell to what extremity such a malicious urchin might have carried his resentment.

He had before served me a scurvy trick, which set the queen a laughing, although at the same time she were heartily vexed, and would have immediately cashiered him, if I had not been so generous as to intercede. Her majesty had taken a marrow-bone upon her plate, and after knocking out the marrow, placed the bone again in the dish erect as it stood before; the dwarf watching his opportunity, while *Glumdalclitch* was gone to the sideboard, mounted upon the stool she stood on to take care of me at meals, took me up in both hands, and squeezing my legs together, wedged them into the marrow-bone above my waist, where I stuck for some time, and made a very ridiculous figure. I believe it was near a minute before anyone knew what was became of me, for I thought it below me to cry out. But, as princes seldom get their meat hot, my legs were not scalded, only my stockings and breeches in a sad condition. The dwarf at my entreaty had no other punishment than a sound whipping.

以前他也曾对我玩过一次卑鄙的恶作剧，博得皇后一笑，不过她也真的很生气，差点把他轰走，还是我宽宏大量帮他求情才留下来。皇后从盘子里拿了一根髓骨，敲出骨髓后又把骨头像原来那样直立在盘子里。格兰姆达尔克立契到餐具架那边去了，那个侏儒见状，就爬上她照顾我用餐时站的凳子，双手举起我，把我的双腿往髓骨里塞，一直塞到我腰部。我在里面卡了半天也动不了，样子十分滑稽。我就这样待了至少一分钟，之后被发现，因为我没敢喊救命，觉得那样未免太没面子了。不过帝王们很少吃滚烫的肉食，所以我的腿并没有被烫伤，只是袜子和裤子被弄得一团糟。而那个侏儒因为我替他求了情，只挨了一顿痛打，再没有受到其他的惩罚。

I was frequently rallied by the queen upon account of my fearfulness, and she used to ask me whether the people of my country were as great cowards as myself. The occasion was this. the kingdom is much pestered with flies in summer, and these odious insects, each of them as big as a *Dunstable* lark, hardly gave me any rest while I sat at dinner, with their continual humming and buzzing about my ears. They would sometimes alight upon my victuals, and leave their loathsome Excrement or spawn behind, which to me was very visible, though not to the Natives of that country, whose large optics were not so acute as mine in viewing smaller objects. Sometimes they would fix upon my nose or forehead, where they stung me to the quick, smelling very offevsively, and I could easily trace that viscous Matter, which our Naturalists tell us enables those creatures to walk with their feet upwards upon a ceiling. I had much ado to defend myself against these detestable animals, and could not forbear starting when they came on my face. It was the common practice of the dwarf, to catch a number of these insects in his hand as schoolboys do among us, and let them out suddenly under my nose on purpose to frighten me, and divert the queen. My remedy was to cut them in pieces with my knife as they flew in the air, wherein my dexterity was much admired.

皇后常常提起这件事来嘲笑我胆小。她总问我，是不是我们国家的人都和我一样胆小如鼠。事情的起因是，夏天时这个国家的苍蝇十分烦人。这些可恶的害虫个个都有邓斯特堡的百灵鸟那么大，我坐在那儿吃饭，它们就在我耳朵边不停地嗡嗡乱叫，吵得我片刻都无法清净。有时候它们还会在我的食物上拉屎产卵，恶心至极。那些东西在我眼里一清二楚，但当地人看不见，因为他们的眼睛太大了，看这些小东西不如我敏锐。有时候这些苍蝇还会落在我的鼻子或额头上，狠狠地咬一口，发出令人难以忍受的气味。苍蝇身上那种令人恶心的黏糊糊的物质我看得一清二楚。据生物学家说，就是因为拥有这种物质，苍蝇才能在天花板上自如地行走。我费尽周折对付这些可恶的动物，使自己免受它们的侵扰，但每当有苍蝇飞到我脸上，我还是会被吓一跳。那个侏儒经常将一把苍蝇抓在手里，凑到我鼻子下面然后忽地松开手将其放飞，就像我们国家喜欢搞恶作剧的小学生一样，故意吓唬我，讨皇后欢心。我的对应策略就是趁苍蝇在空中飞的时候，用刀将它们砍得粉碎，手段之敏捷令他们大为赞赏。

I remember one morning, when *Glumdalclitch* had set me in my box upon a window, as she usually did in fair days to give me air (for I durst not venture to let the box be hung on a nail out of the window, as we do with cages in *England*) after I had lifted up one of my sashes, and sat down at my table to eat a piece of Sweet Cake for my breakfast, above twenty wasps, allured by the smell, came flying into the room, humming louder than the drones of as many Bagpipes. Some of them seized my cake, and carried it piecemeal away, others flew about my head and face, confounding me with the noise, and putting me in the utmost terror of their stings. However I had the courage to rise and draw my hanger, and attack them in the air. I dispatched four of them, but the rest got away, and I presently shut my window. These Insects were as large as partridges, I took out their stings, found them an inch and a half long, and as sharp as needles. I carefully preserved them all, and having since shown them with some other curiosities in several parts of *Europe*; upon my return to *England* I gave three of them to *Gresham College*, and kept the fourth for myself.

记得有一天早晨，格兰姆达尔克立契把我连同我的木箱一起放到窗台上透气。天朗气清时她经常这样做。我不敢让她把箱子挂到窗外的钉子上，像我们英国人挂鸟笼子那样。我打开一扇窗户，坐在桌子旁边，正打算吃甜饼作为早餐。突然，20 几只黄蜂循着甜饼的香味而来，齐刷刷飞进了我的房间，那嗡嗡的叫声比 20 几支风笛同时奏响还要吵。它们有的将甜饼一块块叼走，有的围着我的头和脸飞来飞去，吵吵闹闹地把我烦得不知如何是好，很怕它们会来蛰我。幸好我还有勇气站起来抽出腰刀，与它们展开了一场空中大战。我一共砍死了 4 只黄蜂，剩下的全跑了。我马上关闭了窗户。这些黄蜂都有鹧鸪那么大，我拔下它们的蜂刺，发现它们有 1.5 英寸长，像针一样尖利。我将这些刺小心地收藏起来，后来在欧洲几个地方将它们以及其他一些稀奇古怪的东西一起展出。回到英国后，我送了 3 根给格雷萨姆学院，将第四根作为了自己的珍藏品。

CHAPTER 4

第四章

The Country described. APproposal for correcting modern Maps. The King's Palace, and some Account of the Metropolis.The Author's way of travelling.The chief Temple described.

对这个国家的描述。修改现代地图的建议。国王的宫殿及首都概况。作者的旅途形式。对主要庙宇的描述。

I now intend to give the reader a short description of this country, as far as I travelled in it, which was not above two thousand miles round *Lorbrulgrud* the metropolis. For, the queen, whom I always attended, never went further when she accompanied the king in his progresses, and there stayed till his majesty returned from viewing his frontiers. The whole extent of this prince's dominions reacheth about six thousand miles in length, and from three to five in breadth. From whence I cannot but conclude that our geographers of *Europe* are in a great error, by supposing nothing but sea between *Japan* and *California*; for it was ever my opinion, that there must be a balance of earth to counterpoise the great continent of *Tartary*; and therefore they ought to correct their maps and charts, by joining this vast tract of land to the northwest parts of *America*, wherein I shall be ready

现在我打算给读者简短地介绍一下我在首都洛布鲁格鲁德方圆 2000 英里内的旅行见闻，让大家对这个国家有个大致的了解。皇后陪同国王出巡都不超过这 2000 英里的范围，国王到边境视察时她也在这个范围内等他回来。这时我总是陪着皇后，侍奉其左右。这位君王统辖的领土范围大约为长 6000 英里，宽 3000 到 5000 英里，由此我得知：欧洲的地理学家们犯了一个极大的错误，他们竟然认为日本与加利福尼亚之间只有一片汪洋大海。我则一直觉得，地球上肯定有那么一片大陆与鞑靼大陆相对应。因此他们应该重新修改他们的地图和海图，将这块宽广的陆地绘制在美洲的西北部，在细节上我愿意随时为他们提供帮助。

to lend them my assistance.

The kingdom is a peninsula, terminated to the northeast by a ridge of mountains thirty miles high, which are altogether impassable by reason of the volcanoes upon the tops, neither do the most learned know what sort of mortals inhabit beyond those mountains, or whether they be inhabited at all. On the three other sides it is bounded by the ocean. There is not one seaport in the whole kingdom, and those parts of the coasts into which the rivers issue are so full of pointed rocks, and the sea generally so rough, that there is no venturing with the smallest of their boats; so that these people are wholly excluded from any commerce with the rest of the world. But the large rivers are full of vessels, and abound with excellent fish, for they seldom get any from the sea, because the sea-fish are of the same size with those in *Europe*, and consequently not worth catching whereby it is manifest, that nature, in the production of plants and animals of so extraordinary a bulk, is wholly confined to this continent, of which I leave the reasons to be determined by philosophers. However, now and then they take a whale that happens to be dashed against the rocks, which the common people feed on heartily. These whales I have known so large that a man could hardly carry one upon his shoulders;

这个王国在一个半岛上，东北是一条高 30 英里的山脉作为天然疆界，山顶有火山，根本无法通行。就是最见多识广的人也不知道山那边住着些什么人，或者说究竟有没有人也是个问题。王国 3 面环海。国内无海港，河流入海处的海岸到处布满了尖利的岩石，海上常常是波涛汹涌，没有人敢冒险驾船出海，所以这里与世隔绝，没有任何贸易往来。可是他们的大河里船舶密集，也盛产味道鲜美的鱼。他们几乎从不去海里捕鱼，因为海里的鱼像欧洲的鱼那么小，对他们来说也就不值得捕了。这就表明，这片大陆的自然环境得天独厚，才会生产出如此巨大的动植物来，而只有这片大陆如此的奥秘只有让哲学家们去推断了。不过偶尔他们也会捉到一条碰巧撞到岩石上的鲸鱼，然后就会开心地大吃一顿。但这样的机会很少。据我所知，这些鲸鱼非常大，一个人背不动一条。他们有时候会用带盖的大篮子装着这种鱼当做宝贝送到洛布鲁格鲁德去。在国王的餐桌上我就曾见过一条，盛在一个盘子里，那就是一味珍馐了，不过我也没发现国王多么喜欢吃。我想一定是这鱼太大了，他看着恶心，尽管我在格陵兰还见过一条比这条还大的。

and sometimes for curiosity they are brought in hampers to *Lorbrulgrud*: I saw one of them in a dish at the king's table, which passed for a rarity, but I did not observe he was fond of it; for I think indeed the bigness disgusted him, although I have seen one somewhat larger in *Greenland*.

The country is well inhabited, for it contains fifty-one cities, near an hundred walled towns, and a great number of villages. To satisfy my curious reader, it may be sufficient to describe *Lorbrulgrud*. This city stands upon almost two equal parts on each side the river that passes through. It contains above eighty thousand houses, and about six hundred thousand inhabitants. It is in length three *glomglungs* (which make about fifty-four *English* miles) and two and a half in breadth, as I measured it myself in the royal map made by the king's order, which was laid on the ground on purpose for me, and extended an hundred foot; I paced the diameter and circumference several times barefoot, and computing by the scale, measured it pretty exactly.

这个国家人口密集，有 51 座大城市，有城墙的城镇大约有 100 个，此外还有大量的村庄。为了满足读者们强烈的好奇心，也许我可以把洛布鲁格鲁德描述一下。此城横跨在一条大河上，大河从城中穿流而过，将整个城市分成大小差不多的两半。城中有 8 万多户人家，约 60 万居民。城长 3“格隆格仑”，约合 54 英里，宽 2.5“格隆格仑”。这是我在御制皇家地图上亲自测量出来的。他们特地为我把地图铺在地上，地图展开有 100 英尺长。为了步测其直径和周长，我光着脚在上面来回走了好几遍，又按比例尺计算出来，所以测量的结果应该是相当精确的。

The king's palace is no regular edifice, but an heap of buildings, about seven miles round: the chief rooms are generally two hundred and forty foot high, and broad and long in proportion. A coach was allowed to *Glumdalclitch* and me, wherein

国王的宫殿不太规则，是由许多占地约 7 英里的建筑物集合而成的。主要房间一般都有 240 英尺高，长和宽也都与之成相应的比例。国王赐给格兰姆达尔克立契和我一辆马车。她的女教师时常带她坐车

her governess frequently took her out to see the town, or go among the shops; and I was always of the party, carried in my box; although the girl at my own desire would often take me out, and hold me in her hand, that I might more conveniently view the houses and the people as we passed along the streets I reckoned our coach to be about a square of Westminster Hall, but not altogether so high: however; I cannot be very exact. One day the Governess ordered our Coachman to stop at several Shops, where the Beggars watching their Opportunity, crowed to the sides of the Coach, and gave me the most horrible Spectacles that ever an *European* Eye beheld. There was a woman with a Cancer in her Breast, swelled to a monstrous size, full of Holes, in two or three of which I could have easily crept, and covered my whole Body. There was a Fellow with a Wen in his Neck, larger than five Woolpacks, and another with a couple of wooden Legs, each about twenty foot high. But, the most hateful Sight of all was the Lice crawling on their Clothes. I could see distinctly the Limbs of these Vermin with my naked eye, much better than those of an *European* Louse through a Microscope, and their Snouts with which they rooted like Swine. They were the first I had ever helded, and I should have been curious enough to dissect one of them, if I

出去游玩或者逛街，她们总是顺便带上我和我的箱子。当然，在我的要求下，格兰姆达尔克立契也经常把我从箱子里拿出来放到手上，便于我在我们路过大街时观察沿途的房屋和行人。根据我的估测，我们的马车大概有西敏寺的大厅那么大，但可能比那矮一点。当然这也只是估算，不可能很精确。有一天，女教师吩咐马车夫在几家商店门前停车，乞丐们看准时机，便一窝蜂似的涌到马车边，于是我这个欧洲人就见到了自己从来没有见过的恐怖至极的场面。有个女人乳房上长了毒瘤，肿得叫人害怕，上面布满了洞，其中有两三个洞很大，我轻易就可以爬进去，并把整个身子藏在里面。有一个人脖子上长了一个粉瘤，看样子比 5 个羊毛包还要大。还有一个人装了一副木头做的假腿，每条长约 20 英尺。不过最恶心的还是那些在他们衣服上爬来爬去的虱子。我用肉眼就可以把这些害虫的腿看得一清二楚，比透过显微镜看一只欧洲的虱子还要清楚得多。它们的嘴跟猪嘴一样，我有生以来还是第一次见到这些。如果当时有合适的工具，我一定会好奇地解剖其中的一个，可惜那些工具我都放在船上了。说实话那情景实在太叫人恶心，我的胃一阵翻腾。

had proper Instruments (which I unluchily left behind me in the Ship) although indeed the Sigh was so nauseous, that it perfectly turned my Stomach.

Besides the large box in which I was usually carried, the queen ordered a smaller one to be made for me, of about twelve foot square and ten high, for the convenience of travelling, because the other was somewhat too large for *Glumdalclitch's* lap, and cumbersome in the coach; it was made by the same artist, whom I directed in the whole contrivance. This travelling closet was an exact square, with a window in the middle of three of the squares, and each window was latticed with iron wire on the outside, to prevent accidents in long journeys. On the fourth side, which had no window, two strong staples were fixed, through which the person that carried me, when I had a mind to be on horseback, put in a leathern belt, and buckled it about his waist. This was always the office of some grave trusty servant in whom I could confide, whether I attended the king and queen in their progresses, or were disposed to see the gardens, or pay a visit to some great lady or minister of state in the court, when *Glumdalclitch* happened to be out of Order: for I soon began to be known and esteemed among the greatest officers, I suppose more upon account of their

除了平时带我外出时的那只大箱子外，皇后下令再给我做一只约 12 英尺见方、10 英尺高的小箱子。这主要是为了旅行的便利，原来那只太大了，无法放在格兰姆达尔克立契的膝上，放在马车里也很麻烦。小箱子由原来那个工匠制作，整个过程我都在旁亲自监督。这个旅行用的小屋是个标准的正方体，其中 3 面墙的正中都开了一扇窗，每扇窗户都用格子状铁丝从外面封住，这也是为了防止长途旅行中发生意外。第四面墙上没有安窗户，装了两个结实的铁环。每次当我想骑马旅行，负责带着我的那个人就会在铁环中间穿上一根皮带，再将皮带扣在自己腰间。如果遇到格兰姆达尔克立契身体不适的情况，他们就总是把我交给一位我愿意信赖的办事可靠的仆人。不管我是陪国王和皇后出巡，还是想去逛花园，还是去宫里拜访达官贵妇。显贵们不久就认识并且开始喜爱我了，我想这更多的是他们对我的偏爱，并不是我自身有什么功绩。旅途中，每当我在马车里坐累了，骑着马的一个仆人就会把小箱子扣在他身上，放到他跟前的一块垫子上，这样我就可以透过那 3 扇

majesty's favour than any merit of my own. In journeys, when I was weary of the coach, a servant on horseback would buckle on my box, and place it on a cushion before him; and there I had a full prospect of the country on three sides from my three windows. I had in this closet a field-bed and a hammock hung from the ceiling, two chairs and a table, neatly screwed to the floor, to prevent being tossed about by the agitation of the horse or the coach. And having been long used to sea voyages, those motions, although sometimes very violent, did not much discompose me.

窗户饱览这个国家的风光。我的这间小屋里有一张行军床，一张系在天花板上的吊床，两把椅子和一张桌子。床和桌椅都用螺丝钉牢牢地固定在地板上，不至于被车马颠得东倒西歪。我早已习惯了航海的生活，所以就算有时颠晃得很厉害，我也没觉得多么不安。

Whenever I had a mind to see the town, it was always in my travelling closet, which *Glumdalclitch* held in her lap in a kind of open sedan, after the fashion of the country, borne by four men, and attended by two others in the queen's livery. The people, who had often heard of me, were very curious to crowd about the sedan, and the girl was complaisant enough to make the bearers stop, and to take me in her hand that I might be more conveniently seen.

每次我想到市镇上去逛逛，这间小屋就是我旅行时的容身之所。格兰姆达尔克立契把小屋抱放在膝上，然后坐在当地的一种敞篷轿子里，由四个人抬着，后面还跟着皇后的两名侍从。常常听人说起我的人们，纷纷充满好奇地围到轿子旁边来看我。小姑娘就彬彬有礼地请抬轿子的人停下来，再把我拿在手里让大家看个清楚。

I was very desirous to see the chief temple, and particularly the tower belonging to it, which is reckoned the highest in the kingdom. Accordingly one day my nurse carried me thither, but I must truly say I came back disappointed;

我很想去见识见识这个国家最著名的一座庙宇，特别是它的钟楼，大概是全国最高的。于是有一天我的小保姆就带我去了。不过说实话，我失望而归。因为从地面到最高的尖顶总共不到 3000 英尺。

for, the height is not above three thousand foot, reckoning from the ground to the highest pinnacle top; which allowing for the difference between the size of those people, and us in *Europe*, is no great matter for admiration, nor at all equal in proportion (if I rightly remember), to *Salisbury* steeple. But, not to detract from a nation to which during my life I shall acknowledge myself extremely obliged, it must be allowed that whatever this famous tower wants in height is amply made up in beauty and strength. For the walls are near an hundred foot thick, built of hewn stone, whereof each is about forty foot square, and adorned on all sides with statues of gods and emperors cut in marble larger than the life, placed in their several niches. I measured a little finger which had fallen down from one of these statues, and lay unperceived among some rubbish, and found it exactly four foot and an inch in length. *Glumdalclitch* wrapped it up in a handkerchief and carried it home in her pocket to keep among other trinkets, of which the girl was very fond, as children at her age usually are.

如果按照当地人和我们欧洲人之间在身材上的比例，那这 3000 英尺的钟楼也就算不上宏伟了，按照比例换算下来，如果我没有记错的话，也根本不能与我们的萨立斯波瑞教堂的尖塔相比。但是对于这个国家所给我一切，我应当终生感激不尽，所以我不能贬低它。无论如何，都应该承认这座著名的钟楼虽然在高度上有些欠缺，但其美观与坚固都足以弥补这点不足。这座庙宇的墙壁厚约 100 英尺，全部由 40 英尺左右见方的石头砌成。供奉在四壁的几处壁龛里的是用大理石雕刻而成的、比真人还要大的神像和帝王像。其中一尊神像掉了一根手指，落在垃圾堆里没人发现，我量了一下，正好是 4 英尺 1 英寸长。格兰姆达尔克立契用一个手帕把它包起来，装在口袋里带回了家，和其他的一些小东西放在一起。这个小姑娘和与她同龄的孩子一样，很喜欢收藏这些小东西。

The king's kitchen is indeed a noble building, vaulted at top, and about six hundred foot high. The great oven is not so wide by ten paces as the cupola at St. Paul's: for I measured the latter on purpose after my return. But if I should

国王的厨房堪称一座宏伟的建筑。它的屋顶呈拱形，大约有 600 英尺高。厨房里的炉子比圣保罗教堂的圆顶要小 10 步，我回国以后曾专程去圣保罗教堂量了一次。不过要是让我来描述一下那厨房里

describe the kitchen grate, the prodigious pots and kettles, the joints of meat turning on the spits, with many other particulars, perhaps I should be hardly believed; at least a severe critic would be apt to think I enlarged a little, as travellers are often suspected to do. To avoid which censure, I fear I have run too much into the other extreme; and that if this treatise should happen to be translated into the language of *Brobdingnag* (which is the general name of that kingdom), and transmitted thither, the king and his people would have reason to complain that I had done them an injury by a false and diminutive representation.

的壁炉，那大得惊人的锅和壶，那正在烤架上烤着的大块肉以及其他许许多多的细节，也许很难会有人相信我，至少严厉的批评家肯定会认为我有些夸大其词。旅行家经常受到这样的怀疑。为了避免遭到这样的指责，我担心我又矫枉过正，走向了另一个极端。如果本书碰巧被译成布罗卜丁奈格语，也就是那个王国的语言，再传回那里的话，那里国王和人民就有理由抱怨我污蔑了他们，把他们描写得太过渺小，不够真实。

His majesty seldom keeps above six hundred horses in his stables: they are generally from fifty-four to sixty foot high. But, when he goes abroad on solemn days, he is attended for state by a militia guard of five hundred horse, which indeed I thought was the most splendid sight that could be ever beheld, till I saw part of his army in battalia, whereof I shall find another occasion to speak.

国王陛下的马厩里养了不到600 匹马。这些马的身高基本上是54 到 60 英尺。不过，每逢国王出巡的重大节日，为了彰显国威，总会带上 500 匹马组成的骑兵连。我本以为那就是我所能见到的最壮观的场面了，直到我又看到陆军某军队的演习。关于陆军演习的具体情况，我有机会再谈。

CHAPTER 5

第五章

Several Adventures that happened to the Author. The Execution of a Criminal. The Author shows his Skill in Navigation.

作者的几个奇遇。一名罪犯被处决的经过。作者展示自己的航海技能。

I should have lived happy enough in that country, if my littleness had not exposed me to several ridiculous and troublesome accidents; some of which I shall venture to relate. *Glumdalclitch* often carried me into the gardens of the court in my smaller box, and would sometimes take me out of it and hold me in her hand, or set me down to walk. I remember, before the dwarf left the queen, he followed us one day into those gardens, and my nurse having set me down, he and I being close together, near some dwarf Apple Trees, I must need show my wit by a silly allusion between him and the trees, which happens to hold in their language, as it doth in ours. Whereupon, the malicious rogue watching his opportunity, when I was walking under one of them, shook it directly over my head, by which a dozen apples, each of them near as large as a *Bristol* barrel, came tumbling about my ears; one of them hit me on the back as I chanced to stoop, and knocked me

如果不是身材过于矮小，我本可以在那个国家生活得非常快乐。可是却因此发生了一些滑稽又令人难堪的事，现在我就来叙述其中几件。格兰姆达尔克立契常常用那只比较小的箱子带我去宫廷的花园里玩，有时还会把我从箱子里拿出放在手上，或者让我在地上散步。还记得那个侏儒没被皇后赶走时，有一天，他跟我们一起来到花园。小保姆把我放在地上，侏儒就近在咫尺。旁边有几棵矮苹果树，我想卖弄一下自己的巧思妙想，于是以那几棵矮苹果树来影射他。恰巧他们的语言中也偶尔会使用这种影射的手法。于是，这个恶毒的家伙看准时机，当我走到树底下时，他就拼命摇晃我头顶上的那棵树。他摇掉了 12 只苹果，每只几乎都有布里斯托尔大酒桶那么大，这些苹果朝我劈头盖脸地滚落下来。我弯腰的瞬间，一只苹果正好砸在我背上，我被砸倒在地，幸好没受什么伤。在我的请求下，那个

down flat on my face, but I received no other hurt; and the dwarf was pardoned at my desire, because I had given the provocation.

侏儒才得以赦免，因为毕竟是我挑起了矛盾。

Another day *Glumdalclitch* left me on a smooth grass-plot to divert myself while she walked at some distance with her governess. In the mean time there suddenly fell such a violent shower of hail, that I was immediately, by the force of it struck to the ground: and when I was down, the hailstones gave me such cruel bangs all over the body, as if I had been pelted with tennis balls; however, I made a shift to creep on all four, and shelter myself by lying flat on my face on the Lee side of a border of Lemon Thyme, but so bruised from head to foot that I could not go abroad in ten days. Neither is this at all to be wondered at, because nature in that country observing the same proportion through all her operations, a Hailstone is near eighteen hundred times as large as one in *Europe*, which I can assert upon experience, having been so curious to weigh and measure them.

又一天，格兰姆达尔克立契让我在一块平整的草地上玩，自己和她的女家庭教师去远处散步了。这时，一阵猛烈的冰雹袭来，我立刻被打翻在地。我躺在地上，冰雹重重砸遍全身，像无数网球一起向我袭来。但我还是用尽四肢的力气设法往前爬，一直爬到柠檬树和百里香附近，并趴在下面。我从头到脚伤痕累累，在床上躺了 10 天才能出门。这还不算稀奇，因为这个国家的自然现象都是等比例放大的。这里的一颗冰雹的大小差不多是欧洲冰雹的 1800 倍。这一点我可以用自己的亲身经历来担保，在好奇心的驱使下，我曾称过其重量，测过其大小。

But a more dangerous accident happened to me in the same garden, when my little nurse believing she had put me in a secure place, which I often entreated her to do, that I might enjoy my own thoughts, and having left my box at home to avoid the trouble of carrying it, went to another

然而又一件危险的事发生在了我身上，仍是在这个花园里。当时我的小保姆认为已经给我找到了一个安全的地方，这也是我的要求，因为这样我就可以独自沉思了，为了方便她没有带我的小箱子，放下我之后就和家庭教师及另

part of the gardens with governess and some ladies of her acquaintance. While she was absent and out of hearing, a small white Spaniel belonging to one of the chief gardeners, having got by accident into the garden, happened to range near the place where I lay. the dog following the scent, came directly up, and taking me in his mouth ran straight to his master, wagging his tail, and set me gently on the ground. By good fortune he had been so well taught, that I was carried between his teeth without the least hurt, or even tearing my clothes. But, the poor gardener, who knew me well, and had a great kindness for me, was in a terrible fright. he gently took me up in both his hands, and asked me how I did; but I was so amazed and out of breath, that I could not speak a word. In a few minutes I came to myself, and he carried me safe to my little nurse, who by this time had returned to the place where she left me, and was in cruel agonies when I did not appear, nor answer when she called; She severely reprimanded the gardener on account of his dog. But, the thing was bushed up and never known at court; for the girl was afraid of the queen's anger, and truly as to myself, I thought it would not be for my reputation that such a story should go about.

外几个女孩子到花园的另一边玩去了。她不在我身边，也听不到我声音的这段时间里，一只类似西班牙猎犬的白色小狗突然闯进了花园，这只狗是花园总管的，它正好徘徊在附近。那狗循着气味径直向我走来，把我一口叼到嘴里跑到主人跟前，摇着尾巴，轻轻把我放到地上。幸运的是，这只小狗训练有素，我虽然被它叼在嘴里，却毫发无伤，包括我的衣服也没有弄坏。那位可怜的花园总管和我十分熟悉，平时也对我照顾备至，他吓坏了，将我轻轻放在手心里，问我怎么样。但我被惊得无法呼吸，一个字也吐不出来。几分钟后，我终于恢复正常，他就将我小心地送交给了我的小保姆。她已经回来了，在原地找不到我，喊我也没人回答，正心急如焚。因为那只狗，她严厉地训斥了花园总管。小女孩担心惹怒了皇后，也为了我，毕竟这事传出去对我的名声也是一种损害，此事到此为止了，宫廷并不知情。

This accident absolutely determined

这个意外彻底坚定了格兰姆

Glumdalclitch never to trust me abroad for the future out of her sight. I had been long afraid of this resolution, and therefore concealed from her some little unlucky adventures that happened in those times when I was left by myself. Once a kite hovering over the garden made a stoop at me, and if I had not resolutely drawn my hanger, and run under a thick espalier, he would have certainly carried me away in his talons. Another time walking to the top of a fresh Molehill, I fell to my neck in the hole through which that animal had cast up the earth, and coined some lie not worth remembering, to excuse myself for spoiling my clothes. I likewise broke my right shin against the shell of a snail, which I happened to stumble over, as I was walking alone, and thinking on poor *England*.

达尔克立契从今以后绝不允许我脱离她的视线的决心。我很早就担心会有这样的决定，因此，平时独处时遇到的几个小险境都隐瞒不说。一次，一只盘旋在花园上空的风筝突然向我袭来，如果不是我当机立断，拔出腰刀并跑到一棵枝叶繁茂的树篱下，早就被它的大爪子抓走了。又一次，我走到一个新堆起来的鼹鼠丘上，一头栽进洞里，为自己脏兮兮的衣服编了个不值一提的理由。还有一次，我独自在路上走着，回忆着可怜的英国，撞到蜗牛壳上，摔断了右小腿胫骨。

I cannot tell whether I were more pleased or mortified to observe in those solitary walks, that the smaller birds did not appear to be at all afraid of me, but would hop about within a yard distance, looking for worms, and other food with as much indifference and security as if no creature at all were near them. I remember, a thrush had the confidence to snatch out of my hand with his bill a piece of cake that *Glumdalclitch* had just given me for my breakfast. When I attempted to catch any of these birds, they would

我不知道那些独自散步途中的所见是悲是喜，那些较小的鸟儿似乎一点也不怕我，它们在离我不到一码的地方蹦蹦跳跳，泰然自若地找寻虫子和其他食物，仿佛附近别无其他动物。我记得一只画眉曾神气十足地叼走了我手里的一块蛋糕，那是格兰姆达尔克立契刚刚给我的早饭。我试图抓几只，它们竟敢和我作对，拼命啄我的手指头，我赶紧缩回手。它们又和之前别无二致，若无其事地跳回去寻找虫子或者蜗牛了。不过有一天，我

boldly turn against me, endeavouring to pick my fingers, which I durst not venture within their reach; and then they would turn back unconcerned to hunt for worms or snails, as they did before. But, one day I took a thick cudgel, and threw it with all my strength so luckily at a linnet, that I knocked him down, and seizing him by the neck with both my hands, ran with him in triumph to my nurse. However, the bird who had only been stunned, recovering himself, gave me so many boxes with his wings on both sides of my head and body, though I held him at arm's length and was out of the reach of his claws, that I was twenty times thinking to let him go. But I was soon relieved by one of our servants, who wrung off the bird's neck, and I had him next day for dinner by the queen's command. This linnet, as near as I can remember, seemed to be somewhat larger than an *English* swan.

拿起一根粗重的棒子用尽全力扔出去，非常幸运地打中了一只红雀，于是我双手拎着它的脖子，得意洋洋地跑去给保姆看。不料那只鸟只是被吓晕了，它一有知觉，就扑动翅膀对我展开了劈头盖脸的猛攻。只要我伸直手臂，它的爪子就抓不到我了，但我还是思前想后，是否要放了它。不过一个仆人很快帮我解决了这个困扰，因为他拧断了鸟的脖子。第二天，那只鸟成为了我的晚餐，这是皇后的命令。我记得这只红雀比英国的天鹅还大一些呢。

The Maids of Hounour often invited *Glumdalclitcb* to their Apartments, and desired she would bring me along with her, on purpose to have the plesure of seeing and touching me. They would often strip me naked from top toe, and lay me at full Length in their Bosoms; wherewith I was much disgusted; because, to say the Truth, a very offensive Smell came from their Skins; which I do not mention or intend to the Disadvantage of those

侍奉皇后的宫女们经常邀请格兰姆达尔克立契到她们房间玩儿，并且希望能带我一起去，就是为了看看我、摸摸我，以供娱乐。她们经常把我脱得赤条条的，让我躺在她们怀里。这令我非常恶心，因为说实话，她们的皮肤散发出一股恶臭。这一点我本来不想提，也没打算揭这些美丽的姑娘们的短，我对她们怀有十二分的敬意。但是，可能由于我身材矮小，嗅觉也

excellent Ladies, for whom I have all manner of Respect; but, I conceive that my sence was more acute in proportion on my Littleness, and that those illustrious Persons were no more disagreeable to their Lovers, or to each other, than people of the same Quality are with us in *England*. And, after all, I found their natural Smell was much more supportable than when they used Perfumes, under which I immediately swooned away. I cannot forget that an intimate friend of mine in *Lilliput* took the freedom in a warm Day, when I had used a good deal of Exercise, to complain of a strong Smell about me, although I am as little faulty that way as most of my sex: But I suppose his faculty of smelling was as nice with regard to me, as mine was to that of this people. Upon this point, I cannot forbear doing Justice to the Queen my Mistress, and *Glumdalclitcb* my Nurce, whose persons were as sweet as those of any Lady in *England*.

灵敏得多。而且这群优秀的姑娘们在她们的情人眼里，或者她们之间，就像同样身材的英国人之间一样，是不会互相感觉厌恶的。而且我发现，和香水的气味比起来，她们本来的体香要容易忍受得多，她们的香水简直能令我立即晕过去。我无法忘记在利利普特国，我的一位好朋友竟抱怨说我身上的味道很大。那天天气很暖和，我做了很多运动，虽然我和大多数男人一样，可能多少有一点体味，但我想这是他的嗅觉比我敏锐得多的缘故，就像我的嗅觉比这个国家的人敏锐得多一样。说到这一点，我得称赞一下我的主人皇后和保姆格兰姆达尔克立契，她们身体的芬芳足以和任何一位英国的小姐相媲美。

That which gave me most uneasiness among these Maids of Honour, when my Nurse carried me to visit them, was to see them use me without any manner of Ceremony, Like a Creature who had no sort of Consequence. For, they would strip themselves to the Skin, and put on their Smocks in my Presence, while I was placed on their Toilet directly before their

保姆带我去拜访这些侍女时，最令我不安的是，她们对我非常无礼，好像我是个藐小的小动物。因为她们会把我放在盥洗室里，在我的面前脱光衣服，然后换上工作服。直面她们的裸体，我十分确定这一场景对自己并不具有诱惑力，只会令我感到惊恐和厌恶。她们的皮肤非常粗糙，凹凸不平，近看的

naked Bodies, which, I an sure, to me was very far from being a tempting Sight, or from giving me any other emotions than those of Horror and Disgust. Their Skins appeared so coarse and uneven, so variously coloured when I saw them near, with a Mole here and there as broad as a Trencher, and Hairs hanging from it thicker than Packthreads; to say nothing further concerning the rest of their Persons. Neither did they at all scruple while I was by to discharge what they had drunk, to the quantity of at laest two Hogsheads, in a Vessel that held above three Tuns. The handsomest among these Maids of Honour, a pleasant frolicsome Girl of sixteen, would sometimes set me astride upon one of her Nipples, with many other Tricks, wuerein the Reader will excuse me for not being over particular. But, I was so much displeased, that I entreated *Glumdalclitcb* to contrive some excese for not seeing that young Lady any more.

话颜色极其不均，这儿一颗痣，那儿一颗痣，像切面包用的木盘子一样大。痣上长的毛比粗麻绳还要粗。至于身体其他部位更不必说了。她们还在我面前毫无顾忌地小便，排泄出去的水，一次至少有两大桶，而装小便的容器至少可以装3大桶。侍女中最漂亮的是一位16岁的姑娘，这个讨人喜欢的调皮姑娘竟让我跨在她的乳头上，还有其他各种花样，我不再一一列举了，还请读者原谅。我很生气，于是恳求格兰姆达尔克立契为我找个借口，以后再也不去见那个女孩子了。

One day, a young Gentleman who was Nephew to my Nurse's Governess, came and pressed them both to see an Execution. It was of a Man who had murdered one of that Gentleman's intimate Acquatance. *Glumdalclitcb* was prevailed on to be of the Company, very much against her Inclination, for she was naturally tender hearted: And, as for

一天，一位年轻的绅士来了，他是小保姆的女教师的侄子。他一定要她们两人跟他一起去观看罪犯处决。那名罪犯谋杀了他的一位至交。因为天生心软，格兰姆达尔克立契在大家的说服下勉强决定同去。至于我呢，虽然很讨厌这种场面，但我想一定非同寻常，好奇心驱使我去看一看。那名罪犯被绑

myself, although I abhorred such king of Spectacles, yet my Curiosity tempted me to see something that I though must be extraordinary. The Malefactor was fixed in a Chair upon a Sword of about forty foot long. The Veins and Arteries spouted up such a prodigious quantity of Blood, and so high in the Air, that the great *fet d'Eau at Versailles* was not equal for the time it lasted; and the Head when it fell on the Scaffold Floor, gave such a bounce, as made me start, aithough I were at least half an *English* Mile distant.

在一把椅子上，面前竖着一把大约有40英尺长的行刑刀。手起刀落，大量的血从他的静脉和动脉中喷涌而出，直喷到高空，就是凡尔赛宫的大喷泉也不及它持续的时间长。人头落地时发出一声巨响，虽然至少相距半英里，我还是吓了一跳。

The queen who often used to hear me talk of my Sea Voyages, and took all occasions to divert me when I was melancholy asked me whether I understood how to handle a sail or an oar, and whether a little exercise of rowing might not be convenient for my health. I answered, that I understood both very well. for although my proper employment had been to be surgeon or doctor to the ship, yet upon a pinch, I was forced to work like a common mariner. But, I could not see how this could be done in their country, where the smallest wherry was equal to a first-rate Man of War among us, and such a boat as I could manage would never live in any of their rivers: Her majesty said, if I could contrive a boat, her own joiner should make it, and she would provide a place for me to sail in. The

皇后常常听我讲述航海经历，所以每当我陷入忧郁时，她就会想方设法逗我开心，问我是否会划船，偶尔划一下船是不是有益我的身体健康。我说两个我都很擅长，虽然我在船上的本职工作是医生，但偶尔也会做一般水手的工作。不过如果我想在他们国家划船估计会很难，因为这里最小的舢板就相当于我们一流的军舰大小。而我能驾驭的那种大小的船是无法在他们的河里航行的。皇后说，如果我能设计出一艘自己可以划的船，她的御用工匠就能照样做出来，她还可以给我一个扬帆出航之地。这个心灵手巧的工匠在我的指挥下，仅用了 10 天时间就造成了一艘装备齐全的游艇，足足可容纳8个欧洲人。船造好后，皇后非常欣喜，把它兜在衣服里跑去给国王看。国王

fellow was an ingenious workman, and by my instructions in ten days finished a pleasure-boat with all its tackling, able conveniently to hold eight *Europeans*. When it was finished, the queen was so delighted, that she ran with it in her lap to the king, who ordered it to be put in a cistern full of water, with me in it, by way of trial, where I could not manage my two sculls or little oars for want of room. But, the queen had before contrived another project. She ordered the joiner to make a wooden trough of three hundred foot long, fifty broad, and eight deep; which being well pitched to prevent leaking was placed on the floor along the wall, in an outer room of the palace. It had a cock near the bottom to let out the water when it began to grow stale, and two servants could easily fill it in half an hour. Here I often used to row for my own diversion, as well as that of the queen and her ladies, who thought themselves well entertained with my skill and agility. Sometimes I would put up my sail, and then my business was only to steer, while the ladies gave me a gale with their fans; and when they were weary, some of the pages would blow my sail forward with their breath, while I showed my art by steering starboard or larboard as I pleased. When I had done, Glumdalclitch always carried back my boat into her closet, and hung it on a nail

让我上船试验一下，然后下令把船放入一个满水的水池。可是水池太小了，我根本没办法划那两支短桨。不过皇后早有准备，她吩咐工匠做了一只300英尺长、50英尺宽、8 英尺深的木槽，还涂上沥青以防漏水。那只木槽被安置在王宫外殿的墙边。木槽下部有龙头用来换水，两个仆人半个小时内就可以将木槽换一遍水。于是这里就成为我划船消遣的地方，同时也给皇后及贵妇们带来了很多快乐。她们对我划船的高超技艺和敏捷身手很感兴趣。因为贵妇们会用扇子给我扇风，所以有时候我挂起船帆之后，只需掌握航向即可。如果她们扇得烦了，就让侍从为我的小船吹气做助力，我就随心所欲地展现自己的航海技艺，任我左驶右行。每次划完船，格兰姆达尔克立契都会把船拿回她的房间，挂在一只钉子上晾干。

to dry.

In this exercise I once met an accident which had like to have cost me my life. For, one of the pages having put my boat into the trough, the governess who attended *Glumdalclitch*, very officiously lifted me up to place me in the boat, but I happened to slip through her fingers, and should have infallibly have fallen down forty foot upon the floor, if, by the luckiest chance in the world, I had not been stopped by a corking-pin that stuck in the good gentlewoman's stomacher; the head of the pin passed between my shirt and the waistband of my breeches, and thus I was held by the middle in the air till *Glumdalclitch* ran to my relief.

在划船中曾发生了一次意外，害我差点丢了性命。一名侍从将小船放入木槽，而格兰姆达尔克立契的那个女教师多管闲事，非要帮忙把我拿到船上去，却不小心指尖一滑，我掉了下来。如果不是发生了这世上最幸运的事，我被这位好心的太太胸衣上的一枚别针挡住，毫无疑问我会从 40 英尺的空中一直跌落到地。别针的针头恰巧从我的衬衣和腰带中间穿过，于是我就被拦腰挂在了半空中，直到格兰姆达尔克立契跑过来将我救下。

Another time, one of the servants, whose office it was to fill my trough every third day with fresh water, was so careless to let a huge frog (not perceiving it) slip out of his pail. The frog lay concealed till I was put into my boat, but then seeing a resting place, climbed up, and made it lean so much on one side, that I was forced to balance it with all my weight on the other, to prevent overturning. When the frog was got in, it hopped at once half the length of the boat, and then over my head, backwards and forwards, daubing my Face and clothes with its odious slime. The largeness of its features made it appear the most deformed animal that can

还有一次，一个负责每 3 天给我的水槽换水的仆人一时疏忽，将一只巨大的青蛙一起倒进了水槽。青蛙一直藏在水底，直到我被放进船里，它发现了这个可以休憩之地，于是爬上船来，小船立刻被压歪了，为了保持平衡避免翻船，我只得赶紧跑到船的另一头。青蛙上船后，一跳就跨过了半条船，又在我头上跳来跳去，我的脸上和衣服上到处是它那恶心的黏液。它那巨大的体形看起来丑陋得超乎想象。不过，我请求格兰姆达尔克立契让我独力对付它。我用桨痛打了它很久，终于将它驱逐下了小船。

be conceived. However, I desired *Glumdalclitch* to let me deal with it alone. I banged it a good while with one of my sculls, and at last forced it to leap out of the boat.

But, the greatest danger I ever underwent in that kingdom was from a monkey, who belonged to one of the clerks of the kitchen. *Glumdalclitch* had locked the up in her closet, while she went somewhere upon business or a visit. The weather being very warm, the closet window was left open, as well as the windows and the door of my bigger box, in which I usually lived, because of its largeness and conveniency. As I sat quietly meditating at my table, I heard something bounce in at the closet window, and skip about from one side to the other; whereat although I were much alarmed, yet I ventured to look out, but not stirring from my seat; and then I saw this frolicsome animal, frisking and leaping up and down till at last he came to my box, which he seemed to view with great pleasure and curiosity, peeping in at the door and every window. I retreated to the further corner of my room, or box, but the monkey looking in at every side, put me into such a fright, that I wanted presence of mind to conceal myself under the bed, as I might easily have done. After some time spent in peeping, grinning, and

不过，我在那个王国所遭受的最大的危险源于一只御厨养的猴子。那次，格兰姆达尔克立契可能有事或是见人，把我锁在她的小房间里就出门去了。那天天气很暖和，房间的窗户大开，我自己那只大箱子的门窗也敞开着。我平时都住在大箱子里，因为它宽敞又方便。正当我坐在桌子边静静沉思时，忽然听到一个东西从窗户跳进了房间，满屋东跳西窜。虽然我充满了恐惧，但还是鼓足勇气朝大箱子外看了看，不过我一直坐立不动。然后，我看到了这个调皮的动物，它上蹿下跳，终究跳到了我的箱子边。它似乎很好奇这箱子，还透过门窗朝箱子里窥视。我躲到我的小房间，也就是箱子离门窗最远的角落，那只猴子四处张望，我被吓得手忙脚乱，竟忘了躲到床底下这么容易想到的办法。它一边龇牙咧嘴地笑着偷窥，一边吱吱地叫，我终于被发现了。它从门口伸进来一只爪子，就像猫逗老鼠一样。尽管我拼命躲藏，可终究还是被抓住了上衣的下摆（上衣的布料是这里的，又厚又结实），一把被拽出去。它用右前爪将我抓起抱在怀里，就

chattering, he at last espied me, and reaching one of his paws in at the door, as a cat does when she plays with a mouse, although I often shifted place to avoid him, he at length caught hold of the lappet of my coat (which, being made of that country cloth, was very thick and strong) and dragged me out. He took me up in his right forefoot, and held me as a nurse does a child she is going to suckle, just as I have seen the same sort of creature do with a kitten in *Europe*: and when I offered to struggle, he squeezed me so hard, that I thought it more prudent to submit. I have good reason to believe that he took me for a young one of his own species, by his often stroking my face very gently with his other paw. In these diversions he was interrupted by a noise at the closet door, as if somebody were opening it; whereupon he suddenly leaped up to the window at which he had come in, and thence upon the leads and gutters, walking upon three legs, and holding me in the fourth, till he clambered up to a roof that was next to ours. I heard *Glumdalclitch* give a shriek at the moment he was carrying me out. The poor girl was almost distracted: That quarter of the palace was all in an uproar; the servants ran for ladders; the monkey was seen by hundreds in the court sitting upon the ridge of a building, holding me like a baby

像给孩子喂奶的保姆一样，这情景我在欧洲也见过，大猴就是这样抱小猴的。我试图挣扎，它却把我抱得更紧，我想还是不要轻举妄动比较好。我有充分的理由相信它误以为我是一只小猴子，因为它一直用另一只爪子轻抚我的脸。它正玩得起劲，却被从门口传来的一阵吵闹声打断了，似乎有人正在开门。于是它一下子蹿上来时的窗户，一只前爪抱着我，用另外一只前爪和两条腿走路，沿着导水管和檐槽一直爬上邻屋的屋顶。猴子抱着我离开房间的那一瞬，我听到格兰姆达尔克立契的尖叫。可怜的姑娘简直心急如焚。附近的宫殿全都陷入了一片混乱。仆人们跑去找梯子。宫里有好几百人都看见了那只猴子，它就坐在一座楼的屋脊上，一只前爪像抱孩子似的抱着我，另一只前爪喂我吃东西，将食物嚼碎了再使劲往我嘴里送，见我不肯吃，它就轻轻拍打我，连在下面看着的那些人都忍不住大笑起来。不过我不能怪他们，面对这样滑稽的场景，除了我笑不出来，别人肯定都会忍俊不禁的。有几个人向屋顶上扔石头，希望能逼猴子爬下来，但是这个方法马上就被严厉否决掉了，不然我的脑袋很可能早就已经被打烂了。

in one of his forepaws, and feeding me with the other, by cramming into my Mouth some Victuals she had squeezed out of the Bag on one side of his chaps, and patting me when I would not eat; whereat many of the rabble below could not forbear laughing; neither do I think they justly ought to be blamed, for without question the sight was ridiculous enough to everybody but myself. Some of the people threw up stones, hoping to drive the monkey down; but this was strictly forbidden, or else very probably my brains had been dashed out.

The ladders were now applied, and mounted by several men, which the monkey observing, and finding himself almost encompassed; not being able to make speed enough with his three legs, let me drop on a ridge tile, and made his escape. Here I sat for some time three hundred yards from the ground, expecting every moment to be blown down by the wind, or to fall by my own giddiness, and come tumbling over and over from the ridge to the eaves. but an honest lad, one of my nurse's footmen, climbed up, and putting me into his Breeches Pocket, brought me down safe.

I was almost choked with the filthy stuff the Money had crammed down my Throat; but, my dear little Nurse picked it out of my Mouth with a small Needle, and

终于支好了梯子，几个人爬上来。猴子立刻发现被包围了，来不及用 3 条腿逃跑，于是把我放在屋脊的一片瓦上，就逃掉了。我在这片离地面 300 码的瓦上坐了一段时间，时刻担心被风刮下来，或者由于头昏眼花，从屋脊滚下屋檐。不过就在这时，我的小保姆的一个诚实可靠的男仆爬上了屋顶，把我装到他的马裤裤袋里，安全地带回了地面上。

那只猴子硬塞到我喉咙里的脏东西差点把我噎死。幸好我亲爱的小保姆用一根细针把那些脏东西从我嘴里弄了出来。接下来的呕

then I fell a Vomiting which gave me great Relief. Yet I was so weak and bruised in the sides with the squeezes given me by this odious animal, that I was forced to keep my bed a fortnight. The king, queen and all the court sent every day to inquire after my health, and her majesty made me several visits during my sickness. The monkey was killed, and an order made that no such animal should be kept about the palace.

吐令我轻松了不少。可我还是很虚弱，那可恶的猴子把我的腰都捏青了，我不得不在床上躺了两个星期。国王、皇后以及宫里所有的人每天都派人来查看我的身体状况。在我卧病期间，皇后亲自来过好几次。那只猴子被杀了，同时禁令，以后不准在宫内饲养这类动物。

When I attended the king after my recovery, to return him thanks for his favours, he was pleased to rally me a good deal upon this adventure. He asked me what my thoughts and speculations were while I lay in the monkey's paw, how I liked the Victuals he gave me, his manner of Feeding, and whether the fresh Air on the Roof had sharpened stomach. He desired to know what I would have done upon such an occasion in my own country. I told his majesty, that in *Europe* we had no monkeys, except such as were brought for curiosities from other places, and so small, that I could deal with a dozen of them together, if they presumed to attack me. And as for that monstrous animal with whom I was so lately engaged (it was indeed as large as an elephant), if my fears had suffered me to think so far as to make use of my hanger (looking fiercely and clapping my hand upon the hilt as I spoke)

我身体一康复马上就去拜见了国王，表达他对我的关爱的感谢。见我恢复得很好，他很高兴。他问我，躺在猴子怀里时在想些什么？喜不喜欢吃那只猴子喂给我的食物？它喂我吃东西的方式如何？闻着屋顶的新鲜空气是不是很有胃口？他还想知道，如果我在自己的国家碰到这种事会如何处理？我对国王陛下说，我们欧洲没有猴子，就算有也是由于人们的好奇心而从别处运过去的，而且体形非常小，如果它们胆敢攻击我，我可以同时对付 12 只。至于我最近碰到的那只可怕的大猴子（它几乎相当于一头象那么大），如果我当时再冷静一点，当它把爪子伸进我的大箱子来的时候，想到用我的腰刀（说着这些话时，我一脸坚毅，手轻拍刀柄）。说不定我会狠狠地砍伤它，它缩回爪子都来不及呢，更不要说伸进来了。说这些话的时

when he poked his paw into my chamber, perhaps I should have given him such a wound, as would have made him glad to withdraw it with more haste than he put it in. This I delivered in a firm tone, like a person who was jealous lest his courage should be called in question.

候，我的语气十分坚定，就像一个唯恐别人怀疑他的勇气的人。

However, my speech produced nothing else besides a loud laughter, which all the respect due to his majesty from those about him could not make them contain. This made me reflect how vain an attempt it is for a man to endeavour to doing himself honour among those who are out of all degree of equality or comparison with him. And yet I have seen the moral of my own behaviour very frequent in *England* since my return, where a little contemptible varlet, without the least title to birth, person, wit, or common sense, shall presume to look with importance, and put himself upon a foot with the greatest persons of the kingdom.

然而，我的演讲只换来满堂的笑声，就是国王陛下身边那些本应保持肃静的人都没忍住。这使我想到，当一个人身处毫无平等地位可言的环境中时，如果想要保持尊严，也只能是徒劳。可自从我回到英国后，就见到了不少像我这样的人。有一个卑鄙的无赖，没有高贵的出身，没有相貌，没有智慧，也缺乏常识，却看起来傲慢无礼，总自以为跻身于全国最伟大的人物之中。

I was every day furnishing the court with some ridiculous story; and *Glumdalclitch*, although she loved me to excess, yet was arch enough to inform the queen whenever I committed any folly that she thought would be diverting to her majesty. The girl, who had been out of order, was carried by her governess to take the air about an hour's distance, or thirty miles from town. They alighted out of the

我几乎每天都会发生几件可笑的事情，这为整个皇宫都增添了乐趣。格兰姆达尔克立契很喜爱我，她也很聪明，每当我做出她认为能逗皇后笑的傻事时，就会跑去禀告皇后。有一次她身体不舒服，她的女教师带她出城 30 英里，去呼吸新鲜空气，大约有一个小时的车程。她们停在一条田间小路旁，格兰姆达尔克立契把我乘坐的小

coach near a small footpath in a field, and *Glumdalclitch* setting down my travelling Box, I went out of it to walk. There was a Cow-dung in the path, and I must needs try my activity by attempting to leap over it. I took a run, but unfortunately jumped short, and found myself just in the middle up to my knees. I waded through with some difficulty, and one of the footmen wiped me as clean as he could with his handkerchief; for I was filthily bemired, and my nurse confined me to my box till we returned home; when the queen was soon informed of what had passed, and the footman spread it about the court, so that all the mirth for some days, was at my expense.

箱子放在地上，我就走出来散步。小路上有一堆牛粪，而我偏偏想试试身手。我跑着冲过去，可惜跳得不够远，正好掉进牛粪里面，没到两个膝盖。我吃力地牛粪堆中拔出脚，一个男仆用他的手帕把我擦干净。我浑身脏兮兮的，所以后来小保姆一直把我关在箱子里，到了家里才把我放出来。皇后很快就听说了这件事，那几个男仆也在宫内四处宣扬，所以一连好几天大家都欢笑不停，而这欢笑建立在我的痛苦之上。

CHAPTER 6

第六章

Several Contrivances of the Author to please the King and Queen. He shows his Skill in Music. The King inquires into the State of England, which the Author relates to him. the King's Observations thereon.

作者想出来的讨国王和皇后欢心的几种方法。他展示了自己的音乐才能。国王在作者的介绍下了解了英国国情。国王的意见。

I used to attend the king's levee once or twice a week, and had often seen him under the barber's hand, which indeed was at first very terrible to behold. For, the razor was almost twice as long as an ordinary scythe. His majesty according to the custom of the country was only shaved twice a week. I once prevailed on the barber to give me some of the suds or lather, out of which I picked forty or fifty of the strongest stumps of hair I then took a piece of fine wood, and cut it like the back of a comb, making several holes in it at equal distance with as small a needle as I could get from *Glumdalclitch*. I fixed in the stumps so artificially, scraping and sloping them with my knife towards the points, that I made a very tolerable comb; which was a seasonable supply, my own being so much broken in the teeth that it was almost useless: neither did I know any artist in that country so nice and exact as,

我每周都会有一两天去参加国王的早朝，于是常常会看见理发师给他剃胡子，第一次见到那种情形觉得很可怕，因为那把剃刀差不多是我们平时的长柄大镰刀的两倍长。按照这个国家的惯例，国王每周只刮两次胡子。有一次，我说服理发师给了我一些国王刮胡子用的肥皂沫，从中挑选了四五十根最粗硬的胡子楂。又挑了一块上好的木头，削成梳背状，管格兰姆达尔克立契要了一根最小号的针，在梳背上钻了几个等距离的小孔。将胡子楂精巧地插入小孔，再用小刀削齐，就做成了一把勉强可以用的梳子。这真是一个及时的东西，原来那把梳子的齿大多已经断了，基本上不能用了。我知道这个国家没有哪位艺术家有如此精巧的手艺，能再给我做一把新的。

would undertake to make me another.

And this puts me in mind of an amusement wherein I spent many of my leisure hours. I desired the queen's woman to save for me the combings of her majesty's hair, whereof in time I got a good quantity, and consulting with my friend the cabinet-maker, who had received general orders to do little jobs for me; I directed him to make two chair-frames, no larger than those I had in my box, and then to bore little holes with a fine awl round those parts where I designed the backs and seats; through these holes I wove the strongest hairs I could pick out, just after the manner of cane-chairs in *England*. When they were finished, I made a present of them to her majesty, who kept them in her cabinet, and used to shew them for curiosities, as indeed they were the wonder of everyone that beheld them. The Queen would have had me sit upon one of these chairs, but I absolutely refused to obey her, protesting I would rather die a thousand Deaths than place a dishonourable part of my Body on those precious Hairs that once adorned her Majesty's Head. Of these hairs (as I had always a mechanical genius) I likewise made a neat little purse about five foot long, with her majesty's name deciphered in gold letters, which I gave to *Glumdalclitch*, by the queen's consent. To

这令我回忆起一件趣事，我曾经将很多空闲时间用于此事。我请皇后的侍女把皇后梳头时的掉发收集起来。一段时间后，她给了我一大把。我和一位奉命为我做点零碎物件儿的木匠朋友商量了一下，指挥他制作了两把椅子架，和我的大箱子里那几把椅子差不多大小。然后用尖钻在计划安装椅背和椅面的位置的边框上钻了许多小孔。仿效英国的藤椅的制作方法，将挑选出的最结实的头发穿进孔里。椅子做好以后，我将它们作为礼物献给了皇后。她把它们放在房间里，常常当成新奇玩意儿向别人展示。每一个看到椅子的人都称赞新奇。皇后要我坐在其中一把上，我坚决地违命了，说我就算是死 1000 次也不敢把自己身体那不端庄的部分坐到那些高贵的头发上去，那些头发曾为皇后增添了多少魅力啊！我在制造方面还有一些天赋，又用这些头发做了一只约 5 英尺长的很漂亮的小钱包，并且把皇后的名字用金线绣了上去。得到皇后的允许之后，我把钱包送给了格兰姆达尔克立契。说实话，这个钱包好看却不实用，大一点的硬币都禁不住，所以她只在钱包里放了一些女孩子们喜欢的小玩意，除此之外别无其他。

say the truth, it was more for show than use, being not of strength to bear the weight of the larger coins, and therefore she kept nothing in it, but some little Toys that girls are fond of.

The king, who delighted in music, had frequent consorts at court, to which I was sometimes carried, and set in my box on a table to hear them: but, the noise was so great, that I could hardly distinguish the tunes. I am confident that all the drums and trumpets of a royal army, beating and sounding together just at your ears, could not equal it. My practice was to have my box removed from the places where the performers sat, as far as I could, then to shut the doors and windows of it, and draw the window-curtains, after which I found their music not disagreeable.

I had learnt in my youth to play a little upon the spinet. *Glumdalclitch* kept one in her chamber, and a master attended twice a week to teach her: I called it a spinet, because it somewhat resembled that instrument, and was played upon in the same manner. A fancy came into my head that I would entertain the king and queen with an *English* tune upon this instrument. But this appeared extremely difficult: for, the spinet was near sixty foot long, each key being almost a foot wide, so that, with my arms extended, I could not reach to above five keys, and to press them down

国王非常喜欢音乐，宫里经常举办音乐会。有时候我也会跟他们一起去，他们会把我的箱子放在桌上去，我就在里面听演奏。但是噪声太大了，我几乎听不出演奏的是什么曲子。我敢说就算整个皇家军队都在你的耳边敲鼓吹号，也无法跟这巨大的噪声相比。我习惯让人把我的箱子从演奏者旁边移开，越远越好，然后关上箱子的门窗，放下窗帘，之后才发现他们的音乐并不是无法忍受。

我年轻时曾学过一点古钢琴。格兰姆达尔克立契的房间里就有一架，一个老师每周来给她上两次钢琴课。之所以叫它古钢琴，是因为它的形状有点像那种乐器，而且弹奏的方法也大同小异。我突发奇想，打算用这架古钢琴为国王和皇后弹奏一首英国的曲子。可这似乎有点难办。因为那架古钢琴将近 60 英尺长，每个键就有 1 英尺宽，就算我展开双臂最多也只能够到 5 个琴键，而且得用拳头使劲砸才能将琴键按下去，那样既消耗体力，也徒劳无益。于是我想出了新主意。

required a good smart stroke with my fist, which would be too great a labour, and to no purpose. The method I contrived was this. I prepared two round sticks about the bigness of common cudgels; they were thicker at one end than the other, and I covered the thicker ends with a piece of mouse's skin, that by rapping on them, I might neither damage the tops of the keys nor interrupt the sound. Before the spinet a bench was placed about four foot below the keys, and I was put upon the bench. I ran sideling upon it that way and this, as fast as I could, banging the proper keys with my two sticks, and made a shift to play a jig, to the great satisfaction of both their majesties: but, it was the most violent exercise I ever underwent, and yet I could not strike above sixteen keys, nor consequently, play the bass and treble together, as other artists do; which was a great disadvantage to my performance.

准备两根圆棍，跟普通棍棒差不多即可，一端粗一端细，我把粗的一端用老鼠皮包起来，用它们来敲击琴键，这样既不会损坏琴面，也不会干扰乐声。在钢琴前面放了一张长凳，比键盘大约低 4 英尺。我被放到长凳上，举着那两根圆棍敲击着琴键，斜身在上面快速奔跑，终于想方设法演奏出了一首快步舞曲。国王和皇后听后都很满意，但对我来说，这可是我这辈子所做过的最剧烈的运动。然而就算如此，我最远也只能敲到 16 个键，根本无法像别的艺术家那样，同时弹奏出低音和高音，这是我的演奏中最大的缺陷。

The king, who as I before observed, was a prince of excellent understanding, would frequently order that I should be brought in my box, and set upon the table in his closet. He would then command me to bring one of my chairs out of the box, and sit down within three yards distance upon the top of the cabinet, which brought me almost to a level with his face. In this manner I had several conversations with him. I one day took the freedom to tell his

这位国王，就像我之前提到的，是一位理解能力很强的君主。他经常派人把我和我的大箱子拎到他的房间，放到桌上。他会再下令从我的箱子里搬出一张椅子，放在箱子顶上离边沿 3 码的地方，坐在上面的我就可以和他的脸差不多同一高度了。我们曾以这种方式进行过数次交流。有一天，我坦率地告诉国王，他对欧洲及世界上其他地方的轻视，似乎并不符合他那

majesty, that the contempt he discovered towards *Europe*, and the rest of the world, did not seem answerable to those excellent qualities of mind that he was master of. That, reason did not extend itself with the bulk of the body: on the contrary, we observed in our country that the tallest persons were usually least provided with it. That, among other animals, bees and ants had the reputation of more industry, art, and sagacity than many of the larger kinds. And that, as inconsiderable as he took me to be, I hoped I might live to do his majesty some signal service. The king heard me with attention, and began to conceive a much better opinion of me than he had ever before. He desired I would give him as exact an account of the government of *England* as I possibly could; because, as fond as princes commonly are of their own customs (for he conjectured of other monarchs by my former discourses) he should be glad to hear of anything that might deserve imitation.

过人的智慧。人的智慧并不与个头儿的大小成正比，却有可能成反比，因为在我们国家，我们发现个子最高的人往往最缺乏智慧。其他动物也是如此，蜜蜂与蚂蚁比许多体形比较大的动物们更勤劳，更懂得艺术，更聪明能干。所以，虽然在他看来我只是一个微不足道的小东西，但我希望能够为他做一件显著的功绩。国王认真地听着我的这番话，对我好感倍增。他希望我将英国政府的情况尽可能详细地描述给他听，因为虽然君主们大多喜欢自己的制度（他根据我之前的谈话推测，其他君主也都是如此），如果有一些值得效法之处，也愿意听听。

Imagine with thyself, courteous reader, how often I then wished for the tongue of *Demosthenes or Cicero*, that might have enabled me to celebrate the praise of my own dear native country, in a style equal to its merits and felicity.

亲爱的读者，请为我想想，我当时多么渴望自己能有德谟西尼斯或者西塞罗的口才啊！那样我就能用最美好的词句来形容英国的盛世繁荣，歌颂我亲爱的祖国。

I began my discourse by informing his majesty that our dominions consisted of

我从我国领土由两个岛屿组成开始向国王陛下介绍，在一位君

two islands, which composed three mighty kingdoms under one sovereign, besides our plantations in *America*. I dwelt long upon the fertility of our soil, and the temperature of our climate. I then spoke at large upon the constitution of an *English* parliament, partly made up of an illustrious body called the House of Peers, persons of the noblest blood, and of the most ancient and ample patrimonies. I described that extraordinary care always taken of their education in arts and arms, to qualify them for being counsellors born to the king and kingdom, to have a share in the legislature, to be members of the highest court of judicature from whence there could be no appeal; and to be champions always ready for the defence of their prince and country by their valour, conduct and fidelity. That these were the ornament and bulwark of the kingdom, worthy followers of their most renowned ancestors, whose honour had been the reward of their virtue, from which their posterity were never once known to degenerate. To these were joined several holy persons, as part of that assembly, under the title of bishops, whose peculiar business it is, to take care of religion, and of those who instruct the people therein. These were searched and sought out through the whole nation, by the prince and his wisest counsellors, among such of

主治下，全国分为 3 大王国，此外我们在美洲还有种植园。我详细地叙述了我们那肥沃的土地和温和的气候。接着我又细细介绍了英国议会的体制。议会一部分由一个著名的团体组成，称为上议院，其成员是出身最为显贵的家族，拥有最悠久、最富足的祖业。我又描述了这些人在文武方面所受到的特殊教育，这种特殊的教育使他们有充分的资格做国王或参议员，帮助国家立法，成为最高法庭的法官，使所有上诉都得到合理处理，具有勇敢、公正、忠诚的品格，随时准备为捍卫君主及国家而战。他们是国家的荣耀和中流砥柱，不负先人的盛名。他们的祖先因具有美好的品德而享有盛名，子孙后代也继承了祖先的优点。除此之外，上议院中还有一部分圣职人员，他们享有主教称号，专门负责管理宗教事务，带领教士向全国人民宣传宗教教义。他们从全国范围内选拔出来，由国王和最英明的参政员亲自从品行最美好、学识最渊博的教士搜寻，他们不愧为教士和人民的榜样和领袖。

the priesthood, as were most deservedly distinguished by the sanctity of their lives, and the depth of their erudition; who were indeed the spiritual fathers of the clergy and the people.

That, the other part of the parliament consisted of an assembly called the House of Commons, who were all principal gentlemen, *freely* picked and culled out by the people themselves, for their great abilities, and love of their country, to represent the wisdom of the whole nation. And, these two bodies made up the most august assembly in *Europe*, to whom, in conjunction with the prince, the whole legislature is committed.

I then descended to the courts of justice, over which the judges, those venerable sages and interpreters of the law, presided, for determining the disputed rights and properties of men, as well as for the punishment of vice, and protection of innocence. I mentioned the prudent management of our treasury, the valour and achievements of our forces by sea and land. I computed the number of our people, by reckoning how many millions there might be of each religious sect, or political party among us. I did not omit even our sports and pastimes, or any other particular, which I thought might redound to the honour of my country. And, I finished all with a brief historical account

议会的另一部分由下议院组成，议员都是一些位高权重的绅士，由人民选举产生。这些人拥有超群的才能，对祖国充满了热爱，最能够代表广大人民的智慧。这两院人士共同构成了欧洲最威严的议会，他们和君主一起掌管整个立法机关。

我又开始介绍法庭，那些法官们令人尊敬、德高望重而又精通律法，他们主持案件的审判，判定人们权利和财产纠纷，惩凶除恶，保护无辜。我还提到了我国量入为出的财政管理制度，提到了我国海陆军队的勇猛无敌与辉煌战绩。我根据我国每个教会或政党所获得的支持人数计算出全国的人口总量。我甚至没有遗漏我国的体育和娱乐活动，以及每一件我认为可以作为我国的荣耀来讲述的琐事。最后我对英国近一个世纪以来的历史作了一个简要的总结。

of affairs and events in *England* for about an hundred years past.

This conversation was not ended under five audiences, each of several hours, and the king heard the whole with great attention, frequently taking notes of what I spoke, as well as memorandums of several questions he intended to ask me.

When I had put an end to these long discourses, his majesty in a sixth audience consulting his notes, proposed many doubts, queries, and objections, upon every article. He asked, what methods were used to cultivate the minds and bodies of our young nobility, and in what kind of business they commonly spent the first and teachable part of their lives. What course was taken to supply that assembly when any noble family became extinct. What qualifications were necessary in those who were to be created new lords: whether the humour of the prince, a sum of money to a court-lady or a prime minister, or a design of strengthening a party opposite to the public interest, ever happened to be motives in those advancements. What share of knowledge these lords had in the laws of their country, and how they came by it, so as to enable them to decide the properties of their fellow-subjects in the last resort. Whether they were always so free from avarice, partialities, or want, that a bribe,

这番谈话总共分为5次，每次都谈了好几个小时。国王认真地倾听了我谈及的一切情况，不时将我的谈话内容记录下来，还将他想要问我的问题都写在了备忘录上。

这次长谈结束以后，国王第六次召见了我，他对照着笔记，逐条逐项提出了他的疑惑、问题和异议。他问我们用什么方法来对我们国家年轻贵族的身心进行培养和教育？他们在年轻时那最易于接受教育的时期一般做些什么？一旦某个贵族绝了嗣，议会会采取何种措施来补充这个缺额？那些即将成为新贵的人必须具备一些什么样的资格？国王是否可以一时兴起，送给哪位宫廷贵妇或首相一些奖赏，或者不顾公众利益而支持某一党的势力，将其封为贵族呢？这些新贵对于本国的法律知识了解多少？这些知识是如何获得的？当他们不得不走上法庭主持审理时，又如何评判他们同族人的财产纠纷呢？他们从不贪婪、偏私、不缺钱花也不接受贿赂，是否就不会陷入其他阴谋？我说到的那些圣职官僚是否只是由于具有渊博的宗教知识，品行也十分圣洁，才被选拔到那样高的职位的？他们做普通牧师时从未趋炎附势，

or some other sinister view, could have no place among them. Whether those holy lords I spoke of were always promoted to that rank upon account of their knowledge in religious matters, and the sanctity of their lives, had never been compilers with the times while they were common priests, or slavish prostitute chaplains to some nobleman, whose opinions they continued servilely to follow after they were admitted into that assembly.

从未在某个贵族门下卑躬屈膝，充当低贱堕落的牧师吗？当他们被选进议会后，会不会继续屈从于那些贵族的意志呢？

He then desired to know what arts were practised in electing those whom I called commoners. Whether, a stranger with a strong purse might not influence the vulgar voters to choose him before their own landlord, or the most considerable gentleman in the neighbourhood. How it came to pass, that people were so violently bent upon getting into this assembly, which I allowed to be a great trouble and expense, often to the ruin of their families, without any salary or pension: because this appeared such an exalted strain of virtue and public spirit, that his majesty seemed to doubt it might possibly not be always sincere: and he desired to know whether such zealous gentlemen could have any views of refunding themselves for the charges and trouble they were at, by sacrificing the public good to the designs of a weak and vicious prince in conjunction with a

他还希望了解一下，我所谓的那些被选举为下议员的人，通常会采取何种手段和方法来赢得选票呢？如果一个外乡人财产丰厚，是否就可以收买选民投他的票，而不选举选民自己的地主或周围最有实力的绅士呢？人们为什么会如此强烈地渴望挤进议会呢？毕竟这差使需要耗费大量的精力和金钱，没有薪金和年俸的人往往因此而倾家荡产。这些人看起来似乎品行高尚，愿意为公众服务，但国王却怀疑他们是否出于一片真心？他还想知道，这些热心的绅士们是否会以牺牲公众利益为代价来迎合一位软弱而又堕落的君主以及与其联合为一体的腐败内阁的意志，而自己则能够从中得到金钱的补偿？他提出了无数的问题，并且针对这方面各个部分的问题进行了逐一询问，提出了很多疑问和异议。不过我在此不便复述他的原

corrupted ministry. He multiplied his questions, and sifted me thoroughly upon every part of this head, proposing numberless Enquiries and objections, which I think it not prudent or convenient to repeat.

Upon what I said in relation to our courts of justice, his majesty desired to be satisfied in several points; and this, I was the better able to do, having been formerly almost ruined by a long suit in chancery, which was decreed for me with costs. He asked, what time was usually spent in determining between right and wrong, and what degree of expense. Whether advocates and orators had liberty to plead in causes, manifestly known to be unjust, vexatious, or oppressive. Whether party in religion or politics was observed to be of any weight in the scale of justice. Whether those pleading orators were persons educated in the general knowledge of equity, or only in provincial, national, and other local customs. Whether they or their judges had any part in penning those laws which they assumed the liberty of interpreting and glossing upon at their pleasure. Whether they had ever, at different times pleaded for and against the same cause, and cited precedents to prove contrary opinions. Whether they were a rich or a poor corporation? Whether they received any pecuniary reward for

话。

对于我国法庭的情况，国王陛下有几点想要知晓。关于法庭和法律的情况我还算比较清楚，因为我以前曾在大法官法庭上打过一场官司，历时很久，耗费了大量金钱，几乎破产。他问我审理一件案子一般需要多久？当事人需要花多少钱？如果判决结果明显不公平，故意刁难某人，或者欺压其中一方，辩护人和原告有没有上诉的自由？教派或政党有没有影响执法公正的现象？那些辩护律师是否对公平公正有基本的理解？他们是否只了解某个省、国家或者其他地方性的习俗？律师或者法官是否也参与起草法律呢？如果是这样，他们是否会认为自己有任意解释法律的自由呢？同一桩案子，他们是否会在不同的情况下时而辩护时而反驳，并且援引先例来证明自己意见前后不一致却各有依据？律师富有还是贫穷？他们为人辩护能否获得经济利益？尤其是，他们是否有可能被选为下议院议员？

pleading or delivering their opinions. And particularly whether they were ever admitted as members in the lower senate.

He fell next upon the management of our treasury; and said, he thought my memory had failed me, because I computed our taxes at about five or six millions a year, and, when I came to mention the issues, he found they sometimes amounted to more than double; for the notes he had taken were very particular in this point, because he hoped, as he told me, that the knowledge of our conduct might be useful to him, and he could not be deceived in his calculations. But, if what I told him were true, he was still at a loss how a kingdom could run out of its estate like a private person. He asked me, who were our creditors? and where we should find Money to pay them? He wondered to hear me talk of such chargeable and extensive wars; that, certainly we must be a quarrelsome people, or live among very bad neighbours and that our generals must needs be richer than our kings. He asked what business we had out of our own islands, unless upon the score of trade or treaty, or to defend the coasts with our fleet. Above all, he was amazed to hear me talk of a mercenary standing army in the midst of peace, and among a free people. He said if we were governed by our own consent in

随后他又对我国的财政提出质疑。他说，他觉得我的记忆力不好，因为根据我的计算，我们国家的税收每年五六百万，可根据我接下来提到的各项开支，他发现有时超支不止一倍。他对于这一部分问题记录得非常详尽仔细，他希望据此了解一下，他们或许可以借鉴，统计时不会被人算计。但是，如果我所言属实，他仍旧困惑不解，一个国家如何能够像个人那样超支呢？他问我谁借钱给我们？我们哪儿来的钱还债？他吃惊于我所提及的那些耗资巨大的大规模战争，断言我们必定是一个好斗的民族，不然就是我们的邻国行事恶劣，而且我们的将军肯定比国王更富有。他问，除了贸易往来、签订条约，或者派遣军舰捍卫海岸线之外，我们在自己岛国之外还会做些什么？尤其是当他听我说在和平年代，我们的民族已经获得了自由，却还保留着一支常备军，他说，既然我们是被选举产生的代表所统治，他不明白我们还怕什么，或者说要为反抗谁而战？他想听听我的意见，一个私人家庭难道不应该由这个人自己，或者他的子女，或者其他家人来保护，反而要花一点钱到街上随便找六七个流氓来

the persons of our representatives, he could not imagine of whom we were afraid, or against whom we were to fight, and would hear my opinion, whether a private man's house might not better be defended by himself, his children, and family, than by half a dozen rascals picked up at a venture in the streets, for small wages, who might get an hundred times more by cutting their throats.

保护吗？这些流氓如果把全家人都杀了，不就可以多赚100倍的钱吗？

He laughed at my odd kind of arithmetic (as he was pleased to call it) in reckoning the numbers of our people by a computation drawn from the several sects among us in religion and politics. He said, he knew no reason, why those who entertain opinions prejudicial to the public, should be obliged to change, or should not be obliged to conceal them. And as it was tyranny in any government to require the first, so it was weakness not to enforce the second: for, a man may be allowed to keep poisons in his closet, but not to vend them about as cordials.

他嘲笑我奇怪的计算方法（在他看来很奇怪），我根据几个教派和政党的人数推算出我国的人口总数。他认为那些与公众持不同意见的人没有任何理由改变自己的主张，或者被迫隐藏自己的想法。一方面任何政府如果强迫人改变自己的意见，就是专制；另一方面如果允许人随意公开自己违背大众观点的意见，政府又未免显得太软弱了。这就是为什么允许个人私藏毒药，却不允许拿毒药当兴奋剂去四处兜售。

He observed, that among the diversions of our nobility and gentry, I had mentioned gaming. He desired to know at what age this entertainment was usually taken up, and when it was laid down. how much of their time it employed, whether it ever went so high as to affect their fortunes. whether mean vicious people by their dexterity in that art might not arrive

他注意到，我谈到贵族名流的娱乐活动时涉及了赌博。他想知道，他们多大年龄开始玩这种游戏？要玩到什么时候？要耗费他们多少时间？会不会耗资巨大？品行不端的人会不会因赌博手段高超而成为巨富，令贵族们也要仰仗他们的权势，终日与这些品行低劣的人为伍，从此不思进取？而且

at great riches, and sometimes keep our very nobles in dependence, as well as habituate them to vile companions, wholly take them from the improvement of their minds, and force them by the losses they received, to learn and practise that infamous dexterity upon others.

He was perfectly astonished with the historical account I gave him of our affairs during the last century, protesting it was only a heap of conspiracies, rebellions, murders, massacres, revolutions, banishments, the very worst effects that avarice, faction, hypocrisy, perfidiousness, cruelty, rage, madness, hatred, envy, lust, malice, and ambition, could produce.

His majesty in another audience was at the pains to recapitulate the sum of all I had spoken; compared the questions he made with the answers I had given; then taking me into his hands, and stroking me gently, delivered himself in these words, which I shall never forget, nor the manner he spoke them in. My little friend Grildrig; you have made a most admirable panegyric upon your country. you have clearly proved that ignorance, idleness and vice are the proper ingredients for qualifying a legislator. That laws are best explained, interpreted, and applied by those whose interest and abilities lie in perverting, confounding, and eluding them. I observe among you some lines of

赌输之后，贵族们会不会也去练习那些卑劣手段用来对付别人？

他极其惊叹于我所讲述的上个世纪以来我国的历史。他断言，那些不过是一大堆阴谋、反抗、谋杀、大屠杀、革命和流放，是贪婪、派系之争、虚伪、背信弃义、残酷、愤怒、疯狂、憎恨、嫉妒、欲望、恶意和野心所造成的最可怕的后果。

国王再次召见我的时候又煞费苦心地对我之前所说的话进行了一次总结。他对比了他的所问和我的所答，接着把我放在手里，轻轻地抚摸着我，说了这样一番话，我永远也忘不了，包括他说话的态度："我的小朋友格里尔特里格，你对你的祖国发表了一篇令人钦佩的颂词。你已经清楚地证明，愚昧、懒惰和腐化为立法者必需的特质，能够很好地解释、说明和应用法律的人恰恰也正是那些想要也能够滥用、混淆法律和逃避法律制裁的人。我观察到你们有几条规章制度原本还是可行的，可是一半被废除，剩下的一半也全被腐败玷污了。据你所言，在你们国家，任何

an institution, which in its original might have been tolerable, but these half erased, and the rest wholly blurred and blotted by corruptions. It doth not appear from all you have said, how any one Virtue is required towards the procurement of any one station among you, much less that men are ennobled on account of their virtue, that priests are advanced for their piety or learning, soldiers for their conduct or valour, judges for their integrity, senators for the love of their country, or counsellors for their wisdom. As for yourself (continued the king) who have spent the greatest part of your life in travelling, I am well disposed to hope you may hitherto have escaped many vices of your country. But, by what I have gathered from your own relation, and the answers I have with much pains wringed and extorted from you, I cannot but conclude the bulk of your natives, to be the most pernicious race of little odious vermin that nature ever suffered to crawl upon the surface of the earth.

职位的获得似乎都不需要有何美德，也并非只有品德高尚的人才能封爵。教士升迁不是由于虔诚或博学，军人晋级并非因其品行或英勇，法官升职也不是因为其廉明奉公，入选议员不是因为其爱国，参政大臣也不是因为其智慧而纷纷得到升迁。至于你呢，”国王接着说，“你半生在外旅行，希望你至今还未沾染上你那个国家那么多的恶习。但是，根据你自己的叙述以及我费尽心机才逼问出来的结果来看，我只能产生这样的结论：你的大部分同胞是自古以来，在大自然的宽恕下仍被允许存活在世上的小害虫中最有害的一类。”

CHAPTER 7

第七章

The Author's Love of his Country. He makes a Proposal of much Advantage to the King, which is rejected. the King's great Ignorance in Politics. The Learning of that Country very imperfect and confined. the Laws, and military Affairs, and Parties in the State.

作者的爱国情怀。他向国王提出了一个非常有益的建议却被拒绝了。国王对于政治的一无所知。这个国家的学术存在很多缺陷，且范围狭窄。这个国家的法律、军事和政党情况。

Nothing but an extreme love of truth could have hindered me from concealing this part of my story. It was in vain to discover my resentments, which were always turned into ridicule; and I was forced to rest with patience, while my noble and beloved country was so injuriously treated. I am heartily sorry as any of my readers can possibly be, that such an occasion was given: but this prince happened to be so curious and inquisitive upon every particular, that it could not consist either with gratitude or good manners to refuse giving him what satisfaction I was able. Yet thus much I may be allowed to say in my own vindication, that I artfully eluded many of his questions, and gave to every point a more favourable turn by many degrees than the strictness of truth would allow.

并无其他理由，完全是出于对真理的无比热爱，我才将这段故事公之于众。我表现出自己的怨恨也是徒劳，因为这只会招致更多的嘲笑。我只好耐心聆听我那高贵而可爱的祖国被诋毁。我真的很气愤，相信任何一位读者遇到这种情况都会很气愤。可这位国王恰好好奇心强烈，执著于每个细节，我又不得不怀着感激之情礼貌地一一回答，否则他也不会善罢甘休。不过我要为自己辩解一下，我故意绕开了他的许多问题，在每一个具体问题上，我都采取更加有利于我的祖国的说法。因为我对自己的祖国一向偏袒，这也是值得赞颂的。哈立卡那修斯的狄俄尼索斯就奉劝历史学家这样做。我要掩藏起自己“母亲”的弱点和畸形，而将她的美德和美丽公之于众。在和那位伟

For, I have always borne that laudable partiality to my own country, which *Dionysius Halicarnassensis* with so much justice recommends to an historian. I would hide the frailties and deformities of my political mother, and place her virtues and beauties in the most advantageous light. This was my sincere endeavour, in those many discourses I had with that might monarch, although it unfortunately failed of success.

大的国王的多次谈话中，我曾真心诚意地尽力那样做，然而不幸失败了。

But, great allowances should be given to a king who lives wholly secluded from the rest of the world, and must therefore be altogether unacquainted with the manners and customs that most prevail in other nations: the want of which knowledge will ever produce many *prejudices*, and a certain *narrowness of thinking*, from which we and the politer countries of *Europe* are wholly exempted. And it would be hard indeed, if so remote a prince's notions of virtue and vice were to be offered as a standard for all mankind.

但是，我们也应该谅解这位国王，他生活在这样一个封闭的世界里，因此必然对其他国家十分常见的风俗人情一无所知。这样一种缺乏就导致了许多偏见，以及某种偏执的想法，而我们以及欧洲的其他一些更加文明的国家绝不会如此。如果把如此偏僻国家的一位国王的善恶观作为全人类的范例，的确也太难以实现了。

To confirm what I have now said, and further to show the miserable effects of a *confined education*, I shall here insert a passage which will hardly obtain belief. In hopes to ingratiate myself farther into his majesty's Favour, I told him of an invention discovered between three and four hundred years ago, to make a certain

为了证实我的话，同时也为了进一步说明褊狭的教育会造成什么样的严重后果，我在这里要插入一段几乎令人难以想象的叙述。为了使国王更加喜欢我，我告诉他一项三四百年前的发明，某种粉末堆成一堆，如果有一点小小的火星落进去，也会立刻点着。将堆得像山

powder, into an heap of which the smallest spark of fire falling, would kindle the whole in a moment, although it were as big as a mountain, and make it all fly up in the air together, with a noise and agitation greater than thunder. That, a proper quantity of this powder rammed into an hollow tube of brass or iron, according to its bigness, would drive a ball of iron or lead with such violence and speed as nothing was able to sustain its force. That the largest balls thus discharged, would not only destroy whole ranks of an army at once, but batter the strongest walls to the ground, sink down ships with a thousand men in each, to the bottom of the sea; and, when linked together by a chain, would cut through masts and rigging, divide hundreds of bodies in the middle, and lay all waste before them. That we often put this powder into large hollow balls of iron, and discharged them by an engine into some city we were besieging, which would rip up the pavements, tear the houses to pieces, burst and throw splinters on every side, dashing out the brains of all who came near. That I knew the ingredients very well, which were cheap, and common; I understood the manner of compounding them, and could direct his workmen how to make those tubes of a size proportionable to all other things in his majesty's kingdom, and the

一样高的粉末炸到半空，产生比雷声还要响亮的声音和震动。将这种粉末取一定量放入一根中空的铜管或铁管里，不同大小的管子所产生的力量可以将一枚铁弹或铅弹推出，其力量与速度势不可当。如果粉末的量加大，其产生的威力能够瞬间消灭一支军队，并将最坚固的城墙夷为平地，令载有 1000 名士兵的船只葬身海底。如果把所有的船用链子串到一起，桅杆和船索也会被通通炸断，几千人的身体被炸成两段，一切化为灰烬。我们经常将这种粉末装进空心的大铁球，用一种机器对着我们正在进攻的城市射出去，就可以炸断道路，炸毁房屋，碎片四处纷飞，所到之处人们都会被炸得四分五裂、尸横遍野。我对这种粉末的成分了如指掌，原料不贵而且常见。我了解配制的方法，可以指导国王的工人制造比例合适的炮筒，最长不会超过 100 英尺。如果有了二三十根这样的炮管，装进一定的粉末，再加上铁球，摧毁全国范围内最坚固的城垣也只需要几个小时。无论哪个城市的人胆敢违抗国王的绝对权威，都可以将其炸毁。我谨将这些知识献给陛下，略表寸心，来报答他对我的厚爱和庇护。

largest need not be above an hundred foot long; twenty or thirty of which tubes charged with the proper quantity of powder and balls, would batter down the walls of the strongest town in his dominions in a few hours, or destroy the whole metropolis, if ever it should pretend to dispute his absolute commands. This I humbly offered to his majesty as a small tribute of acknowledgment in return of so many marks that I had received of his royal favour and protection.

The king was struck with horror at the description I had given him of those terrible engines, and the proposal I had made. He was amazed how so impotent and grovelling an insect as I (these were his expressions) could entertain such inhuman ideas, and in so familiar a manner as to appear wholly unmoved at all the scenes of blood and desolation, which I had painted as the common effects of those destructive machines, whereof he said, some evil genius, enemy to mankind, must have been the first contriver. As for himself, he protested, that although few things delighted him so much as new discoveries in art or in nature, yet he would rather lose half his kingdom than be privy to such a secret, which he commanded me, as I valued my life, never to mention any more.

国王对我描述的那些可怕的机器以及我提出的建议感到惊恐万分。他很吃惊，像我这么一只弱小而低贱的昆虫（他就是这样说的），竟然怀有如此残忍的想法，谈起来语气还这么稀松平常。我对自己描绘的那些毁灭性杀伤性武器所造成的血腥和创伤似乎一点也不以为然。他说，这种机器的创始人一定是一个魔鬼，人类公敌。至于他本人，他坚持称，虽然对艺术或自然界的探索进展令他感到无比欣喜，但他宁可失去部分领土，也不愿了解这其中的奥秘。他命令我说，如果我珍惜自己的生命，就不要再提了。

A strange effect of *narrow principles*

这完全是严苛的规则和短浅

and short views! that a prince possessed of every quality which procures veneration, love, and esteem; of strong parts, great wisdom and profound learning, endued with admirable talents for government, and almost adored by his subjects, should from a *nice unnecessary scruple*, whereof in *Europe* we can have no conception, let slip an opportunity put into his hands, that would have made him absolute master of the lives, the liberties, and the fortunes of his people. Neither do I say this with the least intention to detract from the many virtues of that excellent king, whose character I am sensible will on this account be very much lessened in the opinion of an *English* reader: but I take this defect among them to have arisen from their ignorance, they not having hitherto reduced *politics* into a *science*, as the more acute wits of *Europe* have done. For I remember very well, in a discourse one day with the king, when I happened to say there were several thousand books among us written upon the *art of government*, it gave him (directly contrary to my intention) a very mean opinion of our understandings. He professed both to abominate and despise all *mystery*, *refinement*, and *intrigue*, either in a prince or a minister. He could not tell what I meant by *secrets of state*, where an enemy or some rival nation were not in the case.

的目光的奇怪效果！一位国王具有种种令人尊敬、崇拜和仰视的品质，他有非凡的才能，超群的智慧，深厚的学识，令人钦佩的统治才能，赢得了世人的爱戴。他竟然因为一种完全不必要的担心，轻易放掉了到手的机会，这对我们欧洲人来说是不可思议的，不然他完全可以绝对控制他的子民的生命、自由和财产。我这么说绝不是要贬低那位杰出的国王。我心里很清楚，国王的这种性格令英国的读者们很瞧不起。不过我觉得他们的这种性格缺陷可以归结于无知，他们迄今为止还没能像欧洲那些智慧之人一样，把政治发展为一门学科进行研究。因为我很清楚地记得，有一天，在我和国王谈话的时候，偶然谈到，我们写过几千本关于统治的艺术的书。没想到事与愿违，这反而令他特别瞧不起我们的想法。他说他既痛恨又鄙视那些故弄玄虚、附庸风雅和阴谋诡计，不论是君王还是大臣。他无法理解我所说的国家机密是指什么，因为他那里并没有什么外部敌对势力。他所理解的统治，范围非常狭窄，包括情与理，法律制裁与从宽判决，民事、刑事案件的审判效率，以及其他一些不值得考虑的平淡无奇的事务。而且，他还提出了这样的观点：谁能在只生产一串谷穗和一片草叶的土地种出两串谷穗、两片草叶来，

He confined the knowledge of governing within very *narrow bounds*; to common sense and reason, to justice and lenity, to the speedy determination of civil and criminal causes; with some other obvious topics which are not worth considering. And, he gave it for his opinion, that whoever could make two ears of corn, or two blades of grass to grow upon a spot of ground, where only one grew before, would deserve better of mankind, and do more essential service to his country than the whole race of politicians put together.

谁就是国家的功臣，对人类的贡献比所有的政客加起来还要大。

The learning of this people is very defective, consisting only in morality, history, poetry, and mathematics, wherein they must be allowed to excel. But, the last of these is wholly applied to what may be useful in life, to the improvement of agriculture and all mechanical arts; so that among us it would be little esteemed. And as to ideas, entities, abstractions, and transcendentals, I could never drive the least conception into their heads.

这个民族的学术也存在一些缺陷，只有伦理、历史、诗歌和数学几个科目，虽然他们也取得了不错的成果。但他们完全把数学用于生活，比如改良农业以及一切机械技术，这在我们看来不值一提。至于什么意识、本体、抽象、经验，我永远也不可能将这些概念灌输到这些人的脑袋里去。

No law of that country must exceed in words the number of letters in their alphabet, which consists only in two and twenty. But indeed, few of them extend even to that length. They are expressed in the most plain and simple terms, wherein those people are not mercurial enough to discover above one interpretation. and to write a comment upon any law is a capital

这个国家的法律条文都不超过他们的字母表上的字母总数 22 个。不过实际上，绝大部分条文甚至都没有那么长。他们的法律条文全部采取最简洁的措辞，那里的人民也没有那么雄辩，会另外提出不同的解释。写文章评论法律也是死罪。至于民事诉讼的判决或刑事案件的审判程序，他们的判例太少，

crime. As to the decision of civil causes, or proceedings against criminals, their precedents are so few, that they have little reason to boast of any extraordinary skill in either.

没有什么值得自豪的卓越技巧。

They have had the art of printing, as well as the Chinese, time out of mind. but their libraries are not very large; for that of the king's, which is reckoned the biggest, doth not amount to above a thousand volumes, placed in a gallery of twelve hundred foot long, from whence I had liberty to borrow what books I pleased. The queen's joiner had contrived in one of *Glumdalclitch's* rooms a kind of wooden machine five and twenty foot high, formed like a standing ladder, the steps were each fifty foot long: it was indeed a movable pair of stairs, the lowest end placed at ten foot distance from the wall of the chamber. The book I had a mind to read was put up leaning against the wall. I first mounted to the upper step of the ladder, and turning my face towards the book, began at the top of the page, and so walking to the right and left about eight or ten paces according to the length of the lines, till I had gotten a little below the level of my eyes, and then descending gradually till I came to the bottom: after which I mounted again, and began the other page in the same manner, and so turned over the leaf, which I could easily

同中国人一样，他们许久之前就发明了印刷术。他们的图书馆并不大，国王的那一个是最大的了，藏书也不超过 1000 卷，摆放在一条大约 1200 英尺长的长廊里。我在那里可以自由借阅喜欢的书籍。皇后的御用工匠在格兰姆达尔克立契的一个房间里造了一种 25 英尺高的木制机器，形状像一架直立的梯子，每一层踏板有 50 英尺长。这确实是一架可移动的梯子，底端离房间的墙壁 10 英尺。我把打算读的书斜靠在墙上，先爬到梯子最上面的一级，脸对着书，从书页的第一行开始，走到右边，再走回左边，根据每一行文字的长度，来回要走 8 到 10 步，直到文字处于我的视平线以下的时候，我就往下走一级踏板，这样慢慢一级一级走到底层。之后重新爬上梯子，用同样的方法阅读下一页。读完以后就把那一页翻过去。我自己很容易就能翻，因为书页坚硬得如同纸板，最大的对开本也不过 18 到 20 英尺长。

do with both my hands, for it was as thick and stiff as a pasteboard, and in the largest folios not above eighteen or twenty foot long.

Their style is clear, masculine, and smooth, but not florid, for they avoid nothing more than multiplying unnecessary words, or using various expressions. I have perused many of their books, especially those in history and morality. Among the rest I was much diverted with a little old treatise, which always lay in *Glumdalclitch's* bed-chamber, and belonged to her governess, a grave elderly gentlewoman, who dealt in writings of morality and devotion. The book treats of the weakness of human kind, and is in little esteem except among the women and the vulgar. However, I was curious to see what an author of that country could say upon such a subject. This writer went through all the usual topics of *European* moralists, showing how diminutive, contemptible, and helpless an animal was man in his own nature; how unable to defend himself from inclemencies of the air, or the fury of wild beasts. how much he was excelled by one creature in strength, by another in speed, by a third in foresight, by a fourth in industry. He added, that nature was degenerated in these latter declining ages of the world, and could now produce only

他们的文章风格清新豪迈、通顺但不浮华，因为他们最不喜欢作多余的修饰或者加入各种各样的艺术技巧。我详细考察了他们的许多书籍，尤其是历史和伦理方面的。此外，一本比较陈旧的小书为我的生活增添了不少乐趣，这本书一直摆在格兰姆达尔克立契的卧室里，是她的女教师的。这位严肃的老太太喜欢阅读伦理和宗教信仰方面的著作。这本书探讨了人类的弱点，不过只受到女人和底层百姓们的关注。然而，我倒是对这个国家的作家如何探讨这样一个题目感到有点好奇。这位作家论述了欧洲伦理学者经常谈论的所有话题，揭示出人类在本质上是多么渺小、卑微、无能的动物，在严酷的气候和凶猛的野兽面前是多么无能为力。有那么多比人类强大的动物，有的力量更大，有的速度更快，有的更有预见力，有的更勤劳。他还说，大自然在这个近年来日渐衰败的世界中也在退化。现在的大自然只能产生一些发育不全的人，相比之下古代人则要高大得多。他说这不言自明，不仅原始人种比现代人种的体形更魁梧，而且以前也的确有过巨人，这一点在历史和传说

small abortive births in comparison of those in ancient times. He said it was very reasonable to think, not only that the species of man were originally much larger, but also that there must have been giants in former ages, which, as it is asserted by history and tradition, so it hath been confirmed by huge bones and skulls casually dug up in several parts of the kingdom, far exceeding the common dwindled race of man in our days. He argued, that the very laws of nature absolutely required we should have been made in the beginning, of a size more large and robust, not so liable to destruction, from every little accident of a tile falling from an house, or a stone cast from the hand of a boy, or of being drowned in a little brook. From this way of reasoning the author drew several moral applications, useful in the conduct of life, but needless here to repeat. For my own part, I could not avoid reflecting how universally this talent was spread of drawing lectures in morality, or indeed rather matter of discontent and repining from the quarrels we raise with nature. And, I believe upon a strict inquiry, those quarrels might be shown as ill-grounded among us, as they are among that people.

As to their military affairs, they boast that the king's army consists of an hundred and seventy-six thousand foot,

中都可以得到证明，比如王国境内各地偶然挖出的巨型骷髅远超当今人类的骨骼。他指出，在人类发展早期，自然法则要求我们的身材必须高大而强壮得多，那样我们才不会像现在这样在小意外中都可能送命，比如屋顶上掉下来的一片瓦，小男孩扔过来的一块石头，或失足掉进小溪等。根据这一系列的推论，作者提出的几条道德法则对人生大有裨益，但在此不再赘述。我自己却忍不住想，人类宣讲道德的天性如此普遍，或者实际上这关系到人与自然的矛盾，但人们只是抱怨一下来表达一下自己的不满罢了。经过详细的调查，我觉得这个民族与自然之间的矛盾，也和我们的一样，都是自寻烦恼。

至于他们的军事，他们夸耀国王的军队由 17 万 6000 步兵和 32 万骑兵组成。如果这可以称之为一

and thirty-two thousand horse: if that may be called an army which is made up of tradesmen in the several cities, and farmers in the country, whose commanders are only the nobility and gentry without pay or reward. They are indeed perfect enough in their exercises, and under very good discipline, wherein I saw no great merit; for, how should it be otherwise, where every farmer is under the command of his own landlord, and every citizen under that of the principal men in his own city, chosen after the manner of *Venice* by *ballot*?

支军队的话，这支军队由各个城市的商人和乡下的农民组成，由当地的贵族与乡绅指挥，没有军饷。他们的操练非常熟练，纪律严明，不过我没有看到他们的任何功绩。因为每个农民都听凭自己的地主调遣，每个市民都由其所在城市的重要人物率领，这些人都像威尼斯那样投票选举产生，难怪他们的纪律那么好。

I have often seen the militia of Lorbrulgrud drawn out to exercise in a great field near the city, of twenty miles square. They were in all not above twenty-five thousand foot, and six thousand horse; but it was impossible for me to compute their number, considering the space of ground they took up. A cavalier mounted on a large steed might be about an hundred foot high. I have seen this whole body of horse upon a word of command draw their swords at once, and brandish them in the air. Imagination can figure nothing so grand, so surprising and so astonishing. it looked as if ten thousand flashes of lightning were darting at the same time from every quarter of the sky.

我时常看到洛布鲁格鲁德城的民兵到城郊一块 20 平方英里的空地上拉练。这支队伍不超过 2500 名步兵和 6000 名骑兵，不过他们每个人所占的空间太大，我无法统计出确切的数目。一名骑兵骑在一匹大战马上大约有 100 英尺高。我曾见过这样一整队骑兵，指挥官一声令下，他们几乎同时抽出剑刺向空中。这样壮观的场面如此震动人心，简直令人无法想象！就像万道闪电同时从空中各处放出光芒。

I was curious to know how this prince, to whose dominions there is no access

我很好奇这位国王为何想训练军队，或者说要教他的臣民进行

from any other country, came to think of armies, or to teach his people the practice of military discipline. But I was soon informed, both by conversation, and reading their histories. For, in the course of many ages they have been troubled with the same disease to which the whole race of mankind is subject; the nobility often contending for power, the people for liberty, and the king for absolute dominion. All which, however happily tempered by the laws of the kingdom, have been sometimes violated by each of the three parties, and have once or more occasioned civil wars, the last whereof was happily put an end to by this prince's grandfather by a general composition; and the militia then settled with common consent hath been ever since kept in the strictest duty.

军事训练。没有任何一个国家的路可以通到这个国家的领土。不过不久，我通过和别人聊天以及阅读他们的历史，才了解到其中的奥秘。原来，多年以来，他们也被许多其他政府经常犯的通病所困扰：贵族争权，人民要求自由，君王则希望绝对的专制。无论王国的法律对其的规定多么合理，这 3 方势力中总会有一方时而出来破坏，挑起了不止一次的内战。现任国王的祖父曾率大军顺利平定了最近的一次内战。之后 3 方面就此决定设立民兵团，严格履行职责。

CHAPTER 8

第八章

The King and Queen make a Progress to the Frontiers. The Author attends them. The manner in which he leaves the Country very Particularly related. He returns to England.

国王和皇后巡查边境，作者侍驾随行。叙述作者如何离开这个特别的国家，又回到英国。

I had always a strong impulse that I should sometime recover my liberty, though it was impossible to conjecture by what means, or to form any project with the least hope of succeeding. The ship in which I sailed was the first ever known to be driven within sight of the coast, and the king had given strict orders, that if at any time another appeared, it should be taken ashore, and with all its crew and passengers brought in a tumbril to *Lorbrulgrud*. He was strongly bent to get me a woman of my own size, by whom I might propagate the Breed: But I think I should rather have died than undergone the Disgrace of leaving a Posterity to be kept in Cages like tame Canary Birds, and perhaps in time sold about the Kingdom to Persons of Quality for Curiosities. I was indeed treated with much kindness; I was the favourite of a great king and queen, and the delight of the whole court, but it

我的心中一直有一个强有力的声音在告诉自己，终有一天我会重获自由，虽然无法推测以何种手段，也没有制订出有任何成功希望的计划。据说我所乘坐的那艘船是迄今为止第一艘被刮到这一带沿海的船只。国王发出紧急命令，何时再有类似的船只出现，一定要将其带上岸，并用双轮运货车将所有船员和旅客都送到洛布鲁格鲁德来。他非要替我找一个与我身材相当的女人，为我生育后代。但我宁死也不想蒙受那样的羞辱，留下子孙被像温驯的金丝雀那样用笼子豢养起来，后来可能还会被当做珍奇的宝贝在贵族之间交易。我确实受到了礼遇，成为这位伟大的国王及其皇后最恩宠的臣子，得到皇宫上下所有人的喜爱。但那种地位却严重践踏了我作为人类的尊严。我也永远不会忘记我在家人面前立下的誓言。我希望可以与别人平等

was upon such a foot as ill became the dignity of human kind. I could never forget those domestic pledges I had left behind me. I wanted to be among people with whom I could converse upon even terms, and walk about the streets and fields without fear of being trod to death like a frog or a young puppy. But my deliverance came sooner than I expected, and in a manner not very common: the whole story and circumstances of which I shall faithfully relate.

交流，走在道路或田野上也无须担心会像青蛙或小狗那样随时有可能被人踩死。但是，我的自由获得的这么快，而且是以一种不同寻常的方式，超乎了我的想象。这件事的始末稍后我将详尽陈述。

I had now been two years in this country; and, about the beginning of the third, *Glumdalclitch* and I attended the king and queen in a progress to the south coast of the kingdom. I was carried as usual in my travelling-box, which, as I have already described, was a very convenient closet of twelve foot wide. And, I had ordered a hammock to be fixed by silken ropes from the four corners at the top, to break the jolts, when a servant carried me before him on horseback, as I sometimes desired, and would often sleep in my hammock while we were upon the road. On the roof of my closet, just over the middle of the hammock, I ordered the joiner to cut out a hole of a foot square, to give me air in hot weather as I slept, which hole I shut at pleasure with a board that drew backwards and forwards through a groove.

我到这个国家已经两年了。大约第三年年初，格兰姆达尔克立契和我陪同国王和皇后巡查王国的南海岸。和往常一样，他们将我放进旅行箱带在身边。我曾经描述过这箱子，有 12 英尺宽，是个便携的小房间。我吩咐在我的小房间里用 4 根丝绳安装了一张吊床，有时候我还会让骑马的仆人把我的小箱子放在他身前以减轻颠簸。旅行途中，我时常在吊床上睡觉。我让木匠在小箱子的屋顶上挖了一个 1 英尺见方的小洞，正对着吊床中央，以便于在炎热的天气睡觉时能够呼吸到新鲜空气。洞口处还安装了一块木板，我能够沿槽将其来回拉动，随时开闭。

When we came to our journey's end, the king thought proper to pass a few days at a palace he hath near *Flanflasnic*, a city within eighteen *English* Miles of the Sea-side *Glumdalclitch* and I were much fatigued; I had gotten a small cold, but the poor girl was so ill as to be confined to her chamber. I longed to see the ocean, which must be the only scene of my escape, if ever it should happen. I pretended to be worse than I really was, and desired leave to take the fresh air of the sea, with a page whom I was very fond of, and who had sometimes been trusted with me. I shall never forget with what unwillingness *Glumdalclitch* consented, nor the strict charge she gave the page to be careful of me, bursting at the same time into a flood of tears, as if she had some foreboding of what was to happen. The boy took me out of my box about half-an-hour's walk from the palace, towards the rocks on the sea-shore. I ordered him to set me down, and lifting up one of my sashes, cast many a wistful melancholy look towards the sea. I found myself not very well, and told the page that I had a mind to take a nap in my hammock, which I hoped would do me good. I got in, and the boy shut the window close down to keep out the cold. I soon fell asleep, and all I can conjecture is, that while I slept, the page, thinking no danger could happen, went among the

我们的巡行快要结束的时候，国王想去他在弗兰弗拉斯尼克的一座行宫住几天。弗兰弗拉斯尼克是一座距离海边大概 18 英里的城市。我和格兰姆达尔克立契都筋疲力尽。我受了点凉，而可怜的小姑娘则病得出不了门了。我渴望见到大海，如果可能，这也是我唯一的逃生机会。我假装病得很重，要求带一位自己中意的仆人去海边呼吸一下新鲜空气。偶尔他们也曾经把我托他照顾。我永远也忘不了格兰姆达尔克立契当时难分难舍的样子，也永远忘不了她对仆人再三叮嘱要好好照顾我。她顿时泪如泉涌，好像预感到即将发生的事。这个仆人提着我和我的小箱子离开行宫，大概半个小时，就走到了海滨的岩石上。我让他放我下来。我推开一扇窗，满怀渴求而又忧郁地遥望着大海。我感到不太舒服，告诉仆人说我在吊床上小憩片刻可能就会好。我爬上吊床，仆人怕我着凉又放下窗子。我迅速进入了梦乡，我猜仆人看我睡了，觉得不会发生什么危险，就去岩石缝里找鸟蛋了。我刚才从窗口看到他在那里左顾右盼，还确实在岩缝间捡到了一两个。这时，我突然被吵醒了，为了便于携带而安装在箱顶的那个铁环被猛地拉了起来。我感觉箱子一下子飞到了高空，并以迅雷不及掩耳之势飞驰起来。开始的那一

rocks to look for birds' eggs, having before observed him from my window searching about, and picking up one or two in the clefts. Be that as it will, I found myself suddenly awaked with a violent pull upon the ring which was fastened at the top of my box for the conveniency of carriage. I felt my box raised very high in the air, and then borne forward with prodigious speed. The first jolt had like to have shaken me out of my hammock, but afterwards the motion was easy enough. I called out several times as loud as I could raise my voice, but all to no purpose. I looked towards my windows, and could see nothing but the clouds and sky. I heard a noise just over my head like the clapping of wings, and then began to perceive the woeful condition I was in; that some eagle had got the ring of my box in his beak, with an intent to let it fall on a rock like a tortoise in a shell, and then pick out my body and devour it. for the sagacity and smell of this bird enabled him to discover his quarry at a great distance, though better concealed than I could be within a two-inch board.

下颠簸差点儿把我从吊床上震下来，不过之后还算平稳。我用自己最大的音量喊了几声，结果也只是徒劳。我朝窗外看去，只有蓝天白云。我听到头顶有翅膀扇动的声音，才意识到自己正处于什么样的惨境。原来是一只鹰叼起了我箱子上的铁环，打算把箱子扔到岩石上，就像摔碎乌龟壳一样，再把我啄出来吃掉。这种鸟很聪明，嗅觉也非常灵敏，相隔很远就能发现猎物，哪怕猎物躲在再隐蔽的地方也无济于事。

In a little time I observed the noise and flutter of wings to increase very fast, and my box was tossed up and down like a signpost in a windy day. I heard several bangs or buffets, as I thought, given to the eagle (for such I am certain it must have

不一会儿，我感觉到翅膀扇动得越来越快，我的小箱子上下颠簸如同被狂风掀动的路标牌。我听到了几声撞击，那一定是鹰遭到了袭击（我现在已经肯定，叼着我箱子顶上的铁环的是一只鹰）。接着，

been that held the ring of my box in his beak) and then all on a sudden felt myself falling perpendicularly down for above a minute, but with such incredible swiftness that I almost lost my breath. My fall was stopped by a terrible squash, that sounded louder to my ears than the cataract of *Niagara*; after which I was quite in the dark for another minute, and then my box began to rise so high that I could see light from the tops of my windows. I now perceived that I was fallen into the sea. My box, by the weight of my body, the goods that were in, and the broad plates of iron fixed for strength at the four corners of the top and bottom, floated about five foot deep in the water. I did then, and do now suppose that the eagle which flew away with my box was pursued by two or three others, and forced to let me drop while he defended himself against the rest, who hoped to share in the prey. The plates of iron fastened at the bottom of the box (for those were the strongest), preserved the balance while it fell, and hindered it from being broken on the surface of the water. Every joint of it was well grooved, and the door did not move on hinges, but up and down like a sash, which kept my closet so tight that very little water came in. I got with much difficulty out of my hammock, having first ventured to draw back my slip-board on the roof already

我突然感觉自己在径直下坠，这感觉持续了一分多钟，速度快得令人难以置信，我几乎快要窒息了。忽然啪的一声可怕的巨响，我停下来。在我听来，那声音超过尼亚加拉大瀑布发出的水声。其后的一分钟，我的眼前一片黑暗。接着箱子又开始慢慢上浮，从最上面的窗子里透出了一些光亮。这时我感觉到自己已经落入了大海。由于我的体重和箱子里家具的重量，再加上箱顶及底部四角的加固铁板，我的小箱子浸在水中大约 5 英尺。我当时猜想，现在仍然这样想，那只叼着我的箱子飞翔的鹰也许正在被另外两三只鹰追击，它为了自卫被迫将我扔下来，同这几只想要瓜分其猎物的鹰决一胜负。钉在箱底的铁板最坚固，因此箱子下坠时不但保持了平衡，而且没有被水面击得粉碎。所有的接缝处都做成了严丝合缝的沟槽，门不是靠铰链控制，而是像窗户一样可上下拉动，所以我的小房间密不透风，几乎没有渗进一滴水。由于缺氧，我觉得自己快要窒息了，于是冒险拉开屋顶上那块活动的木板才费力爬下吊床，如前所述，这块木板就是用来透气的。

mentioned, contrived on purpose to let in air, for want of which I found myself almost stifled.

How often did I then wish myself with my dear *Glumdalclitch*, from whom one single hour had so far divided me! And I may say with truth that in the midst of my own misfortunes I could not forbear lamenting my poor nurse, the grief she would suffer for my loss, the displeasure of the queen, and the ruin of her fortune. Perhaps many travellers have not been under greater difficulties and distress than I was at juncture, expecting every moment to see my box dashed to pieces, or at least overset by the first violent blast, or rising wave. A breach in one single pane of glass would have been immediate death: nor could anything have preserved the windows, but the strong Lattice wires placed on the outside against accidents in travelling. I saw the water ooze in at several crannies, although the leaks were not considerable, and I endeavoured to stop them as well as I could I was not able to lift up the roof of my closet, which otherwise I certainly should have done, and sat on the top of it, where I might at least preserve myself some hours longer than by being shut up as I may call it, in the hold. Or, if I escaped these dangers for a day or two, what could I expect but a miserable death of cold and hunger! I was

我当时想，如果亲爱的格兰姆达尔克立契在我身边该多好啊！虽然我们才刚刚分离一个小时！说实话，在自身都难保的时候，我还是忍不住要为我那可怜的小保姆难过。把我弄丢了会让她多伤心啊！皇后一怒之下也许会毁了她的前途。也许很多旅行家都不会像我这样经历这么多的磨难和遭遇。我无时无刻不在担心箱子会被撞成碎片，至少也有可能被一阵大风一个浪头打翻。窗户上的一道裂缝也会要了我的命。幸好之前在窗户外安装了结实的铁丝网格，以免旅行时发生意外事故，此外并无其他保护措施。我看到已经有水开始从小房间的角落渗进来，虽然暂无大碍，但我还是竭力堵住漏水的地方。要不是我实在无法掀开小箱子的屋顶，我肯定要坐到箱子上面去，至少可以多支撑几个小时，怎么也比被囚禁起来好多了，我将其称为囚禁。但是，就算我真的熬到一两天之后，又有什么希望呢？最后还不是要在饥寒难耐中痛苦地死掉。我这样坚持了 4 个小时，每一刻都期盼着这是最后一刻。

four hours under these circumstances, expecting and indeed wishing every moment to be my last.

I have already told the reader that there were two strong staples fixed upon that side of my box which had no window, and into which the servant who used to carry me on horseback would put a leathern belt, and buckle it about his waist. Being in this disconsolate state, I heard or at least thought I heard some kind of grating noise on that side of my box where the staples were fixed, and soon after I began to fancy that the box was pulled or towed along in the sea; for I now and then felt a sort of tugging which made the waves rise near the tops of my windows, leaving me almost in the dark. This gave me some faint hopes of relief, although I was not able to imagine how it could be brought about. I ventured to unscrew one of my chairs, which were always fastened to the floor; and having made a hard shift to screw it down again directly under the slipping-board that I had lately opened, I mounted on the chair, and putting my mouth as near as I could to the hole, I called for help in a loud voice, and in all the languages I understood. I then fastened my handkerchief to a stick I usually carried, and thrusting it up the hole, waved it several times in the air, that if any boat or ship were near, the seamen might

读者已经知道，我的小箱子没有窗户的那一面有两个牢固的锁环，常常带我出去骑马的仆人总是把这个锁环穿在皮带上，再绑到腰间。我正在烦恼，忽然听到，至少我自以为听到了，箱子装锁环的那面有摩擦声。我开始幻想，我的箱子被什么东西拖拽着在海面上移动，因为我不时感觉到在一种牵引力的作用下，升起的浪花几乎溅到了箱子顶部的窗户上，我几乎陷入了黑暗。这给了我一些微弱的获救的希望，尽管我无法想象到底发生了什么事。我冒险将一只钉在地板上固定椅子的螺丝拧下来，费力把椅子搬到我刚拉开的木板的正下方，用螺丝重新在地上固定住。我爬上去，尽量把嘴伸到洞口，用我会的所有种语言大声呼救。接着我又把手帕系在我经常带在身边的手杖上，伸出洞口，在空中挥舞了好几下。附近若有大小船只经过，水手们见到了应该能猜到，一个可怜虫被关在了这个箱子里。

conjecture some unhappy mortal to be shut up in this box.

I found no effect from all I could do, but plainly perceived my closet to be moved along; and in the space of an hour, or better, that side of the box where the staples were, and had no window, struck against something that was hard. I apprehended it to be a rock, and found myself tossed more than ever. I plainly heard a noise upon the cover of my closet, like that of a cable, and the grating of it as it passed through the ring. I then found myself hoisted up by degrees at least three foot higher than I was before. Whereupon I again thrust up my stick and handkerchief, calling for help till I was almost hoarse. In return to which, I heard a great shout repeated three times, giving me such transports of joy as are not to be conceived but by those who feel them. I now heard a trampling over my head, and somebody calling through the hole with a loud voice in the *English* tongue: If there be anybody below let them speak. I answered, I was an *Englishman*, drawn by ill fortune into the greatest calamity that ever any creature underwent, and begged, by all that was moving, to be delivered out of the dungeon I was in. The voice replied, I was safe, for my box was fastened to their ship; and the carpenter should immediately come, and saw an hole in the

我感觉自己的所有努力都无济于事，不过明显可以感觉到箱子在移动。大概过了一个小时或者更久，箱子没有窗户、安着锁环的那一面碰到一个硬物。我想恐怕是一块礁石。这时我感到比之前颠簸得更严重了。我清晰地听到有响声从箱子顶上传来，有点像缆绳摩擦铁环的声音。接着我感觉自己在逐渐上升，至少升了 3 英尺。于是我又伸出手杖和手帕，大喊救命，直到嗓音沙哑。外面传来 3 声响亮的回答，终于有人听到了我的呼救，这令我万分惊喜，不曾身临其境的人永远也无法体会我当时的心情。我听到头顶传来脚步声，有人用英语冲着洞口大声喊道："有人在下面吗？说句话！"我回答说我是英国人，不幸遭到了百年不遇的厄运。我请求他们快救我出去。那声音回答我说，现在没事了，他们已经把我的箱子拴到了他们的船上，木匠很快会过来，他会在箱顶锯一个大洞，然后拉我出来。我说不用，那太浪费时间了，只要一名水手用手指钩住铁环，把箱子提上船，送到船长室去就可以了。有人听到我说得这么疯狂以为我疯了，有的捧腹大笑。我的确根本没意识到，现在和我在一起的这帮人的身材和力气都跟我相当。木匠来了，几分钟

cover, large enough to pull me out. I answered, that was needless, and would take up too much time, for there was no more to be done, but let one of the crew put his finger into the ring, and take the box out of the sea into the ship, and so into the captain's cabin. Some of them upon hearing me talk so wildly thought I was mad; others laughed; for indeed it never came into my head that I was now got among people of my own stature and strength. The carpenter came, and in a few minutes sawed a passage about four foot square, then let down a small ladder, upon which I mounted, and from thence was taken into the ship in a very weak condition.

就锯开了一个 4 英尺的口子。接着他们放下一个小梯子，我爬到了船上。此时我已经极其虚弱。

The sailors were all in amazement, and asked me a thousand questions, which I had no inclination to answer. I was equally confounded at the sight of so many pygmies, for such I took them to be, after having so long accustomed mine eyes to the monstrous objects I had left. But the captain, Mr. *Thomas Wilcocks*, an honest worthy *Shropshire* man, observing I was ready to faint, took me into his cabin, gave me a cordial to comfort me, and made me *turn in* upon his own bed, advising me to take a little rest, of which I had great need. Before I went to sleep I gave him to understand that I had some valuable furniture in my box too good to be lost; a

水手们全都非常吃惊，问了我成千上万的问题，我却没有力气回答。长期以来我已经看惯了那些刚刚和我分别的巨人们，现在突然见到这么多和我一样身材矮小的人，觉得他们都像侏儒一样，于是有些惊慌失措。可是船长托马斯·威尔柯克斯先生是个忠诚高尚的什罗普郡人，他看我快要晕了，就把我带进他的船舱，给我服了强心剂让我舒服些，又让我躺在他的床上小睡一会儿，这正合我意。我临睡前告诉他，我的箱子里有几件珍贵的家具，扔掉就太可惜了：一张不错的吊床、一张精致的行军床、两把椅子、一张桌子，还有一个衣橱。

fine hammock, an handsome Field-Bed two chairs, a table, and a cabinet: That my closet was hung on all sides, or rather quilted with silk and cotton: that if he would let one of the crew bring my closet into his cabin, I would open it there before him, and show him my goods. The captain, hearing me utter these absurdities, concluded I was raving: however (I suppose to pacify me), he promised to give order as I desired, and going upon deck, sent some of his men down into my closet, from whence (as I afterwards found) they drew up all my goods, and stripped off the quilting; but the chairs, cabinet and bedstead being screwed to the floor, were much damaged by the ignorance of the seamen, who tore them up by force. Then they knocked off some of the boards for the use of the ship, and when they had got all they had a mind for, let the hull drop into the sea, which by reason of many breaches made in the bottom and sides, sunk to rights. And indeed I was glad not to have been a spectator of the havoc they made; because I am confident it would have sensibly touched me, by bringing former passages into my mind, which I had rather forgot.

小屋的四面都挂着，或者说垫着厚厚的丝绸和棉絮。如果他能派名水手把我的箱子弄到他舱里来，我会当面打开箱子，给他看那些家具。船长听了我这些荒谬的话，推测我是在胡言乱语，但是（我想他当时可能是为了安慰我），他还是答应派人去照我的意思办。他走上甲板，派几个人去我的箱子里搬出所有的东西，扯掉了垫在墙壁上的所有东西（后来我才知晓）。不过椅子、衣橱还有床架都用螺丝钉固定在了地板上，这些无知的水手们只知道用力拽，结果大部分都弄坏了。他们又敲下几块木板，带回船上以备后用，拿走所有他们认为有用的东西后，这个空箱子就被他们扔进了大海。因为四壁和底部有很多缝隙，箱子立刻沉没了。说实话，我很庆幸自己没有亲眼目睹他们的这场破坏。因为我相信，回忆起这一个个过往的片段，我一定会感慨万千，我宁可将其忘记。

I slept some hours, but perpetually disturbed with dreams of the place I had left, and the dangers I had escaped. However, upon waking I found myself

我一睡就是好几个小时，一直不停地做梦，梦见离开的那个地方，梦见自己遭遇的种种灾难。但是醒过来之后，就感觉自己恢复了

much recovered. It was now about eight o'clock at night, and the captain ordered supper immediately, thinking I had already fasted too long. He entertained me with great kindness, observing me not to look wildly, or talk inconsistently; and when we were left alone, desired I would give him a relation of my travels, and by what accident I came to be set adrift in that monstrous wooden chest. He said, that about twelve o'clock at noon, as he was looking through his glass, he spied it at a distance, and thought it was a sail, which he had a mind to make, being not much out of his course, in hopes of buying some biscuit, his own beginning to fall short. That upon coming nearer, and finding his error, he sent out his long-boat to discover what I was; that his men came back in a fright, swearing they had seen a Swimming House. That he laughed at their folly, and went himself in the boat, ordering his men to take a strong cable along with them. That the weather being calm, he rowed round me several times, observed my windows, and wire lattices that defenced them. That he discovered two staples upon one side, which was all of boards, without any passage for light. He then commanded his men to row up to that side, and fastening a cable to one of the staples, ordered them to tow my chest (as they called it) towards the ship. When

很多。这时已是晚上 8 点左右了，船长猜我也许很久没吃东西了，于是马上吩咐开饭。他看我不像是疯子，说起话来也有条有理，就十分友善地招待了我。当只有我们两人时，他要我跟他说说自己旅行的经过，我是怎么跑到那只巨大的木头箱子里，又漂到了海上。他说，中午 12 点左右，他正拿着望远镜瞭望，忽然发现远处有个物体，起初以为是艘帆船，见离他的航线不远，想到自己船上的饼干快吃完了，或许能从那艘船上买些回来。船慢慢靠近，他才发现自己弄错了，于是派人坐小船去看个究竟。水手们惊恐地划回来，发誓说看到了一座移动的房屋。他笑他们太愚蠢，于是亲自乘坐小船去查看，并让随行的水手们带上一根结实的缆绳。当时风平浪静，他围着我划了好几圈，看到箱子上的窗户和保护窗户的铁框，又发现箱子有一面全由木板制成，没有窗户，却有两个锁环。他命令水手们划到那面，把缆绳系在其中的一只锁环上，拖着我的柜子（他称其为柜子）划向大船。到了船边，他下令把一根缆绳系在箱顶的铁环上，然后用滑车将箱子吊起来。可是全体水手一起用力，也只吊起了两三英尺高。他说他们看见我伸出洞口的手杖和手帕，推断肯定有倒霉人被关在那洞里了。我问他刚发现我时，他和

it was there, he gave directions to fasten another cable to the ring fixed in the cover, and to raise up my chest with pullies, which all the sailors were not able to do above two or three foot. He said they saw my stick and handkerchief thrust out of the hole, and concluded, that some unhappy men must be shut up in the cavity. I asked whether he or the crew had seen any prodigious birds in the air about the time he first discovered me. to which he answered, that discoursing this matter with the sailors while I was asleep, one of them said he had *observed* three eagles flying towards the north, but remarked nothing of their being larger than the usual size, which I suppose must be imputed to the great height they were at: and he could not guess the reason of my question. I then asked the captain how far he reckoned we might be from land; he said, by the best computation he could make, we were at least an hundred leagues. I assured him, that he must be mistaken by almost half, for I had not left the country from whence I came above two hours before I dropped into the sea. Whereupon he began again to think that my brain was disturbed, of which he gave me a hint, and advised me to go to bed in a cabin he had provided. I assured him I was well refreshed with his good entertainment and company, and as much in my senses as ever I was in my

水手们是否发现天上有巨鸟飞过。他回答说，在我睡着的这段时间，他已经同水手们谈论过这件事，其中有一个说他看到3只鹰向北飞去了，但他并没说那只鹰比普通的大。我想肯定是因为这些鹰飞得太高的缘故。他不知道我为什么这么问。我接着问，他估计我们现在离陆地多远。他说，据最精确的测量，至少有100海里。我说，他几乎多算了一半的路程，因为我离开出发地还不到2个小时就掉进了海里。一听这话，他又开始怀疑我精神有问题了。他建议我到他为我预备的一间舱房里去休息。我让他放心，他如此热情地招待我、陪我说话，我的精神基本上已经恢复了，思维也灵敏得跟正常状态一样。他换上一副严肃的表情，说想坦白地问我一句，我神志不清是否因为犯了重罪，某个君王下令惩处我，将我锁在那个柜子里，像有的国家那样，将重罪犯放在破船里推到海上漂浮，而且不给任何食物。他说虽然后悔救上来这么一个坏蛋，可他还是会一诺千金，把我安全地送到他们的下一站。他又加了几句，说越来越怀疑我了，从我一开始对水手们说的胡话，到后来对他说的，再加上我的小屋或者说柜子，还有我吃晚饭时古怪的言谈举止，他越来越觉得我不像好人了。

life. He then grew serious, and desired to ask me freely whether I were not troubled in mind by the consciousness of some enormous crime, for which I was punished by the command of some prince, by exposing me in that chest, as great criminals in other countries have been forced to sea in a leaky vessel without provisions: for, although he should be sorry to have taken so ill a man into his ship, yet he would engage his word to set me safe on shore in the first port where we arrived. He added, that his suspicions were much increased by some very absurd speeches I had delivered at first to the sailors, and afterwards to himself, in relation to my closet or chest, as well as by my odd looks and behaviour while I was at supper.

I begged his patience to hear me tell my story, which I faithfully did, from the last time I left *England* to the moment he first discovered me. And, as truth always forceth its way into rational minds; so, this honest worthy gentleman, who had some tincture of learning and very good sense, was immediately convinced of my candour and veracity. But further to confirm all I had said, I entreated him to give order that my cabinet should be brought, of which I had the key in my pocket (for he had already informed me how the seamen disposed of my closet), I

我请求他耐心听完我的故事。于是我实事求是地讲起来，从自己最后一次离开英国讲到他发现我那一刻。事实总是能说服有理性的人。这位正直高尚的先生有些见识，判断力也很强，很快就相信了我说的话。但为了进一步确定，我请求他下令让水手们把我的橱柜搬过来，我的口袋里有钥匙（他已经告诉我水手们如何处理我的箱子了）。我当场打开，向他展示我在那个国家收集到的那点儿宝贝。就是那样一个国家，我竟然被奇迹般地救了出来。其中有一把我用国

opened it in his presence, and showed him the small collection of rarities I made in the country from whence I had been so strangely delivered. There was the comb I had contrived out of the stumps of the king's beard, and another of the same Material, but fixed into a paring of her Majesty's Thumb-nail, which served for the Back. There was a collection of needles and pins from a foot to half a yard long. four wasp stings, like joiners' tacks: some combings of the queen's hair: a gold ring which one day she made me a present of in a most obliging manner, taking it from her little finger, and throwing it over my head like a collar. I desired the captain would please to accept this ring in return of his civilities, which he absolutely refused. I showed him a Corn that I had cut off with my own Hand from a Maid of Honour's Toe; it was about the Bigness of a *Kentisb Pippin*, and grown so hard, that when I returned to *England*, I got it hollowed into a Cup and set in Silver. Lastly I desired him to see the breeches I had then on, which were made of a mouse's skin.

王的胡楂制成的梳子；还有一把同材质，但梳子背用皇后剪下来的一片大拇指指甲做成的；还有几根缝衣针和别针，长度介于一英尺到半码之间；4 根近似于木匠用的平头钉的黄蜂刺；几根皇后的头发；以及一枚金戒指，是皇后某天非常亲切地送给我的，她从自己小指上取下，扔过来直接套到了我头上。为了答谢船长，我提议把这枚戒指送给他，可他一口回绝了。我又拿出一只鸡眼给他看，那是我亲手从一位皇宫婢女脚趾上割下来的。它有肯特郡的苹果那么大，非常坚硬，我回国后将其挖空做成了一只杯子，还镶了白银。最后我还请他参观了当时我身上所穿的裤子，是由一只老鼠的皮制成的。

I could force nothing on him but a footman's tooth, which I observed him to examine with great curiosity, and found he had a fancy for it. He received it with abundance of thanks, more than such a trifle could deserve. It was drawn by an

他不肯接受我的任何礼物，只要了一颗仆人牙齿。我注意到他非常惊奇地打量这颗牙齿，认为他很喜爱，就热情地一再表示要送给他。他接过后不停地道谢，对这么一件小礼物有点小题大做了。那本

unskilful surgeon in a mistake from one of *Glumdalclitch's* men, who was afflicted with the toothache, but it was as sound as any in his head. I got it cleaned, and put it in my cabinet. It was about a foot long, and four inches in diameter.

是一颗好牙，是一位技术不熟练的外科医生为格兰姆达尔克立契的一个牙痛的仆人拔的，却不小心拔错了。我把它清洗干净，收进了橱里。那颗牙齿长约 1 英尺，直径 4 英寸。

The captain was very well satisfied with this plain relation I had given him; and said, he hoped when we returned to *England*, I would oblige the world by putting it in paper, and making it public. My answer was, that I thought we were already overstocked with books of travels: that nothing could now pass which was not extraordinary, wherein I doubted some authors less consulted truth than their own vanity or interest, or the diversion of ignorant readers, that my story could contain little besides common events, without those ornamental descriptions of strange plants, trees, birds, and other animals, or of the barbarous customs and idolatry of savage people, with which most writers abound. However, I thanked him for his good opinion, and promised to take the matter into my thoughts.

船长相信了我这一番简要的叙述。他说希望回国后，我能将这一切记录下来公开出版。我回答说，我想我们的游记已经太多了，如果不写得离奇些根本无法出版。因此我觉得一些作家根本不考虑真实与否，只专注于自身的虚荣和利润，一心只为了吸引庸俗读者的兴趣。我的故事里却只有一些非常平凡的事情，其他很少涉及。我没办法像其他很多作家那样，总是滥用词语，描写各种奇特的草、木、鸟、兽，或者未开化民族的奇风异俗、邪神崇拜，等等。然而，我还是很感谢他的建议，并认真考虑写作的事宜。

He said he wondered at one thing very much, which was to hear me speak so loud, asking me whether the king or queen of that country were thick of hearing. I told him it was what I had been used to for above two years past, and that I admired as much at the voices of him and his men,

他说，有一件事他感到很不可思议，就是我的音量过大，他问我那个国家的国王和皇后是否耳聋。我告诉他，过去的这两年多里我一直这样大声说话。我很钦佩他和水手们说话声音小得就像悄悄话，但我还是能听清楚。我在那个国家同

who seemed to me only to whisper, and yet I could hear them well enough. But, when I spoke in that country, it was like a man talking in the street to another looking out from the top of a steeple, unless when I was placed on a table, or held in any person's hand. I told him I had likewise observed another thing, that when I first got into the ship, and the sailors stood all about me, I thought they were the most contemptible little creatures I had ever beheld. For, indeed, while I was in that little prince's country, I could never endure to look in a glass after my eyes had been accustomed to such prodigious objects, because the comparison gave me so despicable a conceit of myself. The captain said that while we were at supper, he observed me to look at everything with a sort of wonder, and that I often seemed hardly able to contain my laughter, which he knew not well how to take, but imputed it to some disorder in my brain. I answered, it was very true, and I wondered how I could forbear, when I saw his dishes of the size of a silver Three-pence, a leg of pork hardly a mouthful, a cup not so big as a nutshell: and so I went on, describing the rest of his Household-stuff and provisions after the same manner. For although the queen had ordered a little equipage of all things necessary, while I was in her service, yet

别人说话时，就相当于一个站在大街上的人跟另一个在教堂的塔顶的人说话一样，除非他们把我放在桌子上，或者放在某个人的手上才不用那么大声。我告诉他，我还注意到一点，就是我刚被救上来时，所有的水手们都站在我四周，我觉得他们是我所见过的最可鄙的小人。这主要是由于我在那个王国时，已经很久没照镜子了，因为眼睛已经习惯了那些体积巨大的对象，一照镜子就觉得自己和他们相比实在太渺小了。船长说在我们一起吃晚饭的时候，他发现我无论看到什么都是一副吃惊的表情，似乎常常忍俊不禁，他百思不得其解，就估计我精神有问题。我回答说，他观察得很对。我看到他们的盘子只有三便士银币那么大，一条猪腿还不足一口，酒杯没胡桃壳大，怎会不觉得好笑？我接着又将他们的其余家具和食物如此描述了一番。虽然皇后命人给我准备了一整套小型的生活用品，我却只专注于自己周围的那些大物件儿，就像人们面对自己的错误的态度一样，我假装看不到自己的渺小。船长很快就听懂了我的玩笑，借用了一句古老的英国谚语来回复我，说怀疑我眼大肚子小。因为他发现，尽管我已经一天都没吃东西了，我的胃口却并不好。他还继续开玩笑说，他很乐意出100英镑看鹰怎么叼起我

my ideas were wholly taken up with what I saw on every side of me, and I winked at my own littleness as people do at their own faults. The captain understood my raillery very well, and merrily replied with the cold English proverb, that he doubted my eyes were bigger than my Belly, for he did not observe my stomach so good, although I had fasted all day; and continuing in his mirth, protested he would have gladly given an hundred pounds to have seen my closet in the eagle's bill, and afterwards in its fall from so great a height into the sea; which would certainly have been a most astonishing object, worthy to have the description of it transmitted to future ages: and the comparison of *Phaeton* was so obvious, that he could not forbear applying it, although I did not much admire the conceit.

的小屋，再从很高的天上将其丢进海里。他说那场面一定非常精彩，值得记录下来，流芳百世。那显然可以和法厄松的故事相媲美，不过我却不大喜欢他这样夸大其词。

The captain having been at *Tonquin* was in his return to *England* driven North eastward to the latitude of 44 degrees, and of longitude 143. But meeting a Trade wind two days after I came on board him, we sailed Southward a long time, and coasting New-Holland kept our course west-south-west, and then south-south-west till we doubled the *Cape of Good Hope*. Our voyage was very prosperous, but I shall not trouble the reader with a journal of it. The captain

船长之前去了东京，此时正要返回英国。船正驶向东北方，方位是北纬 44°，东经 143°。但我刚上船两天就遇到了信风。我们向正南方向航行了很久，又沿新荷兰海岸航行，之后朝西南偏西方向走，又改为西南偏南方，最后绕过好望角。我们一路顺利，我就不再将每天的航行日记写下来浪费读者的时间和精力了。船长曾在一两个港口靠岸，派人乘小船去采购食品和淡水。不过我一直到唐斯才下船。

called in at one or two ports and sent in his long-boat for provisions and fresh water, but I never went out of the ship till we came into the Downs, which was on the 3d day of *June* 1706, about nine months after my escape. I offered to leave my goods in security for payment of my freight; but the captain protested he would not receive one farthing. We took kind leave of each other, and I made him promise he would come to see me at my house in *Redriff*. I hired a horse and guide for five shillings, which I borrowed of the captain.

我们于1706年6月3日到达唐斯，这时我已经脱险快9个月了。我提出抵押我那些东西作为搭乘他们的船的船费，但船长坚决表示一分不要。我们依依惜别，他答应以后会到我在瑞德里夫的家来拜访。我向船长借了5先令，雇了一匹马和一位向导回家去了。

As I was on the road, observing the littleness of the houses, the trees, the cattle and the people, I began to think myself in *Lilliput*. I was afraid of trampling on every traveller I met, and often called aloud to have them stand out of the way, so that I had like to have gotten one or two broken heads for my impertinence.

回家的路上，我注意到房屋、树木、牲口和人都很小，不禁开始怀疑自己在利利普特国。每遇到一个行人，我都担心会踩到他们，常常大喊让他们让开道路。我如此无礼，以至于有一两次差点被人打破了脑袋。

When I came to my own house, for which I was forced to inquire, one of the servants opened the door, I bent down to go in (like a goose under a gate) for fear of striking my head. My wife ran out to embrace me, but I stooped lower than her knees, thinking she could otherwise never be able to reach my mouth. My daughter kneeled to ask me blessing, but I could not see her till she arose, having been so long used to stand with my head and eyes erect

一番打听之后我终于回到了自己的家。一个用人开门，我怕碰到头，像鹅进窝那样弯着腰走进门去。妻子跑出来和我拥抱，但是我一直把腰弯到比她的膝盖还低，否则总觉得她够不着我的嘴。我的女儿跪下来向我行礼，可是直到她站起来，我才发现她，这时才走上前一手将她拦腰抱起。这都是因为我这么长时间以来已经习惯于站着仰头看60英尺以上的高处的缘故。

to above sixty foot; and then I went to take her up with one hand, by the waist. I looked down upon the servants and one or two friends who were in the house, as if they had been pygmies, and I a giant. I told my wife she had been too thrifty, for I found she had starved herself and her daughter to nothing. In short, I behaved myself so unaccountably, that they were all of the captain's opinion when he first saw me, and concluded I had lost my wits. This I mention as an instance of the great power of habit and prejudice.

我俯视着用人们以及来我家做客的一两个朋友，似乎他们都是矮子，而我则是一个巨人。我说妻子太节俭了，把自己和女儿都饿得快看不见了。总之，我的举止令人无法理解，大家都像船长初次见到我时一样，断定我神经错乱了。我说这些是为了证明，惯性和偏见具有强大的影响力。

In a little time I and my family and friends came to a right understanding: but my wife protested I should never go to sea any more; although my evil destiny so ordered that she had not power to hinder me, as the reader may know hereafter. In the mean time I here conclude the second part of my unfortunate voyages.

很快，我和亲朋好友之间就能够顺利交流了，可是我妻子坚决阻止我再去航海。不过我天生就是无法安顿下来的人，她也无法阻拦我。这一点读者以后就知道了。我的不幸的航行经历的第二部分也就到此为止了。

PART III. A VOYAGE TO LAPUTA, BALNIBARBI, LUGGNAGG, GLUBBDUBDRIB, AND JAPAN

第三部分　拉普他、巴尔尼巴比、拉格奈格、格勒大锥、日本游记

CHAPTER 1

第一章

The Author sets out on his Third Voyage. is taken by Pirates. The Malice of a Dutchman. His Arrival at an island. He is received into Laputa.

作者起程进行第三次航海时，被海盗劫持。一个心肠歹毒的荷兰人。他来到一座小岛，进入拉普他。

I had not been at home above ten days, when Captain *William Robinson*, a *Cornish* man, commander of the *Hope-well*, a stout ship of three hundred tons, came to my house. I had formerly been surgeon of another ship where he was master, and a fourth part owner, in a voyage to the *Levant*; He had always treated me more like a brother than an inferior officer, and hearing of my arrival made me a visit, as I apprehended only out of friendship, for nothing passed more than what is usual after long absences. But repeating his visits often, expressing his joy to find me in good health, asking whether I were now settled for life, adding that he intended a voyage to the *East Indies*, in two months; at last he *plainly* invited me, though with some apologies, to be surgeon of the ship; that I should have another surgeon under me beside our two mates; that my salary should be double to the usual pay; and that having

我在家待了不到 10 天，康沃尔郡人威廉·罗宾逊——载重 300 吨的大船“好望号”的船长——就来拜访了。我曾在他的一艘开往黎凡特的船上当过外科医生，他有那艘船 1/4 的股份。他待我似兄弟而不像下属。听说我航行归来，他就来探望我，我本觉得这不过是出于友情，毕竟这么长时间没见，拜访一下并没什么不寻常。可是他频繁地来我家，说见我身体康健很开心，问我现在是否打算安稳地生活。他特别说明自己正打算这两个月去东印度一带航海。经过一番客套，最后他坦率地邀请我去船上当外科医生。他说，除两名助手外，还有一名外科医生做我的副手，他还会付我双倍薪水。他知晓我对航海事务经验丰富，至少和他不分伯仲，所以他无论做任何决定都会认真听取我的意见，好像我俩共同指挥这艘船一样。

experienced my knowledge in sea-affairs to be at least equal to his, he would enter into any engagement to follow my advice, as much as if I had shared in the command.

He said so many other obliging things, and I knew him to be so honest a man, that I could not reject this proposal; the thirst I had of seeing the world, notwithstanding my past misfortunes, continuing as violent as ever. The only difficulty that remained, was to persuade my wife, whose consent however I at last obtained by the prospect of advantage she proposed to her children.

We set out the 5th day of *August*, 1706 and arrived at Fort *St. George*, the 11th of *April* 1707. We stayed there three weeks to refresh our crew, many of whom were sick. From thence we went to *Tonquin*, where the captain resolved to continue some time, because many of the goods he intended to buy were not ready, nor could he expect them to be dispatched in some months. Therefore in hopes to defray some of the charges he must be at, he bought a sloop, loaded it with several sorts of goods, wherewith the *Tonquinese* usually trade to the neighbouring islands, and putting fourteen men on board, whereof three were of the country, he appointed me master of the sloop, and gave me power to traffic for two Months, while he transacted his affairs at *Tonquin*.

他说了很多客气话，我也知道他为人诚恳，没法拒绝这一邀请了。我要看世界的渴望虽历尽种种不幸，但还与以前一样强烈。所剩的唯一难处就是说服妻子。不过，考虑到儿女们的前途，她最终还是同意了。

我们于 1706 年 8 月 5 日起航，1707 年 4 月 11 日到达军事要塞圣佐治。因为不少船员病倒了，我们在那里停留了 3 周休息整顿。我们从那里开往东京。由于打算购买的一些东西可能在几个月内都很难买到，因此，船长决定在那里继续停靠一段时间。为了支付一部分必要的开支，他买了一艘单桅帆船，在船上囤积了一些东京人和附近岛上居民经常买卖的货物，当时他的船上有 14 名水手，其中 3 名是当地人。他任命我为船长，让我负责近两个月之内的贸易。在这段时间里，他在东京处理自己的事务。

We had not sailed above three days, when a great storm arising, we were driven five days to the north-north-east, and then to the east, after which we had fair weather, but still with a pretty strong gale from the west. Upon the tenth day we were chased by two pirates, who soon overtook us; for my sloop was so deep loaden, that she sailed very slow; neither were we in a condition to defend ourselves.

我们起航不过3天，一场风暴就袭来了。我们向东北偏北方向漂流了5天，后又转东。那时晴空万里，西风强劲。到了第十天，我们被两艘海盗船盯上了，因为我们的单桅帆船负重太大，航行速度慢，根本无法自卫，他们很快就追上了我们。

We were boarded about the same time by both the pirates, who entered furiously at the head of their men, but finding us all prostrate upon our faces (for so I gave order), they pinioned us with strong ropes, and setting guard upon us, went to search the sloop.

这两艘海盗船上的海盗们跟随他们的首领，凶神恶煞地几乎同时登上我们的船时，却发现我们全体俯卧在船板上（这是我的命令）。于是他们用结实的绳子把我们绑起来，留人看守，然后开始搜寻船上的货物。

I observed among them a *Dutchman*, who seemed to be of some authority, though he was not commander of either ship. He knew us by our countenances to be *Englishmen*, and jabbering to us in his own language, swore we should be tied back to back, and thrown into the sea. I spoken *Dutch* tolerably well; I told him who we were, and begged him in consideration of our being Christians and Protestants, of neighbouring countries, in strict alliance, that he would move the captains to take some pity on us. This inflamed his rage, he repeated his threatenings, and turning to his

我注意到这帮人中有一个荷兰人。尽管他并非任何一艘船的头领，但看起来似乎颇有些威信。他根据外表推断我们是英国人，就用荷兰语嘟囔，声称要把我们背对背捆起来扔到海里。我精通荷兰语，就把我们的身份来历告诉他，又请求他，看在我们是基督徒和新教徒，而且荷兰和英国一衣带水的份儿上，帮我们向两位船长求情。这令他雷霆震怒，他再一次恐吓我们，还转身对同伙言辞激烈地说了一番。我猜他说的是日语，又时不时听他提到“基督徒”这个词。

companions, spoke with great vehemence, in the *Japanese* language, as I suppose, often using the word *Christianos*.

The largest of the two pirate ships was commanded by a *Japanese* captain, who spoke a little *Dutch*, but very imperfectly. He came up to me, and after several questions, which I answered in great humility, he said we should not die. I made the captain a very low bow, and then turning to the Dutchman, said, "I was sorry to find more mercy in a heathen, than in a brother christian. But I had soon reason to repent those foolish words; for that malicious reprobate, having often endeavoured in vain to persuade both the captains that I might be thrown into the sea (which they would not yield to after the promise made me, that I should not die), however prevailed so far as to have a punishment inflicted on me, worse, in all human appearance than death itself. My men were sent by an equal division into both the Pirate-Ships, and my sloop new manned. As to myself, it was determined that I should be set adrift, in a small canoe, with paddles and a sail, and four days' provisions, which last, the *Japanese* captain was so kind to double out of his own stores, and would permit no man to search me. I got down into the canoe, while the *Dutchman* standing upon the deck, loaded me with all the curses and

较大的那艘海盗船的船长是一个日本人。他会一点荷兰语，但并不精通。他走到我面前，问了很多问题，我一一谦虚作答后，他说我们不会死。我向这位船长深深地鞠了一躬，接着转身对那荷兰人说："我感到非常失望，一个异教徒竟然比一个基督徒兄弟还要仁慈得多。"但是我很快就为自己说的这几句蠢话而后悔了，因为这个心肠歹毒的无赖三番五次企图说服两位船长把我扔进海里（他们既然已答应不会将我处死，就不会反悔）。但是他的劝说还是起了一定作用，他们要用一种更残酷的惩罚令我求死不能。我的船员被平均分作两队送上了海盗船，那艘单桅帆船则被他们的人占领。至于我，他们决定给我一只独木舟、桨、帆以及4天的给养，让我在海上自生自灭。那位心地善良的日本船长拿出自己的给养帮我多加了一倍，并且不准任何人对我搜身。我踏上独木舟，那个荷兰人还站在甲板上，用荷兰语中所有最恶毒的字眼向我破口大骂。

injurious terms his language could afford.

About an hour before we saw the pirates I had taken an observation, and found we were in the latitude of 46 N. and longitude 183. When I was at some distance from the pirates, I discovered by my Pocket Glass several islands to the south-east. I set up my sail, the wind being fair, with a design to reach the nearest of those islands, which I made a shift to do in about three hours. It was all rocky, however I got many birds' eggs; and striking fire I kindled some heath and dry seaweed, by which I roasted my eggs. I eat no other supper, being resolved to spare my provisions as much as I could. I passed the night under the shelter of a rock, strowing some heath under me, and slept pretty well.

The next day I sailed to another island, and thence to a third and fourth, sometimes using my sail, and sometimes my paddles. But not to trouble the reader with a particular account of my distresses, let it suffice that on the 5th day, I arrived at the last island in my sight, which lay south-south-east to the former.

This island was at a greater distance than I expected, and I did not reach it in less than five hours. I encompassed it almost round before I could find a convenient place to land in, which was a small creek, about three times the

在海盗船出现前大约一小时，我测量过方位，发现我们处于北纬46°，东经183°。离开海盗船一段距离后，我用袖珍望远镜发现东南方有几座小岛。我趁着顺风扬帆，想驶到最近的一座岛上去。我花了将近3个小时才抵达。岛上遍布岩石，但我还是捡到了许多鸟蛋。我打火点着石南草和干海藻烤熟了鸟蛋。晚饭我没再吃别的东西，因为我决定尽量节省随身的干粮。我躲在一块岩石下，把一些石南草铺在身下，就沉沉地睡去了。

第二天，我驶向另一座岛，接着又驶向第三座岛和第四座岛，我有时扬帆，有时划桨。我不一一细说当时的困难处境来令读者厌烦了。总之，第五天我抵达视野内的最后一座岛，它位于前面那些岛的东南偏南方向。

那座小岛比我想象的要远得多，我划了将近5个小时才到达。我围着这座小岛几乎绕了一圈，终于找到一个便于登陆的位置。那是一个小港湾，大约比我的独木舟宽3倍。岛上布满了岩石，只在岩石

wideness of my canoe. I found the island to be all rocky, only a little intermingled with tufts of grass, and sweet-smelling herbs. I took out my small provisions, and after having refreshed myself, I secured the remainder in a cave, whereof there were great numbers. I gathered plenty of eggs upon the rocks, and got a quantity of dry seaweed, and parched grass, which I designed to kindle the next day, and roast my eggs as well as I could (for I had about me my flint, steel, match, and burning-glass.) I lay all night in the cave where I had lodged my provisions. My bed was the same dry grass and seaweed which I intended for fuel. I slept very little, for the disquiets of my mind prevailed over my weariness, and kept me awake. I considered how impossible it was to preserve my life, in so desolate a place, and how miserable my end must be. yet found myself so listless and desponding, that I had not the heart to rise, and before I could get spirits enough to creep out of my cave, the day was far advanced. I walked a while among the rocks, the sky was perfectly clear, and the sun so hot, that I was forced to turn my face from it: when all on a sudden it became obscured, as I thought, in a manner very different from what happens by the interposition of a cloud. I turned back, and perceived a vast opaque body between me and the sun,

缝间散布着星星点点的青草和散发着香味的药草。我把自己那少得可怜的食物拿出来，补充了一下能量，将剩下的全都藏到一个洞穴里，那种洞在这座岛上有很多。我在岩石上捡了许多鸟蛋，又找来大量干海藻和干草。如果可能，我准备第二天点火烤鸟蛋用（我随身带有火石、火镰、火柴和取火镜）。一整晚我就躺在储存食物的那个洞里，预备点火用的干草和干海藻就是我的床。我没怎么睡着，内心的烦躁不安战胜了疲倦，令我睡意全无。我想，在这么荒凉的地方我怎么可能活下去，最后一定会惨不忍睹。我无精打采、意志消沉，根本无心起床。等我振作精神从岩石下面爬出来的时候，天已经大亮了。我在岩石间散了一会儿步，天空澄净无云，阳光晒得发烫，我不得不转过脸去背对着太阳。这时天空突然被什么东西遮住了，却并非云朵飘来的感觉。我转过身，只见一个不透明的巨大物体挡在了我和太阳之间，正向着我所在的小岛飞来。那物体看起来大约高 2 英里，太阳被遮了六七分钟，但我并没发觉变得凉爽了，天色也没变得更暗，仿佛我此时正站在山的背阴一侧。那个物体离我越来越近，看起来像个固体，底部平坦光滑，映着下面的海水闪闪发光。我站在离海边约 200 码的高处，看着这个巨大

moving forwards towards the island: it seemed to be about two miles high, and hid the sun six or seven minutes, but I did not observe the air to be much colder, or the sky more darkened, than if I had stood under the shade of a mountain. As it approached nearer over the place where I was, it appeared to be a firm substance, the bottom flat, smooth, and shining very bright from the reflection of the sea below. I stood upon a height about two hundred yards from the shore, and saw this vast body descending almost to a parallel with me, at less than an English mile distance. I took out my Pocket-Perspective, and could plainly discover numbers of people moving up and down the sides of it, which appeared to be sloping, but what those people where doing, I was not able to distinguish.

的物体在离我相距不到半英里处缓缓降落，落到跟我差不多的高度。我拿出袖珍望远镜，清楚地看到很多人正在那个物体的边缘上下移动。那个边缘像个斜坡，但至于那些人在做什么，我就看不清了。

The natural love of life gave me some inward motions of joy, and I was ready to entertain a hope, that this adventure might some way or other help to deliver me from the desolate place and condition I was in. But at the same time the reader can hardly conceive my astonishment, to behold an island in the air, inhabited by men, who were able (as it should seem) to raise or sink, or put it into progressive motion, as they pleased. But not being at that time in a disposition to Philosophize upon this phenomenon, I rather chose to observe

对生命的天然的热爱之情令我心花怒放。一种希望开始在我心里萌发，这个奇遇说不定能把我从走投无路的境遇中解救出来。不过同时，读者可能很难想象出我当时内心的讶异，看到一座小岛竟然飘在空中，而且有人居住，这些人能够（看起来像是）随意控制这座岛的升降、前进和后退。但是，我当时可没心思从哲学的角度对这个现象进行思考。我只想看看这个奇怪的物体会飞到哪里去，因为它仿佛停下来待了一会儿。很快地，它

what course the island would take, because it seemed for a while to stand still. Yet soon after it advanced nearer, and I could see the sides of it, encompassed with several gradations of galleries, and stairs, at certain intervals, to descend from one to the other. In the lowest gallery, I beheld some people fishing with long angling rods, and others looking on. I waved my cap (for my hat was long since worn out) and my handkerchief towards the island; and upon its nearer approach, I called and shouted with the utmost strength of my voice; and then looking circumspectly, I beheld a crowd gathered to that side which was most in my view. I found by their pointing towards me and to each other, that they plainly discovered me, although they made no return to my shouting. But I could see four or five men running in great haste up the stairs to the top of the island, who then disappeared. I happened rightly to conjecture, that these were sent for orders to some person in authority upon this occasion.

离我更近了，我可以看见它的边缘围绕着一层层的走廊，每隔一段距离就有一段楼梯将这些走廊彼此连接。在底层的走廊上，有人拿着长长的钓竿钓鱼，还有些旁观者。我朝那座岛挥动便帽（我的礼帽早破了）和手帕。在它离我更近的时候，我就扯着嗓子大声喊叫。随后我留心看了看，只见岛上靠近我的这一侧聚集了一群人。我发现他们正朝着我互相指指点点，虽然他们并没有回应，但他们显然已经发现了我。而且我看到四五个人匆忙爬上楼梯跑到岛的最高层就消失了。据我的合理推测，这些人是去向统治者报告了。

The number of people increased, and in less than half an hour, the island was moved and raised in such a manner, that the lowest gallery appeared in a parallel of less then an hundred yards distance from the height where I stood. I then put myself in the most supplicating posture, and spoke in the humblest accent, but received

人越聚越多，不到半个小时，那座岛慢慢移动并上升，底层的走廊已与我所站的位置齐平，相距不到100码。于是我摆出极力恳求的姿势，语气极其谦卑，但无人回应。岛上离我最近的那几个人似乎有些地位，这是我从他们的衣着推测的。他们不时地看向我，彼此间认

no answer. Those who stood nearest over-against me, seemed to be persons of distinction, as I supposed by their habit. They conferred earnestly with each other, looking often upon me. At length one of them called out in a clear, polite, smooth dialect, not unlike in sound to the *Italian*; and therefore I returned an answer in that language, hoping at least that the cadence might be more agreeable to his ears. Although neither of us understood the other, yet my meaning was easily known, for the people saw the distress I was in.

真商议。其中一个人拖着长调喊了一声，声音清晰悦耳，语气彬彬有礼，听起来有点像意大利语。因此我就用意大利语回答了一句，希望这种语调至少在他们听来更顺耳些。虽然我们的语言不通，但他们见我如此狼狈不堪，也很容易就能猜出我的意图。

They made signs for me to come down from the rock, and go towards the shore, which I accordingly did; and the flying island being raised to a convenient height, the verge directly over me, a chain was let down from the lowest gallery, with a seat fastened to the bottom, to which I fixed myself, and was drawn up by Pullies.

他们示意我走下岩石，到海边去。我照做了，那座飞岛上升到一定高度，边缘正对着我的头顶，他们从底层的走廊放下一条链子，链子末端拴着一个座位，我把自己固定在座位上，被他们用滑轮拉了上去。

CHAPTER 2

第二章

The Humours and Dispositions of the Laputians described. An Account of their learning. Of the King and his Court. The Author's Reception there. The Inhabitants subject to Fears and Disquietudes. An Account of the Women.

对拉普他人幽默性情的描述。他们的学术情况。关于国王和整个朝廷。作者在那里的待遇。当地居民惊恐不已。妇女的地位。

At my alighting I was surrounded by a crowd of people, but those who stood nearest seemed to be of better quality. They beheld me with all the marks and circumstances of wonder, neither indeed was I much in their debt; having never till then seen a race of mortals so singular in their shapes, habits, and countenances. Their heads were all reclined either to the right, or the left; one of their eyes turned inward, and the other directly up to the zenith. Their outward garments were adorned with the figures of suns, moons, and stars, interwoven with those of fiddles, flutes, harps, trumpets, guitars, harpsicords, and many more instruments of music, unknown to us in Europe. I observed here and there many in the habit of servants, with a blown bladder fastened like a flail to the end of a short stick, which they carried in their hands. In each

登上飞岛后，我就被一层层的人围住了，不过站在我面前的这几个人似乎有些身份。他们一脸惊奇地端详我。事实上，我比他们更惊奇，因为我从未见过这样一个身材、习俗和相貌都如此古怪的种族。他们的头全部向左或者向右倾斜；一只眼睛内翻，另一只冲着天。他们的外衣上有太阳、月亮和星星的图案；还交织着一些提琴、长笛、竖琴、小号、吉他、羽管键琴，以及许多其他的我在欧洲见所未见的乐器图案。我注意到周围有许多仆人装扮的人，每人手里拿一根一头带有膨胀气囊的短棍，就像一把连枷。每个气囊里都有一点儿干豌豆或者小石子儿（这是我后来得知的）。他们用这些气囊不时地拍打自己旁边人的嘴巴和耳朵，这做法令我百思不得其解。看起来好像这些人正陷入深思，除非对他们的发

bladder was a small quantity of dried peas or little pebbles (as I was afterwards informed). With these bladders they now and then flapped the mouths and ears of those who stood near them, of which practice I could not then conceive the meaning; It seems, the minds of these people are so taken up with intense speculations, that they neither can speak, nor attend to the discourses of others, without being roused by some external taction upon the organs of speech and hearing; for which reason, those persons who are able to afford it always keep a *flapper* (the original is *climenole*) in their family, as one of their domestics, nor ever walk abroad or make visits without him. And the business of this officer is, when two, three, or more persons are in company, gently to strike with his bladder the mouth of him who is to speak, and the right ear of him or them to whom the speaker addresseth himself. This *flapper* is likewise employed diligently to attend his master in his walks, and upon occasion to give him a soft flap on his eyes, because he is always so wrapped up in cogitation, that he is in manifest danger of falling down every precipice, and bouncing his head against every post, and in the streets, of justling others, or being justled himself into the kennel.

It was necessary to give the reader this

音及听觉器官进行一些外部的刺激，否则他们根本无法说话，更无法与别人交流。正因为如此，那些有能力支付这项开支的家庭就会雇用一名拍手（他们称之为“克里门农”）做家仆，无论是出行还是和朋友见面都将其带在身边。当两三个或者更多的人聚在一起时，这名侍从就负责先用拍子轻拍一下发言者的嘴，再拍一下听话者的右耳。这名拍手同样也要在主人走路时从旁服侍，不时轻拍一下主人的眼睛，否则主人很可能会由于陷入深思而不小心掉下悬崖或者将头撞在柱子上，就算走在大街上，也可能撞倒路人或者被别人撞进阴沟。

有必要让读者了解以下情况，

information, without which he would be at the same loss with me, to understand the proceedings of these people, as they conducted me up the stairs, to the top of the island, and from thence to the royal palace. While we were ascending, they forgot several times what they were about, and left me to myself, till their memories were again roused by their *flappers*; for they appeared altogether unmoved by the sight of my foreign habit and countenance, and by the shouts of the vulgar, whose thoughts and minds were more disengaged.

At last we entered the palace, and proceeded into the chamber of presence, where I saw the king seated on his throne, attended on each side by persons of prime quality. Before the throne, was a large table filled with globes and spheres, and mathematical instruments of all kinds. His majesty took not the least notice of us, although our entrance was not without sufficient noise, by the concourse of all persons belonging to the court. But, he was then deep in a problem, and we attended at least an hour, before he could solve it. There stood by him, on each side, a young page, with flaps in their hands, and when they saw he was at leisure, one of them gently struck his mouth, and the other his right ear, at which he started like one awaked on the sudden, and looking

否则大家可能会和我一样一头雾水，无法理解他们的行为。他们带我爬上楼梯，到达飞岛顶端，从那里直奔王宫。在往上爬的过程中，他们有好几次都忘记了自己在做什么，只把我一个人留在那里，直到在拍手们的帮助下才恢复了记忆。他们对我这个外来者的奇特服饰和相貌以及百姓们的惊呼声仿佛视而不见、听而不闻。这些百姓的神志看起来比他们要清醒得多。

终于进入王宫了，我们走进会客厅。只见一位国王正端坐在宝座上，两边侍立着达官贵人。宝座前的大桌子上摆满了地球仪、天球仪以及各种数学仪器。虽然我们的到来已经引起整个宫廷的喧哗，可国王陛下丝毫没有察觉到。他正在思索，当他解决了这个问题时，我们已经等候了一个小时。左右各有一名年轻的侍从手握拍子站在他旁边，一见他忙完，其中一名侍从就轻拍了一下他的嘴，另一名拍了拍他的右耳。国王似乎一下子醒悟过来，看向我以及挤在我周围的人群，想起之前有人向他通报过我们来这里的事情。他说了几句话，一个年轻人立即走到我身旁，手握着拍子轻拍了一下我的右耳。我拼命向他们做手势，表示我不需要拍子

towards me, and the company I was in, recollected the occasion of our coming, whereof he had been informed before. He spoke some words, whereupon immediately a young man with a flap came up to my side, and flapped me gently on the right ear, but I made signs, as well as I could, that I had no occasion for such an instrument; which as I afterwards found gave his majesty and the whole court a very mean opinion of my understanding. The king, as far as I could conjecture, asked me several questions, and I addressed myself to him in all the languages I had. When it was found, I could neither understand nor be understood, I was conducted by the king's order to an apartment in his palace (this prince being distinguished above all his predecessors for his hospitality to strangers), where two servants were appointed to attend me. My dinner was brought, and four persons of quality, whom I remembered to have seen very near the king's person, did me the honour to dine with me. We had two courses, of three dishes each. In the first course, there was a shoulder of mutton, cut into an equilateral triangle, a piece of beef into a Rhomboid, and a pudding into a cycloid. The second course was two ducks, trussed up in the form of fiddles; sausages and puddings resembling flutes and hautboys,

也能听到。后来我才知道，国王和满朝文武都因此对我的理解能力充满蔑视。我尽力推测国王问我的到底是什么问题，然后用自己懂的各种语言回答。后来发现我们都听不懂对方在说什么。国王下令带我去宫殿的客房（这位国王几乎比所有的前任国王都要热情好客），还吩咐两名侍从服侍我。他们很快送来晚餐，荣幸的是，陪我一起用餐的有4个人，我记得他们都是站在国王身边的贵族。晚餐共上了两次菜，每次3道。第一次的菜是一块等边三角形的羊肩肉、一块长菱形的牛肉和一块圆形布丁，第二次上了两只鸭子，被绑成小提琴的形状，此外还有一些长笛和双簧管形状的香肠与布丁，以及一块竖琴形状的小牛胸肉。侍者将面包切成圆锥形、圆柱形、平行四边形和一些其他几何形状。

and a breast of veal in the shape of a harp. The servants cut our bread into cones, cylinders, parallelograms, and several other mathematical figures.

While we were at dinner, I made bold to ask the names of several things in their language; and those noble persons, by the assistance of their *flappers*, delighted to give me answers, hoping to raise my admiration of their great abilities, if I could be brought to converse with them. I was soon able to call for bread, and drink, or whatever else I wanted.

After dinner my company withdrew, and a person was sent to me by the king's order, attended by a *flapper*. He brought with him pen, ink, and paper, and three or four books, giving me to understand by signs, that he was sent to teach me the language. We sat together four hours, in which time I wrote down a great number of words in columns, with the translations over against them. I likewise made a shift to learn several short sentences. for my tutor would order one of my servants to fetch something, to turn about, to make a bow, to sit, or to stand, or walk, and the like. Then I took down the sentence in writing. He showed me also in one of his books, the figures of the sun, moon, and stars, the zodiac, the tropics, and polar circles, together with the denominations of many Figures of Planes and solids. He

用餐时，我冒昧地询问了几种东西用他们的语言怎么说。那几个贵族在拍手们的协助下高兴地作答，他们希望我能同他们交流，以对他们那伟大的才能更加赞赏。我很快就学会怎样叫他们上面包、上酒以及其他我所需要的东西了。

晚饭后这4个人就告辞了。国王又派来一个人，这个人也有一个拍手陪侍左右。他还带来了钢笔、墨水、纸张和三四本书，打手势表示，他是奉命来教我学习他们的语言的。我们在一起待了4个小时，我列出了一大堆单词，并在旁边写上对应的翻译。我的老师让我的一个侍从做出取东西、转身、鞠躬、坐下、起立、走路等各种动作，于是我又设法学会了几个简短的句子，并把这些句子都写了下来。他又拿出一本书，将其上的太阳、月亮、星星、黄道、热带、南北极圈等图案指给我，还向我介绍了许多平面与立体图形的名称。他告诉我各种乐器的名称，并简单对其进行描述，还教给我演奏每一种乐器时所使用的一些专用术语。他离开以后，我将所有的单词连同译文全部

gave me the names and descriptions of all the musical instruments, and the general terms of art in playing on each of them. After he had left me, I placed all my words with their interpretations in alphabetical order. And thus in a few days, by the help of a very faithful memory, I got some insight into their language.

按音序重新排列了一遍。几天之后，凭着自己超强的记忆力，多少听懂了一些他们的语言。

The word, which I interpret the *flying* or *floating island*, is in the original, *Laputa*, whereof I could never learn the true etymology. *Lap* in the old obsolete language signifieth *high*, and *untuh* a governor, from which they say by corruption, was derived *Laputa* from *Lapuntuh*. But I do not approve of this derivation, which seems to be a little strained. I ventured to offer to the learned among them a conjecture of my own, that *Laputa* was *quasi lap outed*; *lap* signifying properly the dancing of the sun beams in the sea, and *outed*, a wing, which however I shall not obtrude, but submit to the judicious reader.

被我翻译成"飞岛"或"浮岛"的原词是"Laputa"（拉普他），我一直没弄明白这个词的词源。在古文中，"Lap"的意思是"高"。"untuh"的意思是"长官"。他们以讹传讹，认为"Laputa"这个词是由"Lapuntuh"派生出来的。我不赞成这种牵强的说法。我曾冒昧地向他们之中的博学之士提出我的观点："拉普他"有点像"quasi lap outed"，"Lap"可能有"阳光在海上舞蹈"的意思，而"outed"则代表"翅膀"。不过我并不想把自己的观点强加于人，还是把这个问题留给智慧的读者自己判断吧。

Those to whom the king had entrusted me, observing how ill I was clad, ordered a tailor to come next morning, and take my measure for a suit of clothes. This operator did his office after a different manner from those of his trade in *Europe*. He first took my altitude by a quadrant, and then with rule and compasses, described the dimensions and outlines of

受国王之命，照顾我的人见我的衣服破烂不堪，就为我预约了一名裁缝第二天来帮我量身裁衣。这位裁缝量身的方法和他那些欧洲同行们完全不同。他先用四分仪测量了我的身高，又用尺子和圆规测量了我身体的长、宽、厚度以及整体轮廓，他将这些数据都记载下来。6 天后衣服送来了，做工极差，

my whole body, all which he entered upon paper, and in six days brought my clothes very ill made, and quite out of shape, by happening to mistake a figure in the calculation. But my comfort was, that I observed such accidents very frequent and little regarded.

During my confinement for want of clothes, and by an indisposition that held me some days longer, I much enlarged my dictionary; and when I went next to court, was able to understand many things the king spoke, and to return him some kind of answers. His majesty had given orders that the island should move north-east and by east, to the vertical point over *Lagado*, the metropolis of the whole kingdom below upon the firm earth. It was about ninety leagues distant, and our voyage lasted four days and an half. I was not in the least sensible of the progressive motion made in the air by the island. On the second morning about eleven o'clock, the king himself in person, attended by his nobility, courtiers, and officers, having prepared all their musical instruments, played on them for three hours without intermission, so that I was quite stunned with the noise; neither could I possibly guess the meaning, till my tutor informed me. He said that the people of their island had their ears adapted to hear the music of the spheres, which always played at

而且完全走样了，因为他不小心计算错了一个数字。不过好在这种事我见多了，也就见怪不怪了。

衣服没做好的这几天，我略感不适，就在家多待了几天，词汇量也增加了不少。当我第二次进宫的时候，已经能听懂国王的很多话了，偶尔还能回几句话。国王已经下令让这个岛向东北偏东方向行进，停到王国的首都——拉格多的正上空位置。我们离那里大约有 90 里格，飞行了 4 天半。我一点也没有意识到这岛正在空中飞行。第二天上午 11 点左右，国王、随行的贵族及满朝官员已经准备好了他们所有的乐器，一连演奏了 3 个小时，乐声震耳欲聋。我百思不得其解，直到后来，我的老师向我解释了其中的原因。他说，住在这座岛上的百姓们已经听惯了来自宫廷的音乐，所以宫廷会定期演奏，届时所有人都会精心准备，演奏自己最拿手的乐器。

certain periods, and the court was now prepared to bear their part in whatever instrument they most excelled.

In our journey towards *Lagado* the capital city, his majesty ordered that the island should stop over certain towns and villages, from whence he might receive the petitions of his subjects. And to this purpose several packthreads were let down with small weights at the bottom. On these packthreads the people strung their petitions, which mounted up directly like the scraps of paper fastened by schoolboys at the end of the string that holds their kite. Sometimes we received wine and victuals from below, which were drawn up by pullies.

The knowledge I had in mathematics gave me great assistance in acquiring their phraseology, which depended much upon that science and music; and in the latter I was not unskilled. Their ideas are perpetually conversant in lines and figures. If they would, for example, praise the beauty of a woman or any other animal, they describe it by rhombs, circles, parallelograms, ellipses, and other geometrical terms, or by words of art drawn from music, needless here to repeat. I observed in the king's kitchen all sorts of mathematical and musical instruments, after the figures of which they cut up the joints that were served to

在飞向首都拉格多的途中，国王下令在某些城镇和乡村上空稍作停留，以听取下方百姓们的意见。为此，他们放下几根和包装线差不多粗的绳子，并在绳子末端系上小小的重物。百姓们将他们的请愿书系到这些绳子上，飞岛上的人就会就像小学生们放纸风筝时收线一样把绳子直接拉上来。有时我们还会收到从下面送上来的酒食，也是系在绳子上拉上来的。

我的数学知识为我学习当地用词提供了有力的帮助。这些词汇部分涉及数学和音乐，我对音乐也并非一窍不通。他们的想法永远和线、图形联系在一起。比如，他们想要赞美一个美貌的女子或者其他动物的时候，就会用菱形、圆形、平行四边形、椭圆形以及其他几何图形，或者一些音乐术语来描述，这里不再赘述。我发现御膳房里有各种各样的数学仪器和乐器，御厨们把大块的肉切成类似的形状，最后摆到国王的餐桌上去。

his majesty's table.

Their houses are very ill built, the walls bevil, without one right angle in any apartment, and this defect ariseth from the contempt they bear to practical geometry; which they despise as vulgar and mechanic; those instructions they give being too refined for the intellectuals of their workmen, which occasions perpetual mistakes. And although they are dextrous enough upon a piece of paper in the management of the rule, the pencil and the divider, yet in the common actions and behaviour of life, I have not seen a more clumsy, awkward, and unhandy people, nor so slow and perplexed in their conceptions upon all other subjects, except those of mathematics and music. They are very bad reasoners, and vehemently given to opposition, unless when they happen to be of the right opinion, which is seldom their case. Imagination, fancy, and invention, they are wholly strangers to, nor have any words in their language by which those ideas can be expressed; the whole compass of their thoughts and mind being shut up within the two forementioned sciences.

他们建造的房屋质量很差，墙壁歪歪斜斜，几乎在任何一个房间里都见不到直角。这种缺陷缘于他们对实用几何学的蔑视，认为其庸俗而机械。可他们的设计又过于精确，工匠们根本无法理解，因此难免出错。虽然他们能够熟练地使用量尺、铅笔和圆规画图纸，但日常行为举止则笨拙得令人难以想象。除了在数学和音乐方面，他们理解其他事物的过程也极其缓慢，常常困惑不已。他们非常武断，听不进其他人的意见，除非他们的意见恰好一致，但这种情况很少发生。想象、幻想和发明创造对他们来说都是毫不相干的东西，他们的语言中甚至没有确切的词语来与之对应。他们所有的思想和精神都完全局限于前面提到的两门学问的范围内。

Most of them, and especially those who deal in the astronomical part, have great faith in judicial astrology, although they are ashamed to own it publicly. But, what I chiefly admired, and thought altogether

尽管他们一直羞于公开承认，但他们中的大部分人，尤其是那些研究天文学的，都坚信“决断占星学”。但更令我吃惊并认为最不可思议的是，他们十分热衷于时事和

unaccountable, was the strong disposition I observed in them towards news and politics, perpetually inquiring into public affairs, giving their judgments in matters of state; and passionately disputing every inch of a party opinion. I have indeed observed the same disposition among most of the mathematicians I have known in *Europe*, although I could never discover the least analogy between the two sciences; unless those people suppose, that because the smallest circle hath as many degrees as the largest, therefore the regulation and management of the world require no more abilities than the handling and turning of a globe. But, I rather take this quality to spring from a very common infirmity of human nature, inclining us to be most curious and conceited in matters where we have least concern, and for which we are least adapted by study or nature.

政治，总喜欢对公众事务穷追不舍，评判国家大事，热烈讨论相关政党的不同政见。我承认欧洲我所认识的大部分数学家也都有同样的兴趣，不过我始终没发现在数学和政治这两种科学之间有丝毫的相似性。除非那些数学家们这样认为：最小的圆也和最大的圆拥有同样的度数，因此管理这个世界无须更多才能，只要会操作和转动一个地球仪就够了。但我宁愿将其归结为一种普遍的人性弱点：人们往往对和自己最不相关以及自己最没有天赋或者后天学习能力的事物更好奇，也更自负。

These people are under continual disquietudes, never enjoying a minute's peace of mind; and their disturbances proceed from causes which very little affect the rest of mortals. Their apprehensions arise from several changes they dread in the celestial bodies. for instance, that the earth by the continual approaches of the sun towards it, must in course of time be absorbed or swallowed up. that the face of the sun will by degrees

这些人内心惶恐不安，片刻也无法冷静下来，而令他们不安的事，对其他地方的人来说根本不算什么。他们担心天体所发生的一些变化。比如，随着太阳不断靠近地球，地球终将会被吸进太阳或者被太阳吞噬。太阳表面将逐渐被自身散发的臭气所笼罩，这层臭气会阻止阳光照射到地球上来。地球上一次勉强逃脱了和彗尾的撞击，否则早已化为灰烬。按照他们的推算，

be encrusted with its own effluvia, and give no more light to the world. That, the earth very narrowly escaped a brush from the tail of the last comet, which would have infallibly reduced it to ashes; and that the next, which they have calculated for one and thirty years hence, will probably destroy us. For, if in its perihelion it should approach within a certain degree of the sun (as by their calculations they have reason to dread), it will conceive a degree of heat ten thousand times more intense than that of Red-hot glowing iron; and in its absence from the sun, carry a blazing tail ten hundred thousand and fourteen miles long; through which if the earth should pass at the distance of one hundred thousand miles from the nucleus or main body of the comet, it must in its passage be set on fire, and reduced to ashes. that the sun daily spending its rays without any nutriment to supply them, will at last be wholly consumed and annihilated; which must be attended with the destruction of this earth, and of all the planets that receive their light from it.

31 年后彗星再次出现时，我们很可能遭遇灭顶之灾（他们有理由担心，因为他们计算出了这个结果）。彗星和太阳的距离在一定范围内时，所吸收的热量是使铁熔化所要吸收的热量的 1 万倍。彗星远离太阳后，身后所闪耀的彗尾大约长达 100 万 14 英里。如果地球运行到距离彗核或者彗星主体 10 万英里的地方，必定会化为灰烬，太阳的热量日益损耗，却没有任何补给，最终全部耗尽的时候，地球以及一切需要太阳光照的行星，也将因此而毁灭。

They are so perpetually alarmed with the apprehensions of these and the like impending dangers, that they can neither sleep quietly in their beds, nor have any relish for the common pleasures and amusements of life. When they meet an

他们长期处于对这些以及其他类似的即将到来的危险的恐惧中，既不能安心入睡，也没心情去感受人生中平凡的快乐。早上起来遇见熟人，大家会先问太阳的生命状况，太阳初升和降落时怎么样，

acquaintance in the morning, the first question is about the sun's health, how he looked at his setting and rising, and what hopes they have to avoid the stroke of the approaching comet. This conversation they are apt to run into with the same temper that boys discover, in delighting to hear terrible stories of spirits and hobgoblins, which they greedily listen to, and dare not go to bed for fear.

可有希望避免即将到来的彗星的撞击。他们谈论这些问题时的心情，就像那些喜欢听恐怖故事的男孩们一样，忍不住想听，听完又怕得要命不敢上床睡觉。

The women of the island have abundance of vivacity; they contemn their husbands, and are exceedingly fond of strangers, whereof there is always a considerable number from the continent below, attending at court, either upon affairs of the several towns and corporations, or their own particular occasions, but are much despised, because they want the same endowments. Among these the ladies choose their gallants: but the vexation is, that they act with too much ease and security, for the husband is always so rapt in speculation, that the mistress and lover may proceed to the greatest familiarities before his face, if he be but provided with paper and implements, and without his *flapper* at his side.

飞岛上的女人都精力充沛，她们蔑视自己的丈夫，却极其喜欢陌生人。常常有大量的陌生人从地面上到岛上来参加会议，要么是为了一些城镇和团体的事，要么是为了自己的私事。但他们总会被鄙视，因为他们不具备岛上人的才能。女人们却常常在这些人中挑选情人。然而令人恼怒的是，他们行动悠闲而安全。因为只要给女人的丈夫提供必要的纸和工具，就可以让他永远在那里思考问题，如果“拍手”也不在身边的话，这对情人就可以当着他的面为所欲为。

The wives and daughters lament their confinement to the island, although I think it the most delicious spot of ground in the world; and although they live here in the

尽管我觉得这座岛已经是世界上最美妙的地方了，但岛上的妻子们和女儿们都为自己被困于此而悲叹不已。她们在这里生活富

greatest plenty and magnificence, and are allowed to do whatever they please, they long to see the world, and take the diversions of the metropolis, which they are not allowed to do without a particular license from the king; and this is not easy to be obtained, because the people of quality have found by frequent experience, how hard it is to persuade their women to return from below. I was told that a great court lady, who had several children, is married to the prime minister, the richest subject in the kingdom, a very graceful person, extremely fond of her, and lives in the finest palace of the island, went down to Lagado, on the pretense of health, there hid herself for several months, till the king sent a warrant to search for her, and she was found in an obscure Eating House all in rags, having pawned her clothes to maintain an old deformed footman, who beat her every day, and in whose company she was taken much against her will. And although her husband received her with all possible kindness, and without the least reproach, she soon after contrived to steal down again with all her jewels, to the same gallant, and hath not been heard of since.

足，物质充裕，随心所欲，但她们还是非常渴望去看看下面的世界，去感受一下大都市的繁华。不过她们必须有国王的特许才能下去。而她们很难获得国王的特许，因为贵族们对此已经很有经验，要想劝说自己的妻子从下面回来非常艰难。有人告诉我，有一位大官的妻子已经是好几个孩子的母亲了，丈夫是首相，也是全国最富有的人，举止优雅得体，对她宠爱有加。她放弃岛上最漂亮的宫殿，却以调养身体为借口，跑到了下面的拉格多。她在那里藏了好几个月，直到国王发布搜查令，才在一家简陋的餐馆里找到穿着破烂的她。为了供养一个又老又丑的男仆，她抵押了自己的衣服。男仆每天都打她，即便如此，被带回来时她竟还依依不舍。她丈夫把她接回来，态度极其友善，连责备的话都没说一句，但没过多久，她竟然又带着自己所有的珠宝溜到下面见她的老情人去了，从那以后音信全无。

This may perhaps pass with the reader rather for an *European* or *English* story, than for one of a country so remote. But

这可能会让读者们觉得，与其说这个故事发生在那个遥远的地方，不如说它就发生在欧洲，也许

he may please to consider, that the caprices of womankind are not limited by any climate or nation, and that they are much more uniform than can be easily imagined.

就在英国。不过您不妨这样想：女人们的善变和任性并不受气候或民族的限制，天下女人的这种共性可能超出了人们的想象。

In about a month's time I had made a tolerable proficiency in their language, and was able to answer most of the king's questions, when I had the honour to attend him. His majesty discovered not the least curiosity to inquire into the laws, government, history, religion, or manners of the countries where I had been but confined his questions to the state of mathematics, and received the account I gave him, with great contempt and indifference, though often roused by his *flapper* on each side.

之后大概一个月的时间里，我已经能够非常熟练地使用他们的语言，当有幸侍驾时也能回答出国王的大部分问题了。国王对我到过的国家的法律、政体、历史、宗教和风土人情一点兴趣也没有，只询问了我一些与数学相关的问题。虽然两边各有一名“拍手”不时地提醒他，但他仍对我的回答一脸鄙夷，不冷不热。

CHAPTER 3

第三章

A Phenomenon solved by modern Philosophy and Astronomy. The Laputians' great Improvements in the Latter. The King's Method of suppressing Insurrections.

一种可以用现代哲学和天文学解释的现象。拉普他人巨大的天文学研究成果。国王镇压暴乱的方式。

I desired leave of this prince to see the curiosities of the island, which he was graciously pleased to grant, and ordered my tutor to attend me. I chiefly wanted to know to what cause in art or in nature, it owed its several motions, whereof I will now give a philosophical account to the reader.

我向君王请求，准许我参观一下这座岛上的新奇景观，他态度和蔼地欣然同意，并下令让我的老师陪我一起去。我最想知道的是，这座飞岛是如何前行的，到底是依靠技术还是依靠自然力，关于这一点我现在就给读者一个哲学上的解释。

The flying or floating island is exactly circular, its diameter 7837 yards, or about four miles and an half, and consequently contains ten thousand acres. It is three hundred yards thick. The bottom or under surface, which appears to those who view it from below, is one even regular plate of adamant, shooting up to the height of about two hundred yards. Above it lie the several minerals in their usual order, and over all is a coat of rich mould ten or twelve foot deep. The declivity of the

这座飞岛或者浮岛是正圆形，直径为 7837 码，换算过来大约 4.5 英里，因此面积约为 10 万英亩。整座岛厚 300 码。从地面上看，岛的底部或者叫下表面是一块形状规则的坚硬的石板，厚约为 200 码。石板上面有各种矿物，按照常规顺序依次排列。最上面是一层肥沃的土壤，10~12 英尺厚。岛的上表面从边缘到中心呈坡状，这使落在岛上的所有雨露都会聚成小河流向飞岛中心，注入 4 个巨大的水塘中，

upper surface, from the circumference to the centre, is the natural cause why all the dews and rains which fall upon the island, are conveyed in small rivulets towards the middle, where they are emptied into four large basins, each of about half a mile in circuit, and two hundred yards distant from the centre. From these basins the water is continually exhaled by the sun in the daytime, which effectually prevents their overflowing. Besides, as it is in the power of the monarch to raise the island above the region of clouds and vapours, he can prevent the falling of dews and rain whenever he pleases. For the highest clouds cannot rise above two miles, as naturalists agree, at least they were never known to do so in that country.

At the centre of the island there is a chasm about fifty yards in diameter, from whence the astronomers descend into a large dome, which is therefore called *flandona gagnole*, or the *astronomer's cave*, situated at the depth of a hundred yards beneath the upper surface of the adamant. In this cave are twenty lamps continually burning, which from the reflection of the adamant cast a strong light into every part. The place is stored with great variety of sextants, quadrants, telescopes, Astrolabs, and other

每个水塘的周长都有半英里左右，大约距离岛中心 200 码。水塘里的水白天在太阳的照射下不断蒸发，因此完全不会溢出。此外，国王还可以将岛上升到对流层上空，随心所欲地控制雨露的降落。自然学家们一致认为，云层根本达不到 2 英里以上，至少这个国家还从来没见过那么高的云。

飞岛的中央有一个直径 50 码左右的裂口，天文学家可以从这里进到一个巨大的圆顶洞里去，名字叫“弗兰多纳·格格诺尔”或者“天文学家之洞”。这个洞位于距离石板上表面 100 码的深处。洞里有 20 盏长明灯，灯光经过石板的反射照亮各个方向。这里存放着各种各样的六分仪、四分仪、望远镜、星盘以及其他天文仪器。但最重要的珍宝，关系到整个飞岛命运的则是一块巨大的形似织布用的梭子的天然磁石。磁石长 6 码，最厚的部分

astronomical instruments. But the greatest curiosity, upon which the fate of the island depends, is a loadstone of a prodigious size, in shape resembling a weaver's shuttle. It is in length six yards, and in the thickest part at least three yards over. This magnet is sustained by a very strong axle of adamant passing through its middle, upon which it plays, and is poised so exactly that the weakest hand can turn it. It is hooped round with an hollow cylinder of adamant, four foot deep, as many thick, and twelve yards in diameter, placed horizontally, and supported by eight adamantine foot, each six yards high. In the middle of the concave side there is a groove twelve inches deep, in which the extremities of the axle are lodged, and turned round as there is occasion.

达 3 码。一块坚硬的石头从磁石中间穿过，磁石可以绕此轴转动。磁石相对于这个石轴来说恰到好处地保持着平衡，所以不费吹灰之力就能将其转动。磁石的外面罩着一个高度和厚度均为 4 英尺、直径 12 码的石质空心圆柱体。圆柱体水平放置，其底部有 8 个 6 码长的石质支架。圆柱体内部正中有一个深 12 英寸的凹槽，与轴的两端相连，随时可以将其转动。

The stone cannot be moved from its place by any force, because the hoop and its foot are one continued piece with that body of adamant which constitutes the bottom of the island.

没有任何力量可以将磁石从原来的位置移开，因为罩在磁石外面的圆柱体和飞岛底部的石板是一体的。

By means of this loadstone, the island is made to rise and fall, and move from one place to another. For, with respect to that part of the earth over which the monarch presides, the stone is endued at one of its sides with an attractive power, and at the other with a repulsive. Upon placing the

借助这块磁石的力量，飞岛得以上升或下降，从一个地方移动到另一个地方。而这块磁石的一端与国王所统治的这片土地互相吸引，另外一端则与其互相排斥。如果把磁石竖直放置，令其与地面互相吸引的一端朝下，岛就下降；如果让

magnet erect with its attracting end towards the earth, the island descends; but when the repelling extremity points downwards, the island mounts directly upwards. When the position of the stone is oblique, the motion of the island is so too. for in this magnet the forces always act in lines parallel to its direction.

By this oblique motion the island is conveyed to different parts of the monarch's dominions. To explain the manner of its progress, let *A B* represent a line drawn across the dominions of *Balnibarbi*, let the line *c d* represent the loadstone, of which let *d* be the repelling end, and *c* the attracting end, the island being over *C*; let the stone be placed in the position *c d* with its repelling end downwards; then the island will be driven upwards obliquely towards *D*. When it is arrived at *D*, let the stone be turned upon its axle till its attracting end points towards *E*, and then the island will be carried obliquely towards *E*; where, if the stone be again turned upon its axle till it stands in the position *E F*, with its repelling point downwards, the island will rise obliquely towards *F*, where by directing the attracting end towards *G*, the island may be carried to *G*, and from *G* to *H*, by turning the stone, so as to make its

其与地面互相排斥的一端朝下，岛就直线上升。假如将磁石倾斜放置，岛也会沿着倾斜的方向行进，因为这块磁石总是在和自身的位置相平行的方向上产生作用力。

飞岛倾斜前进可以到达国王统辖领土的每个地区。为了解释岛的行进原理，假设AB这条线代表横贯巴尔尼巴比领地的位置，cd代表磁石，其中d表示和地面互相排斥的一端，c表示和地面互相吸引的一端，飞岛恰好位于C的上空。如果将磁石的d端倾斜向下，那么，岛就会被倾斜着推移到D。到达D以后，转动磁石的轴，直到磁石的c端恰好指向E的时候停止转动，岛就会倾斜行进到E。这时候如果再转动磁石，令其位于EF，并让磁石的d端朝下，岛就会倾斜着上升到达F的位置。到达F之后，只要磁石的c端指向G，岛就又会向着G处前进了。再转动磁石，令磁石的d端朝下，岛又会从G行进到H。这样随时改变磁石的位置，飞岛也沿着磁石倾斜的方向依次或升或降。通过这种上升和下降的交替进行（倾斜的角度并不是非常大），岛就可以从一片领地上空移动到

repelling extremity to point directly downwards. And thus by changing the situation of the stone as often as there is occasion, the island is made to rise and fall by turns in an oblique direction, and by those alternate risings and fallings (the obliquity being not considerable) is conveyed from one part of the dominions to the other.

另一片领地上空。

But it must be observed, that this island cannot move beyond the extent of the dominions below, nor can it rise above the height of four miles. For which the astronomers (who have written large systems concerning the stone) assign the following reason: that the magnetic virtue does not extend beyond the distance of four miles, and that the mineral which acts upon the stone in the bowels of the earth, and in the sea about six leagues distant from the shore, is not diffused through the whole globe, but terminated with the limits of the king's dominions; and it was easy from the great advantage of such a superior situation, for a prince to bring under his obedience whatever country lay within the attraction of that magnet.

但必须要遵守的是，飞岛不能行进到下面领地的范围之外，也不能超出 4 英里以外的高度。天文学家认为主要有以下原因（他们曾撰写了关于那块磁石的大量系统性论著）：如果距离超过 4 英里，磁性的作用就消失了，它能够对包括地球内部的岩石以及在距离海岸 6 里格以上的海中起作用，而且能和磁石产生作用的矿物只局限于国王的领土范围内，而并非遍布全球。飞岛所处的位置占有这样的优势，国王很容易就能将所有这些处于磁场引力范围内的国家收入治下。

When the stone is put parallel to the plane of the horizon, the island standeth still; for in that case, the extremities of it being at equal distance from the earth, act

如果将磁石水平放置，飞岛就会保持静止。因为此时，磁石的两端与地球的距离相等，一端受到向下的拉力，一端受到向上的推力，

with equal force, the one in drawing downwards, the other in pushing upwards, and consequently no motion can ensue.

This loadstone is under the care of certain astronomers, who from time to time give it such positions as the monarch directs. They spend the greatest part of their lives in observing the celestial bodies, which they do by the assistance of glasses far excelling ours in goodness. For, although their largest telescopes do not exceed three foot, they magnify much more than those of an hundred yards among us, and at the same time show the stars with greater clearness. This advantage has enabled them to extend their discoveries much farther than our astronomers in Europe; for they have made a catalogue of ten thousand fixed stars, whereas the largest of ours do not contain above one third part of that number. They have likewise discovered two lesser stars, or *satellites*, which revolve about *Mars*, whereof the innermost is distant from the centre of the primary planet exactly three of his diameters, and the outermost five; the former revolves in the space of ten hours, and the latter in twenty-one and an half; so that the squares of their periodical times are very near in the same proportion with

两种作用力彼此恰好抵消，因此飞岛也就不会移动了。

这块磁石由几位特定的天文学家专门负责管理，他们按照国王的命令不停转动磁石。他们一生的大多数时间都用于观测天体，他们用来辅助观测的望远镜比我们先进得多。虽然他们最大的望远镜不超过 3 英尺长，却比我们 100 英尺的效果还要好，可以将各种星体看得更清晰。在这一优势的帮助下，他们的发现远领先于欧洲的同行。他们曾编写了一份万颗恒星一览表，而我们最全的恒星表中的恒星数目也不及他们的 1/3。他们还在火星周围发现了两颗微型星星，或者叫卫星。其中更靠近火星的那颗距火星中心正好是火星直径的 3 倍，外面的一颗为 5 倍；前者每 10 小时绕火星运转一周，后者则每 21.5 小时转一周；这样，它们运转周期的平方就和它们距火星中心的距离的立方十分接近。由此也可以证明，它们显然和其他天体一样也遵循万有引力定律。

the cubes of their distance from the centre of *Mars*, which evidently shows them to be governed by the same law of gravitation, that influences the other heavenly bodies.

They have observed ninety-three different comets, and settled their periods with great exactness. If this be true (and they affirm it with great confidence), it is much to be wished that their observations were made public, whereby the theory of comets, which at present is very lame and defective, might be brought to the same perfection with other parts of astronomy.

他们发现了 93 颗彗星，并精确地测量了其运行周期。如果他们的测量无误（他们对此信心十足），我们强烈渴望他们能把其观测结果公之于世，那样目前仍存在许多不足之处的彗星学说或许就能像天文学的其他分支那样，日趋完善。

The king would be the most absolute prince in the universe, if he could but prevail on a ministry to join with him; but these having their estates below on the continent, and considering that the office of a favourite hath a very uncertain tenure, would never consent to the enslaving of their country.

国王如果能说服内阁与其同心协力，他将成为宇宙中最专制的统治者。可那些人都在地面拥有财产，而宠臣的地位又并非稳固，所以永远不会和国王一起对这个国家实行专制。

If any town should engage in rebellion or mutiny, fall into violent factions, or refuse to pay the usual tribute, the king has two methods of reducing them to obedience. The first and the mildest course is by keeping the island hovering over such a town, and the lands about it, whereby he can deprive them of the benefit of the sun and the rain, and

如果哪座城市发生叛乱或者兵变，陷入激烈的内战，或者拒不按照惯例缴纳贡品，国王有两种办法可以令其顺从。第一种办法最温和，就是让飞岛停留在这座城市上空，使这里的居民享受不到阳光和降水，并因此饱受死亡与疾病的威胁。在必要的时候，岛上的人还可以同时向地面扔巨石，而地面上的

consequently afflict the inhabitants with death and diseases. and if the crime deserve it, they are at the same time pelted from above with great stones, against which they have no defence but by creeping into cellars or caves, while the roofs of their houses are beaten to pieces. But if they still continue obstinate, or offer to raise insurrections, he proceeds to the last remedy, by letting the island drop directly upon their heads, which makes a universal destruction both of houses and men. However, this is an extremity to which the prince is seldom driven, neither indeed is he willing to put it in execution; nor dare his ministers advise him to an action, which as it would render them odious to the people, so it would be a great damage to their own estates, which lie all below, for the island is the king's demesne.

But there is still indeed a more weighty reason, why the kings of this country have been always averse from executing so terrible an action, unless upon the utmost necessity. For if the town intended to be destroyed should have in it any tall rocks, as it generally falls out in the larger cities, a situation probably chosen at first with a view to prevent such a catastrophe; or if it abound in high spires or pillars of stone, a

人们只能眼看着自己的房屋被砸成碎片而无法抵抗，只能爬到地窖或洞穴里藏起来。如果他们仍然不知悔改，甚至妄图造反，国王就只好使用撒手锏了：直接让飞岛落在他们头顶上，人和房屋都会遭受灭顶之灾。无论如何，这种极端的办法国王几乎没有用过，其实他也不希望那样做。大臣们也不敢建议国王如此行事，他们的产业都在地面上，那样做不但会招致地面上的人民的仇恨，他们自己的产业也会蒙受巨大损失，而飞岛只是国王的产业。

还有一个更重要的原因令国王不到迫不得已，不敢轻易使用这种恐怖的办法。因为，如果他打算毁灭的城市中竖立着高大的岩石——这种情况在大城市里比较普遍——当初城市选址的时候很可能就已经考虑到了这种大灾难。如果城市里布满高大的尖塔或石柱，那么，飞岛突如其来的降落很有可能就要损害岛的底部或者下表面。虽

sudden fall might endanger the bottom or under surface of the island, which although it consist, as I have said of one entire adamant two hundred yards thick, might happen to crack by too great a shock, or burst by approaching too near the fires from the houses below, as the backs both of iron and stone will often do in our chimneys. Of all this the people are well apprised, and understand how far to carry their obstinacy, where their liberty or property is concerned. And the king, when he is highest provoked, and most determined to press a city to rubbish, orders the island to descend with great gentleness, out of a pretence of tenderness to his people, but indeed for fear of breaking the adamantine bottom; in which case it is the opinion of all their philosophers, that the loadstone could no longer hold it up, and the whole mass would fall to the ground.

About three years before my Arrival among them, while the king was in his Progress over his Dominions, there happened an extraordinary Accident which had like to have put a Period to a fate of that Monarchy, at least as it is now instituted. Lindalio the second City in the kingdom was the first his Majesty visited in his progress.These Days after his

然我前面说过，岛的底部是一整块200码厚的坚硬无比的板，但过于剧烈的冲击也可能把它撞碎。或者由于太过靠近地面房屋中的炉火而爆裂，就像我们的烟囱，虽然由钢铁和石头制成，但如果离火太近的话也会裂开。百姓们对这一切了若指掌，他们知道为了自由和财产，自己可以坚持到什么程度。要是国王被气极了，决心将某个城市压为废墟，他就会假装体恤人民，下令让飞岛以非常缓慢的速度下降，但其实是担心弄坏其坚硬的底板，因为所有哲学家们都一致认定，飞岛的底部如果被损坏了，磁石就再也不能升起这个岛，整个岛就会落到地面上。

在我来到这座飞岛的大约前3年，国王巡视领土的时候发生了一件离奇事，差点毁掉了整个王朝，至少现在的这个王朝差点不复存在了。国王最先巡视了全国的第二大城市林达洛因。国王离开几天之后，那些常常抱怨其压迫的当地居民就紧闭城门，抓住地方长官，同时以不可思议的速度和劳动量，在

Departurn, the inhabitants who had often complained of great Oppressions, shut the Town Gates, seized on the Governor, and with incredible Speed and Labour erected four large Towers one at every Corner of the City (which is an exact Square) equal in Height to a strong pointed Rock that stands directly in the Centre of the City, Upon the Top of each Tower, as well as upon the Rock, they fixed a great Loadstone, and in case their Design should fail, they had provided a vast Quantity of the most combustible Fuel, hoping to burst therewith adamantine Bottom of the Island, if the Loadstone Project should miscarry.

城的四角建造了 4 座巨大的塔楼（这座城是正方形的），差不多和竖立在城区中心的那座坚固的尖顶岩石一样高。在每座塔楼和尖顶岩石的顶端各放置着一块磁石。为了防止他们的磁石计划失败，他们还准备了大量易燃物，希望依靠这些来燃爆飞岛底板。

It was eight Months before the king had perfect Notice that the Lindalinians were in Rebellion. He then commanded that the Island should be wafted over the City. The People were unanimous, and had laid in stone of Provisions, and a great River runs through the middle of the Town. The king hovered over them several Days to deprive them of the Sun and the Rain. He ordered many Packthreads to be let down, yet not a Person offered to send up a Petition, but instead thereof, very bold Demands, the Redressof all their Grievances, great immunities, the Choice of their own Governor, and other the like

8 个月之后国王才获悉林达洛因发生内乱的消息。他命令飞岛在这个城市的上空停下。当地居民团结一心，已经有足够的粮食储备。还有一条大河流经城市中心。国王命飞岛在他们上空盘踞了一段日子，让他们见不到阳光和雨水。他下令向地面放下许多绳子，但没有一个人投降，人们反而提出一些更加大胆的请求。他们要求大规模赦免政府官员，允许民主选举，以及许多其他的过分请求。于是国王命令岛上的全体居民从岛的底层走廊上往下面这座城中投掷巨石，但底下的居民们对这个恶毒的办法

Exorbitances. Upon which his Majesty commanded all the inhabitants of the Island to cast great Stones from the lower Gallery into the Town; but the Citizens had provided against this Mischief by conveying their persons and Effects into four Towers, and other strong Buildings, and Vaults under Ground.

早就有所防备，将人和财物迅速转移到那4座巨塔以及其他坚固的建筑物和地窖中。

The king being now determined to reduce this pround people, ordered that the Island should descend gently within forty Yards of the Top of the Towers and Rock. This was accordingly done; but the Officers employed in that Work found the Descent much speedier than usual, and by turning the Loadstone could not without great Difficulty keep it in a firm position, but found the Island inclining to fall. They sent the king immediate intelligence of this astonishing Event, and begged his Majesty's Permission to raise the Officers of the Loadstone ordered to attend. One of the oldest and expertest among them obtained Leave to try an Experiment. He took a strong Line of an hundred years, and the Island being raised over the Town above the attracting Power they had felt, he fastened a piece of Adamant to the End of his Line which had in it a mixture of Iron miniral, of the same Nature with that whereof the Bottom or lower Surface of

国王决定镇压这帮狂妄的百姓。他命令飞岛慢慢降落到距离巨塔和岩石近40码的上空。开始像这样降落以后，工作人员发现，飞岛比平时下降的速度快得多，而且就算转动磁石也很难令其停下，整个岛都倾斜着往下掉。他们立刻将这种异常报告给国王，请求将岛上升。国王批准了，并立即召集控制磁石的工作人员们参加会议。其中有一位年龄较大而且经验丰富的官员经国王允许做了一个试验。他拿了一根结实的绳子，约100码长，将飞岛上升到城市上空吸引力不是很明显的位置，在这绳子的一头绑上一块与飞岛底部成分一样的含有铁矿的石头，再从飞岛底层的走廊将绳子朝着塔顶缓缓放下。石头才被放下4码，这个官员就感到下面有一股强大的引力在吸引着这块石头，他险些收不回石头了。他又扔下了几块小石头，结果这些石头全被吸到了塔顶上。他又将这

the Island is composed, and from the lower Gallery let it down slowly towards the Top of the Towers. The Adamant was not descent four yards, before the Officer felt it drawn so strongly downwards, that he could hardly pull it back. He then threw down several small pieces of Adamant, and observed that they were all violently attracted by the top of the Tower. The same Experiment was made on the other three Towers, and on the Rock with the same Effect.

个实验在其他3座塔楼以及那岩石上重复了一下，结果都是如此。

This Incident broke entirely the king's Measures and (to dwell no longer on other Circumstances) he was forced to give the Town their own Conditions.

这彻底击败了国王的计划（其他情况就不再赘述了），这个城市提出的条件都得到了批准。

I was assured by a great Minister, that if the Island had descended so near the Town, as not to be able to raise itself, the Citizens were determined to fix it for ever, to kill the king and all his Servants, and entirely change the Government.

一位大臣告诉我，如果那次飞岛降落时距城市再近些，以至于无法再升空，居民们就决心将它永远困在那里，杀掉国王和所有官员，彻底改朝换代。

By a fundamental law of this realm, neither the king nor either of his two eldest sons are permitted to leave the island, nor the queen till she is past child-bearing.

这个国家的一项基本法律规定，国王和他的两位年龄较大的王子都不得离岛，生育年龄内的王后也不能离开。

CHAPTER 4

第四章

The Author leaves Laputa; is conveyed to Balnibarbi; arrives at the Metropolis. A Description of the Metropolis, and the Country adjoining. The Author hospitably received by a great Lord. His Conversation with that Lord.

作者离开拉普他，被送往巴尔尼巴比，到达其首都。首都及其近郊的风景。作者受到一位贵族的亲切招待，与贵族交谈。

Although I cannot say that I was ill treated in this island, yet I must confess I thought myself too much neglected, not without some degree of contempt。 for neither prince nor people appeared to be curious in any part of knowledge, except mathematics and music, wherein I was far their inferior, and upon that account very little regarded.

尽管我不能说自己在岛上受到了虐待，然而我不得不承认，自己是不受重视的，甚至有些被鄙视。无论是国王还是其他人似乎只对数学和音乐感兴趣，这正好是我最不擅长的两门科学，因而一点也得不到大家的尊重。

On the other side, after having seen all the curiosities of the island, I was very desirous to leave it, being heartily weary of those people. They were indeed excellent in two sciences for which I have great esteem, and wherein I am not unversed， but at the same time, so abstracted and involved in speculation that I never met with such disagreeable companions. I conversed only with women, tradesmen, *flappers*, and court-pages, during two months of my

另一方面，遍览了这座飞岛上的一切神奇景观后，我非常渴望离开了，我打心底里厌烦这些人。他们确实非常擅长那两门学问，这学问我也非常尊敬，而且知晓一二。但他们实在太沉迷于此了，总是心不在焉，同这样的人们为伍简直痛苦至极。我在那里待了两个月，其间只能和女人、商人、拍手和宫廷侍卫们交谈，我非常瞧不起自己这样，但也只有从这些人口里才能听到像样一点的回答。

abode here, by which at last I rendered myself extremely contemptible, yet these were the only people from whom I could ever receive a reasonable answer.

I had obtained by hard study a good degree of knowledge in their language; I was weary of being confined to an island where I received so little countenance, and resolved to leave it with the first opportunity.

There was a great lord at court, nearly related to the king, and for that reason alone used with respect. He was universally reckoned the most ignorant and stupid person among them. He had performed many eminent services for the crown, had great natural and acquired parts, adorned with integrity and honour, but so ill an ear for music, that his detractors reported he had been often known to beat time in the wrong place; neither could his tutors without extreme difficulty teach him to demonstrate the most easy proposition in the mathematics. He was pleased to show me many marks of favour, often did me the honour of a visit, desired to be informed in the affairs of *Europe*, the laws and customs, the manners and learning of the several countries where I had travelled. He listened to me with great attention, and made very wise observations on all I spoke. He had two *flappers* attending him

我靠自己的勤奋和努力学会了很多他们的语言知识。我已经烦透了被困在这座岛上受尽轻视。我决定一旦有机会就离开这里。

宫廷里有一位大贵族是皇亲国戚，并因此而受到尊敬。大家都觉得他是全国最无知、最愚蠢的人。他曾为国王立下汗马功劳，无论是先天还是后天都非常优秀，以正直和令人敬仰而出名，但是他五音不全，说他坏话的人说他常常打错拍子。他的老师费尽心思也没办法让他学会证明最简单的数学定理。他很喜欢同在我一起，经常来拜访我，饶有兴致地听我讲述欧洲的情况，以及我所到过的几个国家的法律、风俗、礼仪与学术。我说时他听得很认真，并常能就我所提到的问题发表不凡的见解。他也有两名拍手随身侍候以表明高贵的身份，但他只有在朝廷上或者外出访问时才让他们提醒，当我们俩单独谈话时，他就会让他们退下去。

for state, but never made use of them except at court, and in visits of ceremony, and would always command them to withdraw when we were alone together.

I entreated this illustrious person, to intercede in my behalf with his majesty for leave to depart, which he accordingly did, as he was pleased to tell me, with regret: for, indeed he had made me several offers very advantageous, which however I refused with expressions of the highest acknowledgment.

On the 16th Day of *February*, I took leave of his majesty and the court. The king made me a present to the value of about two hundred pounds *English*, and my protector his kinsman as much more, together with a letter of recommendation to a friend of his in Lagado, the metropolis; The island being then hovering over a mountain about two miles from it, I was let down from the lowest gallery, in the same manner as I had been taken up.

The continent, as far as it is subject to the monarch of the *flying island*, passes under the general name of *Balnibarbi*, and the metropolis, as I said before, is called *Lagado*. I felt some little satisfaction in finding myself on firm ground. I walked to the city without any concern, being clad like one of the natives, and sufficiently instructed to converse with them. I soon

我恳请这位高官帮我求情，求国王让我离开。他照我说的做了，然后告诉我，他非常遗憾。他曾为我推荐了几个很不错的职位，我感激不尽却还是婉言拒绝了。

2月16日，我向国王和满朝文武告辞。国王送给我一份礼物，价值200英镑左右，我的恩人，即那位皇亲，也送给了我一份同样贵重的礼物，以及一封介绍信，让我带给他在首都拉格多的朋友。当时飞岛正停留在一座山的上空，离首都大约有2英里，我被从飞岛底层走廊上放下去，就和上来的时候一样。

飞岛统治下的这块大陆，通常被人们称为巴尔尼巴比，其首都我已经介绍过了，叫拉格多。我发觉自己有些心满意足地迈上这块坚实的土地。穿着和本地人别无二致的服装，说着和他们同样的话，我无所顾虑地走进这座城市。我很快找到了那封介绍信的收信人的家，拿出飞岛上那位贵族的信，于是受

found out the person's house to whom I was recommended, presented my letter from his friend the grandee in the island, and was received with much kindness. This great lord, whose name was Munodi, ordered me an apartment in his own house, where I continued during my stay, and was entertained in a most hospitable manner.

到了他非常热情的接待。这个大贵族叫孟诺迪，在自己家里为我提供了一间屋子，在这里停留的这段时间我一直住在那里，他十分热情友好地款待了我。

The next morning after my arrival he took me in his chariot to see the town, which is about half the bigness of *London*, but the houses very strangely built, and most of them out of repair. The people in the streets walked fast, looked wild, their eyes fixed, and were generally in rags. We passed through one of the Town-Gates, and went about three miles into the country, where I saw many labourers working with several sorts of tools in the ground, but was not able to conjecture what they were about, neither did observe any expectation either of corn or grass, although the soil appeared to be excellent. I could not forbear admiring at these odd appearances both in town and country, and I made bold to desire my conductor, that he would be pleased to explain to me what could be meant by so many busy heads, hands, and faces, both in the streets and the fields, because I did not discover any good effects they produced; but on the contrary, I never knew a soil so unhappily

第二天一早他就带着我乘坐他的双轮马车参观全城。城区有伦敦的一半大，可是建筑风格非常奇特，大部分破败不堪。街上的行人们行色匆忙，看起来非常野蛮，目光呆滞，大多衣衫褴褛。我们走出一座城门，来到大约3英里之外的乡村。我看到许多人拿着各种各样的工具在田里劳动，但推测不出他们到底在干什么，尽管土壤看起来非常肥沃，但看不出地里有任何庄稼或者杂草。我好奇于对这城乡景象的大不相同，于是问了问向导，他非常乐意向我解释为何不管是在大街上还是在田野里都有那么多人在匆匆忙忙地劳动，但却没什么成果。相反，我从没见过哪个地方的田地如此荒芜，也没见过哪个地方的房屋建得如此造作而破败，更没有见过哪个种族的百姓如此困窘。

cultivated, houses so ill contrived and so ruinous, or a people whose countenances and habit expressed so much misery and want.

This lord *Munodi* was a person of the first rank, and had been some years governor of *Lagado*, but, by a cabal of ministers was discharged for insufficiency. However the king treated him with tenderness, as a well-meaning man, but of a low contemptible understanding.

When I gave that free censure of the country and its inhabitants, he made no further answer than by telling me, that I had not been long enough among them to form a judgment; and that the different nations of the world had different customs, with other common topics to the same purpose. But when we returned to his palace, he asked me how I liked the building, what absurdities I observed, and what quarrel I had with the dress and looks of his domestics. This he might safely do, because everything about him was magnificent, regular, and polite. I answered, "that his excellency's prudence, quality, and fortune, had exempted him from those defects which folly and beggary had produced in others. He said if I would go with him to his country House about twenty miles distant, where his estate lay, there would be more leisure for this kind of conversation. I told his

这位贵族孟诺迪是上层人士，曾多年担任拉格多的市政官员，只因其他议员的结党营私和阴谋陷害而被解职。但是国王对他非常和善，认为他心地善良，只不过有点不够世故。

我不客气地说出自己对这个国家及其人民的看法之后，他没有任何回应，只说我来此地和人们相处的时间还太短，现在下结论为时尚早，一方水土养一方人，各有各的风俗，又说了不少相关的话。不过当我们一回到他的宅邸，他又问我是否喜欢他们家的房屋，有什么不合理的地方，家里的装饰有什么可挑剔之处。他完全可以放心，因为他的一切都那么高尚、整齐而文雅。我回答说："阁下如此严谨而德才兼备、幸运，怎么会有那些由愚蠢和贫穷而造成的不妥之处呢？"他认为，如果我愿陪他去约20英里外的乡下——他的产业在那里——住段时间，我们就有足够的时间聊天了。我说听凭安排，因此第二天一早我们就出发了。

excellency that I was entirely at his disposal, and accordingly we set out next morning.

During our journey, he made me observe the several methods used by farmers in managing their lands, which to me were wholly unaccountable, for except in some very few places, I could not discover one ear of corn or blade of grass. But, in three hours travelling, the scene was wholly altered; we came into a most beautiful country; farmers' houses at small distances, neatly built, the fields enclosed, containing vineyards, corn-grounds and meadows. Neither do I remember to have seen a more delightful prospect. His excellency observed my countenance to clear up; he told me with a sigh, that there his estate began, and would continue the same till we should come to his house. that his countrymen ridiculed and despised him for managing his affairs no better, and for setting so ill an example to the kingdom which however was followed by very few, such as were old and wilful, and weak like himself.

We came at length to the house, which was indeed a noble structure, built according to the best rules of ancient architecture. The fountains, gardens, walks, avenues, and groves were all disposed with exact judgment and taste. I gave due praises to everything I saw,

一路上，他要我注意观察农民们耕种土地的种种方式，我却看不出所以然。除了很少的几处，其余的地方看不到一棵谷物和一片草叶。但 3 小时后，完全是另一番风景了。我们进入了一个十分美丽的乡村，家家户户鸡犬相闻，屋舍俨然，田地围绕在中间，其中有葡萄园、麦田和草地。我想不起来自己还在何处见过更美妙的风景了。这位贵族看到我一副神清气爽的样子，叹了一口气告诉我，这一带就是他的产业了，一直到他的房子都是这样的风景。他说自己的同胞们都嘲笑他、轻视他，说他连自己的事情都管不好，更无法成为整个王国的表率。虽然也有很少的一部分人向他学习，但都是一些像他这样衰老而固执的人。

我们最后到达了他在乡村的房子。那可真可谓一座高贵的建筑，严格按照最完美的古建筑范式修建而成。喷泉、花园、小径、林荫大道和小树林被十分合理而有品位地安排部署开来。所见之处我都赞叹不已，而他则不予置评，直

whereof his excellency took not the least notice till after supper, when, there being no third companion, he told me with a very melancholy air, that he doubted he must throw down his houses in town and country, to rebuild them after the present mode, destroy all his plantations, and cast others into such a form as modern usage required, and give the same directions to all his tenants, unless he would submit to incur the censure of pride, singularity, affectation, ignorance, caprice, and perhaps increase his majesty's displeasure.

That the admiration I appeared to be under, would cease or diminish when he had informed me of some particulars, which probably I never heard of at court, the people there being too much taken up in their own speculations, to have regard to what passed here below.

The sum of his discourse was to this effect. That about forty years ago, certain persons went up to *Laputa* either upon business or diversion, and after five months continuance, came back with a very little smattering in mathematics, but full of volatile spirits acquired in that airy region. that these persons upon their return began to dislike the management of every thing below, and fell into schemes of putting all arts, sciences, languages, and mechanics upon a new foot. To this end they procured a royal patent for erecting

到晚饭后所有人都退下了，他才郁郁寡欢地告诉我说，他恐怕得把自己现在在城里和乡下的房子都拆掉了，将其重建成现在的风格，还得拆掉所有的种植园，建造成流行的样式，并令手下的所有佃农都照样改建一番，否则就会招致责备，大家会说他傲慢无礼、特立独行、矫揉造作、目中无人、反复无常，也许还会惹恼国王。

他还说，告诉我详情之后，我的赞赏之情也许就会消失了。可能他要告诉我的这些事在朝廷里我听所未听，他们整天忙着为自己的研究冥思苦想，忽略了地上到底发生了什么。

他所讲述的主要内容是这样的。大约 40 年前，一些人为了公事或者游玩去了拉普他。在那里住了 5 个月，回来的时候略通了一点数学，还染上了那座飞岛上的人反复无常的性情。这些人回来后，就开始觉得地面上的一切都不顺眼，计划将艺术、科学、语言、技术等全部重新设计。为了完成这些目标，他们得到了国王的特许，在拉格多建立了一所设计研究院。这股风迅速吹遍了全国，以至于很快全国范围内每座重要城市都有了这

an academy of PROJECTORS in *Lagado*; and the humour prevailed so strongly among the people, that there is not a town of any consequence in the kingdom without such an academy. In these colleges, the professors contrive new rules and methods of agriculture and building, and new instruments, and tools for all trades and manufactures, whereby, as they undertake, one man shall do the work of ten; a palace may be built in a week, of materials so durable as to last for ever without repairing. All the fruits of the earth shall come to maturity at whatever season we think fit to choose, and increase an hundred fold more than they do at present, with innumerable other happy proposals. The only inconvenience is, that none of these projects are yet brought to perfection, and in the mean time the whole country lies miserably waste, the houses in ruins, and the people without food or clothes. By all which, instead of being discouraged, they are fifty times more violently bent upon prosecuting their schemes, driven equally on by hope and despair; that as for himself, being not of an enterprising spirit, he was content to go on in the old forms, to live in the houses his ancestors had built, and act as they did in every part of life without innovation. That, some few other persons of quality and gentry had done the same, but were

么一所研究院。在这些研究院里，教授们纷纷为农业与建筑学设计出新规范和新方法，并为所有的工商业设计了全新的工具与仪器。他们保证如果使用这些工具和方法，一个人就能干 10 个人的活，一周之内就能建成一座宫殿，而且建筑材料会非常耐用，永远无须修补。他们可以使地里的所有果实在任何他们想要的时间成熟，并且产量是现在的 100 倍。他们还想出了无数其他的奇思妙想。最大的问题就在于，所有这些计划没有一项最后顺利完成。而整个国家却遭到了前所未有的破坏，房屋化为废墟，国民饥寒交迫。他们看在眼里却不气馁，反而在希望与绝望的共同作用下，以 50 倍的热情去推行原来的计划。而他呢，没有那么强烈的进取心，于是满足于继续生活在旧式传统下，居住在祖先们修建的房子里，像他们那样墨守成规，毫无改变。有一少部分贵族和绅士也像我这样，却遭到了众人的鄙夷和谴责，被称之为艺术的敌人，愚昧无知，是国民的公敌，为了自己的舒适和懒惰不顾国家的发展。

looked on with an eye of contempt and Ill will, as enemies to art, ignorant, and ill commonwealth's-men, preferring their own ease and sloth before the general improvement of their country.

His lordship added, That he would not by any further particulars prevent the pleasure I should certainly take in viewing the grand academy, whither he was resolved I should go. He only desired me to observe a ruined building upon the side of a mountain about three miles distant, of which he gave me this account. That he had a very convenient mill within half a mile of his house, turned by a current from a large river, and sufficient for his own family as well as a great number of his tenants. That, about seven years ago, a club of those projectors came to him with proposals to destroy this mill, and build another on the side of that mountain, on the long ridge whereof a long canal must be cut for a repository of water, to be conveyed up by pipes and engines to supply the mill: because the wind and air upon a height agitated the water, and thereby made it fitter for motion: and because the water descending down a declivity would turn the mill with half the current of a river whose course is more upon a level. He said, that being then not very well with the court, and pressed by many of his friends, he complied with the

这位贵族补充说，他绝对不会阻止我去参观那宏伟的研究院，他知道我很想去，所以他就不再赘述了。他只想让我去看一看大约 3 英里外的山坡上一所废弃的房子，并解释说：以前有一座十分便利的水磨坊，距离他的房子不到半英里，以一条大河的水流为动力运作，完全可以供应自己全家使用，还能帮助很多佃农。大约 7 年前，来了一帮研究家，提议拆掉这座磨坊，在那边的山上另外修建一座，而且必须在山顶上开一道长长的水渠，再用管道和发动机将水送到山上存储起来，最后就可以用这些水推动水磨，据说高处的风和空气可以搅动水，可以加速水的流动，又因为水从斜坡上流下，只需要地面上的河水的一半流量就可以推动水磨了。他说自己当时和朝廷之间发生了一些不快，想借此机会表明忠心，再加上朋友们的劝说，于是接受了研究家们的建议。他雇用了 100 个人，用了两年的时间，但整个工程却失败了。研究家们走了，将整件事的责任都归咎于他，并一直对他心怀不满。之后他们又找别人做实验，信心十足会成功，结果

proposal; and after employing an hundred men for two years, the work miscarried, the projectors went off, laying the blame entirely upon him, railing at him ever since, and putting others upon the same experiment, with equal assurance of success, as well as equal disappointment.

仍然是失败和失望。

In a few days we came back to town, and his excellency, considering the bad character he had in the academy, would not go with me himself, but recommended me to a friend of his to bear me company thither. My lord was pleased to represent me as a great admirer of projects, and a person of much curiosity and easy belief, which indeed was not without truth, for I had myself been a sort of projector in my younger days.

过了几天，我们回到城里。考虑到自己在研究院没有留下好印象，他没陪我去，而是介绍了一位朋友陪我前往。这个贵族说我是个工程设计的爱慕者，好奇而轻信。他这样说也并非不符合实情，我年轻的时候真的做过和他们的研究家类似的工作。

CHAPTER 5

第五章

The Author permitted to see the grand Academy of Lagado. The Academy largely described. The Arts wherein the Professors employ themselves.

This academy is not an entire single building, but a continuation of several houses on both sides of a street, which growing waste was purchased and applied to that use.

I was received very kindly by the warden, and went for many days to the academy. Every room has in it one or more projectors, and I believe I could not be in fewer than five hundred rooms.

The first man I saw was of a meagre aspect, with sooty hands and face, his hair and beard long, ragged and singed in several places. His clothes, shirt, and skin, were all of the same colour. He has been eight years upon a project for extracting sunbeams out of cucumbers, which were to be put into Vials hermetically sealed, and let out to warm the air in raw inclement summers. He told me, he did not doubt in eight years more, he should be able to supply the governor's gardens with sunshine at a reasonable rate; but he

作者获准参观拉格多大研究院。研究院的概况。教授们研究的课题。

这所研究院不是一个完全独立的建筑物，而是分布在街道两旁，几所彼此连在一起的房屋。由于快要报废了，才被研究院买下来。

研究院院长非常友好地迎接了我，我还在研究院里住了很多天。每个房间里都住着一位或更多的研究家，而且我敢说我参观过的房间不下 500 间。

我所见到的第一个人骨瘦如柴，手和脸黑得仿佛被烟熏过，头发胡子都很长，衣服破烂，还被火烧焦了好几处，他的外套、衬衣和皮肤全变成了一色的。8 年来他一直在做一项研究，就是把阳光从黄瓜里提取出来，装进密封的小瓶子里，可以在暴雨连连的夏天放出来让空气变得温暖一些。他告诉我，他确信再过 8 年，他就能以一个合适的价格把阳光卖给市长的花园了，不过他又抱怨说存货太少了，恳请我给他一些东西，作为对他此

complained that his stock was low, and entreated me to give him something as an encouragement to ingenuity, especially since this had been a very dear season for cucumbers. I made him a small present, for my lord had furnished me with money on purpose, because he knew their practice of begging from all who go to see them.

项创新的鼓励，尤其是现在这个季节，黄瓜很贵。我就送了他一份薄礼，钱是那位贵族特地给我的，因为他知道，一旦有参观者，他们肯定会要钱的。

I went into another chamber, but was ready to hasten back, being almost overcome with a horrible stink. My conductor pressed me forward, conjuring me in a whisper to give no offence, which would be highly resented, and therefore I durst not so much as stop my nose. The projector of this cell was the most ancient student of the academy. his face and beard were of a pale yellow; his hands and clothes daubed over with filth. When I was presented to him, he gave me a, close embrace (a compliment I could well have excused). His employment from his first coming into the academy was an operation to reduce human excrement to its original food, by separating the several parts, removing the tincture which it receives from the gall, making the odour exhale, and scumming off the saliva. He had a weekly allowance from the society of a vessel filled with human ordure, about the bigness of a *Bristol* barrel.

我走进另外一个房间，却差点被弥漫着的奇臭无比的气味立刻逼出来。我的向导拉着我继续前行，暗示我不要冒犯他们，否则他们肯定会恨我。我吓得都不敢捂鼻子了。这个房间里住的研究家是这所研究院里最资深的学者，他的脸和胡子是淡黄色的。他的手和衣服也都脏兮兮的。当我被介绍给他时，他给了我一个亲密的拥抱（其实我本可以找一个借口换一种方式来表达问候）。自从第一次来到研究院并开始在这里工作以后，他就在研究如何把人类的粪便还原为食物。他把粪便分成几个部分，想办法除去来自胆汁的颜色，把臭气挥发掉，再撇掉表面的唾液。他每星期都会得到人们提供的一桶粪便，大概有布里斯托尔酒桶那么大。

I saw another at work to calcine ice into

我还看到有人试图把冰煅烧

Gun powder, who likewise showed me a treatise he had written concerning the malleability of fire, which he intended to publish.

成火药。他还给我看了一篇他写的关于火的延展性的论文，并打算将其发表。

There was a most ingenious architect who had contrived a new method for building houses, by beginning at the roof and working downwards to the foundation, which he justified to me by the like practice of those two prudent insects the bee and the spider.

有一位最有独创性的建筑师，他创造出了一种修建房屋的新办法，从屋顶开始，从上到下一直修建到地基。他还向我解释说，蜜蜂和蜘蛛这两种最谨慎的昆虫就是这样盖房子的。

There was a man born blind, who had several apprentices in his own condition: their employment was to mix colours for painters, which their master taught them to distinguish by feeling and smelling. It was indeed my misfortune to find them at that time not very perfect in their lessons, and the professor himself happened to be generally mistaken: This artist is much encouraged and esteemed by the whole fraternity.

有一个人先天失明，他还有几个学徒也是这样。他们负责为画家调配颜色，老师教他们凭借触觉和嗅觉来辨色。我的运气真是太差了，当时他们还学艺不精，教授自己都常常犯错。但是这位艺术家在他们的圈子里却十分受人敬仰。

In another apartment I was highly pleased with a projector, who had found a device of plowing the ground with hogs, to save the charges of plows, cattle, and labour. The method is this: in an acre of ground you bury at six inches distance, and eight deep, a quantity of acorns, dates, chesnuts, and other mast or vegetables whereof these animals are fondest; then you drive six hundred or more of them into the field, where in a few days they

在另外一个房间，我和一位研究家相谈甚欢，他发明一种用猪来耕地的办法，以节省人力物力。他的办法是这样的：在一亩地里，每隔 6 英寸，就把一些橡子、枣子、栗子和这种动物最爱吃的其他山毛榉果及蔬菜埋到 8 英寸深的位置，然后把 600 多头猪轰进地里，这些猪为了找吃的，几天之内就可以把所有的土拱一遍，这块地就可以播种了，猪的粪便还给地施肥

will root up the whole ground in search of their food, and make it fit for sowing, at the same time manuring it with their dung; it is true upon experiment they found the charge and trouble very great, and they had little or no crop. However, it is not doubted that this invention may be capable of great improvement.

了。实验中他们遇到了很大的费用问题和实际困难，几乎没有任何成果。不过毫无疑问，这种方法还是可以再改进的。

I went into another room, where the walls and ceiling were all hung round with cobwebs, except a narrow passage for the artist to go in and out. At my entrance he called aloud to me not to disturb his webs. He lamented the fatal mistake the world had been so long in of using silkworms, while we had such plenty of domestic insects, who infinitely excelled the former, because they understood how to weave as well as spin. And he proposed farther, that by employing spiders, the charge of dyeing silks should be wholly saved, whereof I was fully convinced when he showed me a vast number of flies most beautifully coloured, wherewith he fed his spiders, assuring us, that the webs would take a tincture from them; and as he had them of all hues, he hoped to fit everybody's fancy, as soon as he could find proper food for the flies of certain gums, oils, and other glutinous matter to give a strength and consistence to the threads.

我走进另一个房间，墙壁和天花板上都布满了蜘蛛网，只留下一个很小的过道供研究者们进出。我刚一走进去，他就大声喊我让我不要把他的蜘蛛网弄破。他慨叹所有人都犯了个致命的错误，就是这么长时间竟然一直只使用蚕丝，而他这里到处都是家养昆虫，比蚕好得多，因为它们不仅会吐丝还会织网。他进一步提议，如果使用蜘蛛，给丝染色的费用就能全部省下来。当他给我看过大量颜色美丽无比的苍蝇之后，我就完全相信了他。他用这些苍蝇喂他的蜘蛛，他说，蛛网的颜色就来自这些苍蝇，而且各种颜色的苍蝇他都有，他希望能满足每个人的不同喜好。只要他能替苍蝇找到适当的食物，如树脂、油或者其他胶状物质，蛛纺出来的丝线就会强硬而坚固。

There was an astronomer who had

有一位天文学家在市政厅屋

undertaken to place a Sun Dial upon the great weathercock on the Townhouse, by adjusting the annual and diurnal motions of the earth and sun, so as to answer and coincide with all accidental turnings by the wind.

I was complaining of a small fit of the colic, upon which my conductor led me into a room, where a great physician resided, who was famous for curing that disease by contrary operations from the same instrument. He had a large pair of bellows with a long slender muzzle of ivory. this he conveyed eight inches up the anus, and drawing in the wind, he affirmed he could make the guts as lank as a dried bladder. But when the disease was more stubborn and violent, he let in the muzzle while the bellows were full of wind, which he discharged into the body of the patient, then withdrew the instrument to replenish it, clapping his thumb strongly against the orifice of then fundament; and this being repeated three or four times, the adventitious wind would rush out, bringing the noxious along with it (like water put into a pump), and the patient recover. I saw him try both experiments upon a dog, but could not discern any effect from the former. After the latter, the animal was ready to burst, and made so violent a discharge, as was very offensive to me and my companions.

顶的巨大的风标上放置了一架日晷仪，调整地球与太阳每年和每天的运转情况，使其与突转的风向相一致。

我刚想抱怨肚子的一阵疼痛，向导就带我走进一位名医的房间。他以能用同一种器具做功能相反的两种手术以治疗腹痛而出名。他有一个带细长象牙嘴的巨大的手动吹风器。他把这象牙嘴插进肛门8 英寸的位置，把腹中的空气吸出来。他断言这样能将肚子里的凉气全部吸出来，只剩下一个干瘪的膀胱。但是如果病情来势凶猛，他就得先给吹风器充满气再把象牙嘴插入肛门，往病人体内打气，之后再抽出吹风器，并用大拇指紧紧地堵住肛门，再给吹风机重新充好气。这样重复三四次，打进去的气连同毒气也就一起被压出来了（像抽水机抽水一样），病人也就痊愈了。我目睹他给一只狗做了这两种试验，第一次没看出任何反应，第二次做完，那只狗都快要被撑爆了，突然剧烈地排泄起来，我和向导都很不快。狗当场死了，医生企图用同样的手术把它救活时，我们离开了。

The dog died on the spot, and we left the doctor endeavouring to recover him by the same operation.

I visited many other apartments, but shall not trouble my reader with all the curiosities I observed, being studious of brevity.

I had hitherto seen only one side of the academy, the other being appropriated to the advancers of speculative learning, of whom I shall say something when I have mentioned one illustrious person more, who is called among them the *universal artist*. He told us he had been thirty years employing his thoughts for the improvement of human life. He had two large rooms full of wonderful curiosities, and fifty men at work. Some were condensing air into a dry tangible substance, by extracting the nitre, and letting the aqueous or fluid particles percolate; others softening marble for pillows and Pincushions; others petrifying the hoofs of a Living Horse to preserve them from foundering. The artist himself was at that time busy upon two great designs; the first to sow land with chaff, wherein he affirmed the true seminal virtue to be contained, as he demonstrated by several experiments which I was not skilful enough to comprehend. The other was, by a certain composition of gums, minerals, and vegetables outwardly

我参观了很多其他房间，但是为了简洁起见，我就不把我所见的新鲜事给读者们一一分享了。

到此时为止，我只参观了研究院的一半，另外一半主要由擅长勤学深思的学者们占据。我不得不再提到一位名人，他被其他研究家称为“宇宙学者”。他告诉我们他 30 年来一直致力于探索如何改善人类生活。他有两个大房间，里面满是奇妙的宝贝，还有 50 名工作人员。他们有的从空气中提取硝酸钠，并滤掉其中的水蒸气和液体微粒，来将空气压缩成干燥而可感的物质。有的想软化大理石，做成枕头或者针垫。还有的人想将活马的马蹄硬化，这样马在奔跑的时候就不会跌伤了。这位大师自己也正忙于两项伟大的设计：其一是用谷壳播种，他肯定种子的精华全部集中在谷壳，为了证明自己的观点他还做了几项实验，不过我太愚钝了，没看明白；其二是将树脂、矿石和蔬菜的混合物涂在两头小羊身上，阻止羊毛的生长，他希望一段时间之后，能够繁殖出一种无毛羊，并将其推广到整个王国。

applied, to prevent the growth of wool upon two young lambs; and he hoped in a reasonable time to propagate the breed of naked sheep all over the kingdom.

We crossed a walk to the other part of the academy, where, as I have already said, the Projector in speculative learning resided.

The first professor I saw was in a very large room, with forty pupils about him. After salutation, observing me to look earnestly upon a frame, which took up the greatest part of both the length and breadth of the room, he said perhaps I might wonder to see him employed in a project for improving speculative knowledge by practical and mechanical operations. But the world would soon be sensible of its usefulness; and he flattered himself, that a more noble exalted thought never sprung in any other man's head. Everyone knew how laborious the usual method is of attaining to arts and sciences; whereas by his contrivance, the most ignorant person at a reasonable charge, and with a little bodily labour, may write books in philosophy, poetry, politics, law, mathematics and theology, without the least assistance from genius or study. He then led me to the frame, about the sides whereof all his pupils stood in ranks. It was twenty foot square, placed in the middle of the room. The superfices was

我们穿过一条通道来到研究院的另一边，我之前已经说过，那些思索型的设计家们就住在这里。

我见到的第一位教授正在一间很大的屋子里，和他的 40 名学生一起工作。问候之后，他看到我认真地观察那个占据了房间大部分空间的架子，于是说，或许我会对他研究如何通过实践和机械手段来提高人的思考能力感兴趣。不过世人很快就会认识到它的实用性。他又自卖自夸地说，还从来没有谁产生过如此宏伟的想法呢！众所周知，如果想用普通的方法在艺术和科学上取得成就需要付出多少艰辛，但如果使用他的发明，即使是最愚蠢的人，只要缴纳一定的学费，再付出一点劳动，就能够写出关于哲学、诗歌、政治、法律、数学和神学的书，而且不需要任何天赋或者学习能力。他又带我来到架子前，他的学生们都排队在旁边站好。这个架子 20 英尺见方，置于房间正中。其表面由木头组成，差不多每块都如骰子般大小，有的稍微大些。这些木块全部用细绳系在一起，每个木块上面都贴着一张纸，这些纸上写满了他们语言中的

composed of several bits of wood, about the bigness of a die, but some larger than others. They were all linked together by slender wires. These bits of wood were covered on every square with paper pasted on them; and on these papers were written all the words of their language in their several moods, tenses, and declensions, but without any order. The professor then desired me to observe, for he was going to set his engine at work. The pupils at his command took each of them hold of an iron handle, whereof there were forty fixed round the edges of the frame, and giving them a sudden turn, the whole disposition of the words was entirely changed. He then commanded six and thirty of the lads to read the several lines softly as they appeared upon the frame; and where they found three or four words together that might make part of a sentence, they dictated to the four remaining boys who were scribes. This work was repeated three or four times, and at every turn the engine was so contrived, that the words shifted into new places, as the square bits of wood moved upside down.

所有单词及语态、时态和变格，但并没有按照顺序排列。教授让我细致观察，因为他即将发动机器了。他的学生们在他的命令下分别抓住一个铁把手。原来架子的边框上共装有 40 个把手，如果突然转动把手，单词的位置就会全盘变换。然后他又吩咐 36 个学生小声读出架子上恰巧出现的单词，一旦有三四个单词能连成一句话，这 36 个学生就将其读给剩下的 4 名学生听，让他们记录下来。这样重复了三四次，每次扳动机器，这些木方块就会彻底变换到新的位置，重新陷入混乱。

Six hours a day the young students were employed in this labour, and the professor showed me several volumes in large folio, already collected, of broken sentences, which he intended to piece together, and

这些年轻学生每天花费 6 个小时做这项工作。教授给我看了好几卷对开本，全是他们所收集到的断断续续的句子，他计划把这些全都接合在一起，将丰富的材料编写成

out of those rich materials to give the world a complete body of all arts and sciences; which however might be still improved, and much expedited, if the public would raise a fund for making and employing five hundred such frames in *Lagado*, and oblige the managers to contribute in common their several collections.

一部涉及所有文化和科学门类的百科全书，呈献给世人。然而，如果民众筹集齐一笔资金在拉格多制作500个这样的架子，而且令负责人员将自己收集到的材料都贡献出来，这项工作或许能够得以改进，并加快进度。

He assured me, that this invention had employed all his thoughts from his youth, that he had emptied the whole vocabulary into his frame, and made the strictest computation of the general proportion there is in the Books between the numbers of particles, nouns, and verbs, and other parts of speech.

他自信地说，他从年轻时起就致力于这项工作。他把自己所能想到的词汇都写在架子上，并用最严密的方法估算书中虚词、名词和动词与其他词性的词各自所占的一般比例。

I made my humblest acknowledgment to this illustrious person for his great communicativeness, and promised if ever I had the good fortune to return to my native country, that I would do him justice, as the sole inventer of this wonderful machine; the form and contrivance of which I desired leave to delineate upon paper as in the figure here annexed. I told him, although it were the custom of our learned in *Europe* to steal inventions from each other, who had thereby at least this advantage, that it became a controversy which was the right owner, yet I would take such caution, that he should have the honour entire without a

我极其谦恭地表达了自己对这个著名人物所作的详细解释的感谢，又向他保证：如果我有幸回到自己的祖国，我一定会客观公正地说，是他独自发明了这架神奇的机器。我还恳请他让我把这机器形状和构造临摹下来。我告诉他，虽然我们欧洲的学者有互相剽窃发明成果的习俗，在这台机器上他们怎么也得占点好处，到时候谁是真正的发明者就变成一个有争议的问题了。但我一定会采取谨慎的措施，确保他能够独享这份荣誉，没有人敢夺去。

rival.

We next went to the school of Language, where three professors sat in consultation upon improving that of their own country.

The first project was to shorten discourse by cutting polysyllables into one, and leaving out verbs and participles, because in reality all things imaginable are but Nouns.

The other project was a scheme for entirely abolishing all words whatsoever; and this was urged as a great advantage in point of health as well as brevity. For, it is plain, that every word we speak is in some degree a diminution of our lungs by corrosion, and consequently contributes to the shortening of our lives. An expedient was therefore offered, that since words are only names for things, it would be more convenient for all men to carry about them, such *things* as were necessary to express a particular business they are to discourse on. And this invention would certainly have taken place, to the great ease as well as health of the subject, if the women in conjunction with the vulgar and illiterate had not threatened to raise a rebellion, unless they might be allowed the liberty to speak with their tongues, after the manner of their Ancestors; such constant irreconcileable enemies to science are the common people. However,

接着我们进入语言学校。那里有3位教授正在座谈如何改进他们国家的语言。

第一项计划是简化，将多音节词变为单音节词，删除动词和分词，因为实际上只有名词所表述的对象是可想象的。

另一项计划是将所有的词全部废除。这被认为是一项不错的计划，不仅有益于健康，而且简便易行。显而易见，我们所说的每一个词都不同程度地对我们的肺部产生腐蚀作用，会令我们寿命缩短。于是一种权宜之计就应运而生：既然单词只不过是事物的名称，那么所有人都随身携带着自己的谈话中需要谈到的东西就会方便得多。如果不是妇女们联合了平民和文盲提起抗议，要求和他们的祖辈们一样拥有用嘴说话的自由权，这项计划早就得以实施了，还可以令国民们更加轻松和健康。大众往往是科学最大的阻碍者。而很多博学多才的人仍然坚持实行这种以物示意的新方式。这个计划只是有一点不太方便，如果一个人的事情很复杂，涉及各种各样的东西，他就必须得随时背着一大堆东西，除非他有足够的钱能雇用一两个强壮的仆人帮他背。我就见到过两位大研

many of the most learned and wise adhere to the new scheme of expressing themselves by things, which hath only this inconvenience attending it, that if a man's business be very great, and of various kinds, he must be obliged in proportion to carry a greater bundle of *things* upon his back, unless he can afford one or two strong servants to attend him. I have often beheld two of those sages almost sinking under the weight of their packs, like peddlers among us; who when they met in the streets, would lay down their loads, open their sacks and hold conversation for an hour together; then put up their implements, help each other to resume their burthens, and take their leave.

究家，快要被自己背的东西给压趴下了，像极了我们那里的小贩。如果他们在街上碰面了，就会放下背包，拿出东西，在一起交谈一个小时，再把东西都装进包里，互相帮助对方重新背上包，然后再分手。

But for short conversations, a man may carry implements in his pockets and under his arms, enough to supply him, and in his house he cannot be at a loss. Therefore the room where company meet who practise this art, is full of all things ready at hand, requisite to furnish matter for this kind of artificial converse.

对于很简短的谈话来说，一个人通常可以把谈及的事物装在口袋里，或者夹在胳膊下也足够应付了。在自己家里的话也好办。因为人们在室内使用这种办法交谈的时候，到处都是能用的道具。

Another great advantage proposed by this invention, was that it would serve as a universal language to be understood in all civilized nations, whose goods and utensils are generally of the same kind, or nearly resembling, so that their uses might easily be comprehended. And thus ambassadors would be qualified to treat

这项发明还有一个很大的优点：这种语言可以在所有文明国家里通用，因为各个国家的货物和器具通常种类相近，形状相似，因此其用途也就很容易理解。这样，驻外大使们就算不懂外语，也完全可以与他们的君王或国务大臣顺利进行交谈。

with foreign princes or ministers of state to whose tongues they were utter strangers.

I was at the mathematical school, where the master taught his pupils after a method scarce imaginable to us in *Europe*. The proposition and demonstration were fairly written on a thin wafer, with ink composed of a cephalic tincture. This the student was to swallow upon a fasting stomach, and for three days following eat nothing but bread and water. As the wafer digested, the tincture mounted to his brain, bearing the proposition along with it. But the success hath not hitherto been answerable, partly by some error in the *quantum* or composition, and partly by the perverseness of lads, to whom this bolus is so nauseous that they generally steal aside, and discharge it upwards before it can operate, neither have they been yet persuaded to use so long an abstinence as the prescription requires.

我来到数学学校，那里的老师在使用一种在我们欧洲几乎难以想象的方法给学生上课。命题和证明过程都一清二楚地写在一块薄饼上，而且用的是与头皮颜色相近的墨水。学生们得空腹食用这块饼，而且3天之内只能吃面包、喝水。饼干消化后，那墨水的印迹就会留在脑子里。不过现在还没有确凿的证据印证他们的成功，一方面是由于制成墨水的成分总有误差，另一面也因为孩子们不听话，对他们来说这么大一块东西太难以下咽了，通常在药性发作之前就偷溜到旁边，将其吐掉。他们还不顾劝阻，不按照处方的要求节食3天。

CHAPTER 6

第六章

A Further Account of the Academy. The Author proposes some improvements, which are honourably received.

再叙科学院——作者提出的几项改进的意见都有幸被接纳了。

In the school of political projectors I was but ill entertained, the professors appearing in my judgment wholly out of their senses, which is a scene that never fails to make me melancholy. These unhappy people were proposing schemes for persuading monarchs to choose favourites upon the score of their wisdom, capacity and virtue; of teaching ministers to consult the public good; of rewarding merit, great abilities eminent services; of instructing princes to know their true interest by placing it on the same foundation with that of their people: of choosing for employments persons qualified to exercise them; with many other wild impossible chimeras, that never entered before into the heart of man to conceive, and confirmed in me the old observation, that there is nothing so extravagant and irrational which some philosophers have not maintained for

在政治规划家学院，人们对我的态度十分冷淡。在我看来，教授们已经完全丧失理性，一想到那场面我就异常悲哀。这群忧国忧民的人忙着倡议他们的提案，试图说服君王们按照智慧、才干和德行来挑选亲信；教育大臣们为公众利益着想；对那些功绩累累、能力出众、贡献杰出的人予以奖赏；他们想指导君王们与民同心，设身处地为百姓利益着想；想选拔资质符合的人担任相关岗位的工作等其他以前的人们从未想过的不切实际的妄想。这倒让我更加笃信那句老话，有些事不管多么夸张怪诞，都有些哲学家会坚信其为真理。

truth.

But, however I shall so far do justice to this part of the Academy, as to acknowledge that all of them were not so visionary. There was a most ingenious doctor who seemed to be perfectly versed in the whole nature and system of government. This illustrious person had very usefully employed his studies in finding out effectual remedies for all diseases and corruptions, to which the several kinds of public administration are subject by the vices or infirmities of those who govern, as well as by the licentiousness of those who are to obey. For instance; whereas all writers and reasoners have agreed, that there is a strict universal resemblance between the natural and the political body; can there be anything more evident, than that the health of both must be preserved, and the diseases cured, by the same prescriptions? It is allowed, that senates and great councils are often troubled with redundant, ebullient, and other peccant humours, with many diseases of the head, and more of the heart; with strong convulsions, with grievous contractions of the nerves and sinews in both hands, but especially the right: with spleen, flatus, vertigoes, and deliriums; with scrofulous

尽管如此，对于科学院中的这些人，公平地说，他们并非所有人都不切实际。有一位相当天才的医生，他似乎对政府的性质和体系了解颇深。这位出类拔萃的人物非常纯熟地将他的学识应用到为各种公共行政机关易犯的各种罪行和病症寻找特效良方上，这些病症一方面是由于执政者罪孽深重，另一方面是因为被统治者的目无王法。比如说，所有的作者和理论家都同意，人体和政体之间存在着严格类似的关系。那么同一副药方就能起到让二者均保持健康，治愈疾病的作用，这一点再明白不过了。大家心照不宣的是，参议员和大枢密院的官员们常常被啰里啰唆、情绪失控和其他一些病症所困扰，他们的头脑毛病诸多，而心脏的毛病更是数不胜数，他们剧烈地痉挛抽搐，伴随着双手神经和肌肉痛苦地收缩，右手更甚；有时还会肝火旺盛，胀气放屁，头脑发昏，满口胡言；还会生出长满恶臭和脓包的淋巴性结核瘤；他们会将酸臭的暖气喷得到处都是；胃口好得像条狗，内里却又消化不良；其他的许多就更不必提。因此，这位医生提议：每逢参议员开会时，务必请几位医生列席前3天的会议，每天辩论结束，

tumours full of fetid purulent matter; with sour frothy ructations, with canine appetites and crudeness of digestion, besides many others needless to mention. This doctor therefore proposed, that upon the meeting of the senate, certain physicians should attend it the three first days of their sitting, and at the close of each day's debate, feel the pulses of every senator; after which having maturely considered, and consulted upon the nature of the several maladies, and the methods of cure, they should on the fourth day return to the senate house, attended by their apothecaries stored with proper medicines, and before the members sat, administer to each of them lenitives, aperitives, abstersives, corrosives, restringents, palliatives, laxatives, cephalalgicks, ictericks, apophlegmaticks, acousticks, as their several cases required, and according as these medicines should operate, repeat, alter, or omit them at the next meeting.

由他们替每位参议员诊脉；在此之后他们经过深思熟虑，商议各种病灶的性质和治疗方法，第四天，他们在药剂师的陪同下，带着对症的药品回到参议院，在议员们坐下之前，按照各人症状所需分配给他们镇静剂、轻泻剂、去垢剂、腐蚀剂、健脑剂、治标剂、通便剂、头痛剂、黄疸剂、去痰剂、清耳剂，根据这些药的效力在下一次大会的时候再决定是否重复用药，更换药剂，或是停止用药。

This project could not be of any great expense to the public, and would in my poor opinion, be of much use for the dispatch of business in those countries where senates have any share in the legislative power, beget unanimity, shorten debates, open a few mouths which

这项提案并不会给公众造成太大的开销，而依我拙见，在那些参议员参与立法的国家里，这对提高公事效率可大有裨益。它可以让人们团结一致，大大减轻辩论的时间；让沉默的少数发表意见，而让聒噪的多数闭起嘴巴；让年轻人不

are now closed, and close many more which are now open; curb the petulancy of the young, and correct the positiveness of the old; rouse the stupid, and damp the pert.

那么急躁，让老年人不那么刚愎；可以唤醒那些愚蠢的脑瓜，也可以挫挫那些冒失鬼的锐气。

Again, because it is a general complaint that the favourites of princes are troubled with short and weak memories; the same doctor proposed, that whoever attended a first minister, after having told his business with the utmost brevity, and in the plainest words; should at his departure give the said minister a tweak by the nose, or a kick in the belly, or tread on his corns, or lug him thrice by both ears, or run a pin into his breech, or pinch his arm black and blue, to prevent forgetfulness: and at every levee day repeat the same operation, till the business were done or absolutely refused.

还有，由于君王们的亲信忘性极大，引起大众公愤，这位医生又提议不管是谁谒见首相大臣，在用最简明的语言陈述完他要报告的事情之后，临行前都应当拧一下这位大臣的鼻子，或是在他肚子上踹上一脚，还要在他的鸡眼上踩一踩，或者捏住他的两只耳朵扯3下，或者在他屁股上戳上一根大头针，要不就把他的胳膊掐得青紫；免得他再忘记。并且在每一个朝见日都依法炮制，直到事情解决或是彻底被驳回为止。

He likewise directed, that every senator in the great council of a nation, after he had delivered his opinion, and argued in the defence of it, should be obliged to give his vote directly contrary; because if that were done, the result would infallibly terminate in the good of the public.

他还指出，每一位出席全国大会的参议员，在他陈述完自己的意见并作出申辩之后，必须投出与自己意见完全相反的一票，因为如此一来结果必然为公众带来好处。

When parties in a state are violent, he offered a wonderful contrivance to reconcile them. The method is this. You take an hundred leaders of each party, you

当一国党派之间争斗激烈时，他还提供了一个绝妙的让他们和解的巧思。那就是从每个政党之中选出100名首要人物，将脑袋大小

dispose them into couples of such whose heads are nearest of a size; then let two nice operators saw off the *occiput* of each couple at the same time, in such a manner that the brain may be equally divided. Let the occiputs thus cut off be interchanged, applying each to the head of his opposite party-man. It seems indeed to be a work that requireth some exactness, but the professor assured us, "that if it were dexterously performed, the cure would be infallible. For he argued thus; that the two half brains being left to debate the matter between themselves within the space of one skull, would soon come to a good understanding, and produce that moderation as well as regularity of thinking, so much to be wished for in the heads of those, who imagine they come into the world only to watch and govern its motion; and as to the difference of brains in quantity or quality, among those who are directors in faction; the doctor assured us from his own knowledge, that it was a perfect trifle.

差不多的各自两两配对，然后让两位技术高超的外科医生将二人的后脑同时锯下，这样就能将大脑均匀地一分为二。接着将切下来的后脑彼此对换，安在各自的反对党派的人的脑袋上。这个工作需要相当的精确度，然而教授向我们保证，只要手术完成得分毫不差，治疗效果可是绝对信得过的。因为他如此论证，这两个半个大脑现在被放在一个头骨里辩论，很快就能达成共识，如此官员们都会变得脾气温和，思路清晰富有条理，那些梦想来到世界上就是为了俯视它，统治它的人们若是能这样温和而有条不紊该多好！而至于这两派首脑人物的大脑重量和质量上的不同之处，医生向我们保证，据他所知，这种事根本无关紧要。

I heard a very warm debate between two professors, about the most commodious and effectual ways and means of raising money without grieving the subject. The first affirmed the justest method would be to lay a certain tax upon

我听到两位教授热火朝天地辩论，话题是关于怎样筹款才能既不伤害公众的感情又方便而行之有效。第一位认定，最公平的方法是对犯恶和出丑征收一定税额，每人应缴的税款由他邻居组成的陪

vices and folly, and the sum fixed upon every man, to be rated, after the fairest manner by a jury of his neighbours. The second was of an opinion directly contrary, to tax those qualities of body and mind for which men chiefly value themselves; the rate to be more or less according to the degrees of excelling, the decision whereof should be left entirely to their own breast. The highest tax was upon men who are the greatest favourites of the other sex, and the assessments according to the number and natures of the favours they have received; for which they are allowed to be their own vouchers. Wit, valour, and politeness were likewise proposed to be largely taxed, and collected in the same manner, by every person giving his own word for the quantum of what he possessed. But as to honour, justice, wisdom, and learning, they should not be taxed at all; because they are qualifications of so singular a kind, that no man will either allow them in his neighbour, or value them in himself.

审团经过最为公正的裁决判定。另一位的意见则完全相反，他认为应当向那些自认为在体力和智力上都占优势的人征税，根据其才能的水平所征税额的多少，而这决定完全取决于他们自己。最受女性青睐的男子应当被征收最高份额的税款，按照他们所受宠爱的次数和性质评定纳税额的多少；他们可以自行作证。那些聪明的，勇敢的，彬彬有礼的人也应该多缴税，至于这些美德究竟有多少也取决于他们自己的评价。然而对于光荣、正义、智慧和学识渊博的人，他们完全不用缴税，因为这些品质如此罕有，既没人会认可周围的人有这些品德，而这些人自己也对此不屑一顾。

The women were proposed to be taxed according to their beauty and skill in dressing, wherein they had the same privilege with the men, to be determined by their own judgment. But constancy, chastity, good sense, and good nature,

他主张应当根据美貌程度和打扮的本事来对妇女进行征税，她们享有和男子一样的特权，那就是可以自行决定缴税多少。但对于专一、贞洁、有头脑和好脾气的妇女则不征税，因为她们根本无法负担

were not rated, because they would not bear the charge of collecting.

税负。

To keep senators in the interest of the crown, it was proposed that the members should raffle for employment, every man first taking an oath, and giving security that he would vote for the court, whether he won or no, after which the losers had in their turn the liberty of raffling upon the next vacancy. Thus hope and expectation would be kept alive; none would complain of broken promises, but impute their disappointments wholly to fortune, whose shoulders are broader and stronger than those of a ministry.

为了让参议员们效忠王室，他建议议员们用抽签的方式竞选。每个人都先得宣誓一番，保证不管他是否当选，都永远忠于朝廷，这样失败者还能参加下一次空缺职位的抽签竞选。既然希望还在，就没人会抱怨朝廷没有信守承诺，只能将他们的失落归咎于命运不公，后者的肩膀可比朝廷的宽广坚实得多。

Another professor showed me a large paper of instructions for discovering plots and conspiracies against the government. He advised great statesmen to examine into the diet of all suspected persons; their times of eating; upon which side they lay in bed; with which hand they wiped their posteriors; take a strict view of their excrements, and from the colour, the odour, the taste, the consistence, the crudeness, or maturity of digestion, form a judgment of their thoughts and designs. because men are never so serious, thoughtful, and intent, as when they are at stool, which he found by frequent experiment: for in such conjunctures,

另一位教授则给我展示了一份长长的关于如何识破政府的阴谋诡计的论文。他建议大政治家们要对所有可疑人物的饮食进行彻查，他们吃饭的时间，他们睡觉的时候朝向哪边，用哪只手擦屁股，还要严格地检查他们的排泄物，从颜色、气味、稠度、浓度以及消化的程度来形成对他们的想法和预谋的判断，因为他经过反复试验发现，人最认真严肃、思绪纷繁且一心一意的时刻，就是他如厕的时候。因此在这种情况下，如果他在思考怎样才是谋杀国王最好的方法，他的粪便就 会呈现出绿色，但当他仅仅是想到要发起武装叛

when he used merely as a trial, to consider which was the best way of murdering the king, his ordure would have a tincture of green, but quite different when he thought only of raising an insurrection or burning the metropolis.

乱或是烧毁都城，那他粪便的颜色就大为不同。

The whole discourse was written with great acuteness, containing many observations both curious and useful for politicians, but as I conceived not altogether complete. This I ventured to tell the author, and offered if he pleased to supply him with some additions. He received my proposition with more compliance than is usual among writers, especially those of the projecting species, professing he would be glad to receive farther information.

这篇论文的观点十分敏锐，其中包含了很多对政治家来说既新奇又实用的见解。然而在我看来还不够完整。因此我冒昧地向作者提出这一点，并且申明如果他愿意，我可以向他提供些补充建议。他十分乐于接受我的建议，并声明他很愿意听听我的说法。这一点在作家中，尤其是那些空想派作家中可不多见。

I told him that in the kingdom of *Tribnia*, by the natives called *Langden*, where I had sojourned some time in my travels, the bulk of the people consist wholly of discoverers, witnesses, informers, accusers, prosecutors, evidences, swearers, together with their several subservient and subaltern instruments, all under the colours the conduct of ministers of state and their deputies. The plots, in that kingdom are usually the workmanship of those persons who desire to raise their own characters of

我告诉他，我曾在特列不尼亚逗留过一阵子。当地人称它作兰敦。那里的人都是侦探、目击证人、告密者、指控者、检举人、证人、诅咒者以及溜须拍马的走狗。他们全都有正副大臣们做保护伞。在那个国家里，阴谋往往产生于那些想要抬高自己大政治家身份的人之中。他们想让一个摇摇欲坠的政府发生一次大换血，企图压制或者转移公众的不满，企图用没收所得的罚金填满他们自己的口袋，企图控制公众舆论以满足他们的一己私

profound politicians, to restore new vigour to a crazy administration, to stifle or divert general discontents, to fill their Pockets with forfeitures; and raise, or sink the opinion of public credit, as either shall best answer their private advantage. It is first agreed and settled among them what suspected persons shall be accused of a plot: then effectual care is taken to secure all their letters and papers and put the Criminals in chains. These papers are delivered to a set of artists very dexterous in finding out the mysterious meanings of words, syllables, and letters. for instance, they can discover a close stool to signify a privy council, a flock of geese a senate, a lame dog an invader, a Codshead a—[king], the plague a standing army, a buzzard a prime minister, the gout a high priest, a gibbet a secretary of state, a chamber-pot a committee of grandees, a sieve a court lady, a broom a revolution, a mouse-trap an employment, a bottomless pit a treasury, a sink, the court a cap and bells a favourite, a broken reed a court of justice, an empty tun a general, a running sore the administration.

利。他们先在内部取得一致方案，决定先要用图谋不轨的罪名陷害哪一个人，接下来他们动用有效的方法调查这些人的书信文件，然后将他们投入大狱。这些文件被送到一群精于从单词、音节和字母中发掘隐喻含义的高人们手里。例如，他们会破译出“马桶”象征着“枢密院”;“一只鹅”指“一个参议员”;“瘸腿狗”指“侵略者”;“呆头”指“国王”;“瘟疫”指“现役部队”;“秃鹰”指“总理大臣”;“痛风”指“大主教”;“绞刑架”指“国务大臣”;“夜壶”指“贵族委员会”;“筛子”指“宫廷贵妇”;“扫帚”则是“一场革命”;“捕鼠器”指“官职”;“无底洞”指“财政部”;“阴沟”指“朝廷”;“滑稽演员戴的系铃帽”指“宠臣”;“折断的芦苇”指“法庭”;“空酒桶”指“将军”;“流脓的疮”指“当局”。

When this method fails, they have two others more effectual, which the learned among them call acrostics and anagrams. First they can decipher all initial letters

如果这个方法失效的话，他们还有其他两种更加有效的方法，学者叫它们“离合字谜法”和“颠倒字谜法”。采用第一种办法，他们

into political meanings. Thus *N* shall signify a plot, *B* a regiment of horse, *L* a fleet at sea, or secondly, by transposing the letters of the alphabet in any suspected paper, they can discover the deepest designs of a discontented party. So for example, if I should say in a letter to a friend, *Our brother* Tom *has just got the piles*, a skilful decipherer would discover that the same letters which compose that sentence, may be analysed into the following words; Resist, *a plot is brought home, The tour*. And this is the anagrammatic method.

能将所有单词的头文字母破译出政治寓意。因此 N 代表“一场阴谋”，B 指“一个骑兵团”，L 指“海上舰队”。或者采用第二种方法，通过将任何可疑文件的字母拼写顺序颠倒，就能够拆穿对当局不满的政党隐藏最深的阴谋。举个例子，如果我在给朋友的一封信中说，“我们的汤姆兄弟近来患了痔疮。”一个精于此道的破译专家就会发现同一句话里的相同字母可以被解读为如下的句子：“反抗吧！密谋已经成熟。塔。”这就是“颠倒字谜法”。

The professor made me great acknowledgments for communicating these observations, and promised to make honourable mention of me in his treatise.

教授对我提出的意见表示了感激和认可，并承诺会在他的论文中提到我的名字以表敬意。

I saw nothing in this country that could invite me to a longer continuance, and began to think of returning home to *England*.

我在这个国家再也找不到任何值得停留的东西了，于是想到重返英国老家。

CHAPTER 7

第七章

The Author leaves Lagado: arrives at Maldonada. No Ship ready. He takes a short Voyage to Glubbdubdrib. His Reception by the Governor.

作者离开拉格多抵达马尔多纳达。没有现成的船可以搭乘，他于是做了一次短途旅行到达格勒大锥，并受到当地总督的款待。

The continent of which this kingdom is apart, extends itself, as I have reason to believe, eastward to that unknown tract of *America*, westward of *California*, and north to the Pacific Ocean, which is not above a hundred and fifty miles from *Lagado*, where there is a good port and much commerce with the great island of *Luggnagg*, situated to the north-west about 29 degrees north latitude, and 140 longitude. This island of *Luggnagg* stands south-eastwards of *Japan*, about an hundred leagues distant. There is a strict alliance between the *Japanese* emperor and the king of *Luggnagg*, which affords frequent opportunities of sailing from one island to the other. I determined therefore to direct my course this way, in order to my return to *Europe*. I hired two mules with a guide to show me the way and carry my small baggage. I took leave of my noble protector, who had shown me so much favour, and made me a generous

我有理由相信，这个国家所处的这片大陆向东一直延伸至美洲加利福尼亚以西的某片未知地域，向北延伸至太平洋。那里有一处良港，距拉格多只有不到150英里。它与西北方向大约北纬29°、东经140°的拉格奈格大岛之间贸易来往密切。这座拉格奈格岛坐落于日本岛东南方向大约100里格远的位置。日本天皇与拉格奈格国王之间达成了密切的同盟关系，因此两个岛国之间频繁通航。我决心朝着这条线路行进，以便返回欧洲。我雇了一名向导带路，两头骡子扛着我的小行李。我向我尊贵的主人辞别，他一直待我不薄，临行时还送了我一份大礼。

present at my departure.

My journey was without any accident or adventure worth relating. When I arrived at the port of *Maldonada* (for so it is called), there was no ship in the harbour bound for *Luggnagg*, nor like to be in some time. The town is about as large as *Portsmouth*. I soon fell into some acquaintance, and was very hospitably received. A gentleman of distinction said to me, that since the ships bound for *Luggnagg* could not be ready in less than a *month*, it might be no disagreeable amusement for me to take a trip to the little island of *Glubbdubdrib*, about five leagues off to the south-west. He offered himself and a friend to accompany me, and that I should be provided with a small convenient bark for the voyage.

Glubbdubdrib, as nearly as I can interpret the word, signifies the island of *sorcerers* or *magicians*. It is about one third as large as the Isle of *Wight*, and extremely fruitful: it is governed by the head of a certain tribe, who are all magicians. This tribe marries only among each other, and the eldest in succession is prince or governor. He hath a noble palace and a park of about three thousand acres, surrounded by a wall of hewn stone twenty foot high. In this park are several smaller enclosures for cattle, corn, and gardening.

我的旅程波澜不惊，没有什么值得讲述的故事或奇遇。当我来到马尔多纳达港口时（它就叫这个名字），没有看到一只去往拉格奈格的船，而以后也不大可能会有。这镇子和朴次茅斯规模相仿。很快我就结交了些朋友，他们对我都十分热情。其中一位声名显赫的绅士对我说，既然起码一个月内都不会有去拉格奈格的船，那我不妨去距此约 5 里格的格勒大锥小岛玩玩。他表示他自己连同一位友人可以陪我前去，还将提供给我一艘小而轻便的三桅小帆船。

“格勒大锥”，尽我所能来翻译的话，这岛的名字应该是“巫人岛”或是“魔法师岛”。它的面积差不多只及外特岛的 1/3，物产却十分富饶。岛上被一个部落占据，部落居民全是巫人。他们只在部落内部婚配结合，首领或长官均由最年长者接任。首领的宫殿十分富丽堂皇，还有一座占地约 3000 英亩的花园，周围是 20 英尺高的石头围墙。花园里的几处较小些的开阔地用来放牧、种植庄稼和发展园艺。

The governor and his family are served and attended by domestics of a kind somewhat unusual. By his skill in necromancy he hath a power of calling whom he pleaseth from the dead, and commanding their service for twenty-four hours, but no longer; nor can he call the same persons up again in less than three months, except upon very extraordinary occasions.

首领及其一家都被一群有着异于常人的本领的仆人照料着。首领自己精通的巫术是召唤死去的魂魄，并让他们听命于他 24 个小时，然而再长就不行了。而除非是特殊情况，3 个月内他也不能再召唤同一个魂魄。

When we arrived at the island, which was about eleven in the morning, one of the gentlemen who accompanied me, went to the governor, and desired admittance for a stranger, who came on purpose to have the honour of attending on his highness. This was immediately granted, and we all three entered the gate of the palace between two rows of guards, armed and dressed after a very antic manner, and something in their countenances that made my flesh creep with a horror I cannot express. We passed through several apartments between servants of the same sort, ranked on each side as before, till we came to the chamber of presence, where after three profound obeisances, and a few general questions, we were permitted to sit on three stools near the lowest step of his highness's throne. He understood the language of *Balnibarbi*, although it were different from that of his island. He desired me to give him some account of

我们抵达小岛的时候差不多是上午 11 点，陪同我的一位绅士去拜访了首领，请求接见我这样一位特地来敬仰他的陌生访客。首领马上答应了我们的请求，接着我们 3 个人被迎进宫殿大门，大门两旁分别站着一行守卫，装备和服装都十分滑稽，而他们的长相却让我着实胆战心惊。那种恐怖的感觉很难描述。我们穿过几间屋子，两旁都是一模一样的守卫，一直到我们来到接见的大殿上。在深深鞠了 3 个躬，并回答了首领几个通常的问题之后，我们得到允许在离他的宝座下最低一层台阶旁边的 3 个凳子上坐了下来。他听得懂巴尔尼巴比的语言，虽然和他岛上的语言并不一样。他让我将我旅行的见闻讲给他听，为了让我明白我不必拘束于礼节，他动了动手指就让他所有的侍从都退下了，我见到他们转眼之间就消失不见，仿佛从梦里突然惊醒一般，不禁大为骇然。我一时无法

my travels; and to let me see that I should be treated without ceremony, he dismissed all his attendants with a turn of his finger; at which to my great astonishment they vanished in an instant, like visions in a dream, when we awake on a sudden. I could not recover myself in some time, till the governor assured me that I should receive no hurt; and observing my two companions to be under no concern, who had been often entertained in the same manner, I began to take courage, and related to his highness a short history of my several adventures, yet not without some hesitation, and frequently looking behind me to the place where I had seen those domestic spectres. I had the honour to dine with the governor, where a new set of ghosts served up the meat, and waited at table. I now observed myself to be less terrified than I had been in the morning. I stayed till sunset, but humbly desired his highness to excuse me for not accepting his invitation of lodging in the palace. My two friends and I lay at a private house in the town adjoining, which is the capital of this little island; and the next morning we returned to pay our duty to the governor, as he was pleased to command us.

平复，直到首领向我保证我绝不会受到任何伤害，我也发现我的两位同伴面不改色，他们以前经常受到这般款待，我才开始鼓起勇气，向他简短地讲述了我的数番奇遇。然而我还是有些忐忑犹豫，屡屡回头看看之前见到鬼魂护卫的地方。我很荣幸能与首领一同进餐，这时又有一群新的鬼魂端上肉来并在一旁候命。现在我已经没有上午的时候那么战战兢兢了。我一直待到日落时分，不过我还是谦逊地请求首领能原谅我无法留在宫殿里过夜的邀请。我和我的两个朋友当晚下榻在附近镇上的一户人家里，这个镇子也是小岛的首都。次日早上我们返回宫殿去觐见首领，而他也十分乐意接见我们。

After this manner we continued in the island for ten days, most part of every day with the governor, and at night in our lodging. I soon grew so familiarized to the

就这样我们在这座岛上停留了 10 天，每天的大部分时光都陪着首领，到了晚上回到住的地方。很快我就对鬼魂见怪不怪了，三四

sight of spirits, that after the third or fourth time they gave me no emotion at all; or if I had any apprehensions left, my curiosity prevailed over them. For his highness the governor ordered me to call up whatever persons I would choose to name, and in whatever numbers among all the dead from the beginning of the world to the present time, and command them to answer any questions I should think fit to ask; with this condition, that my questions must be confined within the compass of the times they lived in. And one thing I might depend upon, that they would certainly tell me the truth, for lying was a talent of no use in the lower world.

I made my humble acknowledgments to his highness for so great a favour. We were in a chamber, from whence there was a fair prospect into the park. And because my first inclination was to be entertained with scenes of pomp and magnificence, I desired to see *Alexander the Great,* at the head of his army just after the battle of Arbela, which upon a motion of the governor's finger immediately appeared in a large field under the window, where we stood. *Alexander* was called up into the room: it was with great difficulty that I understood his *Greek*, and had but little of my own. He assured me upon his honour that he was not poisoned, but died of a

次之后我已经没什么感觉了。就算我还仅存一丝恐惧，但也被我的好奇所掩盖。因为首领让我可以任意召唤我想叫到的任何一个鬼魂，而且从创世纪以来到现在，所有魂魄他想召唤来多少都可以，而我可以问他们我想问的任何问题，但必须有一个条件，那就是我的问题必须仅限于他们生活的那个年代。而有一点我坚信，那就是他们一定会告诉我实话，因为对于阴间而言撒谎实在是一种无用的本领。

对于首领如此慷慨的恩惠，我万分感激。我们进了一间侧殿，从这里可以将花园的风景一览无余。因为我最想看到的是宏伟壮观的场面，于是我要求看到亚历山大大帝带领着他的军队在艾尔贝拉战役[1]之后的情景。首领只动了动手指这盛大的战场就显现于我们站立的窗下，首领将亚历山大大帝召进屋内。他的希腊语十分晦涩难懂，不过也可能是因为我自己对希腊语知之甚少的缘故。他用他的名誉向我担保说他可不是被毒死的，而是死于过度饮酒引发的一场高烧。

[1] 公元前 331 年发生在亚历山大大帝和大流士三世中间的战役。

fever by excessive drinking.

Next, I saw *Hannibal* passing the *Alps*, who told me he had not a drop of vinegar in his camp.

I saw Caesar and *Pompey* at the head of their troops just ready to engage. I saw the former in his last great triumph. I desired that the senate of *Rome* might appear before me in one large chamber, and a modern Representative, in counterview in another. The first seemed to be an assembly of heroes and demigods; the other a knot of pedlars, Pickpockets, Highwaymen and bullies.

The governor at my request gave the sign for Caesar and *Brutus* to advance towards us. I was struck with a profound veneration at the sight of *Brutus*, and could easily discover the most consummate virtue, the greatest intrepidity and firmness of mind, the truest love of his country, and general benevolence for mankind in every lineament of his countenance. I observed with much pleasure, that these two persons were in good intelligence with each other, and Caesar freely confessed to me, that the greatest actions of his own life were not equal by many degrees to the glory of taking it away. I had the honour to have much conversation with *Brutus*; and was told that his ancestor *Junius*, *Socrates*, *Epaminondas*, *Cato* the younger, Sir

接下来我又见识了正在翻越阿尔卑斯山的汉尼拔。他告诉我他的营地里连一滴醋都没了。

我又看到恺撒和庞贝带领着各自的军队正准备对战。我看到恺撒正沉浸在他最后一次伟大的胜利之中。我要求看一看罗马参议院在我面前的大厅中开会的样子，并且作为对照在另一间屋里召开一场现代的代表大会的情形。前者看起来如同一群英雄和半神半人在集会，后者却是一伙小贩、扒手、劫匪和流氓。

首领在我的要求下向恺撒和布鲁托斯做了个手势让他们走到我们面前。我一见到布鲁托斯，心中就升起一股深深的敬意，我能轻易地从他脸上的每个线条看出他那完美无瑕的德行，刚勇的性格，坚韧的意志，最真诚的爱国情怀和他对人类最无私的仁爱。看到这两个人彼此理解，我感到非常欣慰。恺撒还向我坦承：他此生最伟大的功绩也远远不及布鲁托斯将他的生命了结来得荣耀。而能与布鲁托斯说上这么久也是我莫大的荣幸，他告诉我，他的祖先优尼乌斯、苏格拉底、依帕米浓达斯、小伽图和托马斯·莫尔爵士与他同在，不管全世界哪个年代都找不出第七个人与他们并肩匹敌。

Thomas More and himself, were perpetually together: a *sextumvirate* to which all the ages of the world cannot add a seventh.

It would be tedious to trouble the reader with relating what vast numbers of illustrious persons were called up, to gratify that insatiable desire I had to see the world in every period of antiquity placed before me. I chiefly fed my eyes with beholding the destroyers of tyrants and usurpers, and the restorers of liberty to oppressed and injured nations. But it is impossible to express the satisfaction I received in my own mind, after such a manner as to make it a suitable entertainment to the reader.

为了满足我的贪得无厌，首领将每个时代无数赫赫有名的人物都召唤到我眼前，要将其一一详述将会令读者不厌其烦。我主要看了那些暴政和篡权的终结者们，以及那些解放了被压迫与被损害的民族的人们。然而我却无法将我心中那种满足转化为文字，让读者也能感受到那种酣畅淋漓的快感。

CHAPTER 8

第八章

A Further Account of Glubbdubdrib. Ancient and Modern History corrected.

Having a desire to see those ancients, who were most renowned for wit and learning, I set apart one day on purpose. I proposed that *Homer* and *Aristotle* might appear at the head of all their commentators; but these were so numerous that some hundreds were forced to attend in the court and outward rooms of the palace. I knew and could distinguish those two heroes at first sight, not only from the crowd, but from each other. *Homer* was the taller and comelier person of the two, walked very erect for one of his age, and his eyes were the most quick and piercing I ever beheld. *Aristotle* stooped much, and made use of a staff. His visage was meagre, his hair lank and thin, and his voice hollow. I soon discovered that both of them were perfect strangers to the rest of the company, and had never seen or heard of them before. and I had a whisper from a ghost, who shall be nameless, that these commentators always kept in the most distant quarters from their principals in the

继续讲述格勒大锥的故事，对古今历史的修正。

我特地排出一天来想要见见久负盛名的那些智慧与学识并称的古代圣贤们。我提议让荷马和亚里士多德带领所有他们的评论家现身，但这些人实在是多如牛毛，以至于几百人不得不站在院子里和外殿中。我不但第一眼就将那两位英雄从人群中挑出来，还将他二人分得一清二楚。荷马是二人中较高较英俊的那个，对于他这般年迈的人来说，他走路的姿势可谓十分英挺。而他长了一双我所见过的最犀利灵动的眼睛。亚里士多德的脊背佝偻得厉害，得借助一根拐杖才能站立。他面容瘦削，头发长而稀疏，声如洪钟。很快我就发现这二人对其他人完全陌生，且从未听说或是见过这些人。有一个鬼魂，在此隐去他的名字，他小声告诉我，在阴间，这些评论家永远都离这两位先哲远远的，满心羞愧和懊悔，因为他们竟然将作家的本意完全曲解授予后人。我将迪迭摩斯和尤斯台修斯引荐给荷马，并说服他待他们优厚一些，然而或许他们并不

lower world, through a consciousness of shame and guilt, because they had so horribly misrepresented the meaning of those authors to posterity." I introduced *Didymus* and *Eustathius* to *Homer*, and prevailed on him to treat them better than perhaps they deserved, for he soon found they wanted a genius to enter into the spirit of a poet. But *Aristotle* was out of all patience with the account I gave him of *Scotus* and *Ramus*, as I presented them to him, and he asked them whether the rest of the tribe were as great dunces as themselves.

配受到如此待遇，因为很快他就发现他们没有成为一个诗人的潜质。而当我把司各特斯和拉摩斯[1]介绍给亚里士多德时，在我滔滔不绝介绍的时候他彻底失去了耐心，他问他们其余这群人是否也和他们一样愚蠢得不可救药。

I then desired the governor to call up *Descartes* and *Gassendi*, with whom I prevailed to explain their systems to *Aristotle*. This great philosopher freely acknowledged his own mistakes in natural philosophy, because he proceeded in many things upon conjecture, as all men must do; and he found, that *Gassendi*, who had made the doctrine of *Epicurus* as palatable as he could, and the *vortices* of *Descartes* were equally exploded. He predicted the same fate to *attraction*, whereof the present learned are such zealous asserters. He said, that new systems of nature were but new fashions, which would vary in

然后我又要求首领帮我召唤笛卡儿[2]和伽桑狄[3]。我试图用他们的理论去说服亚里士多德。这位伟大的哲学家坦率地承认自己在自然哲学方面犯下的错误，因为他和平常人一样对许多事也都是想当然的主观臆断罢了。而他还发现，极力宣扬普及伊壁鸠鲁[4]学说的伽桑狄和笛卡儿的涡动说也都一样被推翻了。他预言，当代学者狂热追捧的万有引力学说也必将遭受相同的命运。他说自然哲学的新学说不过是短暂的新流行，随着朝代的更迭也会不断变化，就算是那些自以为可以用数学原理阐述证明

[1] 拉摩斯（1515~1572），法国人类学家，逻辑学家和教育改革家。

[2] 笛卡儿（1596~1650），法国科学家，数学家和哲学家。

[3] 伽桑狄（1592~1655），法国科学家，数学家和哲学家。

[4] 伊壁鸠鲁（公元前 341~公元前 270），古希腊哲学家和伊壁鸠鲁哲学的创始人。

every age; and even those who pretend to demonstrate them from mathematical principles, would flourish but a short period of time, and be out of vogue when that was determined.

I spent five days in conversing with many others of the ancient learned. I saw most of the first Roman emperors. I prevailed on the governor to call up Eliogabulus's cooks to dress us a dinner, but they could not show us much of their skill, for want of materials. A *helot* of *Agesilaus* made us a dish of *Spartan* broth, but I was not able to get down a second spoonful.

The two gentlemen who conducted me to the island were pressed by their private affairs to return in three days, which I employed in seeing some of the modern dead, who had made the greatest figure for two or three hundred years past in our own and other countries of *Europe*; and having been always a great admirer of old illustrious families, I desired the governor would call up a dozen or two of kings with their ancestors in order for eight or nine generations. But my disappointment was grievous and unexpected. For instead of a long train with royal diadems, I saw in one family two fiddlers, three spruce courtiers, and an *Italian* prelate. In another a barber, an abbot, and two cardinals. I have too

自己的学说的人也不过是昙花一现，一旦盖棺定论这些也就成了过眼云烟。

我又花了 5 天时间与其他许多古代的学者畅谈。罗马第一代帝王大部分我都得以亲见。我提议让首领找来伊里欧枷布鲁斯的厨师来为我们准备一顿大餐，然而因为材料不足他们没法完全施展他们的技艺。爱基西劳斯[1]的一个农奴给我们做了一盆斯巴达肉汤，但我喝了一勺就再也没胃口了。

带我来岛上的两位绅士因为一些私人事务被迫在 3 天之内赶回去。而我用这 3 天时间见到了几位近代逝去的伟人，他们都是近二三百年中我国和其他欧洲国家名噪一时的大人物，因为我一直十分敬仰历史悠久显赫的家族，就请求首领把那一二十位国王连同他们上溯八九代的祖先一起召来。然而结果却令我大失所望。因为我并没有看到意想之中的长长的一串皇冠，相反在一个家族中我看到了两名琴师，3 名衣冠整洁的侍臣和一名意大利教长；在另一个家族中，我见到的则是一名理发师、一名修道院院长和两名红衣主教。我对于皇袍加冕的人怀有至高敬意，因此这

[1] 爱基西劳斯（公元前 444~公元前 360），古希腊时期欧里庞提德世系的斯巴达国王。

great a veneration for crowned heads to dwell any longer on so nice a subject. But as to counts, marquesses, dukes, earls, and the like I was not so scrupulous. And I confess it was not without some pleasure that I found myself able to trace the particular features, by which certain families are distinguished up to their originals. I could plainly discover whence one family derives a long chin, why a second hath abounded with knaves for two generations, and fools for two more; why a third happened to be crack-brained, and a fourth to be sharpers. whence it came what *Polydore Virgil* says of a certain great house, *Nec vir fortis, nec faemina casta.* how cruelty, falsehood, and cowardice grew to be characteristics by which certain families are distinguished as much as by their coat of arms. who first brought the pox into a noble house, which hath lineally descended scrofulous tumours to their posterity. Neither could I wonder at all this, when I saw such an interruption of lineages by pages, lackies, valets, coachmen, gamesters, captains, and Pick-pockets.

个讳莫如深的话题就不再继续下去了。然而对于那些公爵、侯爵、伯爵、子爵之流，我可没那么多顾忌了。我得承认我从追溯某些家族从他们祖先之中脱颖而出的一些特质的过程中获得不少乐趣。我看得明明白白，这一家是怎么长出了一个标志的长下巴；那一家为什么两代全是恶棍，接下来的两代又都是傻瓜；为什么第三家人刚好都是疯子；第四家人又偏偏全是骗子；坡里道尔·维吉尔为什么会说某个名门是“男子不勇敢，女子不贞洁”。残暴、欺诈、懦弱是如何成为像家族徽章那样象征某些家族的特征；是谁最先将疱疹传入一个高贵的家族，使得历代子孙都遗传患上堕落的毒瘤。当我看到皇家世袭中断原来是因为出了这么些仆人、用人、走卒、车夫、赌棍、琴师、戏子、军人和扒手，以上种种也就不足为奇了。

I was chiefly disgusted with modern history. For having strictly examined all the persons of greatest name in the courts of princes for an hundred years past, I found how the world had been misled by prostitute writers, to ascribe the greatest

现代历史让我最感到恶心。因为当我严谨地审查了过去100年中帝王宫廷里所有大人物后，发现这帮妓女一样无耻的作家是如何欺骗了整个世界，他们将赫赫战功归功于一群懦夫，将最明智的建议安

exploits in war to cowards, the wisest counsel to fools, sincerity to flatterers, *Roman* virtue to betrayers of their country, piety to atheists, chastity to sodomites, truth to informers. how many innocent and excellent persons had been condemned to death or banishment by the practising of great ministers upon the corruption of judges, and the malice of factions. how many villains had been exalted to the highest places of trust, power, dignity, and profit: how great a share in the motions and events of courts, councils, and senates might be challenged by bawds, whores, pimps, parasites, and buffoons: How low an opinion I had of human wisdom and integrity, when I was truly informed of the springs and motives of great enterprises and revolutions in the world, and of the contemptible accidents to which they owed their success.

到一群白痴头上，他们将拍马屁的阿谀者描绘得真挚无比，还将那些叛国者说成是最具罗马人美德的忠臣。在他们笔下，无神论者最虔诚，鸡奸犯最贞洁，告密者口吐真言。只因为那些权倾朝野的大臣买通了法官，或是党派之间的互相残杀，多少清白无辜的好人被杀害、被流放。多少恶棍爬到最亲信的位子上，被委以重任，手握大权作威作福。朝廷、枢密院和参议院里每日上演的一幕幕事件和鸨母、妓女、皮条客以及小丑的行为是多么相似。当我得知世上这些惊天动地的大事和革命事业背后真正的动机和根源并不那么高尚，而那些成功人士也不过是依赖于卑劣的偶然，不禁对人类的智慧和诚实不屑一顾。

Here I discovered the roguery and ignorance of those who pretend to write *anecdotes*, or secret history, who send so many kings to their graves with a cup of poison; will repeat the discourse between a prince and chief minister, where no witness was by; unlock the thoughts and cabinets of ambassadors and secretaries of state, and have the perpetual misfortune to be mistaken. Here I discovered the secret causes of many great events that have surprised the world. how a whore can

我还发现，那些声称在写什么野史秘闻的人原来是多么险恶无知啊，在他们笔下多少君王都被一杯毒酒送去见了阎王；他们将无人见证的国王和首席大臣的谈话叙述得惟妙惟肖；驻外大使和国务卿脑子里所想的和他们秘密的柜子都被他们敞开了，然而可惜的是他们从来没说对过。我还发现了许多引发令世人震惊的大事的秘密缘由：一名妓女是如何掌控后梯，而后梯又如何掌控议会，议会又如何

govern the back-stairs, the back-stairs a council, and the council a senate. A general confessed in my presence, that he got a victory purely by the force of cowardice and ill conduct: and an admiral that for want of proper intelligence, he beat the enemy to whom he intended to betray the fleet. Three kings protested to me, that in their whole reigns they never did once prefer any person of merit, unless by mistake or treachery of some minister in whom they confided: neither would they do it if they were to live again; and they showed with great strength of reason, that the royal throne could not be supported without corruption, because that positive, confident restive temper, which virtue infused into man, was a perpetual clog to public business.

掌控参议院。一位将军在我面前承认，他纯粹是因为懦弱和糟糕的指挥才赢得一场胜利；而一位海军上将告诉我，他没有得到确凿的情报，他原本打算带领舰队叛逃敌国，却不料击败了敌方。3 位国王向我坦露，在他们统治期间从未提拔过一位贤良之士，除非是搞错了或是中了某个亲信的奸计；而就算他们再活一次也不会这么做的。而且他们还说出了十分有分量的道理，那就是皇权必须由腐败来支撑，因为美德灌输给人类的积极、自信和坚韧的品格对公共事业来说是永久的绊脚石。

I had the curiosity to inquire in a particular manner, by what method great numbers had procured to themselves high titles of honour, and prodigious estates; and I confined my inquiry to a very modern period: however without grating upon present times, because I would be sure to give no offence even to foreigners (for I hope the reader need not be told that I do not in the least intend my own country in what I say upon this occasion) a great number of persons concerned were called up, and upon a very slight examination, discovered such a scene of

我出于好奇就特别提问，那么多人到底是用了什么方法攫取了高官贵爵和万亩良田？我将我提问的范围限制在近代而不考虑现代的情况，因为我必须确保连外国人也不冒犯（因为我希望我所说的情形一点都没针对我的祖国，这一点无须知会读者）。许许多多有关人士被召集前来，我只稍微审视一番就发现这场景多么不堪，以致我每每想起，就十分痛心。伪证、欺压、收买、诈骗、助纣为虐等罪行仅仅是他们提及的最能被原谅的，对于这些我都给予最大的宽容。然

infamy, that I cannot reflect upon it without some seriousness. Perjury, oppression, subornation, fraud, pandarism, and the like *infirmities* were amongst the most excusable arts they had to mention, and for these I gave, as it was reasonable, great allowance. But when some confessed they owed their greatness and wealth to sodomy or incest, others to the prostituting of their own wives and daughters; others to the betraying their country or their prince; some to poisoning, more to the perverting of justice in order to destroy the innocent: I hope I may be pardoned if these discoveries inclined me a little to abate of that profound veneration which I am naturally apt to pay to persons of high rank, who ought to be treated with the utmost respect due to their sublime dignity, by us their inferiors.

而当有人供认他们显赫的地位和财富都是因为他们鸡奸和乱伦，有的则来自逼迫自己的妻女去卖淫，有的是背叛祖国或者君王，有的则是给他人下毒，更多的来自败坏法律陷害无辜者。这些身居高位的人本应自然而然地受到我们这些地位低下的人的尊敬，然而这些发现却让我对他们的印象大打折扣，希望这一点我会得到大家的谅解。

I had often read of some great services done to princes and states, and desired to see the persons by whom those services were performed. Upon inquiry I was told that their names were to be found on no record, except a few of them whom history has represented as the vilest rogues and traitors. As to the rest, I had never once heard of them. They all appeared with dejected looks, and in the meanest habit, most of them telling me they died in poverty and disgrace, and the rest on a scaffold or a gibbet.

我常常读到一些忠君爱国的丰功伟绩，因此十分想见见这些忠义之士。然而一问之下我才知道，没有任何史料记载他们的名字，除了仅有的一些历史记载将他们说成是最邪恶最卑鄙的恶棍和叛徒。而其余的人我根本从未听说。他们都面目忧郁，形容潦倒，大部分人告诉我他们在穷困和耻辱中死去，剩下的人则在断头台或是绞架上了却一生。

Among the rest, there was one person whose case appeared a little singular. He had a youth about eighteen years old standing by his side. He told me he had for many years been commander of a ship, and in the sea fight at *Actium*, had the good fortune to break through the enemy's great line of battle, sink three of their capital ships, and take a fourth, which was the sole cause of *Antony's* flight, and of the victory that ensued; that the youth standing by him, his only son, was killed in the action. He added, that upon the confidence of some merit, the war being at an end, he went to *Rome*, and solicited at the court of *Augustus* to be preferred to a greater ship, whose commander had been killed; but without any regard to his pretensions, it was given to a youth who had never seen the sea, the son of a *Libertina*, who waited on one of the emperor's mistresses. Returning back to his own vessels, he was charged with neglect of duty, and the ship given to a favourite page of *Publicola* the vice-admiral; whereupon he retired to a poor farm, at a great distance from *Rome*, and there ended his life. I was so curious to know the truth of this story, that I desired *Agrippa* might be called, who was admiral in that fight. He appeared and confirmed the whole account, but with much more advantage to the captain,

在这些人中，有一个人稍显不同。他身旁站着一个 18 岁左右的年轻人。他告诉我，他在一艘战舰上当过多年的指挥官，艾克丁姆海战中，曾幸运地突破敌军的强大防线，击沉了 3 艘主力舰，又俘获了一艘，最终导致安东尼的溃败，胜利凯旋，站在他身边的那位青年是他唯一的儿子，在这场战争中身亡。他补充说，他自恃立功，战争刚画上句号他就回到罗马，请求奥古斯都当朝将他派到一艘更大的战舰上去担任指挥，那艘战舰的舰长死了。然而朝廷对他的请求不闻不问，却将这个职位给了一个从未见过大海的年轻人，他是国王的一个情妇的仆人李柏丁那的儿子。回到自己原来的船上，他被控玩忽职守，战船被交付给海军副将帕勃利可拉的一个亲信。从那时起他就退隐到远离罗马的一个穷苦的农场，在那里度过了自己的后半生。我对这个故事的真相太过好奇，因此请求首领召唤来那次战役中任海军上将的阿格瑞帕。他现身之后证实指挥官的话句句属实，而且他还说了船长许多好话，说他因为太过谦虚而略去或是隐瞒了许多他曾立下的功劳。

whose modesty had extenuated or concealed a great part of his merit.

I was surprised to find corruption grown so high and so quick in that empire, by the force of luxury so lately introduced, which made me less wonder at many parallel cases in other countries, where vices of all kinds have reigned so much longer, and where the whole praise as well as pillage hath been engrossed by the chief commander, who perhaps had the least title to either.

我很惊讶地发现在这个新近才引入奢侈之风的国家里，腐败竟会蔓延得如此迅速，程度如此之高，因此对于其他国家里相似的情形，我也感到不那么稀奇了。在那些国家里各种罪恶早已横行已久，而最高统治者坐拥所有的赞扬与财富，而他很可能是最不配拥有这二者的人。

As every person called up made exactly the same appearance he had done in the world, it gave me melancholy reflections to observe how much the race of human kind was degenerated among us, within these hundred years past. how the pox under all its consequences and denominations had altered every lineament of an *English* countenance, shortened the size of bodies, unbraced the nerves, relaxed the sinews and muscles, introduced a sallow complexion, and rendered the flesh loose and *rancid*.

当我看到每一个被召唤来的人与他生前的样子别无二致，而看到在这 100 年里人类竟然退化至此，这让我感到无比难过。梅毒及其变种所引发的一切后果将英国人变得面目全非，将他们变得个子矮小，精神委靡，肌肉松弛，面色蜡黄，浑身的肥肉散发着腐臭气息。

I descended so low, as to desire that some *English* yeomen of the old stamp, might be summoned to appear, once so famous for the simplicity of their manners, diet and dress, for justice in their dealings, for their true spirit of liberty, for their valour and love of their country. Neither could I be wholly unmoved after

我已经堕落到想要召见几个古代英国农夫来见上一见。他们曾以性格淳厚，衣食朴素，公平交易，真正信仰自由和刚勇爱国而著称。在将这些死去的人和现在活着的人对比之后，我无不动容。这些本土民族的纯粹的美德都被他们的子孙为了几个臭钱给糟蹋得精光，

comparing the living with the dead, when I considered how all these pure native virtues were prostituted for a piece of money by their Grandchildren, who, in selling their votes, and managing at elections have acquired every vice and corruption that can possibly be learned in a court.

这些孙子们出卖选票，操纵选举，他们有样学样，将只可能存在于宫廷贵族之中的那些恶行和腐败悉数习得。

CHAPTER 9

第九章

The Author Returns to Maldonada. Sails to the Kingdom of Luggnagg. The Author confined. He is sent for to Court. The Manner of his Admittance. The King's great Lenity to his Subjects.

作者回到马尔多纳达，驶向拉格奈格王国。作者被囚禁起来押送到朝廷。他受到接见的经过。国王对他的子民十分宽厚慈悲。

The day of our departure being come, I took leave of his highness the Governor of *Glubbdubdrib*, and returned with my two companions to *Maldonada*, where after a fortnight's waiting, a ship was ready to sail for *Luggnagg*. The two gentlemen and some others were so generous and kind as to furnish me with provisions, and see me on board. I was a month in this voyage. We had one violent storm, and were under a necessity of steering westward to get into the trade wind which holds for above sixty leagues. On the 21st of *April*, 1709 we sailed in the river of *Clumegnig*, which is a seaport town, at the south-east point of *Luggnagg*. We cast anchor within a league of the town, and made a signal for a pilot. Two of them came on board in less than half an hour, by whom we were guided between certain shoals and rocks which are very dangerous in the passage to a large basin, where a fleet may ride in

到了我们该离开的这天，我向格勒大锥的首领阁下辞别，与我的两位同伴一起回到了马尔多纳达。在那儿等候了两周的时间，终于等到一艘准备出发去往拉格奈格的船。两位先生和其他一些人都十分大方友善，给我带了食物并将我送上船。这次航行历时一个月。我们遭遇了一次非常迅猛的暴风雨，不得不扭转航向向西行驶，信风带着我们又往前驶进了60多里格。1709年4月21日这天，我们驶入了克兰梅格尼格河。这是一座海港城市，位于拉格奈格的东南角。我们在离城一里格以内的地方下锚，并发信号要求派遣一名引航员。不到半个小时两名引航员就来到了船上。在他们的带领下我们驶过部分暗礁与岩石，通往开阔大湾的航道地势十分险恶，这里可以容纳一支舰队安全驶入停泊在距城墙不到一锚链的地方。

safety within a cable's length of the Town Wall.

Some of our sailors, whether out of treachery or inadvertence, had informed the pilots that I was a stranger and a great traveller, whereof these gave notice to a custom-house officer, by whom I was examined very strictly upon my landing. This officer spoke to me in the language of *Balnibarbi*, which, by the force of much commerce is generally understood in that town, especially by seamen, and those employed in the customs. I gave him a short account of some particulars, and made my story as plausible and consistent as I could; but I thought it necessary to disguise my country, and call myself an Hollander, because my intentions were for *Japan*, and I knew the *Dutch* were the only *Europeans* permitted to enter into that kingdom. I therefore told the officer, that having been shipwrecked on the coast of *Balnibarbi*, and cast on a rock, I was received up into *Laputa*, or the flying island (of which he had often heard) and was now endeavouring to get to *Japan*, from whence I might find a convenience of returning to my own country. The officer said I must be confined till he could receive orders from court, for which he would write immediately, and hoped to receive an answer in a fortnight. I was carried to a convenient lodging, with a

我们船上有几个水手，不知是心怀不轨还是不小心说漏了嘴，告诉引航员我是个异乡客，还是个大旅行家，而引航员将这个消息告知了一位海关官员，在我上岸的时候他对我进行了相当严格的盘查。这位官员用巴尔尼巴比语和我交谈，因为两地间通商频繁，因此城里的人，尤其是水手和海关人员都懂不少巴尔尼巴比语。我将我的情况向他简要地说明了一番，尽量将我的经历叙述得可信且前后统一，不过我觉得有必要隐去我真实的国籍，因此声称自己是荷兰人。因为我意图前往日本，而我知道荷兰是欧洲唯一一个被允许进入那里的国家。因此我告诉海关官员，我的船在巴尔尼巴比海岸触礁发生了事故，我流落到岩石滩上，后来被拉普他，也叫飞岛收容（他也常常听说这地方），现在正设法去日本，或许从那里可以找到返回祖国的机会。那官员说，他必须将我囚禁起来直到收到朝廷的命令，他说他会立即写信给朝廷，但愿两星期内能得到回复。我被带到一处附近的便所，门前部署了哨兵看守；然而我可以在里面的一个大花园里自由活动，且得到足够体面的待遇，囚禁期间一切费用都由国王承担。有些人主要出于好奇而来拜访我，因为他们得

sentry placed at the door; however I had the liberty of a large garden, and was treated with humanity enough, being maintained all the time at the king's charge. I was invited by several persons, chiefly out of curiosity, because it was reported that I came from countries very remote of which they had never heard.

知我从非常遥远的地方来，他们从未听说过我的祖国。

I hired a young man who came in the same ship to be an interpreter; he was a native of *Luggnagg*, but had lived some years at *Maldonada*, and was a perfect master of both languages. By his assistance I was able to hold a conversation with those who came to visit me; but this consisted only of their questions, and my answers.

我雇了和我在一条船上的一个年轻人做我的翻译，他是拉格奈格本地人，但在马尔多纳达住过几年，所以对两国语言都非常精通。在他的帮助下我能与那些来拜访我的人对话交谈，但仅限于他们问，我答。

The Dispatch came from court about the time we expected. It contained a warrant for conducting me and my retinue to *Traldragdubb*, or *Trildrogdrib* (for it is pronounced both ways as near as I can remember) by a party of ten horse. All my retinue was that poor lad for an interpreter, whom I persuaded into my service, and at my humble request, we had each of us a mule to ride on. A messenger was dispatched half a day's journey before us, to give the king notice of my approach, and to desire that his majesty would please to appoint a day and hour, when it would by his gracious pleasure that I might have the honour to *lick the dust before his*

来自朝廷的文件如期送达。里面有一张许可证，要求我连同我的随从由 10 名骑兵押解到特拉尔德拉格达布，或者叫特利尔德洛格德利布（因为根据我的印象这个地方的发音有以上两种）。我所有的随从就是那个可怜的翻译小伙，而他还是在我苦苦央求下才同意的。在我低声下气的要求下，我们每人都获得了一匹骡子当坐驾。一位邮差比我们提前半天出发，告知国王我们的行程，并请求国王陛下指定一个日子和时辰，看他何时乐意见我，并让我能有幸“舔他脚凳子前的尘土”。这是宫廷里的规矩，而且我发现这可不是空有形式。因为

footstool. This is the court style, and I found it to be more than matter of form. for upon my admittance two days after my arrival, I was commanded to crawl upon my belly, and lick the floor as I advanced; but on account of my being a stranger, care was taken to have it swept so clean that the dust was not offensive. However, this was a peculiar grace, not allowed to any but persons of the highest rank, when they desire an admittance. Nay, sometimes the floor is strewed with dust on purpose, when the person to be admitted happens to have powerful enemies at court. and I have seen a great lord with his mouth so crammed, that when he had crept to the proper distance from the throne, he was not able to speak a word. Neither is there any remedy, because it is capital for those who receive an audience to spit or wipe their mouths in his majesty's presence. There is indeed another custom, which I cannot altogether approve of. when the king hath a mind to put any of his nobles to death in a gentle indulgent manner, he commands to have the floor strewed with a certain brown powder, of a deadly composition, which being licked up infallibly kills him in twenty-four hours. But in justice to this prince's great clemency, and the care he hath of his subjects' lives (wherein it were much to be wished that the Monarchs of *Europe*

在我抵达后两天被国王接见时，我被命令匍匐着一边前行一边舔地板。不过鉴于我是一个异乡来客，他们特意将地板打扫得十分干净，因此尘土的味道倒并不让人厌恶。尽管如此，这也是一种只有最高官衔的官员要求觐见时才能行使的特殊的恩典。不仅如此，要是被召见的人碰巧有几个位高权重的敌人在朝，地板上就会被故意撒上尘土。我就见过一个大臣爬到宝座前特定的位置时，已经满嘴是土，根本没法说出一个字。这也无可奈何，因为如果谁敢在陛下面前吐一口痰或是擦嘴，就会被处死。事实上还有另一种习俗我也不太赞同。假若国王有想处死一位贵族的心思，那么一种温柔宽大的方法就是他下令在地板上撒满某种致命的褐色粉末，谁舔下这种粉末在 24 小时之内就会必死无疑。不过公平地说，这位君王还是非常仁厚的，十分厚爱他的子民们（这一点我倒希望欧洲的君主们都能效仿他）。为了他的名声，我一定要提到一点：每次用这种方法行刑之后，他都严格命令将沾了毒粉的地板仔细洗净，如果他的侍从们粗心忘记了，就会因触怒了皇威而受到惩罚。我曾亲耳听他下令要把他的一个侍从处以鞭刑，因为一次行刑之后，轮到他去通知将地板洗净，而他却故意没有通知，这个疏忽让一

would imitate him), it must be mentioned for his honour, that strict orders are given to have the infected parts of the floor well washed after every such execution, which if his domestics neglect, they are in danger of incurring his royal displeasure. I myself heard him give directions, that one of his pages should be whipped, whose turn it was to give notice about washing the floor after an execution, but maliciously had omitted it, by which neglect a young lord of great hopes coming to an audience, was unfortunately poisoned, although the king at that time had no design against his life. But this good prince was so gracious, as to forgive the poor page his whipping, upon promise that he would do so no more, without special orders.

位被寄予厚望的年轻贵族不幸被毒死了。而那时国王并未计划要他的命。好在这位好国王十分仁慈，原谅了那位可怜的侍从让他免于鞭笞之苦，只要他发誓今后若无特殊命令不可再犯。

To return from this digression; When I had crept within four yards of the throne, I raised myself gently upon my knees, and then striking my forehead seven times on the ground, I pronounced the following words, as they had been taught me the night before, *Ickpling gloffthrobb squutserumm blhiop mlashnalt zwin tnodbalkguffh slhiophad gurdlubh asht*. This is the compliment established by the laws of the land for all persons admitted to the king's presence. It may be rendered into *English* thus: "*May your celestial majesty outlive the sun, eleven moons and an half*. To this the king returned some

有些离题，话说当我爬到离宝座不到 4 码的地方时，我双膝跪地缓缓抬起上身，在地上磕了 7 个响头，接着按照他们前一天晚上教我的说了下面的话：*Ickpling gloffthrobb squutserumm blhiop mlashnalt zwin tnodbalkguffh slhiophad gurdlubh asht*. 这是由当地法律规定的一句颂词，所有觐见国王的人都必须称颂.如果翻译成英文大概是："祝天皇陛下的寿命比太阳还要长个半月！"对此国王回了一句，虽然我不明白他说了什么，但还是按照别人教我的那样回答道：*Fluft drin yalerick dwuldom*

answer, which although I could not understand, yet I replied as I had been directed: *Fluft drin yalerick dwuldom prastrad mirpush*, which properly signifies, *My tongue is in the mouth of my friend*, and by this expression was meant that I desired leave to bring my interpreter; whereupon the young man already mentioned was accordingly introduced, by whose intervention I answered as many questions as his majesty could put in above an hour. I spoke in the *Balnibarbian* tongue, and my interpreter delivered my meaning in that of *Luggnagg*.

The king was much delighted with my company, and ordered his *bliffmarklub* or high chamberlain, to appoint a lodging in the court for me and my interpreter, with a daily allowance for my table, and a large purse of gold for my common expenses.

I stayed three months in this country out of perfect obedience to his majesty, who was pleased highly to favour me, and made me very honourable offers. But, I thought it more consistent with prudence and justice to pass the remainder of my days with my wife and family.

prastrad mirpush. 这句话正确的意思就是："我的舌头在我朋友的嘴里。"我这么说是意味着我想让国王将我的翻译带来，于是先前提到的那位年轻人就被介绍进来，在他的帮助下我在一个小时之内回答了陛下提出的许多问题。我说巴尔尼巴比语，我的翻译将其译成拉格奈格语。

国王十分乐于与我在一起，他下令他的"bliffmarklub"（内务总管）在宫中给我和我的翻译安排一处住处，提供每天的饮食，还有一大袋金子供我们日常花销。

我完全遵照国王陛下的旨意，在这个国家住了3个月。他十分宠幸我，并提供给我显赫的官职。然而我想，为慎重公平起见我还是和我的妻子家人一起共度余生比较好。

CHAPTER 10

第十章

The Luggnaggians commended. A particular Description of the Struldbrugs, with many Conversations between the Author and some eminent Persons upon that Subject.

作者赞扬拉格奈格人。他对“斯特鲁德布鲁格”的详尽叙述，以及作者与一些名流在这个问题上的谈话。

The *Luggnaggians* are a polite and generous people, and although they are not without some share of that pride which is peculiar to all *Eastern* countries, yet they show themselves courteous to strangers, especially such who are countenanced by the court. I had many acquaintance among persons of the best fashion, and being always attended by my interpreter, the conversation we had was not disagreeable.

拉格奈格这个民族十分礼貌大方，尽管他们身上也不免有几分所有东方国家的人特有的那种傲慢气息，但他们对异乡客，尤其是受到朝廷礼遇的十分客气。我认识了许多位高权重的达官贵人，因为我的翻译一直陪同左右，因此我们之间的交流倒十分顺畅欢快。

One day in much good company I was asked by a person of quality, whether I had seen any of their *struldbrugs*, or immortals. I said I had not, and desired he would explain to me what he meant by such an appellation applied to a mortal creature. He told me, that sometimes, though very rarely, a child happened to be born in a family with a red circular spot in the forehead, directly over the left eyebrow, which was an infallible mark

一天，在许多人的陪同下，有一位贵族问我见没见过他们国家的“斯特鲁德布鲁格”，也就是“长生不老的人”。我说没有，并要求他跟我解释一下这个安在凡人身上的头衔究竟有什么含义。他说，虽然这种情况十分罕见，但有时一家里会刚好生下一个在左眉正上方的前额长着红圆点的孩子，这个标记就表示这个孩子将永不死亡。据他描述，那个圆点大小大约等同

that it should never die. The spot, as he described it, was about the compass of a silver threepence, but in the course of time grew larger, and changed its colour; for at twelve years old it became green, so continued till five and twenty, then turned to a deep blue; at five and forty it grew coal black, and as large as an *English* shilling, but never admitted any farther alteration. He said these births were so rare, that he did not believe there could be above eleven hundred *struldbrugs* of both sexes in the whole kingdom, of which he computed about fifty in the metropolis, and among the rest a young girl born about three years ago. that these productions were not peculiar to any family but a mere effect of chance, and the children of the *struldbruggs* themselves, were equally mortal with the rest of the people.

I freely own myself to have been struck with inexpressible delight upon hearing this account: and the person who gave it me happening to understand the *Balnibarbian* language, which I spoke very well, I could not forbear breaking out into expressions perhaps a little too extravagant. I cried out as in a rapture; Happy nation where every child hath at least a chance for being immortal! Happy people who enjoy so many living examples of ancient virtue, and have

一枚3便士的银币，不过这颗圆点会随着孩子年岁增长而变大变色。到了 12 岁它就变成绿色，一直持续到 25 岁，然后变成深蓝色，在45岁的时候它变成炭黑色，大小如一枚英国先令，之后就再不改变。他说这样的新生儿实在太过罕有，因此他相信整个国家中不论男孩女孩这样的 “斯特鲁德布鲁格”不超过 1100 个，其中他估算有大约 50 名在首都，大约3年前出生的一个小女孩就是其中之一。他说这样的孩子并非是哪一家独有的，而仅仅是因为机缘巧合出生的，而就算是“斯特鲁德布鲁格”自己的子女也和其他人一样只有有限的生命。

听到这番话我毫不掩饰地表露出无法描述的高兴的神色来。而这个人刚好懂得巴尔尼巴比语，而我精通这种语言，于是我不禁喊了几句有些太夸张出格的赞美，我像疯了一般叫嚷道：“幸福的民族啊，你的每一个孩子都有获得永生的机会！幸福的人民啊，你们受到数不尽的古典美德活榜样的熏陶，总有大师愿意将先辈们的智慧传授于你们！但最最幸福的还要数那些杰出的‘斯特鲁德布鲁格’，他们

masters ready to instruct them in the wisdom of all former ages! But, happiest beyond all comparison are those excellent *struldbruggs*, who being born exempt from that universal calamity of human nature, have their minds free and disengaged, without the weight and depression of spirits caused by the continual apprehensions of death. I discovered my admiration that I had not observed any of these illustrious persons at court: the black spot on the forehead, being so remarkable a distinction, that I could not have easily overlooked it: and it was impossible that his majesty, a most judicious prince, should not provide himself with a good number of such wise and able counsellors. Yet perhaps the virtue of those reverend sages was too strict for the corrupt and libertine manners of a court. and we often find by experience, that young men are too opinionative and volatile to be guided by the sober dictates of their seniors. However, since the king was pleased to allow me access to his royal person, I was resolved upon the very first occasion to deliver my opinion to him on this matter freely, and at large by the help of my interpreter; and whether he would please to take my advice or not, yet in one thing I was determined, that his majesty having frequently offered me an establishment in

生来就免于受到困扰全人类的噩运，他们大可无忧无虑，轻松畅快，而无须承担时刻烦忧死神降临的压力。然而令我感到不解的是我却从未在朝廷上见到任何如此卓尔不群的人，前额上的黑痣是如此显眼的特征，我不可能会轻易放过的，而这样一位明智的君王怎么会不找一伙这般聪明能干的帮手在旁辅佐呢？不过或许是因为可敬的圣贤们不能容忍与朝中的贪污腐败分子同流合污，而按我们惯有的经验来看，年轻人往往都太过独断专横，反复无常，因此听不进冷静的年长者的谆谆教诲。然而既然国王欣然同意我与他的皇室成员相近，那我就决定借助我翻译的帮助，一有机会就将我对这个问题的看法向他一五一十坦白，不管他是否乐意接受，但有件事我决心已定，那就是既然国王陛下一而再再而三地要求我留下来帮他治理国家，那我必将怀着莫大的感激接受他的好意，而如果那些超凡的'斯特鲁德布鲁格'人愿意的话，我愿意此生都留在这里与他们交流。"

this country, I would with great thankfulness accept the favour, and pass my life here in the conversation of those superior beings the *struldbruggs*, if they would please to admit me.

The gentleman to whom I addressed my discourse, because (as I have already observed) he spoke the language of *Balnibarbi*, said to me with a sort of a smile, which usually ariseth from pity to the ignorant, that he was glad of any occasion to keep me among them, and desired my permission to explain to the company what I had spoke. He did so, and they talked together for some time in their own language, whereof I understood not a syllable, neither could I observe by their countenances what impression my discourse had made on them. After a short silence the same person told me, that his friends and mine (so he thought fit to express himself) were very much pleased with the judicious remarks I had made on the great happiness and advantages of immortal life, and they were desirous to know in a particular manner, what scheme of living I should have formed to myself, if it had fallen to my lot to have been born a *struldbrugg*.

I answered, it was easy to be eloquent on so copious and delightful a subject, especially to me who have been often apt to amuse myself with visions of what I

在我前文叙述中提到过的那位先生，因为我已经得知他会说巴尔尼巴比语，他在对我说话的时候脸上带着一种通常是出于怜悯无知之人的微笑，他说无论在何种情况下他都愿意让我与他们在一起，并要求我允许他向其他人解释我所说的话。他这么做了之后，他们用本国的语言交谈了一阵子，他们说的话我一个词都没听懂，而我也无法从他们的表情看出他们对我所说的话究竟有何感受。一阵短暂的沉默过后，还是这位先生告诉我，他的朋友们和我的朋友（他认为这样形容他自己再适当不过了）听到我对于长生不老的幸福和优势的一番明智的话语让他们十分欢欣，他们都迫切地想要知道如果我有幸生而成为一个“斯特鲁德布鲁格”，我将如何计划我的人生。

我回答说，这个话题如此内涵丰富令人振奋，大肆发挥并不难。尤其对于我这样一个时常喜欢假想如若我是国王，将军或是大臣的

should do if I were a king, a general, or a great lord: and upon this very case I had frequently run over the whole system how I should employ myself, and pass the time if I were sure to live for ever.

That, if it had been my good fortune to come into the world a *struldbrugg*, as soon as I could discover my own happiness by understanding the difference between life and death, I would first resolve by all arts and methods whatsoever to procure myself riches. In the pursuit of which by thrift and management, I might reasonably expect in about two hundred years, to be the wealthiest man in the kingdom. In the second place, I would from my earliest youth apply myself to the study of arts and sciences, by which I should arrive in time to excel all others in learning. Lastly I would carefully record every action and event of consequence, that happened in the public, impartially draw the characters of the several successions of princes, and great ministers of state, with my own observations on every point. I would exactly set down the several changes in customs, language, fashions, dress, diet and diversions. By all which acquirements, I should be a living treasury of knowledge and wisdom, and certainly become the oracle of the nation.

I would never marry after threescore,

情景的人来说，关于长生不老这件事我也前前后后彻底想过很多遍，如果我能享有不死的生命，我会做些什么，会如何打消没有尽头的时光。

我说，如果我有幸成了一名“斯特鲁德布鲁格”，一旦我辨明生与死的不同，并从中找到属于我自己的幸福，首先我会想方设法绞尽脑汁让我自己成为富人。在追逐财富的过程中我将克己节省努力经营，在大约 200 年的时间里我将大有希望成为该国最富裕的人。其次，我将自小学习研究艺术和科学，这样假以时日我将在学识方面超越其他人。最后，我要将公众发生的每一项活动和每一件重大事件都详细记录下来，并根据我自己细致的观察，不偏不倚地将历代君王和大臣的性格加以记述。我要分毫不差地记下习俗、语言、风尚、装束、饮食和娱乐方面的各种变迁。有了这些所得，我将成为知识和智慧的活宝库，且毫无疑问将成为整个民族的先知。

过了 60 岁我就不用婚娶，而

but live in an hospitable manner, yet still on the saving side. I would entertain myself in forming and directing the minds of hopeful young men, by convincing them from my own remembrance, experience and observation, fortified by numerous examples, of the usefulness of virtue in public and private life. But, my choice and constant companions should be a set of my own immortal brotherhood, among whom I would elect a dozen from the most ancient, down to my own contemporaries. Where any of these wanted fortunes, I would provide them with convenient lodges round my own estate, and have some of them always at my table, only mingling a few of the most valuable among you mortals, whom length of time would harden me to lose with little or no reluctance, and treat your posterity after the same manner, just as a man diverts himself with the annual succession of pinks and tulips in his garden, without regretting the loss of those which withered the preceding year.

我将十分慷慨好客，但绝不铺张浪费，恪守节俭美德。我将教育指导前途光明的年轻人视为己任，用我自身的记忆、经验和所见，用无数例子佐证使他们相信，美德在公共和私人生活中大有用武之地。然而我只会选择和我一样长生不死的兄弟做我终生的伙伴，我要从古代到我同时代的这些人中选出 12 个做我的同伴。如果这些人中谁手头紧迫，我就提供给他我自己住所附近的一套方便的住处，我的同伴中有些会一直是我的座上宾，而我只会和你们这些凡人中极少数几个特别有价值的人交往，而日子久了我也变得铁石心肠，你们去世我也不会感到不舍，而对于你们的后代也是如此，就如同一个每年在花园里种植石竹和郁金香用来消遣的人，对于前年凋零的花儿他并无一丝惋惜与难过。

"These *struldbruggs* and I would mutually communicate our observations and memorials through the course of time, remark the several gradations by which corruption steals into the world, and oppose it in every step, by giving perpetual warning and instruction to mankind; which, added to the strong

我会和这些“斯特鲁德布鲁格”在时间流逝中交流彼此的回忆与见闻，我们谈论腐败是如此悄悄地逐步地侵蚀了这个世界，而我们会在每一阶段不断地警示教导世人，再加上我们自身的榜样作用，或许可以阻止令每朝每代都扼腕叹息的人性的持续堕落。

influence of our own example, would probably prevent that continual degeneracy of human nature so justly complained of in all ages.

Add to all this the pleasure of seeing the various revolutions of states and empires, the changes in the lower and upper world, ancient cities in ruins, and obscure villages become the seats of kings; famous rivers lessening into shallow brooks, the ocean leaving one coast dry, and overwhelming another: the discovery of many countries yet unknown. barbarity overrunning the politest nations, and the most barbarous become civilized. I should then see the discovery of the *longitude, the perpetual motion, the universal medicine*, and many other great inventions brought to the utmost perfection.

除此之外，我还将看到许多国家和政权的变革；上层社会和底层社会发生的种种变化；古老的城市化作废墟；偏僻的村落成为帝王的都城；声名远播的大河化为低浅的溪流；海洋的一边干旱枯竭，另一边则洪水肆虐；许多未被发现的国度为人所知；最文明的国度被野蛮人占据，而最不开化的人逐渐变得文明有礼。目睹这一切的我该是多么欣喜！到那时我将见证经度、永动机和万能灵药以及许多其他伟大的发明发展到至臻化境。

What wonderful discoveries should we make in astronomy, by outliving and confirming our own predictions, by observing the progress and returns of comets, with the changes of motion in the sun, moon, and stars.

在天文学方面我们也将有许多神奇的发现，我们可以活着见证一切，通过观察彗星的运转，以及日月星辰的运动更迭证实自己的预言。

I enlarged upon many other topics which the natural desire of endless life and sublunary happiness could easily furnish me with. When I had ended, and the sum of my discourse had been interpreted as before, to the rest of the company, there was a good deal of talk among them in the language of the country, not without some

出于对无限生命和世俗的美好的自然向往，我又口若悬河地在其他话题上说了不少。等我结束我的演讲，那位先生又像之前那样将我的话总结翻译给其他在场的人，他们用本国话交谈了很久，不时地嘲笑我一番。最后，一直帮忙翻译我的话的那位先生说，他被大家要

laughter at my expense. At last the same gentleman who had been my interpreter said, he was desired by the rest to set me right in a few mistakes, which I had fallen into through the common imbecility of human nature, and upon that allowance was less answerable for them. That, this breed of *struldbruggs* was peculiar to their country, for there were no such people either in *Balnibarbi or Japan*, where he had the honour to be ambassador from his majesty, and found the natives in both those kingdoms very hard to believe that the fact was possible, and it appeared from my astonishment when he first mentioned the matter to me, that I received it as a thing wholly new, and scarcely to be credited. That in the two kingdoms above mentioned, where during his residence he had conversed very much, he observed long life to be the universal desire and wish of mankind. That whoever had one foot in the grave, was sure to hold back the other as strongly as he could. That the oldest had still hopes of living one day longer, and looked on death as the greatest evil, from which nature always prompted him to retreat; only in this island of *Luggnagg*, the appetite for living was not so eager, from the continual example of the *struldbruggs* before their eyes.

That the system of living contrived by me was unreasonable and unjust, because

求要纠正我的几点错误，而我之所以会犯下这些错误无非是因为人性中所共有的痴愚，这一点也无可厚非。他说，“斯特鲁德布鲁格”这种人只在他们国家才有，巴尔尼巴比和日本都没有，他曾有幸受国王陛下派遣作为大使出访这两个国家，发现两国人都不大愿意相信这个事实。而当他初次向我说起这件事时，我也将其看做是全然新奇难以置信的事情。而在他居住在上文提到的两个国家的时间里，他与当地人广泛交流，发现长寿是人类普遍的夙愿。不管是谁哪怕已经半截身子入土，肯定还有着极其强烈的生存下去的欲望。最年长的人依然希望能够多活一天，将死亡看做最可怕的魔鬼，人的天性一直都让他躲避死亡。而只有在拉格奈格岛上，人们才不那么盼着长寿，因为作为活生生的例子，长生不老的“斯特鲁德布鲁格”一直在他们眼前。

他说，我臆想的那种生活体系是有违常理和不公平的，因为这样

it supposed a perpetuity of youth, health, and vigour, which no man could be so foolish to hope, however extravagant he may be in his wishes. That the question therefore was not whether a man would choose to be always in the prime of youth, attended with prosperity and health, but how he would pass a perpetual life under all the usual disadvantages which old age brings along with it. For although few men will avow their desires of being immortal upon such hard conditions, yet in the two kingdoms before mentioned of *Balnibarbi* and *Japan*, he observed that every man desired to put off death some time longer, let it approach ever so late, and he rarely heard of any man who died willingly, except he were incited by the extremity of grief or torture. And he appealed to me whether in those countries I had travelled as well as my own, I had not observed the same general disposition.

做的前提条件是必须永葆青春，健康和活力，一个人再怎么荒唐到做白日梦也不会愚蠢到幻想自己能够拥有这些。因此问题不在于一个人是否能够永远年轻，永远健康富足，而是处于所有伴随衰退老去而来的各种常见的不利情况下，他将如何度过无限的生命。因为尽管几乎没人会愿意在艰难的条件下永生不灭，但在前文提到的巴尔尼巴比和日本这两个国家中，他发现每一个人都希望能推迟死亡的时间，让那一刻来临得越晚越好，他很少听到有人愿意死去，除非他经受着极端的悲伤和痛苦的折磨。他还询问我在我旅行过的国家和我的祖国里，是否也见过此种普遍的心态。

After this preface he gave me a particular account of the *struldbruggs* among them. He said they commonly acted like mortals, till about thirty years old, after which by degrees they grew melancholy and dejected, increasing in both till they came to four-score. This he learned from their own confession; for otherwise there not being above two or three of that species born in an age, they were too few to form a general

以此作为开端，他向我详尽讲述了他们国家“斯特鲁德布鲁格”的情况。他说，在大约30岁之前，他们都和普通人行为一致，30岁之后他们就渐渐变得忧郁沮丧起来，这两种情绪不断加深直到他们到了80岁。他从这些人亲口所言中得知这一点，否则的话这种人一代不出两三个，无法广泛普遍地对他们进行考察。当他们到了80岁（在这个国家80岁被看做是寿命的极

observation by. When they came to four-score years, which is reckoned the extremity of living in this country, they had not only all the follies and infirmities of other old men, but many more which arose from the dreadful prospect of never dying. They were not only opinionative, peevish, covetous, morose, vain, talkative, but uncapable of friendship, and dead to all natural affection, which never descended below their grandchildren. Envy and impotent desires are their prevailing passions. But those objects against which their envy seems principally directed, are the vices of the younger sort, and the deaths of the old. By reflecting on the former, they find themselves cut off from all possibility of pleasure; and whenever they see a funeral, they lament and repine that others are gone to a harbour of rest, to which they themselves never can hope to arrive. They have no remembrance of anything but what they learned and observed in their youth and middle Age, and even that is very imperfect. and for the truth or particulars of any fact, it is safer to depend on common tradition than upon their best recollections. The least miserable among them appear to be those who turn to dotage, and entirely lose their understandings; these meet with more pity and assistance, because they want many

限），他们不但拥有其他老人所具有的所有毛病和缺点，而且因为他们永不会死去这些毛病都变本加厉。他们不仅固执己见、脾气暴躁、贪得无厌、闷闷不乐、自视甚高且唠叨个不停，还连友谊和其他亲情都无法维持，除了对他们的孙子还有些感情。嫉妒和妄想占据了他们的内心。让他们嫉妒的主要是由年轻人的荒淫和年老者的死去引发的。在前者身上他们发觉自己已经丧失了一切享乐的可能，而每当他们见证一场丧葬，他们就怨恨不满旁人去了安宁的港湾休憩，而他们自己却永无宁日。除了青年和中年时期所学到和见识的东西之外他们什么都记不住，就算是那些仅有的记忆也并不完全。因此若想了解任何事实或是真相的细枝末节，依靠常识和传说都比依靠他们最好的记忆要靠谱得多。他们这些人之中悲惨程度最轻的似乎就数那些彻底丧失认知能力的老糊涂蛋了，这些人得到了更多的怜悯和救助，因为他们没有其余人身上那么多恶劣的品格。

bad qualities which abound in others.

If a *struldbrugg* happen to marry one of his own kind, the marriage is dissolved of course by the courtesy of the kingdom, as soon as the younger of the two comes to be four-score. for the law thinks it a reasonable indulgence, that those who are condemned without any fault of their own to a perpetual continuance in the world, should not have their misery doubled by the load of a wife.

如果一个“斯特鲁德布鲁格”刚好与他的同类结婚，按照这个国家的礼制，只要二人之中较为年轻者到了 80 岁，婚姻就可以解除。因为法律认为这是个合情合理的特赦，因为那些并非因为犯错而被惩罚永久地活在世上的人，不该因为受到妻子的拖累而使他们的苦难加倍。

As soon as they have completed the term of eighty years, they are looked on as dead in law; their heirs immediately succeed to their estates, only a small pittance is reserved for their support, and the poor ones are maintained at the public charge. After that period they are held incapable of any employment of trust or profit, they cannot purchase lands or take leases, neither are they allowed to be witnesses in any cause, either civil or criminal, not even for the decision of meers and bounds.

他们一过 80 岁，就被法律认定已经死亡，他们的后代可以立即继承其产业，只留极少的一点钱供他们维持生计，那些贫困的则由公众来养活。过了这个年纪，他们就被认为是丧失了工作能力，且无法给社会带来利益。他们不能购买和租赁土地，也不能成为任何民事或刑事案件中的证人，甚至他们连勘定陆地和海洋的边界都无法参加。

At ninety they lose their teeth and hair, they have at that age no distinction of taste, but eat and drink whatever they can get, without relish or appetite. The diseases they were subject to still continue without increasing or diminishing. In talking they forget the common appellation of things, and the names of persons, even of those who are their

到了 90 岁，他们的牙齿和头发就全都没了，到那时候他们将分辨不出味道，食欲和胃口都已经丧失。他们所患的疾病会一直带在身上，不会加重也不会消退。说话的时候他们记不起东西的名字，也说不上人名，就连那些最亲近的朋友和亲人的名字也忘了。因为这样的原因，他们永远不能通过阅读给自

nearest friends and relations. For the same reason, they never can amuse themselves with reading, because their memory will not serve to carry them from the beginning of a sentence to the end; and by this defect they are deprived of the only entertainment whereof they might otherwise be capable.

己带来些乐趣，因为他们可怜的记忆力连从头到尾看懂一个句子都不行。因为这个缺陷将他们有能力享受的唯一的娱乐也剥夺了。

The language of this country being always upon the flux, the *struldbruggs* of one age do not understand those of another, neither are they able after two hundred years, to hold any conversation (farther than by a few general words) with their neighbours the mortals, and thus they lie under the disadvantage of living like foreigners in their own country.

这个国家的语言一直在不断变化，所以一个时代的“斯特鲁德布鲁格”无法理解另一个时代中他们同类的话，一旦超过 200 年，他们就无法和周围的凡人交流，最多只能说上极少的几个普通的词。因此，他们在自己的国家却生活得如同外国人一样诸多不便。

This was the account given me of the *struldbruggs*, as near as I can remember. I afterwards saw five or six of different ages, the youngest not above two hundred years old, who were brought to me at several times by some of my friends; but although they were told that I was a great traveller, and had seen all the world, they had not the least curiosity to ask me a question; only desired I would give them *slumskudask*, or a token of remembrance, which is a modest way of begging, to avoid the law that strictly forbids it, because they are provided for by the public, although indeed with a very scanty allowance.

这就是我所能记得的他们讲给我的有关“斯特鲁德布鲁格”的事情。后来我见到了五六个生于不同年代的这种人。年纪最小的还不到 200 岁，我的几个朋友带他们来见过我几次，然而虽然人们告诉他们我是个了不起的旅行家，足迹遍布全世界，他们也没有表现出一丁点兴趣向我提问，只是想让我给他们一个“斯兰姆斯库达斯克”，就是一件纪念品。这其实是一种变相的乞讨，为了逃避严令禁止的法律，因为他们是由公众赡养的，就算事实上他们能得到一些非常寒酸的补贴。

They are despised and hated by all sorts of people; when one of them is born, it is reckoned ominous, and their birth is recorded very particularly; so that you may know their age by consulting the registry, which however hath not been kept above a thousand years past, or at least hath been destroyed by time or public disturbances. But the usual way of computing how old they are, is by asking them what kings or great persons they can remember, and then consulting history, for infallibly the last prince in their mind did not begin his reign after they were four-score years old.

他们被各色人等歧视厌恶，他们一经出生就被认为是不祥之兆。他们的出生都有十分详尽的记录，因此只需查询登记档案处就能知晓他们的年龄。然而档案处的记录却没超过一千年，要不就是因为经年累月或是社会动荡记录被破坏了。不过最常用的计算他们年龄的方法，就是问他们还能记得的国王或是大人物，然后再比照历史，因为毫无疑问他们脑海中还记得的最后一位君王起码要在他们过了80岁才登上宝座。

They were the most mortifying sight I ever beheld, and the women more horrible than the men. Besides the usual deformities in extreme old age, they acquired an additional ghastliness in proportion to their number of years, which is not to be described, and among half a dozen I soon distinguished which was the eldest, although there was not above a century or two between them.

他们是我所见过的最伤心懊悔的人，而女人比男人要可怖得多。除了一般极为衰老所引起的毛病之外，随着她们年岁的增长，还会患上其他一些越发严重简直难以形容的可怕毛病，在五六个人当中我能迅速地辨认出最年长的那个，尽管他们彼此不过相差个一二百年。

The reader will easily believe, that from what I had hear and seen, my keen appetite for perpetuity of life was much abated. I grew heartily ashamed of the pleasing visions I had formed and thought no tyrant could invent a death into which I would not run with pleasure from such a life. The king heard of all that had passed

读者很容易相信，自从我亲眼目睹亲耳听闻诸如此类种种事后，我对永生的渴望大大消减。我开始对先前我所抱有的那些美妙的幻想感到真心的惭愧，我想再残暴的君王发明的死法都比这种生不如死的人生要好受得多。与其这样活着真还不如死掉。国王听闻了所有

between me and my friends upon this occasion, and rallied me very pleasantly, wishing I could send a couple of *struldbruggs* to my own country, to arm our people against the fear of death; but this it seems is forbidden by the fundamental laws of the kingdom, or else I should have been well content with the trouble and expense of transporting them.

在这个问题上我和友人的谈话，于是得意洋洋地嘲笑我，说希望我能带一对“斯特鲁德布鲁格”回我的祖国去，让我国人民免于对死亡的恐惧。不过这种行为似乎在该国法律是被禁止的，不然我大概真的很愿意费些力气和金钱将他们运回来。

I could not but agree, that the laws of this kingdom, relating to the *struldbruggs,* were founded upon the strongest reasons, and such as any other country would be under the necessity of enacting in the like circumstances. Otherwise, as avarice is the necessary consequent of old age, those immortals would in time become proprietors of the whole nation, and engross the civil power, which, for want of abilities to manage, must end in the ruin of the public.

我只能无奈同意该国有关“斯特鲁德布鲁格”的法律是最为合情合理的，如果在任何别的国家有这样的情况发生都十分 有必要这样做。不然的话，因为贪婪是老年的必然结果，那些拥有永恒生命的人终有一天会成为整个国家的财富所有人，将所有人民的权力都握在一已之手，而却没有治理国家之能，最终只能落得国破家亡的下场。

CHAPTER 11

第十一章

The Author leaves Luggnagg, and sails to Japan. From thence he returns in a Dutch ship to Amsterdam, and from Amsterdam to England.

作者离开拉格奈格，航行去日本。在那里他乘坐一艘去往阿姆斯特丹的荷兰船只，经由那里回到英国。

I thought this account of the *struldbruggs* might be some entertainment to the reader, because it seems to be a little out of the common way; at least I do not remember to have met the like in any book of travels that hath come to my hands: and if I am deceived, my excuse must be, that it is necessary for travellers, who describe the same country, very often to agree in dwelling on the same particulars, without deserving the censure of having borrowed or transcribed from those who wrote before them.

我想"斯特鲁德布鲁格"的故事应该给读者带来几分乐趣，因为这看起来有些不同寻常，至少我记得从未在我看过的任何一本游记中见过类似的故事，如果我记错了，请大家务必谅解，因为旅行家们的共识是在描绘同一个国家时，总免不了会在相同的细枝末节上花费许多笔墨，而不会被谴责是剽窃或是抄袭改编前人作品。

There is indeed a perpetual commerce between this kingdom and the great empire of *Japan*, and it is very probable that the *Japanese* authors may have given some account of the *struldbruggs*; but my stay in *Japan* was so short, and I was so entirely a stranger to that language, that I was not qualified to make any inquiries. But I hope the *Dutch* upon this notice will be curious and able enough to supply my

在这个国家与大日本帝国之间确实一直有贸易往来关系，因此很可能日本的作家已经讲述过"斯特鲁德布鲁格"的一些事情；不过我在日本停留的时间太短了，而且我对于日语一无所知，因此我无法做出任何调查。但我倒希望在我的说明下荷兰人会生出些好奇，并能对我的缺点和不足提出补充。

defects.

His majesty having often pressed me to accept some employment in his court, and finding me absolutely determined to return to my native country, was pleased to give me his license to depart, and honoured me with a letter of recommendation, under his own hand, to the Emperor of *Japan*. He likewise presented me with four hundred and forty-four large pieces of gold (this nation delighting in even numbers) and a red diamond which I sold in *England* for eleven hundred pounds.

On the sixth Day of *May*, 1709, I took a solemn leave of his majesty, and all my friends. This prince was so gracious as to order a guard to conduct me to *Glanguenstald*, which is a royal port to the *south-west* part of the island. In six days I found a vessel ready to carry me to *Japan*, and spent fifteen days in the voyage. We landed at a small port-town called *Xamoschi*, situated on the south-east part of *Japan*; the town lies on the *western* point where there is a narrow strait, leading northward into a long arm of the sea, upon the *north-west* part of which, Yedo the metropolis, stands. At landing I showed the custom-house officers my letter from the king of Luggnagg to his imperial majesty. They knew the seal perfectly well, it was as broad as the palm of my hand. The impression was, *A king*

国王陛下反复强烈要求我同意接受在朝廷中为他效劳，而当他发现我回国的强烈决心已定，便也不再强求，准许我离开。我有幸获得了一封他亲笔为我书写的给日本天皇的介绍信。他还为我准备了444 块大金子（这个民族喜欢偶数），还有一枚红色钻石，回到英国后我将它卖掉得到了 1100 英镑。

1709 年 5 月 6 日，我郑重向国王陛下和我所有的朋友告别。这位君王十分慷慨仁慈地派了一支卫队护送我去这座岛西南部的皇家港口——格兰古恩斯达尔德。6 天以后，我找到一艘可以将我带往日本的船只。这次航行花了 15 天的时间。我们在位于日本东南部的一个叫滨关的小港口城市上岸，这个城镇坐落在西边，那儿有一条狭窄的海峡，向北通向一个长长的海湾，海湾的西北部就是名为江户的都城。一登陆我就给海关官员看了拉格奈格国王给天皇陛下写的推荐信。他们对上面那印鉴了如指掌。印鉴有我的手掌那么大，图案是一个国王将一个瘸腿乞丐从地上扶起。镇上的地方行政官听闻我的信，便对我施以大臣的礼遇。他们为我备好马车和仆人，免费护送

lifting up a lame beggar from the earth. The magistrates of the town hearing of my letter, received me as a public minister; they provided me with carriages and servants, and bore my charges to Yedo, where I was admitted to an audience, and delivered my letter, which was opened with great ceremony, and explained to the Emperor by an interpreter, who then gave me notice by his majesty's order, that I should signify my request, and whatever it were, it should be granted for the sake of his royal brother of *Luggnagg*. This interpreter was a person employed to transact affairs with the *Hollanders*, He soon conjectured, by my countenance, that I was an *European*, and therefore repeated his majesty's commands in Low-Dutch, which he spoke perfectly well. I answered (as I had before determined) that I was a Dutch merchant, shipwrecked in a very remote country, from whence I travelled by sea and land to *Luggnagg*, and then took shipping for *Japan*, where I knew my countrymen often traded, and with some of these I hoped to get an opportunity of returning into *Europe*: I therefore most humbly entreated his royal favour to give order, that I should be conducted in safety to *Nangasac*: To this I added another petition, that for the sake of my patron the king of *Luggnagg*, his majesty would condescend to excuse my performing the

我去江户。在那里我受到接见。我递上介绍信，他们怀着十分的敬意打开了信，一名翻译将信的内容解释给天皇听。接着翻译向我转达天皇的命令，说我可以提出我的要求，不管是怎样的要求都会得到满足（当然是看在拉格奈格王兄的面子上）。这位翻译是受雇负责与荷兰人交流事宜的，他一看到我的相貌就很快猜出我是个欧洲人，因此又用流利的低地荷兰语向我重复了一下陛下的命令。我按照我事先决定的回答道，我是一名荷兰的商人，航行到一个偏远的国度发生了海难事故，然后坐船到了拉格奈格，接着就坐船来到了日本。我知道我的同胞与这里往来频繁，我寄希望于与他们中的一些人一起返回欧洲。说完我就用最卑微最谦逊的语气请求天皇开恩，希望他能下令把我安全护送到长崎。我还提出了另一个请求，即能否看在我的恩人拉格奈格国王的面上，让我不用行使我同胞们都无法免除的践踏十字架的仪式；因为我是因为种种厄运才流落到他的国家，并非来此做生意的。当后一个请求被翻译给天皇听后，他看起来有些惊讶，说他相信在这个问题上我是第一个质疑这种仪式的荷兰人，因而他开始怀疑我是不是一个真正的荷兰人；但他更怀疑我是个基督徒。尽管如此，出于我提的那些原因，但

ceremony imposed on my countrymen of *trampling upon the crucifix*, because I had been thrown into his kingdom by my misfortunes, without any intention of trading. When this latter petition was interpreted to the Emperor, he seemed a little surprised, and said, he believed I was the first of my countrymen who ever made any scruple in this point, and that he began to doubt whether I was a real *Hollander* or no; but rather suspected I must be a CHRISTIAN. However, for the reasons I had offered, but chiefly to gratify the king of *Luggnagg*, by an uncommon mark of his favour, he would comply with the *singularity* of my humour, but the affair must be managed with dexterity, and his officers should be commanded to let me pass as it were by forgetfulness. For he assured me, that if the secret should be discovered by my countrymen, the Dutch, they would cut my throat in the voyage. I returned my thanks by the interpreter for so unusual a favour, and some troops being at that time on their march to *Nangasac*, the commanding officer had orders to convey me safe thither, with particular instructions about the business of the *crucifix*.

是更主要是看在拉格奈格国王的面上，他可以对我那古怪的脾性法外开恩，不过必须小心机密行事，让他的官员装作是因为健忘而将我错放了过去。因为他告诉我若是秘密一旦败露，被我的同胞荷兰人发现了的话，他们一定会在途中割断我的喉咙。我通过翻译向天皇转达了我对他对我特别恩典的感激之情。那时正好有一支军队要去长崎，天皇就命令指挥官将我安全地送到那里，还附上关于十字架事宜的特别说明。

On the 9th day of *June*, 1709, I arrived at *Nangasac*, after a very long and troublesome journey. I soon fell into the company of some *Dutch* sailors belonging

1709 年 6 月 9 日，经过漫长而折磨的旅行，我抵达长崎。我很快就和几个荷兰水手打成一片，他们都是阿姆斯特丹的载重达 450 吨的

to the *Amboyna of Amsterdam*, a stout ship of 450 tons. I had lived long in *Holland*, pursuing my studies at *Leyden*, and I spoke *Dutch* well. The seamen soon knew from whence I came last: they were curious to inquire into my voyages and course of life. I made up a story as short and probable as I could, but concealed the greatest part. I knew many persons in *Holland*, I was able to invent names for my parents, whom I pretended to be obscure people in the province of *Gelderland*. I would have given the captain (one *Theodorus Vangrult*) what he pleased to ask for my voyage to *Holland*; but understanding I was a surgeon, he was contented to take half the usual rate, on condition that I would serve him in the way of my calling. Before we took shipping, I was often asked by some of the crew, whether I had performed the ceremony above-mentioned? I evaded the question by general answers, that I had satisfied the Emperor and court in all particulars. However, a malicious rogue of a skipper went to an officer, and pointing to me, told him, I had not yet *trampled on the crucifix*: but the other, who had received instructions to let me pass, gave the rascal twenty strokes on the shoulders with a bamboo, after which I was no more troubled with such questions.

Nothing happened worth mentioning in

"阿姆波伊纳号"大商船上的人。我在荷兰住过很长一段时间，在莱登完成学业，所以我能讲不错的荷兰语。水手们很快就知道我是从哪儿来的了。他们都好奇地询问我航海及生活的经历。我尽我所能地编出一个简短而可信的故事，但却隐瞒了最重要的部分。我在荷兰认识很多人，我大可以捏造我父母的姓名，装成他们是生活在盖尔德兰省穷乡僻壤的老百姓。我本来准备付给船长（一个名叫西奥朵拉斯·凡格鲁尔特的人）我应付的到荷兰的船费，可他一听说我是一名外科医生，就说愿意收平常一半的钱，条件是我得操起老本行为他服务。在我们起程之前，我常常被一些水手问到有没有履行前文提到的那种仪式。我回避了这个问题，只含糊大概地回答说，天皇和朝廷提出的所有具体要求我都照做了。然而还是有一个叩头虫一样恶毒的浑蛋跑去一位官员那里告密，指出我没有履行踩踏十字架的仪式。不过官员已经接到放我出境的命令，反而用一根竹子在这流氓的肩膀上打了 20 下；自此之后就再也没有人问我这样的问题了。

此次航海没有发生什么值得

this voyage. We sailed with a fair wind to the *Cape of Good Hope* where we staid only to take in fresh water. On the 16th of *April* we arrived safe at *Amsterdam*, having lost only three men by sickness in the voyage, and a fourth who fell from the foremast into the sea, not far from the coast of *Guinea*. From *Amsterdam* I soon after set sail for *England*, in a small vessel belonging to that city.

On the 10th of *Apirl* 1710, we put in at the *Downs*. I landed the next morning, and saw once more my native country after an absence of five years and six months complete. I went straight to *Redriff*, where I arrived the same day at two in the afternoon, and found my wife and family in good health.

特别提到的事情。我们一路顺风到了好望角，在那儿取了些淡水。4月6日，我们安全抵达阿姆斯特丹，一路上只损失了3名因病去世的海员，还有一名在几内亚海岸附近的地方从前桅上失足掉进了海里。随后很快我就上了阿姆斯特丹的一艘小船从那里起程回英国。

1710年4月10日，我们驶入唐兹锚地。次日早上我上了岸，在阔别整整5年过6个月以后，我终于又一次见到我自己的祖国。我直接回了瑞德里夫，当天下午两点就回到家中，发现我的妻子和家人都身体康健。

PART IV. A VOYAGE TO THE COUNTRY OF THE HOUYHNHNMS

第四部分 慧骃国游记

CHAPTER 1

第一章

The Author sets out as Captain of a Ship. His Men conspire against him, confine him a long Time to his Cabin, and set him on shore in an unknown Land. He travels up into the country. The Yahoos, a strange sort of Animal, described. the Author meets two Houyhnhnms.

本章描述的是作为船长的作者领航出海，却被手下用诡计长时间囚禁在船舱里，而后把他扔到一个无名国家的海岸上，于是他就游历了那个国家。他还描述了一种奇特的动物“雅虎”，还有两只遇见的“慧骃”。

I continued at home with my wife and children about five months in a very happy condition, if I could have learned the lesson of knowing when I was well. I left my poor wife big with child, and accepted an advantageous offer made me to be captain of the *Adventurer*, a stout merchantman of 350 tons: for I understood navigation well, and being weary of a surgeon's employment at sea, which however I could exercise upon occasion, I took a skilful young man of that calling, one *Robert Purefoy*, into my ship. We set sail from *Portsmouth* upon the second day of August, 1710; on the Fourteenth we met with Captain *Pocock of Bristol at Teneriffe*, who was going to the bay of *Campeche* to cut logwood. On the sixteenth, he was parted from us by a storm; I heard since my return, that his

我和妻儿一起度过了将近5个月的幸福时光，如果那时我能意识到，我的生活多么舒适就好了。由于精通航海，很快，我就离开了我那可怜的怀有身孕的妻子，接受了一份薪资丰厚的邀约，成为一艘载重350吨的“冒险号”大商船的船长。此外，尽管我偶尔也可以胜任医生一职，然而对于在航行中充当外科医生，我早已厌倦这样的工作了，因此，我就招了一位技术娴熟的年轻外科大夫罗伯特·漂尔佛伊来船担此重任。1710年8月2号我们从朴次茅斯出发，14号，在特内里费岛，我们遇见了布里斯托尔的坡可克船长，他正打算赶到坎佩切湾采伐苏木。16号，我们被一场风暴吹散了。返航后，我才知道他的船沉没了，除了一个船舱侍应生之外，全部遇难。他是一个正直的人，

ship foundered, and none escaped, but one cabin-boy. He was an honest man, and a good sailor, but a little too positive in his own opinions, which was the cause of his destruction, as it hath been with several others. For, if he had followed my advice, he might have been safe at home with his family at this time, as well as myself.

I had several men who died in my ship of calentures, so that I was forced to get recruits out of *Barbadoes*, and the *Leeward Islands*, where I touched by the direction of the merchants who employed me, which I had soon too much cause to repent; for I found afterwards that most of them had been buccaneers. I had fifty hands on board, and my orders were, that I should trade with the *Indians*, in the *South-Sea*, and make what discoveries I could. These rogues whom I had picked up debauched my other men, and they all formed a conspiracy to seize the ship and secure me; which they did one morning, rushing into my cabin, and binding me hand and foot, threatening to throw me overboard, if I offered to stir. I told them, I was their prisoner, and would submit. This they made me swear to do, and then they unbound me, only fastening one of my legs with a chain near my bed, and placed a sentry at my door with his piece charged, who was commanded to shoot me dead, if I attempted my liberty. They

一个优秀的水手，不过对于自己的看法太过固执，这也促使他同一些这样的水手一样自取灭亡。如果当时他能接受我的意见，也许此时他也和我一样，和家人一起安安稳稳地生活着。

因为得了热病，我的船员死了几个，不得已我只好在巴巴多斯岛和背风群岛雇用新人，在这两个地方招人是我的雇主要求的，但随后我就悔恨起来。因为我很快发现，大部分雇用的新人都做过海盗。我的船上总共有 50 个雇员，雇主命令我到南洋一带和印度人做生意，并尽我所能开拓那一带的新市场，而船上新雇来的这帮浑蛋把原来的船员通通扔到了海里，他们还一起密谋要强占这艘船，囚禁我。某个早晨，他们闯进我的船舱，捆住我的手脚，而且还威胁说，只要我动一下，就把我扔进海里。我告诉他们我愿意投降，被他们囚禁起来。他们就逼我发誓表示服从，随后他们仅仅把我的一条腿用链子拴在床边，松开了其余捆绑，还在门口安排了一个荷枪实弹的人看守，如果我试图逃走，就开枪打死我。他们给我送来吃的喝的，就开始掌管了船上的一切。他们打算做海盗打劫西班牙人，不过他们在召集到更多的船员的时候才可以动

sent me own victuals and drink, and took the government of the ship to themselves. Their design was to turn pirates, and plunder the *Spaniards*, which they could not do, till they got more men. But first they resolved to sell the goods the ship, and then go to *Madagascar* for recruits, several among them having died since my confinement. They sailed many weeks, and traded with the *Indians*, but I knew not what course they took, being kept a close prisoner in my cabin, and expecting nothing less than to be murdered, as they often threatened me.

Upon the ninth day of *May* 1711, one *James Welch* came down to my cabin; and said he had orders from the captain, to set me ashore. I expostulated with him, but in vain; neither would he so much as tell me who their new captain was. They forced me into the long-boat, letting me put on my best suit of clothes, which were as good as new, and a small bundle of linen, but no arms except my hanger; and they were so civil as not to search my pockets, into which I conveyed what money I had, with some other little necessaries. They rowed about a league; and then set me down on a strand. I desired them to tell me, what country it was. They all swore, they knew no more than myself, but said, that the captain (as they called him) was resolved, after they had sold the lading, to

手去做。然而他们决定最先要做的就是卖掉船上的货物，然后去马达加斯加招兵买马。因为我被监禁之后，他们中间就已经有好几个人死掉了。经过数周的航行，他们同印度人做了几笔买卖，但是我一直被严密地看管在船舱里，因此弄不太清楚他们走的究竟是哪条线路。而且他们总是威胁要把我杀死，我也就没有心存任何一丝侥幸能够活下来。

直到1711年5月9号，我的船舱里来了一个叫詹姆斯·威尔契的人，声称他奉船长之命送我上岸。对我的劝告，他都无动于衷，也不愿意让我知道谁是他们的新船长。他们胁迫我上了一艘长舢板，还让我穿上最好的衣服，那可是一套全新的服装，而且让我带上一包内衣，武器只有一把腰刀。幸亏他们还算礼貌，没有搜刮我的口袋，那里面可放着我全部的家当以及少量其他的日用品。划了将近一里格之后，他们就把我遗弃到一片海滩上。我恳请他们让我知道这里是什么地方，但他们全都发誓说他们和我一样不太清楚，只是说船长（他们这么叫他）吩咐他们等船上的货卖光之后，一见到陆地，就打发我下船。他们很快就要划船回

get rid of me in the first place, where they could discover land. They pushed off immediately, advising me to make haste, for fear of being overtaken by the tide, and so bade me farewell.

去，劝我也快点离开，以防被潮水吞没，于是，他们就对我说了再见。

In this desolate condition I advanced forward, and soon got upon firm ground, where I sat down on a bank to rest myself, and consider what I had best, do. When I was a little refreshed, I went up into the country, resolving to deliver myself to the first savages I should meet, and purchase my life from them by some bracelets, glass rings, and other toys, which sailors usually provide themselves with in those voyages, and whereof I had some about me: The land was divided by long rows of trees not regularly planted, but naturally growing; there was great plenty of grass, and several fields of oats. I walked very circumspectly for fear of being surprised, or suddenly shot with an arrow from behind or on either side. I fell into a beaten road, where I saw many tracts of human foot, and some of cows, but most of horses. At last I beheld several animals in a field, and one or two of the same kind sitting in trees. Their shape was very singular, and deformed, which a little discomposed me, so that I lay down behind a thicket to observe them better. Some of them coming forward near the place where I lay, gave me an opportunity

我在这荒岛上一直朝前走，很快就到了安全地带。看到一处浅滩，我就坐下来小憩了一下，顺便想想该怎么办才好。等精力稍微恢复之后，我就走进这个国家，并且决定归顺那些可能会遇到的野人，用这些手镯，玻璃戒指以及其他玩具来换取自己的性命。在那样的航行中，海员们总是随身携带着这些东西，而我也整好带了几件。一长排一长排不是人工种植的，而是自然地毫无规则地生长在那儿的树木，把这里的土地分隔开来。还有大片的野草，几处燕麦田。我异常谨慎地走着，唯恐受到突袭，或是身后或两边突然冒出的冷箭把我射死。我走的是一条被踩踏出来的路，在上面，我看到很多人的脚印，还有一些是母牛的蹄印，不过大多数都是马蹄印。最后，在一块地里，我发现了几只动物，而且还发现其中的一两只坐在树上。它们异常的奇形怪状引起了我的些许不安，于是，我就在一处灌木丛后面躺下，这样就能更好地观摩它们。其中有几只朝我躺着的地方走来，越来越近，这就让我有机会察看它们的模样。一层或浓厚，或卷曲，或笔直

of distinctly marking their form. Their heads and breasts were covered with a thick hair, some frizzled and others lank; they had beards like goats, and a long ridge of hair down their backs, and the fore-parts of their legs and foot, but the rest of their bodies was bare, so that I might see their skins, which were of a brown buff colour. They had no tails, nor any hair at all on their buttocks, except about the *anus*; which, I presume, nature had placed there to defend them as they sat on the ground; for this posture they used, as well as lying down, and often stood on their hind foot. They climbed high trees, as nimbly as a squirrel, for they had strong extended claws before and behind, terminating in sharp points, and hooked. They would often spring, and bound, and leap with prodigious agility. The females were not so large as the males, they had long lank hair on their heads, but none on their faces, nor anything more than a sort of down on the rest of their bodies, except about the *anus* and *pudenda*. The dugs hung between their fore-foot, and often reached almost to the ground as they walked. The hair of both sexes was of several colours, brown, red, black, and yellow. Upon the whole, I never beheld in all my travels so disagreeable an animal, nor one against which I naturally conceived so strong an

的毛发附着在它们的头和胸脯上，还有山羊般的胡子，以及长长的一道毛长在它们的背部和腿脚前部，因为身上别的部分没长毛发，所以我还是能够看到它们那浅褐色的皮肤。而且它们没有尾巴，臀部也都没长毛，只有肛门周围长了些。我推测那是因为它们想要坐在地上的时候，保护肛门不受到伤害。平时，它们就用这样的姿态或坐或躺在地上，也常常会用后腿站立着。它们爬起高树来敏捷得如同松鼠那样，全靠它们前脚和后脚上长着锐利如钩的长爪。而且它们行动极度灵活，常常上蹿下跳。雌性的没有雄性的那样大，它们头上长着又长又直的毛发，但是脸上完全没有，而身上除了肛门和阴部周围之外，其他的地方也都长了一层毛发。它们的乳房垂在两条前腿之间，走路的时候，差不多时常会擦到地面。两种不同性别的野兽都会有几种不同色彩的毛发，比如褐色、红色、黑色、黄色等。总而言之，这还是我这次旅行中，第一次对一种动物产生了厌恶感，而我是不会自然而然对一种动物生发反感之情的。我觉得自己看够了，而心中早就充满了蔑视和反感，于是，我就起身，回到最初那条践踏出来的路上，希望它最后能带我发现某间印第安人住的房子。不过我还未走远，就遇到了其中一只动物

antipathy. So that thinking I had seen enough, full of contempt and aversion, I got up and pursued the beaten road, hoping it might direct me to the cabin of some Indian. I had not got far when I met one of these creatures full in my way, and coming up directly to me. The ugly monster, when he saw me, distorted several ways every feature of his visage, and stared as at an object he had never seen before; then approaching nearer, lifted up his fore-paw, whether out of curiosity or mischief, I could not tell. but I drew my hanger, and gave him a good blow with the flat side of it, for I durst not strike with the edge, fearing the inhabitants might be provoked against me, if they should come to know, that I had killed or maimed any of their cattle. When the beast felt the smart, he drew back, and roared so loud, that a herd of at least forty came flocking about me from the next field, howling and making odious faces; but I ran to the body of a tree, and leaning my back against it, kept them off, by waving my hanger. Several of this cursed brood, getting hold of the branches behind leaped up into the tree, from whence they began to discharge their excrements on my head: however, I escaped pretty well, by sticking close to the stem of the tree, but was almost stifled with the filth, which fell about me on every side.

把我的去路结结实实地拦住了，一路直奔向我。那头怪兽一看见我，就摆出各种鬼脸，然后就像在看一件它从没见过的东西那样，两眼一眨不眨地看着我。随后，它在靠我更近的时候抬起了前爪，我也搞不清楚它到底是出于好奇心或是企图伤害我。因此，我还是拔出了腰刀，只是用刀背对它猛击一阵，并不敢用刀的锋利一面攻击它。因为害怕当地居民知道是我砍死或是砍伤了他们的牲口而被激怒。而那头牲畜受了这样的攻击之后，一面退后，一面高声地狂吼，吼声很快就引得附近的怪兽聚集过来。至少有 40 头这样的怪兽将我团团围在中间，而它们又是嚎叫又是扮怪相。我即刻逃到一棵树下，后背倚着树干，为了不让它们接近，我不停地舞动着腰刀。有几只令人厌恶的畜生攀住我身后的树枝，跳到树上，从上往下，开始在我头上拉屎撒尿。我只好紧紧贴住树干，才算是逃过一劫，但四周落下来的粪便的臭气，还是差点把我熏死了。

In the midst of this distress, I observed them all to run away on a sudden as fast as they could, at which I ventured to leave the tree, and pursue the road, wondering what it was that could put them into this fright. But looking on my left hand, I saw a horse walking softly in the field: which my persecutors having sooner discovered, was the cause of their flight. The horse started a little when he came near me, but soon recovering himself, looked full in my face with manifest tokens of wonder: he viewed my hands and foot, walking round me several times. I would have pursued my journey, but he placed himself directly in the way, yet looking with a very mild aspect, never offering the least violence. We stood gazing at each other for some time; at last I took the boldness, to reach my hand towards his neck, with a design to stroke it, using the common style and whistle of jockies, when they are going to handle a strange horse. But this animal seemed to receive my civilities with disdain shook his head, and bent his brows, softly raising up his right forefoot to remove my hand. Then he neighed three or four times, but in so different a cadence, that I almost began to think he was speaking to himself in some language of his own.

危难关头，我发现这些牲畜突然间尽全力飞速跑开，这样我就大着胆子逃离了那棵树，继续赶路，心里却很想知道让它们感到如此害怕的到底是什么东西。突然，我看到左手边，一匹马正在田野上缓缓地走着，因为那些欺负我的畜生比我先看见它，所以吓得全部跑掉了。当它走近我时，一开始有点吃惊，随即很快就恢复了平静，并且露出异常惊奇的表情，随即察看了我的双手双脚，接着在我的身前身后绕了几个圈。我正打算继续往前走，它却非要挡住去路，然而它看起来倒是很温和，没有一点要强硬的意思。我们相互盯着对方看了一阵子，最后我居然壮着胆子，拿出职业骑师驯服野马的架势，吹着哨子，把手伸向它的脖子，准备去抚摸它。然而，这种动物似乎不屑于我的这番好意，摇摇头，皱皱眉，缓缓地抬起右前蹄推开了我的手。随后，它又用完全不同的音调嘶叫了三四次，让我不禁认为，它是在用它自己的某种语言在自言自语。

While he and I were thus employed, another horse came up; who applying

就在我和它僵持的时候，又过来了一匹马，它规规矩矩地走近第

himself to the first in a very formal manner, they gently struck each other's right hoof before, neighing several times by turns, and varying the sound, which seemed to be almost articulate. They went some paces off, as if it were to confer together, walking side by side, backward and forward, like persons deliberating upon some affair of weight, but often turning their eyes towards me, as it were to watch that I might not escape. I was amazed to see such actions and behaviour in brute beasts, and concluded with myself, that if the inhabitants of this country were endued with a proportionable degree of reason, they must needs be the wisest people upon earth. This thought gave me so much comfort, that I resolved to go forward until I could discover some house or village, or meet with any of the natives, leaving the two horses to discourse together as they pleased. But the first, who was a Dapple-Gray, observing me to steal off, neighed after me in so expressive a tone, that I fancied myself to understand what he meant; whereupon I turned back, and came near to him, to expect his farther commands; but concealing my fear as much as I could, for I began to be in some pain, how this adventure might terminate; and the reader will easily believe I did not much like my present situation.

一匹马，它们的右前蹄先是相互轻轻地触碰了一下，然后它们就如同交谈一般，用变换着的声调相互嘶叫着。它们走得远远的，好像要共同商讨事情，又像在考虑什么大事，一起走来走去，然而眼睛却不停地瞟过来看我这边，似乎在监督我，不要让我逃脱似的。我惊奇于毫无理性的野兽也能够做出这种举动，不禁自己下了推断，如果这个国家有如此理性的头脑的居民，那么世上最睿智的人一定就是他们了。这个想法给了我很大的慰藉，而我决定继续朝前走，试着去找到某间房子或是某个村落，或是遇到一个本地人。于是，我就留那两匹马在那里高兴怎么谈就怎么谈吧。然而第一匹，那只菊花青马发现我要偷溜，就用它那极富感染力的声音在我身后长嘶起来，我想我能明白它要表达的意思。于是，我转过身，靠近它，看看它到底想要干什么。然而我也尽力地掩盖住自己心中的慌乱，因为我开始感到了些许痛楚，却根本不知道到底要怎样摆脱这样的险境。读者也很容易了解，我异常讨厌眼下这样的处境。

The two horses came up close to me, looking with great earnestness upon my face and hands. The gray steed rubbed my hat all round with his right fore-hoof, and discomposed it so much, that I was forced to adjust it better, by taking it off, and settling it again; whereat, both he and his companion (who was a brown bay) appeared to be much surprised, the latter felt the lappet of my coat, and finding it to hang loose about me, they both looked with new signs of wonder. He stroked my right hand, seeming to admire the softness and colour; but he squeezed it so hard between his hoof and his pastern, that I was forced to roar; after which they both touched me with all possible tenderness. They were under great perplexity about my shoes and stockings, which they felt very often, neighing to each other, and using various gestures, not unlike those of a philosopher, when he would attempt to solve some new and difficult phenomenon.

两匹马走近我，认真地打量着我的脸和双手。那匹灰马用右前蹄把我的礼帽摸了一圈，帽子被它弄得乱成了一团，我只得把它取下来，整理好之后，又戴了回去，这让它和它的同伴（一匹棕色的马）感到非常吃惊。棕色的马摸了摸我的上衣襟，发现它居然是松松地在搭我身上时，它俩的神情越发惊奇了。它碰了碰我的右手，似乎非常羡慕它的柔软和颜色，不过它竟然用它的蹄子与蹄骸将我的手放在中间猛夹，让我疼得哇哇大叫，不过这样倒是让它们尽可能温柔地抚摸我。还有，它们对于我的鞋子和袜子也感到十分困惑，时不时地摸一摸，接着又相互嘶叫一番，摆出各种姿势，就像是一位哲学家尝试着去解决某个新的难题似的。

Upon the whole, the behaviour of these animals was so orderly and rational, so acute and judicious, that I at last concluded, they must needs be magicians, who had thus metamorphosed themselves upon some design, and seeing a stranger in the way, were resolved to divert themselves with him; or perhaps were really amazed at the sight of a man so very

总之，看到这两只动物有逻辑，有理性的举动，敏锐的洞察力以及准确的判断力，最终我断言它们肯定是魔术师，见到路上有陌生人，就用魔术把自己掩藏起来，用这样的方式同他寻开心。抑或是见到一个不论是习俗，相貌以及肤色都可能和生活在如此遥远的地方完全不同的人，着实让它们大吃一

different in habit, feature and complexion from those who might probably live in so remote a climate. Upon the strength of this reasoning, I ventured to address them in the following manner: Gentlemen, if you be conjurers, as I have good cause to believe, you can understand any language; therefore I make bold to let your worships know, that I am a poor distressed *Englishman*, driven by his misfortunes upon your coast, and I entreat one of you, to let me ride upon his back, as if he were a real horse, to some house or village, where I can be relieved. In return of which favour, I will make you a present of this knife and bracelet (taking them out of my pocket) The two creatures stood silent while I spoke, seeming to listen with great attention; and when I had ended, they neighed frequently towards each other, as if they were engaged in serious conversation. I plainly observed, that their language expressed the passions very well, and the words might with little pains be resolved into an alphabet more easily than the *Chinese*.

惊。我觉得这样想颇有道理，就大着胆子对它们说了下面的话：先生们，如果你们是魔术师，我有理由相信你们一定可以理解任何语言，因此我斗胆让阁下们知道，我是一名可怜落魄的英国人，遭遇变数而被赶到你们的海岸上，我想恳请你们中任何一位，准许我就像骑真马那样骑到它的背上，把我带到某户人家或是某个村庄，那样我就可以得救了。我将会把这把刀和手镯（说着把它们拿出了口袋）送给你们当做报恩的礼物。而在我说话的时候，这两只动物似乎静静地站在那里专心地聆听。等我讲完以后，它们仿佛在进行一场严肃的对话，互相嘶叫了好一阵子，而且我也能清晰地感觉出它们的对话所传递出的强烈情感，它们所说的话用字母很轻松地就能拼写出来，比中文容易很多。

I could frequently distinguish the word *Yahoo*, which was repeated by each of them several times; and although it was impossible for me to conjecture what it meant, yet while the two horses were busy in conversation, I endeavoured to practise this word upon my tongue; and as soon as

我时不时可以听出的一个词是“雅虎”，它们两个都把这个词重复了好几次，虽然我弄不懂那是什么意思，因此我就趁这两匹马正忙着谈话的空隙，尽力开始练习这个词。在它们的谈话一结束，我就壮着胆子高叫着“雅虎”，同时还

they were silent, I boldly pronounced *Yahoo* in a loud voice, imitating, at the same time, as near as I could, the neighing of a horse; at which they were both visibly surprised, and the gray repeated the same word twice, as if he meant to teach me the right accent, wherein I spoke after him as well as I could, and found myself perceivably to improve every time, though very far from any degree of perfection. Then the bay tried me with a second word, much harder to be pronounced; but reducing it to the *English orthography*, may be spelt thus, *Houyhnhnm*. I did not succeed in this so well as in the former, but after two or three farther trials, I had better fortune; and they both appeared amazed at my capacity.

尽可能地效仿那种马的嘶叫声。听完之后，它们都流露出惊讶之色。灰色的马又重复了两遍，似乎在教我正确的发音，我也就尽量跟着它学，虽然还不可能达到完善的地步，但是每次都能感觉到自己在进步。随后，棕色的马尝试教了我另外一个比第一个发音更难的词，要是按照英语正确写法就是"Houyhnhnm"。这个词的发音不如前一个好，但是多试了三两次之后，也进步了很多。对我有这样的能力，它们都觉得异常吃惊。

After some further discourse, which I then conjectured might relate to me, the two friends took their leaves, with the same compliment of striking each other's hoof; and the gray made me signs that I should walk before him, wherein I thought it prudent to comply, till I could find a better director. When I offered to slacken my pace, he would cry *hhuun, hhuun*; I guessed his meaning, and gave him to understand, as well as I could, that I was weary, and not able to walk faster; upon which, he would stand a while to let me rest.

两位朋友又交谈了一阵子，我想可能和我有关系吧，和之前一样，它们礼节性地相互碰了碰蹄子，之后便要离开，灰色的马示意我走在它前面，我想在找到更好的向导之前，最好还是听它的话好了。我的脚步一放缓，它就会发出"混，混"的低吼声，我能猜出它的意思，但是我也尽量让它知道我太累了，再也走不动了。这样，它只好停下来站着，让我小憩一下。

CHAPTER 2

第二章

The Author conducted by a Houyhnhnm to his House. The House described. the Author's Reception. the Food of the Houyhnhnms. The Author in Distress for want of Meat. is at last relieved. His Manner of feeding in this Country.

Having travelled about three miles, we came to a long kind of building, made of timber, stuck in the ground, and wattled across; the roof was low, and covered with straw. I now began to be a little comforted, and took out some toys, which travellers usually carry for presents to the savage *Indians* of *America* and other parts, in hopes the people of the house would be thereby encouraged to receive me kindly. The horse made me a sign to go in first; it was a large room with a smooth clay floor, and a rack and manger extending the whole length on one side. There were three nags, and two mares, not eating, but some of them sitting down upon their hams, which I very much wondered at; but wondered more to see the rest employed in domestic business. they seemed but ordinary cattle; however this confirmed my first opinion, that a people who could

本章节介绍一只“慧骃”把作者领回家中。这只“慧骃”所住房屋的描绘。作者受到的招待。“慧骃”吃的食物。作者因没有肉吃而感到苦恼，最后还是找到办法解决。还有就是在这个国家里，他是如何吃饭的。

我们走了大约 3 英里之后，就来到一座长房子前。这座房子是将木料插在地上，再在四周编上枝条，然后在低矮的房顶上铺满稻草建成的。此时，我才开始觉得心安了不少，于是就拿出一些旅行家们经常携带送给美洲或其他地方的印第安野人当礼物的几件玩意，期望这些东西能使这家人好好地招待我。那匹马示意我先到房子里去。这是一间有着光滑泥土地面的大房间，在房间的一侧，整整一长条都是饲草架和食槽。房间里还有 3 匹小马和两匹母马没有在吃草，不过让我非常惊奇的是其中几匹用屁股坐在那里。但是更让我吃惊的是，另外几匹马竟然在干家务活。它们看起来只不过是些普通的牲畜，不过这一切更证实了我最初的想法，一个能把野兽驯化成如此的种族，其智慧一定在世上所有种

so far civilise brute animals, must needs excel in wisdom all the nations of the world. The gray came in just after, and thereby prevented any ill treatment, which the others might have given me. He neighed to them several times in a style of authority, and received answers.

Beyond this room there were three others, reaching the length of the house, to which you passed through three doors, opposite to each other, in the manner of a vista; we went through the second room towards the third, here the gray walked in first, beckoning me to attend: I waited in the second room, and got ready my presents, for the master and mistress of the house: they were two knives, three bracelets of false pearl, a small looking-glass, and a bead necklace. The horse neighed three or four times, and I waited to hear some answers in a human voice, but I heard no other returns, than in the same dialect, only one or two a little shriller than his. I began to think that this house must belong to some person of great note among them, because there appeared so much ceremony before I could gain admittance. But, that a man of quality should be served all by horses, was beyond my comprehension. I feared my brain was disturbed by my sufferings and misfortunes: I roused myself, and looked about me in the room where I was left

族之上。灰色的马紧随其后进来了，这样，别的马就不可能再欺负我了。它以一种庄严的姿态向它们嘶叫了几声，它们就嘶叫着回应着。

一直到这座长房的尽头，除了这间房之外，其他 3 个房间连在一起，如果你穿过相对的 3 扇门，就好像走在一条大街上。我们穿过第二间房要到第三间去，此时灰马率先走了进去，招呼我在外面等着。于是，趁在第二间房里等待的工夫，我准备了两把刀，3 副假珍珠手镯，一面小镜子和一串珠子项链，要把它们当礼物送给这家的男女主人。听见那马嘶叫了三四声，我期待着能有人声应答，但我只是听到了一两声比灰色马更尖锐的马叫声，就再也没有听见其他的声音了。而且我开始在心里琢磨着这个房子里住的肯定是他们中的重要人物，因为在召见前要经过如此多的繁文缛节。然而，这位所有事务都由马来打理的高贵人物，却让我摸不着头脑。我害怕自己的遭遇和不幸会让我神志不清，于是便打起精神，四下观察了一下我单独待着的房间，我发现这个房间除了要比第一间更加别致之外，陈设都是一样的。我不停地揉眼睛，见到的却还是一样的东西。于是，我又拧

alone; this was furnished like the first, only after a more elegant manner. I rubbed my eyes often, but the same objects still occurred. I pinched my arms and sides, to awake myself, hoping I might be in a dream. I then absolutely concluded, that all these appearances could be nothing else but necromancy and magic. But I had no time to pursue these reflections; for the gray horse came to the door, and made me a sign to follow him into the third room, where I saw a very comely mare, together with a colt and foal, sitting on their haunches, upon mats of straw, not unartfully made, and perfectly neat and clean.

The mare soon after my entrance, rose from her mat, and coming up close, after having nicely observed my hands and face, gave me a most contemptuous look; and turning to the horse, I heard the word *Yahoo* often repeated betwixt them; the meaning of which word I could not then comprehend, although it was the first I had learned to pronounce; but I was soon better informed, to my everlasting mortification: for the horse beckoning to me with his head, and repeating the *hhuun*, *hhuu*n, as he did upon the road, which I understood was to attend him, led me out into a kind of court, where was another building at some distance from the house. Here we entered, and I saw three of

胳膊，又掐腰，好让自己清醒过来，希望自己只是在做梦。接下来所发生的事情让我确信眼前的一切一定是妖术或是魔法。然而，还没等我来得及细想下去，那匹灰色的马已经走到门口，让我跟着它到第三间房里面去。一进门，我就见到了一匹非常标致的母马，另外就是一匹小公马和一匹小母马，它们一起屁股着地地坐在绝对干净整洁的草席上。

我进去后不久，那匹母马就由草席上站起来，走近我，认真地观察完我的双手和脸之后，异常轻蔑地看着我。随后，它转身对着灰色的马，我听到它们不断地说起“雅虎”这个词。虽然它是我第一个学会说的词，但当时我还是没能领会它的意思。不过很快我就能很好地理解了，却带给我无尽的耻辱感。此时，灰色的马朝我点点头，又像刚才路上那样，不停地发出“混，混”的声音，我就知道它让我跟上它走出房间，来到一个跟院子相像的地方，那里另有一栋离马儿的住房不远的房屋。一走进去，就看见上岸后最先见到的那3只令我厌恶的畜生，正在那里吃着树根和兽

those detestable creatures, which I first met after my landing, feeding upon roots, and the flesh of some animals, which I afterwards found to be that of asses and dogs, and now and then a cow dead by accident or disease. They were all tied by the neck with strong withes fastened to a beam; they held their food between the claws of their forefoot, and tore it with their teeth.

肉。过后，我才知道那竟然是驴肉和狗肉，偶尔也会是遭遇意外或病死的母牛肉。它们的脖子被结实的枝条绑住，枝条的另一头则系在一根横梁上。它们用两只前爪夹住食物，再用牙齿撕下来吃。

The master horse ordered a sorrel nag, one of his servants, to untie the largest of these animals, and take him into the yard. The beast and I were brought close together; and by our countenances diligently compared, both by master and servant, who thereupon repeated several times the word *Yahoo*. My horror and astonishment are not to be described, when I observed, in this abominable animal, a perfect human figure; the face of it indeed was flat and broad, the nose depressed, the lips large, and the mouth wide. but these differences are common to all savage nations, where the lineaments of the countenance are distorted by the natives suffering their infants to lie grovelling on the earth, or by carrying them on their backs, nuzzling with their face against the mother's shoulders. The forefoot of the *Yahoo* differed from my hands in nothing else, but the length of the nails, the coarseness and brownness of the

马主人命令那匹栗色小马——它的一个奴仆去解下它们中最大的一头，带到院子里。然后，主仆两匹马将我和那野兽紧排在一起，随后就开始认真地比较我俩的相貌，紧接着就反复说着“雅虎”这个词。当我发现这只可恶的畜生居然和人长得一模一样的时候，惊恐之情难以言表。它那又扁又宽的脸，塌鼻子，厚嘴唇，大嘴巴，这些差异在所有野蛮族群和人之间很常见，因为土著人总是会让他们的孩子们趴在地上，或是把他们背在背上，这样，孩子的脸就在母亲的肩膀上蹭来蹭去，面部轮廓因此变了形。除了长长的指甲，粗糙的手掌，偏棕黄的颜色，以及手背长毛之外，和我的手相比，“雅虎”的前爪没有太多的差异。而且我们的脚相比较起来，也有着和手一样的异同处。因为我穿了鞋子和袜子，所以我非常清楚这一点，而马却不知道。另外，我们身上的其他

palms, and the hairiness on the backs. There was the same resemblance between our foot, with the same differences, which I knew very well, though the horses did not, because of my shoes and stockings; the same in every part of our bodies except as to hairiness and colour, which I have already described.

部分，除了它是多毛的，颜色不同以外，也都是一样的，我在之前已经提到过这一点。

The great difficulty that seemed to stick with the two horses, was, to see the rest of my body so very different from that of a *Yahoo*, for which I was obliged to my clothes, whereof they had no conception: The sorrel nag offered me a root, which he held (after their manner, as we shall describe in its proper place) between his hoof and pastern; I took it in my hand, and having smelt it, returned it to him again as civilly as I could. He brought out of the *Yahoo*'*s* kennel a piece of ass's flesh, but it smelt so offensively that I turned from it with loathing; he then threw it to the *Yahoo*, by whom it was greedily devoured. He afterwards showed me a whisp of hay, and a fetlock full of oats; but I shook my head, to signify, that neither of these were food for me. And indeed, I now apprehended, that I must absolutely starve, if I did not get to some of my own species: for as to those filthy *Yahoos*, although there were few greater lovers of mankind, at that time, than myself; yet I confess I never saw any sensitive being so

它们看上去对我身体的其他部分和“雅虎”的巨大差异深感困惑，因为这两匹马对衣服没有意识，而我正好穿着衣服。那匹栗色小马递给我一节树根，是用它的蹄子和骹夹给我的（稍后有合适的机会，我会再细说它们拿东西的方式），我把它拿在手上闻了下，又尽可能有礼貌地还给了它。它又从“雅虎”住的地方拿出一块气味十分熏人的驴肉，我更不敢吃，它就把这块肉扔给了“雅虎”，它们就贪婪地吞食起来。随后，对于它给我的一小捆干草和满满一球节燕麦，我都摇头，表明那都不是我吃的食物。说实话，现在我倒是真的有些害怕万一找不到我的同类，那么我肯定会饿死的。虽然那个时候我比任何人都热爱人类，但是不管怎样，我都不会认同那些龌龊的“雅虎”是我的同类，它们是我见过的最令人厌烦的生物。而且我停留在这个国家的那段日子里，越靠近它们，就越发感觉到它们的可憎。从我的举止中，马主人已经感

detestable on all accounts; and the more I came near them, the more hateful they grew, while I stayed in that country. This the master horse observed by my behaviour, and therefore sent the *Yahoo* back to his kennel. He then put his fore-hoof to his mouth, at which I was much surprised, although he did it with ease, and with a motion that appeared perfectly natural, and made other signs to know what I would eat; but I could not return him such an answer as he was able to apprehend; and if he had understood me, I did not see how it was possible to contrive any way for finding myself nourishment. While we were thus engaged, I observed a cow passing by, whereupon I pointed to her, and expressed a desire to let me go and milk her. This had its effect; for he led me back into the house, and ordered a mare-servant to open a room, where a good store of milk lay in earthen and wooden vessels, after a very orderly and cleanly manner. She gave me a large bowl full, of which I drank very heartily, and found myself well refreshed.

觉出来了，因此它命令送“雅虎”回它的住处。随后，它就极其从容自然地把前蹄放到嘴上，这却让我极度吃惊。它又极度轻松自然地摆弄了一些其他姿势，想弄清楚我到底吃什么。然而我没法让它搞懂我的回答，况且就算它明白了，我看它为我找吃的也是无能为力。就在这时，我看到一头母牛从身旁走过，于是，我就指指它，表明我想去喝牛奶。这招倒是奏效了。它很快把我领回房子里，命令一匹母马仆人打开一间房，在那里面，规规矩矩，干干净净地摆放着很多陶盆和木盆，里面满满装着的都是牛奶。母马将满满一大碗牛奶递给我，我一口气喝了下去，立马就来了精神。

About noon I saw coming towards the house a kind of vehicle drawn like a sledge by four *Yahoos*. There was in it an old steed, who seemed to be of quality; he alighted with his Hind foot forward, having by accident got a hurt in his left fore foot. He came to dine with our horse,

将近中午，我瞅见4只“雅虎”拉着如同雪橇似的车子走近这所房子。车上是一匹看起来有些地位的老马，因为无意中伤了左前蹄，因此它下车的时候，后蹄先着了地。它是到我的马主人家聚会的，主人颇有礼貌地招待了它。在最好

who received him with great civility. They dined in the best room, and had oats boiled in milk for the second course, which the old horse eat warm, but the rest cold. Their mangers were placed circular in the middle of the room, and divided into several partitions, round which they sat on their haunches upon bosses of straw. In the middle was a large rack with angles answering to every partition of the manger. so that each horse and mare eat their own hay, and their own mash of oats and milk, with much decency and regularity. The behaviour of the young colt and foal appeared very modest, and that of the master and mistress extremely cheerful and complaisant to their guest. The gray ordered me to stand by him, and much discourse passed between him and his friend concerning me, as I found by the stranger's often looking on me, and the frequent repetition of the word *Yahoo*.

的屋子享用餐点，老马吃到的菜，除了第二道菜牛奶煮燕麦是热菜，其余的都是冷食。在房间中央，它们的食槽围成圈，分成好多格，它们也坐在草堆上，围成一圈。食槽圈的中央摆着一个大草料架，架子上有许多角，每个角都对着食槽的一个格子，这样每匹公马和母马在吃自己的干草和牛奶燕麦糊的时候，就会井然有序。小马驹们行为规矩，马主人夫妇待客的态度也是极其热情而周到的。灰色的马吩咐我站在它身边，它就和它的朋友讲了关于我的很多事情，因为我发现客人时不时看向我，而且还不断地提及“雅虎”这个词。

I happened to wear my gloves, which the master-gray observing, seemed perplexed, discovering signs of wonder what I had done to my forefoot. he put his hoof three or four times to them, as if he would signify, that I should reduce them to their former shape, which I presently did, pulling off both my gloves, and putting them into my pocket. This occasioned farther talk, and I saw the company was pleased with my behaviour, whereof I

那时，我正好戴了一副手套，这在那匹灰色的马主人的眼里，是一件不可思议的事情，而且它也非常想知道我到底对我的前蹄做了些什么。接着，我的手套被它的蹄子碰了三四次，好像在示意我让我把它们变回原来的样子，我立刻脱下手套，把它们放进口袋。这一举动更是引起了它们的热议。我还看得出大家很满意我的做法，并且产生了良好的效应。它们要求我讲出

soon found the good effects. I was ordered to speak the few words I understood, and while they were at dinner; the master taught me the names for oats, milk, fire, water, and some others, which I could readily pronounce after him, having from my youth a great facility in learning languages.

我会的那几个词，在它们吃饭的时候，马主人又教了我燕麦，牛奶，火，水等这些东西的说法。因为打小我就有学语言的天赋，所以很容易就能跟读了。

When dinner was done, the master horse took me aside, and by signs and words made me understand the concern he was in, that I had nothing to eat. Oats in their tongue are called *hlunnh*. This word I pronounced two or three times; for although I had refused them at first, yet upon second thoughts, I considered that I could contrive to make of them a kind of bread, which might be sufficient with milk to keep me alive, till I could make my escape to some other country and to creatures of my own species. The horse immediately ordered a white mare-servant of his family to bring me a good quantity of oats in a sort of wooden tray. These I heated before the fire as well as I could, and rubbed them till the husks came off, which I made a shift to winnow from the grain; I ground and beat them between two stones, then took water, and made them into a paste or cake, which I toasted at the fire, and eat warm with milk. It was at first a very insipid diet, though common enough in many parts of *Europe*, but grew

饭后，我被马主人拉到一边，通过肢体语言以及口头语言想让我知道我没东西可吃，让它很不安。在它们的语言中，“赫伦”就是燕麦的意思，于是我就说了两三遍，因为起初我是拒绝吃这玩意的，可是转念一想，我可以想办法把它变成一种面包，然后伴着牛奶一起吃，或许这样我就可以活命了，再想办法逃往其他国家，找到我的同类。马主人立刻嘱咐一匹白母马仆人给我用木盘子送来了很多的燕麦。我把它们放在火上尽量烤，搓去麦壳，吹掉麦皮，然后用两块石头把它们碾碎，加水后做成类似于糊或饼的东西，接着用火烤熟，趁热就着牛奶吃下去。事实上，虽然在欧洲的很多地方，这种食物相当普遍了，不过一开始吃的时候，还是觉得没什么味道，但是久了也就习惯了。虽然我的一生中，时常会沦落到吃杂食的地步，不过多次经验证明我有一个很容易满足的天性。还有值得一提的是，在这座岛上逗留期间，我没生过一个

tolerable by time; and having been often reduced to hard fare in my life, this was not the first experiment I had made how easily nature is satisfied. And I cannot but observe, that I never had one hour's sickness, while I stayed in this island. 'Its true, I sometimes made a shift to catch a rabbit, or bird, by springes made of *Yahoos'* hairs, and I often gathered wholesome herbs, which I boiled, and eat as salads with my bread, and now and then, for a rarity, I made a little butter, and drank the whey. I was at first at a great loss for salt, but custom soon reconciled the want of it; and I am confident that the frequent use of salt among us is an effect of luxury, and was first introduced only as a provocative to drink; except where it is necessary for preserving of flesh in long voyages, or in places remote from great markets. for we observe no animal to be fond of it but man: and as to myself, when I left this country, it was a great while before I could endure the taste of it in anything that I eat.

小时的病。有时，我会设法用“雅虎”的毛编成网，来抓些兔子或鸟儿之类的。而且时常会去采摘些干净的野菜，煮熟后，和着面包一起吃。还有就是偶尔我也会做些奶油这样的稀罕物，而且我也都会喝光做奶油剩下的乳清。起初，没有盐吃，简直不知所措，可是渐渐习惯了，一段时间之后，不吃它也没什么关系了。我有理由相信我们总是吃盐其实是很奢侈的，因为一开始，饮料中放了盐只是用来提味，因此，食盐除了用于长距离航海，或是要在远离大市场的地方储存肉食之外，并非必需品。我们可以观察到除了人之外，没有哪种动物喜欢吃盐。而我自己也是在离开这个国家很长时间之后，才能接受有咸味的食物。

This is enough to say upon the subject of my diet, wherewith other travellers fill their books, as if the readers were personally concerned, whether we fare well or ill. However, it was necessary to mention this matter, lest the world should think it impossible that I could find sustenance for three years in such a

对于我的饮食问题，已经谈论得够多了。好像所有的读者对我们这些人饮食的好坏都很关心，所以其他的旅行家在他们的作品中大都会提及这个内容。然而还是很有必要谈到这个问题的，否则世人哪会相信我会在这样的国家和这般的居民一起生活了3年。

country, and among such inhabitants.

When it grew towards evening, the master horse ordered a place for me to lodge in; it was but six yards from the house, and separated from the stable of the *Yahoos*. Here I got some straw, and covering myself with my own clothes, slept very sound. But I was in a short time better accommodated, as the reader shall know hereafter, when I come to treat more particularly about my way of living.

傍晚渐渐降临，马主人叮嘱准备一个我能休息的地方。那里相隔马的住所有 6 码远的距离，而且没有和“雅虎”的窝在一起。我铺了一些干草在地上，身上就搭着自己的衣服，睡得很沉。但很快我就有更好的住处了，此后，我还会详细地描述我的生活方式，读者届时就能了解。

CHAPTER 3

第三章

The Author studies to learn the Language. The Houyhnhnm, his Master, assists in teaching him. the Language described. Several Houyhnhnms of Quality come out of Curiosity to see the Author. He gives his Master a short Account of his Voyage.

本章作者主要描写的是在他的"慧骃"主人的帮教下，认真研习它们的语言。对于这种语言的介绍。出于对作者的好奇心，几位"慧骃"贵族都过来探望他。他向主人简单扼要地讲了讲他的航海经历。

My principal endeavour was to learn the language, which my master (for so I shall henceforth call him) and his children, and every servant of his house were desirous to teach me. for they looked upon it as a prodigy that a brute animal should discover such marks of a rational creature. I pointed to every thing, and inquired the name of it, which I wrote down in my *journal-book* when I was alone, and corrected my bad accent, by desiring those of the family to pronounce it often. In this employment, a sorrel nag, one of the under servants, was very ready to assist me.

当时我就想尽最大努力学习那些语言，因为我的主人（此后，我都那么称呼它），它的孩子们以及家中每个仆人都乐意教我。而它们觉得一头畜生居然会有种种理性动物的表现，实属奇迹。我指着每件东西，询问它们的名称，独处时，我就把它们写到我的航海日志中，而且每当遇到发音不准时，我就会请家里的马多发几次，帮我纠正。有匹栗色小马仆人在这个方面随时都准备好帮助我。

In speaking, they pronounced through the nose and throat, and their language approaches nearest to the *High Dutch or German*, of any I know in *Europe*; but is much more graceful and significant. The emperor Charles V made almost the same

它们说话的时候，鼻音和喉音是最主要的，在我所了解的欧洲语言中，高地荷兰语或者德语和它们的语言有相似之处，但是更加优美，意义也更加隽永。查尔斯五世就表达过同样的评论，他说如果他对他

observation, when he said, That if he were to speak to his horse, it should be in *High Dutch*.

The curiosity and impatience of my master were so great, that he spent many hours of his leisure to instruct me. He was convinced (as he afterwards told me) that I must be a *Yahoo*, but my teachableness, civility and cleanliness astonished him; which were qualities altogether opposite to those animals. He was most perplexed about my clothes, reasoning sometimes with himself, whether they were a part of my body; for I never pulled them off till the family were asleep, and got them on before they waked in the morning. My master was eager to learn from whence I came, how I acquired those appearances of reason, which I discovered in all my actions, and to know my story from my own mouth, which he hoped he should soon do by the great proficiency I made in learning and pronouncing their words and sentences. To help my memory, I formed all I learned into the *English* alphabet, and writ the words down with the translations. This last, after some time, I ventured to do in my master's presence. It cost me much trouble to explain to him what I was doing; for the inhabitants have not the least idea of books or literature.

In about ten weeks' time I was able to understand most of his questions, and in

的马说话，用的肯定会是高地荷兰语。

我的主人有很强的好奇心，而且极富耐心，一有空，它就会花很多时间来指导我。对我是一只“雅虎”它深信不疑（这是它事后跟我讲的），但是我是可教的，懂礼貌的，干净的，倒是让它对我和“雅虎”那样的动物有着完全不一样的品格深感惊讶。而且它还对我的衣服深感困惑，有时它自个儿想或许这些就是我身体的一部分呢。因为一般我脱衣服休息的时候，它们一家人都睡着了，而早上穿上的时候，它们都还没睡醒。我的主人急于想弄明白我是从哪里来的，我的一举一动又是如何表现得如此理性的，还有就是因为我已经熟练地学会了说它们的语言，单词和句子，所以它盼望着很快能从我口中听到我的故事。为了帮助自己记忆，我用英文字母把所有学过的单词都拼写好，并且和译文记录在一块。因为这些马全然不清楚什么是书或是文学，所以我花了不少力气向它们解释了我所做的事情，于是，在我主人的面前，我也敢这样做了。

大约 10 周之后，我可以理解出它提的大部分问题，而且 3 个月之

three months could give him some tolerable answers. He was extremely curious to know from what part of the country I came, and how I was taught to imitate a rational creature; because the *Yahoos* (whom he saw I exactly resembled in my head, hands and face, that were only visible) with some appearance of cunning, and the strongest disposition to mischief, were observed to be the most unteachable of all brutes. I answered, That I came over the sea, from a far place, with many others of my own kind, in a great hollow vessel made of the bodies of trees. that my companions forced me to land on this coast, and then left me to shift for myself. It was with some difficulty, and by the help of many signs, that I brought him to understand me. He replied, that I must needs be mistaken, or that I *said the thing which was not*. (for they have no word in their language to express lying or falsehood.) He knew it was impossible that there could be a country beyond the sea, or that a parcel of brutes could move a wooden vessel whither they pleased upon water. He was sure no *Houyhnhnm* alive could make such a vessel, nor would trust *Yahoos* to manage it.

内，我就能够给出一些它能够听懂的答案。它很好奇我是来自这个国家的哪一个部分，还有就是我如何学会仿效理性动物的，因为看起来有些聪慧，但是却最喜欢捣乱的“雅虎”（它只是看我的头，手和脸，就认定我确实和一只“雅虎”相像），传说在所有兽类中是最没可教性的一种。我告诉它，我是和很多其他同类一起，乘着挖空树干所做成的庞大的容器，从一个遥远的地方，远渡而来。而到了这里，我的伙伴硬是把我赶到岸上，扔下我，让我自生自灭。我大费唇舌，还使用了很多的手势语，才让它听懂了我所说的。它回答说，我绝对是搞错了，或者是我所说的事情和事实并不一致（因为在它们的语言中，没有词语去表达谎言或假意这样的意思）。它认为海那边不可能还有任何国家，更不可能有一群畜生能够随便就让一个木质容器在水面上漂动。他确信任何一个活着的“慧骃”都不可能造出这样的容器，也相信“雅虎”不会想办法这样做。

The word *Houyhnhnm*, in their tongue, signifies a *horse*, and in its etymology, the *perfection of nature*. I told my master, that I was at a loss for expression, but would

在它们的语言中，“慧骃”这个词意味着“马”，而从它的词源来看，指的是“完美的大自然”。我告诉主人，我并不能准确地说出自己想说

improve as fast as I could; and hoped in a short time I should be able to tell him wonders: He was pleased to direct his own mare, his colt and foal, and the servants of the family, to take all opportunities of instructing me, and every day for two or three hours, he was at the same pains himself: Several horses and mares of quality in the neighbourhood came often to our house upon the report spread of a wonderful *Yahoo*, that could speak like a *Houyhnhnm*, and seemed, in his words and actions, to discover some glimmerings of reason. These delighted to converse with me; they put many questions, and received such answers, as I was able to return. By all these advantages, I made so great a progress, that in five months from my arrival, I understood whatever was spoke, and could express myself tolerably well.

The *Houyhnhnms* who came to visit my master, out of a design of seeing and talking with me, could hardly believe me to be a right *Yahoo*, because my body had a different covering from others of my kind. They were astonished to observe me without the usual hair or skin, except on my head, face and hands; but I discovered that secret to my master upon an accident, which happened about a fortnight before.

I have already told the reader, that every night when the family were gone to bed, it was my custom to strip and cover myself

的话，但是我会尽我所能提高我的表达能力，希望很快就可以把各种奇奇怪怪的事情都告诉它。因此，它异常开心地要求自己的妻子，子女和家中的仆人抓住一切机会来教导我，与此同时，它自己每天也会花两三个小时来教我。左邻右舍的几位男女马贵族听闻我们家有头奇妙的“雅虎”，既能像“慧骃”一样讲话，举手投足间似乎还能带有些许理性，它们便常常到我家来。这些马贵族很乐意和我交谈。它们问了我很多问题，而我也就知无不言言无不尽。而依靠所有的优势，我得到如此神速的进步，以至于在到这地方的 5 个月之后，它们所说的我通通都听得懂，而且我也能比较清楚地表达出我的意思了。

那些来看望我主人的“慧骃”，都是设法来看我，而且还想和我聊天的，它们几乎全都不信我真的是一只“雅虎”，因为我身体表面所附着的东西让我和“雅虎”不一样。它们感到异常吃惊的是我的身体除了头、脸和手之外，其他没有一处是正常的毛发以及皮肤。然而，大约两周前的偶发事件，却不想让我的主人知道了我的秘密。

我已告知过读者，我每晚都习惯等全家休息之后，才会脱下衣服，然后搭在身上睡觉。某天清晨，作

with my clothes: It happened one morning early, that my master sent for me, by the sorrel nag, who was his valet; when he came, I was fast asleep, my clothes fallen off on one side, and my shirt above my waist. I awaked at the noise he made, and observed him to deliver his message in some disordered; after which he went to my master, and in a great fright gave him a very confused account of what he had seen: This I presently discovered; for going as soon as I was dressed, to pay my attendance upon his honour, he asked me the meaning of what his servant had reported, that I was not the same thing when I slept as I appeared to be at other times; that his valet assured him, some part of me was white, some yellow, at least not so white, and some brown.

为贴身仆人的栗色小马衔主人之令来叫我过去。它进来的时候，我睡得正熟，衣服滑落到一边，衬衫也卷到了腰上方。我被它的声音吵醒了，它有些语无伦次地传达了它主人的命令，随后返回主人那里，极度惶恐地将它所看到的事情乱七八糟地说了一通。我很快知晓了，因为衣服一穿好，我即刻就去拜望我的主人，它开口就问仆人所汇报的情况究竟是怎样一回事，我睡觉时为什么和其他时候不一样呢。它的贴身仆人告诉它我的身体有些部分是白的，有的是黄的，至少没那么白，另外一些部分就是棕色的。

I had hitherto concealed the secret of my dress, in order to distinguish myself as much as possible, from that cursed race of *Yahoos*; but now I found it in vain to do so any longer. Besides, I considered that my clothes and shoes would soon wear out, which already were in a declining condition, and must be supplied by some contrivance from the hides of *Yahoos*, or other brutes; whereby the whole secret would be known. I therefore told my master, that in the country from whence I came, those of my kind always covered their bodies with the hairs of certain

至今，为了尽可能表现出我与那头可恶的“雅虎”不是同一种族，我一直都把我穿衣服的事情当做秘密，不过看来现在秘密根本保守不下去了。除此之外，我的衣服和鞋子越来越烂，就快要穿破了，到时我必须用“雅虎”或者其他兽类的皮另做一套。如果是这样，它们全都会了解这个秘密了。因此，我告诉我的主人，我所在的那个国度里，我的那些同胞们常常会用某种加工后的动物皮毛来包裹住身体，一是为了在糟糕的气候下防暑避寒，另外一个就是为了气派。如果它想要

animals prepared by art, as well for decency, as to avoid the inclemencies of air both hot and cold; of which, as to my own person I would give him immediate conviction, if he pleased to command me: only desiring his excuse, if I did not expose those parts, that nature taught us to conceal. He said my discourse was all very strange, but especially the last part; for he could not understand why nature should teach us to conceal what nature had given. that neither himself nor family were ashamed of any parts of their bodies; but, however I might do as I pleased. Whereupon, I first unbuttoned my coat, and pulled it off. I did the same with my waistcoat; I drew off my shoes, stockings, and breeches. I let my shirt down to my waist, and drew up the bottom, fastening it like a girdle about my middle to hide my nakedness.

看，我即刻就能证实。但是我仅仅恳请它能谅解我不能暴露某些部位，因为这是大自然的教导。它认为我所说的一切都很古怪，尤其是末尾那一句，因为它不能理解大自然为什么要教会我们隐藏起它所赠与我们的东西。而且它说，它和它的家人都对它们身体的每个部分深感骄傲，但它答应我可以按自己的想法去做。既然它这么说，我就先脱下外衣，然后又脱了背心，接着拽下鞋子，袜子和裤子。随后，我放下衬衣遮住腰，接着拉起下摆在腰间打了个结，掩盖住赤身裸体。

My master observed the whole performance with great signs of curiosity and admiration. He took up all my clothes in his pastern, one piece after another, and examined them diligently; he then stroked my body very gently, and looked round me several times, after which he said, it was plain I must be a perfect *Yahoo*; but that I differed very much from the rest of my species, in the softness, whiteness, and smoothness of my skin, my want of hair in several parts of my body, the shape and

我的主人极度惊奇和钦佩地看完了全过程。随后，它用蹄骸拿起所有的衣服，一件又一件认真地打量着，接着它又温柔地摸了摸我的身体，在我身前身后观察了好几次，看完之后，它说我明显就是一只“雅虎”，只不过和同类相比还是有非常大的差异，比如我的皮肤柔软，白皙，润滑，我的身上某些部分没长毛，我的前爪和后爪都很短，而且形状不一样，还有我喜欢用两只后脚走路。因为我冷得一直发抖，它

shortness of my claws behind and before, and my affectation of walking continually on my two hinder-foot. He desired to see no more, and gave me leave to put on my clothes again, for I was shuddering with cold.

允许我重新穿上衣服，不再看了。

I expressed my uneasiness at his giving me so often the appellation of *Yahoo*, an odious animal, for which I had so utter an hatred and contempt. I begged he would forbear applying that word to me, and take the same order in his family, and among his friends whom he suffered to see me. I requested likewise, that the secret of my having a false covering to my body might be known to none but himself, at least as long as my present clothing should last; for as to what the sorrel nag his valet had observed, his honour might command him to conceal it.

它常常喊我“雅虎”，此时我总是很不安。因为我对这种恶劣的动物深恶痛绝和鄙视，所以我恳请它不要再这样喊我，也请求它能够叮嘱它的家人以及被允许来探望我的朋友也不要这样叫了。同时，我还请它至少在我还能穿着这身衣服的时候，除了它之外，不要让任何其他人知道我身上所披着的这层伪装，而对于它的贴身仆人栗色小马所见到的情况，它也得嘱咐它不要说出去。

All this my master very graciously consented to, and thus the secret was kept till my clothes began to wear out, which I was forced to supply by several contrivances, that shall hereafter be mentioned. In the meantime, he desired I would go on with my utmost diligence to learn their language, because he was more astonished at my capacity for speech and reason, than at the figure of my body, whether it were covered or no; adding, that he waited with some impatience to hear the wonders which I promised to tell him."

它真诚地应允了我所有要求，因此，我的秘密一直被保守着，直到我再也不能穿这身衣服，只能想法去置办些衣物，稍后我还会提到此事。而同时，因为惊异于我的演讲以及推断能力，它希望我能继续尽力去研习它们的言语，至于我的身体是否穿衣服的样子，则没有对前者那么强烈的兴趣。它补充说，它已经迫不及待地想听我答应给它讲述的那些奇异事了。

Thenceforward he doubled the pains he had been at to instruct me; he brought me into all company, and made them treat me with civility, because, as he told them privately, this would put me into good humour, and make me more diverting.

从那个时候开始，它双倍用心指导我研习它们的言语，还带我和它所有的伙伴见面，还要求它们对我以礼相待，因为它偷偷跟它们讲这样我会开心，也会变得更加有趣。

Every day when I waited on him, beside the trouble he was at in teaching, he would ask me several questions concerning myself, which I answered as well as I could; and by these means he had already received some general ideas, though very imperfect. It would be tedious to relate the several steps, by which I advanced to a more regular conversation: but the first account I gave of myself in any order and length, was to this purpose:

当我每天服侍它的时候，除了指导我之外，它还会询问一些和我有联系的问题，我也尽全力回答它。虽然它利用这种方式弄清了一些基本情况，但并不全面。对于我是如何逐步提高，能和它做更正式的交流，讲起来会显得很无趣了。然而我第一次较为详尽而有逻辑地讲述我身世的谈话，内容大体如下：

That I came from a very far country, as I already had attempted to tell him, with about fifty more of my own species; that we travelled upon the seas, in a great hollow vessel made of wood, and larger than his honour's house. I described the ship to him in the best terms I could, and explained by the help of my handkerchief displayed, how it was driven forward by the wind. That upon a quarrel among us, I was set on shore on this coast, where I walked forward without knowing whither, till he delivered me from the persecution of those execrable *Yahoos*." He asked me, who made the ship, and how it was possible that the *Houyhnhnms* of my

我早就设法让它知道我和近50个同胞从一个极其遥远的国度来到这里，我们乘着一条大过它的房子，用木头做的容器在海上航行。我用自己所知道的最棒的说辞将船的样子描绘给它听，同时，通过手帕的舞动，让它理解船是如何依靠风前行的。一次争执之后，我就被赶到这个海岸上。我一直向前走，根本不清楚这是什么地方，直到后来它让我摆脱了那些可恶的“雅虎”的困困。它询问我是谁造的船，还有就是在我们的国家里，“慧骃”如何会让一群牲畜打理船务？我告诉它，我不敢继续说下去，除非它能承诺在听完之后不会发脾气，我才

country would leave it to the management of brutes? My answer was, that I durst proceed no farther in my relation, unless he would give me his word and honour that he would not be offended, and then I would tell him the wonders I had so often promised. He agreed; and I went on by assuring him, that the ship was made by creatures like myself, who in all the countries I had travelled, as well as in my own, were the only governing, rational animals; and that upon my arrival hither, I was as much astonished to see the *Houyhnhnms* act like rational beings, as he or his friends could be in finding some marks of reason in a creature he was pleased to call a *Yahoo*, to which I owned my resemblance in every part, but could not account for their degenerate and brutal nature. I said farther, that if good fortune ever restored me to my native country, to relate my travels hither, as I resolved to do, everybody would believe that I said the thing that was not; that I invented the story out of my own head; and with all possible respect to himself, his family, and friends, and under his promise of not being offended, our countrymen would hardly think it probable, that a *Houyhnhnm* should be the presiding creature of a nation, and a *Yahoo* the brute.

会讲曾经答应过要说的奇事。于是，它应承不会发火，有了承诺，我就继续跟它讲述船是由如同我一样的人类修造的。在所有我访问过的国家里，连同我自己的国家都是一样，国家只会被我的同类统治着，而且我们也是仅存的有理性的动物。可是我抵达这里以后，当我看到“慧骃”这样的动物做出如此理智的举动时，深感惊讶，就如同它或是它的同伴在一只原本它们乐意叫做“雅虎”的动物身上觉察出些许理性时会产生的惊讶之情一样。我全身上下确实具有和“雅虎”一样的特征，但是我还是搞不懂它们的本性竟会是如此的颓废和残暴。我接着说，要是我很走运，还可以返回故乡，那么我肯定会告诉大家我在这里的旅行见闻，我已经决定要这样做了，不过所有的人都会觉得我在说谎，这些只是我在脑海中编造出来的故事。虽然我非常尊重它本人以及它的家人和朋友，而且它也应承过不会发脾气，但是我仍然要说我们的同胞应该很难想象，在这个国家里，“慧骃”居然是统治者，而“雅虎”竟是畜生。

CHAPTER 4

第四章

The Houyhnhnm's Notion of Truth and Falsehood. The Author's Discourse disapproved by his Master. The Author gives a more particular Account of himself, and the Accidents of his Voyage.

本章主要描写“慧骃”很有辨别是非的能力。主人怀疑作者的描述。作者更加详细地讲述了自己的身世以及在旅途中的所见所闻。

My master heard me with great appearances of uneasiness in his countenance, because *doubting or not believing*, are so little known in this country, that the inhabitants cannot tell how to behave themselves under such circumstances. And I remember in frequent discourses with my master concerning the nature of manhood, in other parts of the world, having occasion to talk of *lying*, and *false representation*, it was with much difficulty that he comprehended what I meant, although he had otherwise a most acute judgment. For he argued thus; That the use of speech was to make us understand one another, and to receive information of facts; now if any one *said the thing which was not*, these ends were defeated; because I cannot properly be said to understand him, and I am so far from receiving information, that he leaves me worse than in ignorance, for

我的主人面露不安地听着我的诉说，因为在这个国度里，从来都不存在“怀疑”或是“不信任”，居民们一旦遇到这样的情况，根本不知道该如何处理。我记得在和主人多次共同探讨世上其他地区人性的谈话中，偶尔我也会提到“撒谎”或是“说瞎话”，尽管它在其他方面的判断力极强，但是它也很难搞懂我的意思。对此，它是如此争辩的，语言就是让我们彼此能够了解，让我们获取事实的真相的，也就是说，如果一个人把没的说成有的，那么这样的目标就遭到破坏，因为我不能恰如其分地理解对方的意思，我怎么也不能了解事实的真相，它让我比无知更糟糕。因为它让我把白的误认为是黑的，长的认作是短的。这就是它对于“说谎”这种能力的全部认知，而我们人类早就洞悉了这一切。

I am led to believe a thing *black* when it is *white*, and *short* when it is *long*. And these were all the notions he had concerning that faculty of *lying*, so perfectly well understood among human creatures.

To return from this digression; When I asserted that the *Yahoos* were the only governing animals in my country, which my master said was altogether past his conception, he desired to know, whether we had *Houyhnhnms* among us, and what was their employment: I told him, we had great numbers, that in summer they grazed in the fields, and in winter were kept in houses, with hay and oats, where *Yahoo*-Servants were employed to rub their skins smooth, comb their manes, pick their foot, serve them with food, and make their beds. I understand you well, said my master; it is now very plain, from all you have spoken, that whatever share of reason the *Yahoos* pretend to, the *Houyhnhnms* are your masters; I heartily wish our *Yahoos* would be so tractable. I begged his honour would please to excuse me from proceeding any farther, because I was very certain that the account he expected from me would be highly displeasing. But he insisted in commanding me to let him know the best and the worst: I told him, he should be obeyed. I owned, that the *Houyhnhnms* among us, whom we called *horses*, were

言归正传，当我告诉主人唯有“雅虎”这种动物才是我们的国家的主宰时，它说自己完全没有估计到这一点，它急切地想弄清楚我们那里是否会有“慧骃”，它们都会做一些什么事情。我回答它我们那里有很多“慧骃”，夏天，它们就放养在田野里。冬天，它们就留在家里吃干草和燕麦。我们会雇用一些“雅虎”仆人帮它们擦亮身体，梳理鬃毛，清除蹄垢，添加饲料，还要给它们整理床铺。主人对我说：“我已经明白你所说的了，而这一切很容易让我知道，不管‘雅虎’装作自己是多么理智，你们的主人仍旧是‘慧骃’。我满心企盼着我们的‘雅虎’也可以如此温顺。”我请求它谅解我不能继续往下说了，因为我极其确定，它所期待的下面的内容一定会让它很不开心的。不过它要求我继续说下去，不论好坏它都想听。我说我会继续讲下去的。我告诉它在我们那里把“慧骃”叫做“马”，是我们所有的动物中最豪爽，最帅气的一种，而且在动物中，它们的力量与速度也都是最出众的。如果上等人为了骑射，比赛或是拉车而豢养它

the most generous and comely animal we had; that they excelled in strength and swiftness; and when they belonged to persons of quality, employed in travelling, racing, or drawing chariots, they were treated with much kindness and care, till they fell into diseases, or became foundered in the foot; and then they were sold, and used to all kind of drudgery till they died; after which their skins were stripped and sold for what they were worth, and their bodies left to be devoured by dogs and birds of prey. But the common race of horses had not so good fortune, being kept by farmers and carriers and other mean people, who put them to greater labour, and fed them worse. I described as well as I could, our way of riding, the shape and use of a bridle, a saddle, a spur, and a whip, of harness and wheels. I added, that we fastened plates of a certain hard substance called iron at the bottom of their foot, to preserve their hoofs from being broken by the stony ways on which we often travelled.

们，它们就会受到各种更加友善和周到的照顾，直到病倒或是脚跛了，才会被卖掉，到死都在做各种各样的苦力。而它们的皮在死后被剥掉，按价出售，尸身则被扔给狗和飞禽当食物。然而普通的马就没有这么好运了，农夫、搬运工还有其他一些下等人让它们吃得差，出力多。我把尽可能知道的一切讲给它听，比如我们是怎么骑马的，以及缰绳，马鞍，马刺，马鞭，马具和车轮的形状以及用途。我还告诉它，因为我们时常会在石子路上奔走，所以我们就在它们的脚下装上了一种叫做“蹄铁”的硬铁板，这样，它们的蹄子就不会被磨破。

My master, after some expressions of great indignation, wondered how we dared to venture upon a *Houyhnhnm's* back, for he was sure, that the weakest servant in his house would be able to shake off the strongest *Yahoo*; or by lying down, and rolling on his back, squeeze the brute to death. I answered, That our horses were

主人听完之后异常恼怒，想知道我们是如何有胆子骑到“慧骃”的背上，因为它极其确信在它家中，即使是最弱小的仆人也能打倒最强壮的“雅虎”，或者就算躺下来打个滚也能碾死这样的畜生。我解释说我们的马在三四岁的时候，就开始接受训练，学会那些我们需

trained up from three or four years old to the several uses we intended them for; that if any of them proved intolerably vicious, they were employed for carriages; that they were severely beaten while they were young, for any mischievous tricks: that the males, designed for the common use of riding or draught, were generally *castrated* about two years after their birth, to take down their spirits, and make them more tame and gentle; that they were indeed sensible of rewards and punishments; but his honour would please to consider, that they had not the least tincture of reason any more than the *Yahoos* in this country.

要它们做的事情。而那些难以驯服的马就让它去拉车。在马年幼的时候，如果它们敢玩什么诡计，都要接受严厉的鞭刑。通常，那些被训练当做坐骑或是用来拉车的公马，会在两岁左右被阉割，以打消它们的锐气，让它们变得温驯。它们还确实能明辨赏罚。不过，阁下您应该想得到，它们所拥有的理性不会比这个国家的“雅虎”多很多。

It put me to the pains of many circumlocutions, to give my master a right idea of what I spoke; for their language does not abound in variety of words, because their wants and passions are fewer than among us. But it is impossible to express his noble resentment at our savage treatment of the *Houyhnhnm* race, particularly after I had explained the manner and use of *castrating* horses among us, to hinder them from propagating their kind, and to render them more servile. He said, if it were possible there could be any country where *Yahoos* alone were endued with reason, they certainly must be the governing animal, because reason will in time always prevail

我费尽口舌才让我的主人听懂了我的意思。因为它们的索求和欲望比我们少得多，所有它们的词汇比较匮乏。然而，对于我们野蛮对待“慧骃”这一种族，它的愤恨之情无法言表，尤其是我在说明阉马的方法和作用，阻止它们孕育下一代，让它们变得更加温驯，这一点时，让它更是愤慨。它认为在任何国家，如果唯有“雅虎”能够拥有理智，那么毋庸置疑它们就应该统治整个国家，因为野蛮始终要被理性征服的。但是考虑我们的身体构造，尤其是看到我这种状况，它觉得我们是相同大小的动物中体格最糟糕的，而且我们根本没有办法在日常生活中驾驭这些理性。它

against brutal strength. But, considering the frame of our bodies, and especially of mine, he thought no creature of equal bulk was so ill-contrived, for employing that reason in the common offices of life; whereupon he desired to know whether those among whom I lived, resembled me or the *Yahoos* of his country. I assured him, that I was as well shaped as most of my age: but the younger and the females were much more soft and tender, and the skins of the latter generally as white as milk. He said, I differed indeed from other *Yahoos*, being much more cleanly, and not altogether so deformed, but in point of real advantage, he thought I differed for the worse. that my nails were of no use either to my fore or hinder-foot; as to my forefoot, he could not properly call them by that name, for he never observed me to walk upon them; that they were too soft to bear the ground; that I generally went with them uncovered; neither was the covering I sometimes wore on them, of the same shape, or so strong as that on my foot behind. that I could not walk with any security, for if either of my hinder-foot slipped, I must inevitably fail. He then began to find fault with other parts of my body: the flatness of my face, the prominence of my nose, my eyes placed directly in front, so that I could not look on either side without turning my head:

还很好奇，和我生活在一起的那些“雅虎”到底是和我长得一样，还是同它们国家的“雅虎”相像。我让它相信，我和大部分与我一样的年轻人都很健壮，不过年纪稍小一点的以及女人就会长得更加柔嫩，而且大部分女人的皮肤都白若牛奶。它告诉我，我的确不像其他“雅虎”，我身体更加洁净，模样也还不算狰狞，然而它认为要是说到真正的优势，我倒是和其他“雅虎”有些差距，我反而不如它们了，比如我的前脚或者后脚上长的指甲就不起什么作用。而对于我的前脚，它觉得本身就不应该叫它们前脚，因为它从未看到我的前脚走过路。它们如此娇柔，以至于根本不能用来走路，而且平时走路的时候，前脚也不会用东西遮住，偶尔戴上的也是和后脚不同形状的东西，还没有后脚那个扎实。而且我走路时没有稳定性，因为我后脚的任何一只滑一下，就肯定会摔倒。很快，它就开始对我身上别的部分挑挑拣拣起来，什么我的脸太扁，鼻子过高，两眼直视前方，以至于如果我不转头，根本就看不见旁边的东西。它还说如果我不抬起某一只前脚，就不能进食，不过为了达到这个需求，大自然倒是赐予了我那些关节。然而，它还是不能理解我后脚上的几个枝丫有什么用途，它们那么柔软，如果没有用其他兽

that I was not able to feed myself, without lifting one of my forefoot to my mouth: and therefore nature had placed those joints to answer that necessity. He knew not what could be the use of those several clefts and divisions in my foot behind; that these were too soft to bear the hardness and sharpness of stones without a covering made from the skin of some other brute; that my whole body wanted a fence against heat and cold, which I was forced to put on and off every day with tediousness and trouble. and lastly, that he observed every animal in this country naturally to abhor the *Yahoos*, whom the weaker avoided, and the stronger drove from them. So that supposing us to have the gift of reason, he could not see how it were possible to cure that natural antipathy which every creature discovered against us; nor consequently, how we could tame and render them serviceable. However, he would (as he said) debate the matter no farther, because he was more desirous to know my own story, the country where I was born, and the several actions and events of my life before I came hither.

皮做成的套子保护住，根本就不可能走在坚硬而又尖锐的石子路上。我的整个身体需要一种防寒抗热的遮蔽物，每天还要不厌其烦地把那一套衣服脱去穿上。最后它告诉我，它发现在这个国家里，每一只动物生来就对“雅虎”有厌恶感，比它们弱的，就对它们避而远之；比它们强的，就赶走它们。因此，它认为就算老天赐予了我们理智，它也不觉得我们有办法可以让所有的动物消除对我们天生的讨厌情绪，那么我们又怎么可以让它们服从，让它们为我们服务呢？然而，它说它不想再和我争论这件事情了，因为它更多想了解我自己的故事，我所出生的那个国度的状况，以及到这里来之前的生活经历。

I assured him, how extremely desirous I was that he should be satisfied in every point; but I doubted much, whether it would be possible for me to explain myself on several subjects whereof his

我让它确信我非常乐意把所知道的每件事情都讲到它满意为止，但是我还是颇有疑虑，害怕某些事情是否能让它理解，因为，在它们这个国家里，我还没有遇到过

honour could have no conception, because I saw nothing in his country to which I could resemble them. that however, I would do my best, and strive to express myself by similitudes, humbly desiring his assistance when I wanted proper words; which he was pleased to promise me.

I said, my birth was of honest parents, in an island called *England*, which was remote from his country, as many days' journey as the strongest of his honour's servants could travel in the annual course of the sun. that I was bred a surgeon, whose trade it is to cure wounds and hurts in the body, gotten by accident or violence; that my country was governed by a female man, whom we called queen. that I left it to get riches, whereby I might maintain myself and family when I should return. that in my last voyage, I was commander of the ship, and had about fifty *Yahoos* under me, many of which died at sea, and I was forced to supply them by others picked out from several nations. that our ship was twice in danger of being sunk; the first time by a great storm, and the second, by striking against a rock. Here my master interposed, by asking me, how I could persuade strangers out of different countries to venture with me, after the losses I had sustained, and the hazards I had run. I said, they were fellows of desperate fortunes forced to fly

和我所要讲的类似的事情，主人您或许没办法理解。不过即便是这样，我还是会尽力用各种相似的事物来表述我所说的，要是一时找不到合适的词语，还请它提供帮助。它听后高兴地答应了。

我告诉它，我的出生地是在远离这个岛的一个叫做英格兰的岛上，即使是主人最健壮的奴仆也要花上一年时间才可以走到。我的父母都是诚实之辈，他们把我培养成一名外科大夫，这是医治人体所受的种种伤痛的职业，造成伤痛的或许是意外事故，或许是暴力。我们国家的统治者是一位女性，我们都称她“女王”。我离家出海是为了赚钱，回去后凭着这些赚到的钱就可以养家糊口了，在近期的一次出航中，我担当了那艘船的船长，我带领着大约 50 个“雅虎”这样的船员，不过在航行中，他们中的很多人都死掉了，我只好在途经的国家招新成员填补空缺。有两次，我们的船差点儿就沉了，头一次是遭遇大风暴，而第二次则是触礁。讲到这里，主人截住话头，它问我在遭受了这样的损失，又遇到如此的灾难之后，那些来自不同地域的陌生人是如何仍然愿意和我一起外出涉险的？我告诉主人，他们全部是一些不要命的人，因为贫困或者犯了事，只好背井离乡。有的是因

from the places of their birth, on account of their poverty or their crimes. Some were undone by law suits; others spent all they had in drinking, whoring and gaming; others fled for treason; many for murder, theft, poisoning, robbery, perjury, forgery, coining false money, for committing rapes or sodomy, for flying from their colours, or deserting to the enemy, and most of them had broken prison; none of these durst return to their native countries for fear of being hanged, or of starving in a jail; and therefore they were under a necessity of seeking a livelihood in other places.

为官司缠身而家破人亡，有的是因为吃喝嫖赌搞得倾家荡产，有的是叛国，还有很多人是因为凶杀，盗窃，投毒，打劫，作伪证，造假，铸假币，强奸或鸡奸，叛变，或是投敌等这些罪行，不得不外逃。这样的人大部分都是越狱出来的，因此不敢回国，因为他们担心一回去，就会被绞死或是在监狱中被饿死，所以只好是外出谋生。

During this discourse, my master was pleased to interrupt me several times; I had made use of many circumlocutions in describing to him the nature of the several crimes, for which most of our crew had been forced to fly their country. This labour took up several days conversation before he was able to comprehend me. He was wholly at a loss to know what could be the use or necessity of practising those vices. To clear up which I endeavoured to give some ideas of the desire of power and riches; of the terrible effects of lust, intemperance, malice, and envy. All this I was forced to define and describe by putting of cases and making suppositions. After which, like one whose imagination was struck with something never seen or

这次谈话期间，主人好几次打断了我。我费尽周折才跟它解释清楚那几种罪状，因为我船上大多数的船员都是犯了那些罪才被迫离开自己国家的。而我们花费了很多天谈论这件事情，最终它才搞清楚我的意思。它原本完全弄不清做那些邪恶的事究竟有什么好处，或者有何必要。为了让它明晰，我就尽我所能地跟它解释什么是争权夺利、淫欲、放纵、仇恨、妒忌，等等。而在向它说明和讲述所有事情时，我不得不借助一些例子或者做出一些假设。听完我的话，它抬起的双目中满是惊讶和愤怒，如同一个人看到或是听到那些它没有见闻过的事情那样，受到极大的冲击。而在它们的语言中，权力、政

heard of before, he would lift up his eyes with amazement and indignation. Power, government, war, law, punishment, and a thousand other things had no terms, wherein that language could express them, which made the difficulty almost insuperable to give my master any conception of what I meant. But being of an excellent understanding, much improved by contemplation and converse, he at last arrived at a competent knowledge of what human nature in our parts of the world is capable to perform, and desired I would give him some particular account of that land, which we call *Europe*, but especially of my own country.

府、战争、法律、刑罚以及其他许许多多事物根本就没有词语可以表达出来。因此，在这样的状况下，我要让主人理解我所说的话，简直是无法解决的难题。不过，值得一提的是，它有很优秀的理解力，再加上一番认真的思考，另外，我们的谈话也使得它的领悟力进一步提高，这样，它最终彻底地理解了生活在我们那个世界里的人类究竟会做出一些什么事情了。此时，它更是希望我可以给它详细地讲讲那个被我们称作是欧洲的那块土地，尤其是我自己祖国的状况。

CHAPTER 5

第五章

The Author at his Master's Command, informs him of the State of England. The causes of War among the Princes of Europe. The Author begins to explain the English Constitution.

本章描述的是作者按照主人的吩咐，向它汇报英国的情况。欧洲君主之间爆发战争的缘由。还有就是作者开始阐释英国宪法。

The reader may please to observe, that the following extract of many conversations I had with my master, contains a summary of the most material points, which were discoursed at several times for above two years; his honour often desiring fuller satisfaction, as I farther improved in the *Houyhnhnm* tongue. I laid before him, as well as I could, the whole state of *Europe*; I discoursed of trade and manufactures, of arts and sciences; and the answers I gave to all the questions he made, as they arose upon several subjects, were a fund of conversation not to be exhausted. But I shall here only set down the substance of what passed between us concerning my own country, reducing it into order as well as I can, without any regard to time or other circumstances, while I strictly adhere to truth. My only concern is, that I shall hardly be able to do justice to my master's arguments and expressions,

敬请读者关注，下面所记录的是我和我的主人很多次谈话的摘要，其中还包括了我们在两年多的时间里几次非常重要的谈话内容。当我的“慧骃”语有了长足进步的时候，主人就时常希望我能讲得更多，以满足它的好奇心。我就尽量对它描述整个欧洲的状况，我谈论贸易，制造业，艺术以及科学，而且对它提出的所有问题作答，因为它提出的这些问题会涉及多门学科，而且谈话内容庞杂，一时很难言尽。然而在这里，我想记载下来的仅仅是我们谈论的我自己国家的事情，我会尽可能记录得详尽有序，根本不需考虑时间或是其他环境的限制，还有我还会严格尊重事实。我担心只是我或许不能很公正地传达出我主人的观点和想法，因为我的语言能力还很有限，不过我又必须把它所说的话翻译成我们这低俗的英语。

which must needs suffer by my want of capacity, as well as by a translation into our barbarous *English*.

In obedience therefore to his honour's commands, I related to him the *Revolution* under the Prince of *Orange*, the long war with *France* entered into by the said prince, and renewed by his successor, the present queen, wherein the greatest powers of *Christendom* were engaged, and which still continued: I computed at his request, that about a million of *Yahoos* might have been killed in the whole progress of it, and perhaps a hundred or more cities taken, and thrice as many ships burnt or sunk.

因此，按照主人的吩咐，我又给它讲了奥伦治亲王领导的革命，以及亲王亲自发动的同法国的长期战斗，而他的继承人也就是现在的女王重新宣战，基督教世界的强权都加入到这场战役中，而且这场战役还在继续。在它的请求下，我大致估算了一下，整场战争大约会杀死 100 万只“雅虎”，毁掉 100 多座城市，烧毁或是沉没 300 多艘战舰。

He asked me what were the usual causes or motives that made one country go to war with another. I answered they were innumerable, but I should only mention a few of the chief. Sometimes the ambition of princes, who never think they have land or people enough to govern: sometimes the corruption of ministers, who engage their master in a war in order to stifle or divert the clamour of the subjects against their evil administration. Difference in opinions hath cost many millions of lives: for instance, whether *flesh* be *bread*, or *bread* be *flesh*; whether the juice of a certain *berry* be *blood* or *wine*; whether *whistling* be a vice or a virtue; whether it be better to *kiss* a *post*, or throw it into the fire; what is the best

它问我，两国之间的战争一般出于什么缘由或是有什么企图。我告诉它这样的情况不胜枚举，不过我仅仅列举了几个重要的。有时，可能是因为君主们的野心，他们总是觉得自己管辖的土地面积过小或子民过少。有时，是因为臣子腐败，教唆自己的主子发动战争，其实是为了抑制或是转移人们对他们恶劣管理的抵制情绪。意见不一致时也可能会牺牲掉千百万人的性命，打个比方，圣餐中，肉是否就是面包，面包是否就是肉呢？某种浆果的汁到底是血还是酒？吹口哨到底是恶习还是美德？对于那根棍子，是该亲吻，还是该扔到火里呢？什么颜色的外套最好？黑的？白的？红的？或是灰色

colour for a *coat*, whether *black*, *white*, *red* or *gray*; and whether it should be *long* or *short*, *narrow* or *wide*, *dirty* or *clean*, with many more. Neither are any wars so furious and bloody, or of so long continuance, as those occasioned by difference in opinion, especially if it be in things indifferent.

Sometimes the quarrel between two princes is to decide which of them shall dispossess a third of his dominions, where neither of them pretend to any right. Sometimes one prince quarrelleth with another, for fear the other should quarrel with him. Sometimes a war is entered upon, because the enemy is too *strong*, and sometimes because he is too *weak*. Sometimes our neighbours *want* the *things* which we *have*, or *have* the things which we *want*; and we both fight, till they take ours, or give us theirs. It is a very justifiable cause of a war to invade a country after the people have been wasted by famine, destroyed by pestilence, or embroiled by factions amongst themselves. It is justifiable to enter into war against our nearest ally, when one of his towns lies convenient for us, or a territory of land, that would render our dominions round and complete. If a prince sends forces into a nation, where the people are poor and ignorant, he may lawfully put half of them to death, and make slaves of the rest, in order to civilize

的？该长点还是短点的？窄或是宽的？肮脏还是洁净点？像这样的争辩数不胜数。但是没有任何能比因为不同意见而引发如此激烈、血腥，而长久的战争，尤其导致他们不和的事情是无足轻重的时候，所引发的战争更是这样了。

有时，两个君主会争论究竟应该由谁去掠夺另一个君主的领地，而实际上他俩都没有统治权。有时，两位君王争吵是因为害怕其他君王会来同他争论。有时，因为对手太强大而挑起战争，而有时，战争的理由却是对手太懦弱。有时，是因为邻国想掠夺我们的东西，或者他们有我们需要的东西，这样就导致双方发生争斗，战争以双方中任何一方战败为结束。如果哪一国的人民正遭受饥荒，遭遇瘟疫，或者国内党派间分崩离析，这时正有充分的理由对此国发动侵略战争。如果我们最亲密的邻邦有一座我们轻而易举就能得到的城市，或是夺取某块领土就能使我们的疆土更加完整，那么我们同样也有正当的理由同他们交战。如果一个君主派兵进驻一个国家，发现这个国家的人民既贫困又愚昧，那么他处死半数以上的人就是合法的，而余下的就沦为奴隶，这样做是为了让他们开化，摆脱野蛮的生活方式。一国君主恳请另一国君主援助他抵抗外来侵占，而在那位提供帮助的

and reduce them from their barbarous way of living. It is a very kingly, honourable, and frequent practice, when one prince desires the assistance of another to secure him against an invasion, that the assistant, when he hath driven out the invader, should seize on the dominions himself, and kill, imprison or banish the prince he came to relieve. Alliance by blood or marriage, is a frequent cause of war between princes; and the nearer the kindred is, the greater their disposition to quarrel: *poor* nations are *hungry*, and *rich* nations are *proud*, and pride and hunger will ever be at variance. For these reasons, the trade of a soldier is held the most honourable of all others: because a *soldier* is a *Yahoo* hired to kill in cold blood as many of his own species, who have never offended him, as possibly he can.

君主把侵略者赶走后，居然自己强占这片国土，而且还杀死、囚禁、流放了邀请他来施以援手的那位君王，这种事情频繁发生，有辱于那些位高权重的君主。由血缘或是婚姻维系的联盟也常常成为君主间发动战争的导火索，他们之间的关系越紧密，越容易发生争论。穷国忍受饥饿，富国傲慢自大，而傲慢与饥饿永远都是水火不相容的。出于各种缘由，士兵是各类职业中最受人尊重的，其实士兵就是一只招募来当杀手的“雅虎”，虽然它的同类从来没有触犯过它，不过它还是冷血地把它们杀死，而且数量越多越好。

There is likewise a kind of beggarly princes in *Europe*, not able to make war by themselves, who hire out their troops to richer nations, for so much a day to each man; of which they keep three fourths to themselves, and it is the best part of their maintenance; such are those in Germang and other *northern* parts of *Europe*.

在欧洲，有一种君主穷得如同乞丐一般，自己没办法挑起战事，就将自己的部队租借给富庶的国家，而君主会将一个兵士一天租金收入的 3/4 收入囊中，这些收入也是维系他们支出的主要来源，德国以及北欧诸多国家的君主就是这样做的。

What you have told me (said my master) upon the subject of war, does indeed discover most admirably the effects of that reason you pretend to: however, it is happy that the *shame* is greater than the *danger*; and that nature

我的主人说，我所告诉它的和战争有关的一切，确实非常恰当地让它知道了我们自认为拥有的那点理智所带来的恶果，然而值得庆幸的是，廉耻心压倒了危险性，而这一本性压根就让你们没有办法

hath left you utterly incapable of doing much mischief.

进一步做出更多的坏事。

For your mouths lying flat with your faces, you can hardly bite each other to any purpose, unless by consent. Then, as to the claws upon your foot before and behind, they are so short and tender, that one of our *Yahoos* would drive a dozen of yours before him. And therefore in recounting the numbers of those who have been killed in battle, I cannot but think you have *said the thing which is not*.

因为你们脸上长的嘴巴都是扁平的，如果不是出于什么目的，你们几乎不可能相互撕咬对方。更何况，你们的前后脚的爪子短小又柔弱，我们任何一只“雅虎”都能够赶走它们眼前一打这样的你们。所以，我再一次估算了一下战争造成的死亡人数，我觉得你所说的与事实相悖。

I could not forbear shaking my head and smiling a little at his ignorance. And being no stranger to the art of war, I gave him a description of cannons, culverins, muskets, carabines, pistols, bullets, powder, swords, bayonets, battles, sieges, retreats, attacks, undermines, countermines, bombardments, sea fights; ships sunk with a thousand men, twenty thousand killed on each side; dying groans, limbs flying in the air, smoke, noise, confusion, trampling to death under horses' foot; flight, pursuit, victory; fields strewed with carcases left for food to dogs, and wolves, and birds of prey; plundering, stripping, ravishing, burning and destroying. And to set forth the valour of my own dear countrymen, I assured him, that I had seen them blow up a hundred enemies at once in a siege, and as many in a ship, and beheld the dead bodies come down in pieces from the

我忍不住摇了摇头，笑对它的无知。我对战争的情况还算了解，先是跟它讲述了什么是加仑炮、重炮、滑膛枪、卡宾枪、手枪、子弹、火药、剑、刺刀、战役、围攻、撤退、进攻、挖地道、反地道、轰炸、海战，等等。随后，我还给它描述了配有上千士兵的舰船沉没后，双方均有2万人为此丢了性命。还有垂死的低吟，在空中飞舞的残肢，硝烟，喧哗，杂乱，人成了马蹄下的冤魂，逃逸，追捕，获胜，遍地的尸体成了狗、狼以及别的飞禽的腹中食，劫取，抢掠，奸淫，烧杀毁坏。另外，为了体现我亲爱的同胞的胆量，我还让它知道了我曾在一次围剿中亲眼目睹了他们一次就炸死100个敌人，而在一艘船上他们也是如此，而当化成粉末的尸体从空中落下的时候，围观的人觉得大快人心。

clouds, to the great diversion of the spectators.

I was going on to more particulars, when my master commanded me silence. He said, whoever understood the nature of *Yahoos*, might easily believe it possible for so vile an animal, to be capable of every action I had named, if their strength and cunning equalled their malice. But as my discourse had increased his abhorrence of the whole species, so he found it gave him a disturbance in his mind, to which he was wholly a stranger before. He thought his ears being used to such abominable words might by degrees admit them with less detestation. that although he hated the *Yahoos* of this country, yet he no more blamed them for their odious qualities, than he did a *gnnayh* (a bird of prey) for its cruelty, or a sharp stone for cutting his hoof. But when a creature pretending to reason, could be capable of such enormities, he dreaded lest the corruption of that faculty might be worse than brutality itself. He seemed therefore confident, that instead of reason, we were only possessed of some quality fitted to increase our natural vices; as the reflection from a troubled stream returns the image of an ill-shapen body, not only *larger*, but more distorted.

He added, That he had heard too much upon the subject of war, both in this, and some former discourses. There was

我正打算说出更多的事实，主人却吩咐我不要说了。它说，每个了解“雅虎”本质的“慧骃”都很容易相信，“雅虎”这种邪恶的畜生，如果它们的力量与奸诈和残暴的性情一样的话，那么它们说不准就会做出我所说的事情。不过我说的话却让它更加讨厌“雅虎”一族，这样反而让它觉得很不安，而它之前从未遇到过类似的状况。它想如果它的耳朵习惯了这样恶毒的话，也可能会逐渐接受它们，而不会像原先那么厌恶“雅虎”了。它说即使它痛恨这个国家的“雅虎”，讨厌其劣根，也不过是如同憎恨一只凶狠的“格拿耶”（猛禽之一）或是割伤了它蹄子的一块锋利石头一样。然而，当一只自恃有理性的动物犯下如此罪恶滔天的事情时，它很怕理性堕落的结果到最后会比暴力本身更加糟糕。因此，它几乎可以确定我们具有的并非理性，只不过是恰好能够让我们自身固有的恶性更加严重罢了，就像是一条被搅动的溪水，倒映在水中的扭曲的样子不仅比原来的大，而且更加狰狞。

它接着说，它在这次和前几次的交谈中，听了太多有关战争的话题，现在还有一点仍然困扰着它。

another point which a little perplexed him at present. I had informed him, that some of our crew left their country on account of being ruined by *law*; that I had already explained the meaning of the word; but he was at a loss how it should come to pass, that the *law* which was intended for *every* man's preservation, should be any man's ruin. Therefore he desired to be farther satisfied what I meant by *law* and the dispensers thereof, according to the present practice in my own country; because he thought nature and reason were sufficient guides for a reasonable animal, as we pretended to be, in showing us what he ought to do, and what to avoid.

I assured his honour, that law was a science in which I had not much conversed, further than by employing advocates in vain, upon some injustices that had been done me. however, I would give him all the satisfaction I was able.

I said, there was a society of men among us, bred up from their youth in the art of proving by words multiplied for the purpose that white is black, and black is white, according as they are paid. To this society all the rest of the people are slaves. For example, if my neighbour hath a mind to my cow, he hires a lawyer to prove, that he ought to have my cow from me. I must then hire another to defend my right, it being against all rules of law that any man should be allowed to speak for himself.

我曾对它讲，我们的船员中一些人逃离国家是因为法律毁掉了他们，我也已经跟它诠释过法律的含义，然而它茫然不知为何原本是用来维护每个人的法律，竟然把人毁掉？因此它急切地希望知道更多的情况，好弄清楚在我们国家现行的法律实践中，究竟什么才是法律？究竟它受到什么的支配？因为我们自己认定自己是有理性的动物，那么它认为本性和理智足以指导一切有理性的动物做应该做的事情，避免做不该做的事情。

我告诉主人我不太熟知法律这玩意，我所知甚少的那点法律常识，是因为自己受到了数次不公正对待，请律师才知道的，不过请他们也是白搭。然而，我对它还是知无不言，言无不尽。

我说，我们的生活中就有这么一群人，他们在很年轻时就接受教育，学会玩弄文字，颠倒黑白，他们所说的完全要看你所支付的钱数。对这个社会而言，其余的人都是奴隶。打个比方，我的邻居想打我的一头母牛的主意，他会请来一个律师为他打官司，证实他应该从我这里拿回牛。因为任何人都不得为自己辩护，否则就是违背了法律的一切准则，所以我肯定要另请一位律师为自己打官司。就拿这个案

Now, in this case, I who am the true owner lie under two great disadvantages. first, my lawyer being practised almost from his cradle in defending falsehood, is quite out of his element when he would be an advocate for justice, which as an Office unnatural, he always attempts with great awkwardness, if not with ill will. The second disadvantage is, that my lawyer must proceed with great caution, or else he will be reprimanded by the judges, and abhorred by his brethren, as one that would lessen the practice of the law. And therefore I have but two methods to preserve my cow. The first is to gain over my adversary's lawyer with a double fee, who will then betray his client by insinuating that he hath justice on his side. The second way is for my lawyer to make my cause appear as unjust as he can, by allowing the cow to belong to my adversary; and this, if it be skilfully done, will certainly bespeak the favour of the bench. Now, your honour is to know that these judges are persons appointed to decide all controversies of property, as well as for the trial of criminals, and picked out from the most dexterous lawyers, who are grown old or lazy, and having been biased all their lives against truth and equity lie under such a fatal necessity of favouring fraud, perjury, and oppression, that I have known several of them refuse a large bribe from the side

子来说，我作为母牛真正的拥有者却有两个劣势。一方面是我的律师打娘胎出来几乎就在为假象辩护，现在突然让他伸张正义，让他感到异常不适，因为与他往日的行径不一致。虽然他对我并没有恶意，然而这样辩护起来，肯定不能驾轻就熟。另一个方面的劣势是，我的律师还必须行事小心，否则他这么做既会遭到法官们的谴责，也必然会引起其他律师的同仇敌忾，因为这样做减弱了法律的作用。在此情况下，我则有两个方法保住我那头母牛。一个是用双倍价格收买帮我对手的律师，因为我非常确信他受到金钱的诱惑而倒戈到我这边。另一个就是让我的律师尽量让人觉得我是无理取闹，承认我的对手就好像应该是那头母牛的主人。如果这个办法处理得当，我最后肯定能够获得有利的判决。尊敬的主人现在应该知道法官能够裁定财产分配，给罪犯判刑，而这些法官都是从最聪慧的律师中挑选出来的，这帮人年老多病又懒散，而且他们终生都对真相和平等抱有偏见，因此非常需要施仁慈，作伪证，搞镇压，而且据我所知，他们中的一些人宁愿拒绝公正一方的大笔贿赂，也不做任何有悖于他们的天性或职业道德的事，以免伤害任何人。

where justice lay, rather than injure the *faculty* by doing anything unbecoming their nature or their office.

It is a maxim among these lawyers, that whatever hath been done before, may legally be done again: and therefore they take special care to record all the decisions formerly made against common justice, and the general reason of mankind. These, under the name of precedents they produce as authorities to justify the most iniquitous opinions; and the judges never fail of decreeing accordingly.

In pleading, they studiously avoid entering into the *merits* of the cause; but are loud, violent and tedious in dwelling upon all *circumstances* which are not to the purpose. For instance, in the case already mentioned; they never desire to know what claim or title my adversary hath to my cow, but whether the said *cow* were red or black, her horns long or short; whether the field I graze her in be round or square, whether she was milked at home or abroad, what diseases she is subject to, and the like; after which they consult *precedents*, adjourn the cause, from time to time, and in ten, twenty, or thirty years come to an issue.

It is likewise to be observed that this society hath a peculiar cant and jargon of their own, that no other mortal can understand, and wherein all their laws are written, which they take special care to

这些律师会遵循一条原则，不管他们之前做过什么事，那么再多做一次，也都算是合法的。因此，他们特意记载下过往发生的一切违背普遍真理和人类共同准则的裁决，把这些“判例”当成是权威的依据，依靠它们去纠正最不公正的观点，而且法官依据这些典据也从未作出错误的裁定。

他们在抗辩时故意不谈案情的实质，而是大声地，激昂地，无聊地深入讨论一切和案件毫无瓜葛的其他状况。就拿之前讲到的那个案子来说，他们压根都不想弄明白究竟是什么原因或是特权让我的对手可以霸占我的母牛，而是问那头母牛是红的还是黑的，牛角究竟是长的还是短的，我放牛的地方是圆的还是方的，我是在家里还是在外面挤奶，牛经常感染什么疾病，诸如此类。他们问完后，就会去查询先例，致使这桩案子一再拖延，可能过了10年，20年，30年也不会有结论。

另外值得留意的一点是，这个圈子里的人拥有他们自己能够理解而不被外人所知的行话，他们用这样的术语编写全部的法律条文，而且他们会特别关注修补这些条

multiply; whereby they have wholly confounded the very essence of truth and falsehood, of right and wrong; so that it will take thirty years to decide whether the field, left me by my ancestors for six generations, belongs to me or to a stranger three hundred miles off.

文。凭借这些玩意，他们几乎混淆了是非的本质，以至于他们需要用30年的时间来决定那块传了6代才到我手上的土地，到底判给我还是给那个远在300英里外的外乡人。

In the trial of persons accused for crimes against the state the method is much more short and commendable: the judge first sends to sound the disposition of those in power, after which he can easily hang or save the criminal, strictly preserving all due forms of law.

他们对于叛国犯的审理就异常简化，这一点值得赞赏。法官最先询问了权威人士的想法，随后就很容易裁定是绞死还是赦免犯罪人，而且还能说他是严格按照法律程序办事的。

Here my master interposing, said it was a pity, that creatures endowed with such prodigious abilities of mind as these lawyers by the description I gave of them must certainly be, were not rather encouraged to be instructors of others in wisdom and knowledge. In answer to which I assured his honour, that in all points out of their own trade they were usually the most ignorant and stupid generation among us, the most despicable in common conversation, avowed enemies to all knowledge and learning, and equally disposed to pervert the general reason of mankind in every other subject of discourse, as in that of their own profession.

主人在我讲到这里时接过话头说，据我讲的来看，这些律师的能耐实在不得了，不过你们并没有激励他们传授智慧和知识，教育其他人，太浪费了。我告诉他，律师们除了他们的本职工作之外，在别的方面是我们中间最愚昧无知的。在一般的闲谈中，他们也表现得比其他行业中的人更令人鄙夷，他们是公认的所有知识和学问的公敌，和他们探讨每一门学问的时候，他们表现出来的都和自己的业务那样，违背人类的常规理性。

CHAPTER 6

第六章

A Continuation of the State of England under Queen Anne. The Character of a first Minister of State in European Courts.

本章继续描述安妮女王治理下的英格兰。欧洲皇廷中一位首相大臣的性格。

My master was yet wholly at a loss to understand what motives could incite this race of lawyers to perplex, disquiet, and weary themselves, and engage in a confederacy of injustice, merely for the sake of injuring their Fellow Animals; neither could he comprehend what I meant in saying they did it for hire. Whereupon I was at much pains to describe to him the use of *money*, the materials it was made of, and the value of the metals; that when a *Yahoo* had got a great store of this precious substance, he was able to purchase whatever he had a mind to, the finest clothing, the noblest houses, great tracts of land, the most costly meats and drinks, and have his choice of the most beautiful females. Therefore since *money* alone, was able to perform all these feats, our *Yahoos* thought, they could never have enough of it to spend or to save, as they found themselves inclined from their natural bent either to profusion or avarice. that the rich man enjoyed the fruit of the

我的主人仍然不能理解，这帮律师究竟出于什么目的让自己困惑不安，疲惫，参与到不道义的阴谋中，难道仅仅是为了伤害自己的同类？还有它不是很清楚，为什么我说是别人雇用他们去做这样的事情。于是，我就只有耐心地跟它讲解钱的用途，制作钱的材质，以及各类金属不同的价值。我告诉它，当一只“雅虎”储存了大笔这样的贵金属后，它就可以买到一切它想得到的东西，比方说最好的衣服，最豪华的房子，甚至大面积的土地，最昂贵的酒肉，而且还能选到最靓丽的女子。因此，因为金钱本身就可以让人受惠良多，所以我们的“雅虎”就会觉得钱怎么都不够花，钱怎么也存不够，永远都不能得到满足。因为他们觉得这个是自己的天性使然，要么随意挥霍要么贪婪吝啬。富人享用穷人辛勤的劳动果实，而穷富在人数上的比例高达1000:1。我们中大部分人为生活所迫，过得很凄惨，每天为微薄

poor man's labour, and the latter were a thousand to one in proportion to the former. that the bulk of our people were forced to live miserably, by labouring every day for small wages to make a few live plentifully. I enlarged myself much on these and many other particulars to the same purpose: but his honour was still to seek: for he went upon a supposition that all animals had a title to their share in the productions of the earth, and especially those who presided over the rest. Therefore he desired I would let him know, "what these costly meats were, and how any of us happened to want them. Whereupon I enumerated as many sorts as came into my head, with the various methods of dressing them, which could not be done without sending vessels by sea to every part of the world, as well for liquors to drink, as for sauces, and innumerable other conveniences. I assured him that this whole globe of earth must be at least three times gone round, before one of our better female *Yahoos* could get her breakfast, or a cup to put it in. He said, that must needs be a miserable country which cannot furnish food for its own inhabitants. But what he chiefly wondered at was how such vast tracts of ground as I described should be wholly without *fresh water*, and the people put to the necessity of sending over the sea for drink. I replied,

的薪水而辛苦工作，而让极少数的人富裕生活。我就此问题还有很多其他相似的内容进行了详细的描述，不过尊敬的主人还要继续发问，因为它自己的推论是，所有动物都有权分享地球上的产物，特别是那些统治其他动物的动物更应享有这项权利。因此它想知道这些如此贵的肉到底是什么？我们如何会吃不到它们呢？我就告诉它我脑子中能记起的各种肉类，而且还讲了多种烹饪它们的方式，不过要不是有到世界各地航行的船去采购各类酒水，作料还有无数其他类别的食物，这所有的都是不可能做到的。我告诉它要让我们中一只比较富有的雌“雅虎”做一份早餐或是搞一只杯子装早餐，最少围着地球绕 3 圈才可以做到。它认为一个国家竟然让生活在它里面的居民吃不上饭，必然是一个令人悲哀的国家。但让它更为惊讶的是，在如同我描绘的如此广袤的大地上居然完全会不产任何淡水，而人们一定要航海去外国寻找这样的饮品。我回答说，英国（它就是我可爱的诞生地）本地所出产的粮食大约能够满足当地居民将近 3 倍的需求量，而且从当地的谷类或是某种树木的果实中所提炼或是压榨出的一些液体可酿制出非常不错的饮品，它们同其他每一种日常用品一样，都能够提供将近 3 倍的量给

that *England* (the dear place of my nativity) was computed to produce three times the quantity of food, more than its inhabitants are able to consume, as well as liquors extracted from grain, or pressed out of the fruit of certain trees, which made excellent drink, and the same proportion in every other convenience of life. But in order to feed the luxury and intemperance of the males, and the vanity of the females, we sent away the greatest part of our necessary things to other countries, from whence in return we brought the materials of diseases, folly, and vice, to spend among ourselves. Hence it follows of necessity, that vast numbers of our people are compelled to seek their livelihood by begging, robbing, stealing, cheating, pimping, Forswearing flattering, suborning, forging, gaming, lying, fawning, hectoring, voting, scribbling, stargazing, poisoning, whoring, canting, libelling, free-thinking, and the like occupations: every one of which terms, I was at much pains to make him understand.

居民饮用。然而，为了满足男人们的随意挥霍以及女人们的爱慕虚荣，我们只得把我们大多数的生活必需品送到其他国家去，而作为回报，我们从其他国家得到了一些能够引起疾病，诱发愚昧，滋生罪恶的物质供自己享用。于是我们大部分的人就失去了生活的倚靠，迫于生存的压力，他们只得靠乞讨、打劫、扒窃、欺诈、拉皮条、讲假话、奉承、教唆、造假、赌博、撒谎、献殷勤、恫吓、拉选票、乱涂乱画、算卦、投毒，卖淫、讲大话、诽谤、胡思乱想以及诸如此类的事情来养家糊口。以上所说的每一个术语我都花了很多工夫来解释它们的意思，最终它才理解了。

That *wine* was not imported among us from foreign countries, to supply the want of water or other drinks, but because it was a sort of liquid which made us merry, by putting us out of our senses; diverted all melancholy thoughts, begat wild extravagant imaginations in the brain,

我还告诉它，我们的酒水需要从外国引进，并不是由于我们缺乏淡水或别的饮品，而是因为喝了酒这种液体可以让人开心，它让我们毫无知觉，分散一切困扰我们的忧虑，唤醒我们脑中豪放的影像，增添期望，消除恐慌，让我们暂时丧

raised our hopes, and banished our fears, suspended every office of reason for a time, and deprived us of the use of our limbs, untill we fell into a profound sleep; although it must be confessed, that we always awaked sick and dispirited, and that the use of this liquor filled us with diseases, which made our lives uncomfortable and short.

But beside all this, the bulk of our people supported themselves by furnishing the necessities or conveniences of life to the rich, and to each other. For instance, when I am at home and dressed as I ought to be, I carry on my body the workmanship of an hundred tradesmen; the building and furniture of my house employ as many more and five times the number to adorn my wife.

I was going on to tell him of another sort of people, who get their livelihood by attending the sick, having upon some occasions informed his honour that many of my crew had died of diseases. But here it was with the utmost difficulty, that I brought him to apprehend what I meant. He could easily conceive, that a *Houyhnhnm* grew weak and heavy a few days before his death, or by some accident might hurt a limb. but that nature, who works all things to perfection, should suffer any pains to breed in our bodies, he thought impossible, and desired to know

失全部的理智，四肢不能动弹，直到最后醉得不省人事。不过我们还得承认每次这样醒来后，精神总是很差，而经常喝这种液体会让我们染上各种疾病，让我们的生命变得苦楚而短暂。

不过除了以上所说的这些之外，我们中大部分的人通过供应各种生活所需给富人，或是相互交换这些必需品来维系自己的生活。打个比方，我在家的时候，衣着讲究，而那一套衣服需要100名裁缝来完成，我的房屋以及里面的家具也需要雇用100个工人来修建，而我妻子的装扮则需要500名工人付出劳动。

紧接着，我又同它讲了另一类人，他们通过照顾病人来养活自己，我曾数次告诉过主人，我船上很多船员是得病才死掉的。不过我可是费尽周折才让它搞清楚那是怎么一回事。它很容易明白在一头“慧骃”快要死掉之前，会逐渐变得虚弱，动作缓慢，或者它遭受不幸伤到一条腿。但是，大自然既然创造了如此完美的万事万物，却为何还会让我们饱尝身体痛苦的折磨呢。它觉得这是不可能的，因此它就想了解究竟是怎样不能够解释的厄运。我告诉它，我们吃下上

the reason of so unaccountable an evil. I told him, we fed on a thousand things which operated contrary to each other; that we ate when we were not hungry, and drank without the provocation of thirst; that we sat whole nights drinking strong liquors without eating a bit, which disposed us to sloth, enflamed our bodies, and precipitated or prevented digestion. that prostitute female *Yahoos* acquired a certain malady, which bred rottenness in the bones of those, who fell into their embraces; that this and many other diseases, were propagated from father to son, so that great numbers came into the world with complicated maladies upon them; that it would be endless to give him a catalogue of all diseases incident to human bodies; for they would not be fewer than five or six hundred, spread over every limb, and joint; in short, every part, external and intestine, having diseases appropriated to them. To remedy which, there was a sort of people bred up among us, in the profession or pretence of curing the sick. And because I had some skill in the faculty, I would in gratitude to his honour, let him know the whole mystery and method by which they proceed.

千种互相克制的东西，而且我们会在肚子不饿时吃东西，嘴巴不干时喝东西，我们还会呆坐整晚只是喝烈性酒，而不吃任何东西，使得人变得懒散，点燃我们的身体，反正要么加速消化要么消化不良。卖淫的女“雅虎”身上有一种疾病，和她们拥抱的人骨头都会溃烂，而这种病同很多其他疾病一样都是遗传的，以至于很多人一降生到这个世界上，就已经身患各种疑难杂症了。要让我把人体患有的一切疾病全部告诉它，恐怕会没完没了，因为这样的疾病不少于五六百种，遍布我们人体的四肢以及各个关节。简而言之，我们身体的每个部分都可能会有各类疾病。为了治愈这些病痛，我们中间就会培养出一批人，他们专门是来治愈人类疾病的，当然也会有的是弄虚作假的。因为我还是掌握这行的一些技能，所以为了答谢主人的大恩大德，我非常乐意让它了解医者所有的奥秘和疗法。

Their fundamental is, that all diseases arise from *repletion*, from whence they conclude, that a great *evacuation* of the

他们的基本信条是，饮食不当是引发一切病痛的根源，从中总结出以下论断，我们需要对人体内部

body is necessary, either through the natural passage, or upwards at the mouth. Their next business is from herbs, minerals, gums, oils, shells, salts, juices, seaweed, excrements, barks of trees, serpents, toads, frogs, spiders, dead men's flesh and bones, birds, beasts, and fishes, to form a composition for smell and taste the most abominable, nauseous and detestable, they can possibly contrive, which the stomach immediately rejects with loathing; and this they call a *vomit*; or else from the same storehouse, with some other poisonous additions, they command us to take in at the orifice *above* or *below* (just as the physician then happens to be disposed) a medicine equally annoying and disgustful to the bowels, which relaxing the belly, drives down all before it, and this they call a *purge*, or a *clyster*. For nature (as the physicians allege) having intended the superior anterior orifice only for the *intromission* of solids and liquids, and the inferior posterior for ejection, these artists ingeniously considering that in all diseases nature is forced out of her seat; therefore to replace her in it, the body must be treated in a manner directly contrary, by interchanging the use of each orifice, forcing solids and liquids in at the *anus*, and making evacuations at the mouth.

进行大扫除，要么是自然排泄，要么从嘴里吐出来。接着他们要做的就是把草药、矿物元素、树脂、甘油、贝壳、盐巴、果汁、海草、排泄物、树皮、蛇类、蟾蜍、青蛙、蜘蛛、死人的骨肉、鸟类、兽类、鱼类等混合起来，尽力把它们变成一种在气味和味道上都是最让人厌恶，令人作呕，使人嫌恶的东西，吃到胃里后立马就让人恶心得想吐，他们给它取名催吐剂。或者用上述相同的药材，另外加入几样其他的有毒的物质，合成的药也会让人反胃，他们会要求我们从上面的孔（嘴）或是下面的孔（肛门）灌入（医生会决定应该从哪个孔灌入）。这种药可以清理肠道，让肚子里的东西全都排泄出来，他们称它是泻药或者灌肠剂。这些医生宣称，我们吃喝的时候，原本应该使用长在前面的上孔（嘴），而后面的下孔（肛门）是用来排泄的，这帮聪慧的医生认为，当发生疾病时，造物主的一切安排都被迫改变了，因此让一切都恢复到常规上，就一定要用一种彻底相悖的办法来治愈身体的病痛，那就是调节上下孔的作用，在肛门中强行灌入固体和液体，让嘴把它们吐出来。

But, besides real diseases, we are

然而，除了这些真实的病痛，

subject to many that are only imaginary, for which the physicians have invented imaginary cures; these have their several names, and so have the drugs that are proper for them, and with these our female *Yahoos* are always infested.

One great excellency in this tribe is their skill at *prognostics*, wherein they seldom fail; their predictions in real diseases, when they rise to any degree of malignity, generally portending *death*, which is always in their power, when recovery is not: and therefore, upon any unexpected signs of amendment, after they have pronounced their sentence, rather than be accused as false prophets, they know how to approve their sagacity to the world by a seasonable dose.

They are likewise of special use to husbands and wives, who are grown weary of their mates, to eldest sons, to great ministers of state, and often to princes.

I had formerly upon occasion, discoursed with my master upon the nature of *government* in general, and particularly of our own *excellent constitution*, deservedly the wonder and envy of the whole world. But having here accidentally mentioned a minister of state; he commanded me some time after to inform him, what species of *Yahoo* I particularly meant by that appellation.

我们还会受到很多仅仅是凭空想象出来的疾病的困扰，而针对空想症，医师们不仅找出了治疗方法，给这些病起名字，还发明了治疗它们的各种药物。我们中女“雅虎”们就总是会患上这样的空想症。

这帮人最出众的本领就是能够预计出疾病的结果，而且很少失败。因为真实的疾病一旦恶化，很快就会濒临死亡，无法治愈，那么他们的预测肯定是不会出错。因此，即使他们早已宣告患有不治之症的病人突然出现好转的迹象，他们也不会坐以待毙，任人辱骂他们是骗子，他们很清楚适时给病患注射一剂抢救药就能够让世人了解他们的洞察力。

对于对自己另一半渐生反感的丈夫或是妻子，长子，重臣，时常还有君王，他们都会起到特殊作用。

我先前已经同我的主人讲述过政府的普遍特性，尤其是我们那卓越的宪法，它足以让全世界都惊叹和嫉妒。然而，在此，我不经意间说到了大臣这个词语，它就要求我接下来花点时间跟它聊聊我口中所提到的“大臣”究竟是怎样一种“雅虎”呢。

I told him, that a first or *chief minister of state*, who was the person I intended to describe, was a creature wholly exempt from joy and grief, love and hatred, pity and anger; at least, makes use of no other passions but a violent desire of wealth, power, and titles; that he applies his words to all uses, except to the indication of his mind; that he never tells a truth, but with an intent that you should take it for a *lie*; nor a *lie*, but with a design that you should take it for a *truth*; that those he speaks worst of behind their backs, are in the surest way of preferment; and whenever he begins to praise you to others or to yourself, you are from that day forlorn. The worst mark you can receive is a *promise*, especially when it is confirmed with an oath; after which every wise man retires, and gives over all hopes.

我告诉它，我想要讲的这位首相大臣是这样一个人，他整个人都没有喜怒哀乐，没有爱憎，不会动情也不会发怒，你至少能够了解的是，他只对金钱、权势和爵位抱有强烈的渴望，对其他一切都没什么感情。他所说的能够表明一切，除了他的真心之外。但总是想要人们把这当成是实话，而不是谎言。喜欢背后说是非的那些人事实上是他觉得最完美的人，而无论何时，他开始跟别人或是当面赞扬你，自那天始，你就要倒霉了。最不幸的是他承诺你什么，而且尤其不幸的是他承诺的时候，还发了誓。自此后，每个聪明人都会撤退，舍弃所有希望。

There are three methods by which a man may rise to be chief minister: The first is, by knowing how with prudence to dispose of a wife, a daughter, or a sister: the second, by betraying or undermining his predecessor: and the third is, by a *furious zeal* in public assemblies against the corruptions of the court. But a wise prince would rather choose to employ those who practise the last of these methods; because such zealots prove always the most obsequious and subservient to the will and passions of

有3种方法能够升任到首相大臣的职位。首先就是要懂得如何巧妙地安排自己的妻女或者姐妹。其次是出卖或是暗害上任首相。最后是在公开集聚地，对政府的种种腐败行为进行猛烈的抨击。不过凡是有眼光的君王必定很乐意挑选那些善于运用第三种方式的人，因为事实告诉他们，那些狂热的人往往最遵从他们主子的意思，最了解他们的爱好。而这些权臣在位时会掌控一切要职，他们利用贿赂笼络了元老院或是大枢密院中的大部分

their master. That these *ministers*, having all employments at their disposal, preserve themselves in power by bribing the majority of a senate or great council; and at last by an expedient called an *act of indemnity* (whereof I described the nature to him) they secured themselves from after Reckonings, and retired from the public, laden with the spoils of the nation.

人，这样才能巩固自身地位。最后，他们还有一条权宜之计叫做“免责法”（我向它阐释了这则法令的实质）以保障日后东窗事发，他引咎辞职时，还可以盆满钵满地带走贪污来的一切。

The palace of a *chief minister*, is a seminary to breed up others in his own trade: the pages, lackies, and porters, by imitating their master, become *ministers of state* in their several districts, and learn to excel in the three principal *ingredients*, of *insolence*, *lying*, and *bribery*. Accordingly, they have a *subaltern* court paid to them by persons of the best rank, and sometimes by the force of dexterity and impudence, arrive through several gradations to be successors to their lord.

首相府邸是他栽培同僚的场所。而他的随从、仆人还有看门的人都会模仿他们的主子，在他们各自的领域中混得有头有脸。他们跟自己的主人学了3种要领，耍蛮、撒谎和贿赂，但是青出于蓝而胜于蓝，这样他们就形成了自己的一套小班底接受贵族的追捧。有时，他们还能依靠机敏和无耻步步为营，最后成为他们主人的接班人。

He is usually governed by a decayed wench or favourite footman, who are the tunnels through which all graces are conveyed, and may properly be called, *in the last resort*, the governors of the kingdom.

首相常常会受到色衰的荡妇或是亲信奴仆的钳制，所有试图攀龙附凤的人都要打通这条渠道，因此最终如果说是他们统治着这个国家，也再恰当不过了。

One day in discourse my master, having heard me mention the *nobility* of my country, was pleased to make me a compliment which I could not pretend to deserve: that he was sure, I must have been born of some noble family, because I

某天，在和主人谈论我国贵族的时候，它赞扬了我，但是我不敢接受。它说它能够确定，我一定生长在一个贵族家庭里，因为我生得俊美，皮肤白皙，身体洁净，而这几个方面比它们国家里全部的“雅

far exceeded in shape, colour, and cleanliness, all the *Yahoos* of his nation, although I seemed to fail in strength, and agility, which must be imputed to my different way of living from those other brutes, and besides, I was not only endowed with the faculty of speech, but likewise with some rudiments of reason, to a degree, that with all his acquaintance I passed for a prodigy.

虎”都要好很多。即使我看起来好像没有它们那么健壮，行动也并不矫捷，不过那是出于我和它们完全不同的生活方式。此外，我不仅能够说话，而且似乎还有些理性，因此它所有的熟人都觉得我是一个奇才。

He made me observe, that among the *Houyhnhnms*, the *white*, the *sorrel*, and the *iron-gray*, were not so exactly shaped as the *bay*, the *dapple-gray*, and the *black*; nor born with equal talents of mind, or a capacity to improve them; and therefore continued always in the condition of servants, without ever aspiring to match out of their own race, which in that country would be reckoned monstrous and unnatural.

它认为我应当注意的是，“慧骃”中的白马、栗色的马、铁青色的马和火红的马、深灰色的斑纹马以及黑马长得不一样，而这些都是与生俱来的，没有办法好转，因此它们永远只能当仆人。如果它们企图高人一等，在这个国家就会被当做是一件异常可怕而且不寻常的事情。

I made his honour my most humble acknowledgments for the good opinion he was pleased to conceive of me; but assured him at the same time, that my birth was of the lower sort, having been born of plain honest parents, who were just able to give me a tolerable education: that *nobility* among us was altogether a different thing from the idea he had of it; that our young *noblemen* are bred from their childhood in idleness and luxury; that as soon as years will permit, they

我的主人能如此抬举我，我无限感激，然而我还是告诉它我的出身并不高贵，我的父母只是一般的百姓，只能让我受到一些勉强还可以的教育。而我口中的那些贵族和它所想到的绝对不是一回事，我们那些年轻贵族从他们还是孩子的时候就过着无所事事，奢华无度的生活。成年后，他们就在淫贱的女人中消耗体力，感染一身恶疾，等到他们的产业快挥霍一空时，就会迎娶某个出身低微，脾气暴躁并且

consume their vigour, and contract odious diseases among lewd females; and when their fortunes are almost ruined, they marry some woman of mean birth, disagreeable person, and unsound constitution, merely for the sake of money, whom they hate and despise. That the productions of such marriages are generally scrofulous, rickety, or deformed children, by which means the family seldom continues above three generations, unless the wife takes care to provide a healthy father among her neighbours, or domestics in order to improve and continue the breed. That a weak diseased body, a meagre countenance, and sallow complexion, are the true marks of noble blood; and a healthy robust appearance is so disgraceful in a man of quality, that the world concludes his real father to have been a groom, or a *coachman*. The imperfections of his mind run parallel with those of his body being a composition of spleen, Dulness, ignorance, caprice, sensuality, and pride.

身体糟糕的女人做太太，只是为了她的钱财。事实上，他们既憎恶又鄙视这样的女人。他们这种婚姻所生下的孩子常常都是身患结核病、佝偻病，要不就是畸形人。而且通常这样的家庭不会延续到第三代就绝灭了，除非做妻子的会留意她们的邻居或是仆人中身强体壮的人做孩子的爸爸，这样才能够改良基因传宗接代。体弱多病、面容消瘦、面色苍白通常是一个贵族的体征。而健壮的外表对一位贵族而言，有可能是一种奇耻大辱，因为外人可能会觉得他真正的父亲肯定是一个马夫或是车夫。他的大脑和他的身体一样，也会极不完善，肯定是那种坏脾气、反应迟钝、毫无常识、异想天开、淫荡而且自大的混合品。

Without the consent of *this illustrious body* no law can be made, repealed, or altered, and these have the decision of all our possessions without appeal.

任何法令未经这帮贵族的批准都不得发布、废除或是修订。这些贵族对我们所有的财产都有支配权，而无须征得我们的同意。

CHAPTER 7

第七章

The Author's great Love of his Native Country. His Master's Observations upon the Constitution and Administration of England, as described by the Author, with parallel cases and Comparisons. His Master's Observations upon Human Nature.

本章描述了作者对祖国的深情厚爱。主人依据作者的陈述，表达了对英国的宪法和行政的意见，并指出类似的事件予以相互比较。主人对人性的观点。

The reader may be disposed to wonder how I could prevail on myself to give so free a representation of my own species, among a race of mortals who are already too apt to conceive the vilest opinion of human kind, from that entire congruity betwixt me and their *Yahoos*. But I must freely confess, that the many virtues of those excellent quadrupeds placed in opposite view to human corruptions, had so far opened my eyes and enlarged my understanding, that I began to view the actions and passions of man in a very different light, and to think the honour of my own kind not worth managing; which, besides, it was impossible for me to do before a person of so acute a judgment as my master, who daily convinced me of a thousand faults in myself, whereof I had not the least perception before, and which with us would never be numbered even

读者可能会很好奇，我怎么可能在如此低俗的生物面前，这样坦诚地讲出自己同类的一切，它们应该早就认定我和它们的"雅虎"是一样的，而且早就对人类有了最糟糕的评价。但是我不得不认同，这些优秀的四足动物的多种美德确实同人类的腐败有巨大的差异，而且它们开拓了我的视野，拓展了我的知识面，让我从不同视角去看待人类的举止和情感，而且还使得我认为想办法维护同类的尊严是没有必要的。再说，在一位如同我的主人这样有着机敏辨识能力的"慧骃"面前，我根本没法维系我们的尊严，它每天都会让我觉察出自身的很多缺点，而在此之前，我对此毫无认识。而且对我们来讲，这些可能也不算是人类的不足之处。与此同时，我在它的榜样作用下，学会了完全地憎恶所有的虚伪和伪

among human infirmities, I had likewise learned from his example an utter detestation of all falsehood or disguise; and *truth* appeared so amiable to me, that I determined upon sacrificing everything to it.

Let me deal so candidly with the reader, as to confess, that there was yet a much stronger motive for the freedom I took in my representation of things. I had not been a year in this country, before I contracted such a love and veneration for the inhabitants, that I entered on a firm resolution never to return to human kind, but to pass the rest of my life among these admirable *Houyhnhnms* in the contemplation and practice of every virtue; where I could have no example or incitement to vice. But it was decreed by fortune, my perpetual enemy, that so great a felicity should not fall to my share. However, it is now some comfort to reflect, that in what I said of my countrymen, I *extenuated* their faults as much as I durst before so strict an examiner, and upon every article, gave as *favourable* a turn as the matter would bear. For, indeed, who is there alive that will not be swayed by his bias and partiality to the place of his birth?

I have related the substance of several conversations I had with my master, during the greatest part of the time I had the honour to be in his service, but have

善，而真理对我来讲，是如此可爱以至于我决定为此牺牲一切。

可以更加坦诚地告诉读者，我胆敢向它们透露那些事，还有一个更大的目的。虽然我到此还不满一年，但是早就极度爱护和尊重它的居民了，同时我还决定再也不会返回人类世界，要在这些值得尊重的“慧骃”中了却我的一生，不断地思考和实践它们的种种美德。在这里，我不会有坏榜样，更没有诱因让我去干坏事。但是命运总和我作对，它不会让好运降临到我的身上。然而，现在回忆起来多少还是有些欣慰，因为在那位如此苛刻的考官面前，我在谈论我的同类时，居然还敢尽力为他们的缺点辩解，一旦条件应允，我会尽量在每件事情上为他们说好话。不过说实话，哪个活在世间的人不会对自己的故乡有些许偏袒之心呢？

在我伺候主人的大多数时间里，我们都会轮番谈论这些话题，这些话题前面已经提到过了。不过，我为了精简内容，在此记载的

indeed for brevity sake omitted much more than is here set down.

When I had answered all his questions, and his curiosity seemed to be fully satisfied he sent for me one morning early, and commanded me to sit down at some distance (an honour which he had never before conferred upon me) he said, he had been very seriously considering my whole story, as far as it related both to myself and my country: that he looked upon us as a sort of animals to whose share, by what accident he could not conjecture, some small pittance of *reason* had fallen, whereof we made no other use than by its assistance to aggravate our *natural* corruptions, and to acquire new ones, which nature had not given us. that we disarmed ourselves of the few abilities she had bestowed, had been very successful in multiplying our original wants, and seemed to spend our whole lives in vain endeavours to supply them by our own inventions. that as to myself, it was manifest I had neither the strength nor agility of a common *Yahoo*, that I walked infirmly on my hinder foot, had found out a contrivance to make my claws of no use or defence, and to remove the hair from my chin, which was intended as a shelter from the sun and the weather. lastly, that I could neither run with speed, nor climb trees like my brethren (as he called them) the *Yahoos* in this country.

内容比省略的还要少得多。

在我回答完它提出的所有问题后，看起来好像彻底满足了它的好奇心，这样在某天的清晨，它派人请我过去，命令我在靠它很近的地方坐下（在此之前，我还从未受到过这样的礼遇）。它告诉我，它一直都在深思我所说的一切有关我本人以及我的国家的事情。它说，它觉得我们这种动物所拥有的那点理性是偶然得到的，不过，它还是没办法弄清楚我们是如何在机缘巧合下得到那点理性的。而我们利用这点理性什么也没做，只是依靠它们膨胀和获取了恶习。我们放弃了老天赐给我们的极少的几样本领，而原始的欲念却在不断地成倍增长，而且我们看上去好像要荒废我们个人毕生的精力，发明各式各样的东西来满足这些欲望。而我本人很明显在体力和身手矫捷上都比不上一只寻常的“雅虎”，我用后脚走路的时候摇摇晃晃，而且想方设法让自己的爪子不仅不起什么作用，而且还毫无防御能力。还有就是剃光了长在下巴上那些用来抵挡阳光和恶劣气候的毛发。最后一点就是我跑不快，又不会爬树，完全不同于生活在这个国家的“雅虎”同胞们（它是这样叫它们的）。

That our institutions of *government* and *law* were plainly owing to our gross defects in *reason*, and by consequence, in *virtue*; because *reason* alone is sufficient to govern a *rational* creature; which was therefore a character we had no pretence to challenge, even from the account I had given of my own people although he manifestly perceived, that in order to favour them, I had concealed many particulars, and often *said the thing which was not*.

我们设立行政和司法机构，很明显是缘于我们在理智和道德上有严重的缺陷。而事实上，只需依靠理智就能管束一只理性的动物，所以虽然我极力为我的同胞开脱，但是我们仍旧没有资格号称自己是理性的。它显然已经觉察出我为了袒护自己的同胞，我对它欺瞒了很多具体的事件，而且还会捏造一些根本不纯正的事情。

He was the more confirmed in this opinion, because he observed, that as I agreed in every feature of my body with other *Yahoos*, except where it was to my real disadvantage in point of strength, speed and activity, the shortness of my claws, and some other particulars where nature had no part; so from the representation I had given him of our lives, our manners, and our actions, he found as near a resemblance in the disposition of our minds. He said the *Yahoos* were known to hate one another more than they did any different species of animals; and the reason usually assigned, was, the odiousness of their own shapes, which all could see in the rest, but not in themselves. He had therefore begun to think it not unwise in us to *cover* our bodies, and by that invention, conceal many of our deformities from each other, which would else be hardly supportable.

这样它就更加坚定自己的想法是正确的，因为它发觉我身上每一种特质都和“雅虎”相同，有所区别的是我力气没它们大，跑得比它们慢，动作不灵活，爪子短小，还有某些与上天的赐予毫无联系的缺点。它这样认为是根据我给它描述的有关我们的生活，习俗还有行动来判断的，因此也就发现我们和“雅虎”的性情很接近。它说，众所周知，“雅虎”之间的仇视远比它们对任何别的动物的仇视大得多，究其原因，通常会认定那缘于它们狰狞的面貌，而“雅虎”们却只在同伴身上见到这种恐怖的样子，却看不见自己也是如此。因此，它开始觉得我们发明衣服来遮蔽身体是一种多么明智的方法，而这个方法让我们掩盖了互相不能容忍的各自所拥有的缺陷。不过它此时才明白它之前完全搞错了，其实在它们国家生活的这些畜生，它

But, he now found he had been mistaken, and that the dissensions of those brutes in his country were owing to the same causes with ours, as I had described them. For, if (said he) you throw among five *Yahoos* as much food as would be sufficient for fifty, they will, instead of eating peaceably, fall together by the ears, each single one impatient to *have all to itself*; and therefore a servant was usually employed to stand by while they were feeding abroad, and those kept at home were tied at a distance from each other, that if a cow died of age or accident, before a *Houyhnhnm* could secure it for his own *Yahoos*, those in the neighbourhood, would come in herds to seize it, and then would ensue such a battle as I had described, with terrible wounds made by their claws on both sides, although they seldom were able to kill one another, for want of such convenient instruments of death as we had invented. At other times the like battles have been fought between the *Yahoos* of several neighbourhoods without any visible cause: those of one district watching all opportunities to surprise the next before they are prepared. But if they find their project has miscarried, they return home, and, for want of enemies, engage in what I call a *civil war* among themselves.

That in some fields of his country, there are certain *shining stones* of several

们相互间产生矛盾的缘由和我们的相同，就和我讲述的一样。它说如果给 5 只“雅虎”提供足够 50 只“雅虎”吃的东西，它们根本不会心平气和地享用，每只“雅虎”都急不可待地想要吃独食，而这样也就引起它们的争斗。所以，它们在户外进食的时候，总是要有一名仆人站在旁边看管它们，而在房间里关着的那些就肯定要用绳子系住，相互间隔开一定的距离。要是一头母牛老死或是因意外死掉了，在“慧骃”把它扔给自己的“雅虎”吃之前，邻近的“雅虎”早已群起而抢起来了，紧接着就会发生如同我所叙述的战争。双方都会被对方的爪子抓得伤痕累累，但是因为它们并未拥有我们发明的那种即刻置人于死地的装备，所以很难杀掉对方。还有就是，有时，住得很近的“雅虎”在毫无任何征兆的情况下，也会大打出手。而且住在一个地区的“雅虎”会抓住所有机会，在住在另一个地区的“雅虎”疏于防备之时，对它们发动突袭。不过一旦它们发现自己的计划失败，就撤退回去，没有了敌人，它们之间就陷入了一场我所称作内战的那种争斗中。

它说，在它的国家的某些地方存在着某些颜色各异，发光的石

colours, whereof the *Yahoos* are violently fond, and when part of these *stones* is fixed in the earth, as it sometimes happenth, they will dig with their claws for whole days to get them out, then carry them away, and hide them by heaps in their kennels; but still looking round with great caution, for fear their comrades should find out their treasure. My master said, he could never discover the reason of this unnatural appetite, or how these *stones* could be of any use to a *Yahoo*; but now he believed it might proceed from the same principle of *avarice*, which I had ascribed to mankind; That he had once, by way of experiment, privately removed a heap of these *stones* from the place where one of his *Yahoos* had buried it whereupon, the sordid animal missing his treasure, by his loud lamenting brought the whole herd to the place, there miserably howled, then fell to biting and tearing the rest, began to pine away, would neither eat, nor sleep, nor work, till he ordered a servant privately to convey the *stones* into the same hole, and hide them as before; which, when his *Yahoo* had found, he presently recovered his spirits and good humour, but took care to remove them to a better hiding-place, and hath ever since been a very serviceable brute.

My master farther assured me, which I also observed myself, that in the fields where these *shining stones* abound, the

头，“雅虎”们异常喜欢，这些石头有时候会被泥土掩盖一部分，它们就会没日没夜地用爪子刨出石头，把它们带回自己的窝，成堆地储藏在那里，不过在把它们藏起来的时候，还要警惕地关注周遭的情况，害怕自己的同伴会找到它们的宝贝。我的主人说它一直都不能理解它们是如何滋生这种有悖于本性的欲念，而且“雅虎”要这些石头又有什么用呢。不过此刻它确信，这一切可能是源于我所说的人类所有的贪婪的本性。它告诉我，它曾做了一次试探，它偷偷搬走了一只“雅虎”埋在某个地方的一堆这样的石头。那只贪婪的畜生发觉它的宝贝不见了，就悲恸地嚎叫起来，引得所有的“雅虎”都聚集到这个地方来。它一边凄惨地低吼着，一边开始撕咬其他同伴，此后便一蹶不振，不吃东西，不睡觉，还不做事情。此时它就让一个仆人悄悄地把这些石头搬回原先的那个坑，并且要埋得和之前一模一样。这只“雅虎”发现后，精神和脾气都恢复如初了。不过为了安全起见，它把这些石头埋到了另一个更稳妥的地方。此后，它也一直十分听话。

主人还让我知道，它发现在有大量这种发光的石头的地方，因为附近的“雅虎”会时不时来侵扰，

fiercest and most frequent battles are fought, occasioned by perpetual inroads of the neighbouring *Yahoos*.

所以时常会引发最猛烈，次数最多的战争。

He said, it was common when two *Yahoos* discovered such a *stone* in a field, and were contending which of them should be the proprietor, a third would take the advantage, and carry it away from them both; which my master would needs contend to have some kind of resemblance with our *suits at law*; wherein I thought it for our credit not to undeceive him; since the decision he mentioned was much more equitable than many decrees among us: because the plaintiff and defendant there lost nothing beside the *stone* they contended for, whereas our courts of equity, would never have dismissed the cause while either of them had anything left.

它还说两只“雅虎”在这个地方找到了一块发光的石头，当它们在争论这块石头的归属权时，另一只就会趁机带走这块石头，这种事情时有发生。我的主人非要认为这和我们上法庭打官司有点像，而我认为我们的公正并不能蒙骗它，因为它所提及的那种制裁方式比我们的很多法典都要公正很多。在它的这个裁定中，原告和被告并未遭受任何损失，只是弄丢了它们争抢的石头，而我们宣扬公平的法庭如果不让原告或是被告任何一方破产的话，它是坚决不会结案的。

My master continuing his discourse, said, there was nothing that rendered the *Yahoos* more odious, than their undistinguishing appetite to devour everything that came in their way, whether herbs, roots, berries, the corrupted flesh of animals, or all mingled together: and it was peculiar in their temper, that they were fonder of what they could get by rapine or stealth at a greater distance, than much better food provided for them at home. If their prey held out, they would eat till they were ready to burst, after which nature had pointed out to them a

主人接着讲下去，它说，“雅虎”最让人不可理喻的地方就是它们并不会去分辨食物的好坏，无论是草、根、浆果、腐坏的兽肉，还是把杂七杂八的东西混合在一起的东西，它们都会咽下去。它们的脾气也很古怪，不愿意在家吃为它们准备好的食物，却乐意跑到很远的地方偷吃或者抢着吃。如果偷抢来的食物没有那么快吃完，它们会一直吃到肚子爆炸为止，随后它们的本性会引导它们去吃某种草根，吃下这种草根之后，就会拉空肚子。

certain *root* that gave them a general evacuation.

There was also another kind of *root* very *juicy*, but somewhat rare and difficult to be found, which the *Yahoos* sought for with much eagerness, and would suck it with great delight; it produced in them the same effects that wine hath upon us. It would make them sometimes hug, and sometimes tear one another; they would howl and grin, and chatter, and reel and you, and tumble, and then fall asleep in the Dirt.

I did indeed observe, that the *Yahoos* were the only animals in this country subject to any diseases; which however, were much fewer than horses have among us, and contracted not by any ill Treatment they meet with, but by the nastiness, and greediness of that sordid brute. Neither has their language any more than a general appellation for those maladies, which is borrowed from the name of the beast, and called *Hnea-Yahoo*, or *Yahoo's-Evil*; and the cure prescribed is a mixture of *their own dung* and *urine* forcibly put down the *Yahoo's* throat. This I have since often known to have been taken with success and do here freely recommend it to my countrymen for the public good, as an admirable specific against all diseases produced by repletion.

As to learning, government, arts, manufactures, and the like, my master

另外，还有一种多汁的草根，不过比较少见很难找到，"雅虎"们会兴致勃勃地寻找这种草根，一旦发现，就会兴高采烈地吮吸起来。而这些草根对它们所起的作用，同酒对我们的作用极其相似。它们一会儿抱在一起，一会儿又撕咬起来，它们还会嗥叫，狂笑，喃喃自语，感到眩晕，打滚，最后昏睡在烂泥地里。

我发现在这个国家中唯有"雅虎"这种动物会染上疾病，只是它们感染的病痛远远少于我们的马所得的病，并且它们的病因都不是受虐所致，而只是因为它们好吃邋遢。这些疾病用它们的语言有一个统一的称谓，它是借用这个牲畜的名字而来的，被称作"赫尼•雅虎"，简言之就是雅虎病。治愈这种疾病的办法就是把"雅虎"自己的尿液混合物从喉咙中强行灌入。而我所了解到的是这种治疗方法总是很奏效，同时为了让大众受益，我在这里免费给我的同胞们介绍这种能够治愈所有由于吃得太饱而引发的病痛，不过这种特效的疗法的确有推广的必要性。

我的主人坦言，它并不能察觉出它们国家的"雅虎"和我们在学

confessed he could find little or no resemblance between the *Yahoos* of that country and those in ours. For, he only meant to observe what parity there was in our natures. He had heard indeed some curious *Houyhnhnms* observe, that in most herds there was a sort of ruling *Yahoo* (as among us there is generally some leading or principal stag in a park) who was always more deformed in body, and *mischievous in disposition*, than any of the rest. that this *leader* had usually a favourite as *like himself as* he could get, whose employment was to *lick his master's foot and posteriors, and drive the female Yahoos* to his *kennel*; for which he was now and then rewarded with a piece of ass's flesh. This *favourite* is hated by the whole herd, and therefore to protect himself, keeps always near *the person of his leader*. He usually continues in office till a worse can be found; but the very moment he is discarded, his successor, at the head of all the *Yahoos* in that district, young and old, male and female, come in a body, and discharge their excrements upon him from head to foot. But how far this might be applicable to *our courts* and *favourites*, and *ministers of state*, my master said I could best determine.

I *durst* make no return to this malicious insinuation, which debased human understanding below the sagacity of a common *hound*, who has judgment

术、政治、艺术以及工艺等方面的差异。因为它唯一想了解的是我们在自然性上的共通之处。以前的确有一些奇异的“慧骃”告诉它，大部分“雅虎”生活的群落中，总有那么一头统治着它们（就如同我们中间的某些人常常会是某一方的领导者），而这种“雅虎”常常会比其他“雅虎”更丑陋，脾气更古怪。这个领头人通常会想办法找一只和自己相像的替代品，让替代者跟在主人鞍前马后地伺候着，还要把母“雅虎”赶到它的窝里，而为此时不时会获得主人赏赐的一块驴肉吃。然而这个宠儿却受到大伙的敌视，所以它为了保护好自己，不得不紧跟着它的主人。它通常都会一直担任这个职位，除非能够找到比它更加恶劣的“雅虎”，它一旦被解职，接替它的“雅虎”就会偕同这一带男女老少的“雅虎”们一起让它浑身上下都淋上屎尿。然而这种状况和与我们那里的朝廷、宠臣和大臣究竟有几分相似之处，我的主人说唯有我能分析得最准确。

我根本都不敢驳斥这种毒辣的讥讽。它贬低人类的智慧还比不上一头普通的猎犬，因为猎犬有极佳的洞察力，能够在一群狗中辨别

enough to distinguish and follow the cry of the *ablest dog in the pack*, without being ever mistaken.

My master told me, there were some qualities remarkable in the *Yahoos*, which he had not observed me to mention, or at least very slightly, in the accounts I had given of human kind. he said, those animals, like other brutes, had their females in common; but in this they differed, that the she-*Yahoo* would admit the males, while she was pregnant, and that the hees would quarrel and fight with the females as fiercely as with each other. both which practices were such degrees of infamous brutality, that no other sensitive creature ever arrived at.

Another thing he wondered at in the *Yahoos*, was their strange disposition to nastiness and dirt, whereas there appears to be a natural love of cleanliness in all other animals. As to the two former accusations, I was glad to let them pass without any reply, because I had not a word to offer upon them in defence of my species, which otherwise I certainly had done from my own inclinations. But I could have easily vindicated human kind from the imputation of singularity upon the last article, if there had been any *swine* in that country (as unluckily for me there were not) which although it may be a *sweeter quadruped* than a *Yahoo*, cannot I humbly conceive in justice pretend to

出最有能耐的那只，并且跟着它叫，从未失误过。

我的主人还告诉了我“雅虎”的几种显著的特征，它在我谈人性的时候，并未听我提到过，即使提起过，也最多蜻蜓点水地说了一下。它认为那些动物在拥有雌性这一点上和其他畜生没有任何差别，而不同之处就在于怀孕的母“雅虎”还照样同公“雅虎”交配，还有就是公“雅虎”和母“雅虎”也会和两只公“雅虎”吵得一样凶，打得一样猛，它们把吵架和斗殴做到了不可理喻的残忍，凡是其他有感情的动物永远都不可能办到。

它还想了解“雅虎”的一个情况，那就是它们居然会钟爱肮脏同污浊，而其他的动物看起来都天生喜欢整洁干净。对于它的前两项指责，我宁愿不回答，敷衍了事，因为我实在说不出任何话语去给自己的同类辩解了，要不是这样，我一定会按照我的意愿替他们做一番辩护。不过它对我们最后一条的指责，认为我们偏爱污秽这个说法，要是这个国家有猪的话（不幸的是它们没有），我就能够为我们人类开脱一番，尽管猪这种四脚动物可能会比“雅虎”更温和，但公平来讲，我认为它绝对没理由说自己比“雅虎”更讲卫生。如果主人亲眼目睹过猪进食时那副肮脏的

more cleanliness; and so his honour himself must have owned, if he had seen their filthy way of feeding, and their custom of wallowing and sleeping in the mud.

My master likewise mentioned another quality which his servants had discovered in several Yahoos, and to him was wholly unaccountable. He said, "a fancy would sometimes take a *Yahoo,* to retire into a corner, to lie down and howl, and groan, and spurn away all that came near him, although he were young and fat, wanted neither food nor water; nor did the servants imagine what could possibly ail him. And the only remedy they found was to set him to hard work, after which he would infallibly come to himself. To this I was silent out of partiality to my own kind; yet here I could plainly discover the true seeds of spleen, which only seizeth on the *lazy*, the *luxurious*, and the *rich*; who, if they were forced to undergo the *same regimen* I would undertake for the cure.

His honour had further observed, that a female *Yahoo* would often stand behind a bank or a bush, to gaze on the young males passing by, and then appear, and hide, using many antic gestures and grimaces, at which time it was observed, that she had a most *offensive smell*; and when any of the males advanced, would slowly retire, looking often back, and with a counterfeit show of fear, run off into

样子，见到它们惯于在污泥中打滚睡觉，肯定会赞同我所说的话。

在此，我的主人还提出了其他的特征，那是它的仆人从几只“雅虎”身上看出来的，而它却根本不能理解。它说“雅虎”偶尔胡思乱想着就会退缩到一个角落里，就地躺下，不停地低吼哀鸣，而且会踢开所有靠近它的人。虽然它又小又肥，却能够不吃不喝，仆人们也看不出它究竟出了什么毛病。随后它们看出唯一疗法就是派它去干体力活，一干这样的活，它们必然就恢复正常了。因为我对同类有袒护之心，所以听完之后就沉默了。而这也让我发现了忧郁症的病因，唯有懒散、铺张浪费和富有的人才会染上这样的疾病，如果迫使他们接受一样的疗法，我可以担保他们立马就能痊愈。

主人继续说，一只母“雅虎”时常会驻足在土堆或是灌木的后面，两眼直勾勾地看着来来去去的年轻的公“雅虎”，躲躲藏藏，扮着各种丑态和怪相，据称此时的它身上会散发一股恶臭。如果一只公“雅虎”上前搭讪，它就会缓缓地退后，但是会不断地回头望，假装很惶恐，随后跑到一个便利的地方，它知道那只公“雅虎”一定会

some convenient place where she knew the male would follow her.

At other times if a female stranger came among them, three or four of her own sex would get about her, and stare and chatter, and grin, and smell her all over and then turn off with gestures, that seemed to express contempt and disdain.

Perhaps my master might refine a little in these speculations, which he had drawn from what he observed himself, or had been told him by others: however, I could not reflect without some amazement, and much sorrow, that the rudiments of *lewdness, coquetry, censure,* and *scandal*, should have place by instinct in womankind.

I expected every moment that my master would accuse the *Yahoos* of those unnatural appetites in both sexes, so common among us. But nature it seems hath not been so expert a schoolmistress; and these politer pleasures are entirely the productions of art and reason, on our side of the globe.

跟着它去的。

有时不知从哪里蹿出一只不熟识的母“雅虎”，三四只母“雅虎”就会围住它盯着看，唧唧喳喳地讨论，在讥笑的同时把它全身闻个遍，接着故作姿态地走开，好像在表示它们看不起它。

这些可能都是我主人它自己看到的，或是别人转告它的情况，虽然可能在讲的时候用词可以更加文雅一点，但是我回想的时候还是难免感到一些惊讶，同时还有一种悲凉之感，因为在女性的天性中，居然都能够看出淫荡、风骚、刻薄和造谣的苗头。

我无时无刻不期待着我的主人控诉男女“雅虎”身上那些违反自然天性的欲望，尽管那在我们中间极其平常，不过自然似乎并不是一位技艺高超的教师，在我们生活的这个半球上，这些更为文雅的享乐全部都是艺术和理性的结晶。

CHAPTER 8

第八章

The Author relates several Particulars of the Yahoos. The great Virtues of the Houyhnhnms. The Education and Exercise of their Youth. Their general Assembly.

作者对“雅虎”的情况的详细描述——“慧骃”的美德——小“慧骃”受到的教育和运动——它们的大会。

As I ought to have understood human nature much better than I supposed it possible for my master to do, so it was easy to apply the character he gave of the *Yahoos* to myself and my countrymen, and I believed I could yet make farther discoveries from my own observation. I therefore often begged his Favour to let me go among the herds of *Yahoos* in the neighbourhood, to which he always very graciously consented, being perfectly convinced that the hatred I bore these brutes would never suffer me to be corrupted by them; and his honour ordered one of his servants, a strong sorrel nag, very honest and good-natured, to be my guard, without whose protection I durst not undertake such adventures. For I have already told the reader how much I was pestered by th0se odious animals upon my first arrival. and I afterwards failed very narrowly three or four times of falling into their clutches, when I happened to stray at

因为我觉得关于人性这一点，我比我主人可能了解得要深刻得多，因此我很容易就将它描述的“雅虎”的特性联想到了我自己以及我的同胞们身上，而且我相信从我自己的观察也无法得出更多的结论了。因此我经常乞求它准许我到附近的“雅虎”群中去。对此它总是十分大方地同意我的要求，我对这些畜生们有如此深的仇恨，我永远不可能被它们引诱，对此它深信不疑。而且它还派自己的一名仆人，一匹强壮忠诚又好脾气的栗色马儿，当我的警卫，要不是它保护我，我可不敢如此冒险。因为我已经告诉过读者，我刚到这里的时候，可没少被这群该死的畜生们欺负。之后有三四次我也差点就落在它们手里。那几次我碰巧没带腰刀走失了。我有理由相信它们怀有一些认为我是它们的同类的想象，因此当我和我的警卫在一起的时候，经常在它们面前虚张声势地卷起

any distance without my hanger. And I have reason to believe they had some imagination that I was of their own species, which I often assisted myself, by stripping up my sleeves, and showing my naked arms and Breast in their sight, when my protector was with me: At which times they would approach as near as they durst, and imitate my actions after the manner of monkeys, but ever with great signs of hatred, as a tame jack-Daw with cap and stockings, is always persecuted by the wild ones, when he happens to be got among them.

袖子裸露着胳膊和胸膛。这时它们就会大着胆子靠近我，像猴子一样模仿我的动作，但也带着很强烈的仇视，我倒像一只穿戴整齐的被驯化的八哥不巧闯入了野生的鸟群里，总会被它们群起而攻之。

They are prodigiously nimble from their infancy; however, I once caught a young male of three years old, and endeavoured by all marks of tenderness to make it quiet; but the little imp fell a squalling, and scratching, and biting with such violence, that I was forced to let it go, and it was high time, for a whole troop of old ones came about us at the noise, but finding the cub was safe (for away it ran) and my sorrel nag being by, they durst not venture near us. I observed the young animal's flesh to smell very rank, and the stink was somewhat between a *weasel* and a *fox*, but much more disagreeable. I forgot another circumstance (and perhaps I might have the reader's pardon, if it were wholly omitted) that while I held the odious vermin in my hands, it voided its

它们生下来的时候就惊人的机灵敏捷。然而有一次我还是抓到了一只 3 岁的幼小的“雅虎”，为了让它安静一点，我大费周章地作出各种温柔的讨好，但那小家伙不停地吵闹，到处乱抓，还狠狠地咬了我，我不得不放它走，而就在这时一大群老“雅虎”听到声音而聚拢过来，不过它们发现小东西安然无恙（因为它已跑得远远的），我那栗色小马又在近旁，因此没敢冒险接近。我觉察到这小东西的肉有股恶臭，有点像黄鼠狼的味儿，又有点狐狸的骚臭，但要比这两种更加难以忍受。我还忘了一件事（如果我能彻底省略掉这件事的话，或许能博得读者们的原谅），那就是当我把那只讨厌的畜生抓在手里时，它拉了一泡黄色的稀屎，溅了

filthy excrements of a yellow liquid substance, all over my clothes; but by good fortune there was a small brook hard by, where I washed myself as clean as I could, although I durst not come into my master's presence, until I were sufficiently aired.

我一身，还好我运气好，附近有条小河，我在那儿把自己彻底洗了个干净，一直到身上完全没有臭气之后，我才敢出现在主人面前。

By what I could discover, the *Yahoos* appear to be the most unteachable of all animals, their capacities never reaching higher than to draw or carry burdens. Yet I am of opinion this defect ariseth chiefly from a perverse, restive disposition. for they are cunning, malicious, treacherous, and revengeful. They are strong and hardy, but of a cowardly spirit, and by consequence, insolent, abject, and cruel. It is observed, that the red-haired of both sexes are more libidinous and mischievous than the rest, whom yet they much exceed in strength and activity.

从我的发现来看，“雅虎”似乎是所有动物中最难教化的，它们除了拖、拽、扛东西之外就没有别的本事了。然而我却认为它们这个缺点主要还是源于它们倔犟易怒，难以驾驭的性格特征。因为它们是非常狡猾恶毒，背信弃义，报复心强的生物。它们十分强壮，可是却胆小如鼠，因此它们就表现得傲慢粗野，卑鄙残忍。据我观察，红色皮毛的公母“雅虎”比别的“雅虎”更加淫荡恶毒，而且在力量和活力方面，它们也比其他同类更胜一筹。

The *Houyhnhnms* keep the *Yahoos* for present use in huts not far from the house; but the rest are sent abroad to certain fields, where they dig up roots, eat several kinds of herbs, and search about for carrion, or sometimes catch *weasels* and *luhimuhs* (a sort of *wild rat*) which they greedily devour. Nature hath taught them to dig deep holes with their nails on the side of a rising ground, wherein they lie by themselves; only the kennels of the females are larger, sufficient to hold two

“慧骃”将眼下用得到的“雅虎”养在屋子附近的茅屋里，剩下的都被赶到外面的田野里，在那里它们刨树根，以杂草为食，四处找寻动物的腐尸，有时还去捕猎黄鼠狼和“鲁黑木斯”（一种野鼠），猎物都被它们贪婪地吞噬个精光。造物主赋予了它们用爪子在土坡的一边挖出深洞的本领，它们就生活在这样的洞穴中，只不过母“雅虎”的窝要大一些，足够容纳 2 到 3 只幼崽。

or three cubs.

They swim from their infancy like frogs, and are able to continue long under water, where they often take fish, which the females carry home to their young. And upon this occasion, I hope the reader will pardon my relating an odd adventure.

Being one day abroad with my protector the sorrel nag, and the weather exceeding hot, I entreated him to let me bathe in a river that was near. He consented, and I immediately stripped myself stark naked, and went down softly into the stream. It happened that a young female *Yahoo*, standing behind a bank, saw the whole proceeding, and inflamed by desire, as the nag and I conjectured, came running with all speed, and leaped into the water within five yards of the place where I bathed. I was never in my life so terribly frightened; the nag was grazing at some distance, not suspecting any harm. She embraced me after a most fulsome manner; I roared as loud as I could, and the nag came galloping towards me, whereupon she quitted her grasp, with the utmost reluctancy, and leaped upon the opposite bank, where she stood gazing and howling all the time I was putting on my clothes.

This was a matter of diversion to my master and his family, as well as of mortification to myself. For now I could

像青蛙那样，它们天生就会游泳，可以在水底待上相当长的时间。它们经常在水里捉鱼，母“雅虎”将捉到的鱼带回家给幼崽吃。提到这个，我还要提到一件奇遇，希望读者能够原谅。

有一天，我跟我的警卫栗色小马在外面，天气热得厉害，我央求他让我去附近的一条小河里洗个澡。它同意了，于是我马上将自己脱得赤条条的，缓缓地走进河里。就在这时，一只站在土堆后面的母“雅虎”目睹了整个经过，它燃烧的欲火难以抑制（我和小马均作此推断），全速奔了过来，一头扎进距离我洗澡处不到5码的地方。我此生中头一次如此惊惧，小马在远处吃着草，压根没怀疑出了什么事。它用最最令人作呕的姿态紧紧抱住我，我用最大声音叫喊着呼救，小马闻声奔来，这时它才极不情愿地放开手，跳到对岸去了，当我在穿衣服的时候它还一直站在那儿盯着我高声嚎叫。

我的主人和它的亲戚都把这件事当成是个笑话，而对我却是天大的耻辱。因为现在我再也没法否

no longer deny, that I was a real *Yahoo,* in every limb and feature, since the females had a natural propensity to me as one of their own species: Neither was the hair of this brute of a red colour (which might have been some excuse for an appetite a little irregular) but black as a sloe, and her countenance did not make an appearance altogether so hideous as the rest of the kind; for, I think she could not be above eleven years old.

认我从头到脚都是一只真正的“雅虎”，因为母 “雅虎”将我视为它们的同类且对我产生了自然的爱慕之情。这畜生的毛可不是红色的（因此它的行为也就不能用古怪的欲求旺盛来解释），而是像黑刺李一般黑，相貌也不像其他的“雅虎”那般丑得骇人，因为我觉得它的年纪应该不超过 11 岁。

Having lived three years in this country, the reader I suppose will expect, that I should, like other travellers, give him some account of the manners and customs of its inhabitants, which it was indeed my principal study to learn.

在这个国家我已生活了 3 年，我想读者们会期待我能像别的旅行家那样讲讲当地居民的习俗和规矩，而事实上这也是我最想弄明白的东西。

As these noble *Houyhnhnms* are endowed by nature with a general disposition to all virtues, and have no conceptions or ideas of what is evil in a rational creature, so their grand maxim is, to cultivate *reason*, and to be wholly governed by it. Neither is *reason* among them a point problematical as with us, where men can argue with plausibility on both sides of a question; but strikes you with immediate conviction; as it must needs do where it is not mingled, obscured, or discoloured by passion and interest. I remember it was with extreme difficulty that I could bring my master to understand the meaning of the word

由于“慧骃”这种高贵的生物与生俱来的种种美德，它们对理性动物的恶习完全没有概念，因此它们最伟大的格言就是，培养理性思维，一切受到理性的支配。在它们看来，理性不容争辩，不像我们，可以从问题的两面展开辩论，它们的理性必然顷刻间令你折服，因为它不会与感情和利益相混淆，也不会被二者蒙蔽或扭曲。我记得为了让我的主人理解 “意见”这个词的含义我费了好大劲儿，我也很难让它理解为什么一个问题会引发争论，因为理性教会我们只对我们确定的事物表示肯定或否定，然而超出我们认知的范围我们就无法

opinion, or how a point could be disputable; because *reason* taught us to affirm or deny only where we are certain; and beyond our knowledge we cannot do either. So that controversies, wranglings, disputes, and positiveness in false or dubious propositions are evils unknown among the *Houyhnhnms*. In the like manner when I used to explain to him our several systems of *natural philosophy*, he would laugh that a creature pretending to *reason*, should value itself upon the knowledge of other people's conjectures, and in things, where that knowledge, if it were certain, could be of no use. Wherein he agreed entirely with the sentiments of *Socrates, as Plato* delivers them; which I mention as the highest honour I can do that prince of philosophers. I have often since reflected what destruction such a doctrine would make in the libraries of *Europe*, and how many paths to fame would be then shut up in the learned world.

做出判断。因此对于"慧骃"来说，争论、吵闹、争端以及对虚假的模棱两可的事物的肯定都是它们无法理解的恶。每当我向它解释我们关于自然哲学的几种体系的时候，它都会嘲笑我们这种假装具有理性的生物竟然也会珍视别人的构想，而就算对那些东西的认知是确切的，也毫无用处。这方面它完全同意经由柏拉图阐述的苏格拉底的思想。我之所以提到苏格拉底是为了向这位哲学之王致以我最崇高的敬意。自从那时我时常想到这种学说将会给欧洲的图书馆造成怎样的破坏，又将会让多少条学术界的成名之道因此破灭。

Friendship and *benevolence* are the two principal virtues among the *Houyhnhnms*, and these not confined to particular objects, but universal to the whole race. for a stranger from the remotest part is equally treated with the nearest neighbour, and wherever he goes, looks upon himself as at home. They preserve *decency* and *civility* in the highest degrees, but are

友谊和仁爱是"慧骃"的两种主要美德，它们并不局限于个别的"慧骃"而是适用于整个族群。它们对自远方来的客人和近在毗邻的友人都一视同仁。而无论它到了哪儿都会受到殷勤的接待。它们将正派和文明保持在最高的水准，但却从不拘泥于繁文缛节。它们从不溺爱小马，然而它们的教育理念完

altogether ignorant of *ceremony*. They have no fondness for their colts or foals, but the care they take in educating them proceeds entirely from the dictates of *reason*. And I observed my master to show the same affection to his neighbour's issue that he had for his own. They will have it that *nature* teaches them to love the whole species, and it is *reason* only that maketh a distinction of persons, where there is a superior degree of virtue.

全服从理性的准绳。而我观察到我的主人对它邻居的孩子与对自己的孩子别无二致。它们永远遵从自然教会他们的事，爱自己所有的同类，而当美德有高下之分的时候，唯有理性能够将人区分开来。

When the matron *Houyhnhnms* have produced one of each sex, they no longer accompany with their consorts, except they lose one of their issue by some casualty, which very seldom happens: but in such a case they meet again, or when the like accident befalls a person, whose wife is past bearing, some other couple bestows on him one of their own colts, and then go together again until the mother is pregnant. This caution is necessary to prevent the country from being overburdened with numbers. But the race of inferior *Houyhnhnms*, bred up to be servants is not so strictly limited upon this article; these are allowed to produce three of each sex, to be domestics in the noble families.

当母“慧骃”产下一对子女后，就不与配偶居住在一起了，除非因为某种意外它们其中一个孩子夭折，这种情况十分少见，但只有在这时它们才会再度同居，或是当别的“慧骃”也遭遇了相同的事故而它的妻子已无法生养，这时别的夫妇就会将它们其中一个孩子过继给它们，而它们再同居到母亲怀孕为止。这项措施对于防止国家人口过剩十分必要。然而那些低等的生来就是仆人阶层的“慧骃”则不受这么严格的管制，它们每对夫妇可以生育 3 对子女，作为贵族家庭中的家仆。

In their marriages they are exactly careful to choose such colours as will not make any disagreeable mixture in the breed. *Strength* is chiefly valued in the

在婚姻中它们对挑选毛色十分谨慎，为了防止血统的混乱。力量是衡量男方的最主要因素，而漂亮的外表则是衡量女方的最主要

male, and *comeliness* in the female, not upon the account of *love*, but to preserve the race from degenerating; for where a female happens to excel in *strength*, a consort is chosen with regard to *comeliness*. Courtship, love, presents, jointures, settlements, have no place in their thoughts; or terms whereby to express them in their language. The young couple meet and are joined, merely because it is the determination of their parents and friends: it is what they see done every day, and they look upon it as one of the necessary actions of a rational being. But the violation of marriage, or any other unchastity, was never heard of: and the married pair pass their lives with the same friendship, and mutual benevolence, that they bear to all others of the same species, who come in their way; without jealousy, fondness, quarrelling, or discontent.

In educating the youth of both sexes, their method is admirable, and highly deserves our imitation. These are not suffered to taste a grain of *oats*, except upon certain days, till eighteen years old; nor *milk*, but very rarely; and in summer they graze two hours in the morning, and as long in the evening, which their parents likewise observe; but the servants are not allowed above half that time, and a great part of their grass is brought home, which

因素。并不是从爱情的角度，而是为了防止种族退化，因为若是女性碰巧力气过人，那么就会挑选一个外表英俊的伴侣与它相配。它们的观念中没有求偶、爱情、礼物、寡妇、遗产或是财产继承这样的事，它们的语言中也没有可以形容这些的词语。年轻伴侣相遇结合，仅仅因为这都是它们父母和朋友做出的决定，它们日日如此，并将其视为理性动物必有的行为之一。然而却从未听闻婚姻破裂或是任何不贞行为，伴侣们像对待遇到的所有同类那样，友爱如一，相敬如宾地度过一生，毫无嫉妒、溺爱之心，从不争执，彼此满足。

在教育男女青年方面，它们的方法令人起敬，十分值得我们效仿。孩子们在 18 岁以前，只有在某些特定的日子里才能吃到一点点燕麦，能喝到牛奶的日子也十分罕见。而在夏天早晚它们各有两个小时时间可以在外面吃草，它们的父母也同样在旁监督，但仆人们吃草的时间不到它们的一半，它们将大部分青草带回家，在干活的空闲时拿出来享用。

they eat at the most convenient hours, when they can be best spared from work.

Temperance, industry, exercise and *cleanliness*, are the lessons equally enjoined to the young ones of both sexes: and my master thought it monstrous in us to give the females a different kind of education from the males, except in some articles of domestic management; whereby as he truly observed, one half of our natives were good for nothing but bringing children into the world; and to trust the care of our children to such useless animals, he said was yet a greater instance of brutality.

节欲、勤劳、运动和清洁是青年男女都必须学习的课程。我的主人认为我们在除了家政功课之外的其他方面对女子施以与男子不同的教育，这一点十分可怕。这一点他完全正确，我们的人有一半除了生小孩就什么都不会干，而听任这些无用的动物来照看我们的子女，我的主人说这是一种更大的残忍。

But the *Houyhnhnms* train up their youth to strength, speed, and hardiness, by exercising them in running races up and down steep hills, and over hard stony grounds, and when they are all in a sweat, they are ordered to leap over head and ears, into a pond or river. Four times a year the youth of a certain district meet to show their proficiency in running, and leaping, and other feats of strength and agility, where the victor is rewarded, with a song in his or her praise. On this festival the servants drive a herd of *Yahoos* into the field, laden with hay, and oats, and milk for a repast to the *Houyhnhnms*; after which, these brutes are immediately driven back again, for fear of being noisome to the assembly.

可是“慧骃”却让它们的孩子在陡峭的山峰上上下奔跑，或是越过坚硬的石滩地，以此来磨炼它们的力量，速度和耐力，当它们大汗淋漓的时候，就命令它们一头扎进池塘或是小河之中。一年中有4次某个地区的年轻的“慧骃”要会聚起来展示它们奔跑、跳跃和其他力量和灵敏度方面的本领，优胜者将会得到大家对它或它的歌颂。每逢这样的节日，仆人们就赶着一群驮着干草、燕麦和牛奶的“雅虎”到场地给“慧骃”享用。之后这些畜生们就立即被赶回去，免得它们给会场带来吵闹的噪声。

Every fourth year at the *vernal equinox*, there is a representative council of the whole nation, which meets in a plain about twenty miles from our house, and continues about five or six days. Here they inquire into the state and condition of the several districts; whether they abound or be deficient in hay or oats, or cows or *Yahoos*? and wherever there is any want (which is but seldom) it is immediately supplied by unanimous consent and contribution. Here likewise the regulation of children is settled: as for instance, if a *Houyhnhnm* has two males, he changeth one of them with another that hath two females: and when a child hath been lost by any casualty, where the mother is past breeding, it is determined what family in the district shall breed another to supply the loss.

每隔 4 年的春分时节，都要召开一次全国代表大会，地点在距离我主人家 20 英里的平原上，持续五六天。会上它们询问各个地区的状况，它们的干草、燕麦、母牛、“雅虎”是富余还是不足？不管哪里出现短缺（不过这种情况很少见），全体成员就意见一致地决定立即捐助。在会上关于子女的规划也得以解决，比如，如果一个“慧骃”有两个男孩子，那么它用其中一个可以与有两个女孩子的“慧骃”交换。当有一个孩子因为意外而夭折，而母亲又无法再生育时，就由大会来决定地区里的哪一家再生一个来补充损失。

CHAPTER 9

第九章

A Grand Debate at the General Assembly of the Houyhnhnms, and how it was determined. The Learning of the Houyhnhnms. Their Buildings. Their manner of Burials. The Defectiveness of their Language.

"慧骃"全国代表大会进行大辩论及其结果。"慧骃"的学术，建筑及葬礼的习俗。它们语言的缺陷。

One of these grand assemblies was held in my time, about three months before my departure, whither my master went as the representative of our district. In this council was resumed their old debate, and indeed, the only debate which ever happened in that country; whereof my master after his return give me a very particular account.

其中一次代表大会在我离开之前的 3 个月召开，作为我们地区的代表，我的主人参加了此次大会。在这次会议上它们老调重弹，而事实上这也是在这个国家唯一有争论的话题，我主人回来之后向我详述了辩论的经过。

The question to be debated, was, whether the *Yahoos* should be exterminated from the face of the earth. One of the *members* for the affirmative offered several arguments of great strength and weight, alleging, that as the *Yahoos* were the most filthy, noisome, and deformed animal which nature ever produced, so they were the most restive and indocible, mischievous and malicious: they would privately suck the teats of the *Houyhnhnms'* cows, kill and devour their

辩论的话题是：是否应该将"雅虎"从世界上彻底灭除。支持方的一位代表提出了数个有力且站得住脚的论点。它声称，"雅虎"是世上最肮脏、最恶臭、最丑陋的动物，因此它们最难管束，最难驯化，爱耍花招且恶毒。如果不时时盯着它们，它们就会趁人不备偷喝"慧骃"母牛的奶，杀死并吃掉它们的猫儿，践踏它们的燕麦和青草，诸如此类无法无天的恶行。此外，它还注意到一个广泛认可的传

cats, trample down their oats and grass, if they were not continually watched, and commit a thousand other Extravagances. He took notice of a general tradition, that *Yahoos* had not been always in their country: but, that many ages ago, two of these brutes appeared together upon a mountain; whether produced by the heat of the sun upon corrupted mud and slime, or from the ooze and froth of the sea, was never known that these *Yahoos* engendered, and their brood in a short time, grew so numerous as to overrun and infest the whole nation. that the *Houyhnhnms* to get rid of this evil, made a general hunting, and at last enclosed the whole herd, and destroying the elder, every *Houyhnhnm* kept two young ones in a kennel, and brought them to such a degree of tameness, as an animal, so savage by nature, can be capable of acquiring, using them for draught and carriage; that there seemed to be much truth in this tradition, and that those creatures could not be *yinhniamshy* (or *aborigines* of the land) because of the violent hatred the *Houyhnhnms*, as well as all other animals, bore them; which, although their evil disposition sufficiently deserved, could never have arrived at so high a degree, if they had been *aborigines*, or else they would have long since been rooted out. that the inhabitants taking a

说，那就是“雅虎”并不是一直就有的，而是许多年前有一对畜生突然就出现在一座山上，至于它们究竟是太阳照射着淤泥生出来的还是从海中的软泥和泡沫生出来的就成了一个永远的谜。然后这对“雅虎”开始繁殖，很快它们的子孙数量就变得越来越庞大，以至于肆虐全国。是“慧骃”为了除掉这种害畜而举行了一次盛大的狩猎，最后将整个“雅虎”群团团包围，杀掉年长的，每个“慧骃”只留两只小的豢养起来，将它们这种本性刁蛮的动物驯服到如此听话的地步，能够取物，拖拽、搬运东西。这种传说似乎很有些道理，因为那动物不可能是“依林赫尼阿姆锡”（意思是当地的土著），因为“慧骃”和所有别的动物都对它们怀着深切的仇恨，尽管它们生性恶劣仇恨也理所应当，但若它们是原住民的话大家也不会如此痛恨它们，否则它们早就被彻底扫除了。当地居民还莫名其妙地喜好培养“雅虎”来为自己服务，而这一鲁莽的举动致使对驴的培养被忽略了。驴子是种很不错的动物，它们容易饲养，更加温驯听话，不会臭气熏天，虽然它们不够机敏灵活，但力气够大，用来干活绰绰有余。就算它们的叫声有些难听，但比起“雅虎”那可怕的嚎叫声来简直算得上是天籁了。

fancy to use the service of the *Yahoos*, had very imprudently neglected to cultivate the breed of *asses*, which were a comely animal, easily kept, more tame and orderly, without any offensive smell, strong enough for labour, although they yield to the other in agility of body; and if their braying be no agreeable sound, it is far preferable to the horrible howlings of the *Yahoos*.

Several others declared their sentiments to the same purpose, when my master proposed an expedient to the assembly, whereof he had indeed borrowed the hint from me. He approved of the tradition, mentioned by the *honourable member*, who spoke before, and affirmed that the two *Yahoos* said to be first seen among them had been driven thither over the sea; that coming to land, and being forsaken by their companions, they retired to the mountains, and degenerating by degrees, became in process of time, much more savage than those of their own species in the country from whence these two originals came. The reason of his assertion was, that he had now in his possession, a certain wonderful *Yahoo* (meaning myself) which most of them had heard of, and many of them had seen. He then related to them, how he first found me; that my body was all covered with an artificial composure of the skins and hairs of other

还有好几个代表也宣称了同样的看法，这时我的主人向大会提出一个权宜之计，事实上这个点子是它受我启发才想到的。它对前面那位尊贵的代表的发言表示了赞同，且认可了最先看到的两只“雅虎”是从海上漂流而来的传说，它们被同伴抛弃上了陆地，躲进山林隐居，一代代繁衍下去就变得比它们那些在祖国的同类要野蛮得多。它做出此番声明的理由是现在它就拥有这样一只神奇的“雅虎”(也就是我)，这一点大多数代表都曾耳闻，许多代表也都亲眼见过我。接着它向它们讲述了当初它是如何发现我的，那时我周身包裹着别的动物的毛皮，说着自己的语言，也完全能够理解它们的语言。我向它讲述了我是如何意外来到这里，当它见到我卸去遮盖原本的样子时，我是只彻头彻尾的“雅虎”，只是较白一些，毛少一些，爪子更短罢了。它还补充说，我曾大费周

animals: that I spoke a language of my own, and had thoroughly learned theirs: that I had related to him the accidents which brought me thither: that when he saw me without my covering, I was an exact *Yahoo* in every part, only of a whiter colour, less hairy, and with shorter claws. He added, how I had endeavoured to persuade him, that in my own and other countries the *Yahoos* acted as the governing, rational animal, and held the *Houyhnhnms* in servitude: that he observed in me all the qualities of a *Yahoo*, only a little more civilized by some tincture of reason, which however was in a degree as far inferior to the *Houyhnhnm* race, as the *Yahoos* of their country were to me: that, among other things, I mentioned a custom we had of *castrating Houyhnhnms* when they were young, in order to render them tame; that the operation was easy and safe; that it was no shame to learn wisdom from brutes, as industry is taught by the ant, and building by the swallow (for so I translate the word *lyhannh*, although it be a much larger fowl). that this invention might be practised upon the younger *Yahoos* here, which, besides rendering them tractable and fitter for use, would in an age put an end to the whole species without destroying life. That, in the mean time the *Houyhnhnms* should be *exhorted* to

章地想要说服他，在我自己的祖国和其他一些国家里，“雅虎”是占据支配地位的理性动物，在这些地方他们将“慧骃”当做奴隶。它说它在我身上找到了“雅虎”的全部特征，只不过我比其他“雅虎”略显文明、稍有理性而已。然而比起“慧骃”来还差得远，就像他们国家的“雅虎”远不如我一样。除了这些，我还向它提起我们有种在“慧骃”幼年时就将它们阉割的习惯，这样就可以让他们变得温驯，手术简单风险小，他说学习畜生们的智慧也并不丢脸，正如蚂蚁教会我们勤劳，而燕子教会我们筑窝（我把“利航赫”这个词译作燕子，但其实它是比燕子个头大许多的飞禽）。因此这个发明也可以应用到这里的小“雅虎”身上，这样做的好处除了可以让它们更易驾驭，更能为它们所用，而且可以在一代中就让整个种群灭绝而不用杀生。与此同时，“慧骃”也应当积极地培育驴这种生物，因为从各方面来说，驴都比别的畜生更有价值，且它们有一个优势，那就是长到 5 岁就可以派上用场，而其他的动物起码要等到 12 岁。

cultivate the breed of asses, which, as they are in all respects more valuable brutes, so they have this advantage, to be fit for service at five years old, which the others are not till twelve.

This was all my master thought fit to tell me at that time, of what passed in the grand council. But he was pleased to conceal one particular, which related personally to myself, whereof I soon felt the unhappy effect, as the reader will know in its proper place, and whence I date all the succeeding misfortunes of my life.

以上就是我主人那时认为可以告诉我的、发生在全国代表大会的事。但它却隐瞒了一件关乎我自身的事，很快我就体验到了它所带来的不幸，而随后我生命中接踵而来的厄运也随之开始。读者将会在后文中适当的时候读到这些。

The *Houyhnhnms* have no letters, and consequently, their knowledge is all traditional. But there happening few events of any moment among a people so well united, naturally disposed to every virtue, wholly governed by reason, and cut off from all commerce with other nations, the historical part is easily preserved without burdening their memories. I have already observed, that they are subject to no diseases, and therefore can have no need of physicians. However, they have excellent medicines composed of herbs, to cure accidental bruises and cuts in the pastern or frog of the foot by sharp stones, as well as other maims and hurts in the several parts of the body.

"慧骃"们没有文字，因此它们的知识都靠口耳相传。然而在这样一个非常团结，天性具有各种美德且完全被理性支配，与其他国家毫无往来的民族中，几乎发生什么重大事故，历史的部分也无须太多耗费记忆力就能传承下来。我还发现它们不会患病，因此也就不需要医生。然而它们却拥有草药制成的灵丹妙药，用来治疗意外被尖利的石头划伤的趾关节或脚掌，以及其他身体各部位受到的伤残和损害。

They calculate the year by the revolution of the sun and moon, but use no

它们根据日月更迭来记年，但却没有星期的细分。它们对太阳和

subdivisions into weeks. They are well enough acquainted with the motions of those two luminaries, and understand the nature of *eclipses*; and this is the utmost progress of their *astronomy*.

月亮这两个天体的运动了解得十分透彻，也懂得日食和月食的原理，而这就是他们在天文学领域取得的最高成就了。

In *poetry* they must be allowed to excel all other mortals; wherein the justness of their similes, and the minuteness, as well as exactness of their descriptions, are indeed inimitable. Their verses abound very much in both of these, and usually contain either some exalted notions of friendship and benevolence, or the praises of those who were victors in races, and other bodily exercises. Their buildings, although very rude and simple, are not inconvenient, but well contrived to defend them from all injuries of cold and heat. They have a kind of tree, which at forty years old loosens in the root, and falls with the first storm; they grow very straight, and being pointed like stakes with a sharp stone (for the *Houyhnhnms* know not the use of iron), they stick them erect in the ground about ten inches asunder, and then weave in oat-straw, or sometimes wattles betwixt them. The roof is made after the same manner, and so are the doors.

在诗歌方面，它们比其他的生物具有更高的天赋，它们贴切而形象的比喻和细致入微的准确描述都是我们望尘莫及的。它们的诗歌运用丰富的比喻和描绘，内容经常是关于崇高的友谊和仁爱，以及歌颂那些赛跑和其他体力运动中的获胜者。尽管它们的建筑物都粗放而简陋，但却十分便利，巧妙地解决了它们抗热抗寒的需要。它们有一种树，这种树的树根到 40 岁就松动了，第一场风暴到来的时候就会倒下。它们生长得十分笔直，“慧骃”就用锋利的石头将它们削成木桩（因为“慧骃”不会使用铁器），它们将木桩间隔 10 英寸左右插在地上，然后用燕麦秸编织其中，有时也用合欢的枝条代替。屋顶和门也如法炮制。

The *Houyhnhnms* use the hollow part between the pastern and the hoof of their forefeet, as we do our hands, and this with greater dexterity, than I could at first

“慧骃”用趾节和前蹄之间中空的部分拿东西，就像我们用手一样，比我最初想象的要灵活得多。我曾见过我家一匹白色母马用那

imagine. I have seen a white mare of our family thread a needle (which I lent her on purpose) with that joint. They milk their cows, reap their oats, and do all the work which requires hands, in the same manner. They have a kind of hard flints, which by grinding against other stones, they form into instruments, that serve instead of wedges, axes, and hammers. With tools made of these flints, they likewise cut their hay, and reap their oats, which there groweth naturally in several fields: the *Yahoos* draw home the sheaves in carriages, and the servants tread them in certain covered huts, to get out the grain, which is kept in stores. They make a rude kind of earthen and wooden vessels, and bake the former in the sun.

个关节穿针（针线是我故意借给它的）。它们挤牛奶，收割燕麦，做其他一切需要手的工作，都是如此。它们有一种坚硬的火石，只需用这种火石和别的石头摩擦，就能制成各种可以替代楔子、斧子、锤子等的工具。它们同样也用火石打磨出的工具割干草，收燕麦。燕麦是许多田地里自然生长出来的，“雅虎”将一束束燕麦驮回家，仆人们在茅屋里踩踏它们，将麦粒弄出来储藏起来。它们还制造粗质的陶器和木器，前者被置于阳光下烘干。

If they can avoid casualties, they die only of old age, and are buried in the obscurest places that can be found, their friends and relations expressing neither joy nor grief at their departure, nor does the dying person discover the least regret that he is leaving the world, any more than if he were upon returning home from a visit to one of his neighbours. I remember my master having once made an appointment with a friend and his family to come to his house upon some affair of importance, on the day fixed, the mistress and her two children came very late; she made two excuses, first for her husband,

如果它们没有死于意外，那么就只会老死，之后被埋葬在最僻静的地方，对于它们的离世它们的朋友和亲戚既不欢喜也无悲伤，临死的人也丝毫不会对离开这个世界感到一丝遗憾，就如同刚刚拜访一位邻居准备归家一般自然。我记得我的主人有一次和一位朋友以及它的家人约好到它家商讨要事，在约定的那天，女客人和它的两个孩子来得很晚，它道了两次歉，第一次是代它丈夫，据它说它早上刚巧“西奴思赫”了。这个词语在它们的语言中有很深的含意，但却很难译成英语，它的意思是：“回到它

who, as she said, happened that very morning to *lhnuwnh*. The word is strongly expressive in their language, but not easily rendered into *English*, it signifies, *to retire to his first mother*. Her excuse for not coming sooner, was that her husband dying late in the morning, she was a good while consulting her servants about a convenient place where his body should be laid; and I observed she behaved herself at our house, as cheerfully as the rest, and died about three months after.

的第一个母亲那儿去了。”它又为自己来晚了而表示歉意，因为它丈夫今天早上去世的时候已经不早了，它和仆人商议了好一会儿挑选一个便利的地方好将它丈夫下葬，而我观察到它在我家十分自如，和其他人一样兴致高昂，而它也在 3 个月之后去世了。

They live generally to seventy or seventy-five years, very seldom to fourscore: Some weeks before their death they feel a gradual decay; but without pain. During this time they are much visited by their friends, because they cannot go abroad, with their usual ease and satisfaction. However, about ten days before their death, which they seldom fail in computing, they return the visits that have been made them by those who are nearest in the neighbourhood, being carried in a convenient sledge drawn by *Yahoos*, which vehicle they use, not only upon this occasion, but when they grow old, upon long journeys, or when they are lamed by any accident. and therefore when the dying *Houyhnhnms* return those visits, they take a solemn leave of their friends, as if they were going to some remote part of the country, where they

它们通常都能活到 70 或者 75 岁，极少有活到 80 岁的。在它们死前几周，它们会感到身体逐渐衰颓，但却并不痛苦。在这段时间里它们的朋友会频繁探访，因为它们不能像平时那样安然适意地外出。然而在它们死前 10 天左右（它们的算术很少出差错），它们就坐在“雅虎”拉着的便利的雪橇里去探访最近的亲朋好友，它们不但只有这种时候才用到雪橇，当它们年纪大了，要长途旅行或是意外摔坏了腿都要用到它。因此当濒死的“慧骃”回访之时，都会向它们的朋友庄重地道别，仿佛它们要去离这个国家非常遥远的地方，并准备在那里度过余生。

designed to pass the rest of their lives.

I know not whether it may be worth observing, that the *Houyhnhnms* have no word in their language to express anything that is *evil*, except what they borrow from the deformities or ill qualities of the *Yahoos*. Thus they denote the folly of a servant, an omission of a child, a stone that cuts their foot, a continuance of foul or unseasonable weather, and the like, by adding to each the epithet of *Yahoo*. For instance, *hhnm Yahoo*, *whnaholm Yahoo*, *ynlhmndwihlma Yahoo*, and an ill-contrived house *ynholmhnmrohlnw Yahoo*.

I could with great pleasure enlarge farther upon the manners and virtues of this excellent people; but intending in a short time to publish a volume by itself, expressly upon that subject, I refer the reader thither. and in the mean time, proceed to relate my own sad catastrophe.

我不知道这是否值得一提，那就是在“慧骃”的语言中没有用来表示“恶”的词语，除了它们从“雅虎”的丑态和恶行之中借来的。因此如果它们要表示仆人太愚笨，小孩偷懒，脚被石头划伤，反常的持久的恶劣天气等，就在其后加上“雅虎”一词。例如，“赫恩姆·雅虎”、“呼纳霍尔姆·雅虎”、“银尔赫姆思德威赫尔玛·雅虎”。一幢盖得很糟的房子就叫做“银霍尔姆赫恩姆罗赫尔思乌·雅虎”。

我很乐意继续讲述这个优异的民族的高贵行为和美好品德，不过就这个问题我准备在不久的将来专门出一本书来详细叙述，有兴趣的读者可以参考。而这时我要继续讲述我自己悲惨的遭遇。

CHAPTER 10

第十章

The Author's Economy, and happy Life, among the Houyhnhnms. His great Improvement in Virtue by conversing with them. Their Conversations. The Author has notice given him by his Master, that he must depart from the Country. He falls into a Swoon for Grief; but submits. He contrives and finishes a Canoe by the help of a Fellow-Servant, and puts to Sea at a venture.

作者的日常生活以及他跟"慧骃"快乐的生活。与他们的对话让作者的品格有了极大的提升。他们之间的对话。作者的主人通知他必须离开这个国家。他因为悲伤而晕厥过去，但他服从了这个指令。他在仆人的帮助下想办法制成了一艘小船，开始了他的航海探险。

I had settled my little economy to my own heart's content. My master had ordered a room to be made for me after their manner, about six yards from the house the sides and floors of which I plastered with clay, and covered with rush mats of my own contriving; I had beaten hemp, which there grows wild, and made of it a sort of ticking: this I filled with the feathers of several birds I had taken with springes made of *Yahoos'* hairs, and were excellent food. I had worked two chairs with my knife, the sorrel nag helping me in the grosser and more laborious part. When my clothes were worn to rags, I made myself others with the skins of rabbits, and of a certain beautiful animal

我的小日子过得十分滋润。我主人在离家大约6码远的地方照着它们房子的规格给我盖了间小屋，我将墙壁和地板刷上黏土，然后盖上我自己编织的草席。我将随处生长的大麻柏松做成被罩，然后用"雅虎"毛制成的圈套捕到的各种鸟的羽毛填充进去，这些鸟的肉也是非常美味的食物。我用自己的小刀做了两把椅子，栗色小马则帮我分担了脏活累活。当我的衣服磨烂了，我就用兔子皮和另一种和兔子差不多大的美丽的动物的皮毛做了几身新衣服，这种动物名叫"奴赫诺赫"，它的皮上覆盖着一层柔软的绒毛。我还用这两种皮做了几双非常结实的袜子。我的鞋底是用

about the same size, called *nnuhnoh*, the skin of which is covered with a fine down. Of these I also made very tolerable stockings. I soled my shoes with wood which I cut from a tree, and fitted to the upper leather; and when this was worn out, I supplied it with the skins of *Yahoos* dried in the sun. I often got honey out of hollow trees, which I mingled with water, or ate with my bread. No man could more verify the truth of these two maxims, *That nature is very easily satisfied*; and, *That necessity is the mother of invention*. I enjoyed perfect health of body and tranquillity of mind; I did not find the treachery or inconstancy of a friend, nor the injuries of a secret or open enemy. I had no occasion of bribing, flattering or pimping, to procure the favour of any great man or of his minion. I wanted no fence against fraud or oppression: here was neither physician to destroy my body, nor lawyer to ruin my fortune; no informer to watch my words and actions, or forge accusations against me for hire: here were no gibers, censurers, backbiters, pick-pockets, highwaymen, housebreakers, attorneys, bawds, buffoons, gamesters, politicians, wits, splenetics, tedious talkers, controvertists, ravishers, murderers, robbers, virtuosos; no leaders or followers of party and faction; no encouragers to vice, by

树上砍下来的木片做成的，安在皮质的鞋面底下，鞋皮烂了我就用晒干的“雅虎”皮来填充。我经常从中空的树中找到蜂蜜，兑些水喝或是就面包吃。没人能比我更好地诠释这两句箴言，“人的需要很容易满足”，还有“需要是发明之母”。我体格康健，心平气和，我身边没有一个背信弃义反复无常的朋友，也没有暗中谋害的小人或是光明正大的仇敌。我也无须用行使贿赂，阿谀奉承或是拉皮条等下作的手段去博得任何大人物或是它们下属的欢心。我无须防范别人的欺诈或迫害。没有给我身体造成伤害的庸医，也没有让我倾家荡产的律师；没有时刻监视我言行的奸细，也没有捏造指控诽谤我的受雇者。这里没有人对他人讥笑讽刺，横加指责，背后诽谤；也没有人小偷小摸，拦路抢劫，入室行窃；没有律师、鸨母、小丑、赌棍、政客、才子、怪胎；也没有乏味的演说家、辩论者、强奸犯、杀人犯、强盗、艺术大师；没有政党和宗派的领导及其走狗；也没有用坏榜样引诱犯罪的教唆犯；没有地牢、斧头、绞架、鞭笞刑柱或颈手枷，也没有欺诈的店主和技师；没有傲慢、虚荣、假模假样；没有纨绔子弟、流氓恶棍、醉鬼、站街妓女和梅毒病人；没有夸夸其谈挥金如土的淫荡的贵妇；没有愚蠢却又自以为是的学

seducement or examples: no dungeon, axes, gibbets, whipping-posts, or pillories: no cheating shopkeepers or mechanics: no pride, vanity or affectation: no fops, bullies, drunkards, strolling whores, or poxes: no ranting, lewd, expensive wives: no stupid, proud pedants: no importunate, overbearing, quarrelsome, noisy, roaring, empty, conceited, swearing companions: no scoundrels, raised from the dust for the sake of their vices, or nobility thrown into it on account of their virtues: no lords, fiddlers, judges or dancing-masters.

究；没有纠缠不休、蛮横无理、寻衅滋事、吵吵嚷嚷、大吼大叫、脑袋空空、自负自大、口出秽言的同伴；没有恶贯满盈却平步青云的无赖，也没有因为品德高尚却被贬为平民的贵族；没有官人老爷、提琴家、法官和舞蹈老师。

I had the favour of being admitted to several *Houyhnhnms*, who came to visit or dine with my master, where his honour graciously suffered me to wait in the room, and listen to their discourse. Both he and his company would often descend to ask me questions, and receive my answers. I had also sometimes the honour of attending my master in his visits to others. I never presumed to speak, except in answer to a question, and then I did it with inward regret, because it was a loss of so much time for improving myself: but I was infinitely delighted, with the station of an humble auditor in such conversations, where nothing passed but what was useful, expressed in the fewest and most significant words; where the greatest *decency* was observed, without the least degree of ceremony; where no

我有幸被允许见到那些来拜访我主人并一起吃饭的“慧骃”，它十分慷慨地允许我留在房间候命，并聆听它们的交谈。它和它的客人经常屈尊向我提问，并认真听取我的答案。有时我也十分荣幸能与我主人一起出访它的朋友。我从不敢妄言，除非有问题需要我回答，即便如此我也感到满心羞愧，因为这让我失去了如此多的改进自我的时间，但我却对能在这样的对话中做一个谦虚的听众感到无比欣喜。它们从不说一句废话，语言极简却极具分量；它们举止万分体面却一点都不流于形式；说话者总是既能满足自己也能取悦别人；没有人中途打断，没有冗长乏味的对话，不会发生争执，也不会观点不一。它们达成一个共识，那就是当人们聚在一起，短时间的沉默会

person spoke without being pleased himself, and pleasing his companions: where there was no interruption, tediousness, heat, or difference of sentiments. They have a notion, that when people are met together, a short silence doth much improve conversation: this I found to be true; for during those little intermissions of talk, new ideas would arise in their minds, which very much enlivened the discourse. Their subjects are generally on friendship and benevolence, on order and economy, sometimes upon the visible operations of nature, or ancient traditions; upon the bounds and limits of virtue, upon the unerring rules of reason, or upon some determinations, to be taken at the next great assembly; and often upon the various excellencies of *poetry*. I may add without vanity, that my presence often gave them sufficient matter for discourse, because it afforded my master an occasion of letting his friends into the history of me and my country, upon which they were all pleased to descant in a manner not very advantageous to human kind; and for that reason I shall not repeat what they said: only I may be allowed to observe, that his honour, to my great admiration, appeared to understand the nature of *Yahoos* in all countries, much better than myself. He went through all our vices and follies, and discovered many which I had never

让对话更加丰富。这一点我深以为然，因为在谈话中短暂的间隔里，它们的脑海中会浮现出新的想法，而这使得对谈格外生动活力。它们的话题基本上集中于友谊和仁爱，秩序与经济，有时会谈到大自然中可见的活动，或是自古以来的传统；它们畅谈美德的界限和范畴；理性、不偏不倚的正确法则；它们还会谈到下一次全国代表大会会做出哪些决议；还常常探讨诗歌的种种美妙。我可以毫不虚荣地补充，我的出席也为它们的对话带来了丰富的谈资，因为这给了我主人向它的朋友们介绍我和我的祖国历史的机会，它们都十分乐于详细地谈起这些，而这对于人类而言并不十分中听；因此我对它们的话不再赘述。不过有一点我想请大家允许我提到，那就是令我万分敬佩的是，我的主人似乎比我还要了解所有国家里“雅虎”的特性。它将我们所有的罪行和蠢事一一道来，还发现了许多我从未向它提起过的事，它仅仅通过设想在它国家里的“雅虎”们若是具有一点点理性的话，将会发展到何等地步，它还颇为肯定地总结道：这是一种多么邪恶而可怜的生物！

mentioned to him, by only supposing what qualities a *Yahoo* of their country, with a small proportion of reason, might be capable of exerting; and concluded, with too much probability, how vile as well as miserable such a creature must be.

I freely confess, that all the little knowledge I have of any value, was acquired by the lectures I received from my master, and from hearing the discourses of him and his friends; to which I should be prouder to listen, than to dictate to the greatest and wisest assembly in *Europe*. I admired the strength, comeliness, and speed of the inhabitants; and such a constellation of virtues in such amiable persons produced in me the highest veneration. At first, indeed, I did not feel that natural awe, which the *Yahoos* and all other animals bear toward them, but it grew upon me by decrees, much sooner than I imagined, and was mingled with a respectful love and gratitude, that they would condescend to distinguish me from the rest of my species.

我直率地坦承，我所有的那点有用的知识都来源于我的主人和它与它朋友们的对话，比起聆听欧洲那些最伟大最睿智的人们的话语，能够聆听它们的对话我要更为自豪。对这个国家居民的力量、美丽与速度，我敬佩不已；这样一个有着璀璨星辰一般美德的民族使我油然而生最崇高的敬意。事实上，一开始我确实无法理解为什么“雅虎”和其他的动物会如此自然地敬畏它们，然而之后，我对它们生出敬畏比我想象的要快许多，而且这敬畏中还夹杂着敬爱和感激，因为它们愿意俯就认为我与我的同类们并不相同。

When I thought of my family, my friends, my countrymen, or the human race in general, I considered them as they really were, *Yahoos* in shape and disposition, perhaps a little more civilized, and qualified with the gift of speech, but making no other use of reason, than to

当我想起我的家人、朋友、同胞或是整个人类时，我认为他们从形体和性格来看，依然是真正的“雅虎”，或许只是略微文明开化，更能言会道罢了，但他们的理性却只用来加倍犯下的恶。而相比之下在这个国家中他们的兄弟却只具

improve and multiply those vices, whereof their brethren in this country had only the share that nature allotted them. When I happened to behold the reflection of my own form in a lake or fountain, I turned away my face in horror and detestation of myself, and could better endure the sight of a common *Yahoo,* than of my own person. By conversing with the *Houyhnhnms*, and looking upon them with delight, I fell to imitate their gait and gesture, which is now grown into an habit, and my friends often tell me in a blunt way, that *I trot like a horse*; which, however, I take for a great compliment: Neither shall I disown, that in speaking I am apt to fall into the voice and manner of the *Houyhnhnms*, and hear myself ridiculed on that account without the least mortification.

有一些天性的恶。当我恰好在一面湖或是一口泉旁边看到自己的倒影时，就会因为恐惧和厌憎别过脸去，我宁愿忍受一只普通“雅虎”的模样也好过现在自己的样子。因为常常跟“慧骃”交谈，我很喜欢看到它们的样子，我开始模仿它们的步态和姿势，如今已经养成了习惯，我的朋友们经常开门见山地告诉我，我走起来像一匹马，而我却将这视为是对我极大的赞美。我也不得不承认，我说话的语调和习惯也常常模仿“慧骃”的样子，就算人们因此而讥笑我，我也一点也不觉得羞耻。

In the midst of all this happiness, and when I looked upon myself to be fully settled for life, my master sent for me one morning a little earlier than his usual hour. I observed by his countenance that he was in some perplexity, and at a loss how to begin what he had to speak. After a short silence, he told me, he did not know how I would take what he was going to say: that in the last general assembly, when the affair of the *Yahoos* was entered upon, the representatives had taken offence at his keeping a *Yahoo* (meaning myself) in his

然而，就在我泡在蜜罐里以为自己会舒适安定地度过一生时，一天早上比通常要早的时间，主人叫我过去。我从它的面容看出它正被什么事困扰着，不知如何开口。一阵短暂的沉默过去了，它说，它不知道听了它将要说的话我听了会是怎样的心情：上次全国代表大会当“雅虎”的话题被提起时，代表们都对于它家养了一只“雅虎”（也就是我）而表示不满，而且它对待我更像是对待“慧骃”而不是对待一只畜生。人们都知道它时常与我

family more like a *Houyhnhnm,* than a brute animal. that he was known frequently to converse with me, as if he could receive some advantage or pleasure in my company: that such a practice was not agreeable to reason or nature, nor a thing ever heard of before among them. the assembly did therefore *exhort* him, either to employ me like the rest of my species, or command me to swim back to the place from whence I came. that the first of these expedients was utterly rejected by all the *Houyhnhnms,* who had ever seen me at his house or their own: for they alleged, that because I had some rudiments of reason, added to the natural pravity of those animals, it was to be feared, I might be able to seduce them into the woody and mountainous parts of the country, and bring them in troops by night to destroy the *Houyhnhnms'* cattle, as being naturally of the ravenous kind, and averse from labour.

交谈，仿佛它与我在一起就能受益良多且乐趣非凡一样。它们认为它这番做法与常理和天性相悖，且前所未闻。因此大会劝诫它，要么像对待我同类那样奴役我，要么就命我游回我原来的地方。第一种计策受到所有曾经在主人家或是他们家见过我的“慧骃”们的彻底反对，那是因为我身上除了动物生来具有的野性之外，还有几分理智，它们得提防这一点，我可能会将“雅虎”们引诱到这个国家的山林里，到了夜晚再将它们聚集到一起去破坏“慧骃”们的家畜，因为我们天性就十分贪婪，不愿付出劳动。

My master added, that he was daily pressed by the *Houyhnhnms* of the neighbourhood to have the assembly's *exhortation* executed, which he could not put off much longer. He doubted it would be impossible for me to swim to another country, and therefore wished I would contrive some sort of vehicle resembling those I had described to him, that might carry me on the sea, in which work I

我的主人还说，附近的“慧骃”每日都来施压，让它遵循代表大会的告诫，它再也没法拖下去了。它对于我能否游到另一个国家十分怀疑，因此它希望我能设法造出那种我曾向它描述过的交通工具，可以载着我漂洋过海，而它可以让它自己的仆人和它邻居家的仆人帮助我完成这项工作。它还总结说，它自己倒是很乐意让我留在它身

should have the assistance of his own servants, as well as those of his neighbours. He concluded, that for his own part he could have been content to keep me in his service as long as I lived, because he found I had cured myself of some bad habits and dispositions, by endeavouring, as far as my inferior nature was capable, to imitate the *Houyhnhnms*.

边一辈子服侍它，因为它发现我尽管天性卑劣，但却努力学习“慧骃”而摒弃了自身的坏毛病和坏品行。

I should here observe to the reader, that a decree of the general assembly in this country, is expressed by the word *hnhloayn*, which signifies an exhortation; as near as I can render it: for they have no conception how a rational creature can be *compelled*, but only advised, or *exhorted*, because no person can disobey reason, without giving up his claim to be a rational creature.

这里我要向读者们声明，这个国家的全国代表大会的法令叫做“赫恩赫娄阿乌恩”，这意味着一种“郑重劝告”，这是我所能想到的最近似的含义了。因为它们对于如何强迫一种理性动物没有任何概念，只能建议或是劝告，因为没人会违背理性，否则就代表着它放弃做理性动物的权利。

I was struck with the utmost grief and despair at my master's discourse, and being unable to support the agonies I was under, I fell into a swoon at his foot; When I came to myself, he told me that he concluded I had been dead. (for these people are subject to no such imbecilities of nature.) I answered, in a faint voice, that death would have been too great an happiness; that although I could not blame the assembly's *exhortation*, or the urgency of his friends; yet, in my weak and corrupt judgment, I thought it might consist with reason to have been less rigorous. that I

听完主人的一番话，我万分悲痛绝望，我实在无法承受我所遭遇的痛苦，晕倒在它脚下。当我恢复意识之后，它告诉我它以为我已经死了（因为“慧骃”们不可能如此低能）。我用微弱的声音回答说，要是能死的话倒是莫大的幸福了。虽然我不能责怪大会作出这样的劝告，也无法责怪它的朋友的督促，然而以我微弱而不太正确的判断来说，它们对我没有那么严厉也算是理性吧。我连一里格都游不了，而离它们最近的陆地距离也超过100里格。而要想做一艘小小的

could not swim a league, and probably the nearest land to theirs might be distant above an hundred: that many materials, necessary for making a small vessel to carry me off, were wholly wanting in this country, which, however, I would attempt in obedience and gratitude to his honour, although I concluded the thing to be impossible, and therefore looked on myself as already devoted to destruction. that the certain prospect of an unnatural death, was the least of my evils: for, supposing I should escape with life by some strange adventure, how could I think with temper, of passing my days among *Yahoos*, and relapsing into my old corruptions, for want of examples to lead and keep me within the paths of virtue. that I knew too well upon what solid reasons all the determinations of the wise *Houyhnhnms* were founded, not to be shaken by arguments of mine, a miserable *Yahoo*; and therefore after presenting him with my humble thanks for the offer of his servants' assistance in making a vessel, and desiring a reasonable time for so difficult a work, I told him I would endeavour to preserve a wretched being; and if ever I returned to *England*, was not without hopes of being useful to my own species, by celebrating the praises of the renowned *Houyhnhnms*, and proposing their virtues to the imitation of mankind.

船离开所需要的许多原料都无法在这个国家找到，然而我还是要试着服从我的主人，虽然我认定这些事都做不到，而我自己肯定也会走上毁灭之路。然而不得善终还算得上是最好的结果呢，因为设想我若能因得什么奇缘幸免一死，想到没有榜样指引我永远在美德的道路上前行，我将要在“雅虎”群中度过一生，重拾以前的恶习和秉性，想到这里我又如何能高兴得起来呢。而我也相当清楚，智慧的“慧骃”们所作出的一切决定都是基于充分而可靠的理由，不可能会被我这样一只可悲的小“雅虎”的说法而动摇，因此对于它大方地提供它的仆人帮助我建造一艘小船，我向它表示了我最谦恭的感谢。同时我乞求它能给我足够的时间来完成这项困难的工作，之后我告诉它，我一定会尽力保住我的小命，如果我还能回到英国，或者还有希望为我的同类们带来些益处；我会讴歌众所周知的“慧骃”的美德，并号召全人类都效仿它们。

My master in a few words made me a very gracious reply, allowed me the space of two *months* to finish my boat; and ordered the sorrel nag, my fellow servant (for so at this distance I may presume to call him) to follow my instruction, because I told my master, that his help would be sufficient, and I knew he had a tenderness for me.

我的主人宽厚地给了我简短的答复，它批准我在两个月的时间里完成小船的制造，命令那匹栗色小马也就是我的随行仆人（我们已经如此遥远我因此冒昧地如此叫它）听候我的吩咐，因为我告诉过主人，有它帮忙就足够了，而我知道它对我十分亲厚。

In his company, my first business was to go to that part of the coast, where my rebellious crew had ordered me to be set on shore. I got upon a height, and looking on every side into the sea, fancied I saw a small island, towards the north-east: I took out my pocket-glass, and could then clearly distinguish it above five leagues off, as I computed; but it appeared to the sorrel nag to be only a blue cloud: for, as he had no conception of any country beside his own, so he could not be as expert in distinguishing remote objects at sea, as we who so much converse in that element.

在它的陪伴下，我第一件事就是去被我那群叛徒水手们逼着上岸的海滩去。我站在高处眺望大海的各个方向，我好像看到东北方向有一座小岛，我掏出我的口袋望远镜，然后就清晰地辨明它就在距离我 5 里格的地方（我估算），但对栗色小马来说那不过是一块蓝色的云，因为它除了自己的国家完全不知道还有别的国家，所以它不能辨明大海远处的物体，而我们则不同，在这方面我们十分在行。

After I had discovered this island, I considered no farther; but resolved, it should, if possible, be the first place of my banishment, leaving the consequence to fortune.

在我发现这座小岛之后，我就再无他想，而是决心如果可能的话，那里将是我被放逐的第一个所在，结果如何就交给老天吧。

I returned home, and consulting with the sorrel nag, we went into a copse at some distance, where I with my knife, and he with a sharp flint fastened very

回到家，我和栗色小马商议了一下，我们就来到不远处的一块杂树林里，我用小刀，它用一块尖利的火石（用他们的方式十分巧妙地

artificially, after their manner, to a wooden handle, cut down several oak wattles about the thickness of a walking-staff, and some larger pieces. But I shall not trouble the reader with a particular description of my own mechanics; let it suffice to say, that in six weeks time, with the help of the sorrel nag, who performed the parts that required most labour, I finished a sort of *Indian* canoe, but much larger, covering it with the skins of *Yahoos* well stitched together, with hempen threads of my own making. My sail was likewise composed of the skins of the same animal; but I made use of the youngest I could get, the older being too tough and thick, and I likewise provided myself with four paddles. I laid in a stock of boiled flesh, of rabbits and fowls, and took with me two vessels, one filled with milk, and the other with water.

将它绑在一根木条上），砍下了几根大约有手杖那么粗的橡树枝，还有一些更粗的树枝。不过我不想详述我如何完成苦工而令读者厌烦，简要地说，就是在6周的时间里，在栗色小马的鼎力相助之下（它干了最重的活儿），我完成了一只印第安式的小船，不过规模要大许多。我用自己搓的麻线将一张张“雅虎”皮穿在一起将船完整地包裹起来。我的帆也是用“雅虎”皮制作的，不过是用我所能找到的最幼小的“雅虎”的皮，因为老“雅虎”的皮毛太粗太厚。我还给自己做了4支桨。我储存了一些煮熟的兔肉和禽肉，带上两只罐子，一只装着牛奶，一只装着水。

I tried my canoe in a large pond near my master's house, and then corrected in it what was amiss; stopping all the chinks with *Yahoos'* tallow, till I found it staunch, and able to bear me, and my freight. and when it was as complete as I could possibly make it, I had it drawn on a carriage very gently by *Yahoos* to the seaside, under the conduct of the sorrel nag, and another servant.

我在我主人屋子旁边的一个大池塘里试了一下我的小船，改善了不足的地方，再用“雅虎”的油脂把所有的裂缝都封住。直到小船已经十分牢固，足以承受我和我的货物。当我做完了我所能做的一切之后，我让“雅虎”们将小船十分小心地放到一架车上，在栗色小马和另一名仆人的指挥下拉到了海边。

When all was ready, and the day came for my departure, I took leave of my

万事俱备，就到了我要离开的日子。我告别了我的主人夫妇一

master and lady, and the whole family, my eyes flowing with tears and my heart quite sunk with grief. But his honour, out of curiosity, and perhaps, (if I may speak without vanity) partly out of kindness, was determined to see me in my canoe, and got several of his neighbouring friends to accompany him. I was forced to wait above an hour for the tide, and then observing the wind very fortunately bearing towards the island, to which I intended to steer my course, I took a second leave of my master: but as I was going to prostrate myself to kiss his hoof, he did me the honour to raise it gently to my mouth. I am not ignorant how much I have been censured for mentioning this last particular. For my Detractors are pleased to think it improbable, that so illustrious a person should descend to give so great a mark of distinction to a creature so inferior as I. Neither have I forgot, how apt some travellers are to boast of extraordinary favours they have received. But, if these censurers were better acquainted with the noble and courteous disposition of the *Houyhnhnms*, they would soon change their opinion.

I paid my respects to the rest of the *Houyhnhnms* in his honour's company; then getting into my canoe, I pushed off from shore.

家，眼里溢满了泪水，心里充满了无尽哀伤。然而我的主人一方面出于好奇心驱使，或是出于对我的善待（我这么说可不是因为虚荣），决定叫上它附近的朋友一起前去看看我的小船。我被迫等了一个多小时才盼来涨潮，然后我发现幸运的是风向正好朝着我准备起程前往的小岛。我再一次告别我的主人，然而就当我准备俯身亲吻它的蹄子时，它格外赏光将蹄子轻轻举到我的嘴边。我很清楚正因我提到最后这件事而遭受了许多非难。因为诋毁我的人认为这简直是天方夜谭，如此杰出的“慧骃”怎么可能屈尊对我这样低等的生物青眼相待。而我也未曾忘记有些旅行者是多么乐于吹嘘他们所受到的特殊的优待。但是如果这些非难者更了解“慧骃”那高贵礼貌的性格，他们立即就会大为改观的。

我向我主人的同伴们致敬之后，就上了小船离开了海岸。

CHAPTER 11

第十一章

The Author's dangerous Voyage. He arrives at New-Holland, hoping to settle there. Is wounded with an Arrow by one of the Natives. Is seized and carried by Force into a Portuguese Ship. The great Civilities of the Captain. The Author arrives at England.

作者的危难重重的航行。他抵达新荷兰，希望能够安居于此。他被其中一个当地土著用箭射伤，被人抓住并强行带往一艘葡萄牙人的船上。船长热情地款待了他。作者到达了英国。

I began this desperate voyage on *February* 15, 1714/15, at 9 o'clock in the morning. The wind was very favourable; however, I made use at first only of my paddles, but considering I should soon be weary, and that the wind might chop about, I ventured to set up my little sail; and thus, with the help of the tide, I went at the rate of a league and a half an hour, as near as I could guess. My master and his friends continued on the shore, till I was almost out of sight; and I often heard the sorrel nag (who always loved me) crying out, *Hnuy illa nyha majah Yahoo*, Take care of thyself, gentle *Yahoo*.

我于1714年（也许是1715年）2月15日，上午9时开始了这次铤而走险的旅程。风向十分合意，然而一开始我只敢用桨划，但想到这样下去我会很快疲惫不堪，而风也可能会转向，于是我冒险扯起了我的小帆。因此在潮水的推动下，我以每小时一里格半的速度前进着（这是我最接近的估计了）。我的主人和它的朋友还在岸边一直到我已经消失在视线之外才离开。我还时时听到那匹栗色小马在喊（它一直很喜欢我）："赫奴伊·伊拉·奴哈·玛加赫·雅虎。多保重，温顺的'雅虎'！"

My design was, if possible, to discover some small island uninhabited, yet sufficient by my labour to furnish me with the necessaries of life, which I would have thought a greater happiness than to be first

我的计划是，如果可能，就找到一座无人占领的小岛，即使只有我一个人也足以自给自足，这样的生活在我看来可比那些欧洲最优雅的宫廷里的首相大臣幸福多了。

minister in the politest court of *Europe*; so horrible was the idea I conceived of returning to live in the society, and under the government of *Yahoos*. For in such a solitude as I desired, I could at least enjoy my own thoughts, and reflect with delight on the virtues of those inimitable *Houyhnhnms*, without an opportunity of degenerating into the vices and corruptions of my own species.

一想到回到那个社会就要臣服于“雅虎”的统治之下，我就觉得十分恐惧。因为要是能过上我所期待的隐居生活，至少我能尽情地思考，从那些令我无法望其项背的“慧骃”的美德中获得深远的影响，而免于和我的同类同流合污一起作恶。

The reader may remember what I related when my crew conspired against me, and confined me to my cabin. how I continued there several weeks without knowing what course we took; and when I was put ashore in the long-boat, how the sailors told me with oaths, whether true or false, that they knew not in what part of the world we were. However, I did then believe us to be about ten degrees *southward* of the *Cape of Good Hope*, or about 45 degrees *southern* latitude, as I gathered from some general words I overheard among them, being I supposed to the *south-east* in their intended voyage to *Madagascar*. And although this were little better than conjecture, yet I resolved to steer my course *eastward*, hoping to reach the *south-west* coast of *New Holland*, and perhaps some such island as I desired, lying *westward* of it. The wind was full *west*, and by six in the evening I computed I had gone *eastward* at least

读者可能记得，我之前曾提到过，我的那些水手是如何密谋背叛我，将我关在船舱里。我待在那儿好几个星期，完全不知道我们朝着哪个方向去了，当我被押上舢板送上岸时，那些水手还指天发誓说他们也不知道我们身处何方，鬼知道是真是假。然而从我听到的他们对话的只言片语推断，我们应该是位于好望角以东大约 10°的地方或者南纬 45°左右，我想他们是准备一路向东南方到马达加斯加去。虽然这仅仅是有待考证的猜想，但我还是决定向东行驶，希望能够到达新荷兰的西南岸，或许我想要的那种无人小岛就在新荷兰西岸的某个地方。这时风向正西，到晚上 6 点时，我估算我已经至少向东行了 18 里格。这时我发现在大约半里格外有一座非常小的岛屿，很快我就到了那里。这座岛只由一块岩石构成，有一处由暴雨天然冲刷出的港湾。我将我的小船停泊在港湾里，

eighteen leagues, when I spied a very small island about half a league off, which I soon reached. It was nothing but a rock with one creek naturally arched by the force of tempests. Here I put in my canoe, and climbing a part of the rock, I could plainly discover land to the *east*, extending from *south* to *north*. I lay all night in my canoe; and repeating my voyage early in the morning, I arrived in seven hours to the *south-east* point of *New Holland*. This confirmed me in the opinion I have long entertained, that the *maps* and *charts* place this country at least three degrees more to the *east* than it really is; which thought I communicated many years ago to my worthy friend Mr. *Herman Moll*, and gave him my reasons for it, although he hath rather chosen to follow other authors.

爬上一处岩石，看得明明白白，小岛的东面有一块从南延伸到北的陆地。我在小船上过了一夜，次日早上继续航行，7 小时之后我到达了新荷兰的西南角。这使我长时间以来持有的想法得到证实，那就是地图和海图把这个国家的位置标错了，比实际情况向东至少偏移了 3°。这一点在许多年前我就和我的好友赫尔曼·莫尔[1]先生谈过，向他阐述了我的理由，然而他还是更愿意听从别的作者的意见。

I saw no inhabitants in the place where I landed, and being unarmed, I was afraid of venturing far into the country. I found some shellfish on the shore, and eat them raw, not daring to kindle a fire, for fear of being discovered by the natives. I continued three days feeding on oysters and limpets, to save my own provisions; and I fortunately found a brook of excellent water, which gave me great relief.

我登陆之后没有发现一个居民，但是因为手无寸铁我不敢深入太远。我在海滩上发现了一些蚌蛤，因为害怕点火被当地居民发觉我只能生吞了它们。为了将自己的补给省下来，连着 3 天我都只吃些牡蛎和虫戚子。而我的运气很好，发现了一溪极好的淡水，这让我大感欣慰。

On the fourth day, venturing out early a

第四天的时候，我走得有些

[1] 赫尔曼·莫尔（1654~1732）英国绘图师、雕刻师和出版商。

little too far, I saw twenty or thirty natives upon a height, not above five hundred yards from me. They were stark naked, men, women, and children, round a fire, as I could discover by the smoke. One of them spied me, and gave notice to the rest; five of them advanced towards me leaving the women and children at the fire. I made what haste I could to the shore, and getting into my canoe, shoved off: the savages observing me retreat, ran after me; and before I could get far enough into the sea, discharged an arrow, which wounded me deeply on the inside of my left knee (I shall carry the mark to my grave). I apprehended the arrow might be poisoned, and paddling out of the reach of their darts (being a calm day) I made a shift to suck the wound, and dress it as well as I could.

远，看到离我不到500码的地方有二三十个土著居民站在高处，全都赤条条的，从烟雾判断男女老少都围着一团火。他们中的一个发现了我，通知了其他人，他们中的5个男人丢下妇女和小孩留在火旁，向我走来。我用最快的速度冲向岸边，跳上小船驶离，这些野人发现我要逃跑就跟在我后面跑，我还没来得及划开多远，他们就放箭深深地射中了我的左膝（这个伤疤要跟着我入土了）。我担心箭上有毒，划离他们的射程之后（好在那天没风），就迅速地将伤口的血吸出然后尽可能地包扎好。

I was at a loss what to do, for I durst not return to the same landing-place, but stood to the *north*, and was forced to paddle; for the wind although very gentle was against me, blowing *north-west*. As I was looking about for a secure landing-place, I saw a sail to the *north north-east*, which appearing every minute more visible, I was in some doubt, whether I should wait for them or no, but at last my detestation of the *Yahoo* race prevailed, and turning my canoe, I sailed and paddled together to the *south*, and got into the same creek

我完全不知道接下去该怎么办，因为我没胆再回到原来登陆的地点，不得不划桨向北驶去。风虽然不大但却是从西北方向迎面吹向我。就在我四处寻找一个安全的着陆地点时，我看到一艘船正驶向正北以东，它正越来越近。我有些犹豫要不要停下来等他们，但最终我对于“雅虎”一族的憎恶占了上风，我掉转小船帆桨并用地向南驶去，又到了我早上出发的那个港湾。要知道我宁肯把我自己交到那群野人手中也不愿意与欧洲的“雅

from whence I set out in the morning, choosing rather to trust myself among these *barbarians*, than live with *European Yahoos*. I drew up my canoe as close as I could to the shore, and hid myself behind a stone by the little brook, which, as I have already said, was excellent water.

虎”们生活在一起。我尽量靠岸停船，自己则藏身于小溪旁的一块石头 后面，我已经说过，那条小溪的水十分清冽。

The ship came within half a league of this creek, and sent her long-boat with vessels to take in fresh water (for the place it seems was very well known) but I did not observe it till the boat was almost on shore and it was too late to seek another hiding-place. The seamen at their landing observed my canoe, and rummaging it all over, easily conjectured that the owner could not be far off. Four of them well-armed, searched every cranny and lurking-hole, till at last they found me flat on my face behind the stone. They gazed a while in admiration at my strange uncouth dress, my coat made of skins, my wooden-soled shoes, and my furred stockings; from whence, however, they concluded I was not a native of the place, who all go naked. One of the seamen, in Portuguese bid me rise, and asked who I was. I understood that language very well, and getting upon my foot, said, I was a poor *Yahoo* banished from the *Houyhnhnms*, and desired they would please to let me depart. They admired to hear me answer them in their own tongue,

那条船距离港湾不到半里格，水手们放下舢板带着容器前来取淡水（这水似乎众人皆知）。然而我一直到水手们快上了岸才发现它，而这时再找另一处藏身地已经太迟。水手们一上岸就发现了我的小船，他们将小船从头到尾搜查了一番，不费吹灰之力就想到船的主人肯定就在附近。4 个全副武装的水手没有放过任何一处岩缝和可掩藏的洞穴，终于他们发现了石头后面脸朝下趴着的我。他们羡慕地盯着我奇特而粗陋的衣服看了好一会儿，我的外套是毛皮做的，我的鞋子是木底的，我还穿着绒毛袜子。而从这些他们得出结论，我不是当地土著，因为他们都一丝不挂。其中一个水手用葡萄牙语把我喊了起来，并问我是什么人。我精通葡萄牙语，于是我站起来说道，我是一只可怜的“雅虎”，被“慧骃”放逐了，希望他们能好心放了我。他们听到我用他们的语言回答他们十分惊讶，而从我的长相来看我应该是个欧洲人，但却不明白我所说的“雅虎”和“慧骃”是什么

and saw by my complexion I must be an *European*; but were at a loss to know what I meant by *Yahoos* and *Houyhnhnms*, and at the same time fell a laughing at my strange tone in speaking, which resembled the neighing of a horse. I trembled all the while betwixt fear and hatred: I again desired leave to depart, and was gently moving to my canoe; but they laid hold of me, desiring to know, what country I was of? whence I came? with many other questions. I told them "I was born in *England*, from whence I came about five years ago, and then their country and ours were at peace. I therefore hoped they would not treat me as an enemy, since I meant them no harm, but was a poor *Yahoo,* seeking some desolate place where to pass the remainder of his unfortunate life.

东西。并且与此同时，因为我说话的腔调很奇怪，活像一匹马在嘶吼，他们全都轰然大笑。我又怕又恨不禁发起抖来，我又一次乞求他们能放我离开，并且慢慢地向我的小船移去，但他们抓牢我追问我来自哪个国家，从哪里来，等等许多问题。我告诉他们，我生于英国，大约 5 年前离开那里，那时他们国家和我的祖国十分和睦。因此我希望他们不要将我看做敌人，因为我对他们并无恶意，只是一只可怜的"雅虎"罢了，想要找到一处僻静的所在度过他那不幸的余生。

When they began to talk, I thought I never heard or saw anything so unnatural; for it appeared to me as monstrous as if a dog or a cow should speak in England, or a *Yahoo* in *Houyhnhnm-land*. The honest *Portuguese* were equally amazed at my strange dress, and the odd manner of delivering my words, which however they understood very well. They spoke to me with great humanity, and said they were sure their captain would carry me *gratis* to *Lisbon*, from whence I might return to my own country; that two of the seamen

当他们一开口说话，我觉得我从未听过或是见过如此不同寻常的事情，因为这对于我就如同在英国一只狗或一头牛会说话，或者在"慧骃"国的一只"雅虎会说话一样令人匪夷所思。"那些老实的葡萄牙人也同样对于我奇怪的打扮和古怪的说话方式感到惊奇，然而尽管如此他们还是毫无困难地听懂了。他们和我说话的口气十分友好，并且说他们敢肯定他们的船长乐意无偿将我带回里斯本，在那里我就能回到我自己的国家。他们派

would go back to the ship, inform the captain of what they had seen, and receive his orders; in the mean time, unless I would give my solemn oath not to fly, they would secure me by force. I thought it best to comply with their proposal. They were very curious to know my story, but I gave them very little satisfaction; and they all conjectured, that my misfortunes had impaired my reason. In two hours the boat, which went laden with vessels of water, returned with the captain's commands to fetch me on board. I fell on my knees to preserve my liberty; but all was in vain, and the men having tied me with cords, heaved me into the boat, from whence I was taken into the ship, and from thence into the captain's cabin.

了两名水手返回船上，将他们所见告知船长，然后接到他的命令，与此同时他们表示除非我郑重发誓绝不逃跑，不然他们就用武力将我制伏。我想还是听从他们的要求为妙。他们都对我的经历十分好奇，但我却不愿满足他们，因此他们全都猜想是我不幸的际遇毁掉了我的理智。两小时之后，装满淡水返程的小船回来了，还带来了船长的指令要抓我上船。我双膝跪地，祈求他们放我自由，然而一切都是徒劳，这些人用绳子将我捆起来丢上小船，接着我就被带上大船，进到船长的船舱里去。

His name was *Pedro de Mendez*, he was a very courteous and generous person; he entreated me to give some account of myself, and desired to know what I would eat or drink; said, "I should be used as well as himself, and spoke so many obliging things, that I wondered to find such civilities from a *Yahoo*. However, I remained silent and sullen; I was ready to faint at the very smell of him and his men. At last I desired something to eat out of my own canoe; but he ordered me a chicken and some excellent wine, and then directed that I should be put to bed in a very clean cabin. I would not undress

船长的名字叫彼得罗·德·孟德斯，是个彬彬有礼又豪爽大方的人。他请我简单地介绍了自己，然后问我想吃什么或是喝点什么。他还说我的地位和他一样，还有许多客气话，我对这样一只“雅虎”也能如此文明有礼而感到十分奇怪。然而我还是一言不发闷闷不乐。一闻到他和他手下身上的味道，我就几乎要昏过去。最后我想要一些我自己小船上的食物来吃，他却给我要了一只鸡和好酒，还下令将我带到一间非常干净的船舱去下榻。我不想脱去衣服，只好穿戴整齐地躺了下来。又过了半个小时，我估摸

myself, but lay on the bedclothes, and in half an hour stole out, when I thought the crew was at dinner, and getting to the side of the ship was going to leap into the sea, and swim for my life, rather than continue among *Yahoos*. But one of the seamen prevented me, and having informed the captain, I was chained to my cabin.

着水手们都在吃饭就溜了出去，跑到船边准备跳进海里；我宁愿在海上漂一辈子，也不愿和“雅虎”们生活。然而一名船员制止了我，并通报了船长，我就被锁在我的船舱里。

After dinner *Don Pedro* came to me, and desired to know my reason for so desperate an attempt: assured me he only meant to do me all the service he was able; and spoke so very movingly, that at last I descended to treat him like an animal which had some little portion of reason. I gave him a very short relation of my voyage; of the conspiracy against me by my own men, of the country where they set me on shore, and of my three years residence there. All which he looked upon as if it were a dream or a vision; whereat I took great offence; for I had quite forgot the faculty of lying, so peculiar to *Yahoos*, in all countries where they preside, and consequently the disposition of suspecting truth in others of their own species. I asked him, whether it were the custom in his country to *say the thing that was not?* I assured him, “I had almost forgot what he meant by falsehood, and if I had lived a thousand years in *Houyhnhnmland*, I should never have heard a lie from the meanest servant; that I

晚饭后，彼得罗先生来见我，想知道我为何要奋不顾身地逃走。他向我保证，他只想尽可能地帮助我，他的言语非常打动人，最后我勉强将他也看做是有几分理性的动物。我十分简要地向他讲述了我航海的经历，告诉他我的水手是如何背叛了我，他们将我丢到一个国家的海岸上，而我在那儿生活了 3 年。他将我的话都视作是梦境或是臆想，这让我十分愤恨，因为我差不多已经忘了如何撒谎，说谎是“雅虎”独有的本领，存在于所有由他们统治的国度里，以至于他们连同类所说的话也抱有怀疑。我问他在他的国家里是不是有着说些“莫须有”的风俗？我向他保证说，我几乎已经忘了他所谓的“虚假”的意思了，而就算我在“慧骃”国住上 1000 年，也不会听到最卑贱的仆人口中有一句谎言。我可不在乎他是不是相信我的话，但尽管如此，为了回报他的厚爱，我也可以原谅他腐朽的本性。而他若提出任何异议我也会尽可能地回答，这

was altogether indifferent whether he believed me or not; but however, in return for his favours, I would give so much allowance to the corruption of his nature, as to answer any objection he would please to make, and then he might easily discover the truth.

样他就能很容易地发现事实真相。

The captain, a wise man, after many endeavours to catch me tripping in some part of my story, at last began to have a better opinion of my veracity. But he added, that since I professed so inviolable an attachment to truth, I must give him my word and honour to bear him company in this voyage without attempting any thing against my life, or else he would continue me a prisoner till we arrived at *Lisbon*. I gave him the promise he required; but at the same time protested that I would suffer the greatest hardships rather than return to live among *Yahoos*.

船长是位十分有智慧的人，他绞尽脑汁想要从我的故事里找到些漏洞，然而最终却开始相信我所言的真实性了。但他也补充说，既然我已经宣誓所说的每一句话都是真的，那我必须恪守诺言，答应和他一起走完这段航程，绝不再试图轻生，不然他就一直将我囚禁在里斯本。我按他所说的立下誓言，但是同时我还是重申我宁愿忍受最大的困难也不愿意回去和“雅虎”们一起生活。

Our voyage passed without any considerable accident. In gratitude to the captain I sometimes sat with him at his earnest request, and strove to conceal my antipathy against to human kind, although it often broke out, which he suffered to pass without observation. But the greatest part of the day, I confined myself to my cabin, to avoid seeing any of the crew. The captain had often entreated me to strip myself of my savage dress, and offered to lend me the best suit of clothes he had.

我们的航程一路波澜不惊。为了报答船长，有时我也会接受他真诚的请求和他坐在一起，并竭力将我对人类的反感掩藏起来，然而我的厌憎还是常常暴露，好在船长总是装作没有发现。不过一天的绝大部分时间里，我还是待在我的船舱里避免见到任何水手。船长时时恳求我脱下我那身野蛮人的装束，并愿意借给我他最好的衣服。但我却毫不领情，我对于身着“雅虎”穿过的任何东西都相当抵触。我仅仅

This I would not be prevailed on to accept, abhorring to cover myself with any thing that had been on the back of a *Yahoo*. I only desired he would lend me two clean shirts, which having been washed since he wore them, I believed would not so much defile me. These I changed every second day, and washed them myself.

要求他能借给我两件干净的衬衫，在他穿过之后洗过，我想这样就不太会弄脏我的身体。这两件衣服我每两天一换，并亲自清洗它们。

We arrived at *Lisbon*, Nov. 5, 1715. At our landing, the captain forced me to cover myself with his cloak, to prevent the rabble from crowding about me. I was conveyed to his own house, and at my earnest request, he led me up to the highest room backwards. I conjured him to conceal from all persons what I had told him of the *Houyhnhnms*, because the least hint of such a story would not only draw numbers of people to see me, but probably, put me in danger of being imprisoned, or burnt by the *Inquisition*. The captain persuaded me to accept a suit of clothes newly made, but I would not suffer the tailor to take my measure; however, *Don Pedro* being almost of my size, they fitted me well enough. He accoutred me with other necessaries all new, which I aired for twenty-four hours before I would use them.

我们于1715年11月5日抵达里斯本。上岸时，为了防止那群暴民围观我，船长强迫我穿上他的外套。我被带到他自己的家里，在我最诚挚的请求下，他将我安置到屋后最高的一个房间里。我请求他不要向任何人透露我曾告诉过他的有关“慧骃”的事，因为哪怕泄露出一丝一毫，不仅会吸引大批的人来围观，而且我很可能会陷入被宗教法庭囚禁或烧死的危险。船长试图说服我接受一套新做的衣服，但我不能接受裁缝计量我的尺寸，不过还好彼得罗先生和我身量相仿，他给我的两件衣服非常合身。他还给我准备了其他一些全新的必需品，我将它们晾了24小时才使用。

The captain had no wife, nor above three servants, none of which were suffered to attend at meals, and his whole deportment was so obliging, added to very

船长没有妻子，只有3个仆人，他们都不用在吃饭的时候列席待命。他风度翩翩，举止有礼，再加上十分善解人意，以至于我真的开

good *human* understanding, that I really began to tolerate his company. He gained so far upon me, that I ventured to look out of the back window. By degrees I was brought into another room, from whence I peeped into the street, but drew my head back in a fright. In a week's time he seduced me down to the door. I found my terror gradually lessened, but my hatred and contempt seemed to increase. I was at last bold enough to walk the street in his company, but kept my nose well stopped with rue, or sometimes with tobacco.

始喜欢他的陪伴了。他赢得了我极大的好感，以至于我开始大着胆子朝后窗外面张望了。渐渐地我搬进了另一间屋子，从那开始我也敢偷偷向街上看了，但常常看一眼就害怕得把头缩回去。又过了一个星期，我已经可以在他的诱导下走到门口了。我发现我的恐惧渐渐减轻，但我的憎恨和厌恶却与日俱增。最后我已经胆大到可以和他一起在街上散步，但我一直用芸香或是烟草将鼻孔捂得严严实实的。

In ten days, *Don Pedro*, to whom I had given some account of my domestic affairs, put it upon me as a matter of honour and conscience, that I ought to return to my native country, and live at home with my wife and children. He told me, there was an *English* ship in the port just ready to sail, and he would furnish me with all things necessary. It would be tedious to repeat his arguments, and my contradictions. He said it was altogether impossible to find such a solitary island as I had desired to live in; but I might command in my own house, and pass my time in a manner as recluse as I pleased.

由于我已经跟彼得罗先生提到过我家里的一些事情，因此 10 天后他说为了我的名誉和良知，我应该回到我的祖国与我的妻子和孩子生活在一起。他告诉我，港口有一艘去往英国的船就要起航了，他会帮我安排好一切。重复他和我之间的争论太过枯燥无趣。他说根本找不到我想要居住的孤岛，而我完全可以在自己家中获得自主，我想过怎样的隐居生活都可以。

I complied at last, finding I could not do better. I left *Lisbon* the 24th day of November, in an *English* merchant-man, but who was the master I never inquired. *Don Pedro* accompanied me to the ship,

最后我发现，我确实也没有更好的方案，只好妥协。我在 11 月 24 日这天乘坐一艘英国商船离开里斯本，但对于谁是船长我却一无所知。彼得罗先生送我到船上，并

and lent me twenty pounds. He took kind leave of me, and embraced me at parting, which I bore as well as I could. During this last voyage I had no commerce with the master or any of his men, but pretending I was sick kept close in my cabin. On the fifth of *December*, 1715, we cast anchor in the *Downs*, about nine in the morning, and at three in the afternoon I got safe to my house at *Redriff*.

借给我 20 英镑。他十分友好地同我告别，分别的时候还给了我一个拥抱，我只能尽可能忍受。在这最后的旅程中，我从不和船长或是任何水手交谈，而是假装生病一直待在船舱里。1715 年 12 月 5 日上午 9 点钟左右，我们在唐兹抛锚。等到下午 3 点的时候我已经安全抵达我在瑞德里夫的家中。

My wife and family received me with great surprise and joy, because they concluded me certainly dead; but I must freely confess the sight of them filled me only with hatred, disgust, and contempt, and the more by reflecting on the near alliance I had to them. For, although since my unfortunate exile from the *Houyhnhnm* country, I had compelled myself to tolerate the sight of *Yahoos*, and to converse with Don Pedro de Mendez; yet my memory and imaginations were perpetually filled with the virtues and ideas of those exalted *Houyhnhnms*. And when I began to consider, that by copulating with one of the *Yahoo* species I had become a parent of more, it struck me with the utmost shame, confusion, and horror.

我的妻子和家人万分惊讶，欢喜地迎接了我，因为他们以为我肯定已经死了，但我必须坦承，一见到他们，我的心中满满的只有憎恨，恶心和厌恶，且这种感觉因为他们与我是如此亲密的关系而越发严重。因为尽管我已经不幸地被“慧骃”国驱逐出境，不得不忍受见到“雅虎”们，还得同彼得罗·德·孟德斯先生交谈，但那些高贵的“慧骃”们的美德和思想却永远地留在我的记忆和想象之中。每当我想到我曾与一只“雅虎”交配而成了好几只“雅虎”的父亲，我就感到莫大的羞耻，茫然和恐惧。

As soon as I entered the house, my wife took me in her arms, and kissed me, at which having not been used to the touch of that odious animal for so many years, I

我一走进家门，妻子就紧紧抱住我并亲吻我。我已太多年没有触碰这些丑恶的动物了，以至于我昏迷了有将近一个钟头。在我写这本

fell into a swoon for almost an hour. At the time I am writing it is five years since my last return to *England*: During the first year, I could not endure my wife or children in my presence, the very smell of them was intolerable; much less could I suffer them to eat in the same room. To this hour they dare not presume to touch my bread, or drink out of the same cup, neither was I ever able to let one of them take me by the hand. The first money I laid out was to buy two young stone-horses, which I keep in a good stable, and next to them the groom is my greatest favourite; for I feel my spirits revived by the smell he contracts in the stable. My horses understand me tolerably well; I converse with them at least four hours every day. They are strangers to bridle or saddle they live in great amity with me, and friendship to each other.

书的时候，我已经回到英国5年了，在第一年里，我无法忍受妻子或孩子出现在我面前，他们那种特有的气味让我无法忍受，更不要说和他们在一间房里吃饭了。直至此刻他们都不敢碰一下我的面包，或是从我的杯子里喝水，我也从来不和他们中任何一个牵手。我的第一笔花销用来买了两匹小公马，我将它们养在优良的马厩里。除了它们，我最喜欢的就是马夫了，因为他身上那种马厩的气味让我神清气爽。我的马儿很懂我，每天我都要和它们至少说上4个小时的话。我从不给它们佩戴辔头和马鞍。我们相处得其乐融融，它们彼此也有着深厚的友谊。

CHAPTER 12

第十二章

The Author's Veracity. His Design in publishing this Work. His Censure of those Travellers who swerve from the Truth. The Author clears himself from any sinister Ends in writing. An Objection answered. The Method of planting Colonies. His Native Country commended. The Right of the Crown to those Countries described by the Author is justified. The Difficulty of conquering them. The Author takes his last leave of the Reader; proposes his Manner of Living for the future; gives good Advice, and concludes.

作者所叙的真实性。他出版此书的计划。他对于那些颠倒黑白的旅行家的谴责。作者澄清自己在写作中并没有抱有任何不良居心。作者对一则反对的申辩。扩展殖民地的方法。作者赞美自己的祖国。他认为国王有权占领他所描述的那些国家。攻占这些国家的困难之处。作者对读者们的最后道别，提出他日后将如何生活，给出好的建议，全文结束。

Thus, gentle reader, I have given thee a faithful history of my travels for sixteen years and, above seven months, wherein I have not been so studious of ornament as truth. I could perhaps like others have astonished thee with strange improbable tales; but I rather chose to relate plain matter of fact in the simplest manner and style; because my principal design was to inform, and not to amuse thee.

那么亲爱的读者们，我已经将我这 16 年过 7 个月的旅行经历原原本本地讲给你们了。我从未如此忠于事实。我本来可以像别的旅行家那样用荒谬无稽的故事让你们吃惊不已，但我宁愿选择最简单的叙事方式和风格来讲述直白的事实，因为我的初衷是为了传述事实，而非哗众取宠。

It is easy for us who travel into remote countries, which are seldom visited by *Englishmen* or other *Europeans*, to form descriptions of wonderful animals both at

对我们来说，去那些少有英国人和欧洲人旅行的偏远国家旅行并非难事，而描摹那些奇异的海洋陆地生物也轻而易举。然而一个旅

sea and land. Whereas a traveller's chief aim should be to make men wiser and better, and to improve their minds by the bad as well as good example of what they deliver concerning foreign places.

I could heartily wish a law was enacted, that every traveller before he were permitted to publish his voyages, should be obliged to make oath before the *Lord High Chancellor* that all he intended to print was absolutely true to the best of his knowledge; for then the world would no longer be deceived as it usually is, while some writers, to make their works pass the better upon the public, impose the grossest falsities on the unwary reader. I have perused several books of travels with great delight in my younger days; but having since gone over most parts of the globe, and been able to contradict many fabulous accounts from my own observation, it hath given me a great disgust against this part of reading, and some indignation to see the credulity of mankind so impudently abused. Therefore, since my acquaintance were pleased to think my poor endeavours might not be unacceptable to my country, I imposed on myself as a maxim, never to be swerved from, that I would *strictly adhere to truth*; neither indeed can I be ever under the least temptation to vary from it, while I retain in my mind the lectures and example of my noble master,

行家最主要的目的应该是让人们更聪慧，更善良，并且通过讲述外国的善与恶，美与丑来改进人们的思想。

我多么希望能颁布这样一项法律，那就是每一位旅行家在获准发表他的游记之前，都应当在大法官面前宣誓，所要出版的东西全部真实可靠。只有如此世人才不会像往常那样被欺瞒，有些作者为了让他们的作品被更多大众接受，不惜编造弥天大谎欺骗那些不够警惕的读者。在我年轻的时候也曾饶有兴致地细读过许多游记，然而自从我自己走南闯北踏遍地球上大部分地方，并能够根据自己的所见所闻驳斥那些不可信的叙述之后，我见到此类读物就十分倒胃口，并对于有人会如此轻易地被这些骗倒而感到十分愤慨。因此，既然我的朋友们都认为我这本拙劣的心血还可以被我的国家所接受，我就给自己立下一则誓言，永不歪曲事实，忠于真相。事实上我也永远不会被引诱而歪曲事实的本来面目，因为我一直将我那尊贵的主人和其他那些卓越的“慧骃”们的话语和榜样铭记在心，曾经有幸能够虚心倾听它们的教诲，我感到十分荣幸。

and the other illustrious *Houyhnhnms,* of whom I had so long the honour to be an humble hearer.

– Nec si miserum Fortuna Sinonem Finxit, vanum etiam, mendacemque improba finget.

I know very well how little reputation is to be got by writings which require neither genius nor learning, nor indeed any other talent, except a good memory, or an exact *journal*. I know likewise, that writers of travels, like *dictionary*-makers, are sunk into oblivion by the weight and bulk of those who come after, and therefore lie uppermost. And it is highly probable, that such travellers who shall hereafter visit the countries described in this work of mine, may by detecting my errors (if there be any) and adding many new discoveries of their own, justle me out of vogue, and stand in my place, making the world forget that I was ever an author. This indeed would be too great a mortification if I wrote for fame: but, as my sole intention was the PUBLIC GOOD, I cannot be altogether disappointed. For who can read of the virtues I have mentioned in the glorious *Houyhnhnms*, without being ashamed of his own vices, when he considers himself as the reasoning, governing animal of his country? I shall say nothing of those

"……虽然恶运使西农落难，却不能强使他诳语欺人。"

写出这样一本书，除过好记性和准确的日记之外，并不需要多少天才和学识或是其他什么禀赋，也收获不了什么赞誉，这一点我再清楚不过。我还十分清楚，游记作家和编撰字典的人没什么两样，都会被淹没在后来者的更有分量、更浩瀚的作品当中，所谓"长江后浪推前浪"。更有很可能会发生的情况，即那些在我之后去造访我书中所描述的那些国家的旅行家就会发现我所犯下的谬误（如果有的话），然后加上他们自己的许多新发现，如此我就被挤出潮流之外，他们取代我的位置，而我曾也是个作家这一点就渐渐被世界所遗忘。如果说我是为了成名而写作无疑对我来说是莫大的屈辱，实际上我唯一的目的就是为了公众利益。如此我才不会失落。因为那些自认是理智的，统治着我的国家的动物们，读到我提到的那些光辉的"慧骃"的各种美德的人，谁会不为自己犯下的罪恶而感到羞愧呢？对于"雅虎"统治的那些遥远的国度我再也不会多说一个字了，在那里布罗卜

remote nations where *Yahoos* preside, amongst which the least corrupted are the *Brobdingnagians*, whose wise maxims in morality and government, it would be our happiness to observe. But I forbear descanting farther, and rather leave the judicious reader to his own remarks and Applications.

I am not a little pleased that this work of mine can possibly meet with no censurers: for what objections can be made against a writer who relates only plain facts that happened in such distant countries, where we have not the least interest with respect either to trade or negotiations? I have carefully avoided every fault with which common writers of travels are often too justly charged. Besides, I meddle not the least with any *party*, but write without passion, prejudice, or ill will against any man or number of men whatsoever. I write for the noblest end, to inform and instruct mankind, over whom I may, without breach of modesty, pretend to some superiority from the advantages I received by conversing so long among the most accomplished *Houyhnhnms*. I write without any view to profit or praise. I never suffer a word to pass that may look like reflection, or possibly give the least offence even to those who are most ready to take it. So that I hope I may with justice

丁奈格人算得上是最不腐朽的了，如果我们可以学习他们在道德和治理国家方面的种种智慧的准则，那么将是我们莫大的福祉。然而我不想说得太多，让英明公正的读者们自行判断吧。

我的这本书并未遇到什么非难，这让我十分欣慰。不过对于这样一个只是描述发生在如此遥远的国家里的平凡无趣的事实的作者，有什么值得批判的呢？要知道我们对于和他们谈判或是开展贸易都毫无兴趣。我谨慎地避免普通的游记作者经常犯下的错误，当然他们也受到公正的指责。除此之外我对任何政党都退避三舍，我不带任何个人色彩和偏见写作，也并没有掺杂对任何个体或是人群的敌意。我最为高尚的写作目的，是向人们普及见闻，提供指导。毫不谦虚地讲，我的见解超出了普通人的认识，这都源于我曾长时间地和最聪明的“慧骃”们交谈。我不为利益或是赞誉而写作。我从不肯使用任何看起来像是责难的字眼，就连那些总是疑心自己受到批评的人我也尽可能地不去冒犯他们。因此，我希望我能公正无愧地宣称我是一个完全挑不出毛病的作者，任何答辩者、思想家、观察家、批评家、检验家和评论员，都永远对我

pronounce myself an author perfectly blameless, against whom the tribes of Answerers, Considerers, Observers, Reflectors, Detectors, Remarkers, will never be able to find matter for exercising their talents.

的书无计可施，一筹莫展。

I confess, it was whispered to me, that I was bound in duty as a subject of *England*, to have given in a memorial to a secretary of state, at my first coming over; because, whatever lands are discovered by a subject belong to the crown. But I doubt whether our conquests in the countries I treat of, would be as easy as those of *Ferdinando Cortez* over the naked *Americans*. The *Lilliputians* I think, are hardly worth the charge of a fleet and army to reduce them, and I question whether it might be prudent or safe to attempt the *Brobdingnagians*. or whether an *English* army would be much at their ease with the Flying Island over their heads. The *Houyhnhnms,* indeed, appear not to be so well prepared for war, a science to which they are perfect strangers, and especially against missive weapons. However, supposing myself to be a minister of state, I could never give my advice for invading them. Their prudence, unanimity, unacquaintedness with fear, and their love of their country would amply supply all defects in the military art. Imagine twenty thousand of

我承认，有人曾私下对我说作为大英帝国的子民，我有义务在回国之后立即提交一份报告给国务卿，因为一个英国子民所发现的任何土地都属于国王。然而我对我们能否像费迪南多·柯太兹征服赤身裸体的美洲人那样，轻而易举地攻克这些国家心存怀疑。我认为征服利利普特国所获得的好处连派遣一支军队的损耗都比不上，而对于征服巨人国的想法我则怀疑这是否慎重而安全；我也十分怀疑如果有一座飞岛在英国军队头顶上方他们是否还能谈笑风生。说实话，“慧骃”国倒确实不太能应付战争，它们对于战争这门学问，特别是大规模武器完全一无所知。然而假如我是国务卿，我可不会主张去入侵它们。它们稳健、团结、大无畏，且热爱自己的祖国，这些足以弥补它们在军事上的不足。想象一下2万“慧骃”冲进一支欧洲的军队，冲垮队列，掀翻战车，用它们的后蹄将士兵们的脸踩个稀巴烂的样子。因为它们完全称得上拥有奥古斯都的性格：*Recalcitrat undique tutus*。不过与其提议去攻占

them breaking into the midst of an *European* army, confounding the ranks, overturning the carriages, battering the warriors' faces into mummy, by terrible yerks from their hinder hoofs. for they would well deserve the character given to *Augustus; Recalcitrat undique tutus*. But instead of proposals for conquering that magnanimous nation, I rather wish they were in a capacity or disposition to send a sufficient number of their inhabitants for civilizing *Europe*, by teaching us the first principles of honour, justice, truth, temperance, public spirit, fortitude, chastity, friendship, benevolence, and fidelity. The *names* of all which virtues are still retained among us in most languages, and are to be met with in modern as well as ancient authors; which I am able to assert from my own small reading.

But I had another reason which made me less forward to enlarge his majesty's dominions by my discoveries. To say the truth, I had conceived a few scruples with relation to the distributive justice of princes upon those occasions. For instance, a crew of pirates are driven by a storm they know not whither; at length a boy discovers land from the topmast; they go on shore to rob and plunder; they see an harmless people, are entertained with kindness, they give the country a new name, they take formal possession of it for

这个宽宏大量的民族，相反我更愿意它们可以或是乐于派出一支拥有足够的“慧骃”的队伍给欧洲带来先进文明，教会我们有关荣耀、正义、真理、节制、公德、坚韧、贞洁、友谊、仁爱和忠诚等基本原则。这些美德的名字依然保留在我们大多数的语言中，在从古至今的作家作品中也常有提到，就算是我这样只有粗浅阅读量的人也敢断言。

然而对于并不赞成国王陛下将我发现的陆地扩张为他的领地，我还有别的理由。老实说，我对分派诸侯去统辖那些地方颇有些微词。举例来说，一群海盗被飓风刮到了一个未知的地方，最后一名水手爬上主桅发现了陆地，于是他们纷纷上岸强取豪夺。他们看到一个温良无害的民族热情款待他们，而他们却赋予这个国家一个新的名字，为了国王将此地正式侵占，还要立上一块烂木碑或是石头当做记号。他们杀掉二三十个土著居

their king, they set up a rotten plank or a stone for a memorial, they murder two or three dozen of the natives, bring away a couple more by force for a sample, return home, and get their pardon. Here commences a new dominion acquired with a title by *divine right*. Ships are sent with the first opportunity, the natives driven out or destroyed, their princes tortured to discover their gold; a free license given to all acts of inhumanity and lust, the earth reeking with the blood of its inhabitants: and this execrable crew of butchers employed in so pious an expedition, is a *modern colony* sent to convert and civilize an idolatrous and barbarous people.

民，强行带走几个当做样本，返回祖国就获得赦免。如此以“神圣”的名义获得一片新的疆土。国王第一时间派出船队，土著被赶尽杀绝，为了淘金百般折磨他们的头领，所有灭绝人性荒淫无度的行为都被允许，整片土地都被当地居民的鲜血沾染。这帮进行虚伪的所谓探险的穷凶极恶的屠夫们，正是被派往改造开化那些偶像崇拜的野蛮人的现代殖民者。

But this description, I confess, doth by no means affect the *British nation*, who may be an example to the whole world for their wisdom, care, and justice in planting colonies; their liberal endowments for the advancement of religion and learning; their choice of devout and able pastors to propagate *Christianity*, their caution in stocking their provinces with people of sober lives and conversations from this the mother kingdom; their strict regard to the distribution of justice, in supplying the civil administration through all their colonies with officers of the greatest abilities, utter strangers to corruption; and to crown all, by sending the most vigilant and virtuous governors, who have no other

但是我得承认，这段话可并无影射大英帝国的意思，从世界范围的殖民扩张来看，英国人的智慧、关怀和公正都可以算得上是榜样和楷模。他们开明地推行宗教和知识；挑选虔诚能干的牧师传播基督教；他们谨慎地从本国挑选出头脑清晰说话富有条理的人派往驻地；他们严格遵守公平分配的原则，指派最有能力，最清正廉明的官员去管理殖民地；更好的是，他们派遣最警惕最有德行的官员去统治殖民地，这些人只一心一意为管辖的子民谋幸福，为他们的主人大英国王效劳终生。

views than the happiness of the people over whom they preside, and the honour of the king their master.

But, as those countries which I have described, do not appear to have any desire of being conquered, and enslaved, murdered or driven out by colonies, nor abound either in gold, silver, sugar, or tobacco; I did humbly conceive they were by no means proper objects of our zeal, our valour, or our interest. However, if those whom it more concerns, think fit to be of another opinion, I am ready to depose, when I shall be lawfully called, that no *European* did ever visit these countries before me. I mean, if the inhabitants ought to be believed; unless a dispute may arise concerning the two *Yahoos*, said to have been seen many Ages ago on a mountain in *Houyhnhnmland*, from whence the Opinion is , that the Race of those Brutes hath descented; and these, for anything I know, may have been *English*, which indeed I was apt to suspect from the Lineaments of their Posterity's Countenances, although very much defaced. But, how far that will go to make out a Title, I leave to the Learned in Colony-Law.

然而那些我所提到的国家不见得愿意被占领，被奴役或是被侵略者杀害驱逐，而这些国家也并不盛产黄金、白银、食糖和烟草，因此我谦逊地设想，他们无论如何都不该算作我们发泄一腔热情、勇猛神武或是大捞好处的对象。然而，如果那些利害关系人士对此持有另一种看法，那么我已做好被合法传唤时宣誓作证的准备，我会说，还没有一个欧洲人先我之前去过那些国家。我的意思是，如果当地居民是值得信赖的，那么唯一能引发争议的大概只有那两只传说许多年前出现在“慧骃”国一座山上的“雅虎”了。而从这种意见来看，这些畜生就是这两只“雅虎”的后裔，而据我所知这两只“雅虎”可能就是英国人。虽然很丢脸，但实际上从他们后代的面部特征来看我对这种观点倾向于持怀疑态度。然而这一点是否就能成为我们占有“慧骃”国的证据，就留给那些殖民法的学究们判断了。

But as to the formality of taking possession in my sovereign's name, it never came once into my thoughts; and if it had, yet as my affairs then stood, I

但至于以国王陛下的名义正式占领那些地方的想法却一次都没出现在我脑海里，就算有，考虑到我当时的处境，出于慎重和明哲

should perhaps in point of prudence and self-preservation, have put it off to a better opportunity.

保身的考虑，我或许还是应当另觅良机再说。

Having thus answered the only objection that can ever be raised against me as a traveller, I here take a final leave of all my courteous readers, and return to enjoy my own speculations in my little garden at *Redriff*; to apply those excellent lessons of virtue which I learned among the *Houyhnhnms*, to instruct the *Yahoos* of my own family as far as I shall find them docible animals, to behold my figure often in a glass, and thus if possible habituate myself by time to tolerate the sight of a human creature: to lament the brutality to *Houyhnhnms* in my own country, but always treat their persons with respect, for the sake of my noble master, his family, his friends, and the whole *Houyhnhnm* race, whom these of ours have the honour to resemble in all their lineaments, however their intellectuals came to degenerate.

既然我已经回答了作为一个旅行家唯一可能受到的责难，在此我将向我所有有礼貌的读者做出最后的道别。之后，我将回到我在瑞德里夫的小花园中享受独自思考的快乐，我会将"慧骃"教给我的美德的经验学以致用，直到将我家里的那几只"雅虎"教导成温良顺从的动物为止。我会常常照镜以省吾身，如果有可能，我要让自己今后慢慢习惯忍受人类出现在我面前，我对于我自己国家里的"慧骃"的粗野而感到悲哀，但看在我那尊贵的主人和它的家人朋友以及整个"慧骃"族的分上，我依然对它们以礼相待。我国的"慧骃"们有幸长着和"慧骃"国的"慧骃"相同的样貌，但它们的智力却走了下坡路。

I began last week to permit my wife to sit at dinner with me, at the farthest end of a long table, and to answer (but with the utmost brevity) the few questions I asked her. Yet the smell of a *Yahoo* continuing very offensive, I always keep my nose well stopped with rue, lavender, or tobacco leaves. And although it be hard for a man late in life to remove old habits,

从上星期开始，我已经允许我妻子与我一起吃饭，她坐在长桌最远的另一端，只能回答我问她的几个问题（但是必须用最简明的语言）。然而"雅虎"的气味依然十分难闻，我总是用芸香、熏衣草或者烟草将鼻子堵得严严实实的。尽管对于一个迟暮的人来说要改掉旧习惯可不容易，但我还尚存一丝

I am not altogether out of hopes in some time to suffer a neighbour *Yahoo* in my company without the apprehensions I am yet under of his teeth or his claws.

My reconcilement to the *Yahoo* kind in general might not be so difficult, if they would be content with those vices and follies only, which nature hath entitled them to. I am not in the least provoked at the sight of a lawyer, a pick-pocket, a colonel, a fool, a lord, a gamester, a politician, a whore-monger, a physician, an evidence, a suborner, an attorney, a traitor, or the like: this is all according to the due course of things: but when I behold a lump of deformity, and diseases both in body and mind, smitten with *pride*, it immediately breaks all the measures of my patience; neither shall I be ever able to comprehend how such an animal and such a vice could tally together. The wise and virtuous *Houyhnhnms*, who abound in all excellencies that can adorn a rational creature, have no name for this vice in their language, which hath no terms to express anything that is evil, except those whereby they describe the detestable qualities of their *Yahoos*, among which they were not able to distinguish this of pride, for want of thoroughly understanding human nature, as it showeth itself in other countries, where that animal presides. But I, who had more experience,

希望，再过上一段日子，就能忍受紧邻的“雅虎”在我身边，而不像现在时刻担心着我会被他的牙齿和利爪所伤。

假若一般的“雅虎”仅有那些天性中的罪恶和愚蠢，我与他们之间的和解也就不至于如此艰难了。律师、扒手、上校、傻瓜、老爷、赌棍、政客、嫖客、医生、证人、教唆犯、讼棍、叛国者等，这些人倒一点都不会触怒我，这些都是天经地义的事，然而当我看到一个畸形的怪胎，不但身体残疾，还心理扭曲，却还得意洋洋，我的耐性就瞬间瓦解，我无论如何都搞不懂，这样一种动物竟然会有着如此的罪恶。睿智而又品行高贵的“慧骃”们富有理性动物所能拥有的一切美德，它们的语言里却没有一个可以用来形容这种罪恶的名词，它们的语言中，除了那些用来描述“雅虎”令人憎恶的特性的名词外，没有任何形容恶的词语。它们缺乏对人性深刻而透彻的理解，以至于它们无法区分这种自大的罪恶，然而在“雅虎”这种动物统治的别的国家中，这恶行随处可见。然而我比“慧骃”们有更多的经验，就能明白地发现“雅虎”身上自大的因子。

could plainly observe some rudiments of it among the wild *Yahoos*.

But the *Houyhnhnms*, who live under the government of reason, are no more proud of the good qualities they possess, than I should be for not wanting a leg or an arm, which no man in his wits would boast of, although he must be miserable without them. I dwell the longer upon this subject from the desire I have to make the society of an *English Yahoo* by any means not insupportable, and therefore I here entreat those who have any tincture of this absurd vice, that they will not presume to come in my sight.

然而，那些基于理性而生存的"慧骃"们却从不为它们拥有的那些美好品德而自满，就如同我亦不会因为缺条腿或一条胳膊而自豪一样。一个聪明人是不会吹嘘自己四肢齐全的，即使他如果失去它们亦会十分痛苦。我在这个话题上停留比较久，因为我必须想方设法让英国的"雅虎"们不那么面目可憎。因此在这里我想请求那些哪怕只沾了一点这种愚蠢的罪恶的人们，千万别自作主张地出现在我眼前。

（完）